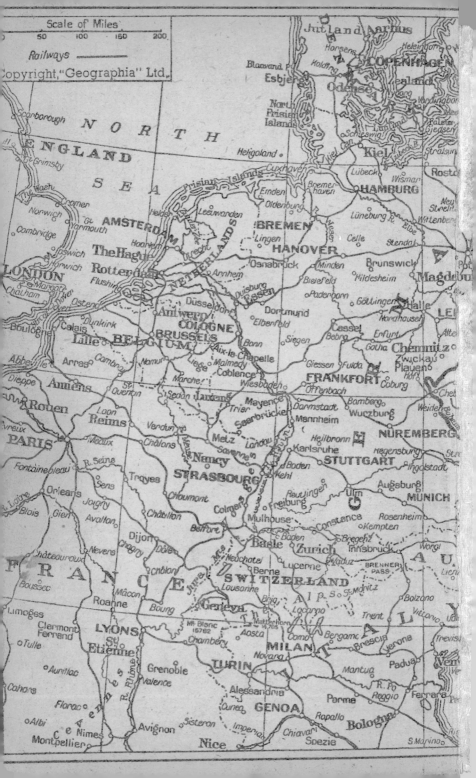

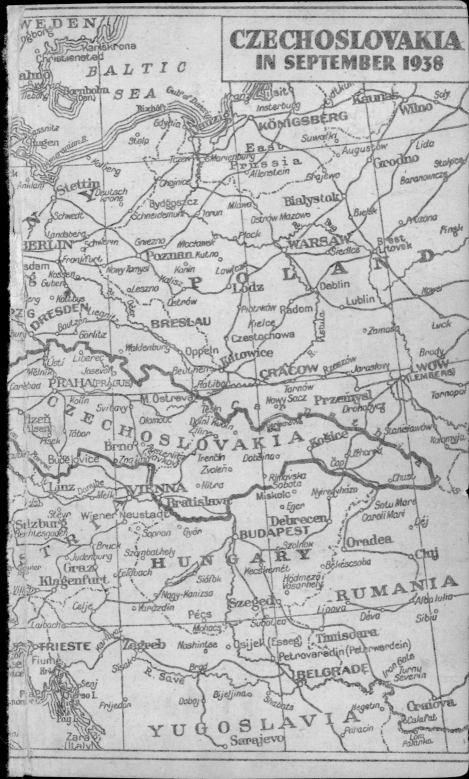

CZECHOSLOVAKIA
IN SEPTEMBER 1938

A HISTORY OF THE CZECHS AND SLOVAKS

A HISTORY OF THE CZECHS AND SLOVAKS

By

R. W. SETON-WATSON

D.Litt. (Oxon), Hon. Ph.D. (Prague and Bratislava), F.B.A.

*Masaryk Professor of Central European History
in the University of London*

' People of whom we know nothing '

HUTCHINSON & CO. (Publishers) LTD.

LONDON : NEW YORK : MELBOURNE

1943

THIS BOOK
IS DEDICATED
TO
THE CZECH PEOPLE
LOYAL AND STEADFAST

Made and Printed in Great Britain at St. Albans by *The Mayflower Press (of Plymouth)*. William Brendon & Son, Ltd.

FOREWORD

On September 11, 1918, the British Prime Minister, Mr. Lloyd George, telegraphed to Professor Masaryk, as President of the Czechoslovak National Council, "Your nation has rendered inestimable service to Russia and to the Allies in this struggle to free the world from despotism ; we shall never forget it." On September 27, 1938 (almost exactly twenty years later) another British Prime Minister, broadcasting to the Empire, tried to justify his surrender by describing the Czechoslovaks as "people of whom we know nothing."

The present volume is an attempt to deprive future politicians of any excuse for repeating this ineptitude. No one is more conscious than its author, of its imperfections and improvisations. It was originally planned as a companion to *A History of the Roumanians* (published in 1934), and to a still unfinished History of Jugoslav Unity ; and it also incorporates fragments from a History of Austria-Hungary under the Dual System, begun before the last war. The only valid excuse for its completion at high pressure and its production in time of war, is that for good or for ill it is the first history which covers the whole ground, from the earliest times right on to the Gestapo Terror of to-day, and that it contains a collection of facts which, if fully accessible at the time and clearly interpreted, might have served as a timely warning.

Czechoslovakia was in many ways the most promising and normal of the political creations of the Great War, full of life and ideals, led by men of high purpose and intellectual calibre. None the less this reconstituted State was the subject of many misconceptions and even calumnies, and these can only be cleared away by a study of its history and origins. From this study Bohemia emerges as one of the earliest national states in Europe, with a highly developed consciousness at a time when not only Germany and Italy, but even France and Spain were still disunited. On the one hand she possessed one of the best natural frontiers in Europe, only inferior to the Alps and the Pyrenees—one which till its overthrow in 1938 had stood for more than ten centuries. On the other hand she was handicapped by her landlocked position ; her attempts to reach the Baltic or the Adriatic inevitably failed. The fatal legacy bestowed upon her by geography made of the Czechs an exposed salient jutting far into the German positions ; and this became all the more marked as with the centuries the tenfold more numerous Germans pushed their frontiers eastwards from the Elbe and Saale to the Oder and on towards the Vistula, at the expense of the Slavs, applying the alternate methods of extermination and assimilation. But on the physical map of Europe Bohemia still stands out lozenge-shaped in the very centre of the picture. Bismarck used to call Bohemia "a natural fortress erected in the centre of our Continent." Let those who ignored this warning in 1938 be careful to complete the quotation in 1943–44 ; "Bohemia in the hands of Russia," he said, "would be Germany's enslavement, Bohemia in our hands would be war without mercy or truce with the Empire of the Czars." A free and independent Czechoslovakia offers the only true solution.

'The great object in trying to understand history, political, religious, literary or scientific,' wrote Lord Acton, 'is to get behind men and to grasp ideas.' The history of Bohemia is that of a small nation which has from early times stood in the van of intellectual, religious and political freedom. What gave its conflict with the Germans an added bitterness was that it almost always found them on the side of reaction, from the Council of Constance till the Protectorate and the Heydrich Terror. Politically there have always been 'ragged fringes' between German and Czech, between Magyar and Slovak ; and as a 'clean cut' proved impossible in 1918, the new Republic of necessity rested upon two conflicting principles—in Bohemia the historic rights of the Crown of St. Wenceslas, in Slovakia the principle of Nationality, which led logically to Czechoslovak Unity. Above all, there stands out from the pages of Czech history a marked preference for leaders of the intellectual rather than the military or narrowly political type, and a no less marked capacity for recognizing and following such leaders when they appear. The reader will, it is hoped, be able to trace a clear continuity of political thought, on what are to-day somewhat arbitrarily called 'democratic' lines. It will be for him to decide whether Czechoslovakia was (as its enemies contend) a mere passing aberration, at whose door some of our present ills might fairly be laid, or whether on the contrary it was a natural evolution from a long historic past, a noteworthy experiment in political and social progress, such as has already won for it a key-position amid the vast schemes of European reconstruction which must follow the agonies of war.

For my part, I have endeavoured to follow the example set by a revered colleague, the late Ernest Denis, who prefaced his History of *Bohemia since the White Mountain* with these words :—*Je n'ai dissimulé aucune des erreurs des patriotes tchèques ; je crois malgré tout qu'ils ont écrit une des plus belles pages de l'histoire de l'humanité.*

R. W. SETON-WATSON.

September 3, 1943.

76 - 89

CONTENTS

CHAPTER I

ORIGINS OF THE BOHEMIAN STATE

Since the beginning of our national independence we have always been surrounded by the Germanic sea, and we have always known how to protect ourselves, whether by alliances or military defence, or political ententes.

Dr. E. Beneš (1934).

THE earliest records of Bohemia and the Czechs are extremely scanty, and lie outside the scope of such a work as the present. The name Bohemia certainly seems to come from the Celtic Boii, but it is very difficult to decide what are the relative proportions of Boian and Marcoman, of Celtic and Teutonic blood in the population of to-day. Legend gives the name of Čech to their first mythical leader, just as Magyar is claimed as the first mythical leader of Hungary, and Hrvat of the Croats. This may well be a myth of the first Czech chronicler, Cosmas, who admits that he had no real data earlier than the ninth century. The first migration of the Czechs to their present home is variously assigned to the middle of the fifth or the beginning of the sixth century. They were soon followed and subjected by a non-Aryan tribe, the Avars, who made their centre in the Pannonian Plain—what is now Hungary.

About the year 620 a certain Samo threw off the Avar yoke and made his capital on the Vyšehrad, now a suburb of modern Prague[1]; and he is alleged to have held sway as far as the Baltic in the north and Carinthia in the south. But this assertion is quite incapable of proof; Samo remains a semi-mythical figure, whose death was followed by dissolution and obscurity.

In the late eighth century, however, there arose a national Czech dynasty, the Přemysl family, which was to rule for five centuries, and to make of Bohemia one of the earliest national states of Europe. At first we are dependent upon mere legends, those infantine chronicles which surround the first dawn of history in every country. The frontiers are entirely vague, the names of princes and warriors are but shadows on the screen. During the eighth and ninth centuries the whole of Central Europe was in a state of transition; there were no settled conditions. Tribes and nations rose and fell, frontiers swayed to and fro, in all the lands between the Baltic and the Adriatic and Ægean; and little is to be gained by establishing the full facts. Their doings have passed into the same limbo as those of their contemporaries, pale ghosts from Mercia, Deira, Dalriada or Strathclyde. Let it suffice that Charles the Great tried to conquer Bohemia with very limited success, that he imposed a kind of loose vassalage upon the Czechs; and that his son and successor, Louis the Pious, concentrated his efforts against the neighbouring Slav state of Moravia.

---

[1] The date is given by Count Lützow as 623, by Peisker, the Graz historian, as 603 (*Cambridge Medieval History*, Vol. I).

The 'Great Moravian State'

In the ninth century Bohemia almost vanishes from the map, and Moravia takes its place, under two Princes, Mojmir and Rostislav, who, to judge by the scanty records that have survived, must have been men of very remarkable talents. Under them there is a long series of struggles against Germanic invasion. But though the records of these wars are utterly barren and do not belong to a brief general survey such as the present, it is necessary to dwell for a moment upon two events of that period which were fraught with consequences of supreme importance, not only for the Czechs and Slovaks themselves, but indeed for the whole history of Europe. These are the introduction of Christianity and the coming of the Magyars.

The German leaders, Louis the Pious and his son Louis the German, were prompted in their assaults upon Bohemia and Moravia probably at least as much by religious as by political motives. With the German soldier came the German priest and monk. Bohemia fell gradually under the influence of the Bishop of Regensburg, in whose town Louis the German held his court, while Moravia owned allegiance to the Archbishop of Salzburg and the Bishop of Passau. It is superfluous to point out the great part played by the medieval Church in the colonization of Eastern Europe, which eventually stemmed back the Slavonic tide from the Elbe and the Oder, from the middle Danube and from the Alps, and planted the German language and German culture in many ancient Slavonic strongholds.

The heathen Prince Rostislav found himself between two advancing tides, from west and east, and he turned to the latter as a more distant and less immediate danger. At this moment—when Egbert was uniting the Saxon heptarchy, and when the East and West Franks were falling finally apart—there was as yet no such thing as a Hungarian state. The old Pannonia, comprising the plain of the Middle Danube, was occupied by various tribes of predominantly Slav character, some of whom were destined to be completely merged. Notably the Bulgars, who in the Migration of the Nations followed the Avars and preceded the Magyars, and who shared the Asiatic origin of both, stretched the whole way from the Lower Danube to what in modern times has been known as 'the Banat.' Thus the Bulgaria of those days was a fairly near neighbour of the Moravian state, and some have even concluded that the two states bordered upon each other, though this is scarcely susceptible of proof.

The Slav Apostles

In 863 Rostislav of Moravia found himself in the same position as so many other heathen monarchs of those crucial centuries, almost driven by a sort of *force majeure* to accept Christianity, finding an identity of interest between kingship and Church, and faced with the need for deciding whence he was to select teachers of the new faith—or, stated in political terms, the need for deciding on which of the major Powers of the day he was to lean. The missionaries of the West, the successors of Boniface, with whom Christianity and Germanism went hand in hand, were already a menace to his survival as an independent ruler : and he seems to have calculated that remote Byzantium was a far safer ally. He therefore sent a special mission to the Emperor Michael, appealing in particular for clergy capable of expounding the Christian faith in the language of the country. In response Michael sent two missionaries who had already won fame by their visits to the Khazars and Saracens, the brothers Constantine and Methodius, sons of a high official at Salonica. If not themselves Slavs, they were at any rate well acquainted with the most southerly branch of the Slavs, and presumably with other Slav dialects. The two brothers accompanied the Moravian envoys homewards and became the first Apostles of the Western, no less than of the Southern, Slavs; their labours have left an indelible mark not merely on the religious or ecclesiastical, but even on the national or political development of Europe.

Their triumph at the Court of Moravia was rapid and was undoubtedly facilitated by their successful invention of a new Slavonic script, based upon the Greek but adapted to suit certain Slav peculiarities. Needless to say, this is the origin of the famous Cyrillic alphabet, upon which the modern Russian, Serbian and Bulgarian orthography is based; Cyril was the name in religion assumed by Constantine. This script, and its liturgical developments, exercised a profound influence over all Slavs and lies at the root of those special affinities and sense of kinship which in modern times acquired a certain political tinge, blending militant Orthodoxy with the so-called 'Pan-slav Idea.'

The German party, acting especially in the interests of the Archbishop of Salzburg, under whose jurisdiction all Pannonia had been since Charles the Great, left no stone unturned to counteract the influence of the two apostles at the Moravian Court, and at the same time to poison the Holy See against them. But this was only partially successful. The schism between the Eastern and Western Churches was at this time dormant. The brothers, when on the point of returning to Constantinople, received an invitation from Pope Nicholas to visit Rome. Cyril himself died there in 869, but Methodius received at the hands of the Pope his investiture as Archbishop of Moravia and Pannonia. Despite all the research of modern students, it is not really possible to identify the exact scene of his labours. The place popularly associated with it is the small town of Nitra, in Western Slovakia; but alternative theories point to Velehrad in modern Moravia, or to another site close to the River Morava (March). Even the date of Methodius' consecration is uncertain; it may have been in 868, before his brother's death, or not till 871. Even when he enjoyed the full Papal sanction, he had determined opposition to encounter from the Germans, being cited before a mixed ecclesiastical and lay assembly under Louis the German, and imprisoned in Swabia for eighteen months on the charge of exercising episcopal functions in the diocese of another. His position became even more difficult after the overthrow of Prince Rostislav by his treacherous nephew Svatopluk, who had the backing of the German king and of the German episcopate. Such all too scanty evidence as we possess goes to show that Svatopluk, the Slavonic champion of modern romantic legend, in reality plotted with Louis the German, gave his backing to Bishop Wiching of Nitra against Methodius, and opposed the latter's attempts to secure the succession to his own see for one of the foremost Slav clergy, Gorazd. Methodius was subjected to much insult and obloquy during his captivity in Germany, but resisted every effort to force him into resignation, and at last secured the active support of Pope John VIII, and was allowed to return to Moravia. He was, it is true, forbidden to employ Slavonic as the language of the liturgy, but at once set himself to reverse this decision. The stern apostle and the dissolute Svatopluk had little in common, and the latter, seemingly above all for personal reasons, allied himself with the German clergy in their campaign against the Slav liturgy. When, however, he urged the Pope to summon Methodius to Rome to explain his policy, he found that he had overreached himself. The journey to Rome was completely successful, and the apostle returned with a Bull confirming once more the Slav liturgy (880), and extending his jurisdiction as Archbishop of all Moravia.

Even now Methodius' success was only transitory. He never overcame the enmity of Svatopluk, and after his death in 885 Pope Stephen V reimposed the veto upon the Slav liturgy and threw his weight in favour of Bishop Wiching against Gorazd. This time the result was decisive and permanent. The influence of Byzantium and Kiev proved far too remote to assert itself, the Slav liturgy and script were driven eastwards, and Bohemia and Moravia definitely entered the sphere of Rome. The most that can be said is that certain Eastern affinities survived, which it would be rash to exaggerate, but which indicate at the very least a difference of mentality and psychological outlook. Henceforth the Czech lands belong to the West, while constantly endeavouring to maintain their contacts with the East.

The quarrel between German and Slav churchmen was still raging unabated, when a new danger arose and submerged the young Moravian state before it could consolidate itself. The frontiers of Svatopluk's realm were still fluid when he died in 894, stretching at their utmost to the River Saale on the north-west, and to the Danube on the south. His three sons fought among themselves, and the German king, Arnulf, for his own selfish aims, first fanned the flames within, then sowed discord between Bohemia and Moravia, and finally called in the help of the Magyars, then still a nomadic heathen horde moving westwards from the steppes of Russia into what is now Galicia. It was the last of the great migrations of the peoples, that was to leave a permanent mark upon Europe.

The Coming of the Magyars

At the last moment the Germans realized the danger to themselves and joined forces with the Slav forces, but it was too late. A decisive battle took place not far from Posonium (the modern Pressburg or Bratislava), and sealed the fate of the loosely knit structure which is somewhat illogically known as the 'Great Moravian Empire.' The exact date remains uncertain. It seems probable that the first Magyar irruption took place in 892, two years before Svatopluk's death ; but in modern times the Magyars themselves, in organizing their Millenary Exhibition, strongly tinged with political and expansionist theory, committed themselves to the year 896 as the decisive date. Svatopluk's eldest son, Mojmir II, still held his ground in 902, but by 906 at the latest the Magyar conquest was an accomplished fact. For a couple of centuries to come the fate of what we now know as Moravia and Slovakia (Slovensko) remained in the balance between Hungary and Bohemia, with frontiers still fluid or ill-defined. But in effect a single blow had virtually decided the course of history for nine centuries. Henceforth Slovakia remained a part of Hungary, and the two kinsmen went different ways, save for brief interludes in the thirteenth and fifteenth centuries. Palacký,

Bohemia's greatest historian, was not exaggerating when he described the establishment of the Magyars in Hungary as 'the greatest misfortune that has befallen the Slavonic world for thousands of years.' For it cut the Slav family of nations into two unequal portions, creating a separation which history has rendered permanent, and which not even the Great War could annul. Czechs, Slovaks, Poles, Ukrainians, Great and White Russians belong to the northern and western groups, Slovenes, Croats, Serbs and Bulgars to the southern; between the two, Germans, Magyars and Roumanians form a non-Slavonic *bloc* linking the Baltic with the Black Sea.

The Rise of Bohemia

During Moravia's brief period of glory Bohemia plays an entirely subordinate part. The break-up of this strong united state was all the more unfortunate for the Slavs because it coincided with the final stages of a long movement lasting from the ninth to the fourteenth century, in which the Teutonic element turned again eastwards, setting the seal of German blood and language and culture upon wide territories east of the Elbe and the Saale, and along the whole Baltic coast. Pomerania, Mecklenburg, the Mark of Brandenburg, Lusatia, Prussia, Silesia, are so many landmarks on the road of aggressive and triumphant Germanism; and at the same time German settlers penetrated into Bohemia, Hungary and Transylvania, down the middle Danube and even into Croatia and Bosnia.

During the tenth century Bohemia slowly swims back into the field. At first the main feature of its history is the consolidation of Christianity. St. Methodius appears to have baptized Prince Bořivoj, at a date unknown; and a generation later the Royal House gave two martyrs to the Church, who were duly canonized. St. Ludmila, after the death of her husband, Prince Bořivoj, and of two sons who succeeded him as reigning princes, came into conflict, over the education of her young grandson Wenceslas (Václav), with her own daughter-in-law, the masterful Drahomíra, and was murdered by her under circumstances which have remained obscure. Wenceslas assumed the reins of government a few years later, at the age of seventeen, and showed great piety and energy in his brief reign. It was marked by a determined effort to establish cordial relations with Germany, now recovering under Henry the Fowler, forerunner of the great Saxon dynasty of the Ottos, after shaking off the trammels of the degenerate Carolings. Round the very scanty facts which confirm this tendency on the part of Wenceslas, certain historians of National Socialist opinion have clumsily woven elaborate theories, and would fain place him on a level with the greatest of the Czech national heroes, alone conscious of the compelling necessity of a German orientation for Bohemia. In reality the royal Saint—whom a popular carol has wrongly designated as 'Good *King* Wenceslas'—was a man perhaps not more important than Edward the Martyr, of the English royal house, but of whom recent research has formed a rather higher opinion. His murder in 929, at the age of twenty-two, cast a certain spell upon the imagination of the Czechs; and under the Republic the cult of St. Wenceslas was skilfully developed as a counter-attraction to that of the heretical Hus and of the fatally compromised Nepomuk.

His brother and successor, who was also his murderer, was known as Boleslav the Cruel. He held his own for fourteen years against the

Germans, but in later life co-operated with Otto the Great, and shared in the latter's great victory over the Magyars on the Lechfeld, near Augsburg (955). This was one of the decisive battles of the Middle Ages, which rolled back the heathen invaders from Germany and Italy ; and it marks their transition from the nomadic to the settled stage.

His son Boleslav II (967–999) maintained good relations with the Germans, and it was in large measure owing to this that the favourite project of his father was realized in 973. The Bishopric of Prague was founded, and the Bohemian Church detached from its dependence upon the great German see of Regensburg—a see which had played a part only secondary to those of Magdeburg and Lübeck in the expansion of Germanism at the expense of Slavdom. It was under the jurisdiction of the primatial see of Mainz, but this was too remote to be effective. Its first holder, Detmar, was a Saxon monk, conversant with the language and customs of his adopted country, and enjoying due respect, but still absorbed by a burning zeal for the final extirpation of heathendom on the Bohemian and Polish borders. His successor, Adalbert or Vojtěch, belonged to the great Slav family of the Slavníkovci, who at times enjoyed a princely power hardly inferior to that of the reigning Přemyslide Dukes. His missionary efforts completed the conversion of Bohemia, and he is credited with having baptized the son of the Magyar Prince Vajk, the future St. Stephen, first king of Hungary. After an absence of five years, devoted to proselytizing Hungary, he returned in 992 to his neglected diocese, but found his Slavníkovci kinsmen in conflict with Boleslav, and soon began to look for a more congenial sphere of activity. In 997 he was put to death by the heathen Prussians, and his body was interred with great ceremony by King Boleslaw the Brave of Poland at the future primatial see of Gniezno (Gnesen). Thus one of the greatest churchmen in Czech history is identified no less intimately with Hungary and Poland than with his native Bohemia.

Christianization and political development went side by side, and after a long series of wars with Germans and Poles, Bohemia may be said to have found her natural boundaries by the beginning of the eleventh century—boundaries which received their first rough definition by the Treaty of 1013 with the Emperor Henry II.

Bohemia and the Empire

In this very brief historical outline it is impossible to do more than indicate a few outstanding features of the opening period. From its mythical origin under the Princess Libuše and her peasant husband Přemysl, down to its extinction in 1306, there were thirty-one rulers of that House. If the essence of that history may be summed up in a few sentences, it must be as one long and stubborn struggle to hold Germany at arms' length. The fate of the two countries had already become inseparable : and just as the German monarchs took advantage of the ever-recurring dissensions in Bohemia in order to assert their influence, so, on the other hand, the Princes of Bohemia, whenever they found themselves secure upon the throne, meddled in their turn in German home politics. Some centuries elapsed before the position was stabilized, and there were many ups and downs, which, however, belong to medieval constitutional history.

The Emperor asserted from time to time his suzerainty over Bohemia, and sometimes even the right to nominate or confirm each holder of the Bohemian Crown ; this claim Bohemia was generally strong enough to resist.   On three occasions between the tenth and thirteenth centuries he offered the royal dignity to the reigning prince ; to St. Wenceslas (921–929), who refused it ; in 1086 to Vratislav II, who was made king by Henry IV of Canossa fame, in return for the military assistance which he had rendered in the German and Italian wars, but only for his own lifetime ; and, in 1156, to Vladislav II, whom Frederick Barbarossa thought it politic not so much to reward for past services, as to win over as a future auxiliary.   This time the title fell into abeyance owing to the anarchy in which Vratislav's reign ended.   But though the succession in the Přemyslide House was at times uncertain, and though Bohemia was acknowledged as a fief of the Empire, it proved possible to check the inroads of the Imperial administration and to maintain native forms and practice.

At the same time the Princes of Bohemia gradually asserted a place among the seven Electors of the Empire.   Bohemia thus acquired a hybrid character, being at once inside and outside—of course at a period when every kingdom in Europe was still technically, though only technically, under the civil supremacy of the Holy Roman Emperor.   At least as early as 1114 the Duke of Bohemia became hereditary cup-bearer, and henceforward the sovereigns of Bohemia invariably shared in, sometimes even turned the scale at, the elections.   Thus from an early date we find the rival currents of dynastic ambition and national hatred now promoting, now checking, the growth of German influence in the country.

The German Colonists

There was first of all the fact, for which parallels could be found elsewhere, that foreign elements secured a foothold by allying themselves with one or other of the rival factions.   Moreover, Bohemia in these centuries had to face the most powerful rulers of the Middle Ages—the Saxon, Franconian and Hohenstauffen Emperors.   There was also frequent intermarriage with German princesses, from Saxony, Swabia, Meissen, leading naturally to the adoption of German manners ;   there was the influence of the German clergy, who favoured their own nationality, and there was a steady influx of German colonists to the towns and to the mining districts, bringing with them their own code of laws—notably the famous 'Magdeburger Recht.'   Thus the Germans came to form something not far removed from a state within a state :   and this was no less true of Hungary, where the towns of Slovakia and Transylvania in particular lived their own narrow life till far on into modern times.   There is a certain irony in the fact that it was the three most powerful sovereigns of the Czech national dynasty who were above all responsible for augmenting the non-Slav elements in the country.

Přemysl Otakar I (1198–1230)

It was Otakar I who most effectively asserted Bohemian independence, taking sides very skilfully in the German civil war that filled the first decade of the thirteenth century, and shifting from one side to the other, winning new concessions at every change, until in 1212 he extracted from the Emperor a Golden Bull, confirming the Royal title to Otakar and his descendants, and at the same time renouncing the double Imperial claim to ratify each succession to the Crown and to appoint the Bishop of Prague. Thus Bohemia became a hereditary kingdom under its own national dynasty.

Otakar had been crowned King of Bohemia at Mainz in 1198, at the same time that Philip of Hohenstauffen was crowned King of the Romans ; and in 1213 he was present at the coronation of Frederick II, the last great medieval Emperor. But he made good the claim to be dispensed from attending the Imperial Diet, except when it was held in certain specified towns along the western border, such as Nürnberg and Bamberg. Control from Germany grew more and more shadowy, even before the downfall of the Hohenstauffen and the long period of interregnum made fatal inroads into the central authority of the Empire.

Wenceslas I (1230–1253) : *Otakar II* (1253–1278)

Otakar was succeeded by his son, Wenceslas I, who was throughout his reign preoccupied by disputes with Austria and the Empire—with one hideous interlude, the Tartar invasion of 1241, which for a time threatened to submerge Hungary altogether but whose waters began to subside as they reached the borders of Moravia. The last male representative of the famous house of Babenberg, Frederick the Warlike, was killed in battle in 1246 ; but it may be supposed that the combative nature to which he owed his nickname had not been diminished by the knowledge that his succession was in doubt, and that the eagles, Imperial and lesser, were gathering round the Austrian carcass. Vladislav, the eldest son of Wenceslas, had been married to the Babenberg Princess Gertrude, but had predeceased his father in 1247. The great Emperor Frederick II—'Wonder of the World,' as his contemporaries called him —died in 1250, without carrying into effect his designs upon Austria as a lapsed fief, well calculated to supplement the Hohenstauffen patrimony. In 1251, then, Wenceslas's surviving son Otakar married Frederick's sister Margaret, a woman nearly twenty years his senior, and was accepted by the Austrians as their Duke ; and succeeding in 1253 to his father's throne, he soon showed himself as the most powerful ruler whom Bohemia had as yet produced. He profited by the long interregnum in the Empire to make his position still more unassailable, playing off Richard of Cornwall and Alfonso of Castile against each other—a relatively easy task in the case of aspirants who had no territorial background within the Empire. He also enjoyed the support of the Papacy, the implacable foe of the tottering Hohenstauffen dynasty, and indeed curried favour with it by conducting, on Innocent IV's initiative, a crusade against the heathen Prussians. This diversion deserves more than a passing mention, since it led to the foundation of Königsberg by the Teutonic Knights ; for there is no slight piquancy in the fact that this stronghold and symbol of German aggression in its most blatant form was named after a Czech king !

In the first years of his reign he had found it necessary to make a bargain with his jealous Hungarian neighbours, who were allowed to occupy Styria, while leaving the rest of Austria to Otakar. But the latent quarrel broke out afresh and in 1260 Otakar inflicted a smashing defeat upon the Hungarian king at Kressenbrunn—sometimes called the first battle of the March. As the result, Styria was added to his Austrian possessions. When in 1269 he acquired Carinthia, Carniola and Istria, also, he ruled from Silesia to the Adriatic: and thus for a brief span Bohemia had the seaboard with which Shakespeare credits her.

The jealousy and alarm aroused among the German princes by this great access of strength to a Slav sovereign, certainly not diminished by his second crusade against the heathen Lithuanians, were unquestionably one of the chief contributing causes of the election of Count Rudolf of Habsburg as Emperor in the year 1273.

It is an all too common mistake to regard Rudolf as an insignificant figure among the princes of his day. He already belonged to one of the more powerful Houses, which had been prominent even in the eleventh century, had given a bishop to Strasburg in 1027, had gradually acquired wide lands in Alsace and practically all the southern bank of the Rhine from Basel to the Lake of Constance, and had enjoyed the favour of the later Hohenstauffen. Incidentally, this was the first occasion on which the College of Electors asserted its sole right to choose the Emperor, to the exclusion of the princes as a whole; and their first act after the election was to revoke as invalid the grant of lands in fief since the deposition of Frederick II by the Council of Lyon in 1245. This was, of course, specially aimed at Otakar II, as heir to the extinct Babenbergs: it was a challenge of which Rudolf boldly made himself the spokesman, and to his scheming mind a golden opportunity for turning the lapsed Austrian lands into a hereditary dominion for his own family.

From the outset the rival tendencies were unmistakable, and war to the knife between Rudolf and Otakar was soon inevitable. In 1274 the challenge was given a precise form, when Otakar's rights over Austria, Styria and Carinthia were formally annulled by the Diet of Regensburg. In 1275 Otakar himself was placed under the ban of the Empire; and in 1276 Rudolf led an army against him, having taken care to secure the help of Hungary and to deflect the Papacy from its old alliance with Bohemia. The Emperor also profited by the growing hostility of the great nobles to Otakar's rule; and this hostility in its turn was largely due to the ironic fact that the ambitious and masterful Slav monarch was of all the rulers of his time the one who did most to encourage German settlers in his dominions. His aim was, of course, to counteract the growing power of the nobility by forming a middle class, developing the towns and incidentally ensuring their dependence upon the Crown. He therefore invited Flemish, Franconian and Saxon settlers and brought in German miners, especially to Kutná Hora, to the east of Prague.

Step by step Rudolf gathered round him all the many enemies of Otakar; one defection followed another among the high nobility, not merely of Styria and Carinthia, but even of Bohemia and Moravia, and on the urgent advice of his loyal supporters, he found it advisable to send delegates to negotiate with Rudolf outside Vienna. The outcome of these discussions was that Otakar renounced altogether Austria, Styria, Carinthia and Carniola as well as the Mark of Eger in north-west Bohemia, and even consented to do homage for the kingdom of Bohemia. The contracting of a double marriage between Habsburg and Přemysl did not conceal the humiliation to which Otakar had been subjected, the more so as he had to provide the dowry of his daughter Cunigunda by the cession of large private estates, and had at the same time to grant a free pardon to the rebels who had helped to turn the scale against him. It soon became clear that Otakar's surrender was purely tactical; he was searching everywhere for friends and allies, and there is a striking letter extant, which he addressed to the Polish and Silesian dukes, and which there is no reason to refuse to take at its face value—bidding them raise the standard of common Slav interests against 'the insatiable lusts of the Germans' and warning them that he alone was a bulwark of a free Poland in face of German tyranny.[1]

In 1278, then, the Bohemian king renewed the struggle and marched against Vienna. But he showed indecision and faulty strategy and gave the Hungarians time to send reinforcements to the help of Rudolf. On August 26, 1278, it came to a decisive battle at Dürnkrut, on the Marchfeld; the Bohemian cavalry was borne down by a charge of heavy German riders, and Otakar himself was left dead upon the field. Habsburg rule over Austria was solidly established for centuries, and Bohemia, though not deprived of her independence, was restricted to definite frontiers, especially towards the valley of the Danube.

Geography had already endowed Bohemia with frontiers almost as well-defined and immovable as those of Poland were fluid and incapable of definition. To the north the Ore Mountains (Krušné Horý or Erzgebirge), to the north-east the Giant Mountains (Krkonoše, Riesengebirge), to the east the Sudetian Hills, which have in recent times, not very accurately, become a generic name for all the German districts of Bohemia; to the west and south-west the Bohemian Forest (Šumava), to the south-east the valley of the Morava, formed the rim of that lozenge-shaped plateau which stands out so boldly upon every physical map of Europe, and which justifies Bismarck's reference to Bohemia as a fortress set by God Himself in the heart of the Continent. Otakar's was not the last attempt to extend further afield; we shall see that Silesia and Lusatia played at times their parts in a game of monarchical expansion. But never—even in the darkest period of Habsburg subjection—were Bohemia's natural frontiers erased from the map, until in our own day two panic-stricken statesmen from the West tried to purchase from triumphant gangsters a peace that was no peace.

The Last of the Přemyslides
(Wenceslas II, 1278–1305 : Wenceslas III, 1305–1306)

Wencelas II was only a boy of seven when disaster overcame his father; and the Regency fell into the detested hands of Rudolf's son-in-law, Margrave Otto of Brandenburg. Against him was ranged the refractory Czech nobility, led by Zavis of Rosenberg, who married the Queen-Mother Cunigunda, and using her to assert control of the boy-King and his associates, was for some years the effective ruler of Bohemia. With her death the Habsburg party regained the ascendancy; Rudolf's daughter Guta, or Judith, became Wenceslas's queen, and Zavis died upon the scaffold in 1290. But with the death of Rudolf a year later the rising Habsburg power suffered a serious setback. His two attractive and talented younger sons, Hartmann and Rudolf, were removed by death; and his new heir Albert roused the hostility of the Electors by his territorial ambitions and his harshness of character, with the result that they elected Adolf of Nassau as King of the Romans (1292). The young King of Bohemia helped to turn the scale against his brother-in-law.

For some years the Habsburgs were absorbed by internal dissensions in Austria, and it was not till 1297 that, thanks largely to the efforts of

[1] See Huber, *Gesch. Oesterreichs*, I, p. 608.

Queen Guta, Wenceslas and Albert were reconciled. In that year there was a coronation ceremony of unusual pomp in Prague, which the Duke of Austria attended with 10,000 horse; but at the same time elaborate plans were discussed for the overthrow of Adolf. In 1298 there was a joint offensive westwards; Adolf fell at the battle of Gollheim, and Albert was elected to the vacant throne and solemnly crowned at Aachen (July-August, 1298). Once more Czech military help probably turned the scale.

The Polish Crown

The real interests of Wenceslas, however, lay in another direction, and it was his settled policy, while urging the Habsburgs westwards, to secure for himself a free hand in the east. During the last decade of the thirteenth century the anarchical dissensions of Poland reached a further acute stage, and after the deaths of Leszek the Black and Henry IV of Breslau, a large section of the Polish nobility, together with the citizens of Krakow, offered themselves to the Přemyslide dynasty. Step by step Wenceslas established himself in Krakow and in Silesia, drove the rival candidates on to the defensive, and at last was crowned King of Poland at Gniezno (Gnesen) in 1300. The dream of a united Slav state stretching from the Danube to the Baltic seemed to have been achieved, though in a somewhat altered form from that of earlier experiments. That Wenceslas, however, was not a man of strong calibre is shown by his action in first securing the approval of Albert for his enterprise, and also for his second marriage with a Polish princess, and still more in accepting investiture of Poland as a fief of the German Crown (July 3, 1300). This was a needlessly heavy price to pay for the continued support of the new King of the Romans.

The End of the Árpád and Přemyslide Dynasties

The first decade of the fourteenth century witnessed far-reaching dynastic changes alike in Bohemia, Hungary and the Empire, and a fresh series of kaleidoscopic attempts at union. Already in 1301 the House of Árpád became extinct after four centuries, and Wenceslas obtained the Hungarian Crown for his son and namesake, as the descendant of Béla IV, and now betrothed him to Elizabeth, only daughter of the last King Andrew III. He was crowned at Stuhlweissemburg and won a large section of the nobility by liberal grants of money and office. But the scale was turned against him by the Papal Legate, who on instructions from Boniface VIII supported the rival candidature of Charles Robert of Anjou, heir in the male line of the redoubtable Charles of Anjou, King of Naples and through his grandmother descended from Stephen V of Hungary. Hungary was ravaged by a long civil war, and Albert was induced to side with the Pope and the Angevins, as leaders of the Guelf faction. It is not, indeed, surprising that the German king should have viewed with alarm the prospect of the Přemyslides adding the Crown of Hungary to those of Bohemia and Poland; for then Bohemia's secession from the Empire would only be a matter of time, and it might even be doubted whether Habsburg would be able to maintain its hold upon its Austrian possessions. In 1304 Wenceslas was diverted from his plans for strengthening his son's hold upon Hungary by a serious invasion of Bohemia by Albert and a number of powerful German princes. A gallant defence of Kutná Hora was followed by the retreat of the invaders. But Wenceslas only survived his victory by a few months, dying on June 21, 1305, at the early age of thirty-four ; consumption and excess are variously assigned as the cause.

Wenceslas III, as yet only a boy of sixteen, promptly made peace with his uncle Albert, to whom he ceded the Egerland. He also renounced his claims upon the Hungarian Crown in favour of his cousin Otto of Bavaria, proving his indifference in the most practical manner by renouncing his plighted bride Elizabeth and marrying a Silesian Princess. But before he had time to demonstrate whether this was a wise concentration of effort or a mere irresponsible whim, the young king was murdered at Olmütz under circumstances which have never been cleared up (August 4, 1306). With him ended the romantic Přemyslide dynasty, whose origins, though lost in saga, compared in antiquity with any of their contemporaries. The last king, it is true, left four sisters, but female succession had never been recognized in Bohemia, there were no exact norms for meeting such a situation, and the great nobles were disposed to claim for themselves the unrestricted right of free election.

Meanwhile Bohemia and Hungary at once fell apart, the latter after a prolonged civil war submitting to the new Angevin dynasty. Worse still, Poland promptly shook off the Bohemian connection and found in Władisław Łokietek, no longer a dissolute youth, but tempered by exile and misfortune, a sovereign capable of relaying the foundations of a strong Polish national state. The project of wider Slav unity, still more of a triple union of Czech, Pole and Magyar, rested on far too artificial foundations to become a permanent reality, though more than one effort was still to be made in that direction.

Albert of Habsburg

At this point King Albert asserted his right to nominate a successor to the vacant Imperial fief, arguing that the privilege conceded by Frederick II—by which the Emperor was bound to invest each successive Přemyslide as elected by the Bohemian nation—did not apply in the case of an entirely new dynasty. He then proceeded to appoint his own son Rudolf, and as a conciliatory gesture to marry him to Elizabeth, the widowed queen of Wenceslas II. Rudolf was able and discreet, though unduly parsimonious, and had already won a considerable section of the nobility to his side, when he suddenly fell ill of dysentery, and died on July 4, 1307, at the age of twenty-six, and without leaving heirs. Albert's desire to secure the succession for his second son Frederick met with growing resistance ; and a strong party grouped itself round Duke Henry of Carinthia, who was married to Anne, the elder sister of Wenceslas III. Albert invaded Bohemia, but failed in the attempt to capture Kutná Hora and Kolín, and found it necessary to retreat. For the present the Habsburg luck had very definitely turned ; for in May, 1308, Albert himself was treacherously murdered by his own nephew John, known in the chronicles as 'Parracida.' No question of high policy was involved, but simply the resentment of a cross-grained youth at his unfair exclusion from a share in the Habsburg heritage—secretly fanned, it is true, by some of Albert's numerous enemies.

CHAPTER II

THE HOUSE OF LUXEMBURG. THE GOLDEN AGE
(1346–1378)

EVEN students of the vagaries of dynastic succession and their bearing upon the fate of whole nations will find it hard to produce any parallel to the series of premature deaths which robbed Bohemia of the two Wenceslas's, the young King Rudolf, and finally his father Albert, all within the space of barely three years. The first attempt at achieving a 'personal union' between Bohemia, Hungary and Poland was thus nipped in the bud ; and for the time being the Habsburg family was too disunited and leaderless to continue the expansive policy of Rudolf and Albert, radiating from the Danubian valley. For a time Albert's five sons were driven on to the defensive and were in only too frequent discord among themselves. The German Electors, and especially the three Rhenish Archbishops, looked askance upon a family whose obvious policy it had become to link up its Alsatian and Swabian lands with the Babenberg inheritance, and they directly encouraged Swiss resistance to the Habsburgs. Their motives in electing Count Henry of Luxemburg as King of the Romans were not dissimilar to those which decided the choice of Rudolf of Habsburg a generation earlier. While anxious to prevent a recrudescence of the old anarchy, they viewed with great suspicion a concentration of power in the hands of the foremost princely families, and therefore thought it safer to choose one who belonged to the second rank. It was Archbishop Baldwin of Trier who turned the scale in favour of his own brother Henry.

Henry VII, by blood, tradition and association, was French rather than German ; from the first he neglected his German kingdom and set his heart upon the phantom of Imperial power. Almost the whole of his short reign was spent in Italy, where he was heralded with high hopes by the Ghibelline faction and became involved in adventures with which we are not concerned. But that he in his turn should have sought to make good the deficiencies of the central power by building up a territorial *Hausmacht* was inherent in the German situation ; and before he left for Italy he took action which was to place the House of Luxemburg among the great dynasties of the late Middle Ages.

Henry of Carinthia had proved quite incompetent to govern Bohemia ; he had the support of the towns, which were mainly German, but for that very reason had to face the hostility of the Czech nobles. A powerful party therefore addressed itself to Henry VII and offered to his eldest son John the Crown of Bohemia, and with it the hand of Elizabeth, the youngest sister of the last Přemyslide king and of the Duchess of Carinthia. His acceptance was largely influenced by Peter of Aspelt, Archbishop of Mainz, who had been Chancellor to Wenceslas II and an old opponent of the Habsburgs. Prince John was only fourteen, though, like so many medieval princes, precocious for his age ; and his bride had to be kidnapped from a castle belonging to the Carinthian party. But in September, 1310, she was brought to Speier and there married to John by Archbishop Peter, as 'the lawful heiress of Bohemia.' An expedition was at once sent to Bohemia, Henry of Carinthia was driven out of Prague, and special privileges were granted to the estates in the name of the new king, who promised to rule in love and not in severity. On February 7, 1311, John was solemnly crowned King of Bohemia.

Yet again death was to play havoc with dynastic plans. The new king's father had meanwhile pursued his messianic designs in Italy, and had received the Imperial Crown in Rome from the delegate of a refugee pope (June, 1312) ; but difficulties multiplied round him, and, able and energetic though he was, it is doubtful whether he could have maintained himself successfully in the Peninsula. His disappearance from the scene was a blow from which the Ghibelline cause never altogether recovered. It soon became apparent that John was too young to secure his father's succession ; and his two supporters among the Electors—his uncle of Trier and Peter of Mainz—had to content themselves with turning the scale against the Habsburgs and in favour of Duke Louis of Bavaria. There followed a double election, and eight years of civil war between Habsburg and Wittelsbach, ending in a decisive defeat for Frederick of Austria, only seven years after his brother Leopold's overthrow at Morgarten by the rising Swiss Confederacy. Nearly a century was to pass before the Habsburgs could again hope to win the German Crown.

The Knight-errant King

In all this John was *tertius gaudens*, but he failed to profit as he might have done. He was a man of mercurial temperament, incapable of settling down to the drudgery of administration and for ever tilting at windmills ; and these predispositions were strengthened by the some-what hybrid position of his dynasty, Germanic in blood, French in culture and now Slavonic by adoption. As a youth he was a constant visitor at the French Court, his sister being Queen to Charles IV ; in later life he married as his second wife a daughter of the Duke of Bourbon. The best proof of his French outlook is that he brought up his son and heir, the future Emperor Charles, in Paris, and even changed his original name of Wenceslas to Charles in honour of the boy's royal uncle, and in due course married him to a sister of the first Valois king, Philip VI. His constant absences from Bohemia were much resented and weakened his prestige, the more so as he spent very lavishly and imposed heavy taxa-tion, and in particular squeezed the clergy in right of a special title upon ecclesiastical income conceded to him by Pope John.

His successive adventures against the heathen Russians and Lithuan-ians, then in Tirol and among the Lombard cities (out of which he at one time hoped to carve an Italian sovereignty for his House), need not detain us here. The only concrete result was to create a coalition of Austria, Brandenburg, Bavaria and the Palatinate against him. When at last he realized the hopelessness of the Italian enterprise he did not return home to Bohemia, except at rare intervals, preferring to spend his time in France and Luxemburg in tournaments and other knightly festivities. His quarrels with the House of Wittelsbach, whose head, Louis IV, was Emperor from 1314 to 1346, brought John and his far abler son Charles—at first appointed Margrave of Moravia under his father—into ever closer alliance with France and with the Papacy of the Avignon captivity, in whose eyes Louis was a patron of heretical and subversive elements. The election of Charles's former tutor as Pope

Clement VI in 1342 set a seal to the process ; and Charles himself has
put on record how they had once met at Avignon in the days of Pope
Benedict, and how the cleric had prophesied that Charles would one day
be King of the Romans, to which the Prince countered : "Before that
happens, you will be Pope." "Both of these things came to pass" is
Charles's own terse comment. One momentous favour was granted by
Clement VI to King John : in 1344 the see of Prague was erected into an
archbishopric, henceforth free from the jurisdiction of Mainz and the
Empire, and its occupant thus received the right of crowning the Bohemian
kings.

In later life John undertook two further crusades against the
Lithuanian heathen—the last in 1344, despite the blindness that came
upon him as the result of a wound, aggravated by the treatment of a
quack doctor. But even before this the reins of government were passing,
by a natural process, into the hands of his son Charles. The one contribution to the consolidation of his kingdom which can be placed to John's
credit is his consistent plan for the absorption of Silesia, then split into
a large number of petty duchies under collaterals of the Polish royal
house. From 1327 onwards John induced them, one by one,[1] to acknowledge the suzerainty of the Bohemian Crown ; and at last in 1335 this
was ratified by the King of Poland, in return for John's express renunciation of all inherited claims upon the Polish Crown. The first step was thus
taken towards the incorporation of Silesia by Bohemia.

John's son, Charles of Moravia, differed fundamentally in character
from his father ; fate had separated him early from his mother, and he
had grown up among his French relations, probably himself studying at
the famous University of Paris, or at any rate drinking in impressions
which led him at the very outset of his own reign to create a similar
foundation in Prague, with momentous results for the whole of Central
Europe. Already precocious for his age, he learned in the school of his
Italian experience the value of an ancient culture and at the same time
acquired a preference for diplomacy rather than arms. He thus had a
thoroughly international outlook, having spent his youth almost equally
in France, Germany and Italy, and speaking Latin, French, German,
Czech and Italian with equal fluency. It is all the more remarkable that
he should have so quickly assimilated the tradition of his long neglected
kingdom, and shown himself far more Czech in sentiment than his
Přemyslide forbears Otakar and Wenceslas II.

Charles is the first modern sovereign to have attempted his own
autobiography, thereby proving himself akin to the new culture and
mentality, on the border line between the medieval and modern times.
Bald and naïve as it often is, it also shows a sober realism that was to
stand him in good stead. 'I found Bohemia desolate,' he tells us, 'not a
castle free that was not pledged, so I had nowhere to lodge except in
cities like any other citizen. Prague had been desolated and destroyed
since the days of King Otakar. So I decided to build a new palace which
should be large and handsome.' Thus the most practical motives urged
him upon an unexampled career of building ; and after nearly six centuries
Prague bears his mark more truly than any great European capital that
of any of his contemporaries.

The long feud between the Houses of Wittelsbach and Luxemburg

---

[1] In 1327 Teschen, Ratibor, Falkenberg, Aufschwitz, Oppeln ; in 1328 Breslau ;
in 1329 Liegnitz, Brieg, Sagan, Ols ; in 1331 Glogau.

reached its height in 1346, when **Louis IV** was placed under the ban of the Church and denounced as a heretic and schismatic, and the Electors were openly invited to elect Charles to the now vacant throne. Scarcely had the five Electors[1] taken their decision in July of that year than King John dashed off to the assistance of his friend and cousin Philip of France, who had to meet Edward III's invasion. His advice was cast soberly enough against the ill-conceived strategy of the French nobles at Crecy, but when it was disregarded John became once more the true knight-errant, and giving the reins of his horse to two of his companions, and shouting the battle-cry of 'Prague,' he charged into the thick of the fray and, blind as he was, soon went down fighting (August 26, 1346). His son Charles was also wounded in the battle and only escaped with difficulty. King Edward did all honour to the dead king, placed his body in his own tent, and then sent it to Germany for burial. It was on this memorable occasion that the Black Prince assumed the crest and insignia of his fallen enemy ; and the three ostrich feathers and the motto *Ich Dien* may be regarded as the first direct link between England and Bohemia.

Thus within the space of a few weeks Charles acquired two of the chief Crowns of Europe ; though still barely thirty, he was already ripened by years of experience and responsibility.

Charles and the Church

It is natural enough that Charles's dual tenure of the German and Bohemian Crowns should have given rise to much misapprehension, and in particular should have earned him the repute of neglecting the one at the expense of the other. This attitude was picturesquely expressed by one of his most versatile successors, Maximilian I, who said that though he was the father of Bohemia, he was 'the arch-stepfather' of the Reich ; and as the first half of the phrase stood beyond all challenge, the second and far more questionable also crept into common usage. Outside Bohemia few were concerned to defend one whose Slav proclivities and known devotion to the Church rendered him doubly suspect ; and it is only in quite modern times that historians have done him tardy justice and dispelled the foolish legend of 'the Parson's Emperor' (*Pfaffenkaiser*). It is perfectly true that, unlike his Bavarian predecessor, he steadily cultivated friendship with the Holy See ; this rested partly on policy, but also on strong religious conviction. He may have been superstitious, as the importance he attached to dreams suggests, and he certainly was an inveterate collector of every imaginable relic; but he was also able to expound the Gospels and to hold his own in theological disputations. He was never a bigot, and showed a critical tolerance towards honest differences of opinion such as was most unusual in that age. Thus, though he frowned upon the anti-clerical tendencies which Louis had furthered, and showed no sympathy for such popular religious currents as those of Tauler and the German mystics, he gave his protection to some of the earlier Czech reformers in their attacks upon corruption in the Church. He had already had his fill of warlike adventures, and took to heart the warnings of his father's career ; henceforward he showed a marked preference for diplomacy and alliances rather than war.

[1] The other two were the two Wittelsbach, Louis and the Count Palatine.

The University of Prague

His leaning towards the Church had both a legal and cultural background. Ever since he first came to Bohemia he had aimed at the improvement of the barbarous laws still prevalent ; and soon after his accession, with the aid of the new Archbishop of Prague, he procured the abolition of the ordeal by fire or by branding. His attempt to establish a new legal code, known as the *Maiestas Carolina*, was resisted by the Bohemian Estates as unduly favourable to the royal power, and eventually withdrawn by him as unworkable. But his efforts in the sphere of education were more successful, and indeed epoch-making ; and his genuine zeal is shown by the fact that the main decisions were taken at the very beginning of his reign. A recent writer is quite right in claiming him as 'a pupil of Dominican scholasticism.'[1] Already in June, 1347, he obtained from the Pope a Bull permitting the erection of a high school, or *Studium Generale*, at Prague ; and on April 7, 1348, he signed the charter of a university enjoying all the rights and liberties of its Parisian model. It was divided into the usual four faculties of theology, law, medicine and arts, but also for administrative and voting purposes into four nations—the Bohemian (including, of course, Moravia, but also Hungary and the South Slav countries), the Polish (including Silesia, Lithuania and Russia), the Bavarian (for Southern Germany and the Rhine), and the Saxon (for Thuringia and North Germany, together with Scandinavia.) It was not until a whole generation had passed that the full effect of this peculiar constitution was to become apparent ; but it is obvious that from the very outset the native Bohemians found themselves in a minority and could be invariably outvoted by the foreign elements.

The University of Prague, as the first foundation of its kind in Central Europe, at once sprang to fame, and for over half a century was a worthy rival of the three great seats of medieval learning, Bologna, Paris and Oxford. The original aim had been to enable natives of Bohemia to study without undertaking distant journeys, and most of its first teachers were Czechs. But as a contemporary writer points out, 'the University became so great that nothing equal to it existed in Germany, and students came there from all parts of the world—from England, France, Lombardy and Poland and all surrounding countries—sons of nobles and princes and prelates of the Church.' Fresh teachers of standing were summoned from outside, and first the Carolinum, then a series of other colleges, were founded by Charles and his son Wenceslas IV, while the great Orders—the Dominicans, enjoying Charles's especial favour, the Cistercians and the Minorites—formed similar centres of teaching in Prague. In 1373, as the result of learned disputes, the jurists were allowed to set up what was in effect a separate university, with statutes modelled on those of Bologna.

The wandering students of the Middle Ages were a *mixtum compositum*, some penurious and erudite, others dissolute and obstreperous, and the New Town of Prague, now rising between the river and the Castle Hill, contained both elements. They were of every class and age, the younger often serving as famuli of the more wealthy, eking out a livelihood by singing and the collection of arms, and being subject to the strenuous discipline of the rod. Brawls between students and townsmen led to

[1] Jarrett, *The Emperor Charles IV*, p. 170.

constant disputes of jurisdiction between the University and the municipal authorities. Some idea of Prague's importance as an intellectual centre may be gathered from the bare register of the jurists, which in the first thirty-six years of its separate existence enrolled a bishop, an abbot, 36 deans and provosts, 209 canons, 187 parish priests and 103 clergy of inferior rank.

Charles as Builder

While, then, men of learning flocked from all parts of Europe, Charles sought to make of Prague an artistic centre also, and developed ambitious architectural plans. When he began to restore the ruined Hrad or castle, perched steeply above the Vltava, he appears to have had before him the model of the Louvre ; but later additions of the sixteenth and seventeenth centuries have changed his plan out of all recognition. On the other hand, the Cathedral of St. Vitus, as at last completed in our own day, owes its main conception to him and to the foreign builders whom he invited to his court—first of all Master Matthew of Arras, whom Pope Clement had recommended to him at Avignon in 1344, and after his death in 1352 a young Swabian named Peter Parler, noted not only as an architect, but for his wood-carving, sculpture and metal work. As a specimen of late and somewhat ornate Gothic, St. Vitus, with its tall spire and buttressed choir, is in its own way unique in Central Europe. The two men also worked successively on the 'Charles Bridge,' linking the old town with the so-called 'Malá Strana' (or Small Side) ; and after nearly six centuries it still gives a distinctive character to the Czech capital, and is the most famous stone bridge surviving from medieval times. We may fairly quote the words of Scaliger :

> *Omnia turrigeræ concedant oppida Pragæ.*
> *Natura hic posuit quidquid in orbe fuit.*

Two other notable buildings date from Charles's reign—the strongly fortified Castle of Karlstein, twenty miles to the west of Prague, where he deposited the regalia and the archives, and whose decoration he entrusted to foreign artists ; and the Benedictine Monastery of Emmäus, on the outskirts of Prague itself. This last has an interest all its own, for it was established according to the Slavonic rite, with the deliberate object of strengthening ecclesiastical ties with the Eastern Church. Croat monks were brought to it from Croatia, Bosnia and Dalmatia, and Charles was in correspondence with the Serbian Tsar, Stephen Dushan. He was, moreover, devoted to the memory and traditions of Slavonic Saints, notably of the Apostles Cyril and Methodius, and of his own ancestors Wenceslas and Ludmila.

Charles and Foreign Policy

In foreign policy Charles was a realist, never allowing romantic hopes to obscure the hard facts of the situation. Maximilian's famous phrase, already quoted, rests on a misconception : for in fortifying his position in Bohemia he was merely following the precedent set up by other dynasties. Long before his day it must have been apparent to all thoughtful men that for the holder of the German Crown the only hope lay in building upon a territorial and family basis, and thus acquiring an instrument by which to win hereditary power in the Empire. That this aim was eventually realized by the Habsburgs was due very largely to the accidents of personality ; for if Charles's sons had been more apt for government or had in their turn left behind them sons of Charles's calibre, it is quite possible that Luxemburg would have succeeded in establishing a powerful national kingdom in Central Europe. On the other hand, it may of course be argued that the latent conflict of Slav and German, to which the events of the Hussite period were to give such devastating force, would in any case have prevented such a development.

Charles's attitude to England is a good illustration of his realism. Despite the memories of Crecy he expressed his readiness to support Edward III against all comers, save only in his designs for the destruction of the French throne, to which he himself was so closely allied ; and on these terms he would have liked to contract an English marriage. His approach to the chief reigning houses of the Empire was somewhat similar. He married two of his daughters to Rudolf IV and Albert III of Austria, thereby as it were immunizing the Habsburgs. But his own marriages were also made instruments of policy. Within a year of the death of his first wife, Blanche of Valois, he had married a daughter of the Count Palatine Rudolf, and thus at once won over his most dangerous opponent among the Electors and separated the two branches of the House of Wittelsbach. His hope of thus acquiring some territorial extension was disappointed ; for Anna did not bring him an heir, and indeed died childless before her father in 1353. His third venture was more successful ; for Anna of Schweidnitz not only bore him a son, but as heiress of her uncle linked up with the Bohemian Crown the last of the independent duchies of Silesia.

Closely linked up with this was Charles's policy of expansion northwards. Upper Lusatia (the Mark of Budissin or Bautzen) was acquired in 1355 ; and in 1368 Lower Lusatia also fell in, after having been pawned by the Elector of Brandenburg to his neighbour of Meissen, then redeemed by Charles and left in the temporary possession of his father-in-law Bolko of Schweidnitz. But Charles was after bigger game, and after a series of skilful moves upon the chess-board detached the Mark of Brandenburg from the Wittelsbach family and secured it for his own. In the long process he had married one of his daughters to Margrave Otto, but then contrived at one and the same time to set him at variance with his cousins of Lower Bavaria and to leave him isolated and without allies in Northern Germany. In 1373 Otto definitely renounced the electoral dignity in return for a large cash indemnity, while Lower Bavaria was bought off with some border territory and the hand of yet another daughter in marriage.[1]

Without reading into Charles's motives a modern racial policy entirely alien to his age, it is quite clear that his attempts at expansion were directed towards the wide debatable land that then still existed between the German and Slav. For some two centuries a process of Germanization had been in full swing in the countries lying east of the Elbe ; it had, of course, gone farthest in Brandenburg and Meissen, but the Silesian duchies were already more and more affected, and it was Lusatia—the link between Brandenburg and Silesia—which resisted longest and indeed remains Slav in patches even to the present day. Ardent champions

[1] When the old Ascanian dynasty of Brandenburg died out in 1323, Emperor Louis of Bavaria granted it to his eldest son Louis, from whom it passed to two younger brothers, Louis the Roman and Otto.

of the extreme German or Czech thesis have tried to claim Charles wholly for their theories ; but it would seem more probable that he sought to build deliberately upon a dual basis. In his day it was still quite possible to find a higher Bohemian unity transcending the feud of Czech and German ; the fatal cleavage was first wrought by the prolonged religious conflict of the coming century.

In two other directions Charles pursued an ambitious dynastic policy. He concluded with the Habsburgs one of those mutual pacts of inheritance so frequent in German history ; and by an irony of fate it was a Habsburg prince who eventually became heir to the House of Luxemburg and applied its matrimonial methods with even greater success. Meanwhile the fact that Louis the Great of Hungary was without male heirs led Charles to entertain hopes of a fresh dynastic union such as had followed the extinction of the Árpád and Přemyslide families. In 1365, then, Charles's heir Wenceslas, then only a boy of four, was betrothed to Louis' niece ; but when the King remarried and had two daughters, the original project was abandoned, and for it was substituted in 1374 the betrothal of Louis' elder child and Sigismund, Charles's son by his fourth wife.

All these complicated schemes clearly illustrate the importance attaching to dynastic policy in the fourteenth century, and the extent to which it formed the basis of all territorial aggrandizement. It is strange to see a sovereign who had built up the structure with such persevering sagacity, endanger its results by the action of his later years. Not without many difficulties and the expenditure of judicious bribes, he secured the election of his son Wenceslas as King of the Romans (June 10, 1376) ; but he now committed the blunder of dividing up his patrimony, making Sigismund Elector of Brandenburg and his youngest son John Duke of Görlitz in Lusatia (with the addition of the Neumark), while his own brother John Henry, who predeceased the Emperor by three years, also divided his own Mark of Moravia between three sons, Jost, Soběslav and Prokop. Family dissensions were thus rendered chronic in the House of Luxemburg.

The Empire and Reform

With Charles's Imperial policy we are not directly concerned. It must suffice to point out that it was by no means the feeble and feckless thing imagined by early historians, but rested upon a clear comprehension of changing values. He was fully conscious that nothing could bring back the days of the Hohenstauffen, and that the German Crown lacked the financial resources and the administrative machinery by which alone it could impose its full authority. He therefore, as it were, fell back upon a second line of defence, and sought to give the Empire a constitution such as would arrest disintegration, make disputed elections henceforth impossible, and ensure a minimum of internal order. The Golden Bull of 1356 was doubtless an abandonment of prerogatives once enjoyed, but it was also a concentration of all that it was still possible to save. To say that 'he legalized anarchy and called it a constitution'[1] is a highly misleading epigram ; in actual fact he stabilized the German constitution for over four centuries. But it is, of course, true that this involved a strengthening of the princely power, a blow to the prospects of popular liberty, and in particular an act of hostility to the towns and such organiza-

[1] James Bryce, *Holy Roman Empire*, p. 246.

tions as the Swabian League. At the same time it regulated the status of the seven Electors, assured to them all the privileges hitherto reserved to the Emperor, and insisted upon primogeniture and indivisibility of territory in the case of the four lay Electors. The position of the three great Rhenish Archbishoprics had never been in dispute; Charles was eager and able to define that of his native kingdom of Bohemia. It remained ostensibly to assign lay Electorates to the four great German nations—Franconian, Swabian, Saxon and Bavarian; but here Charles's personal motives turned the scale. Of the three main possessions of the powerful House of Wittelsbach the Palatinate was definitely associated with the electoral dignity; Bavaria was as definitely excluded, while, as we saw, Luxemburg contrived to supplant Wittelsbach in the Mark of Brandenburg. Austria was no less deliberately excluded, to the great anger of her Dukes, though she came in time to enjoy a special position of her own and indeed ended by almost monopolizing the Imperial dignity. It is also important to bear in mind that nowhere in the Golden Bull is there any acknowledgment of the Papal claim to confirm elections, much less to administer the Empire during a vacancy; it is, of course, also true that it is not challenged in so many words. It may reasonably be claimed that Charles had laid foundations upon which worthy successors, following in his tradition, could have re-established the royal power in Germany; but his son Wenceslas was the most incompetent and negative of all the Emperors, Sigismund was really more concerned with Hungary and Bohemia, Albert lived but two years and Frederick was futile and powerless.

Charles and Italy

In yet another respect Charles showed a wise realism, and those who criticize him stand self-condemned. With the example of his grandfather and so many others before him, he steadily refused to be drawn into Italian adventure on a grand scale. In 1354–1355 he visited Milan and was peacefully crowned in Rome, fulfilling to the letter his pledge not to linger in the Imperial city; yet even with all his restraint and caution he became involved in faction fighting at Pisa, and with his wife barely escaped from a burning house. His second visit, in 1368, was closely connected with his constant efforts to bring back the Papacy from exile, and thus free it from a dependence upon France which was disturbing even to the Francophile Charles. On this occasion his readiness to be bought off by one commune after another did not increase his reputation, and at Siena he was besieged by the mob and had to fly with ignominy. As Matteo Villani contemptuously records, Charles's progress was not that of an emperor, but of a merchant journeying to a fair.

His sober outlook upon things Italian is revealed in his relations with Rienzi. When that strange Tribune of the People, after bathing in the basin of Constantine, cited the rival Emperors-elect before himself and the Papal delegate (1347), Charles was still deeply absorbed in consolidating his position at home and naturally remained entirely unmoved. In 1350 the fallen Rienzi found his way in disguise to Prague and in vague ecstatic language preached the Ghibelline doctrine and high Italian adventure to the grandson of Henry VII. Pope, Emperor and Tribune were then to represent the Trinity upon earth; the clergy would be stripped of their inordinate wealth, the Church would be reformed, and an Universal

Temple of the Holy Ghost would be constructed. Charles was shocked at Rienzi's questionable views, but showed a certain respect and admiration for the friend of Petrarch, the greatest humanist of the age. For a whole year the Tribune was confined at the Castle of Roudnice, on the Elbe, and was only surrendered to the Pope when Archbishop Ernest publicly condemned his utterances as heretical (1352). Charles presumably used his influence at Avignon in favour of clemency ; but he himself remained unmoved by Rienzi's oratory, and also by the shrill summons of Petrarch to the 'God-sent saviour and liberator,' to whom all Italy looked, 'that thy glance may shine on us as a star.' In 1356 Petrarch visited Prague, and was loaded with favours and attentions ; but his political views were politely ignored.

CHAPTER III

THE AGE OF JOHN HUS

Woe on me, if I were silent ! It is better for me to die than not to oppose such wickedness.

—John Hus.

If this man was not a noble, strong and dauntless martyr and confessor of Christ, then will it be hard indeed for anyone to obtain salvation.

—Martin Luther.

Ferment in the Bohemian Church

IT remains to consider Charles's attitude to those new currents of opinion that were so soon to transform the Bohemian situation. For over a century the Church had been growing rapidly in wealth and power, and its separation from the jurisdiction of Mainz hastened the process still further. Despite the high character and reforming zeal of Archbishop Ernest, corruption spread through the Bohemian clergy ; on the one hand there was simony and the traffic in benefices, from which the Curia derived its own financial profit, on the other concubinage and all the grosser forms of immorality. Under Charles St. Vitus was served by no fewer than 300 clergy, so that the Hrad, of which it was the central point, came to be described as *mons clericorum*.

The statutes of Archbishop Ernest show clearly by their prohibitions what was the common practice of the day—the frequenting of taverns and wearing of lay dress and weapons by priests, their refusal to marry, bury, confess or administer the sacraments save in return for money payments, and much else beside. An archidiaconal inspection of the year 1380 revealed that of the thirty-two parish priests of Prague itself, sixteen were living in open scandal ; while charges of theft and even highway robbery against the lower clergy were far from uncommon ; the canons and prebendaries openly defied the rulings of the hierarchy.

The combined efforts of Charles and Ernest failed to repress these tendencies, but they showed their goodwill by encouraging certain popular preachers of the day who represented the first stirrings of conscience among the masses. Conrad Waldhauser, a German Augustinian, who had for years been Court preacher in Vienna, came to Prague at Charles's instance and soon caused a great sensation by his attacks upon luxury and evil living. His main stress was laid upon the morality of the rising generation : to be a good teacher, he argued, one must first of all be a good man. He thus became involved in fierce controversy with the Mendicant Orders, which, at any rate in Bohemia, had lost all trace of their pristine love of poverty and had for that and other reasons become the foremost opponents of Church reform. Their attempts to convict him of heresy entirely failed, and Conrad remained undisturbed as Rector of the famous Týn Church ; but neither Emperor nor Archbishop could help him to prevail against the Orders, which of course held direct from the Holy See itself, and his dispute with them, to promote which he made the journey to Rome, was still pending at his death in 1369.

33

He first stirred the waters, but there is nothing to show that he achieved any kind of reform.

Still more remarkable was the young Moravian priest, Jan Milič[1] of Kroměříž (Kremsier), whose ascetic life, devotion to the Scriptures and fiery eloquence drew crowds to hear him. His was the life of the true medieval mystic; his *Treatise on Antichrist* was the outcome at once of self-imposed privations and of the plagues and omens of his time, which seemed to him to portend judgment upon a corrupt world. Once when preaching before the Emperor he had even gone so far as to point at him as Antichrist; and no more signal proof of Charles's tolerance can be found than the fact that the culprit escaped with a short term of imprisonment, and was absolved from all charges of heresy. But the fear of Antichrist had burned itself upon his brain, and drove him to Rome at the time of Urban V's impending return from exile; imprisoned by the Inquisition, he appealed to the Pope 'to bring back the Church to the state of salvation,' and was able to convince Urban of his essential orthodoxy. After his return to Prague he dwelt less upon public affairs and devoted himself to a life of self-denial and good works. Succeeding Conrad Waldhauser as rector of the Týn, he gathered a band of social workers round him, organized the rescue of fallen women amid the marked disapproval of both the parish clergy and the mendicant friars, and in 1372 opened a sort of hostel bearing the name of Jerusalem. Towards the end of his life charges of heresy were trumped up against him, but after a searching enquiry in the Archbishop's court he was allowed to proceed to Avignon, where he triumphantly vindicated himself, preached before the assembled cardinals, but then contracted a fatal illness and never returned to his native Bohemia. His 'Jerusalem' foundation died with him, but its memory was treasured in Prague and it was soon revived in a new and more memorable form. It is necessary to emphasize that both Waldhauser and Milič found their real support among the masses, alike German and Czech, who were increasingly alienated from the corrupt and worldly Church of their day, but responded to true apostolic teaching. To Milič, with his belief in the impending Judgment, the main end of life was to achieve oneness with Christ: as the raindrops in the river, so must the faithful become one with God.

It is sometimes argued that the tradition of a married clergy had never died out among the Czechs, and that the imposition of celibacy was therefore still more difficult than in other countries of the West. But this theory—and it is little more—probably belongs to the same category as the legend that Hussitism derives from the Orthodox Church of Russia, and is essentially Slav in its origin. Clerical immorality in Bohemia, as in other countries of the West, is sufficiently accounted for by the excessive and all too rapid accumulation of wealth, and especially landed wealth, in the hands of the clergy—coinciding as this did with a general growth of material prosperity since the political consolidation of the early thirteenth century. If Hus and his successors were especially attracted by Wyclif's doctrine that the clergy should not have worldly possessions,[2] and pushed it to exaggerated lengths, they were but following the path along which bitter experience in their native Bohemia seemed to point.

---

[1] Translated by his contemporaries as 'carissimus.'

[2] Article X of the Wyclifian tenets condemned at London in 1380 runs: *'contra sacram scripturam est, quod viri ecclesiastici habeant possessiones temporales.'*

The reign of Charles IV has been rightly called the Golden Age of Bohemia ; for under him it enjoyed a hitherto unexampled peace and prosperity, and the deep cleavage of social, religious and political life still lay in the future. Charles himself lacked the robust physique and assertive personality of certain of the Hohenstauffen or Habsburg rulers, but in patient statecraft and planned diplomacy he had few equals, while he showed a versatility then rare upon a throne by holding his own with experts upon many subjects. A modern apologist has, by no means unfairly, described him as 'the most patent example of the new type of ruler' ; his affinities were not with his own father or with Edward III, but far rather with such practical sovereigns as Henry of Lancaster or Charles V of France.

Wenceslas IV

Charles's death coincided fairly closely with other momentous changes in Europe. A year earlier a boy of twelve had replaced the victor of Creçy and Poitiers on the English throne ; in 1380 the statesmanlike Charles V of France was followed by a weak king who suffered from periodic fits of madness ; in 1382 the death of Louis the Great separated the crowns of Hungary and Poland, and plunged the former kingdom into a long period of anarchy. The lack of outstanding rulers during the last two decades of the fourteenth century undoubtedly contributed to the deadlock in public affairs, and above all to the prolonged schism in the Church, which broke out only a few months before Charles's death. He had repeatedly used all his influence to induce the Pope to return to Rome ; for, Francophil as he was, he did not wish to see the Holy See become a mere dependency of the French Crown. He had paid a second visit to Rome in 1368 with the special purpose of welcoming back Urban V, and was deeply chagrined when the latter decided to return to Avignon ; and he had encouraged Gregory XI in his turn to put an end to the 'Captivity.' He now gave emphatic support to Urban VI ; and it is quite possible that if he had lived his prestige might have outweighed the brutal tactlessness of the Neapolitan Pope and prevented the dissensions between the two rival groups of cardinals from widening into an almost irreparable breach.

Wencelas IV, who was now both German King and King of Bohemia, offered a lamentable contrast to his father. Headstrong yet irresolute, impulsive and indolent by turns, he utterly lacked the stability of character demanded by so grave a situation. He was far from being the drunken and sadistic tyrant depicted by certain chroniclers of his own era and of the following century ; but there is no doubt that he indulged in heavy bouts of drinking, that the habit steadily grew upon him and sometimes vented itself in ferocious outbursts. The stories that he roasted an incompetent cook on his own spit, shot down a monk during one of his hunting *battues* and himself on occasion helped the executioner at his work, are almost certainly spiteful myths, as unreliable as the tale that he saw the words 'Wenzeslaus, alter Nero' scrawled upon a wall and himself added : '*Si non fui adhoc, ero.*' On the other hand, he disliked great parade, had a warm feeling for the common people, and was equally hostile to the land-hunger of the great barons and the luxury of the Church. That he surrounded himself with lowborn favourites only rendered him all the more suspect in high quarters.

In the first two years of his reign he tried to assert himself in German affairs and at the Imperial Diet pressed strongly for the recognition of Urban VI. But meeting with strong resistance—exemplified by the miniature schism that arose in the primatial see of Mainz—and doubtless influenced by the support given by his French kinsmen to the rival Pope in Avignon, Wenceslas gradually desisted from his efforts, and for ten whole years left the Reich unvisited, with the result that anarchy again raised its head, and in particular feuds between the princes and the towns were the order of the day. At the same time he more than once planned a coronation visit to Rome, but each time the uncertainty of the German situation seemed a reason for abandoning it, and he contented himself with nominating his cousin Jost of Moravia as his Vicar-General in Italy. Meanwhile he could point to two concrete achievements in the sphere of foreign policy. In 1381 his sister Anne was married to Richard II of England, thereby putting the relations of the two countries on a new footing and preparing the way for an ever memorable intercourse in the intellectual sphere. In the meantime the king's brother Sigismund had been betrothed to Maria, heiress to the Hungarian throne, and in 1384 started out upon his long and stormy wooing. A strong party opposed his marriage and welcomed as king Maria's cousin Charles III of Naples. Sigismund was driven across the Moravian frontier ; the young queen and her scheming and imperious mother Elizabeth were forced to attend the coronation of Charles, and avenged themselves by the treacherous murder of their rival in the Castle of Buda. The Neapolitan party retorted by imprisoning the two queens at Novigrad in Croatia and putting Elizabeth to death ; and it was only with the help of Wenceslas's army that Sigismund could at last rescue his wife and assert their joint authority. Incidentally, this involved the cession of the Mark of Brandenburg to his cousin Jost of Moravia, who was certainly the best of the Luxemburgs of that generation. A still more momentous result of this prolonged Hungarian anarchy was that the Polish nobility, already restive in the last years of Louis the Great, broke away from union with Hungary and substituted the more natural union with Lithuania, by arranging the marriage of Hedwig, Maria's much abler sister, with the hitherto heathen Grand Duke Wladislaw Jagiello. Thus failed yet another attempt to attract Poland within the Danubian orbit and away from its proper sphere on the Vistula and the Njemen. As for Sigismund, he was left with more than his fill of problems inside his new kingdom and along its southern borders, where a new and expansive force, the Ottoman Turks, was also threatening the very existence of the Serbian, Bulgarian and Wallachian states.

At home in Bohemia Wenceslas's authority steadily weakened, but it was probably no accident that his first violent collision was with the hierarchy. The Archbishop of Prague, John of Jenstein, was a man of arrogant and unbalanced character, who after a lax and frivolous youth had plunged into the opposite extreme of rigorous asceticism. There had already been friction owing to the protection accorded by the Archbishop to university students who had incurred the royal displeasure. But in 1393 an acute quarrel broke out between King and prelate, over the former's desire to create a new episcopal see, the endowment for which was to be found in the revenues of the monastery of Kladruby, whose abbot had just died. But Archbishop John, though fully aware of the royal plans, encouraged the monks to elect a new head, and instructed his Vicar-General, John of Pomuk, to confirm the election. Wenceslas fell into one of his ungovernable rages, ordered the arrest of the Archbishop, the Vicar-General, and some other high clerics, and put the latter to the torture—it is sometimes alleged, with his own hand. In the end John of Jenstein was released, but the others were sentenced to death by drowning, and only reprieved on giving written pledges of secrecy as to their treatment. The unfortunate John of Pomuk, however, was so broken down by his tortures that he could not sign the necessary document; and he was then dragged down to the famous Charles Bridge, bound hand and foot, and ruthlessly flung into the Vltava (March 20, 1393). Three centuries later, under the name of St. John Nepomuk, this cruelly wronged, but quite insignificant, prelate was to be made the object of a zealous cult by the Jesuits, and to serve with the masses as a counter-attraction to the heretic Hus. At the time the incident had no significance, save as showing the brutal folly of the King and the tactlessness of the Archbishop, who found it impossible to remain in Bohemia and carried his grievances to the Papal Court. But the weak Boniface IX was still too dependent upon the support of the Reich to risk a quarrel with Wenceslas: and John of Jenstein found it expedient to resign office in 1395 and to remain in Rome, where he died five years later.

How far this incident roused the nobility to action is not altogether clear. But within a year Wenceslas was faced by a formidable league of the great lords under Henry of Rosenberg, who were openly supported by Jost of Moravia, King Sigismund, and finally Duke Albert of Austria. Their demands were a curious blend of personal and national interests— on the one hand the dismissal of upstart counsellors such as the hated Huler and Pflug von Rabstein, on the other the journey for the Imperial Crown, the restoration of Church unity, the reform of the Court and the administration, of course in an oligarchic sense. For some months Wenceslas was the prisoner of his barons, until a royal party slowly formed itself round his youngest brother, Duke John of Görlitz (Zhořelec), and secured his release. Soon there were fresh discords and fresh demands, and Duke John died suddenly at the age of twenty-six (March, 1396), just as he seemed to be acquiring a real position as mediator, such as caused Sigismund and Jost no little anxiety. Sigismund stepped into John's place, and might well have asserted himself as effective Regent of Bohemia; but, as ever throughout his long reign, he allowed himself to be diverted by other still more pressing issues. Never was there a sovereign who so well illustrated the motto: *Qui trop embrasse, mal étreint*; and this was aggravated by his two outstanding qualities, the true spendthrift's inability to husband his resources or plan ahead, and a profligacy which neither honour, shame nor policy could restrain. In 1395 death removed the unfortunate Maria, after a long series of incredible adventures; she had seen her cousin treacherously murdered, her mother flung from the battlements, her life had been in constant danger, and she had even thought it necessary to connive at a conspiracy for the murder of her husband in the royal bedchamber, in order the more effectually to warn him and secure the punishment of the plotters. That Sigismund was now able to hold the Hungarian Crown in his own right and to dissuade his sister-in-law, Hedwig of Poland, from pushing a rival claim, was probably due in the main to the gathering of the Turkish danger and to Sigismund's success in recruiting help from Western Europe. Thus in the summer of 1396 he advanced into Bulgaria, with the flower of French and Burgundian chivalry in his army, deaf to all strategic con-

siderations and arrogantly expecting to drive the Turks into the sea.
The battle of Nicopolis, which ended in a crushing victory for the Janis-
saries, was decisive in many directions · it brought Bulgaria to final
subjection, destroyed all hope of Serbia recovering from the disintegration
ushered in at Kosovo seven years earlier, and firmly entrenched the
Turks along the Danube river front. Henceforward the Roumanian
Principalities and Hungary were permanently menaced.

For Sigismund, and for the House of Luxemburg, this reverse was
scarcely less decisive. Sultan Bayezid's defeat might well have been
followed by the expulsion of the Turks from Europe and the revival of
Byzantium ; and it would certainly have increased Hungary's prestige
and power as against Serbia, Bosnia and Wallachia. As it was, he returned
as a fugitive, and so far from dictating Bohemian policy to his feckless
brother, had his own hands full for some years in Hungary and Croatia,
and perforce left events to take their course in Prague and in the
Reich.

During this period friction between Wenceslas and his subjects grew
even more acute and culminated in the murder of three of his chief
favourites at Karlstein by order of the barons—an insult which he seemed
powerless to avenge. Meanwhile the discontent was steadily ripening in
Germany against his absentee rule. After ten whole years he attended
an Imperial Diet and then visited his cousin Charles VI at Rheims, to
discuss a settlement of the Papal Schism. But nothing practical came of
this, and the German Princes were finally roused to a long premeditated
action by Wenceslas's grant of the Dukedom of Milan to that sinister
but supremely able adventurer, Galeazzo Visconti. In February, 1400,
the Electors openly proclaimed their intention of deposing Wenceslas as
'a useless, dilatory, ill-esteemed dissolver and unworthy disposer of the
Holy Roman Empire,' and this revolutionary step they justified by a long
list of personal misdeeds. Wenceslas not unnaturally ignored their
summons to appear before them, but after the first burst of rage remained
entirely inactive, with the result that on August 21 the Electors carried
out their threat, and elected in his place the only layman amongst them,
the Rhenish Count Palatine Rupert. It is easy for modern historians to
say that Wenceslas had justified this by his exclusive devotion to dynastic,
as opposed to national, interests, but in this he only differed in degree
from all his immediate predecessors and successors. His real fault was
gross incompetence. The Electors on their side bound the new king to
abolish all dues and customs set up by Wenceslas, but to leave their own
untouched. Rupert also stood pledged to reconquer Lombardy from the
Visconti and to end the Schism. But with all his energy and goodwill he
lacked the resources for either. He had to abandon his attack upon
Bohemia ; in 1401 he was decisively defeated outside Brescia and driven
across the Alps ; he could effect nothing whatsoever in the matter of
the Schism, while inside Germany his authority was persistently defied,
until in 1406 he had to recognize the right of the Estates to form unions
and confederacies without the royal permission. Wenceslas had lost all
control over German affairs, but his successor was no less impotent, and
the anarchy was for a time complete.

In Bohemia the years following Rupert's bid for power were full of
barren and kaleidoscopic disputes between Wenceslas and Sigismund,
with their cousins Jost and Prokop each playing a lone hand. At first
Sigismund set an exorbitant price upon his help—Silesia and Lusatia in

pledge, unconditional succession to the Bohemian Crown and meanwhile the Regency—and on Wenceslas's refusal, led his troops back to Hungary. But by degrees Wenceslas, realizing his impotence in Germany, accorded to Sigismund the Regency, both there and in Bohemia ; Wenceslas was at last to be crowned Emperor, Rupert overthrown and Sigismund elected to the Crown of the Romans, and thus in the end to step into his brother's shoes. Sigismund's idea of loyalty was to place Wenceslas under restraint and even to send him for safer keeping to a castle of the Duke of Austria, and then to conclude a family pact with Albert IV and to solve his own perennial shortage of money by selling the Neumark of Brandenburg to the Teutonic Order for hard cash. In 1403 Wenceslas escaped from his prison and issued a flaming indictment against his treacherous brother. For some years to come there were sporadic hostilities between them ; and Wenceslas owed his relative success on the one hand to a working alliance with Jost and Prokop, but still more to Sigismund's absorption in the internal affairs of Hungary, hostilities with Naples, Venice, Bosnia and the Turks, and busy intervention between Poland and the Teutonic Order. It was not until 1409 that anything like reconciliation between the brothers was effected, and this owing to the vital need of co-operation in the all-important question of the Schism, and to the conviction spreading in Germany that Rupert was as impossible as Wenceslas, and that Sigismund, despite his many faults, was the only serious candidate for the Crown.

Towards the end of his reign Rupert was in an impossible position in Church affairs. His one hope was an alliance with Gregory XII, but of course he was thereby openly promoting the Schism, and this turned public opinion increasingly against him and helped Wenceslas, who sided with the reforming cardinals. The Council of Pisa, meeting in the summer of 1409, solemnly deposed both the rival popes, and elected to their place the noted Greek humanist, Peter Filargi, as Alexander V. Incidentally, it recognized Wenceslas as lawful King of the Romans, and Rupert, after a strong protest, was making armed preparations, when he suddenly died in May, 1410. Acute dissensions broke out among the Electors, only one of them admitting Wenceslas's view that no fresh election was needed ; and so, while the Archbishop of Trier and the Count Palatine, with Sigismund's Brandenburg proxy, proceeded to elect the King of Hungary, the other Electors, with proxies of Saxony and Bohemia, elected the Margrave Jost (September 20—October 1, 1410). Thus to the scandal of three popes contending for the voice of Christendom there was added the scarcely less crying scandal of three rival kings of the Romans, all members of the House of Luxemburg. It is true that already in 1411 Jost died at Brno, his margravate reverting automatically to the Bohemian Crown ; and that in the following summer there was a reconciliation of Wenceslas and Sigismund, resulting in the latter's election at Frankfurt by a majority of the Electors (July 21, 1411). It is typical of the ceaseless distractions of his eastern policy—which aroused much discontent in the Reich—that three years and a half elapsed before he could present himself for coronation at Aachen. That he abandoned his one-time intention of renouncing the Crown and concentrating upon Hungary was above all due to the urgent advice of his chief counsellor, Frederick of Nürnberg, whom in 1411 he rewarded by the cession of Brandenburg.

The Forerunners : Thomas of Štitný and Adalbert Ranků

The dreary misrule of Wenceslas and his prolonged family brawls form a necessary background for the great spiritual movement of which Bohemia was now to become the scene. The sympathetic response with which the teachings of Waldhauser and Milič were met was no mere isolated phenomenon : their vineyard was fruitful and found fresh labourers. But it is not without significance that Thomas of Štitný, Matthew of Janov and Adalbert Ranků all belonged to the lesser nobility, and wrote much more in Czech than in Latin—which accounts for their almost total neglect, or at best their very cursory treatment, by all historians up to, and even many since, the days of Palacký. One thing is common to all these 'forerunners'—as they fully deserve to be called, despite the sarcasm with which some writers use the word—and this is an intense devotion to the Scriptures and a zeal for primitive Christianity which leads naturally to a denunciation of worldliness in the Church of to-day and fears of the coming Antichrist. Štitný, it must be emphasized, was of a retiring and cautious character, and in his two major works, *Of General Christian Matters* (*O obečných věcech Kreštánských*) and *Learned Entertainments* (*Besední Reči*), stops far short of his more daring successors. He died in 1401, leaving an only daughter who, with several other pious Czech ladies, lived in community near the Bethlehem Chapel at Prague.

Of Master Adalbert Ranků (Adalbertus Ranconis de Ericinio) much less is known, despite his high academic distinction. He had been Rector of Paris University in 1355, and afterwards visited Oxford, where he entered into relations with FitzRalph, Archbishop of Armagh, the opponent of the Mendicant Orders. But from 1364, with but few interruptions, until his death in 1388, he was a Canon of St. Vitus' Cathedral, and as a man of combative nature and an ardent advocate of the Czech language became involved in many controversies with German scholars. His fame as a preacher led to his selection for the funeral oration upon the Emperor Charles ; and Loserth calls him, not without reason, 'the most learned Bohemian of his time.' Late in life he openly opposed the proposals of the Archbishop for an additional festival in honour of the Virgin, but on technical grounds rather than *in merito* ; and both in this and in the sacramental controversies of his day he took up an attitude of reserve which prevents us from ranking him decisively among the 'heretics.' But he gave free expression to a view held by Wyclif, and afterwards elaborated in Protestant theology—that in the days of Schism it was not to be believed that the Church had no Head, for it still had Christ. Ranků founded bursaries for poor students at Paris and Oxford, and if we but knew more of him, would undoubtedly rank as one of the first intellectual links between Bohemia and England.

Matthew of Janov

A very special interest attaches to Matthew of Janov, whom modern research has revealed as the true forerunner of Utraquist doctrine. After studying at Paris as a member of the English 'nation'—like all Bohemians —he became an honorary Canon at the Cathedral of Prague, then penitentiary to the Archbishop, and a popular preacher, in both Latin and

Czech, at the Church of St. Nicholas. In his sermons he attacked the
excessive veneration of pictures and statues, and also the intercession of
Saints, while on the other hand he laid great stress upon the practice of
daily communion. It is not surprising that though his devout way of
life contrasted markedly with that of many of his fellow-priests in Prague,
he was in 1389 summoned before the Archbishop and constrained to
retract these questionable views, but only, it would appear, reluctantly
and under secret protest. But he continued to teach on the old lines,
and his latest biographer and editor, Dr. Kybal, has shown that towards
the end of his life he was passing through a keen spiritual crisis. It was
perhaps well for him that he died in 1394, while the Archbishop was
absorbed in his open quarrel with the king. Matthew's tenets are contained in his *Regulæ Veteris et Novi Testamenti*, the work of a lifetime,
which exercised a deep influence upon the first generation of Hussites,
but remained unpublished until the twentieth century. In this book,
which really consists of a number of independent treatises, the main
themes are the means of defining true, as opposed to false, Christianity,
the depraved state of the Church and the imminent coming of Antichrist,
and also—with constant yet reverent insistence—the desirability of
frequent, if not even daily, communion for the laity, as the truest means
of achieving a mystical union between God and man. To him the Scriptures were 'the mother of love, of understanding, of fear and of holy
hope'; while every Christian who held this world in affection was 'a
member of the body of Antichrist.' Like so many of his contemporaries
he read in the Schism a sign that the Second Coming was near at hand,
and he turned from the corruption round him to the primitive Church,
to the Scriptures as a guide to true living, and to the 'simple in Christ' as
his hope for the future. More and more he preached in the vernacular,
and his sermons, though full of quotations, were less scholastic in tone
than was as yet customary. That Matthew ever advocated the granting
of the Cup to the laity would appear to have been definitely disproved,
and he cannot therefore be claimed as having anticipated the fundamental Hussite tenet. But Count Lützow and Dr. Kybal are obviously
right in pointing out 'how close is the connection between the principle
of the frequent communion of laymen, as maintained by Janov, and the
utraquism of the fifteenth century. Both claims were founded on a
democratic basis and were protests against the theory of the inferiority
of laymen which the priests—and often the most unworthy priests—
were maintaining in Bohemia at this period.' The contrast between their
own unregenerate times and the primitive age of the Church, as their
imagination pictured it, was a vital factor which we must bear constantly
in mind if we are to understand what now follows.

John Hus

With such examples before our eyes it is impossible to resist the conclusion that Bohemian soil was favourable to the growth of men of
saintly life and endeavour, to whom the reform of public and private
morals was a vital issue. But to none of them was vouchsafed that gift
of inspired leadership which John Hus possessed in so eminent a degree.
This man, who gave his name to a great religious movement and ushered
in a new era in European thought, was born of peasant parents in the
village of Husinec, close to the linguistic frontier between Czech and

German, about the year 1369. Controversialists have sometimes had
the temerity to treat his admitted poverty as a disproof of his learning,
though of course poverty was the glory of many medieval scholars, right
down to the days of Erasmus ; and it is quite true that Hus had not the
advantages of a Parisian education or of foreign travel, like his close
friend Jerome of Prague. That his learning was less profound and all-
embracing than that of Wyclif seems certain, but a poet does not cease
to be a poet if he does not attain to the rank of a Dante or a Shakespeare.
Hus passed Magister in 1396 at Prague, then at the height of its international repute ; two years later he became a regular lecturer, then dean
of the philosophic faculty, and in 1403 Rector. In 1402 he was appointed
preacher at the Bethlehem Chapel, the foundation of two pious Czech
citizens, Kreuz and Mülheim—definitely Czech despite their German
names—taking its name from the earlier chapel of Milič. The fame of
Hus's own teacher, John of Stěkna, had already gone before him, and
among his colleagues there were men like the restless and eloquent
Jerome, and Jakob of Stříbro, known as Jacobellus de Misa for his minute
stature, but afterwards a giant of the infant Utraquist Church. But
with Hus's appointment the Chapel at once became a centre of outspoken
thought and teaching, and ere long the focusing point of the reforming
party. Moreover, his position as the stern corrector of morals was greatly
strengthened by the fact that Queen Sophie made him her confessor and
never lost her confidence in him.

There is no manner of doubt that Hus during his earlier career was
in full accord with the prevalent theology of the day ; and there is an
apparently authentic story of his having spent his last penny upon the
purchase of an indulgence during the first public traffic in Prague in the
year 1393. The first sign of any clash with his ecclesiastical superiors
came in 1403, when a party at the University demanded the condemnation
of forty-five articles from the works of Wyclif, as heretical. The main
assault came from the German Masters, while the Czechs rallied round
Hus and his friends : thus early did the growing conflict of nationality
react upon the issues of Church Reform. Hus did not so much defend
the articles as contend that many of them were a gross and self-evident
distortion of what Wyclif had said ; and his trenchant comments culminated in the enquiry whether the forgery of opinions were not a still
worse crime than the adulteration of saffron dyes, for which some tradesmen of Prague had recently been burnt at the stake ! The strictly
orthodox party carried the day, and the teaching and distribution of the
forty-five articles were forbidden to all members of the University, under
pain of broken allegiance.

Hus and Wyclif

From that day to this a controversy has raged as to how the doctrines
of Wyclif first penetrated to Bohemia. One story widely believed during
the Hussite wars is that Hus and Jerome themselves brought them from
Oxford : but it is notorious that Hus never went there, and almost
certain that Jerome only went long after Wyclif's works were widely
known in Prague. The most plausible theory—which will, however,
always remain a theory for lack of positive proof—is that a close connection was established between the English and Bohemian courts by the
marriage of Anne with Richard II in 1382, and that members of her

suite[1] brought back news of the Lollard movement and copies of Wyclif's works. In reality it might easily have happened without this : for quite apart from direct contacts, both Prague and Oxford were then closely linked with Paris, where Wyclif's teachings were keenly debated, and where the Czechs were enrolled as members of the 'English' nation.[2]

That Wyclifite doctrine was the point of departure for the whole subsequent Hussite movement can hardly be contested, but unfortunately the facts have been greatly obscured by the racial and religious bias of modern controversialists. On the one hand, Hus, as the arch-heretic, has been credited with many doctrines which he never held, and notably on the subject of the Eucharist ; on the other hand, he has been contemptuously treated as the merest plagiarist of Wyclif, without original ideas of his own, or much claim to real culture. Dr. Loserth, in his latest volume upon *Hus and Wyclif*, has proved beyond all question that Hus, in writing his *De Ecclesia*, lifted whole passages from Wyclif's book of the same name, that the same is true of practically all his works, both in Latin and Czech (including that to which all modern Czech scholars attach special importance, *Super IV Sententiarum*), and that these transcriptions often embody extracts from the Fathers which Hus may, or may not, have known at first hand. Hus's attitude to Wyclif may, however, be best expressed in his own words, in a polemic with the Englishman Stokes, a fanatical enemy of Wyclif. 'I am drawn to Wyclif,' he says, 'by his reputation, not with the bad, but with the good, priests, and with the University of Oxford and generally among the people, though not among evil, rapacious, indulgent prelates and priests. I am drawn to him by his writings, by which he seeks to bring all men back to

[1] Her maid of honour, Anna (?) of Lancekrona, married Richard's favourite, De Vere, Duke of Ireland. Peter of Wartenberg, Bohemian envoy to England was the father of Zdislav, one of the foremost Hussites, while Vuk of Waldstein stood in cordial relations with Sir John Oldcastle, the Lollard chief. All this is purely circumstantial.

[2] It would seem that even at the time the manner in which Wyclif's teachings first reached Bohemia was uncertain ; for Abbot Ludolf, in his *Tractatus de longevo schismate*, writes of Wyclif's '*mendosa volumina cum ad Bohemiam* nescio quo portante *pervenerunt*' (Loserth, *Beiträge*, iii, p. 84). In 1411, however, in his controversy with the Englishman Stokes, Hus speaks of having 'possessed and read those works for twenty years now and more' (Loserth, *Hus and Wyclif* : Workman, *Wyclif*, i, p. 17). It is known that one Paul Slavikovič, B.A., of Prague, in 1395, himself possessed fifteen works of Wyclif. It can be no accident that most of the available MSS. of Wyclif should have been found in Prague and Vienna, and should have proved to be, as a rule, the work of Czech scribes, 'oftentimes copying from a Czech rather than an English source' (*De off. Reg.*, Wyclif Society, p. xxix : Workman, *Wyclif*, i, p. 16). One of the earliest of Hus's own works is a Czech translation of Wyclif's *Trialogus* (Lützow, *Jan Hus*, p. 79). Jerome of Prague is known to have copied with his own hand both the *Dialogus* and *Trialogus*. Finally Professor Loserth, that most valiant pioneer of Wyclifite lore, points to MS. 1294 in the Hofbibliothek of Vienna (comprising the *De Ecclesia* and two other works of Wyclif) as bearing the inscription of having been copied '*per Nicolaum Faulfiss et Georgium de Kniechnicz*' in 1407 and showing signs of much careful revision. Aeneas Sylvius was thus wrong in crediting Faulfisch, who may have been one of Ranků's scholars, with having first brought Wyclif to Prague.

See also O. Odložilík, *Wycliffe's Influence upon Central and Eastern Europe* (*Slavonic Review*, No. 21, March, 1929), and also his *Wyclif and Bohemia* (1935).

The latest contribution before the War is the paper of Prof. R. R. Betts in *Transactions* of the Royal Histor. Soc., Vol. XXI (1939), entitled : 'English and Czech Influences on the Hussite Movement.' This is all the more valuable because it is the first English study based upon the numerous Czech publications since 1918. See also the same author's essay upon John Hus in *History*.

the Law of Christ, and especially the clergy to leave the pomp and rule of this world, and to live with the Apostles according to Christ's life. I am drawn by the love which he shows for Christ's law, when he maintains that it cannot be false even in the smallest point.'[1] He once spoke of 'benedicta Anglia,' the blessed land of England. None the less it should be borne in mind that, in the words of Professor Betts : 'Hus only adopted that in Wyclif which was congenial, which harmonized with the genius of Bohemia, and rejected all that was inapt and unsympathetic.'

The capital importance of Wyclifite doctrine in the whole Bohemian struggle is abundantly shown by the course of events from 1403 onwards. There was a growing cleavage at the University between the German party, which adhered to the strictly orthodox and 'nominalist' tradition of the Schoolmen, and at the same time enjoyed an undue share of the fat livings and privileged positions of that time, and the Czechs, who leant more and more towards the 'realist' school, and felt themselves to be in the position of an aggrieved minority. Friction was augmented by the general position of the Church ; for the support given by Innocent VII and his successor Gregory XII to King Rupert served, naturally enough, to increase the leaning of Wenceslas towards the conciliar and reformist movement. The new Archbishop of Prague, Zbynek, of the ancient family of Zajic of Hasenburg, had been more of a soldier and a politician than of a churchman, and though correct in behaviour and by no means uncultured, was not interested in theological controversy. Judging Hus as a man of piety and eloquence who possessed the further advantage of great influence at Court, he at first looked on him with high favour. The mission with which he entrusted Hus in 1405 had a decisive effect on the latter's career ; for it revealed to him the credulity of the masses and their unscrupulous exploitation by the clergy. The bleeding wafers in the Mass and the miracles wrought upon pilgrims to the little German town of Wilsnack were shown to be an impudent imposture, which Hus was not slow to denounce publicly. The feeling thus aroused is yet another proof of the keen interest with which all questions relating to the Eucharist were already being discussed in Bohemia, not merely among the learned, but among the common people. The idea of frequent Communion, as put forward by Matthew of Janov and by one or two contemporary German thinkers, again aroused widespread sympathy. Two of Hus's earliest Latin works deal with the sacramental dispute. Hus certainly had not then, and probably never, adopted Wyclif's sacramental doctrine, but to the last upheld transubstantiation in its unabated form.

Meanwhile Zbynek had received an earnest appeal from the Pope for greater zeal in extirpating the Wyclifite error in Bohemia, and found it expedient to issue a pastoral defining the true doctrine of the Eucharist. In May, 1408, while preparations for a Church Council were at last taking definite shape, Wenceslas, with his eye upon his possible recognition by the assembled fathers, and eager to clear his country of the spreading taint of heresy, induced the University of Prague to issue a fresh condemnation of Wyclifite doctrines. It is highly significant that on this occasion only the Bohemian nation was summoned to take action, the fact being that

---

[1] In the words of Dr. Odložilík, Hus 'was not so much attracted by Wyclif's dogmatic ideas as by his zeal for reform in the Church and more especially in the life of the priests.' The same writer propounds the interesting theory that 'it was only through its transportation to Bohemia that Wyclif's doctrine was saved from extinction and oblivion.'

the other three, in all of which the German element predominated, were virtually unanimous against Wyclif. This incident therefore marks a further widening of the gulf between the German and Czech parties. The Archbishop followed it up by suspending certain suspect preachers, and the protest which Hus then addressed to Zbynek was couched in language which it is hard to approve as addressed to an ecclesiastical superior, and began the estrangement between the two men.

The University Quarrel

What followed was materially influenced by wider European events. Almost all the Cardinals of the rival obediences had at last abandoned the rival Popes and convoked a Council at Pisa for March 25, 1409. While Rupert was allied with Gregory XII, the Conciliar party needed Wenceslas's help and were ready to recognize him as lawful King of the Romans. But to Wenceslas's rage and discomfiture, Archbishop Zbynek adhered rigidly to the cause of Gregory, and was backed in this by the German Masters of Prague University. Its verdict was of scarcely less moment than that of Paris, whence proceeded the leaders of the whole Conciliar movement. The deadlock brought into high relief the old grievance of the Bohemian 'nation,' which, sympathizing with Wenceslas and the Council, found itself in a minority of one to three in its favour. Already in 1384 there had been stormy rioting in favour of a change in the proportion of votes in the University, and now the Czechs saw a chance of winning over the impatient King to some such action. The University had become a mirror of the wider national quarrel between the Czech supporters of Wenceslas and the German supporters of Rupert and Gregory.

On January 18, 1409, then, urged on by his chief counsellor, Nicholas of Lobkovicz, Wenceslas issued the famous decree of Kutná Hora, which abruptly inverted the position by assigning to the Czechs as 'the true heir of this Kingdom' (*ejusdem regni iusta heres*) three votes, and to the foreign nations combined only a single vote ; the former status he characterized as 'unjust and indeed indecent,' and justified his action by the powerful analogy of the French nation (*natio gallica*) at Paris and similar practices at the Italian universities.

The news caused extreme ferment among the Germans, and from the first there was no one capable of mediating, and much tactlessness on both sides. Indeed, when the German Masters and students individually bound themselves by oath to abandon Prague rather than give in, and there was a last hope of compromise on the basis of complete equality and alternation of office between the native Bohemians and foreigners, the king himself, on his royal authority, superseded the rector and dean, nominated Czechs in their place and sent to the malcontents a detailed statement, entirely endorsing the Czech case and enjoining submission. Among other arguments he claimed that his father, in the original charter of foundation, had wished above all to benefit his Bohemian subjects ; at first they had been inferior to the Germans in learning, but now that with God's help this was no longer so, the time had come to make a change.

On this the dispossessed Rector, Henning von Baltenhagen, handed over the insignia of office, the registers and keys (May 9) ; and there at once began an exodus of the German Masters and students from

Prague.[1] The majority of them found their way to Leipzig and there founded a new university, while others scattered among the recently founded German seats of learning, Heidelberg, Vienna, Köln and Erfurt. There can be little doubt that their resentment and sense of grievance, compounded of racial prejudice and theological zeal, did much to give Bohemia a bad name as a breeding ground of heresy, and so to stimulate the long series of crusades against the Hussites. Meanwhile the international character of Prague University vanished at one blow ; henceforth it was to be narrowly national, and increasingly isolated from the rest of Europe. That Prague had been the intellectual centre of the whole Reich under Charles IV is true ; that it was no longer so after the lapse of a generation is equally certain. Whether, then, the breach could have been averted if Wenceslas had shown greater tact and had not long since wrecked his reputation in the Reich, or whether an open conflict between the two nations was not altogether inevitable from the moment when they became virtually identified with the two rival tendencies in the Church, will always remain a matter of opinion. For German learning the effect of the great exodus was centrifugal : and a stimulus was given to those local and particularist tendencies which were to give such a many-sided character to German culture until the victory of *Gleichschaltung* in our own day. Certain it is that the cause of Bohemia now came to be linked with that of ecclesiastical reform in a manner which has left permanent traces upon the national character. All the latent sources of unrest and discontent, spiritual and social no less than political, now welled up without restraint and found expression in the inspired figure of John Hus.

Hus, Zbynek and Wyclifism

The Council of Pisa elected Alexander V as Pope ; and, as we saw, Europe was for a short time confronted by the revolting spectacle of three rival candidates competing alike for the Papal and for the Imperial throne. Nowhere did the poison of Schism work more potently than in Bohemia. Zbynek refused to recognize the conciliar Pope till late in the year; he even laid Prague under an interdict, and only yielded when Wenceslas proceeded to confiscate the goods of refractory clergy.

Intense popular feeling was aroused by this conflict and there were charges and countercharges. But on December 20, 1409, a Papal Bull enjoined Zbynek to form a commission of six doctors for the extirpation of heresy throughout the kingdom ; only declared opponents were appointed, and the result was a foregone conclusion. In June, 1410, it was laid down that certain specified writings of Wyclif[2] were heretical, that all who possessed them must hand them over for destruction, and the teaching of Wyclifite doctrine was henceforth strictly forbidden.

More and more the situation centred upon a duel between the Arch-

---

[1] Estimates as to the number of seceders have varied very greatly. It may be presumed that between 3,000 and 5,000 left Prague ; the figure of 20,000 is, of course, ridiculous. Tomek (*op. cit.*, p. 39) holds that up to 1389 the number of students at Prague approximated to 11,000, but that since then they gradually declined, owing to the foundation of rival universities. Between 1366 and 1409 we possess the names of 234 Masters lecturing in the Arts faculty alone, while in the same period 834 Masters and 3,823 Bachelors are known to have been promoted. The Saxon nation formed nearly half the total, whereas the Bavarian had shrunk to a ninth. The Bohemian formed about a fifth (*ibid.*, p. 47).

[2] Seventeen by name, beginning with the *Dialogus* and *Trialogus*.

bishop and Hus, who had been made the first Rector of the truncated national university, and had not only it, but the Czech masses, solidly behind him. The university had already challenged the view that Wyclif was a heretic, and now Hus, who had for some time past disregarded the Archbishop's veto upon his sermons at the Bethlehem Chapel, launched a frontal attack before a crowded congregation. He denounced as false the charges against Wyclif contained in the Bull, quoted Zbynek's own recent declaration that there were no heretics in Bohemia, and made the famous medieval appeal 'from a Pope ill-informed to a Pope better informed.' Zbynek was inexorable, and on July 16 himself set a light to the pile of Wyclif's books outside the Cathedral; two days later he excommunicated Hus and all those who joined in his protest. The excitement was so great in Prague that the Archbishop found it expedient to withdraw to Roudnice. A street ballad satirized his hasty action and lack of learning in doggerel words :

> Zbynek, Bishop, A.B.C.,
> Burnt the books, but ne'er knew he
> What was in them written.

These incidents represent the parting of the ways. Hus, encouraged by popular support and the keen sympathy of Queen Sophie,[1] resisted the prohibition upon preaching, and declared that 'We must obey God rather than men in things which are necessary for salvation ' He was thus already appealing from the authority of the Church to that of the individual conscience.

In the meantime Alexander V was succeeded by John XXIII, a man of infamous private character, 'possessing all the qualities of a successful *condottiere* general,[2] whose early acts of piracy were overshadowed by the terrorism of his rule as Legate in Bologna. It was obvious that this sinister figure would have but scanty sympathy for one who had denounced so outspokenly as Hus the corrupt and immoral lives of the clergy. In actual fact, John was not at first interested in the affairs of Bohemia, and entrusted Cardinal Colonna (the future Martin V) with the necessary enquiry. As a result, Zbynek's policy was confirmed, and Hus was cited before the Papal tribunal; and when the latter's friends at Court very wisely dissuaded him from setting out on a journey from which he might never be allowed to return, he was excommunicated (February, 1411). For a time it seemed as though Zbynek would become involved in a conflict with Wenceslas no less irreconcilable than that of his predecessor, John of Jenstein; but the precedent was doubtless ever before his eyes, and the king's improved position after the death of Jost and the reconciliation with Sigismund enjoined caution upon Zbynek. In the summer of 1411 arbitrators were appointed and it was agreed that the Archbishop should make his submission to the King, assure the Pope that there was no heresy in Bohemia, and revoke all excommunications, while the King was to collaborate in checking the growth of error and to restore the clergy whom he had suspended. Hus on his side wrote to the Pope, confidently affirming that he had spoken and written nothing contrary to the Catholic faith and repudiating certain sacramental views attributed

---

[1] The Queen wrote to the Cardinals that the veto was contrary to Scripture, since 'the word of God must not be filtered, but should be preached in hamlets, streets, houses, and indeed wherever necessity arises.' (Lutzow, p. 128.)

[2] Creighton, *History of the Papacy*, I, p. 268.

to him ;[1] before despatching the letter, he read it to the assembled University, whose seal was affixed as a sign of approval.

Zbynek was only half-hearted in his submission and, complaining that his opponents had not kept their side of the bargain, set out for the Hungarian court, in the hope of enlisting the support of Sigismund His death at Pressburg on the journey (September 28, 1411) was followed by a brief lull ; but his successor as Archbishop, Albik, a weak and avaricious old man, who as the Royal Physician had amassed a fortune and by his chemical experiments earned the reputation of a 'necromancer,' was in no way equal to so difficult a situation. Trouble was in the very air, and a fresh ground of quarrel soon presented itself. John XXIII, not content with denouncing his rival Gregory XII as a heretic, included in the ban the latter's chief supporter, King Ladislas of Naples, and offered plenary absolution to all who took their share in the 'crusade' against Ladislas. Indulgences for this purpose were put up for sale, and in due course a German prelate, Wenzel Thiem, arrived in Prague and proceeded to organize the traffic in very much the same way as his more famous successor, Tetzel, on the eve of the German Reformation. This was a most unusual proceeding in Bohemia, and the only precedent for it, in the year 1393, had caused no little scandal and heart-burning. In June, 1412, then, Hus publicly protested against the traffic in indulgences and opened a stormy discussion at the University. The excited state of public opinion is shown by the demonstration staged by Vuk of Waldstein, one of Wenceslas's favourite courtiers. A student decked out as a prostitute, and wearing silver bells, carried a bogus papal bull through the streets and then burnt it in front of an applauding crowd. More serious were the public protests against indulgences made in several of the leading Prague churches ; for this time the civil authorities acted swiftly, seized three young men who had led the protest, and hurried them off to execution. The crowd took possession of the bodies, carried them to the Bethlehem Chapel and chanted the Martyr's Mass. 'Many students also, common people, lords and ladies, followed the bodies with much crying and lamenting, but with great piety and while accompanying them to their graves, they heartily pitied the young men, saying they had not deserved to die.' It seems probable that but for Hus's restraint and moderation an armed conflict between the opposing factions could hardly have been avoided.

In August fresh papal bulls reached Prague, confirming the ex-communication of Hus and forbidding all contact with him ; he was to be seized and handed over to the Archbishop for execution, and Bethlehem, as 'a nest of heretics,' was to be levelled to the ground. Prague, too, was laid under an interdict, but Pope John still hesitated to excommunicate the King and Queen, whose help he needed in the struggle against Gregory. Even at this stage Hus retained the royal favour, but Wenceslas made a personal appeal to him to withdraw from Prague for a time, in the hope that some compromise might be reached. Thus the next two years of Hus's life offer a curious parallel to Luther's period of retirement on the Wartburg, and gave him for the last time real leisure for literary achievement.

Meanwhile the triple schism of the Church continued. The conscience of Europe was deeply stirred, the reforming party could not be brought

---

[1] 'I have been wrongfully defamed to the Apostolic See by those heresy hunters.' (Workman, *Letters*, p. 51.)

to silence, and it is significant that even the worldly, licentious and un-scrupulous Sigismund came to feel that his whole reputation must be staked upon reunion and reform. It is indeed only just to point out that he pursued this aim with a fixity of purpose lacking in so many of his political projects, and did not rest until Pope John had been reluctantly manœuvred into sanctioning a new council of the Church, to meet at Constance in November, 1414. No such representative assembly had been seen for many generations, and though intrigue, vice and even crime lingered in its antechambers, its leaders showed real statesmanship and a common front, and from the first drove the three rival pontiffs on to the defensive. Gregory and Benedict were already isolated and well-nigh helpless, and John, after five months of evasion and plotting, fled ignominiously from Constance, only to be surrendered to the jurisdiction of the Council and solemnly deposed (May 29, 1415).

Hus at Constance

It was already obvious at the time that the issue of the Council would have a decisive influence upon the course of events in Bohemia. Hus and his supporters, and with them King Wenceslas, hoped for their vindication by the party of reform : while Sigismund calculated that success at Constance might well give him an irresistible position in Bohemia, as heir to the childless and somewhat ineffective Wenceslas and Sophie, who were already suspected of heresy. Pope John on his side saw in a concentration upon doctrinal disputes his only respite from the problem of unity. So hardened a cynic may well have doubted whether the Bohemians would win much sympathy from the type of prelate largely represented at Constance ; but it seems doubtful whether he was much interested in the question, save merely as a means of tactical diversion. Thus a chain of circumstances combined to render Hus's appearance before the Council well-nigh inevitable, despite the obstacle presented by canon law in the case of an excommunicated person. Hus had the foreboding that he would not see Prague again,[1] and he only left for Constance after his safe return had been definitely guaranteed by Sigismund ;[2] the expenses of the journey were found for him, and he was escorted through Germany by loyal friends, notably the two Czech lords, Wenceslas of Duba and John of Chlum.

But he had to contend with many determined enemies, such as John the Iron, Bishop of Litomyšl, a man of great wealth who had made a determined effort to buy the Archbishopric of Prague at the last vacancy and whose notorious simony stood in sharpest contrast to the tenets of the Bethlehem group ; Wenzel Thiem, whose indulgence campaign had ended in financial disaster, thanks to Hus's agitation ; Hus's former friend, Stephen Palec, who had at one time gone further than Hus ever did in expounding Wyclifite doctrine ; and a certain papal official of Bohemian origin, colloquially known as Michael 'de Causis.' These and others spared no effort to poison the minds of the Council against Hus, and this was all the easier because its real directing force came from the University of Paris, which had latterly broken off its old intimacy with Prague, and, as the headquarters of nominalist teaching, was emphatic

---

[1] Letter of October 12, 1414. See *Letters*, p. 146.

[2] Hus left Prague without the document, which was fetched by one of his friends from Speier, where Sigismund was then holding his court, on the way from his coronation at Aachen to Constance.

in its denunciation of Wyclifite heresy. D'Ailly and Gerson, equally eminent as thinkers and as constructive statesmen, were already hostile ; the former had been offended by Hus's teaching on the poverty of the clergy, while the latter had already in the previous summer been corresponding with Archbishop Conrad of Prague and denouncing Hus's teaching on predestination. On November 28, therefore, Hus was arrested by order of the Council and kept in close confinement, despite the angry protests of Sigismund himself. The latter, indeed, found himself in a most delicate position ; his insistence upon respect for the royal safe-conduct was met by the claim that nothing could absolve the Council from examining one suspect of heresy ; his threat to leave Constance unless Hus were released was countered by the argument that the Council, if hampered in its performance of so fundamental a duty, would have no choice but to dissolve. In the end Sigismund gave way, left Hus to his fate, and saved his conscience with the thought that the healing of the schism stood higher than his personal word of honour, and with such medieval arguments as that adduced by the King of Aragon, that it was impossible to break faith with one who had already broken faith with God.

An account of Hus's memorable trial at Constance would far exceed the scope of this volume, and could hardly fail to impinge upon the theological field ; it is only possible to indicate the more salient points. After the flight of John XXIII on March 20, 1415, Hus was the prisoner of the Council, and no longer technically of the Pope ; and only four days later Sigismund sealed his perfidy by formally surrendering his victim to the Bishop of Constance, as nominee of the Council. Special commissioners were appointed to examine the charge of heresy ; and on May 4 Wyclif's doctrines—not only the forty-five articles over which controversy had so long raged, but 206 others, compiled by his enemies, now predominant at his old University of Oxford—were solemnly condemned and ordered to be burnt. In May the demands of the Bohemian nobles for the release of Hus, in accordance with the safe-conduct, was deliberately rejected, but a public examination was promised. He was three times called before the Council, but was constantly interrupted and never allowed to refute the charges against him, still less to expound his views. It may freely be admitted that Hus more than once showed great tactlessness and even arrogance of phrase—when, for instance, he said that he had 'expected to find in the Council more piety, reverence and order,' and again when he maintained the view that a pope or a bishop who was in mortal sin was no true pope or bishop, and that the same applied to a secular sovereign. Nor did he improve matters by drawing the scholastic distinction between *quoad officium* and *quoad meritum*. He still further affronted Sigismund by the reminder that he had come to Constance of his own free will, and that there were many lords in Bohemia who loved him, in whose castles he could have been hidden, so that neither king could have compelled him ; and bluff John of Chlum made matters even worse by affirming that he himself, though but a poor knight, could have kept him in safety for a whole year, but that many were the powerful lords who could protect him for as long as they pleased. It is easy to see that in several directions such an attitude seemed subversive to authority in Church and State.

Various forms of recantation were put before him,[1] but one and all

---

[1] Probably the nearest to success was that proposed by the Cardinal of Ostia. 'Apart from the declaration which I have already given and now repeat, I declare

were shattered by his refusal to perjure himself by renouncing doctrines which he did not hold. "I stand," he declared, "at the judgment seat of Christ, to Whom I have appealed, knowing that He will judge every man, not according to false or erroneous witness, but according to the truth and to each one's deserts." And to the last he was unconscious of any guilt. 'I, Master John Hus, in chains and in prison,' so he bade farewell to the University of Prague, 'now standing on the shore of this present life and expecting on the morrow a dreadful death, which will I hope purge away my sins, find no heresy in myself, and accept with all my heart any truth whatsoever that is worthy of belief.' On July 6, 1415—at the last so-called hearing, or rather jeering[1]—formal sentence was pronounced against him, and on the same day he was burnt at the stake, his ashes being scattered to prevent all possibility of relics of the martyr reaching Bohemia.

Ardent Protestant writers have laid great stress on the farcical nature of the trial and contrasted the pure and lofty character of Hus with the men who occupied the two supreme dignities in Christendom, John the ex-*condottiere* and the licentious Sigismund; but this betrays both a lack of perspective and a wrong emphasis. It is quite true that no other than Gerson himself admitted that Hus, if he had been permitted an advocate, would never have been convicted, and added that he himself would rather be tried by Jews and pagans than by the members of the Council. It is also true that Hus was hampered at every turn, that his appeals to Christ's teaching were greeted with mocking laughter,[2] that the use of unchecked translations from his Czech works opened a door to much confusion and misrepresentation, and that he was accused not merely of opinions which he never held, and publicly denied, but even of such grotesque and self-evident falsehoods as that he had claimed to be the fourth person of the Trinity. But it is also true that every effort was made to secure his submission, and that the Council would much have preferred it to his execution. Though neither Hus nor his adversaries may have been fully conscious of all that was involved, we can see clearly, after the lapse of five centuries, that a fundamental issue had been raised between the medieval and the modern world. In the words of Bishop Creighton: 'It is the glory of Hus that he first deliberately asserted the rights of the individual conscience against ecclesiastical authority, and sealed his assertion by his own lifeblood.'[3]

The supreme tragedy of Constance is that Hus's condemnation was

anew that though much was ascribed to me of which I never thought, I none the less—in all that is ascribed to me or charged against me, and in extracts from my books or in evidence given—do submit to the most merciful ruling and decision of the most holy General Council, with a view to abjure, revoke and recall, and to merciful atonement, and to do everything which the most holy Council may see fit to order for my salvation and according to its grace, recommending myself to it most humbly.' (Höfler, *op. cit.*, p. 109.)

[1] These are the words of Hus's faithful friend Peter Mladenovič—*ultima audientia dicta, veriusque derisio.* (Lützow, *op. cit.*, p. 252.)

[2] 'All cried out at me,' wrote Hus himself, 'as the Jews against Jesus.' (*Letters.*)

[3] Let us add the verdict of Ernest Denis, in *Huss et la Guerre des Hussites*, pp. 160–161, v. ii, p. 51 : 'La pensée humaine s'indique de nos jours contre l'intolérance, elle réclame pour tous le droit de défendre et de prêcher ses croyances, elle voit dans la persécution une offense à la dignité humaine, une injure même à la religion. Mais ces idées, qui forment comme le capital moral de la civilisation moderne, les hommes du quinzième siècle n'en avaient pas conscience, et il n'est pas permis de sé servir d'elles pour condamner Gerson, d'Ailly et leurs compagnons. Les lois morales pas plus que les lois civiles n'ont d'effet rétroactif.'

not the work of an ill-living Pope whom the Council had already deposed for his crimes, nor of a time-serving monarch who, with all his short-comings, worked valiantly for the cause of union, but of the Council itself, the highest expression of Christian idealism in those days. Hus, in Creighton's words, 'had no wish to attack the system of the Roman Church, no wish to act in opposition to its established rules, he maintained conscientiously to the last that he was a faithful son of the Roman Church. But the necessity of attacking abuses led him on step by step to set up the law of Christ as superior to all other enactments, as sufficient in itself for the regulation of the Church : and this law of Christ he defined as the law of the Gospel, as laid down by Christ during the sojourn on earth of Himself and the Apostles. His adversaries at once pointed out that, starting from this principle, he maintained the right of each individual to interpret Scripture according to his own pleasure, and so introduced disorder into the Church.'[1]

Ever since Luther made the astonished avowal, 'We have all been Hussites unawares,' Hus has been claimed as one of the chief forerunners of the Reformation ; and Luther's monument at Worms is flanked by the four figures of Petrus Waldus, Wyclif, Hus and Savonarola. But if Hus was, despite all his fervid denials, a heretic, it was not in the field of dogma, but rather in the still undefined sphere of authority, where the relations of Church and State were still keenly contested, and many of their implications as yet lay in the future. It would be presumptuous of me to attempt any exact definition of Hus's theological views : the more so since after five centuries the field has only been partially explored. It must suffice to remind the reader that many of the teachings which afterwards came to be regarded as specifically 'Hussite' were certainly not held by Hus himself (this applies specially to the controversy on the Eucharist), while others were only condemned by the Roman Church at a much later date and could not therefore be described as then heretical, even from the standpoint of Rome. Thus it came about that in our own day the solemn revocation of the sentence upon Hus has been tentatively suggested, on the ground that so much of the evidence was false and the trial itself an obvious travesty of justice. The rehabilitation of Joan of Arc provides an obvious precedent, and if Rome is unlikely to undertake similar action on behalf of Hus, it is not because of any inherent obstacle in the facts of the case, but rather because, in the political and social outlook of our own times, Hus and the very different 'Hussitism' of his successors have become inextricably interwoven.[2]

[1] Vol. ii, p. 20.

[2] Fifty years have passed since Bishop Creighton wrote his account of Hus in Vol. ii of *A History of the Papacy*; and no more restrained or balanced estimate has ever been penned. I have no desire to strike a polemical note, but I am bound in fairness to point out the striking contrast offered by the comments of the two foremost Catholic historians—Janssen and Pastor—two scholars for whom I have the highest respect and admiration, and whose work has in their own sphere been no less epoch-making than that of Lingard and Gasquet in England. Pastor (*Geschichte der Päpste*, i, p. 162) treats the teachings of Wyclif as having necessarily led to a social revolution, and affirms that Hus 'declared war on the social order.' Janssen, in his *Geschichte des deutschen Volkes*, ii, p. 421, declares that 'Hus put in question all spiritual and state power by his thesis that no man who has committed mortal sin can be a bishop or temporal ruler . . .': he also 'declared war on the whole social order by the claim that all those who use their property contrary to divine ordinance have no right to this property.' Such verdicts carry their own condemnation with them, and are altogether unworthy of serious historians. All this, however, pales before the dictum of Albert Hauck, the distinguished author of

Hus as National Leader

If the name of Hus has given to Bohemia a pre-eminence in the history of religious thought, the special flavour which it conveys derives undoubtedly from his Slav temperament. He is less rugged and downright than Luther, more mystical than Calvin or Zwingli, less stern and domineering than Knox. Moreover, he differs from them all in that he was a teacher of high academic distinction, holding a position for which Wyclif is the sole parallel among the reformers. But above all, he did for the language and literature of his people all that Luther did for the German. His Latin works have long since lost any literary significance which they may ever have possessed, and are to be judged according to theological standards. Some modern writers have shown a curious lack of perspective by setting themselves to convict him of plagiarism (that besetting sin of all medieval writers, which indeed has only come to weigh upon the literary conscience in comparatively modern times). The inference thus drawn is that Hus was a mere imitator of Wyclif, entirely lacking in originality. The absurdity of such a thesis is best demonstrated by placing in conjunction Luther's famous conclusion, 'Paul and Augustine are Hussites to the letter,' and Professor Loserth's reference to Wyclif as 'the man for whose doctrine Hus went to the stake.' Hus went to the stake for no man's doctrines, but for what, rightly or wrongly, he conceived to be the eternal and divine verities ; and his influence upon his own people and upon succeeding generations far beyond the narrow bounds of Bohemia was direct, personal and profound.

Far more important than his Latin are his Czech writings, though the political development of his country condemned them to centuries of neglect and they have only received attention since the dawn of Czech historical criticism under Palacký. Hus deliberately wrote the language as it was habitually spoken in his day, in order to be as widely understood as possible ; and he chose the Prague dialect in particular as the basis of those orthographic reforms which stand as a pioneer achievement in the history of the Western Slav tongues, and gave the first impetus in the direction of diacritic signs. The most important of these writings are a series of Expositions (*Výklad*, 'The Daughter', *Dcerka*), addressed to the pious ladies near the Bethlehem Chapel: the *Postilla* (1413), which was long regarded as Hus's testament ; the treatise on Simony, and, above all, '*Super IV Sententiarum*,' a commentary upon a once famous medieval textbook of Peter Lombard, which gives the best insight into Hus's outlook and teaching. To the modern reader, however, the most living portion of his writings are his Letters, both in Latin and in Czech, especially those written from his prison in Constance. That which he addressed 'To the Bohemian Nation' is one of the most moving documents in all Bohemian history, blending a calm faith with ardent patriotism, taking equal account of all classes of the faithful, and towards its close earnestly commending his beloved Bethlehem Chapel to the people of Prague.

'Faithful and beloved of God,' he writes, 'Lords and Ladies, rich and poor. I entreat and exhort you to love God, to spread abroad His Word,

---

Kirchengeschichte Deutschlands, in five ponderous volumes ; '*Für Kirche und Christentum haben die Tschechen so wenig geleistet wie die übrigen slavischen Stämme*.' Here speaks the Pan German Chauvinist, abandoning all pretence of historical impartiality (v. ii, p. 870).

and to hear and observe it more willingly. I entreat you to hold fast the truth of God, which I have written and preached to you from the Holy Scriptures and the utterances of the Saints. I entreat you also, if any have heard in my preaching or private conversations that which is opposed to God's truth, or if I have ever written anything of that kind— I trust God it is not so—not to hold to it. I entreat you, if any have noticed frivolity in my words or actions, not to imitate it, but to pray God that it may please Him to pardon me. I entreat you to love and commend and cultivate priests of good life, especially those who are earnest students of Holy Writ. I entreat you to beware of deceitful men, and particularly of wicked priests, of whom the Saviour saith that they are in sheeps' clothing, but inwardly are ravening wolves. I entreat you to be kind to the poor and to rule them justly. I entreat all citizens to be righteous in their business dealings. I entreat all artisans faithfully to follow their craft and take delight in it. I entreat all servants to be faithful servants of their masters and mistresses. I entreat masters to live a good life and faithfully to instruct their scholars, especially that they may love God and learn to give themselves to knowledge, in order to promote His honour, the welfare of the state and their own salvation, but not for the sake of avarice or the praise of men. I entreat students of letters and other scholars to obey their masters in things good, to imitate them and diligently apply themselves to letters for the sake of God's honour and their own salvation and that of other men.'

Hus's patriotism was something wider than the narrow interpretation placed upon it by friend and foe alike. Fate willed it that the struggle between the two great parties in Church and University should follow the same lines as the far narrower racial and linguistic quarrel between German and Czech, and the growing social rivalry of town and country. But this vindication of the Czech vernacular, like the devotion of Luther and Cranmer a century later to a tongue 'easily understood of the people,' was no mere act of racial prejudice, but proceeded from a desire to shake off the shackles of Latin scholasticism and open wide the gates of faith and learning. Translating cautiously into modern terms, we may detect traces alike of the missionary and of the democrat. Much depends indeed upon which aspect of his career receives the most emphasis ; and it cannot, of course, be denied that he was the real soul of the party which achieved the Czechization of the University, and thus narrowed it from one of the four *Studia Generalia* of Europe to an institution of intensely national aspect. Nor must it be forgotten that he condemned in unmeasured phrase intermarriage with the Germans, as likely to endanger the purity of the Czech language. On the other hand, there stands his much-quoted saying : 'If I saw a foreigner of any country who loved God and strove for the good more than my own brother, I would love him more. Therefore good English priests are dearer to me than faint-hearted Bohemian ones, and a good German is dearer to me than a bad brother.'[1] This is but in accord with his constant motto : 'Let God be true and every man a liar.'

That Hus, though not a travelled man, saw beyond the frontiers of

[1] *Christus scit quod plus diligo bonum Teutonicum quam malum Bohemicum, etiamsi sit frater meus germanus.* (cit. Loserth.)

his own country, is revealed in his correspondence with King Wladislaw Jagiello of Poland, whom he congratulated on the great victory of Tannenberg (1410), and to whom he appealed in the cause of extirpating simony. His initiative was largely responsible for the close and cordial relations between Poland and Bohemia during the Hussite period.

No survey of Hus's career would be complete without a brief reference to his influence upon music. Coming as he did from one of the most spontaneously musical of peoples, he was an ardent promoter of congregational singing, and made it a special feature of the services at the Bethlehem Chapel. He established a 'school' of singing and himself wrote a number of hymns, though many seem to have been wrongly attributed to him. Music provides yet another common trait between Hus and Luther, but while the tradition of the German chorale, as inaugurated at Wittenberg, has flowed uninterruptedly till our own day, the hymns and songs which played so unique a part in the Hussite movement and fired a whole nation in resistance to the invaders, suffered a fatal interruption in the period of national eclipse during the seventeenth and eighteenth centuries.

CHAPTER IV

THE HUSSITE MOVEMENT

*The condemnation of Hus was not merely a matter of faith ; it was a step
towards suppressing the movement of the Czechs against the Germans in
Eastern Europe.* —*Bishop Creighton.*

*One school of historians, to which I have the honour to belong, has main-
tained that the Hussite War is the first war in history that was fought,
not for material interests, but for intellectual ones, that is to say, for ideals.*
—*Palacký.*

THE execution of Hus roused intense indignation in his native country :
'it branded Bohemia in the eyes of Christendom as the home of heresy,'
and this was doubly resented as an injustice and as a national insult.
Czech resentment was specially directed against Sigismund, whose broken
pledge towards Hus was in full accord with his perfidy in the past. His
difficult position towards the Council, which had given no corresponding
pledge, was clearly realized, but unfortunately for Sigismund he had been
overheard by the Bohemian lords Chlum and Duba, advising the leaders
of the Council never to allow Hus to return home,[1] and everything points
to his having calculated that without its leader the movement in Bohemia
would die a natural death, and that its collapse would give him political
advantage over his brother Wenceslas. His famous blush before the
Council[2] when the safe conduct was mentioned at Hus's final condemnation, and the prisoner looked him straight in the face, has gone down
to history.

On the news from Constance reaching Prague, there were rioting and
attacks on the Iron Bishop's property, which was partly seized by the
local nobility ; the King was at first irresolute, but Queen Sophie and
the ladies of her court were open in their indignation. In September the
Diet met and addressed an angry letter to the Council, rebutting the
charges of heresy and 'the eternal insult' offered to Bohemia. Hus, they
declared, was 'a man of pure manners and unsullied fame, who taught the
precepts of the Gospel according to the doctrines of the Fathers and the
Church, abhorred all errors and heresies and earnestly exhorted us and
all the faithful to peace and neighbourly love, both in word, writing and
deed, and set the example by his own tranquil and edifying manner of
life.' Any who charged him with heresy was 'a liar, traitor and enemy of
our land and people, yea even a grave heretic and a son of the Devil, the
father of lies.' On this shrill note they proceeded to frame a kind of
Solemn League and Covenant—pledging themselves to joint action in
defence of free preaching, in resistance to the ban of the Council and in
acceptance of the University's opinion in dogmatic matters. This was at
first signed by 69 nobles, but their number soon swelled to 452, led by
Čenek of Wartenberg, Lacek of Kravář and Boček of Poděbrad. A rival

---

[1] This incident, which played a decisive part at the time, is dramatically reported
by Peter of Mladenovič, but was lost sight of by historians, and only rediscovered
after the publication of the latter's chronicle in modern times.
[2] *Ille statim vehementer erubuit . . .*

Catholic League was also formed, but made little headway, and John the Iron found himself dangerously isolated. Archbishop Konrad fell in with the exhortations of the Council and laid Bohemia once more under an interdict : but in Prague most of the churches fell into Hussite hands, and all parts of the country were soon affected.

Jerome of Prague

The conflict was still further widened by fresh action on the part of the Council. Hus's friend and follower, Jerome of Prague, was still in their hands, and after a long and rigorous imprisonment, had been induced on September 10, to sign a humiliating recantation, admitting his master's heresy. Jerome was a very different character from Hus—impulsive, variable, led away by passion and mercurial temperament ; indeed he was more of a humanist than a reformer, and was infected by the 'Wanderlust' and adventurous spirit that animated the medieval student. He had played a vital part in propagating the works of Wyclif, but he himself wrote but little and lacked the sober mood of a theologian. Finding that recantation did not spell freedom, and that the Council had no intention of letting such a firebrand return to Bohemia, he grew resigned to his fate, and when again summoned to a public hearing in May, 1416, withdrew his former words. In a defence of fiery eloquence he was obviously following the model of St. Stephen, whom priestly contemporaries had also condemned as subversive and seditious ; and he now boldly reaffirmed the opinions of Hus, though expressly endorsing the Church's teaching on the Eucharist. "Hus," he said, "spoke not against the Church of God, but against the abuses of the clergy, the pride and pomp of prelates." All the efforts of the more moderate party were unavailing, nothing could now shake him, and on May 30 he suffered death at the same spot, with a calm heroism worthy of Hus. The famous Italian humanist, Poggio Bracciolini, has left on record a vivid and penetrating study of his friend Jerome's character and martyrdom.

The Utraquist Party

Not content with this, the Council sharply challenged the 452 Bohemian lords and summoned them to appear before it ; indeed, it could with difficulty be restrained by Sigismund from citing King Wenceslas and Queen Sophie also. Its choice of Bishop John of Litomyšl as its delegate to the King was the most unfortunate which it could conceivably have made, and Wenceslas's flat refusal to admit him to the vacant see of Olomouc (Olmütz) widened the growing gap. Soon there was a complete breach : the interdict was completely disregarded, and almost from the first the clergy of the anti-Conciliar party proceeded to dispense the Communion in both kinds in the leading churches of Prague. Nothing shows more clearly the idealist character of the early Hussites than their adoption of the Chalice as the symbol of their faith. Frequency of Communion and equal rights for the laity were to become distinguishing features of the movement—the first, as we saw, having had many advocates from the days of Conrad Waldhauser onwards, while the exact origin of the second has never been fully explained. All that can be affirmed with certainty is that it was not put forward by Hus himself, but that it was almost from the first universally adopted by his followers, moderate and radical alike. The main line of division lay between the

Catholic 'one kind' and the Hussite 'two kinds'; and the name of 'Calixtine,' or adherent of the Chalice for the laity, was overshadowed by the commoner 'Utraquist' (from the Latin phrase : '*sub utraque specie.*'[1]

During the three years following Jerome's death the breach steadily widened, and the Council by its unconciliatory attitude, and notably by its manifesto of July, 1417, to the nobles, knights and tradesmen of Bohemia, made matters still worse. The University, which had come to occupy the position of arbiter on all doctrinal issues, and set its face against the extremists, none the less took up an uncompromising view on the Sacrament, declaring Communion in both kinds to be necessary to salvation, proclaiming Hus a martyr for the faith and ordering the annual commemoration of his death. But a new party was rapidly forming to the left of the Utraquists, which rejected the Mass, purgatory and all but two of the Sacraments, and above all insisted upon the Bible as the sole authority in all matters of belief, to the exclusion of the oral tradition of the Church as upheld by the University. The more fanatical congregated in the southern districts of Bohemia, and held conventicles in the open air : their chief centre was the small town of Ústi, to which they gave the Biblical name of Tabor.

The course of events at Constance served to revive the courage of the Catholic party in Bohemia. Sigismund, who had certainly devoted long and unsparing efforts to the cause of Church Unity, at last saw the election of Martin V as unchallengeable head of Western Christendom. But unity in a sense triumphed over reform, and Martin lost no time in dissolving the Council, with its second great task still unachieved ; and he himself, as a Roman noble, turned to the more selfish problem of the Temporal Power. These events increased Bohemia's isolation ; for he not merely confirmed all the Council's decrees against heresy, but incited Sigismund to drastic interference in his elder brother's kingdom. Sigismund needed but little pressing, and in a letter to Wenceslas, whose contents were made public, included a warning to 'every Czech, German and Latin, that we can hardly await the day when I shall drown all Wyclifites and Hussites.'

The Death of Wenceslas

The irresolute and now rapidly failing Wenceslas was alarmed at the prospect of a general crusade which might be expected to rally the more conservative nobles and the influential German element in the towns. He therefore set himself to check the Hussite movement and issued a decree permitting the return of all priests who had been expelled from their charges for opposing Utraquism, and restricting to three the churches at the disposal of the Utraquists in Prague. This only increased the general unrest, which found expression in a monster meeting of the Taborites, gathered from all parts of the country, on a hill near Ústi (July 22, 1419). A week later a procession of Utraquists, led by the demagogue priest John of Želivo carrying the monstrance, passed through the streets of Prague. Stones were thrown from a window of the new town hall. The angry mob stormed the building, and flung down the Mayor and several of his councillors, to be done to death in the square below. This was the first of the two famous Defenestrations which were

---

[1] Contemporary writers were in the habit of distinguishing between the rival factions by adding the description '*sub utraque,*' or '*sub una.*'

to mark an epoch in Bohemian history. Wenceslas's fury at these incidents brought on an apoplectic stroke, from the effects of which he died on August 16—'roaring like a lion,' says a contemporary chronicler.[1]

Modern historians have hardly exaggerated in referring to Wenceslas as the most incompetent ruler whom Bohemia had hitherto known. Witty and gay on occasion, and not without the charm of all his House, he also had a certain sympathy for the down-trodden masses, and resented the ambitions and selfish quarrels of the greater barons : but the men upon whom he bestowed his favours were mere court favourites or upstarts, unequal to, perhaps hardly conscious of, the tasks before them, and the King himself was fickle and moody, 'to one thing constant never.' His utter neglect and mismanagement had lost him the German Crown and, it is sometimes plausibly argued, left permanent traces for evil upon the relations of Bohemia and Germany. In the dispute which rent the University and culminated in the breach with Rome, he saved himself by taking the national side, but there is no trace of tact or statesmanship in his conduct of affairs, and it may well be doubted whether his father would ever have allowed it to come to so open a breach.

Wenceslas left no children, and thus his death at once produced an acute crisis, for Sigismund, his lawful heir, was notoriously hostile to the Hussite cause. Not merely was he opposed to all compromise and inclined to insist upon complete submission, but his perfidious conduct at Constance and the stories that circulated about him were widely quoted as an argument against any dealings whatsoever with him. In the lively imagination of John of Želivo, Sigismund of Hungary, the founder of the Order of the Dragon, was no other than the dragon of the Apocalypse. In reality he was a man of great versatility and charm, but licentious, lacking in character, utterly thriftless, yet always in pursuit of a score of important objects, and thus inevitably forced, by the very nature of things, always to skimp, postpone or leave much unfinished ; eager to sip from every flower and driven equally by ambition and pleasure. Thus when the news of his brother's death came, he was deeply involved in Balkan and Venetian negotiations, and preparing for war upon the Turks, who were already a grave menace to his Hungarian kingdom. If then the postponement of his coming to Bohemia was a blunder which bore bitter fruit in central Europe, it had its explanation in the political situation with which he had already been mainly concerned for nearly a generation.

In the meantime Queen Sophie was made Regent, but though widely respected, she was not equal to so difficult a situation. There were immediate outbreaks in Prague, many cloisters were stormed, there was a fresh flight of Catholic clergy, and the Royalists found it necessary to take refuge inside the fortified castle of Hradčaný ; while on the other hand the German population of Kutná Hora massacred the Hussites and flung them wholesale down the mine-shafts. The Estates gave a very clear definition of their standpoint ; they demanded full freedom for the Hussites, and Communion in both kinds, the exclusion of clerics from all lay offices, the strict abolition of simony, the freedom of the University, and an end to the abuse levelled at Hus and Jerome—all this based upon an appeal to a future Church Council. These terms were laid by special delegates before Sigismund at the Court of Hungary ; but he answered evasively that he would govern like his father of glorious memory, and his

[1] *Cum magno clamore et rugitu quasi leonis.*—Laurence of Březina.

ungracious manner confirmed even the moderate party in the belief that no compromise was possible.

John Žižka

As usual in crises of such a nature the real leadership showed itself among the extremists. Čenek of Wartenberg, to whom Queen Sophie soon made over the Regency, was a man of high character, now torn between loyalty to the new king and adherence to moderate Hussite tenets ; but the only result of his efforts was a constant wavering from side to side which confused the issue and undermined his own prestige. Very different were the two men who now came to the front as leaders of the Taborite party—Nicholas of Hus and John Žižka of Tročnov. The former seems to have been possessed of real statesmanship, and formed the main link between Prague and Tabor ; in his day he was widely credited with designs upon the Crown, and certainly he might have gone far, if a fall from his horse had not proved fatal to him at an early stage of the struggle. But Žižka's name is only second to that of Hus himself, of whom he was an ardent and faithful admirer. Little or nothing is known of Žižka's birth or lineage, save that he came of a family of the lesser nobility in the south of Bohemia and that he held a post at the court of Queen Sophie and attracted the notice of Wenceslas by his earnest manner of life. The story that he fought in the Polish ranks at the battle of Tannenberg remains unverified ; it was obviously put about as a proof of what would now be called his Slavophil outlook.

It is highly characteristic of the rugged scruples which lay behind their creed that Žižka and Nicholas of Hus should have addressed to the University the enquiry whether material welfare was permissible for the Word of God. Only in extreme need, was the reply ; it was un-Christian to spread the Gospel sword in hand, and adherents must be won by love and patience, but against violence and persecution armed defence was enjoined. It was in this spirit that the Taborite leaders prepared to resist Sigismund, while the town council of Prague made its surrender to his deputy. Žižka had at first intended to make Pilsen his centre, but found himself dangerously outnumbered by all his opponents, and established a new stronghold on the hill of Hradiště, near Ústi, transferring to it the original name of Tabor, and soon making of it a place of refuge for all the irreconcilables of the country. It was now that he first emerged as a great military leader, following entirely original tactics, inspiring the masses with his own enthusiasm and welding peasants and townsfolk into a disciplined army capable of resisting in the open field the mounted chivalry of Bohemia and Hungary. Attacked at Sudoměř by greatly superior forces on March 25, 1420, he achieved victory by a new formation of mobile wagons, which checked hostile attacks and offered a base for sudden sorties. 'At first he used ordinary peasant wagons with sides and bottoms protected by boards, afterwards the outside or wing-of-battle wagons were improved to suit the military purposes required of them. When on the defensive they were parked in such a way as to form a huge rectangle, thus providing Žižka's men with *points d'appui* like those offered by the ramparts of a fort. On the march the supply and commissariat wagons were placed between the outside files, and in the event of an unexpected attack by cavalry the wings were able to close up and reproduce the rectangular formation. To do this successfully order was an essential condition, and was still more necessary when the laager moved up for a surprise attack. A sudden sortie of massed bands from the wagons would then turn an attack into a rout, if the enemy had previously been physically and morally shaken by heavy firing. Unless the enemy's discipline was strict and the leader in effective control of his forces, the effect of such sorties was frequently devastating.'[1]

Meanwhile Sigismund himself, who had come as far as Brno, remained as intransigeant as ever and even used threatening language to a fresh deputation from Prague. But instead of trying to establish himself at Prague, he went to Breslau, whither he had summoned the Reichstag, and here he committed a series of blunders which were to have fatal effects. He had been named an arbiter in the long quarrel between King Wladislaw of Poland the Teutonic Order, and now by his one-sided findings seriously undermined his good relations with Wladislaw and the latter's cousin Witold of Lithuania who, as recent converts to Christianity, looked askance at papal intolerance, and saw in the Slav sentiments of the Czechs a political asset not to be despised. He followed up the execution of twenty-three Silesian democrats by the savage torture and burning of a much respected Prague citizen named Kasa, solely for his Hussite tenets. He flatly refused an amnesty to the Praguers, and demanded absolute submission ;[2] and he crowned all by his public endorsement of the papal bull summoning all Christendom to a crusade for the extirpation of Wyclifite and Hussite heresy. It thus became only too obvious what fate awaited all ranks of the Hussites if Sigismund could once again regain control of his hereditary kingdom. Even the moderates were now thoroughly alarmed by his ill-judged show of severity.

By the end of June, 1420, large crusading armies began to converge upon Prague, drawn from almost every nation in Europe and therefore lacking in any real corporate spirit, but convinced of the hideous wickedness of the Bohemians and ready enough to massacre first, and enquire into the religious beliefs of their victims afterwards. Typical of the legends that circulated in Western Europe was the story that the Praguers openly worshipped the Evil Spirit in the form of a white lamb upon the Great Ring of the City. Self-preservation drove the rival parties to united action, and at the height of the crisis Žižka and a chosen band of Taborites became the soul of the defence. On July 14, 1420, after desperate fighting, he repelled the onslaught of the Crusaders on the hill of Vitkov outside the city ; the flails and maces of the Taborites did great execution, and many fugitives perished in the River Vltava. The religious exaltation which inspired the Hussites was revealed when they knelt upon the field of victory and intoned the *Te Deum*. The battle was a turning-point in the struggle, breathing fresh confidence into the Hussite ranks and forcing the Crusaders to renounce their designs upon Prague ; and from that day to this the hill has justly borne the name of the victorious Žižka. Sigismund, before retreating to Moravia, was crowned in the Cathedral of St. Vitus, but with a hurried and curtailed ceremony, which his opponents long affected to regard as invalidating it altogether.

The Four Articles

The signal advantages of combined action now encouraged the victors to attempt a compromise of opinion ; and the result was the promulgation

[1] R. Urbànek, *Jan Žižka* (*Slavonic Review*, No. 8, December, 1924, p. 278).
[2] '*In superbam velut alter elatus Lucifer.*' (Březova, p. 36.)

of the famous Four Articles of Prague, which were to remain the veritable Charter of the Hussite faith. Their preamble announced to the whole world that 'the Bohemian nation and its Christians trusting loyally in God, stand with all their goods, for life and death, as best they may, against everyone, for the following four Christian Articles, resting upon the New Testament of Jesus Christ :

'I. That the Word of God shall be freely and without hindrance proclaimed and preached by Christian priests in the kingdom of Bohemia.

'II. That the Holy Sacrament of the Body and Blood of Christ under the two kinds of bread and wine, shall be freely dispensed to all true Christians who are not shut off by mortal sin.

'III. That since many priests and monks held many earthly possessions, against Christ's command and to the disadvantage of their spiritual office and also of the temporal estates, such priests shall be deprived of this illegal power and shall live model lives according to Holy Scripture, and following the way of Christ and the Apostles.

'IV. That all mortal sins, and especially those that are public, as also other disorders contrary to the divine law, shall be prohibited and punished by those whose office it is, and that so the evil and false repute of this country may be removed and the well-being of the kingdom and of the Bohemian nation may be promoted.'[1]

This document deserves a high place among the spiritual charters of mankind, and a greater emphasis than historians are wont to lay upon it. It was no mere sudden and passing sentiment, but the logical outcome of that sense of sin and yearning for reform which had already obsessed the Czech nation for at least two generations. It was at once ideal and practical, exalting the preaching of the Word, but upholding the Chalice as the highest symbol of Christian mysticism, and linking reform with social order and justice in the State. But it was far more than this, for in the words of Bishop Creighton, 'these articles were a worthy exposition of the principles of the Reformation ; the first asserted the freedom of man to search the Scriptures for himself ; the second attacked one of the great outposts of sacerdotalism, the denial of the cup to the laity ; the third cut at the root of the abuses of the ecclesiastical system ; and the fourth claimed for Christianity the power to regenerate and regulate society.' The torch first kindled by Wyclif, but by this time quenched

---

[1] There is a Puritanic ring about the concluding paragraph :

'But should anyone write or speak or charge evil, erroneous, shameful or abusive things against us, we beg that he should not be believed, as speaking from and lack of charity, and as a false witness. For we boldly confess before God and the world, that with God's grace no other feeling rules in our heart, than to serve Jesus Christ with all our strength and power and means, to dedicate ourselves to Him and follow and fulfil His commands and laws, as befits every good Christian —but every opponent and all who would force us away from the good we must resist according to God's law and truth, and according to our profession we must protect with secular arm both the truth and ourselves. And if through the wickedness of any among us any evil should befall, we declare that this is not our will, for with God's help we stand against every mortal sin ; and should anyone suffer injury from our side, this happens either in necessary self-defence, or as an enemy of God and our enemy, since we must defend God's Law and us from his violence and cruelty. And in general we declare that should anyone think of us that we are doing wrong, we are ready to make it good and in all things to accept from the heart the correction and teaching of Holy Scripture.'

in blood throughout his native land, was now taken up by the Czechs, and kept burning by them for a whole century, until the Germans and other northern nations were ready to take up the task of reform on a wider scale.

Sigismund did not at once give up the struggle, and in the autumn gathered a fresh army for the relief of the besieged fortresses. But there was again no leadership or competence on the royal side and on October 31 Žižka won a still more decisive victory on the Vyšehrad, inflicting desperate losses on the Moravian nobles and German townsmen, and driving Sigismund himself into such ignominious retreat that he was widely accused of treachery by both the contending parties. The garrison at once surrendered, and the wilder elements in Prague sacked the royal castle, purged the churches of their rich ornaments, and destroyed the houses of the Cathedral clergy. Sigismund vented his rage at this new episode of iconoclasm by burning and killing on the estates of the Hussite lords, but this only stiffened opposition against him, and some of his foremost adherents like Ulrich of Rosenberg and Wenceslas of Duba now consented to Taborite services in the districts still under their control. A very large share of the blame for the savage character assumed by hostilities must lie on the shoulders of the King.

Taborites and Crusaders

The victory of Vyšehrad assured to Prague for a time the virtual hegemony over Bohemia—as Palacký has described it, in 'the form of a theocratic Republic.' The Utraquists possessed a number of men whose undoubted ability took a form rather more academic than practical, and the brief lull that followed the battle enabled them to indulge their passion for theological discussion. John of Želivo, commonly known as 'Priest John,' had originally belonged to the Præmonstratensian Order and distinguished himself for his demagogy ; but latterly his chief desire was to seal the passing reconciliation of Utraquist and Taborite. Among his colleagues may be mentioned Jacobellus of Mies, one of Hus's own most intimate pupils, John of Reinstein, sometimes nicknamed 'Cardinal,' the chronicler Peter of Mladenovič, Magister Peter Payne, the wandering Lollard humanist, who since 1417 had played a notable part in the University of Prague, and the preacher John of Rokycan, who was soon to out-distance all the others as a practical statesman. An early bone of contention was provided by a new Taborite programme, which, not content with demanding the strict fulfilment of the Four Articles, insisted that all laws, whether 'heathen or German,' should be replaced by the sole standard of 'the Law and Judgment of God,' that superfluous cloisters and churches should be pulled down, and that decorations and vestments should be forbidden. On December 10 a public disputation was held at the house of Peter Zrmžlik of Svojšin, former master of the mint under Wenceslas ; and the scanty records which have survived enable us to form some opinion as to the true Taborite doctrines, though only in the distorting mirror of their opponents' charges. There can be no doubt of their dislike of all elaborate ceremonial, of incense and vestments, of making the sign of the Cross ; and they were content to read Mass in ordinary dress and in other places than a church. They insisted upon the vernacular for all church services ; they rejected fasting, purgatory, relics, prayers or dedications to Saints, and held firmly the view that no priest in deadly sin might dispense the Sacraments. Their Bishop, Nicholas of Pilgram, pleaded eloquently for a return to the observances of the primitive church, and this remained the ideal of every section of the Hussites. But it soon became clear that the Utraquists, apart from their fundamental insistence on the Chalice and the changes of administration which events forced upon them, scarcely differed doctrinally from their Catholic opponents, and it must be added that they showed exactly the same narrow intolerance towards all who differed from them ; whereas the Taborites, for a time roused by Žižka to a frenzy that vented itself in massacre, afterwards adopted a far milder tone and applied to their enemies the tenets of the New rather than the Old Testament.

During the first few months of 1421 civil war raged in Bohemia, but the triumph of the Hussites was completed by the surrender of Kutná Hora (April 25) and the reconciliation of its inhabitants—hitherto ardent royalists—with the Praguers. Two further signs of the times were a public recantation of anti-national feelings by the ever vacillating Čenek of Wartenberg, and the acceptance of the Four Articles by Archbishop Conrad, which was received with horror in many parts of Christendom, but could not fail to increase Bohemian prestige, the more so as he was no Czech, but a German born and bred. On June 3 the Bohemian Diet met at Čáslav, on the joint summons of the Prague magistracy and of the Archbishop, to restore ordered conditions. The Four Articles were formally accepted, and King Sigismund was excluded from the throne as 'unworthy' by his acts, as a 'blasphemer of sacred truths,' and as the deadly enemy of the Bohemian nation. A Commission of Regency was then appointed, consisting of twenty members—five lords, five knights, four members of the Prague Council, four delegates of the other towns and two representatives of the community of the Taborites. In religious matters they were to take the advice of two clergy—John of Příbram and John of Želivo, and a synod was summoned to regulate Church affairs.

Dissensions were, however, already rending the Hussite ranks. While the election of Nicholas of Pilgram as Taborite Bishop seemed a success for more conservative principles, there was a rapid growth of extreme sectarian opinions. Martinek Hauska, one of the most eloquent of the Taborite priests, preached the purely commemorative view of the Eucharist, and denounced the use of the monstrance and even of the chalice. In August, 1421, Hauska and several others were put to the torture and finally burnt as heretics by the dominant party. More excusable, no doubt, was the drastic action taken against the Nicolaitan sect, so-called after the priest who led them, but better known under the name of Adamites. These unhappy visionaries developed the strange incoherent doctrine that to follow a natural inclination could not be sinful, so long as man remained one with God and not in wilful isolation—from which some drew the conclusion that everything should be shared in common, and therefore women also. There was no God and no devil, save in a good or evil man : God's law was in every man's heart, and he therefore could obey no commands nor follow written injunctions. Marriage was a sin, and clothes were contrary to nature. The centre of this madness was near Veselý, on a small river island ; and here they were assailed by Žižka's troops in October, 1421, and virtually exterminated, exclaiming as they entered the flames that they would reign that day with Christ in Heaven. The contemporary world, which was of course in no way shocked by such methods of dealing with an objectionable sect, did not scruple to identify the Hussites as a whole with its doctrines, and these tactics have even been upheld by some modern historians who lacked the excuse of ignorance or legend.

Meanwhile Sigismund was roused to fresh efforts by the very widespread criticism which his repeated failures provoked, and summoned the Imperial Diet to Nürnberg to rouse Germany against the heretics. It is but fair to add that it was almost impossible for him to concentrate his attention upon Bohemia while Venice was bent upon the conquest of Dalmatia, while the Turks took the offensive on the Danube and even raided Transylvania, and the alarmed Hungarians insisted that he should organize their defences on the south and leave the Bohemian problem to the Princes of the Empire. This time the Papal Legate Branda met with considerable response in Germany, and the crusading armies which assembled in the autumn of 1421 have sometimes been estimated at the high figure of 200,000 men. Five of the seven Electors appeared in person, but there was no recognized commander and no real plan of campaign, while Sigismund and Albert of Austria failed to keep their promise of a simultaneous advance from the south. The crusaders stopped to besiege Saaz, and on the mere report of the redoubtable Žižka's approach, broke up in confusion and withdrew ignominiously beyond the German frontier, apportioning the blame almost equally between Sigismund and the Elector Frederick of Brandenburg.

During the summer serious overtures were made to Poland by the moderate Hussites, with whom on this point Žižka was in agreement.[1] It is always dangerous to read modern conceptions into a medieval period of history, yet there seems no reasonable doubt that feelings of Slav solidarity already played their part in the relations between Czechs and Poles, and that many on both sides desired a union of the two Slav kingdoms and Lithuania in a common defence against German aggressors. Wladislaw played with the idea, but probably more for tactical reasons than from real conviction ; Bohemia could always be used as a counter in Poland's wars against the Teutonic Knights. Moreover, the higher Polish clergy spared no effort to dissuade him from accepting the Four Articles as the condition of union. The fact that Sigismund was his brother-in-law doubtless served less as a deterrent ; he had many grounds for distrusting that treacherous and volatile ruler. In any case, Wladislaw declined the Bohemian Crown, but raised no obstacle to the candidature of Witold, his cousin[2] and successor on the Lithuanian throne, and one of the ablest rulers of those days. Indeed, it is sometimes alleged that Witold had glimmerings of the idea of a Slav Confederation, in which Orthodox and Hussite would find a common basis, and which would oppose an invincible barrier to German aggression eastwards.

The delegation of nobles sent to offer the crown to Witold were waylaid by the Duke of Troppau and handed over to Sigismund ; but this naturally put the Grand Duke on his mettle, and he sent Prince Sigismund Korybut, his own and Wladislaw's nephew, as his deputy in Bohemia, with a retinue of two to three thousand men, and even the Taborites speedily recognized him as 'Lieutenant and Governor.' The enraged Sigismund hired the services of Pipo of Ozora, a noted Italian *condottiere*, who

[1] The first soundings date back to 1420, but had been steadily blocked by the influential Nicholas of Hus, and of course by the extreme Taborites, who were republican in sentiment.

[2] Bachmann. *Gesch Böhmens*, (ii, p. 276) says, Brother.

ravaged the estates of the Moravian Hussite nobles, and was for a time confident that he could reduce the heretics to submission. But his advance upon Prague ended in fresh disaster ; the Hussites were again victorious at the battle of Německý Brod (January 10, 1422), secured a huge booty and avenged upon the town of Kutná Hora the cruelties of Sigismund, who again only saved himself by precipitate flight.

The young Prince Korybut's first difficulties were with the Hussites themselves ; his coming coincided with a rally of conservative forces, and on March 8, John of Želivo, who during the winter had virtually ruled Prague by demagogic methods, was treacherously arrested and beheaded. Žižka wavered between the two extremes, showing a restraint which in itself suffices to refute the legend of his wild and passionate character ; far rather was he a man of simple, straightforward, devout views, ready to make many sacrifices in the cause of national unity, and therefore not carrying his implacable hostility to Sigismund to the length of rejecting monarchy altogether. But he was essentially a soldier by disposition, and in that iron age his stern sense of discipline brought him into growing conflict with the wilder sectaries. His own immediate followers never adopted extreme Taborite views, but adhered strictly to transubstantiation, fasted, and held the Saints in honour, and retained the use of vestments.

The enraged Sigismund incited the Teutonic Order against the 'protectors of the Hussites' in Poland and Lithuania, but Elector Frederick, whose relations with his former friend and benefactor were steadily deteriorating, mediated between the Order and Poland, and indeed henceforth sought the friendship of the Polish Court. The Imperial Diet, however, still displayed some zeal against the heretics, and sent a request to Wladislaw that he would recall his nephew and join the crusade. The Legate Branda gave Sigismund a crusading banner blessed by Pope Martin, and the Elector Frederick was assigned command of an army 'against the Wyclifites who are called "Hussen".' Frederick advanced as far as Tachau in October, 1422, but many of the princes failed to join him or, worse still, withdrew prematurely, while Sigismund and his son-in-law, Albert of Austria, remained inactive in Vienna. By December Frederick found it advisable to retreat from Bohemia without accomplishing anything, and only owed immunity from attack to the acute dissensions in the Hussite ranks and the pressure exercised from Cracow upon Korybut. Sigismund, indeed, had very adroitly made his peace with Wladislaw and Witold, and early in 1423 the latter recalled their reluctant nephew from Bohemia and openly rebuffed their would-be allies. A year later Sigismund even visited Cracow and attended the coronation of Wladislaw's second wife ; and friendship with Poland was now the order of the day. But a deep mutual distrust remained, and Sigismund inspired this attitude not only in the Hussites, whom he still further alienated by investing their deadly foe Albert of Austria as Margrave of Moravia, but among the princes of the Empire, several of whom resented the grant of the Saxon Electorate to Frederick of Meissen, and even in Martin V, who was bluntly critical of King Sigismund's whole policy and tactics.

The years 1423 and 1424, then, were a transitional period of internal dissension in Bohemia, but at least of immunity from invasion. The one outstanding event was the death of the blind hero Žižka (October 11, 1424), during an epidemic of the plague, at the very moment when he was again reconciled with his opponents in the capital, and was planning joint action between Taborites, Praguers and moderate Utraquists, against the foes once more gathering beyond the frontier. Žižka was neither a statesman nor a religious leader in the ordinary sense of the terms, but Bezold is right in describing him as 'the ideal of "God's Warrior," for whom there are only two points of view, the religious and the military.' What made his death so irreparable was his dynamic force, coupled with a sincere, unbending character and real military genius. The legend that his followers, at his own request, used his skin for their war-drums was doubtless put about by his enemies to prove his barbarous and pagan outlook, but it is also a testimony to the terror which his name inspired. There is much to be said for the seductive theory put forward by Count Lützow that this was the only moment at which it might have been possible 'to establish in Bohemia a national Church and a national Kingdom under a Slavic dynasty.'[1]

Certainly dissensions speedily revived, and the more rigid section of the Taborites broke away and assumed the name of Horebites, or 'Orphans,' to indicate their belief that no one could take the place of their lost leader, certainly not the perfidious Sigismund, or even the well-meaning but not very reliable Sigismund Korybut. It is significant that the command of the Hussite armies passed, after a short interval, from Žižka to Prokop, one of those warrior priests whom necessity had driven to bear arms and study tactics. When at a later date he was sent to Basel as delegate, his credentials included the phrase : 'Procopius, exercitum Taboritarum in spiritualibus rector' ; but popular feeling named him : 'Procopius the Great.'

From Ústi to Domažlice

Early in 1426 a number of leading German princes, for the most part bent upon narrow aims of territorial aggrandizement, met Sigismund at Vienna, and responded to the Papal message 'to drive out these swine from the vineyard of the Lord, which they have trodden all too long.' Prokop and his men were ready for the new German invasion, and his skilful use of chained wagons turned the battle of Ústi (June 16, 1426) from a defeat to a rout and a massacre. Some of the defeated nobles knelt to beg their lives, and the dead, we are told, lay like sheaves upon the field. Elector Frederick of Brandenburg would fain have rallied a fresh army, but there were dissensions in the German ranks ; and Prokop followed the virile tactics of counter-attacking deep into German territory, with a view to extracting recognition, however unwilling. Korybut, meanwhile, without abandoning his Utraquist views, hugged the illusion that a direct agreement might be reached with Rome behind the backs of both Sigismund and the German princes. Both contemporaries and modern writers have judged Korybut with great severity and blamed him for not pursuing to the uttermost the policy of aggression and ravaging ; but though the full facts are not available, it is at least probable that he acted in the best of faith, and realized the strain that prolonged war was placing upon the Czech nation. In any case he had clearly lost the confidence of the majority ; for in April, 1427, he was suddenly seized and spirited away to Prague, and after a certain interval sent back to his native Lithuania, thus accepting his fate and fading out of the Bohemian picture.

[1] *The Hussite Wars*, p. 170.

In the summer of 1427 fresh crusading armies began to assemble, preparatory to a simultaneous attack from four quarters; but it is curious that their most eminent leader, the Elector Frederick of Brandenburg, who six years earlier had favoured the massacre of all save small children, now formally offered mediation to Prague, and deplored the ravages of so prolonged a war. When this failed the crusaders moved into Bohemia, but without any real co-ordination of effort, and indeed without observing the not unskilful plan of concerted action which had been drawn up. Cardinal Henry of Beaufort, uncle of the infant Henry VI, arrived as Papal Legate, but found himself involved, through no fault of his own, in the shameful collapse of the siege of Stříbro (Mies) and the panic-stricken flight of the German army to Tachov (August 5–11). He found his right to military command challenged by the Elector Frederick and other leaders, and publicly lost his temper, flinging his banner to the ground in the sight of some of the troops. After sharing the inevitable retreat into Germany, the Legate tried to rally the Imperial Diet to further efforts and openly reproved the princes for their quarrels; but there was a general lack of enthusiasm, it was difficult to raise more *Hussengeld* or equip armies, and Sigismund was meanwhile plunging into the bottomless pit of Balkan adventure.

During 1428 Prokop overran Silesia, brought its dukes to terms, and thus made Bohemia less vulnerable on the east. By the end of that year the ground was sufficiently prepared for one of the chief Hussite nobles, Menhard of Neuhaus, to set on foot negotiations with the Emperor on his return to Central Europe. In April, 1429, then, a delegation consisting of Prokop himself, some of the Utraquist lords, and the English Hussite Peter Payne, waited upon Sigismund at Pressburg (Bratislava); they offered to acknowledge him as king if he would adopt their faith, and asked him to secure them a hearing before all Christendom. Sigismund was furious at what he felt to be a reflection upon his orthodoxy, and spoke freely in private of renewed war and extermination. The deadlock was complete. The Bohemian Diet was invoked in May, to give its decision upon the negotiations, and went the length of accepting the principle of a new Council, but on condition that the Eastern Churches were also represented there and that those lords who had espoused the Utraquist faith, but afterwards departed from it, should be definitely excluded. They also demanded that Moravia should be placed in the hands of a prince 'of Slav blood.' This, of course, led to nothing; Sigismund was almost equally distrusted by the Hussites and by the German princes and towns, and Pope Martin did all he could behind the scenes to wreck the prospects of a Council. In the autumn of 1429 hostilities broke out more fiercely than ever, and this time Prokop and his armies carried fire and sword into Saxony and Thuringia, and for the first time forced the Germans to negotiate on equal terms, instead of demanding unconditional surrender. In passing it is to be noted that such German chroniclers as Windecke put on record that amid the savagery of captured and burning castles it was the Hussite practice to spare the women.

Early in 1430 the Elector Frederick,[1] who as a statesman stands head and shoulders above his contemporaries, met and negotiated with Prokop in person, but both Sigismund and Pope Martin opposed all plans for a compromise with Bohemia, and the former introduced fresh

[1] The first Elector of the Hohenzollern House, he was the direct ancestor of the Emperor William II.

complications by his alternate parleys and quarrels with King Wladislaw Jagiellon of Poland and his interference in Lithuanian problems. At the same time there are grounds for the view that Hussite victories, and especially their successful inroads into the Reich, were reacting upon the German masses, and even further afield, in France and other countries ; and this would account on the one hand for Frederick's eagerness for peace, and for that curious incident, the publication of a letter from Joan of Arc, denouncing the 'obscene superstition' of the Czechs.[1] Moreover, the spread of so-called 'heretic letters' (*Ketzerbriefe*), challenging the whole Papal system and urging the deposition of Pope and Cardinals should they block the summons of the Council, appears to have gravely alarmed Martin V and convinced him that to summon a Council was a lesser evil than to leave the cauldron seething. A document threatening him with the consequences of further evasion was even affixed to the gate of his palace and attributed to certain of the German princes. Droysen, the great historian of Prussian policy, does not hesitate to write of 'the wild effervescence' of the peasantry in all countries bordering on Bohemia, and of the 'immeasurable danger in which Germany stood,' and adds : 'Only a summons from an invading band of Hussites seemed to be needed, in order to unleash the mass of the German people.' This would seem to provide the background for a manifesto issued in 1430 by Prokop and his friends to 'honourable, clear-sighted, honest lords, magistrates, and the whole community, rich and poor.' To its demand for the final recognition of the Four Articles and its recapitulation of Hussite grievances against the Roman Church, was appended the telling argument that the partisans of Rome had never granted the Hussites a hearing or allowed them to state their doctrine in open discussion. Yet Our Lord had listened even to the Devil, and 'Catholic priests are not better than Christ, and we not worse than the Devil.'

Martin V was incorrigible to the last. Shortly before he died in February, 1431, he had nominated Cardinal Julian Cesarini first as Legate for the next Crusade, and then as president of the new Council ; and he continued to hope for and advocate a final victorious campaign, which would have led automatically to a collapse of the Conciliar agitation. On the other hand, both Sigismund, who by now was tired of waiting for the Bohemian crown, but whose idea of negotiation was simply dictation, and Wladislaw, who had been induced to take a hand in the Hussite dispute and to organize a disputation at Cracow, insisted that the Hussites should give in advance an unconditional pledge to accept all the future Council's decisions. This was rejected by all shades of opinion and roused the more extreme Taborites to a still more irreconcilable attitude. One Taborite preacher denounced Archbishop Conrad for necromancy, simony and hypocrisy, adding : "What is more, he is a German, a natural enemy of our nation."

Meanwhile Cesarini overbore all attempts at compromise, and after investing the Elector Frederick and his knights with the Cross in the Church of St. Sebaldus at Nürnberg, issued a manifesto bidding the Hussites return to the bosom of the Church. One of the largest crusading armies ever launched against Bohemia crossed the western frontier in August, 1431, repeating all the previous errors of strategy and rousing the war-weary population to resistance by indiscriminate burning and massacre. In the words of Aeneas Silvius, 'they had undertaken to root

[1] Its authentichity as always remained in doubt.

out the whole Bohemian nation.' But there was the same failure of generalship on the German side as in former invasions ; a week was wasted in the siege of the relatively unimportant town of Tachov, and when on August 14 the armies joined near Domažlice, the Czechs, chanting 'Ye Warriors of God,' and sounding their drums and trumpets, speedily drove the Germans in headlong flight across the Bohemian Forest and gathered a huge booty on the field. 'They scattered like smoke, they melted like wax,' sang a Hussite poet. The Legate in particular escaped with difficulty, leaving behind him his cardinal's robes and the Bull which he had brought from the Pope, and disguising himself against the anger of his fellow-fugitives. The *Hussenflucht* remained one of the most painful memories of the fifteenth century in Germany.

The Last Years of the Taborites

Cesarini was welcomed by Sigismund at Nürnberg, but this time he was in chastened mood, and declared that there was no other remedy save the Council, by which the spread of the Hussite heresy could still be checked. The Czechs, it has been well said, had now 'attained the summit of their military glory ; at no period was the fate of Europe so completely in their hands.' Their leaders showed no little moderation, but also nothing very constructive in the sense of political plans. But when the newly constituted Council of Basel invited the Czechs to take their part in the promotion of Christian unity and assured them of that free hearing which had hitherto always been denied them (October, 1431), there was a very widespread desire for acceptance. The death of Archbishop Conrad removed a powerful enemy of compromise, and the fact that the Council had to face the open hostility of the new Pope Eugenius IV was treated in Prague as a proof that the reformers were at last in earnest. After somewhat stormy debates the Diet decided in the first instance to send delegates to meet the Council's envoys at Eger (Cheb), with a view to regulating the delicate problem of a safe conduct before there could be any question of their proceeding to Basel. The Hussite envoys included Prokop, John of Rokycan, now rapidly coming to the front as the most eminent Utraquist churchman, and Peter Payne, commonly known as 'the English Master.' They were satisfied with the personal guarantees offered, and exacted the right to express their opinions freely, to censure the abuses of the Church and to defend the Four Articles ; and in January, 1433, the same envoys, attended by several of the leading Utraquist nobles, arrived in Basel. There had been a significant incident on their way through Germany, one of the party having displayed a Taborite battle flag showing on one side the portrait of Christ and on the other a representation of the Chalice, bearing the inscription *Veritas omnia vincit.* It is not surprising that this evoked painful memories of Czech prowess.

The negotiations of the Council with the Hussites lie outside the scope of this narrative. It may suffice to affirm that never did the yearnings of devout men in Christendom come nearer to their fulfilment than in the two opening years at Basel. There were occasional outbursts against the permission enjoyed by the Czech envoys to hold religious services according to their own rite, as liable to pervert the good people of Basel itself ; and there were clever attempts to create dissensions between the Utraquists, Taborites and Orphans. Moreover, Peter Payne's glorification of Wyclif and his teachings led to altercations with the

English ecclesiastics present. But the main protagonists were able to state their case very fully, and there seems to have grown up a certain mutual esteem between Cesarini and Prokop, that strange and somewhat enigmatic figure, whose qualities of leadership belonged now to the political, now to the military, and now to the religious, sphere. A more worldly note is struck by the anecdotes of a cardinal who saw at least one bond of union between the two sides : "If the Pope had us in his power," he told Prokop, "he would hang us both."

For a time, however, the current of events was set strongly against papal intransigeance and in favour of pacification. When the Bohemian envoys returned to Prague in April, 1433, they were followed by delegates of the Council, led by Bishop Philibert of Coutances, and friendly discussions followed. In the end they returned to Basel with concrete proposals relative to the Four Articles. Unhappily the long delays had had a disintegrating effect upon opinion in Bohemia, and civil war had broken out during the summer of 1433 between those who desired an understanding with the Council and those who feared that this would lead to the reimposition of Romanist doctrine. Cause and effect operated in a vicious circle, for at Basel there were many who urged postponement, as likely to augment the discord between the three rival currents of opinion. The only basis on which all three could agree was that Communion in both kinds should be obligatory throughout Bohemia : but it was difficult for the Council to concede this so long as Pilsen and other towns were in the hands of the Catholic party, which was of course opposed to the granting of the Cup to the laity. There was thus a most obvious motive for the attempt made by the extremists in July, 1433, to reduce Pilsen to submission.

The circumstances under which Prokop broke away from the moderates and early in 1434 placed himself at the head of the Taborite armies will always remain obscure. The appointment of Aleš of Riesenburg as Regent, and the increase in the power of the great nobles which this implied, was certainly not without influence on his decision ; there doubtless also were personal issues between Prokop and John of Rokycan, who now had a majority of the Diet and all the Utraquist clergy solidly behind him. It is dangerous to transplant such watchwords as democracy to a remote century and radically different problems ; but it is abundantly clear that Prokop and the Orphans led a popular movement recruited among the masses, prompted to increasing fanaticism, alike in the social and religious sphere, by the strain of a prolonged and often savage war. It is also fairly certain that there had been latterly a marked decay of discipline among the extremists, which explains the sudden crash, and that parallel with this had gone a deterioration in the character of Prokop that alienated him from many with whom he had hitherto co-operated.

The threat to Pilsen failed, but it evoked a working coalition between the Utraquist nobles and the Catholic minority ; the siege had to be raised, while on the other hand the new allies seized the New Town of Prague and marshalled their forces for the final struggle. On May 30, 1434, the two armies met at Lipany, near Kolín, in the heart of Bohemia, and the battle, thanks very largely to the skilful generalship of Bořek of Miletinek, ended in a crushing defeat of the Taborites and Orphans. The defeated army was almost wiped out, and Prokop the Great and his ablest lieutenant, Prokupek, perished with many others.

The Czech historian Prokeš has, with very considerable exaggeration, called Lipany 'the saddest day in Bohemian history' and 'a deadly blow to pure Hussitism.' It certainly ended the phase of civil war and religious exaltation and ushered in a new period of compromise. At the time the first reactions were to claim the battle as a victory for the Council, but this proved fallacious, as the Utraquists had only joined hands with the Catholics to check the growing anarchy, and soon showed that they had no intention of returning without conditions to the old Church. The real gainers were Rokycana and the conservative lords, who gradually found it expedient, and indeed necessary, to drop their demand for a sort of Utraquist conformity throughout the whole kingdom. At the same time they were able to exploit the impatience of the ardent but ageing Sigismund to secure the allegiance of Bohemia before he died. One of the main questions which delayed the final settlement was that of appointing John of Rokycan to the vacant Archbishopric of Prague, and of accepting his election through the medium of the Bohemian Diet. It is characteristic of Sigismund that while these protracted negotiations were at their height, he, the champion of orthodoxy and Christian unity, remarked that he did not care if the Bohemians were to elect a donkey ; it was not he who would have to ordain him !

The Council of Basel and the Compactata

The final stages of agreement really belong to the history of the Conciliar movement, round which the fate of Europe then still revolved. Suffice it to say that at last, on July 5, 1436, the Bohemian delegates accepted the 'Compacts' which had formed the main basis of discussion between them and the Council ; and Sigismund's recognition as King of Bohemia, and the tacit recognition of Rokycana, immediately followed. At the age of sixty-eight, and seventeen disastrous years after his brother's death, Sigismund was welcomed in Prague as undisputed sovereign. Early in 1437 the Council's formal sanction arrived, and a decree was read out officially in four languages in one of the churches of Prague, declaring that those who partook of the Sacrament according to the Utraquist rite were 'true Christians and genuine sons of the Church.'

The so-called 'Compactata' deserve to be quoted in full, as one of the most remarkable documents of their time—the more so as they remained one of the foundations of the Bohemian Constitution for over a century to come and might, under happier circumstances, have served as a signpost towards religious, and so towards political, conciliation. They are an undying witness to the idealism which inspired a small nation to stake its all upon questions of principle.

'I. The Holy Sacrament is to be given freely in both kinds to all Christians in Bohemia and Moravia, and to those elsewhere who adhere to the faith of those countries.

'II. All mortal sins shall be punished and extirpated by those whose office it is to do so.

'III. The Word of the Lord is to be freely and truthfully preached by the priests of the Lord and by worthy deacons.

'IV. The priests in the time of the law of grace shall claim ownership of no worldly possessions.'

Sigismund's self-seeking and unprincipled character was well illustrated in the brief time that remained to him. The 'Compacts' were to him a mere means to an end, his own recognition as King of Bohemia ; henceforth he lost all interest in the Council, and no longer supported it against the Pope, feeling that it was adopting dangerously 'democratic' ideas, subversive to the whole monarchical order in Europe. Meanwhile Bohemia had won for herself a peculiar hybrid position between the two extremes of ecclesiastical opinion, and was to retain it for a century and a half to come, her heresy condoned and covered up by a grudging and conditional recognition of her right to the Cup for the laity, and to married clergy. But she paid dearly for this privilege in the undoubted overstrain of the Hussite wars, and a position of isolation among the European nations which she found it difficult to shake off, and which certainly contributed to her eventual downfall.

An Outline of Hussite Tenets

The close of the Hussite Wars offers a point of vantage from which to survey briefly the ideas which gave impetus and endurance to the rival combatants. More than one historian has stressed the strange contrast between the Bohemia of Charles IV, reputed as a bulwark of the faith and offering more hopeful signs of consolidation than the nebula of small self-governing principalities and towns into which Germany had fallen since the fall of the Hohenstauffen and the Bohemia of Žižka and Prokop, filled with the din and uproar of warring sects and moving towards dissolution. In the eyes of contemporary Europe Bohemia incorporated the ideas of social upheaval, in very much the same way as Russia in the first *élan* of the Soviet regime ; but though the conflict between German and Slav was always one of the major elements involved, yet it is utterly false to suggest that the Hussite movement was mere cover for national fanaticism. The religious issue dominated Czech national life, just as in the literature of the period it drove all other issues into the background. In one sense, it may be said that the Czechs were a mere mouthpiece of a wellnigh universal movement of revolt against the corruption of the medieval Church ; but it is equally true to say that Czech interest in religious and ecclesiastical questions is a thread running through their entire history, up to the present day, and that from the first reformist tendencies found specially fertile soil in Bohemia. It is true that there was deplorably little tolerance on either side ; a classic instance is the long list of punishments by which Žižka's famous regulations of war sought to enforce the principles of Christian discipline upon recalcitrants. Yet the Taborites, in their manifesto of 1431, expressly reject the persecution of heretics, on the ground that he who persecutes others is himself a heretic, and again that such punishment is contrary to the Gospel and the primitive Church. Often enough they used language of extreme crudity, but this was then, and long after, the common practice of all rival theological controversialists. It may be noted in passing that the Taborites were often reproached for the relative tolerance which they showed towards the Jews.

The Taborite synods were constantly warning against uncritical interpretation of the Scriptures ; and all sections of the movement were agreed in attaching capital importance to free preaching of the word, and in maintaining that the New Testament contained all that was necessary for salvation. Next to this tenet came their insistence upon frequent

Communion even for children. It was the practice of the more radical-clergy to dispense the Sacrament in the open air, kneeling, reciting the Lord's Prayer, then blessing the elements and giving to all present ; in battle the Host was placed in a monstrance, and attached to a high pole, which made it conspicuous to the whole army. In view of the extreme importance attached to the Communion, it was doubtless inevitable that there should be acute controversy and divergence of interpretation, as in the period of the Reformation. It will suffice to point out that the Utraquist majority upheld the doctrine of the Real Presence as taught by Hus, that Žižka and the leading Taborites held the same view, while Peter Payne (influenced by memories of the 'evangelical doctor' Wyclif) inclined towards the commemorative view, and this was stressed much more crudely by the small group of sectaries known as Picards, who took refuge in Bohemia from Flanders.

There was in all the sectaries a strikingly Puritanic trait ; adultery was treated with special severity and one of the first acts of the Hussite authorities after occupying a town was to close and destroy all houses of ill fame. The excesses of the Adamites and other similar small bodies were as little characteristic of the movement as a whole as were those of the Anabaptists of Münster characteristic of the German Reformation as a whole. There were at times iconoclastic outbreaks, and dancing was often denounced as sinful. As in other religious movements, a considerable amount of energy was expended upon the barren issues of vestments and ceremonial ; but it may be noted that the Taborites did not condemn them as sinful, but only as a useless and hurtful tradition, contrary to the practice of the primitive Church, to which it was their paramount desire to return.

Though their German opponents, sometimes deliberately, sometimes quite unconsciously, exaggerated the threat involved to the social order, it would be absurd to deny that the movement as a whole speedily went far beyond the ideas of Hus, and took on a distinctly anti-monarchical and levelling (in our modern parlance, democratic) character. The Legate Branda on one occasion tried to convince Wladislaw of Poland that 'the salvation of human society' demanded the destruction of Hussitism, while Sigismund once tried to make the Diet believe that 'the extermination of the whole nobility' was a deliberate Hussite aim. The truth is that its original appeal to the peasantry was closely bound up with a desire to improve its status as against the feudal lords, just as on the other hand these latter, step by step, as the war dragged on, set themselves to appropriate the former Church lands and to strengthen their powers over the simple man. In the final stage the nobles and the moderate Utraquist clergy secured more and more the direction of the movement and un-doubtedly exploited it for their own ends, to prepare the reversion of a free and self-conscious peasantry to eventual serfdom. The towns appear to have shared in the distribution of Church property, and the burghers of Prague in particular played a great part in the early period of these troubles. But this does not apply to the German element which was still very strong in them, and which, being unable to disguise its hostility to Hussite tenets, found it wiser to withdraw to Germany, often after the confiscation of their property and something in the nature of forced sales, to persons who had done special service in the 'Holy War.' The heightened friction between German and Slav was an important factor in the whole struggle. The withdrawal of the Germans from the University simultaneously strengthened the Czech element in Prague and other cities and led to attempts at Czechization. The fact that in 1421 a single Church in Prague was assigned to the Germans of the city, with permission to use their own language, was already regarded as a concession. In 1435 a demand was put forward for the exclusion of all Germans from office ;[1] and though it did not come to this, Czech tended to replace Latin in the administration, the courts, and the Diet. Meanwhile it is possible to trace at times the growth of wider Slav sympathies, notably, of course, with Poland ; the occasional relations with Wladislaw Jagiello are symptomatic, and still more the sympathetic, though not very effective, part played by his nephew Sigismund Korybut. The Hussites more than once made more general appeals for the sympathy and co-operation of the outer world ; but never succeeded in giving them such concrete form as would pierce the wall of suspicion and isolation produced by obloquy and abuse.

Dr. Krofta has pointed out that the Hussite struggle permanently affected the national character by kindling in their minds 'the idea of some special character attaching to the Czech nation, of its call to great deeds in the service of God and the divine law. The national consciousness of the Czechs thus acquired a special mystical tinge and impressive fervour, and the Czech national idea was enriched by the thought that the nation, apart from its defensive struggle against the German menace, had had a great positive task laid upon it—a fight for the pure truth of God.'[2] To this may be appended the words of the most discerning of German writers on this period, Friedrich von Bezold : 'It is the tragic fate of certain peoples to fight out terrible struggles for the advantage of all mankind, but by the sacrifice of their whole strength and blood.'

[1] Palacký, in his *Documente*, p. 357, quotes the demand : '*Natio bohemica debet in regno Bohemiæ regere nationes exteras, ipsis præsidere et eos tanquam servos incolarum compati.*'
[2] *Cambridge Medieval History*, viii, p. 86.

CHAPTER V

BOHEMIA'S NATIONAL KING

In alle Fernen trug ich Böhmens Namen,
Aus allen Fernen tönt zurück sein Ruhm.
                                    —*Grillparzer.*

Albert and Ladislas

SIGISMUND died in December, 1437, on his way back to Hungary, where he had always felt most at home, and where he desired to be buried. He left behind him, besides the ripe fruits of long years of perfidy and prevarication, the awkward legacy of an unregulated succession. His only daughter Elizabeth was the wife of Albert II of Austria, a man of great ability and considerable charm, but distrusted in Bohemia both as a militant German and as an ardent supporter of the Papacy against the Hussites. Albert was unanimously elected King of Hungary in December, within a month of his father-in-law's death ; but his election in Bohemia was opposed by a strong section of the nobility, which favoured Prince Casimir of Poland. Albert was crowned in Prague, but declined to appease Casimir by offering his daughter's hand in marriage. He had also won the support of the Electors, and was thus the first ruler of Austria to unite the Crowns of Bohemia and Hungary with the dignity of King of the Romans. Scarcely had peace been patched up again with Poland than he was called back hastily to organize the defence of Hungary's southern frontier against the growing Turkish menace. His death, as the result of an attack of dysentery, removed a ruler who was rapidly making himself felt, and bade fair to be the heaven-sent leader to unite Europe against the Turks. He was only forty-two, but contemporary chroniclers bear witness to his high capacity ; in the words of one, a Czech, 'he was, though a German, good, brave and gentle.' It was as fatal a blow to the Habsburg power, and indeed to the peaceful development of all Central Europe, as was the premature death, again after a brief reign of two years, of his lineal descendant Leopold II, after an interval of 350 years. Both events are crowning examples of the influence of the personal factor upon the course of history, and a profound mystery to those who believe in historic continuity and in the Providence which that phrase implies.

Four months later his wife Elizabeth gave birth to a son, whom history knows as Ladislas Posthumus. The times were too uncertain for the rule of an infant in arms, and national feeling and personal ambition, combined with the desire of the nobility to exploit this occasion for curtailing the royal power. Hungary, then, elected King Wladislaw III of Poland, in the hope that Polish resources, added to Hungarian, would suffice to repel the Turks ; and as the new king had the backing of the great national hero, John Hunyady, he was able after a famous march through the heart of the Balkan Peninsula, to dictate peace to the Sultan, by which Wallachia was ceded to Hungary and George Branković recognized as independent King of Serbia. These events lie outside the scope of the present narrative ; and it must suffice to remind the reader that Wladislaw, in an evil hour for all Europe, allowed himself to be persuaded by the

Papal Legate, Cesarini (whose behaviour on this occasion was far from worthy of the man who had striven so earnestly at Basel for a real appeasement), that faith need not be kept with infidels. He therefore resumed the attack, thinking that he would drive the Sultan out of Europe. Instead of this, he was defeated and killed at the disastrous battle of Varna, on November 10, 1444 ; the Legate shared his fate and Hunyady barely escaped with his life.

It is important to bear in mind that this Christian defeat ushered in the great period of Turkish expansion. In 1453 Constantinople fell, in 1459 what was still left of Serbia, in 1463 Bosnia, and during the next two decades the last points of resistance in Hercegovina and Albania. Hungary thus became a border state, open to the persistent attacks of a great military empire, whose appetite was whetted by the political ambitions of a series of very great monarchs, and by the religious fanaticism and hopes of plunder of their armies. Yet instead of increasing unity, the states most directly menaced fell more and more apart, and the pathetic figure of Pope Pius II stands like one crying in the wilderness, pleading for a union of Christendom against the advancing Crescent, and vainly warning Europe of the dire consequences of disregarding his advice.

Meanwhile Bohemia had held almost equally aloof from Hungary and from Austria. The vacant crown of the Romans fell to Frederick of Austria, whom his cousin had designated as guardian of his unborn child, and who, though a man of considerable culture and high personal character, was sluggish and apathetic, unable to rouse himself to action though dreaming day-dreams of vast ambition, which his descendants were to realize (A.E.I.O.U.—*Austriæ Est Imperare Orbi Universo*—was his favourite anagram). But he was also stubborn and grasping, and he refused to hand over the custody of the child to the Bohemian lords, who consequently turned elsewhere for a king, and when Duke Albert of Bavaria declined their offer of the Crown, governed the country through a Regent elected by the Diet.

The most powerful of these oligarchs, Ptáček of Pirkstein, died prematurely in 1444, but in his place there arose one of the few really gifted political leaders in Czech history, George of Poděbrad—son of Viktorin of Poděbrad, the leader of the Praguers during the late wars. Though barely twenty-four, he soon became the acknowledged head of the so-called 'Union of Poděbrad,' which was strong enough to keep the reviving Catholic party at bay. The mission of Cardinal Carvajal, in the name of the new Pope Nicholas V, brought matters to a head, for he announced the Pope's categorical refusal to recognize the Utraquist Archbishop Rokycana—whose enforced withdrawal from Prague had been one of the last acts of the dying Sigismund. Worse still, the Legate took one of those grotesque steps only possible before the age of printing ; after denying all knowledge of the 'Compactata,' he decamped from Prague with the original document in his baggage, and was made to disgorge it to messengers despatched post-haste in his pursuit. Poděbrad shared the general embitterment, and in the early autumn made himself master of Prague, driving out the Catholic party and restoring Rokycana to his functions as leader of the Utraquist clergy. In the civil war that followed Poděbrad threw his whole weight into the Utraquist scale, and was able to hold at bay the lords of the Austrian and Catholic party until in 1451 Frederick, in his capacity as guardian of Ladislas, recognized Poděbrad as *de facto* ruler of Bohemia until the young king was ready to

assume power ; and in April, 1452, the Diet formally confirmed the
Regency which he had already exercised for several years past. He was
challenged from two sides, but ere long reduced the stronghold of Tabor
and with it the last attempt at organized Taborite resistance, and soon
after compelled the Catholic leader Ulrich of Rosenberg to make his submission. Henceforth it was no longer possible to exploit one section of
the Utraquists against the other ; those who desired an accord with
Rome and those to whom the Compactata were the *ne plus ultra* of
concession, were united on a national basis.

Meanwhile Frederick had gone to Rome to receive the Imperial
Crown, taking Ladislas in his train, and in Hungary, John Hunyady,
though more keenly alive than ever to the need for concentrating against
the Turks, found it advisable to lay down the office of Governor. By
1453 Frederick was no longer in a position to restrain the boy's liberty
of action, owing to the open resistance of Vienna, aided by the powerful
Count Ulrich of Cilli, and by sections of the Austrian, Hungarian and
Bohemian nobility. Ladislas was therefore allowed to visit first Vienna,
where he fell from Frederick's hands into Cilli's, and then Prague, but
only after he had promised to recognize the 'Compactata' and the Utraquist Archbishop. On October 28, 1453, he was crowned in St. Vitus'
Cathedral.

The real power remained in the hands of George of Poděbrad, who
contrived to maintain the most cordial relations with the young king.
They addressed each other as 'My Father' and 'My Son' ; and for a time
it was hoped in Rome that between them they would steer the heretic
kingdom back to its allegiance. In the words of Aeneas Silvius, who
wrote with intimate personal knowledge : 'By his efforts all Bohemia
became one people. Each was allowed his rite and those were punished
who accused others of heresy. Thus the wolf lies down with the sheep,
the panther with the lion-cub.'

King George of Poděbrad

The fall of Constantinople in 1453 was too lightly regarded in Europe,
but to Hunyady, though not to the selfish magnates of his day, it was
only too apparent that Hungary would soon have to bear the full brunt
of the Ottoman advance. His heroism saved Belgrade from Mohammed
the Conqueror, and made it possible for his successors to hold the line of
the Danube against the Turks for two more generations ; but he himself
died of the plague before the critical operations were completed. Only
a year later (November 29, 1457) the same disease removed the boy king
Ladislas, and re-opened the question of the succession in all three countries. In January, 1458, the Hungarian Diet elected Hunyady's son,
Matthias Corvinus, not as Regent but as king, and two months later
the Diet of Bohemia elected George of Poděbrad. He was backed by the
whole influence of the Utraquists and Rokycana, who declared from
the pulpit that "it would be better to follow the example of the judges of
Israel and transform Bohemia into a Republic, if there were no native
worthy to bear the royal crown." None the less, in the opening years
of his reign George pursued a distinctly tortuous policy, which may
doubtless be excused by a knowledge of his precarious and isolated
position, as the first heretic and elected king in the Europe of his day.
The disregard of hereditary claims shown equally by Bohemia and

Hungary seemed to mark an epoch in European history and alarmed both Emperor and Pope. Yet Frederick, in spite of his being the legitimate heir of Ladislas, needed help against his recalcitrant Austrian subjects, his cantankerous brother Albert VI and a strong anti-German party among the Hungarian magnates. He therefore himself invested George with the royal insignia. This did not prevent George from sounding several of the German Electors as to the possibility of ousting Frederick from the Crown of the Romans ; but he soon found that the balance was heavily weighted against one who was both a Slav and a heretic, and wisely abandoned his efforts. On the other hand, he played an elaborate diplomatic game with the new Pope, Pius II, who as Aeneas Sylvius Piccolomini had an intimate personal acquaintance with the long Bohemian contest. Each hoped to extract the essential concessions from the other ; and when George was crowned in St. Vitus' Cathedral he took a secret oath to the papal delegates, promising 'to uphold obedience to the Papal See and in agreement with Rome to lead his subjects away from all error.'[1] There can be no doubt that this ambiguous phrase expressed George's resolve to secure papal recognition for the Compactata, just as to the Pope it meant their eventual renunciation. Pius II impatiently expected the arrival of Bohemian envoys and for a time he had the illusion that George was on the point of abjuring heresy and heading a crusade against the Turks. It was already felt in Rome to be a bad sign that of the two chief envoys one was a Utraquist and one a Catholic, and that the two worked amicably together ; but when they demanded sanction for the Compactata, it came to a public disputation not unlike those in the Council, and the Pope, in the presence of 4,000 people, flatly rejected all idea of recognition.

This made a deplorable impression in Bohemia, and George promptly forestalled the complaints of the Utraquists that he was playing a double game. As the German historian Voigt has neatly put it ; 'He desired the favour of the Catholics, but the favour of the Utraquists was a necessity to him.' George read aloud publicly the much-canvassed coronation oath, and added the categorical declaration that 'since we were born, brought up and raised by God's will to the throne in this faith, we swear to maintain it, to defend it and to live and die in it. . . . And we believe there is no other way to the salvation of all souls, than to die in the Compactata and to partake of both kinds according to the Saviour's injunction.' He thus rallied the whole body of Utraquists solidly behind him, and the Catholic nobles, influenced by national considerations, were ready with their support 'where his and the kingdom's honour was at stake.' The deadlock was all the greater because Frederick found himself dependent upon the politic George's help against his own rebellious Austrian subjects. "Poor Germany," lamented Pius, "whose Emperor can only be saved by a heretic king. . . . The Bohemian will not let thee either be destroyed or win the day, he wishes to fan eternal hatred among the Austrians, in order to be first arbiter and then master."

On the eve of his departure for Ancona to head the Crusade, Pius threatened George with excommunication, and gave him 180 days in which to make submission in person in Rome. But Pius did not return alive, and his successor, Paul II, at first tried to sow dissension among the Czechs by underground methods. After a rising of the malcontent nobles had failed, George made in 1466 a last attempt at compromise

[1] Krofta, *C. M. H.*, viii, p. 96.

with the Holy See, offering to accept a Catholic as Archbishop of Prague, if he were a Czech by birth and if he were authorized to ordain as priests those who celebrated *sub utraque* as well as *sub una*. But Paul publicly denounced King George's envoy as 'an audacious beast' and 'a ribald heretic,' flinging his credentials unread upon the floor. Thereupon the Pope formally excommunicated King George, and followed this up by deposing him from the Bohemian Crown and bidding all his subjects renounce their allegiance.

It was in this situation that George countered with a highly original and interesting project for a League of European Princes, which has sometimes been claimed as the first germ of the idea of a League of Nations and certainly deserves a place in the introductory chapter of any treatise on international government. His idea was to bring together Bohemia, Poland, Hungary, France, Burgundy and Venice, with the object of removing the Turkish question from the hands of the Holy See —in modern parlance, to give it a purely political character. There was to be a General Council for the reform of the Church, something in the nature of an international assembly or 'Parliament,' from which the Papacy would be excluded. The constitution of the decaying Empire was also to be reformed. The King of France was to be head of the Union, and thus in some sense the political head of the Christian world. The scheme was a blend of selfish interest and of constructive statesmanship, the one obvious enough to render it suspect to sceptical and grasping neighbours, the other far in advance of what was possible in that age of transition, or in the despotic eras that were to follow it.

The papal offer of Bohemia to King Casimir of Poland (whose wife, as daughter of Albert and grand-daughter of Sigismund, was the lineal heiress of the original Přemyslide House) met with a polite refusal. But the Papacy found a ready instrument for the enforcing of its aims in the ambitions of the Hungarian king, and this time it suited Frederick to join him in an attack upon Bohemia, even though the Turks were knocking at the door.

Matthias, during his first precarious tenure of the Hungarian throne, had been befriended by George, whose daughter he had married ; but his ambition could not resist the invitation to become the Pope's mandatory against the heretic king, and he swallowed the convenient doctrine that a campaign against the Hussites, who asked nothing more than to be left alone, was as meritorious as against the infidel armies which were flooding, year by year, into the Danubian basin. He, of course, also hoped that when once the doughty George had been overthrown it would be a relatively easier task to deprive Frederick of the crown of the Romans. Early in 1468, therefore, Matthias, helped by the dissident Czech lords, made himself master of Moravia. Carried away by initial success, Matthias found himself surrounded by superior Czech forces and had to surrender near Kutná Hora. King George's generous action in releasing him from captivity, on receiving a solemn promise of mediation in favour of peace with Rome, did not meet with its due reward. Matthias was all the time playing false, and within three months of his release had himself proclaimed King of Bohemia by George's enemies (May 3, 1469). George was almost equally indignant with Frederick, whom he had helped 'when he sat like a bird in a cage,' but who was playing again with Hungary. But it is only fair to point out that all three monarchs had rung the changes of intrigue and calculation at each other's expense, and that Frederick felt that he had more than once paid through the nose, and owed no gratitude. Needless to say, it suited the ruler of Austria admirably to see Hungary and Bohemia cutting each other's throats.

In the straits to which he was thus reduced, George showed his realism by renouncing the ambition of handing on the Crown to his sons, and he encouraged the Diet to offer it to Prince Vladislav, the second son of King Casimir III of Poland, thus countering the danger of a coalition between Hungary and Poland. During 1470 Matthias found himself driven on to the defensive in Moravia, he fell out with the Emperor, he met with growing opposition at home in Hungary owing to his neglect of the Turkish danger, and he must needs involve himself in a conflict with Venice in Dalmatia. A compromise already seemed near at hand, when George died of dropsy, at the early age of fifty-one, on March 21, 1471, having been preceded one month earlier by Archbishop Rokycana. For Bohemia this was an irreparable loss, and his short reign of thirteen years became enshrined in the national memory as one of the great periods of Czech history. He was not a man of much education, he wrote with difficulty, his German was halting and he had no Latin at all ; but he was a master of statecraft, singularly free from intolerance both in a religious and a national sense, and bent on following a middle path between two extremes, realizing Bohemia's dangerous situation and the horror with which pious Europe regarded her. One of the most judicious of Czech historians, Dr. Kamil Krofta, has admirably summed up the contribution of the great Hussite king. 'Although there was within him none of that sacred passion for the Hussite cause which had inspired the Czech 'warriors of God' in the preceding era, he had nevertheless been reared in so Hussite an atmosphere that it proved impossible to induce him to purchase the religious unity of the Czech state and its reconciliation with the Church by any surrender of the fundamental principles of Hussitism or a denial of the great Hussite past. On the contrary, he assisted his nation to defend, in face of practically the whole world, the spiritual and moral heritage of the Hussite movement—a movement which, though it had not made the life of the nation more comfortable or easy, was certainly richer in content and more characteristic than the life of the majority of nations of that day.'[1]

Peter Chelčický

If we survey the fifteenth century from our own distant perspective, there stands beside King George of Poděbrad another figure, too little regarded in his own day, but now accepted even by those who reject his social and religious views, as in the true line of succession from Hus to Masaryk, and as one of the most original thinkers of the now closing Middle Ages. Little is known of the personality of Peter of Chelčic, the real founder of the Bohemian Brethren, and thus one of the spiritual forerunners of the Society of Friends, and of another great Slav thinker, Leo Tolstoy. He was probably born about 1390, but the exact date of both birth and death is unknown. He was almost certainly of peasant stock, though some would have it that he belonged to the lesser nobility. There is even doubt about his profession, though he is generally described as having been a tailor. He probably studied at Prague without taking a degree, he was certainly not a priest, he did not know very much Latin,

[1] *Cambridge Medieval History*, viii, p. 102.

he was for most of his life out of reach of libraries, living in poverty and obscurity. His main writings seem to date from 1433 to 1443. The most famous of them, *Sít Víry* (The Net of Faith), was probably not written till 1450[1] and was first printed in 1521. His most ambitious work is *Postilla : or a Book of Interpretations of the Gospel for the whole Year ;* others are *On God's Grace, On the Picture of Antichrist, On Faith and Religion.*

His teaching, though obviously derived from Hus and Wyclif, was carried very much further. Most characteristic of all was his condemnation of the use of force in religious matters—the germ of the modern idea of non-resistance. 'Thou shalt not kill' was to him a supreme overriding command. On this point he challenged the whole Taborite 'Old Testament' outlook, just as he challenged the more orthodox Utraquist view, in a public disputation with the Hussite theologian Jacobellus. At the same time he held very strongly to Hus's doctrine of the Real Presence, but also the Cup for the laity. Where he again went further than Hus was in his exclusive reliance upon the Bible, subjected to the most rigid and literal interpretation of which even that age was capable. His aim was a reversion to the practices of the primitive Church, a very special stress being laid upon the Christian teachings of humility and the equality of all men. He thus opened the way to a kind of Christian Communism, from which there peeped out on occasion a certain anarchic strain. For he shows a deep and ineradicable distrust, amounting often to hatred, of the priestly caste, and still more of the nobles, whom he accuses of tyranny, evil manners, superstition and arrogance. He doubts whether the true Christian can hold public office, or make war, or impose the death penalty. He looks on the towns as the work of Cain and of fratricidal tendencies. He regards the oath as an accursed institution, like the little eighteenth-century Scottish sect of Antiburghers ; and his views on the Scarlet Woman of Babylon are quite as drastic as those of Richard Cameron or of Peden, the *éxalté* Covenanting prophet. Church and State are to him almost incompatible, since Constantine's entry into the Church has demoralized the original true conception. In *The Net of Faith,* of which he writes in allegorical language, the meshes have been torn by those two giant whales, the Emperor Constantine and Pope Sylvester, who have abandoned the Church's pristine poverty and divided her between the opposing currents of masters and defenders, of priests and oppressed workers. And thus Chelčický finds himself in conflict with both spiritual and temporal authority, without having fully faced up to the inevitable implications of his own teaching. In the words of President Masaryk : "Chelčický is an example to the Czechs—a clear, consistent, fearless thinker and worker, and yet an enemy to violence, a Žižka and a Comenius in one soul."

Chelčický had close relations with Rokycana, and it was the latter's own nephew, Gregory (originally a mendicant friar), who took the first definite steps towards the foundation of a separate Church community at Kunwald in 1459 ; and it was with his uncle's help that he did so. Yet only two years later Rokycana stained his reputation for tolerance in an intolerant age by persecuting the infant sect and putting Gregory and some of his closest colleagues to the torture. One effect was to extract from them all a declaration of renewed faith in the Real Presence and in the Seven Sacraments. In 1467 they invoked a Synod at Lhota near

---

[1] There is a German, but no English translation.

Reichenau, and here, drawing lots according to Apostolic practice, they elected their first three priests. It has been alleged that the Brethren derive from the Waldensians, and Professor Goll, the first serious investigator of their origins, holds that negotiations for union with the Waldensians did actually take place, and that though these broke down, the succession was obtained from the Italian community. On the other hand, it is clear that they themselves regarded their priesthood as an independent creation, not connected with existing Church organisms ; such was, for instance, the view expounded by Brother Lukas of Prague, their most eminent preacher and writer in the early sixteenth century.

Steeled and strengthened by periodic persecution, the new sect survived under the name of the 'Jednota Bratřska,' or 'Unitas Fratrum.' Best known to the outside world under the erroneous name of the Moravian Brethren—in reality it never struck such strong roots in Moravia as in Bohemia proper—it has from the outset exercised an influence far beyond its numbers, and may be regarded as one of the most original contributions of the Czech mind to religious and social development.

The hostile verdicts of German historians have been fittingly corrected by the greatest of them all, Leopold von Ranke, who after a passing reference to the infiltration of Wyclifite and Hussite doctrine in Germany (even as far as Prussia) adds this phrase : 'All the more striking was it that from all the wild waves of Hussite opinions and parties there should have emerged the community of Bohemian Brethren, which once more showed forth a Christian fellowship in the innocence and simplicity of its first origin, and gave an unexpected religious content to the opposition principle that Christ Himself was the rock upon which the Church had been founded, and not Peter nor his successors.'[1]

[1] *Deutsche Geschichte im Zeitalter der Reformation* (Gesamtausgabe), i, p. 204.

CHAPTER VI

BOHEMIA UNDER THE JAGIELLON KINGS (1471–1526)

IF the year 1471 is described as a turning point in Czech history, there is far more excuse than in many cases where the phrase is habitually applied. The amazing energy which the nation had displayed in the earlier part of the century was by now evaporating ; the wilder sectaries were exhausted ; the peasantry was in marked decline, and the oligarchy was turning to its own selfish advantage the changes due to so many sturdy peasants and yeomen having left their holdings for service in the long wars, and to so many of their survivors having eventually drifted to the towns. Even George himself was an oligarch, though one of genius, and his successors lacked his vision and were at once rapacious, factious and short-sighted.

George's sons, even though possessing wealthy appanages, had no party at their backs ; and Prince Vladislav of Poland was duly elected to the vacant throne, partly because he was George's own designated candidate, and partly because of his maternal descent from the Luxemburg, and so also from the Přemyslide house. The only possible rival was Matthias of Hungary, whose cause really suffered rather than gained when Pope Sixtus IV carried his support to the extent of excommunicating both Vladislav and his father Casimir, whose Slav blood outweighed their ardently Catholic sympathies. In the eyes of the Utraquist masses a friendly Slav king was more acceptable than the Hungarian invader. Moreover, it soon transpired that Vladislav, who was only fifteen at his accession, was a man of more than mediocre attainments, lacking the energy or the resources to resist his all too powerful barons ; he earned the nickname of 'King All-right,' because he always said '*Dobře*' to any proposal or demand.

Hostilities between Bohemia and Hungary dragged on for seven years, until in December, 1478, Matthias, by the Peace of Olomouc, renounced Bohemia, but retained possession of Moravia, Lusatia and Silesia. Frederick played a vacillating part between the two rivals, and in 1480 Matthias, again neglecting the marauding inroads of the Turks on his southern border, overran the greater part of Austria ; in 1483 he forced Frederick to withdraw from Vienna to Graz, and for the last five years of his reign made Vienna his own chief residence, by no means to the edification of his Hungarian subjects. He evidently was in no manner of doubt as to the proper strategic point from which to govern his motley dominions. He aimed openly at the union of Hungary, Bohemia and Austria, and indeed this might well have been achieved but for the irony of fate, that like George of Bohemia, he had no heir capable of carrying on the arduous task of welding a strong dynastic power in the Danubian valley, much less of imitating the expansion of the Árpáds or the Angevins.

Matthias was only forty-seven at his death in 1490, which speedily transformed the whole situation. Frederick was now old and more immobile than ever, suitably nicknamed 'the Imperial Nightcap' ; but his brilliant son Maximilian, already elected King of the Romans, made a bid for the vacant Hungarian throne, though rather as one of a long series of romantic adventures than as a serious and well-planned enterprise. In the end the Hungarian magnates, who cared little about Moravian conquest, but a great deal about their own feudal rights, fell back upon the highly unsensational candidature of Vladislav of Bohemia. They had doubtless had ample means of observing his helplessness in face of his own great lords ; as one of their number frankly admitted : "We want a king whom we can hold by the hair," and in choosing him they had shown admirable judgment. The Personal Union between Bohemia and Hungary thus became a fact from 1490 onwards, and the question of the Moravian frontier, though still unregulated, no longer possessed the same importance.

The reign of Vladislav II was marked by a few outstanding events and can be passed rapidly in review. It was a period of compromise between the rival Utraquist and Romanist factions. Vladislav, though his own preference for Rome was never in doubt, and though he often encouraged, tacitly or otherwise, encroachments upon the pure Utraquist order, was never strong enough to attempt its overthrow. The Olomouc settlement had permitted the return of the Prague Chapter, banished since 1467, and they enlisted the support of the monastic Orders in an attempt to turn away the masses from their allegiance to the Cup. The unrest which this generated unloaded itself in considerable disorders at Prague in 1483. As a result, in 1485 a last serious effort was made to check the eternal bickerings between the two main factions, a religious truce being concluded for a period of thirty-one years. By it the Compactata were reaffirmed ; equal privileges were assured to Catholic and Utraquist ; Communion might be dispensed freely under either rite ; each side pledged itself not to persecute the other, and to be content with such churches as it had held at Vladislav's accession. Though this compromise worked none too well, it encouraged Cola di Castro, an Italian noble with many personal contacts with the Czechs, to attempt mediation between the more conservative wing of the Utraquists and Pope Alexander VI ; but as the latter rejected *a limine* the idea that the Compactata should form the basis of the new settlement, negotiations were stillborn, and any faint hope of their renewal was destroyed when the Pope established a zealous Dominican as censor of all books published in Bohemia, with orders to burn whatever struck him as heretical.

While in religious matters the two sides were too nearly balanced to risk the revival of earlier conflicts, a decision was taken by the Diet of 1487 which had the most fateful results for the future of the Czech nation. It henceforth became illegal for anyone to aid or conceal a fugitive peasant, and those who did so were liable to fines and other punishment. In 1497 a royal decree went a stage further, by forbidding villeins to migrate, either to the towns or to other estates. Thus a gradual process by which, for almost a century past, the great lords had sought to strengthen their hold over the agricultural population, was crowned with success. It is not too much to describe the work of this Diet as the triumph of serfdom, and this in its turn sapped the vitality of the whole nation and prepared its paralysis and downfall. A country where neither peasant nor townsman is free is marked out in advance for slavery.

There was a parallel decline in the fortunes of Hungary. In the words of an Austrian historian : "In Matthias the conqueror swallowed up the moderate ruler, concerned only for the prosperous future of his own kingdom. The struggle for Bohemia, for the possessions of the House of Austria, was a mere war of ambition and land-grabbing, which could not awaken any echo in the hearts of the people." Matthias had raised Hungary to unprecedented power and prosperity. He had introduced vital judicial reforms, he had laid the foundation of an efficient official class, he had been an eager patron of arts and letters amid a semi-barbarous nobility and corrupt hierarchy. Moreover, he had been a genuine constitutional monarch, governing through the Diet despite its unruly and selfish tendencies. He had reorganized Hungary's military strength and restored her to the position of a Great Power ; but he had been unable to resist the temptation to use the weapon which he had forged. Thus he involved Hungary in long wars of aggression against her western neighbours, instead of concentrating and husbanding all her resources against the rising Turkish danger on her southern borders—already the most formidable military power of that age—and dire were the consequences for all the Danubian countries.

This first union of the Bohemian and Hungarian Crowns is a foretaste of the wider dynastic and constitutional union to be effected by the Habsburgs. Henceforward Vladislav spends the greater part of his time in Hungary, and only pays occasional visits to Prague. Perhaps his strongly Catholic sentiments are the key to his very marked preference for Buda ; and the fact that he spoke a Slav tongue was no obstacle, for Slav seems to have been far more widely employed in Hungary then than it was a century later, and was even used in the Hungarian Diet. Speaking generally, the situation under the two Jagiellon kings was almost equally deplorable in Bohemia and in Hungary ; it is not too much to speak of slow disintegration, without which all the military prowess and religious fanaticism of the Turks would hardly have achieved such sensational success. The extent to which the great nobles disregarded the wishes of the Crown is well illustrated by the answer given to a royal appeal for united action against the Turks ; even if the King sent a cartful of such letters and wrote them in gold, they would not listen. The reverse of this medal was the increasing ferocity of their behaviour towards their own peasantry, who were rapidly sinking in the social scale, and who in their despair plunged periodically into such desperate upheavals as the rising of George Dózsa in 1514. Their captured leader was bound upon a throne of red-hot iron and crowned with a red-hot crown, and a starving mob of gipsies was then encouraged to carve cutlets from his living flesh. When authority relied on such hideous inhumanity, it is hardly surprising that the masses lacked all incentive to resist the invader and may even have looked to him to alleviate their intolerable lot. In the coming century religious intolerance perpetuated savage punishments, and it may be questioned which motive force was the more repulsive, the bigotry of an inquisitor or the sadism of a factious anarch.

As Vladislav II had married late in life and did not live to be an old man, his son Louis II was only a child of ten when in March, 1516, he succeeded to the two Crowns. Shortly before his death Vladislav had concluded with the Emperor Maximilian, in Vienna, one of the most momentous marriage contracts in history (July 23, 1515)—the Emperor's second grandson, Archduke Ferdinand, becoming the husband of Louis' sister Anne, while Louis took Ferdinand's second sister Mary to wife. In the event of Louis dying childless, it was agreed that the Bohemian Crown should pass to the descendants of Anne, though, characteristically enough, the Estates were not consulted, and did not give their assent.

This double marriage set the seal upon the amazing match-making achievements of the House of Habsburg. Maximilian himself had married the heiress of Burgundy and the Netherlands, their son Philip I in his turn married the heiress of Spain, Naples, Milan and the Indies, and now this second grandson was destined by fate to establish Habsburg power on the Middle Danube.

Spread of Lutheran Doctrine

Under an absentee child-king it was inevitable that the great nobles should dominate Bohemian politics, and in particular Zdenek Lev of Rožmital, who held his own against King George's grandson, Bartholomew, Duke of Münsterberg. When at last the young king visited Prague in 1522, he deprived Lev and entrusted another leading oligarch, Pašek of Vrat, with the supreme power, but he was quite unable to suppress what amounted to civil war. The situation was further complicated by the penetration and rapid spread of Lutheran doctrines in Bohemia to the almost equal alarm of Catholics and Utraquists. The latter in particular fell into two groups, the one intensely conservative and hostile to the slightest modification of existing ritual or liturgy. National prejudice still undoubtedly played its part ; ever since the days of Hus there had been a sharp conflict, ideological no less than political, between Germanism and Hussitism, and the latter had been anathema in Germany. Now, as it were, the scales began to fall from many eyes. Already in 1520 Luther, who had till recently detested the Hussites as arch-heretics, was writing to his venerated mentor Spalatin : 'Fool that I am, without knowing it, I have taught and held all the teachings of John Hus. We are all Hussites without having been conscious of it. Yes, Paul and Augustine are literally Hussites.' In this he was not shaken by the warning of the Catholic polemist, Hieronymus Emser : 'See that you do not lead us Germans into such a game as that into which Hus miserably led away the Bohemians.'[1] There can be no doubt that Luther's doctrine of the universal priesthood of all Christians came to him from Hus ; and Emser argued that Luther's errors came, not from his own quiver, but from the books of his forerunners, Wyclif and Hus. Luther's own view is to be found in a well-known passage from the *Table Talk*, in which he said : 'Hus cut down and rooted out some thorns and thickets from the vineyard of Christ, and chastized the abuses and evil life of the Pope ; but I, Dr. Martin Luther, have come into an open, flat and well-ploughed field, and have attacked and overthrown the doctrine of the Pope.'

Luther, then, addressed to the Bohemian Estates an exhortation to remain faithful to the spirit of Hus and to their opposition to Rome. Two years later he sent the Czechs the advice to separate themselves finally from the Church of Rome ; and his most ardent Czech supporter, Gallus Cahera, then priest of the famous Týn Church in Prague, played a leading part in stiffening the so-called 'Neo-Utraquist' tendencies, and rejecting ordination for Utraquist priests by Catholic bishops. Unhappily, when the conservative current gained the upper hand again, with the aid of Pašek, and when some of the chief innovators were actually sent to the stake, Cahera lost his nerve and submitted, thereby doing considerable harm, not only to the Protestant cause but to the rapidly reviving relations of Czechs and Germans.

It is but natural that in such a situation the 'Brethren' should be

[1] About the same time Ulrich von Hutten, that scholar-knight-errant, was writing of Žižka, hailing the latter as the true prototype of a liberator, and urging Sickingen to follow in his steps and start a Hussite *Religionssturm* on German soil.

increasingly in evidence, as in some degree holding the balance between rival extremes. Persecuted under George and Rokycana, they were, for reasons not altogether obvious, treated with a certain mildness by Vladislav. In 1496 there was a split in their ranks ; the more radical section, known as 'Amosites,' after its leader, and laying its main stress on an ultra-literal interpretation of Holy Scripture, seceded altogether, and slowly languished in isolation, while the majority, led by Brother Lukas, continued to steer a middle course. In his correspondence with the Brethren, Luther showed an unusual mildness, especially in view of the fact that Lukas defended Transubstantiation, the seven Sacraments and celibacy, and polemized against justification by faith. For these views Lukas had to defend himself, not merely against Wittenberg, but also against an active minority within his own fold, which adhered to the purely commemorative doctrine of Zwingli. Lukas was in no sense the equal of Luther, but his tireless energy and resolute views make of him the second founder of the Brethren, but for whom the little sect might have merged its identity in either Utraquism or Lutheranism.

Mohács

King Louis' attention was diverted from the religious situation in Bohemia by an urgent signal of alarm from Hungary. Sultan Suleiman, at the head of a splendid army of at least 200,000 men, had followed up his earlier capture of Belgrade and Šabac by reducing the scarcely less important fortress of Peterwardein on the Danube, fifty miles to the north of Belgrade. A hopelessly inferior Hungarian army flung itself in his path, regardless of strategy or common sense, and without waiting for the Croat reinforcements which were already on their way, and the Bohemian army for which the King had urgently appealed. At the battle of Mohács (August 29) the Hungarian army was almost wiped out ; the two Archbishops and five other Bishops and many of the leading magnates were left dead upon the field, and King Louis in his flight was unhorsed and drowned in a neighbouring swamp. Within a fortnight Hungary's defenceless capital was in the Sultan's hands.

The year 1526 is a decisive landmark, not only in Bohemian history, but in the whole history of Central Europe, for it is the real birthday of the Habsburg Monarchy, of the Great Power which weathered the storms of four centuries, but succumbed in 1918 to the strain of four years of world war. Throughout this period the fate of Bohemia and Hungary is closely linked together, and also with that of the hereditary Austrian dominions. Bohemia avoided the supreme disaster that overcame Hungary, which was partitioned into three uneven portions between the Habsburgs, driven altogether on to the defensive, the native Magyar princes of Transylvania and of the easterly counties, balancing uneasily between the Emperor, the Sultan and the King of Poland, and the Ottoman conquerors, holding the great plain of the Danube and the Tisza, and making the fortress of Buda their capital. This condition was to last for 160 years, and it was not till the closing year of the seventeenth century that Central Hungary and Transylvania could be reunited with the northern and western districts, and indeed not till 1718 that the work of recovery was finally completed by the victories of Prince Eugene. Bohemia in the meantime retained her national identity and political unity, but when she fell, almost a century later, her ruin was more sudden and thorough, and for a time seemed irretrievable.

CHAPTER VII

THE FIRST FOUR HABSBURG KINGS

AT first a whole crowd of candidates were spoken of for the vacant Bohemian throne—the Dukes of Bavaria; Vladislav's nephew, King Sigismund of Poland; the Saxon Elector; Francis I of France; and even George's grandson, the Duke of Münsterberg and Lev of Rožmital. In the end the Archduke Ferdinand outbid all others; after lengthy negotiations the special committee of twenty-four appointed by the Diet unanimously elected him as king (October 23, 1526) and delegates were sent to Vienna to acquaint him with the conditions which they demanded in return. For instance, no one, not even his heir and successor, might be crowned until he had taken the coronation oath and confirmed the liberties of the Estates. The king should live mainly in Bohemia and during absence entrust authority to natives only, and on the advice of the Estates. All offices were to be reserved for citizens of the kingdom, and the two confessions were to enjoy equal consideration from him.[1] Ferdinand was obviously acting in his own interests in giving a prompt declaration that the Estates had elected him freely; but he declined to accept their interpretation of the Golden Bull of Charles IV—namely, that only male descendants or an unmarried daughter of the last king possessed a hereditary title. Other unsolved points he promised to discuss with the Diet after his arrival in Prague, and in due course he obtained their consent to the coronation of his eldest son on attaining his majority, in his own lifetime. They even withdrew their unrestricted veto on foreign counsellors, and no longer insisted upon their advice being taken before the appointment of royal officials. Thus, although he had not secured recognition of his hereditary right, he had already laid the basis for an augmentation of the royal power. He and Anne were crowned in Prague with immense pomp on February 24, 1527; and meanwhile the Estates of Moravia, always not a little jealous of their Bohemian colleagues, had freely recognized the hereditary rights of Queen Anne, while Silesia and Lusatia, not to be outdone, extended this recognition to husband as well as wife. But in Hungary not even Mohács could avail to reunite the warring factions, and it came to a double election—in November John Zápolya, and then in December Ferdinand, who was not crowned until November of the following year. As a further complication, the Croatian Estates unanimously elected Ferdinand on January 1, 1527, whereas the Slavonian adhered to the Zápolya faction.

Ferdinand's Efforts towards Reunion

Ferdinand thus became the symbol of unity and strong government against faction at home and foreign invasion, and from the first it was clear that he aimed at converting the link of Personal Union between his somewhat heterogeneous dominions into something less exiguous, and at making his own contribution to Church reunion. Though not possessed

[1] Incidentally, the Estates expressed the prophetic opinion that it was not desirable that the King of Bohemia should be ruler of Hungary also, because its defence would cost huge sums and compel him to spend much of his time there.

of outstanding ability, he was a man of sterling character, autocratic, yet less so than many of his kinsmen and contemporaries in a hard and increasingly autocratic age ; and his enduring loyalty to his brother the Emperor, so utterly different in temperament, though not in his ultimate objectives, is a strong testimonial in his favour. They had, it is true, both realized the geographical impossibility of governing from a single point the huge and disjointed possessions inherited by Charles V ; and already in 1522 Charles had freely made over to Ferdinand the hereditary Austrian dominions. It followed logically that to Ferdinand's hands should be entrusted the arduous task of stemming the Turkish tide, which in 1529 burst in all its fury against the gates of Vienna. Confronted by the sustained aggression of the Turks, by the rapid spread of Lutheran doctrine, by occasional co-operation of Turk and Protestant, by a rival king in Hungary, by the mortal enmity and perpetual intrigues of Francis I, and by difficulties with the Papacy itself after the iniquitous Imperialist sack of Rome, Ferdinand was for some years in a position of very real peril, in which his restive teams needed cautious driving and none too tight a rein. But after 1531, when Charles used all his influence to secure his brother's election as King of the Romans, Ferdinand's position improved, and he could devote himself to the triple task of holding the battered frontiers of Hungary, checking the ambition of the Estates in his here- ditary lands, extending in a centralizing sense the administrative reforms which his grandfather Maximilian had introduced, and endeavouring to build up the broken morale of the Church, above all in matters of the parochial clergy and the schools. Though brought up in Spain, under the most rigid Castilian etiquette, he was on the whole able to acclimatize himself in Central Europe, in a way that neither his brother Charles nor his inflexible cousin Philip could ever have achieved.

Meanwhile Bohemia held aloof alike from the Turkish wars and from German affairs : the oligarchy which controlled the Estates was mainly concerned in consolidating their power both against the peasantry and against the Crown. Utraquism, handicapped by a shortage of priests and the old difficulties about ordination, was by now definitely in decline, and the religious position centred round the rivalry of Catholic and Lutheran with the 'Unity of the Brethren' as an important minority. The leader of the latter group, Bishop Augusta, was in personal contact with Luther and enjoyed his sympathy ; but the Brethren were unable to accept his views on justification, and were doubtful as to the institution of marriage of the clergy, while their insistence on the re-baptism of new members seemed to identify them with the Anabaptists, to whom, in every other respect, they formed the antithesis. Augusta took to Luther at Wittenberg the newly drafted Confession of the Brethren, which was mainly based on the Confession of Augsburg ;[1] but no definite agreement was reached, though on one occasion Luther urged upon them to 'be the Apostles of the Bohemians ; I and mine will be the Apostles of the Germans.' In passing, it may be noted that the Reformation had worked a transformation in the relations of Czech and German ; never perhaps were those relations more cordial than in the sixteenth century.

It was Ferdinand's constant aim to bring the enfeebled Utraquists back to the bosom of the Church, and to this end he would have been ready to accept the Compactata ; but here he was foiled on the one hand by the stiffening attitude of Rome, in the earlier stages of the Council

[1] He also visited Calvin and Bucer at Geneva.

of Trent, and by the corresponding stiffening of the Utraquists, who made a last attempt to revert to the Four Articles, of which the Compactata may be said to have been a watered-down version. As the breach between Catholic and Protestant grew more violent inside Germany, Ferdinand naturally did all in his power to enlist the forces of Bohemia on the side of his brother Charles, and this caused fresh dissensions and heart-burnings.

Ferdinand and Charles V

In the ensuing War of Schmalkalden all calculations were upset by Charles V's victory at Mühlberg (April 24, 1547), and his capture of the two Protestant ringleaders, the Saxon Elector John Frederick and Philip of Hesse. The loyal Ferdinand shared, as it were, the profits of victory, and immediately demanded the submission of the recalcitrant elements in Bohemia. The short-lived League for the defence of Bohemian liberties collapsed, and the so-called 'Bloody Diet' obeyed his behests. On July 2 King Ferdinand occupied the Castle of Prague, and ordered the execution of the four ringleaders, two knights and two burghers, and the confiscation of considerable properties. One specially unhappy sequel was the renewed persecution of the Church of the Brethren, who seem to have been deliberately made the scapegoat. Many of its members were banished to Poland ; Augusta himself was twice put to the torture, and spent the greater part of sixteen years in prison. The Lutheran party in Bohemia fell into the background, and the more conservative section of the Utraquists, which still favoured an accord with the Holy See, retained the upper hand, though by now reduced to a negative and defensive attitude.

After Mühlberg Charles seemed to be master of Germany ; but the treacherous Maurice of Saxony was an instrument that turned in his hand, and the intractable attitude of the Papacy, at first under the worldly Paul III and later under that grim bigot Paul IV, introduced a further complication. The so-called 'Interim' project of 1548, by which Charles hoped to restore the unity of the Church as a kind of patchwork quilt, was almost equally displeasing to both sides ; at times Ferdinand evidently hoped that the Utraquist tradition might produce an intermediate formula, but there was neither good will nor leadership. Bohemia maintained its passive attitude to German affairs, and after the strange incident of 1552, when Charles and Ferdinand were forced into ignominious flight from Innsbruck, before the bold raid of the Elector Maurice, there was little or no prospect of a religious accord. The Religious Peace of Augsburg (1555) was an open and final confession of failure to restore the lost religious unity ; in effect Germany was partitioned into two unequal portions between Catholic and Protestant and the famous political doctrine of 'cuius regio, eius religio' (i.e. the assertion of the reigning sovereign's right in each case to dictate the religious allegiance of his subjects) seemed to stereotype the status quo, but in reality left the door open for drastic reversal. For over sixty years the truce was maintained, but in the Thirty Years' War a determined effort was made to upset the balance established in 1555—with disastrous consequences for all. Charles's abdication in 1556 was the result of broken health, religious melancholia and a longing to end his days in Spain ; but it was also the tacit acknowledgment of his failure in what had been the dearest hope of his reign—even dearer than the constant aggrandizement of his House —namely, the reunion of Christendom, or at least of German Christians.

Ferdinand and Bohemia

It is characteristic of Ferdinand I that though a man of lesser calibre than his brother, he did not give up the struggle, and took due advantage of the increased prestige which his accession to the Empire assured to him. Henceforth his attitude to the Protestants, and also to the Brethren, was milder, but in this later period of his reign he was responsible for two measures of great advantage for the Catholic cause. In 1556 he invited the Jesuits to settle in Prague, and assigned to them the former Dominican cloister, known as the Clementinum. They were already the torch-bearers of the new system of education, for which their gifted leader Peter Canisius was responsible, and which contributed probably more than any other factor to the triumph of the Catholic Counter-Reformation. Their house in Prague at once became a rival to the now decadent Utraquist University, and a focus of aggressive teaching. In 1561 the Archbishopric of Prague, after remaining vacant for 140 years,[1] was again filled by a Catholic prelate, Anton Brus of Möglitz ; and this weighting of the scales against the Utraquists was increased a year later, when Ferdinand withdrew from the Diet its ancient right of nomination to the Utraquist consistory.

Ferdinand's patient efforts to achieve a compromise seemed for a brief moment to have succeeded, when on April 16, 1564, Pius IV authorized all German bishops to grant the Cup to all laymen who wished to receive it. But the opponents of this concession speedily regained the ascendancy at the Council of Trent, and before the end of the year it was again withdrawn. In any case it almost certainly came too late ; it was received without enthusiasm and regarded by many as a trap or a device for dividing the Protestant ranks, within which the breach between Lutheran and Calvinist was already unbridgeable. Moreover, on the equally burning question of marriage of the clergy there was no longer any real hope of concession from Rome. The shocking immorality of the clergy throughout his hereditary dominions had long been Ferdinand's highly practical motive in pressing for this reform ; but by now the zeal of the Orders and the new methods of education were working wonders in restoring priestly morale, and at Rome the view prevailed, that celibacy could safely be upheld, and that its advantages fully outweighed its drawbacks.

Ferdinand's Centralist Policy

Ferdinand died on July 25, 1564, after a reign of only partially realized aims, but also one which had given to many causes an impetus which could no longer be arrested. Above all, his plans for a centralized bureaucracy were already beginning to bear fruit before he died. The Hofkanzlei (or Aulic Chancellery) which he set up in 1528 was as yet divided into a number of separate sections (*Expeditionen*)—for Germany and Austria proper, for Lower Austria, for Hungary and for the Bohemian Crown-lands ; and the legality of the machine was sharply challenged by the Hungarian Estates, and less sharply in Bohemia. His next step was to make a will in 1532, providing, in the event of his son succeeding as a minor, for 'a supreme government (*ain oberste Regierung*) for all our kingdoms and lands,' consisting of fourteen members (four from Bohemia

[1] Since the death of Archbishop Conrad in 1421 ; his Utraquist successor, Rokycana, was never recognized.

as against three each from Hungary and Austria and two each from Tirol and the lesser provinces). This was revoked, but during the next twenty years there grew up the practice of joint meetings representing all his various dominions ; and though this was discontinued after 1547, events ere long set it again in motion. He also set up a Privy Council of his immediate advisers in matters of general policy, and the new Aulic Chamber (*Hofkammer*) was the foundation on which eventually common finances were to be built up.

A Relapse into Partition

In one direction he administered a set-back to his whole policy, by ordering a fresh partition of the hereditary dominions between his three sons—Maximilian receiving Upper and Lower Austria ('above' and 'below' the Enns), Ferdinand the Tirol and Vorarlberg, and Charles 'Inner Austria' (Styria, Carinthia, Carniola and Istria). It is, of course, true that the eldest, as the wearer of the German, Bohemian and Hungarian Crowns, was far stronger than his two brothers, but the decision opened up the way for all kinds of dissensions and abandoned the Habsburg tradition of consolidating the hereditary provinces as a groundwork for major dynastic policy in the Reich and in Europe. Not the least obvious flaw was that it left the defence of the whole heritage against the Turks mainly in the hands of the Styrian Archduke, instead of pooling all resources for the purpose. Fortunately for the House, the four sons of Maximilian II all died without male issue, while Ferdinand of Tirol married morganatically, with the result that on the death of Matthias in 1619 the three lines were again united under a single head.

The Habsburg Dilemma

Ferdinand is one of those secondary figures which have filled a great place in history, and whose merits, or at least their influence in shaping their times, have not always received due attention. His contribution to the defence of the Danubian lands against Ottoman invasion belongs rather to Hungarian than to Bohemian history ; despite all handicaps and failures it is not to be dismissed as merely negative. But under him we first see clearly the tendency which was for the next four centuries to leave so strong a mark on Austrian history, and of which the Imperialist arms may be taken as a symbol—the double-headed eagle, facing both ways, westwards and eastwards, to Germany and to the Balkans. It is the history of repeated diversions which left one or other of its tasks unfinished. By his election to the Imperial throne, Ferdinand and his heirs became increasingly involved in the internal politics and disputes of Germany, and found one hand tied when it was a question of a major effort against the Turks.

There was another direction in which these dual tendencies had a no less paralysing effect on Habsburg will power. That dynasty, for all its faults, has amply earned a place in history as champion of Christendom against the invading Crescent. But this great mission it interpreted in a narrow sectarian spirit, making itself the mouthpiece of Catholicism in its most vindictive and aggressive form, under the impulse of Loyola and the Counter-Reformation. It was thus on the horns of a permanent dilemma, the ever-recurring need for concentrating against the infidel invader, or against heresy at home ; it was a choice between defending

Europe against the Crescent, or the Church against schism and false doctrine. Its persecuting zeal envenomed the situation still further, since it drove the Protestants of Germany and Hungary into many a compact or working alliance with the Turks.

It cannot, then, be emphasized too strongly that the religious feud was the chief cause of the long delay of a century and a half in liberating South-eastern Europe from its conquerors.

Maximilian II

The short reign of Maximilian II has few features that need detain us long. Almost alone among the Habsburg princes, he stands out as a man of lukewarm and vacillating views upon the great issues of his day. Long before his accession he had passed as an active sympathizer with Protestant doctrines ; and it is highly probable that he would have become a Protestant if he had not been deterred on the one hand by his personal dislike of the Calvinist princes—every whit as arrogant and intolerant as their Catholic contemporaries, and possessing considerably less excuse— and above all by considerations of international and dynastic policy. As a young man he once thought seriously of flying from his father's court, and he showed marked favour to many Protestants. For years he attended Mass, but never communicated. But in response to his father's appeal, and under the influence of his devout brothers Ferdinand and Charles, he gave a pledge to live and die within the Catholic Church, and this facilitated, and was meant to facilitate, his election as King of the Romans ; and though he insisted on the omission of the Mass from the coronation ceremony rather than partake of Communion in one kind, and though he openly disapproved of the work of the Council of Trent, he kept his word to the end. He doubtless saw that if he once gave formal recognition to Protestantism in the Empire, he would find himself almost forced into the position of leading the Protestant cause in Europe, and this, he realized, would almost inevitably have conjured up a fresh religious war, and split the House of Habsburg into two conflicting groups. Bound up with this were his eagerness to secure for his son Rudolf the succession to the Empire ; and he was on increasingly good terms with his Spanish cousins, in proportion as Philip II renounced all idea of the Imperial throne. His own wife was Spanish-bred, as the daughter of his uncle, Charles V, and now he wanted his own daughter to become her uncle Philip's fourth wife. The decisive factor with Maximilian, however, was a superficiality of character which made it impossible for him to stake everything upon belief and principles, and led him to prefer an uneasy and ill-defined *status quo*. This stands out most clearly in his foreign policy. Like his father, he was involved in the Turkish Wars, and marshalled his forces against Suleiman, who in 1566 headed his thirteenth and last campaign against the West. But if this formidable invasion failed, the merit lay not with Maximilian, but with the heroic defence of the fortress of Sziget by Count Zrinski. Instead of profiting by Suleiman's death and by the utter incompetence of the new Sultan, 'Selim the Sot,' he concluded in 1568 an eight years' peace with the Porte ; and even the great naval victory of Lepanto in 1571 and the readiness of Spain and Venice to carry the offensive further, did not rouse him to action. On the contrary, he allowed his main interest to be diverted from the defence of Hungary to the wooing of Poland, when, as a result of the extinction of the Jagiellon dynasty in 1572, there were two elections to the vacant throne within two years. Needless to say, Maximilian lacked the energy to push his claim and did not inspire sufficient confidence among the Polish nobles.

Maximilian's Religious Policy

So far as Bohemia was directly concerned, the main interests of Maximilian's reign belong to the religious sphere. As king he would fain have maintained a neutral attitude between the rival sects, and was, reasonably enough, anxious to prevent the disordered conditions that prevailed in Austria spreading to Bohemia also. In his own words, everything there was 'threatening to go topsy-turvy' (*drunter und drüber*) ; many parishes and churches being vacant or filled with drunken ignoramuses, living in open concubinage, and the educational system having broken down altogether. Early in the reign no other than Canisius himself expressed the view that barely an eighth of the population was 'really Catholic.' The Estates of Lower Austria upheld the Confession of Augsburg, and demanded a uniform church service, without the old ceremonies, while those of Upper Austria demanded the free preaching of the word, in the vernacular. In 1571 Maximilian found it necessary to grant the so-called *Assekuration*, or Assurance, by which the right of Protestant worship was conceded to the nobles in their castles and lands, while in return the Estates were not to allow action against the Catholics.

With such a situation next door in Austria, it was useless to suppose that the Bohemian Estates would exclude religious affairs from their discussions ; and indeed the Neo-Utraquist party, much to Maximilian's disgust, assumed the offensive, and instead of pushing the now almost traditional claim for a recognition of the Compactata as the basis of reconciliation with Rome, now insisted upon a reversion to the much more categorical and less conciliatory Articles of Prague. Meanwhile there was a renewed tendency to find a scapegoat in the Brethren, despite a certain benevolent interest shown by the Emperor in their fate ; and in 1568 he was persuaded to order the closing of their churches. While the Estates put forward a demand for religious liberty based upon the Confession of Augsburg, the Lutherans themselves urged the Brethren to adopt that Confession as their own, and thus in effect accept absorption in the Lutheran body. The chief advocate of this course was Augusta, now set free from prison, but old and broken in health as the result of his sufferings. That he found himself almost isolated within his own communion was largely due to the influence of Jan Blahoslav, the immediate forerunner of Comenius, and certainly the most gifted writer whom the Unity of Brethren has produced. Blahoslav's first claim to the gratitude of posterity is his version of the New Testament, which was eventually incorporated in the Czech Bible known as that of Kralice. As we shall see later this Bible acquired a very special position among the Slovak Protestants. In addition to his fiery eloquence, Blahoslav was noted for the purity of his Czech style, standing midway between Hus and Comenius ; he was the author of the first Czech grammar and of the first serious Czech book on music. He was an ardent champion of Czech nationality, and of the specifically Czech character and content of the Church of the Brethren.

Blahoslav and Augusta both died in 1572, within not many weeks of each other, and the dispute took a less acrimonious turn. When Maxi-

milian met the Bohemian Diet in 1575 for the last time, the so-called
'Czech Confession' (*Confessio Bohemica*) was submitted for its approval.
It was an attempt to graft the tenets of Augsburg upon the parent tree of
Prague and Constance. The full Lutheran attitude towards justification
was accepted, but the interpretation of the Real Presence inclined rather
to Calvin than to Hus or Luther. In matters of administration it was
laid down that the Consistory which had ruled the Utraquist Church since
the death of Rokycana should be retained, but that all its members,
including the 'Administrator,' or President, should henceforth be
appointed by the Estates. Maximilian ended by assuring to the Protestants full liberty of worship and allowing them to appoint fifteen
'Defenders' (*Defensores*), not subject to the Consistory's jurisdiction ;
but with his usual preference for half-measures he shrank back from the
step that followed most logically on the 'Czech Confession'—namely, the
setting up of a new constitution for the whole Bohemian Church. Thus
the last moment at which religious unity might have been restored in
Bohemia, was lost for ever. The sects fell apart again, the Old Utraquists
gravitated slowly towards reviving Catholicism, the Neo-Utraquists and
Protestants tended to mark time, while the Brethren were again subjected by Maximilian to repressive measures. Indeed, the decree which
he issued against them from Regensburg early in 1576 was part of the
price he paid for smoothing the election of his son Rudolf to the Crown
of the Romans.

Maximilian died on October 12, 1576, after steadfastly refusing the
last sacraments. What were his real sentiments was a secret that perished
with him ; as Duke Albert of Bavaria wrote to the Elector Augustus of
Saxony : 'His Majesty behaved at the end as he had done in life—so that
no one could really know whether he was a Catholic or of the (Augsburg)
Confession, and declared neither for the one opinion nor for the other,
but passed away without many words.' "My happiest hour has come,"
he is reported to have exclaimed, and the comment of the Spanish
Ambassador was that "the unhappy man has died as he had lived."

'A natural benevolence, a winning openness of mien, charming manners,
delight in conversation,' gave him, in Droysen's opinion, a wide popularity. He was, moreover, 'very gifted, highly cultured, full of interest
and, like his father, very industrious,' so that his Vice-Chancellor said of
him : "If he had been a secretary or chancellor, he would have put us
bureaucrats to shame." But he was also easy-going, soft, easily influenced,
quickly interested and then not easy to hold, either in thoughts or words.
Rich in talent rather than a measured, firm character.'

Rudolf II

The reign of Rudolf II, who succeeded at the age of twenty-four and
reigned for thirty-five years, was in many ways one of decisive importance
for Bohemia, not for any constructive achievement on his part, but for
the very fact that he initiated nothing and paralysed all government,
leaving an accumulation of neglect and negation that rendered an explosion inevitable. At the very outset his contemporaries realized his
incompetence : as the Chancellor of Brunswick bluntly put it : "We shall
soon have the French War in German lands." The House of Habsburg
has produced a rich variety of types, but never in its long history anything so pitiable or so eccentric as Rudolf. He was certainly a man of wide

knowledge, taste and versatility ; he spoke six languages and was well versed in mathematics and science. He was a genuine lover and patron of the arts, and soon developed into a passionate collector of pictures, coins, precious stones, antiquities, and so on. He also devoted much time to the laying out of gardens, and had a magnificent stud of thorough-bred horses. But it was typical of him that he very rarely rode his horses or allowed others to ride them, though he spent hours in the stables and riding-school of the Hrad. His favourite study was astronomy, and the Prague Observatory was placed in the charge of two noted scientists, Tycho de Brahe and Keppler ; but here again his own interest in the stars degenerated into astrology and superstition, and chemical research became alchemy and a search for the elixir of life. His lofty conception of the royal power did not deter him from gross neglect of his duties ; for months at a time he would be inaccessible even to his foremost advisers, and he constantly revoked decisions after they had been made, or ruth-lessly laid aside matters of the utmost urgency. He soon transferred himself from Vienna to Prague, and perched in solitary state in the famous Hrad, high above the ancient city, practically never leaving its precincts. The fact is that he was not merely a recluse, but had inherited the deep melancholia of his Spanish great-grandmother, Joanna the Mad ; his hallucinations and periodical fits of persecution mania showed him to be not far from the borderline of insanity. It was obvious that such a ruler was not only utterly unequal to his position but was likely to en-venom still further the burning controversies of his day. His sympathies were strongly Catholic, and the Jesuits and other champions of the Counter-Reformation found it easy to exploit his bigotry and superstition.

The Counter-Reformation in Bohemia

Under such a ruler it was but natural that the role of his brothers and cousins of the House of Habsburg should have assumed increased importance. The most zealous of all was his uncle Ferdinand of Tirol, who succeeded in winning back that province to the allegiance of Rome, without serious disturbance or bloodshed ; it was, of course, the most remote from German Protestant influences, and the nearest to Trent and to Northern Italy. In Vienna and Lower Austria the Archduke Ernest acted as Rudolf's deputy until 1593, when he was transferred to the Netherlands ; and he set himself wherever possible to root out the Protestant clergy, but found a very serious handicap in the lack of worthy candidates for the priesthood. With every year, however, this problem was eased by the educational achievements of the Jesuits and other Orders. In 'Inner Austria' the resistance to the Counter-Reformation was much more determined and had the support of a majority of the nobility. Rudolf's youngest uncle, Charles of Styria, yielded to no one in his zeal for the Church, but as the defence of the borderlands against the Turks was absolutely vital and as the main weight of it was placed on Charles's shoulders by the Gallio-like Rudolf, reform could not be pursued to the limit of alienating the Estates. As an example of this, in 1572, while admitting the first twelve Jesuits to Graz, he also had to promise not to eject the Lutheran preachers. In 1578 he was even obliged by the Estates to renew his earlier concessions to Protestantism, subject to a pledge on the part of the preachers to refrain from public abuse of the old Church. Thus in Graz, Laibach and Klagenfurt they remained un-

touched, despite the protests of the Pope and the zealous incitements of
Charles's Bavarian wife. In 1581 the Town Council of Graz was still able
to impose a fine upon those who attended a Catholic sermon, but in the
next year Charles put the Mayor under arrest and issued a decree making
attendance at the town church obligatory. In 1587 he imposed a veto
upon the erection of new Protestant churches, and insisted that all judges
must be Catholics. His death in 1590 was a set-back to the cause of the
militants, for his son Ferdinand was a boy of twelve, and the Estates
pressed their advantage with Ernest as Regent. When they demanded
'freedom of religion,' they really meant freedom for Lutheran teaching,
and, much more justifiably, the same rights for the towns as had been
secured by the nobles. Neither Ernest nor Rudolf could be won over for
such a concession, but once again the danger on their southerly frontiers
and the need for money grants compelled them to humour the Estates.
Some idea of the tension between the contending parties may be gathered
from an incident in the year 1593, when Archduchess Maria ordered three
days of prayer and procession in face of imminent Turkish invasion, and
the Protestant preachers must needs denounce this as 'pure idolatry.'
"The Turk is the Lutheran's fortune," said a court preacher before the
Archduke Charles at Judenburg in 1577 ; "otherwise one would treat
them very differently."

The year 1595 may be said to have opened the second and more
vigorous stage of the Counter-Reformation in the Habsburg dominions.
It was then that Ferdinand of Styria, at the age of eighteen, returned from
his studies at the Bavarian Court and at the reconstituted Catholic
University of Ingolstadt, to take up the government of 'Inner Austria.'
He is credited with saying on his return : "Rather would I let country
and people go, and leave nothing but my shirt, than consent to promises
which might be injurious to religion." He was firmly resolved to apply
the principle of *cuius regio* to his duchies, and as a first measure not to
tolerate the preachers ; and it is characteristic of the man that he began by
paying a pilgrimage to the famous shrine of Loreto and taking oath, at
the knees of Pope Clement VIII, to restore Catholicism, even at the peril of
his life. In 1598, then, he issued a decree ordering the departure of the
Protestant preachers from Graz and other towns within a fortnight ; and
a month later, seeing doubtless that he was strong enough to carry out his
decisions, he also decreed that all townsmen in Inner Austria must return
to the Catholic faith or sell their goods, hand over a tenth part, and then
emigrate. When the Estates protested, he told them flatly that there
were too many appeals to the distant Emperor, that this was an infringement of the rights of the *Landesfürst*, and that he was free to act as he
pleased in his own lands. A series of commissions appointed by him
proceeded to restore Catholic worship in one place after another, to burn
Protestant books by the thousand, to expel Protestant teachers and to
exact a public oath and church attendance. When the Estates renewed
their protest, Ferdinand abused them for their 'refractory, unseemly and
quite abusive proposals,' and refused to receive a deputation. Year by
year he went on his way, and before the first decade of the new century
Austria was a changed world. In the early seventies it had been the
practice of young gallants of the nobility to show their disrespect for the
Catholic religion by riding their horses from one transept to the other,
past the high altar of St. Stephen's Cathedral in Vienna, but within a
very few years Opitz, one of the most popular of Lutheran divines, was

not allowed to preach within the walls of the capital. When Ferdinand first assumed power at Graz he and his immediate entourage were the only communicants on Easter Sunday, but within ten years all Protestant services in Styria had been suppressed. There is no more dramatic transformation in history than the recovery of Austria for Catholicism.

The Decline of Utraquism

It is against this background that the situation in Bohemia during the first three decades of Rudolf must be viewed. It shows how strongly the tide was setting in favour of authoritative principles both in Church and State, that so grotesque and mischievous a figure as Rudolf should have been for so long its foremost representative in Central Europe. As in neighbouring Austria, the Catholic party, and especially the Jesuits, was steadily assuming the offensive, while in the Utraquist ranks there was marked decay and irresolution. In 1580 the Utraquist Consistory, led by the Administrator, Fabian, actually took an oath of obedience to the Catholic Archbishop, abandoning all their distinctive tenets save that of the Cup for the laity; and after an interval of some years Fabian renounced the Hussite faith and was admitted to the Catholic Church. Some writers date from this the decline of Utraquism, but in reality it evoked a temporary revulsion of feeling, and in 1594 Rudolf found it advisable to consent to the re-establishment of the Consistory on its original lines. The lack of leadership, however, led to a strengthening of the Lutherans at the expense of the Utraquists, and a still closer association with Germany. The Brethren, on the other hand, disappointed at the increasingly oligarchic tendencies which were asserting themselves, leant rather towards the Calvinists. But the decree issued by Rudolf in 1602 against the Brethren (reviving the persecuting edict of 1508) roused very general indignation, and remained for the most part inoperative; and the complete disregard shown by Rudolf for the 'Remonstrance' prepared by the Diet increased still further the tension in religious matters.

The Turkish Wars

For thirty years Rudolf had pursued a policy of inactivity alike at home and abroad; he could not even make up his mind whether to marry his Spanish cousin, and in the end remained a bachelor, perhaps deterred by the hideous perverted career of one of his illegitimate sons. As so often, it was foreign affairs which brought the long crisis to a head. The treaty concluded by Maximilian II with the Turks in 1568 was followed by years of uneasy peace; the Habsburgs used the respite given by the besotted Selim II, and by a series of diversions in Persia and Georgia, in order to strengthen the defences of Styria and Croatia. Charles of Styria was responsible for the erection of the 'Military Frontiers' under a hereditary caste of Croat 'Frontiersmen,' and gave his name to the new key-fortress of Karlovac, or Karlstadt, thirty miles to the west of Zagreb. But Rudolf did nothing whatsoever of his own initiative for the delivery of Hungary, and it was not until 1592 that the Turkish War flared up more fiercely than ever. The fortunes of war swayed to and fro, but at last it was clear that the Imperialists were no longer incapable of taking the offensive. The battle of Mezökeresztés in 1596 was a serious blow, but it was counterbalanced by the recovery of Esztergom (Gran), the primatial see of Hungary, and of Raab, in 1598.

This is not the place to tell the complicated story of the Báthory princes in Transylvania, of their triangular relations with Sultan and Emperor and with the great Voivode Michael, who for a brief space united all the Roumanian lands under his sceptre. Michael professed readiness to become the Emperor's vassal, assumed the title of 'His Imperial Majesty's Statthalter and Commander in the field,' and he even paid a hurried visit of homage to the immovable Rudolf in his castle of Prague. But Michael did not retain the allegiance of the Magyar nobility, nor was he a match in treachery for the Imperialist General Basta, and was foully murdered by the latter's orders. This left Transylvania and parts of Northern Hungary once more in the hands of the Emperor. But though Rudolf's armies were on two occasions able to lay siege to Pest, the war on the whole was allowed to languish, and Ahmed I's accession in 1603 was followed by tentative peace feelers. Rudolf was less interested in the task of completing the emancipation of Central Hungary from the Turkish stranglehold than in extending the Counter-Reformation to the northern and western districts already under his rule. In Transylvania he was not able to overthrow the religious settlement which had already been fifty years in operation, for the Catholics at this period were only fourth in influence, as against the other three 'Received Religions'—the Calvinists, Lutherans and Unitarians. But in the Slovak counties he took the offensive, and the forcible transfer of the Cathedral of Košice (Kassa) from Protestant to Catholic hands in November, 1603, was hailed on both sides as a signal of the coming struggle. When the Hungarian Diet met at Pressburg a few weeks later, Rudolf committed the folly of ignoring their protests, and of adding to the twenty-one Articles passed by the Diet another of his own composition, and therefore entirely illegal—condemning in the future the introduction of religious *gravamina* as an act of treason. Basta, Belgioioso and Rudolf's other foreign commanders were instructed to enforce obedience, but met with open resistance ; the gates of Kassa were shut in their face, and they had to retreat in disorder from the scene of their terrorist activities to Moravia. Hungarian resistance, stiffened by the double motive, religious and national, found its expression in the insurrection of Stephen Bocskay, who not merely allied himself with the Sultan but appeared before the Grand Vizier in his camp at Pest, kissed his hand and knee, and accepted from his hands the royal crown of Hungary.

In face of this dangerous situation, Rudolf remained inert and indifferent ; and his four nearest kinsmen—his brothers Matthias and Maximilian, and his cousins Ferdinand and Max Ernest—encouraged by the Pope, the King of Spain and Archduke Albert of the Netherlands—met at Linz in April, 1605, to consider a joint *démarche* in favour of Rudolf's abdication. Meanwhile Matthias's trusted adviser, Bishop Melchoir Khlesl of Vienna, set on foot negotiations with Hungary and the Turks. But the suspicious Rudolf, though nearer than ever to the verge of madness, indulging in periodical outbursts of rage, in which he struck his ministers or his attendants and even threatened to take his own life, obstinately resisted all idea of relinquishing the control of affairs or regulating the succession. He saw in the suggestion nothing but the personal ambitions of Matthias ; and he was influenced by the prophecy of one of his astrologers that he would be murdered like Henry III of France. He kept Matthias's envoy waiting two whole months for an audience, and it was only when Gran again fell into Turkish hands that he grudgingly granted to his brother the necessary authority for waging war in Hungary and negotiating both with Bocskay and with the Sultan. An Armistice was concluded with the former on January 15, 1606, but it took six months longer to negotiate the Treaty of Vienna, by which Bocskay received Transylvania and eight other counties of Hungary, for his own lifetime, and his son's if he should have one. The main delay was caused by the religious issue. It was useless to expect the Estates to accept less than what Transylvania already enjoyed ; but it was only with great hesitation and in the teeth of Jesuit and Papal admonitions that Matthias conceded free exercise of religion for Catholic, Lutheran and Calvinist on equal footing. There was to be a religious *status quo* as in the time of Ferdinand, Maximilian, 'and the other kings' ; and the obnoxious Article XXII of 1604 was abrogated. A modern historian has put forward the plausible enough theory that this treaty was the first *Ausgleich* between Austria and Hungary, for the reason that the latter secured its guarantee not only by the Emperor and by the Archduke Ferdinand, but also by the Estates of Bohemia, Moravia, Silesia, Upper and Lower Austria and Styria.[1]

The Treaty of Zsitva Török

Rudolf only consented with the utmost reluctance, and two days later drew up a secret document declaring that he had acted under duress and was not bound by his oath. But the Treaty gave a further stimulus to the negotiations with the Porte, and on October 29 the Treaty of Zsitva Török was signed at a small village near Komárom. Though based territorially upon the *status quo* of the moment, it marks an altogether new departure. For the first time the two Emperors negotiate on an equal footing ; never again is there a message 'from the victorious Sultan to the ever defeated King of Vienna,' and the envoys of Vienna and Prague are at last received with fitting honour at the Porte, instead of languishing in the prison of the Seven Towers.[2] Moreover, the peace is valid for twenty years, and after a century of humiliation the Emperor makes his last payment of tribute—200,000 gulden in hard cash, but 'once and not again.' The Treaty was a clear sign that Turkey, though still formidable, was in decline, and that Habsburg military power was no less steadily gaining ground, concurrently with the growth of royal, as opposed to oligarchic, power.

Rudolf, out of jealousy towards Matthias, at first refused his signature ; and it is characteristic of the impossible situation, that what neither his kinsmen nor his advisers could obtain from him was secured by judicious bribes offered to the Emperor's body-servant, Philip Lang. It was not till May, 1607, that he sent to Matthias the ratification of the Turkish Treaty. He summoned the Hungarian Estates to Pressburg in the summer of that year, but withheld from his brother the authority without which he could not present himself before him ; and the result was that after waiting in vain for two months they protested and went home, more furious and discontented than ever. By this time an open breach between

[1] Richard von Kralik, *Oesterreichische Geschichte*, p. 110. In reality this guarantee was essentially a sign of justified suspicion towards the Imperial House ; needless to say the famous Ausgleich of 1867 does not contain any such guarantee. The only semblance of a parallel is the attempt of Hungary in 1867 to make the newly won constitutional position of Austria inviolable (in the well-grounded calculation that the loss of Austria's liberties would endanger Hungary's also, or vice versa).

[2] Under conditions graphically recorded by the Czech diplomat Wratislaw.

the two brothers was merely a matter of time and occasion ; one proof out of many was Rudolf's demand that on pain of his 'highest displeasure' Matthias should dismiss Bishop Khlesl and his other most trusted advisers —a demand which was, of course, flatly refused. The only remaining choice was between abject surrender and armed resistance ; and mediocre as was the Archduke Matthias in character and attainments, it is hardly too much to say that his firmness in these critical years saved the House of Habsburg from utter ruin.

Protestant Union and Catholic League

The first decade of the seventeenth century witnessed a marshalling of rival tendencies, leading inevitably to an unexampled explosion. In the Reich also friction was growing between Catholic and Protestant ; neither side was satisfied with the Religious Peace of Augsburg, and there was much manœuvring for the possession of the ecclesiastical sees, some of whose holders had seceded to the Protestants, without, however, always being able to apply the principle of *cuius regio*. The Protestants were in a majority and held the three lay Electorates, but they were fatally weakened by the disputes of Lutheran and Calvinist, and by the opportunist attitude of the Elector of Saxony, who gave his support to the Emperor. For this very reason the Calvinists were inclined to ally themselves with Holland and the still powerful French Calvinist party. There was much indignation at the suppression of Protestantism in Inner-Austria ; and the selection of its chief author, Ferdinand of Styria, as the Emperor's envoy to the Diet of Regensburg in 1607, was regarded as nothing less than a provocation. The events of the Austrian Counter-Reformation, the Turkish Wars and the Hungarian rebellion, which we have briefly described above, reacted almost equally upon Germany and upon Bohemia ; and during the summer of 1608 the Reich fell very rapidly into two armed camps—the Protestant Union, led by the Elector Palatine, and the Catholic League, led by Duke Max of Bavaria and the ecclesiastical princes. The latter was ostensibly the champion of the *status quo*, but in reality no one on either side was ready to respect it where changes in his own favour could be effected.

We need not concern ourselves here with the details of the German situation. Suffice it to say that it was so precarious and artificial that the least spark might have fired the train. The disputed succession to the Duchies of Jülich and Cleves, with its bearing both upon the principle of *cuius regio* and the balance of power in the Rhenish provinces, brought about an alliance between the Protestant Union and France, while Holland and England also seemed on the point of intervening. But the murder of King Henry IV of France (May 14, 1610), disastrous as it was for the immediate development in his own country, probably averted a great conflagration. In October, 1610, the Union and the League came to terms and war was averted, but was still balanced on the razor's edge.

Rudolf and Matthias

It will already be clear that the tragedy is approaching its climax, and that the course of events in Bohemia at this period can only be understood if treated in connection with parallel events in Austria, Hungary and Germany.

In January, 1608, the Hungarian Estates met at Pressburg and elected Matthias as 'hereditary Gubernator,' simply ignoring the protests of Rudolf's special envoy. This was followed by the formation of a Confederacy between Hungary, Austria and Moravia, the latter's adherence being largely due to the efforts of that able Moravian Conservative, Charles of Žerotin, in the teeth of resistance from Cardinal Dietrichstein of Olomouc and Rudolf's faithful courtier Slavata. While the two latter pressed for mediation by the Princes of the Reich, Matthias boldly grasped the nettle and demanded Rudolf's immediate abdication : and this had the backing of Žerotin and the Moravian Estates. There emerges the clear aim of deposing the impossible Rudolf, very much as Wenceslas had been deposed two centuries earlier.

While Matthias marched into Bohemia as far as Čásláv, the Bohemian Estates, showing all their proverbial jealousy of their Moravian colleagues, forced the unwilling Rudolf to receive them in audience ; and on June 24, 1608, an agreement was reached by which Rudolf was to renounce Hungary, Austria and Moravia in favour of Matthias, and while retaining Bohemia for himself, to recognize his brother as his heir there also. Matthias, for his part, refused the demand of the Moravian Estates that he should sign a document granting unrestricted liberty of religion : the most that he would concede was a verbal pledge not to persecute any man for his religion. Charles of Žerotin induced his colleagues not to press further for the moment, but the Austrian Protestants, led by Georg von Tschernembl and Richard von Starhemberg, took up a much more extreme position and formed the so-called League of Horn, which made the rendering of homage to the new sovereign contingent upon the restoration of all rights enjoyed under Maximilian II in 1575. On November 16 Matthias was elected King of Hungary and crowned three days later ; but the Estates imposed so many restrictions and conditions as to amount to a virtual capitulation on the part of the Crown.

During the critical year of 1609 the struggle centred more than ever round the person of Rudolf, who had the backing of the Nuncio and the Spanish Ambassador, but had a positive gift for alienating all support among his own subjects. The mischief was increased still further by his attempt to play off his young Styrian cousin Leopold against Matthias, as a possible candidate for the Imperial Crown. On April 1 his ministers, on his orders, illegally dissolved the Diet, but this led them, before separating, to take the semi-revolutionary step of fixing a new meeting in a month's time, and they now found in Budovec, a noble belonging to the Brethren, a fiery, eloquent and quite unconciliatory leader who was not afraid to make open attacks upon Rudolf. As part of his piecemeal bargaining, the Emperor next offered to restore the religious position that prevailed under Ferdinand I ; and when this was rejected as altogether unacceptable both to the Lutherans and to the Brethren, he offered the position under Maximilian II, or alternately arbitration by the six Electors, among whom he would have been almost certain of a majority. The Diet retorted by appointing three generals under its direct control, and thirty directors, chosen from its own members, for the conduct of affairs. This step was the equivalent, in modern parlance, of the appointment of a Provisional Government, and the historian, Alfons Huber, hardly goes too far in speaking of 'the proclamation of the permanent Revolution.'

The Letter of Majesty

Rudolf now found himself with his back against the wall, and lacked the military force without which continued resistance was impossible. On July 9, 1609, he signed the momentous 'Letter of Majesty,' amounting to a surrender of the absolutist pretensions of the Crown. Its main provisions assured the free exercise of religion to all who professed the 'Confessio Bohemica.' No one, neither townsman nor peasant, might henceforth be compelled to change his religion. The Estates obtained control of the Utraquist Consistory and its ordination of clergy, and at the same time control of the University of Prague, which had been steadily falling into the hands of the Catholics and Jesuits. Finally, the right to build new churches and schools was granted to the lords, knights and royal cities, though not to the rank and file. The only modification which Rudolf could obtain from his opponents was that where the document demanded liberty for the 'Evangelicals' (i.e. the Protestants), the word 'Utraquists' was substituted.

On the same day as the Letter of Majesty, and at the express instance of Rudolf himself, an agreement was signed between the Catholic and Protestant Estates and given full legal form ; this extended to each confession the right of building churches or schools in any place where it did not yet possess any. We have the testimony of Slavata, Rudolf's most trusted counsellor and author of a valuable contemporary history, that this was intended to apply equally to lay and ecclesiastical property ; and it thus transpired that the veto placed upon the building of Protestant churches at Braunau and Klostergrab—an incident which contributed very materially to the outbreak of the Thirty Years' War—was a definite infringement of the agreement of 1609, which had equal validity with the Letter of Majesty.

For the brief remainder of his life Rudolf's main energies were directed to intrigue against his brother. Early in 1610 the family and their allies in the Reich, conscious of the injury done to their cause and that of the Church, arranged a meeting of princes in Prague—the Electors of Mainz, Köln and Saxony, and the Archdukes Maximilian and Ferdinand—with a view to reconciliation. But while Matthias was ready to sue for pardon and to make a formal recognition of the Emperor as head of Christendom and of the Arch-House, Rudolf obstinately withheld his consent to Matthias' succession to the Empire, and babbled seriously in a project for substituting Ferdinand's younger brother Leopold. This intrigue assumed a serious character in the winter of 1610, when Leopold, as Bishop of Passau, used the territory of his see for massing an army that was to come to Rudolf's aid. Led by a foreign soldier of fortune, this army occupied Budějovice (Budweis) and even forced its way into Prague ; but the arrival of Matthias in March, 1611, forced it to withdraw from Bohemian soil, and soon disband. Henceforward the ultimate issue could not be in doubt. The Estates demanded to be released from their oath to him, and on May 23 Matthias was proclaimed King of Bohemia and crowned next day in St. Vitus' by Cardinal Dietrichstein. On August 11 Rudolf abdicated, and was allowed to retain the Imperial title and possession of the Castle of Prague, with an allowance adequate for the maintenance of its vast spaces. He was by now incorrigible, and feeling that he had been abandoned by his friends, developed a violent antipathy for the

League and intrigued actively with the Protestant Union. From such futilities he was removed by death on January 20, 1612. That summer Matthias was elected Emperor without serious opposition.

Of all the Habsburg rulers Rudolf II was the most incompetent and negative, and had the most baneful influence upon Bohemia and upon Europe. In one direction only can he be said to have left something positive behind him. He was a genuine lover and patron of the arts, and the steady encouragement which he gave to them was responsible for the century of Catholic Baroque, of which Prague is the most perfect and still unspoilt example.

CHAPTER VIII

THE CATASTROPHE

Und dieses böhmsche Land um das wir fechten,
Das hat kein Herz fur seinen Herrn, den ihm
Der Waffen Glück, nicht eigne Wahl gegeben.
Mit Murren frägt's des Glaubens Tyrannei.

—Schiller, *Wallenstein.*

Persecution has often won in human history : often has a violent hand
dashed out the lamp of truth.

—John Morley.

FOR the moment the unanimous acceptance of Matthias as the holder of
all three Crowns was greeted as a favourable omen. There was much
anti-Habsburg feeling in the Reich, not confined to the Protestants
alone, but there was no other candidate capable of uniting the votes of
the Electors, and inside the Habsburg family Matthias was infinitely the
less objectionable to the Protestants, who detested Ferdinand, distrusted
the unstable Leopold and dismissed Albert as one whom long absence
abroad had rendered unsuitable for the task. Matthias was only fifty-
three, but he had lived well and was by now old and enfeebled, not a
recluse like his brother, and indeed attached to the domestic hearth (in
1611 he had married Ferdinand of Tirol's daughter Anne), a lover of music
and art, and fond of the quips and buffooneries of court jesters. But he
was lazy and remiss in the performance of official duties ; his minister,
Cardinal Khlesl, who now contrived to make himself more indispensable
than ever, said of Matthias that 'he generally says yes, because he won't
take the trouble to think things over.'

The new Emperor, living mainly in Vienna rather than in Prague,
proved quite unable to win the confidence of his subjects, and the Estates
in each of his dominions tended to go each their own way. In a letter to
his cousin Ferdinand he lamented his own helplessness, while in Upper
Austria there was an open threat of choosing a foreign Prince in his
place, while the Bohemian *defensores* controlled the summons of the
Estates and all financial decisions, and while in Hungary, Moravia and
Silesia respectively the Palatine Count Thurzo, Charles of Žerotin and
the Duke of Jägerndorff had made themselves all-powerful. Žerotin, the
only really far-sighted man among them, continued to advocate a Confederacy for joint defence against religious or political encroachment ;
but the spirit of oligarchy was stronger than that of unity, and the
oligarchs, while defending their rights against the Crown, were equally
bent upon extending their already excessive power over the peasantry.
Meanwhile all Germany was ranging itself into two armed camps ; on all
sides the question of the succession exercised men's minds, and there was
already much loose talk of the need for another dynasty and for 'finding
another master.' In Hungary there was danger of fresh Turkish invasion ;
and Gabriel Báthory, the prince who had succeeded Bocskay on the
throne of Transylvania and was on friendly terms with Matthias, was
murdered and replaced by Gabriel Bethlen, who on the contrary allied

himself with the Turks and made himself an open champion of the Protestant cause among all his neighbours.

Matthias and the Succession

Matthias in his alarm took the remarkable step of convoking, at Graz in August, 1614, a General Diet for all the Austrian Lands (for which precedents already existed from the years 1518 and 1541). But his main purpose—to obtain money grants for a renewed conflict with the Turks and their allies in Hungary—met with very little response; and the Emperor found it necessary to come to terms with Bethlen, who promised never to separate Transylvania from Hungary or to make war on the House of Austria. In June, 1615, another General Diet was summoned to Prague, but the Hungarians jealously held aloof, and the zeal displayed at Prague for the Czechization of the whole administration and the insistence upon a knowledge of Czech as a condition of citizenship, and upon Czech, not German, sermons in the churches, naturally enough helped to create a certain coolness on the part of the Austrian Estates.

The question of the succession now threw all others into the shade. Maximilian and Albert formally renounced their rights, and Philip III of Spain, who for a time had played with the unpromising idea of reuniting the two branches of the House of Habsburg and establishing a 'Universal Monarchy,' allowed himself to be bought off by Ferdinand's secret promise of territorial concessions in Italy and in Alsace. On June 6, 1617, the Bohemian Estates accepted Ferdinand as their future king, recognizing him not merely as 'elected,' but as 'accepted,' in other words admitting the hereditary claim of the Habsburgs. A fortnight later he was crowned in St. Vitus's Cathedral, duly confirming the obnoxious Letter of Majesty, and, as events were to show, not feeling bound to observe it a day longer than was necessary. Only two votes were cast against him, by Count Thurn and Colonna de Fels. This yielding attitude on the part of the Estates has always seemed inexplicable, for it placed their most implacable enemy in the central strategic position of the coming struggle and automatically put his opponents in the wrong. Henceforth there was a clear choice between submission and rebellion. A year later Ferdinand fortified his position still further; for Matthias being too ill to attend the Hungarian Diet at Pressburg, a compromise was agreed upon by which Ferdinand was elected as King of Hungary (May 16, 1618) and crowned six weeks later.

The Defenestration

This was the signal for a counter-offensive against the Protestants throughout the Habsburg dominions; in Bohemia in particular there were constant and systematic infringements of the Letter of Majesty on the part of Lobkovic, Martinic and Slavata, in whose hands the administration lay. The incident which actually provoked an explosion was of no very special significance. The citizens of two small towns, Braunau and Klostergrab, acting in accordance with the Agreement concluded simultaneously with the Letter of Majesty, proceeded to erect Protestant churches; they were now ordered to desist by the Archbishop and by the Abbot to whose domains they respectively belonged. The former actually pulled down what had been built, and when the Protestants persisted, a number were thrown into prison. Failing redress from the proper authorities, the Defensores convoked in Prague a General Assembly of the Bohemian Protestants, and when the remonstrances which they addressed to Matthias in Vienna met with a most ungracious and even menacing retort and a direct veto upon further meetings, they none the less re-assembled in greater numbers than ever, under the leadership of Count Thurn and soon resolved upon drastic action. On May 23, 1618, over a hundred Protestant nobles and knights made their way to the Castle of Prague, and after violent altercations flung Martinic, Slavata and their secretary, Fabricius, headlong out of the window of the council chamber. That they escaped with their lives was due to the medieval neglect of hygiene, which permitted the refuse heaps of the Castle to pile up in deep ditches some fifty feet below the state apartments ! Known as the 'Defenestration,' this dramatic act of violence was a deliberate imitation of that earlier defenestration that had set the Hussite troubles in motion in 1419. From it it is usual to date the outbreak of what was till then the most widespread and devastating of wars.

The die was now cast, and the Estates promptly took the further revolutionary steps of setting up a sort of provisional government, consisting of thirty directors, ten from each Estate, and of expelling the Jesuits from Bohemia, as guilty of deliberate incitement of the sovereign and his subjects, of encouragement to the murder of kings who resisted their advice, of the acquisition of vast temporal estates, and finally of openly preaching the doctrine that no faith need be kept with heretics. Quite undismayed, the Jesuits retorted from their place of exile that it was impossible to tolerate different religions in a single country and that it was their chief aim to reduce the whole world to the papal obedience. In taking such drastic action against his teachers and favourites, the directors must have fully realized that they were entering upon war to the knife with Ferdinand, and this explains their immediate mustering of troops and their negotiations with the Protestant Union in Germany. On the other hand, they still hoped to come to terms with Matthias, now fast failing in health, and with his astute adviser Cardinal Khlesl, ever a lover of compromise and tortuous bargaining. A further last effort at appeasement was also made by Charles of Žerotin on behalf of the Moravian Estates. But this only spurred on the reactionaries who surrounded Ferdinand and who calculated that their opponents, by their revolutionary acts, were offering him a final chance of forcible repression. On July 20 Ferdinand visited Vienna, and over the head of Matthias dismissed Khlesl and sent him to close confinement for a number of years. He then prepared the invasion of Bohemia under two Spanish generals, Bucquoy and Dampierre, selected as tried veterans of war in the Low Countries.

Ferdinand was not a man of any real ability, his natural interests lay in the direction of hunting and music, he was a bad manager, frequently in financial difficulties, and he had no military talent or ambition, coming thus to rely upon his generals to an inordinate degree. But he had one dominating passion, which never left him : he was at all costs resolved to re-establish Catholicism, first in his own dominions, but if possible in Germany also. In this he never wavered, and his constancy was rewarded.

Ferdinand's army found Bohemia better prepared for resistance than it had expected and made a timely withdrawal ; the Bohemians for their part received German reinforcements from Ernest von Mansfeld, and also from the Duke of Savoy, Charles Emanuel, who was a strong personal enemy of the Habsburgs, and with their help they stormed Pilsen, the only Bohemian city which still recognized the Emperor.

Ferdinand II and Bohemia

The death of Matthias (March 20, 1619) made the issue clearer than ever. Ferdinand sent to Prague a written pledge to respect Bohemia's rights and the Letter of Majesty ; but it was pretty obvious that both sides were almost equally insincere and merely manœuvring for position, and the Directors did not even send an answer. In passing, it is important to note that the old line of cleavage between Czech and German no longer held good, but was replaced by what we now call divergent ideologies. Lutheranism had become a link rather than a barrier, as was shown by the eager support given to Prague by Protestant and German Silesia, at a time when predominantly Czech Moravia was still hesitant. Upper Austria also, under Tschernembl and Starhemberg, actively sympathized with Czech resistance. But it must be admitted that nowhere in the Protestant ranks was there a leader of vision and *élan*, such as the Czechs had possessed two centuries before in Žižka and Prokop. Žerotin, it is true, was a man of high character and broad political conceptions, groping towards some kind of triple confederacy—Austria, Bohemia and Hungary ; but he was too cautious, too conservative to push the idea home to the logical conclusion that it could only be achieved through the expulsion of the Habsburgs and Jesuits, and perhaps on republican lines quite unsuited to that authoritative age.

In April, 1619, Count Schlick invaded Moravia, and speedily helped the more radical party into the saddle under a directorate of thirty members, on the Prague model. Encouraged by the ease of this operation, Count Thurn in June pressed on to the very gates of Vienna, expecting to have the active support of the Austrian nobility and perhaps even to seize the person of Ferdinand. But Ferdinand, at this crisis of his fate, showed the most unflinching courage ; he refused to yield one inch to the Estates, who, led by Paul von Starhemberg, demanded the grant of full religious liberty, and at the very last moment he was saved by the arrival of reinforcements from Dampierre. Thurn lacked the resources for a siege and withdrew again to Bohemia ; a chance had been lost which never again presented itself.

Ferdinand undoubtedly believed in the direct guidance of Providence, and he saw clearly that he must act quickly if the Imperial succession was to be saved for his House. Fortunately for him there was no other very serious candidate ; the Duke of Savoy asked too much and soon found himself without backers, while Duke Maximilian of Bavaria, for all his jealousy of the Habsburgs, refused to take up so dangerous and doubtful a challenge. The moment Vienna was out of danger Ferdinand hastened to Frankfurt ; his own vote (whose exercise by Ferdinand the Bohemian Estates challenged, but of course to no purpose) and those of the three ecclesiastical Electors already gave him a majority, Saxony was friendly, Brandenburg drew back into a shell of neutrality, with the result that the Elector Palatine, who for months past had been in secret parley with Prague and had even paid a special visit to Munich in order to induce Duke Maximilian to become a candidate, found himself quite alone and lacked the courage to withhold his vote. Thus on August 28 Ferdinand was unanimously elected Emperor.

Meanwhile, however, Bohemia had launched upon a wholly revolutionary course. On July 1 a General Diet was opened in Prague, with Protestant delegates from Upper and Lower Austria, and began by proclaiming an alliance or 'confederation' between all the lands of the Crown of St. Wenceslas. Bohemia was proclaimed an elective, and no longer a hereditary, kingdom ; at an election to the vacant throne Bohemia was to have two votes, Moravia, Silesia, Upper and Lower Lusatia one each. A series of restrictions were imposed upon the royal power ; without the approval of the Estates he could neither make war nor introduce foreign troops, neither build fortresses nor incur debts, nor even appoint high officials. Finally, in each province *Defensores* were appointed to watch over the liberties of the Estates, and the highest offices were reserved to Protestants. Protestants might build churches on Catholic lands, but not Catholics on Protestant lands. It followed logically that on August 19 Ferdinand was deposed, as a pupil of the Jesuits and an arch-enemy of the Evangelical faith, as having only obtained the Crown illegally by threats and bribes, and then not having kept his promises.

The Winter King

A week later Frederick V of the Palatinate was elected to the vacant throne ; the Duke of Savoy and the Elector of Saxony were only mentioned to be rejected. He hesitated to accept, having placed himself in a weak position by his recognition of Ferdinand's title to the Bohemian crown on the occasion of the recent Imperial election. His wife, Elizabeth Stuart, the fascinating but unfortunate daughter of James I, was widely credited by contemporaries with whetting her husband's ambition. But there is not much evidence for this beyond the obvious fact that Frederick owed a considerable part of his prestige to his marriage with a British princess. Moreover, it is certain that James himself disapproved and tried to hold Frederick back—an attitude that was quite logical in a monarch with such exalted ideas upon the royal power.

Good evidence suggests that it was the intriguing Christian of Anhalt who turned the scale in favour of acceptance. In October Frederick and Elizabeth arrived in Prague, and on November 4 were crowned, the ceremony being performed by the Administrator of the Protestant Consistory and the Senior of the Unity of Brethren. It is useless to pretend that the selection was a happy one. Without accepting the caustic contemporary gibe that a people which could commit the folly of electing such a mediocrity deserved anything that might come to it, it must be admitted that Frederick was in no way equal to his position as the foremost Calvinist Prince in Germany, still less as defender of the most exposed bastion of Protestantism.

Frederick's anxieties were for the moment gravely increased by the reserved attitude of the Styrian and Tirolese Estates, but still more by events in Hungary, where Gabriel Bethlen, having consolidated his position in Transylvania, openly allied himself with Thurzo and the other Protestant magnates of Slovakia, found much active support in Kassa and the mining towns, and on October 14 occupied Pressburg. He came too late, however, to join Thurn in his attack upon Vienna, and soon had to retire eastwards again. A second vital opportunity of united action between Hungary and Bohemia had thus been lost and did not recur again ; and Bethlen, though elected 'Prince' of Hungary in January,

1620, and openly aiming at the Crown of St. Stephen, and perhaps also of Styria and Austria, decided not to break irreparably with the new Emperor, and allowed himself to be bought off by the promised cession of additional Hungarian counties, and of the Silesian duchies of Oppeln and Ratibor to his heirs. He ended by contenting himself with the title of 'Elected King' ; 'Cobbler, keep to your last,' is one of his alleged sayings. He recognized the common bond of Calvinism, but Frederick's extravagant ambition made him hold back.

Frederick spent a year in his new kingdom, seemingly incapable of any initiative, and awaiting the gathering storm. Hungary had failed ; Poland, under that ardent proselyte Sigismund Vasa, was directly un-friendly ; Denmark and Sweden were not yet conscious of the issues ; James was reluctant even to support his own son-in-law against the Em-peror's authority, and the wide sympathy which the Bohemian cause enjoyed in English Puritan circles only served to augment his doubts. Worst of all, the Lutheran leader, John George of Saxony, in his petty, grudging jealousy, threw his weight into the Catholic scale rather than help his foremost Calvinist rival to maintain himself as king. John George was more to blame than any other for the Protestant Union's pitiable failure to comprehend the probable consequences for Germany and for the Protestant cause throughout Europe of Ferdinand's success over Bohemia. Frederick himself showed a lack of tact towards his new subjects, notably by encouraging Calvinist vandalism against the pictures and ornaments of St. Vitus' Cathedral and both Catholic and Utraquist Churches. He was no soldier himself, he had no soldier of ability to lead his army, and his troops, thanks to ill-discipline and arrears of pay, were always on the verge of mutiny. On the other hand, the Catholic League had practical help from Spain and the Pope and possessed a most com-petent leader in Maximilian of Bavaria, supported by Bucquoy, Dampierre and above all the fanatical Tilly. Incredible as it may seem, Maximilian was able to negotiate an arrangement with the Protestant Union based upon the clown's principle : 'Heads I win, tails *you* lose'—by which the Union and League were to live at peace with each other, but this was not extended to Bohemia and Hungary, with the result that Maximilian had his flanks secured against both sections of the Palatinate, while himself free to concentrate against Bohemia. The spirit in which Ferdi-nand marshalled his forces is clearly revealed in the instructions sent to Maximilian on the eve of his advance : his first step must be to 'clear the preachers, with their damned heresy, out of Upper Austria.' Another and no less characteristic anecdote relates to an audience during which Ferdinand demurred to a more than usually extravagant outburst of the Spanish Ambassador against the heretics. If Ferdinand hesitated, the envoy boldly declared, 'his place in hell would be deeper than those of Calvin and Luther.'

The White Mountain

On August 4, 1620, Maximilian occupied Linz and forced the Upper Austrian Estates to do immediate homage to Ferdinand, thirty of their number being deprived of their lands. By the end of September he and Bucquoy were ready to cross the Bohemian frontier, and pushing on towards Prague gave battle a couple of miles outside the city, on the so-called White Mountain, on November 8, 1620. As battles go, it was the merest skirmish ; Christian of Anhalt fought gallantly, and 1,600 of his men were killed. But the rest of the Czech army broke into a disordered flight, and in a few hours all was over.[1] But the defeat was far from irretrievable ; the Hrad and the Malá Strana of Prague were well fortified and capable of defence, while a contingent of 8,000 men sent by Bethlen were within four miles of the city. If Prague had held out, help would certainly have come from Germany, and eventually from Denmark and perhaps even from England. But Frederick and his generals—even Anhalt and Thurn—fell into utter panic and set out that very afternoon in headlong flight towards the Silesian border, leaving the dismayed citizens to note the long lines of carriages and baggage wagons which they were still able to remove. The strong fortress of Karlstein, with its English garrison of 2,000 men, was surrendered at the first summons by Mansfeld, who fled back to Germany. Pilsen and Eger surrendered, and long before the close of the year Ferdinand's occupation of Bohemia was complete. Frederick, by his pusillanimity, lost not merely his new-won kingdom, but also his hereditary dominions ; and Ferdinand, after placing him under ban of the Empire as a rebel, induced the other Electors to transfer the Palatinate and its voting power from the Calvinist Frederick to Maximilian of Bavaria, the champion of militant Catholicism, a step which very materially altered the whole balance in Germany to the detriment of the Protestants. Queen Elizabeth survived her husband by many years, but she and her children lived and died in exile. The 'Winter Queen' is the second and the sadder of the dynastic links between Bohemia and England ; and she, like Richard II's charming young Queen Anne, rests in Westminster Abbey. Henry Wootton's apostrophe, 'Ye meaner beauties of the night,' has given her a permanent niche in every anthology of English poetry. Her sons, Rupert and Maurice, play a military part in England's civil war very different from that of their unwarlike father.

The victory of the White Mountain was received with consternation in the Protestant North, but hailed with the most exuberant joy in Vienna, Rome and Madrid, and with every reason, for it seemed to mark a decisive turn in the fortunes of the Counter-Reformation. The Protestants were driven on to the defensive, and were only rescued from their precarious plight after nearly ten years of war, with the coming of Gustavus Adolphus. At the first moment the Capuchin preacher Sabinus, in the presence of the Emperor, declaimed the Psalmist's words : 'Thou shalt chastise them with a rod of iron, and shalt break them in pieces like a potter's vessel,' and claimed that now was the time to extirpate the heretics and that failure to do so would bring upon the sovereign's head the fate of Ahab. Ferdinand did not allow his zeal to outrun his discretion and only proceeded step by step in introducing his 'New Order' in Bohemia ; but there was never the slightest doubt as to his ultimate intentions. Already in May, 1621, some two hundred Calvinist preachers were summarily expelled, but there was as yet no general decision, and it was not till the following December that the edict of banishment against the Jesuits was revoked. Meanwhile an Imperial Commission had come to Prague and sentenced forty-five persons out of all three Estates as rebels guilty of death. On June 21, 1621, twenty-six of these ringleaders were executed in front of the Town Hall of Prague. Among them were

---

[1] The story that the battle only lasted an hour seems to have been put about by the Jesuits, who ascribed their well-nigh miraculous victory to the direct intervention of the Virgin, and to render this plausible the collapse had to be swift and sudden.

Count Schlick (whom the Saxon Elector had basely handed over), the already ageing Budovec, and ten other Directors, one of them, Gaspar Kapliř, being a man of eighty-six. All died with courage and dignity, laying the main stress of their parting words upon their devotion to the reformed faith. In view of the importance rightly attached by Czech writers to what is one of the crowning tragedies of Bohemian Independence, it is important to point out that these executions have a much wider significance from the national than even from the religious point of view. For just as there were Utraquists, Lutherans, Calvinists and Brethren among them (the latter being expressly refused access to their clergy on the scaffold), so also there were Germans side by side with the Czechs. The most notable of them was Dr. Jessenius, Rector of the University, one of the pioneers of the modern school of anatomy and a noted orator, who had often been employed by Matthias upon diplomatic missions in Hungary. By a refinement of cruelty his tongue was torn out and nailed upon the scaffold, before he was beheaded. Another German, Martin Frühwein, a Prague advocate, escaped execution by flinging himself from a high window. Those of the Moravian Directors who had not saved themselves by flight were also sentenced to death, but reprieved by Ferdinand, who seems to have had very genuine scruples about executions. Special severity, however, was shown to the priest of the famous Týn Church, in Prague, Lecika, who boldly continued to celebrate *sub utraque* and to preach Utraquist doctrine.

In passing, it is surely but right to draw a contrast between these twenty-seven executions, ordered by the legitimate sovereign of Bohemia against undoubted rebels, and the many hundreds of executions ordered in 1941 by the butcher Heydrich in the name of a foreign conqueror who had no claim to Czech allegiance, and who by seizing Prague had violated the pledges he had freely given before all Europe less than six months earlier. The worst excesses of Ferdinand and his Jesuit advisers pale before the systematic reprisals against thousands of innocent Czechs by the Gestapo henchmen of Hitler and Daluege.

Ferdinand was now free to devote himself to the paramount task of re-Catholicization, and a series of decrees against the Protestants of Bohemia were issued in 1624. But he found it expedient to go warily in order not to alienate his Lutheran ally, John George of Saxony, and also not to drive Northern Hungary needlessly into the arms of Gabriel Bethlen. He actually sent assurances to the Elector that the punishments inflicted were purely political and were in no way directed against adherents of the Augsburg Confession. The double series of victories in 1626, by Tilly over Christian IV of Denmark, by Wallenstein over Bethlen, encouraged Ferdinand in the belief that Protestant Germany had been driven finally on to the defensive, and had no serious hope of military assistance from abroad. He therefore felt that the moment had come for drastic action in Bohemia. Among those advisers to whose persistent pressure he may be said to have yielded (though in reality the issue between them was never one of principle, but only of choosing the psychological moment) were Archbishop Lohelius of Prague and Questenberg, abbot of the great Præmonstratensian monastery of Strahov (less than a mile from the Castle of Prague), Prince Liechtenstein, whom Ferdinand had appointed Governor of Bohemia and who had to prove the completeness of his own conversion to Catholicism by stern repression of heresy ; but above all his own confessor, Lamormain, and the Papal

Nuncio in Vienna, Carlo Caraffa, who would hear of no compromise or concession. Under their auspices the Jesuits were given a free hand in the great task of proselytizing ; and if there were no more executions, it was because on the one hand Ferdinand, with his tender conscience, preferred to stop short of actual bloodshed, and because unhappy Bohemia was now in the grip of irresistible strategic forces. The Jesuits re-echoed the appeal addressed by one of their order to Rudolf II :

> *'Utere iure tuo, Cæsar, servosqve Lutheri*
> *Ense, rota, ponto, funibus, igne neca.'*
> (Exercise thy rights, O Cæear, and kill the servants of
> Luther by sword, and wheel, by water, rope and fire).

As second best they contented themselves with the less expeditious but highly effective methods of confiscation, re-education and delation, on a scale not again attained till our own day. Once more we may pause to note that the methods of enforced emigration applied by Ferdinand's ministers were less drastic than those applied by Hitler's minions of the Gestapo to hundreds of thousands of Jews, Poles, Slovenes and others, who were given an hour or two to collect a few belongings, and then sent off in cattle trucks to an unknown destination, without the possibility of disposing of their property or taking money with them. Truly our own enlightened age can teach our most barbarous ancestors methods of sadistic torture such as they had hardly dreamt of.

On May 10, 1627, Ferdinand issued his famous 'Renewed Ordinance' (*Vernewerte Landesordnung*), wiping out the Letter of Majesty—the original document may still be seen in the Vienna Archives, mangled by the august scissors of Ferdinand himself—and placing the constitution of Bohemia on an entirely new footing. In the preamble it is made clear that Bohemia is undergoing the fate of a rebellious and conquered country. 'Having by the help of Almighty God brought our hereditary Kingdom of Bohemia by the sword once more into our power and obedience,' Ferdinand had 'no higher task' than to 're-establish God's honour and justice' against 'most loathsome rebellion,' to 'correct and remove the weaknesses due to previous disorder,' and to leave as far as possible 'the old customs'—corrected, however, 'according to the principles (*gewöhnliche Satzungen*) of the Empire and our kingdoms and lands.' It is quite true, then, that Ferdinand believed himself to be reverting to an earlier tradition, and that some of his changes were directed against oligarchic or feudal innovations in the Utraquist period at the expense of the masses. But it is also only necessary to sum up the essential points of the new statute in order to see that the Renewed Ordinance in its turn was a far-reaching experiment in the expansion of the royal power.

In the first place the Crown was made hereditary—a necessary first step towards the projected fusion with the Austrian 'hereditary dominions' : henceforth the Diet could only elect a king, if the dynasty were entirely extinct in the female as well as male line—a contingency, no doubt, which cannot have seemed so academic to contemporaries, who knew that Ferdinand owed his accession to the death of five male cousins without issue.[1]

Thus even the ceremony of 'reception' by which the heir of the last four sovereigns had been elected King of Bohemia in his predecessor's lifetime, became superfluous, and the *Huldigung*, or act of allegiance,

---

[1] Rudolf II and his four brothers, Matthias, Albert, Ernest and Maximilian.

became an unimportant ceremonial connected with the Coronation of the heir (*Erbherr*) of an almost absolute sovereign. This is not materially altered by the imposition of a coronation oath to maintain the Catholic religion, to administer justice and to leave the Estates 'in their confirmed and well-established privileges'—privileges which had in reality vanished like smoke.

The fourth Estate—the ecclesiastical—recovered its lost place and was assigned special precedence over the other three. The Diet lost its right of initiative and was restricted to proposals submitted by the Crown; it lost also the right to attach conditions to money grants. The Crown, in addition to this extension of its legislative powers (*ius legis ferendæ*), took into its own hands all the higher official appointments and acquired complete control of the bureaucracy. Incidentally, the high office of Burggrave was abolished. The Bohemian Chancellery (*Böhmische Hofkanzlei*) in Vienna acquired added importance and, it is true, served for a century to come as a barrier against complete centralization; but it was all the time performing a merely intermediate function and could be easily swept aside in the eighteenth century, when the time for more far-reaching administrative reforms seemed to have arrived.

Finally, the Ordinance expressly annulled all the successive privileges granted in favour of the Utraquists or other non-Catholics, and in particular the Letter of Majesty of 1609, and it placed the German language on a footing of equality with Czech throughout Bohemia.

Ferdinand and the Jesuits

Even more important in the eyes of Ferdinand and his advisers than the secular changes was the regulation of ecclesiastical affairs. This culminated in the Decree of July 31, 1627, the anniversary of St. Ignatius Loyola being deliberately chosen for its promulgation, as a special compliment to the all-powerful Order of Jesus. By it a space of six months was granted to all members of the noble and knightly Estates who had not yet conformed to the Roman Church,[1] in which to sell their lands and houses, gather together their cash and movable property and leave the country with them. Two months later similar measures were prescribed for the royal towns, but in their case there was no respite, but immediate and harsh enforcement.[2]

It will suffice to treat as a whole the various decrees issued between 1620 and 1627, beginning with the weaker members of the community and applied finally to the class which had dominated Bohemian politics for over a century past. There can be no doubt that between them Ferdinand and his advisers pursued the double aim of transforming the existing social and political order in Bohemia and extirpating the religious faith upon which it had been built up. From the outset, then, absolute uniformity was the aim: there was to be 'a crusade of extermination'

---

[1] An extension was eventually granted till May, 1628.

[2] Perhaps the most surprising feature of the persecution is the number of persons in all ranks of life who preferred exile and poverty to surrender of their faith; but that there was an undercurrent of stubborn passive resistance which baffled all the zeal and interference of the Jesuits, backed by the whole force of the secular arm, is shown by the amount of repressive measures still considered necessary a whole generation later, after the Peace of Westphalia, and above all by the extent of crypto-Hussite doctrine brought to light by the scandalized authorities in the second and third decades of the eighteenth century.

against Utraquism no less than Lutheranism or the other Protestant sects. This was speedily applied to the clergy, though for many years to come it was found difficult to fill so many vacancies with fully qualified priests, and a certain number of Utraquist clergy saw themselves not merely forced into acts of conformity resembling those imposed in England or Scotland under Elizabeth or the Stuarts, but also into a humiliating repudiation of their lawful wives and children.

First the shepherds, then their flocks ; and this extension of the field of operations was enforced by wholesale confiscation of property. Already in the summer of 1623, 12,000 persons are known to have emigrated from Prague, Litoměřice and Neubunzlau ; and the historian Slavata, who, as one of the most exposed and most influential adherents of Ferdinand, had very special means of informing himself, has estimated that by 1628 36,000 families had emigrated from Bohemia, 180 of these belonging to the nobility, and that the confiscations amounted to 40–45,000,000 gulden. The first of these figures has on the whole been endorsed by modern historians, but the second is far below the truth ; indeed, Bílek, the principal authority on this question, maintains that the value of the confiscated property was certainly not lower than 100,000,000, and that out of 936 noble domains nearly 500 were forfeited.

In a letter addressed to Liechtenstein, Ferdinand denied that it had ever been his intention 'to expel and destroy the Bohemian nobility,' and this may have originally been true of himself, though never, of course, of the Jesuits ; but the extinction of the knightly order, from whom so many of the most redoubtable Hussites had been recruited, was certainly planned from the first, and most successfully achieved. But the back of the old nobility was also effectively broken, and from this period dates the influx of numerous alien families, which won the favour of the Emperor during the long wars and received from him generous grants of land. There are names from almost every country in Europe, though Germans, Spaniards and Walloons predominate—Bucquoy, Trautmannsdorf, Dietrichstein, Clary, Verdugo, Piccolomini, Paravicini, Clam-Gallas, Leslie, Nugent, Marradas, Colloredo. Ferdinand was all his life long in urgent need of money, and more than ever since the spread of the war to Germany, and this added a fresh incentive in favour of confiscation. But, as in so many other historical cases where land-ownership was one of the keys to political motive, there was infinite squandering of resources, gross speculation and even depreciation of the coinage. Some of Liechtenstein's creatures actually obtained the royal assent to the formation of what was in effect a syndicate of false coiners, who melted down old money and reminted it at the rate of 79 gulden to 32. The misery and confusion resulting from all this aroused the indignant protests of Maximilian of Bavaria, whose bigotry did not outweigh his common sense or sense of justice.

Meanwhile the zeal of the Jesuits in the cultural sphere knew no bounds, and there followed in their footsteps a crowd of eager competitors—Carmelites, Barnabites, Dominicans and other preaching and teaching Orders. But the Jesuits, firmly rooted in the royal favour, overshadowed all others ; they dominated the University, enjoyed a virtual monopoly in the faculties of philosophy and theology, imposed their ideas of education on the whole school system of the country, and were entrusted with the censorship. This last privilege was of very special importance, for it not merely put a strait-jacket upon all literary output for two centuries to come, but it extended into the past, leading to a thorough purge of existing libraries, and regular holocausts of books in the Czech vernacular, most of which were, at any rate in Jesuit eyes, tinged with Hussite heresy. The Jesuit historian Balbín—whose relative tolerance and critical faculty, no less than his genuine attachment to his native Czech tongue, favourably distinguish him from all his colleagues —tells us that he 'could name more than 300 of our Fathers, each of whom had converted several thousands of heretics ; one has converted more than 6,000,' and that a certain Peter Kravarský claimed no fewer than 33,140 to his credit. The Jesuit Koniaš, who maintained in the more frigid atmosphere of the eighteenth century the incendiary zeal of the seventeenth, is generally allowed to have achieved the record for those times in burning of Czech books, though whether his own figure of 60,000 was strictly accurate it is impossible to determine.

To sum up the situation, within a few years of the White Mountain Bohemia was bound helplessly to the Habsburg war chariot, and exploited in the interests of absolutism and militant Catholicism ; so militant as to frighten a Roman pontiff and a French cardinal, Urban VIII and Richelieu, into giving political support to the Protestant North. Moreover, the broad outline of these events may help us to an understanding of our own times ; for it is no exaggeration to say that just as the seizure of Czechoslovakia opened up to Hitler the path of strategic ascendancy in Europe, so the collapse of Bohemia in 1620 turned the scale in favour of Ferdinand and the Counter-Reformation, as against the Protestant Union, drove Protestantism on to the defensive and infinitely prolonged the struggle.

These years provide eloquent testimony to Bismarck's famous definition of Bohemia as a fortress whose possession meant the mastery of Central Europe.

Bohemia's Role in the Thirty Years' War

The sudden downfall of Bohemia in the struggle against the Counter-Reformation is one of the most dramatic incidents in her whole history, the chief example of that catastrophic element which is to be found in the history of all the Slavonic nations. Moreover, the fact that for the second time she stands in the very forefront of events in Europe is due not merely to geographical reasons, but, as in the Hussite wars, to her alert and ardent response to the call of religious and political liberty, which placed her in earlier centuries ahead of intellectual opinion in most other countries. Certainly the Defenestration, the election of a foreign king and the imposition of elaborate constitutional restraints, must be regarded as even more revolutionary in intention than the corresponding actions of the Hussite period. But if we look below the surface, we can soon detect on this second occasion a narrower conception, less idealism, and less solidarity among the classes. In the first case Bohemia successfully held the world at bay, in the second she collapsed at a single blow. That is no mere accident, but is due above all to the fact that in 1620 the conduct of affairs was in the hands of an oligarchy, out of sympathy with the peasant masses whose ancestors had formed the backbone of Hussite resistance, and engaged in a feud of their own with the expanding royal power. It would be monstrous to suggest that their leaders were not genuinely devoted to their religion, and ready to seal their devotion with their blood ; the dying utterances of Budovec,[1] Schlick and others afford the proof. But none the less their cause was tinged with a narrowly aristocratic flavour ; and as in other countries in the Reformation period, the question of Church lands and their future ownership played a very vital part on both sides. In passing, it is germane to add that what first turned the scale against Ferdinand in the long German wars was his promulgation of the notorious 'Edict of Restitution' of 1629, which, coming from above, was quite as revolutionary in its implications as earlier transfers of landed property effected from below, and which turned many waverers against the fanatical Emperor.

If in the sixteenth century it was increasingly difficult to disentangle Bohemian and Austrian history, after the events of 1620–1627 it becomes altogether impossible to do so. The fate of Bohemia is swallowed up in the wider fate of the Habsburg monarchy and of Germany itself. Had Frederick been able to maintain himself on the throne, there can be little doubt that the cause of the Habsburgs would have suffered speedy eclipse, and that the many elements hostile to them in Hungary and in Austria would have asserted themselves. That is why the action of Frederick, as the leading lay Elector, and champion of the German Calvinists, was a challenge which Ferdinand could not possibly disregard. Once conquered, Bohemia became his strongest key-position, a base from which his generals could penetrate the Upper Palatinate and force the Protestants of North Germany on to the defensive. It was to remain for three centuries the granary and storehouse of the Monarchy, whose resources were relatively greater than those of any other province, and whose exploitation was less open to objection, in view of its recalcitrant past and doubtful loyalty.

It would lead far beyond the scope of this volume to attempt even a general survey of the Thirty Years' War : it must suffice to indicate the moments at which Bohemia was most directly involved. And here there is one name which throws all others into the shade, a name still surrounded by mystery, treachery and speculation, and likely to defy to all time the researches of archivist and pathologist alike. Albrecht von Waldstein, best known as Wallenstein, belonged to the lesser Czech nobility, being related to the Moravian statesman, Charles of Žerotin, and was at first brought up as a member of the Brethren ; but losing his parents at an early age, he was placed by his uncle, Albert of Slavata,[2] in a Jesuit College and afterwards sent on foreign travel. From the first he developed on a-national rather than either Czech or German national lines, and was swayed entirely by his ambitions, utterly devoid of principle, always preferring tortuous to straightforward methods, taking a natural delight in political intrigue and completely immune from religious feeling. To this must be added ruthless and untiring energy, but also the fatal quality of superstition, resting upon elaborate astrological studies which, as he grew older, sapped his powers of decision and placed him at the mercy of quacks and plotters. From the time when he married a wealthy widow and inherited her property, he showed an astonishing aptitude of the kind associated in modern times with company promotion or speculation on the bourse ; and quite early in life, by judicious manipulations and by buying up forfeited estates at derisory prices, he had accumulated

---

[1] "I am weary of my days. May God deign to receive my soul, so that I may not behold the disaster which, as I know, has overcome my country."

[2] A cousin of William of Slavata, of Defenestration fame.

a vast fortune which grew in snowball fashion, and enabled him to become a creditor of the hard-pressed and unbusiness-like Emperor, and thus to purchase still more rapid advancement and heap title upon title. As Häusser puts it : 'He had no more respect for tradition, usage or legal rights than a successful soldier is likely to have,' and he has not unfairly been described as the greatest army contractor of all time. His gifts of leadership and organization rallied round him soldiers of fortune from every land and of every type, allured by the splendid prospects of a career open to talent and indifferent to scruple. His armies lived like locusts, adopting as their motto : 'War must live by war ' (*sich ernähren*).

For this adventurer, who successively became Duke of Friedland and Mecklenburg, and already by 1625 had built up a domain of over fifty Bohemian castles and villages, Bohemia was at one and the same time the strategic centre from which to conduct war—*his* war no less than the Emperor's—and the goal of his own soaring ambitions. His success against Christian of Denmark, which may be said to have ended the first stage of the war, set him dreaming of a goal which had eluded the Houses of Přemysl and Luxemburg—the union of all the lands from the Baltic to the Adriatic under a single ruler throned in Prague—at first perhaps as a new appanage of the Habsburgs, with a place of fitting dignity reserved for himself, and then, as Mars or Saturn suggested, as a kingdom carved by his own good sword from the bleeding body of Europe. In the north Denmark and Sweden, in the south Venice, were to be robbed of their sea-power, and perhaps the crown of the whole enterprise would be a concentration of effort against the Turks and the establishment of a Habsburg world-empire. But Wallenstein aroused a host of enemies by playing so obviously for his own hand, and the devout Ferdinand resented his persistent subordination of the religious to the political issue. His attitude to the cause that lay nearest to the Emperor's heart is indicated by his occasional outbursts : 'The devil and hell-fire take the priests !' Ferdinand, it is true, owed his emancipation from Spain and Bavaria to Wallenstein's redoubtable New Model army, but found that he had escaped from the frying-pan into the fire, and hated to be at the mercy of his own general. Wallenstein's failure before the Baltic port of Stralsund upset his whole Baltic plan, while his own seizure of Mecklenburg as a fief of the Empire alarmed the whole Protestant north and, following on the defeat of Denmark, made the intervention of Sweden only a matter of time. The second stage of the war closes with the Edict of Restitution (March 6, 1629) which roused all the secularized states of Northern Germany (Bohemia had shown them the fate which awaited them in the event of Ferdinand's victory), and with the dismissal of Wallenstein from his command (June, 1630).

The second of these acts of folly occurred at the most dramatic moment of the whole war, when Gustavus Adolphus landed on the Baltic coast and rallied the whole Protestant North round the banner of Sweden against Ferdinand and the Catholic League. It is true that he stood virtually alone, his negotiations with France not having gone much beyond their initial stages ; and the phrase ascribed to Ferdinand on the first reception of the news : 'So we've got another wee enemy' (*ein Feindel mehr*), corresponds with the contemporary view that it was a desperate venture. The sack of Magdeburg by Tilly (May, 1631) marked the lowest depths of the Protestant cause ; but it also called for a supreme effort. The victory of Gustavus over Tilly at Breitenfeld (September 17,

1631) again transformed the whole situation, opening the King's path
both eastwards and westwards, averting danger from the North German
secularized sees and placing the Middle German bishoprics in their turn
in grave danger. Encouraged by this, the Elector of Saxony promptly
invaded and overran Bohemia, reaching Prague in November and receiving there the oath of loyalty on March 17, 1632. With him returned a
large number of the Czech exiles, notably Count Thurn and Wenceslas
of Ruppa, by whose orders the heads of their slaughtered comrades were
removed after ten years from the Charles Bridge and solemnly interred.
Corresponding to their high hope of restoration was the influx of Utraquist
and Lutheran clergy and also of the Brethren, and the suspicious immunity enjoyed by Wallenstein during the Saxon occupation has often
been regarded as proof of his treason. In reality it may be that in listening
to his brother-in-law Trčka, and to the exiled Czech patriot, Count Thurn,
he was merely indulging his passion for intrigue and testing every line of
advance or retreat before taking an irrevocable decision.

Meanwhile Gustavus pushed southwards and occupied Munich and
Augsburg ; Ferdinand therefore had no choice but to reinstate Wallenstein after two years of inaction, and invite him to form a new army.
The terms on which he consented were such as few generals have ever
even dreamt of dictating to their master—including as they did a veto
upon either the Emperor or his heir visiting the army. There was nothing
save the deepest distrust on both sides, for Ferdinand knew that Wallenstein had been negotiating secretly with Saxons, Swedes and French, and
would have parleyed with the Devil if the stars had seemed to favour
the enterprise. Once the decision was made, Wallenstein showed all his
old energy, fell upon the Saxon invader and in three weeks had driven
them out of Bohemia and re-established the Habsburg regime in Prague,
and with it, to his disgust, the Jesuits.

During the summer of 1632 the two great generals faced each other,
and then in November came the battle of Lützen, in which Gustavus was
victorious, but died upon the field. Once more there was a shifting of
all values. The Swedes remained in Germany under their Chancellor
Oxenstierna and a bevy of conflicting generals ; but the *élan*, the dominant personality, and the high idealism which outweighed the undoubted
designs of personal and national aggrandizement, were gone for ever.
Bernhard of Mansfeld, the foremost Protestant general, was playing for
his own hand, still more Cardinal Richelieu, who was equally opposed
to the Habsburgs and to German Unity, and fanned the discord by all
the means in his power. Of Wallenstein's contribution to this labyrinth
of intrigue and perfidy it is impossible to write further. All those who
have explored its paths most thoroughly—and the story of Wallenstein,
like that of Mary Stuart, has become one of the test cases for a historian's
acumen and combined powers of research and deduction—are sooner or
later confronted with facts and designs redolent of abnormality and
superstition. Moreover, just as it is certain that the Casket Letters have
been tampered with, so is it virtually certain that essential documents
are missing from the Wallenstein dossier. Let it suffice to say that
Wallenstein played with every side in turn, and often simultaneously
with all, and that the ultimate prize was the Bohemian Crown ; but that
Bohemia, though the closing events of his career took place on her soil,
was an entirely passive instrument in the hands of the chief actors, for
the most part reckless soldiers of fortune. The only persons to whom

the Czech cause meant anything were the exiled leaders, congregated mainly in Dresden ; but in looking to such a quarter as Wallenstein's camp for the restoration of lost liberties they may be said to have displayed either their own lack of judgment or the utterly desperate plight to which they had been reduced. Wallenstein's death by assassination at the hands of four British soldiers of fortune[1] (February 25, 1634), followed logically from his undoubted treason. Nor is it possible to judge Ferdinand too severely for his ultra-secret transactions with the adversaries of a general who, he well knew, would let no man's life stand between him and the supreme goal of his ambition. It is at least possible to argue that he did not in any way exceed the limits permissible in that age to an absolute sovereign against a proved traitor : and he at any rate had the decency to recognize the need for explanations and the courage to assume responsibility afterwards.

Thus within eighteen months of each other the two chief protagonists had both met a violent death ; but the war dragged on interminably. The battle of Nördlingen (August 27, 1634) gave another kaleidoscopic turn to the German situation, and this check to Swedish prestige resulted nine months later in the Peace of Prague (June 15, 1635), between the Emperor and Saxony, which closes the second phase of the war. It rested on a narrowly Lutheran and Conservative basis, taking no account of the interests of the Calvinists, of whom one of John George's chief clerical advisers roundly declared that they were 'not our brethren in Christ, but God's enemies,' originating from the devil ! But Ferdinand, though most reluctantly, consented to revoke the Edict of Restitution in respect of all transactions earlier than 1627, and this saved most of the northern bishoprics for Protestantism. Moreover, John George was won over by the attractive bribe of Lusatia, which, with its Slavonic population of Sorbs or Wends, was now finally separated from the Crown of St. Wenceslas. None the less, Saxony and Brandenburg by their selfish policy did not escape from the plague of war, which plunged Germany into ever-growing misery. We now enter the final phase of the war, less rich in dramatic events or striking personalities, but characterized by a savagery that appalled even the cynical Swedish generals. In this phase Germany ere long found herself at the mercy of the allied French and Swedes.

Ferdinand II outlived Wallenstein by three years, leaving to his son another eleven years of war. For all his mediocrity he had shown, in adversity as in success, a steadfastness of purpose and a zeal for the Catholic faith such as few monarchs of that age possessed. His policy had three fundamental aims—to recover Hungary from the Turks, to reimpose Catholicism upon the recovered territories, and to entrench the royal prerogative no less in Hungary and Bohemia than in the hereditary dominions, at the expense of all existing rights. In his earlier years he had been distinctly reserved towards unitary tendencies, as then favoured by the Estates, and had even denounced these 'highly mischievous' (*hochschädliche*) ideas as 'the mother of the Bohemian rebellion.' But after the downfall of Bohemia he quite logically reverted to the centralist and aggrandizing traditions of his House ; and his Will expounds quite clearly the theory that all his dominions were to be regarded as an unitary and indivisible hereditary monarchy. None the less he repeated the error committed by his great-grandfather, Ferdinand I, and yielded to the

[1] Butler the Irishman, Leslie and Gordon the Scots, and Devereux the Englishman.

demands of his two younger brothers, Leopold and Charles, for appanages, to be carved out of the hereditary dominions. Thus it came about that Leopold received Tirol, Vorarlberg and all the wide Habsburg lands in Schwabia and Alsace, while Charles was consoled with a whole series of rich bishoprics, in gross defiance of the newly introduced measures against simony. Fortunately for Habsburg unity, Charles died prematurely, while Leopold's line became extinct in 1665 and the possibility of a disputed succession was solved by his heir in the female line, Claudia Felicitas, becoming the second wife of her cousin, Emperor Leopold. Henceforward partition was avoided, and the Habsburgs reverted to their earlier tactics, '*Tu, felix Austria, nube,*' by marrying the younger Archdukes to Italian heiresses. Hence the *secundo-genitur* of Tuscany and the *tertio-genitur* of Modena and Parma.

Ferdinand III

Ferdinand III followed closely in his father's footsteps, as a man of mild manners and simple tastes, less extravagant, but also no less passionately fond of the chase and of music. Above all he was a devout servant of the Church and its aggrandizement though considerably less under the thumb of the Jesuits than either his predecessor or successor. His share in the battle of Nördlingen gave him a moderate reputation as a soldier, such as his father could never claim : but in plain truth, according to his principal biographer, M. Koch, his contribution was to attend mass in a tent, together with the Cardinal-Infant, and to join him in reciting the All-Saints Litany ! Until poor health undermined his will power he showed that aptitude for bureaucratic labours which so many Habsburg rulers, from Frederick to Francis Joseph have developed. In one other respect he was an improvement on his improvident father ; he set himself by thrift and personal economy to reduce the alarming expenditure of the long wars. But he made but little mark upon his times, and is left strangely in the background by both contemporary and modern historians.

The Last Phase of the War

By this time the war had passed altogether beyond the control of Germany herself, just as the atrocities committed by the rival soldiery seem quite genuinely to have passed beyond the control of their generals. Richelieu, when he heard that Saxony had made peace, commented : "But that will have no effect on us, except to make us renew our efforts to *keep all in train*"—an ominous phrase that spelt prolonged disaster for Europe. This was more than ever the case after 1639, when the death of Bernard of Weimar removed the only soldier of real eminence among the Germans themselves ; and the war, in Miss Wedgwood's words, 'now degenerated altogether into a contest between the Kings of France and Spain, fought on German soil.' So far as Bohemia was concerned, she had been reduced to complete passivity, and from 1639 to 1648 served almost uninterruptedly as the battle ground of Swede and Imperialist. Banér and his successor Torstenssen drained dry whatever moisture remained in the unhappy country, and in 1645 the latter, in alliance with George Rákóczy, Prince of Transylvania, brought the Emperor to the verge of disaster. Torstenssen followed up his victory at Jankov, near Tabor (March 6, 1645), by laying siege to the Moravian capital, Brünn (Brno) ; in Vienna there was a panic flight of many citizens when the news arrived that the Magyar army had crossed the March at Hodonín, and was about to join hands with the advancing Swedes. The Imperial family found it advisable to withdraw to Graz. But Brünn held, the Swedish advance was checked, and Rákóczy, yielding to Turkish intimidation and dire threats of invasion, drew closer to the Emperor and consented to a separate peace. Thus by the Treaty of Vienna (August 8) he renounced his alliance with France and Sweden, and by the Treaty of Linz (September 16) he reaped his reward in concessions which revealed the straits to which Ferdinand was reduced ; on the one hand he guaranteed the absolute equality of Catholics and Protestants in Hungary, and on the other a sort of double autonomy as between Transylvania and those northern and western counties of Hungary which were under Ferdinand's direct rule. This compromise was of the utmost importance for the whole future development of Hungary, and not least of all for the Slovaks. It represented a check to the system of aggressive proselytism which had been set up by Cardinal Pázmány and his Jesuit protégés ; and it meant that Hungary was never subjected to the same thorough dragooning as Bohemia. Ironically enough, it was really the triple partition that saved Hungary from Bohemia's fate, for the Counter-Reformation could not penetrate either Turkish Hungary or Transylvania, and the latter's existence gave the Protestants of Slovakia something to lean against and something that could intervene on their behalf. By the time that Hungary was again united under the Habsburgs the age of enlightenment was already dawning, and dragooning was no longer possible.

After a generation of war it took five long years of negotiation to make peace. Richelieu had lived to see the temporary collapse of Spain as a Great Power ; but after his death in December, 1642, the war was entirely lacking in directive or unity of purpose, and became an orgy of conflicting interests. In its last two years there was really no outstanding commander in the field, and no diplomatist of the front rank made his mark in the negotiations. Bavaria's attempt to steal a march by concluding a separate peace with France (March, 1647) only resulted in fresh devastation of the south, on lines as drastic as in the centre and east ; and after the defeat of the Imperialists at Zusmarhausen (May, 1648) the Swedes once more carried fire and sword through ravaged and almost helpless Bohemia. After thirty years the war may be said to have ended at the gates of Prague, but with this ominous change, that when the Swedes had seized the Malá Strana, they met with determined resistance on the Charles Bridge from a generation which had grown up under Jesuit influence and was quite impervious to the appeals of the Czech exiles in the Swedish camp.

The Peace of Westphalia

The details of the Treaty of Westphalia need not concern us here. But its most salient features must be placed on record, since they gave a new shape to Europe and sealed the fate of Bohemia for two centuries to come. In a certain sense it was a reversion to the Augsburg compromise of 1555. The attempt to reimpose the old religion upon the Protestant north had definitely failed, and this had fatal consequences for German unity. The Reich was henceforth divided, roughly speaking,

along the line of the River Main, into two unequal halves, the Protestant
North and the Catholic South. Even the last nominal connections of
Switzerland and the Netherlands with the Reich were severed, and the wide
Habsburg lands in Alsace were ceded to France. This meant the virtual
disintegration of the old Empire, and the end of the Imperial power,
even in the curtailed form in which it had entered upon modern times.
The title and ceremonial remained, but lacked any real substance ;
henceforth the power rested with the territorial princes—Brandenburg,
Saxony and Bavaria, the medium Swabian states, and a fine spray of
petty principalities and free cities. So far as the House of Habsburg was
concerned, it maintained control of the Imperial dignity to the very end
(with one brief interval from 1740 to 1747), but its power and prestige
depended entirely upon the kingdoms and territories of the Habsburg
Crown, of which Bohemia had once more become hereditary, and Hungary
was to become so a generation later. There were many in Germany who
held the Habsburgs responsible for her sad eclipse, and one early publicist
clamoured for 'domus Austriacæ extirpatio.' Certainly 'Austria'—the
generic name conveniently though erroneously used to designate the whole
monarchy—was henceforth separated from the Reich in all but name.

Inside the Habsburg dominions the Treaty meant the triumph of the
absolute power of the Crown in Austria and Bohemia, and marked a fresh
stage in the process by which the latter was gradually absorbed into the
system of the former. The maxim *Cuius regio* had proved incapable of
universal application, but so far as Austria and Bohemia were concerned
it was completely successful, what we now call the totalitarian principle
being applied in favour of the Catholic religion. Combined with this went
a further impetus towards a centralized administration. The separation
of the Austrian, Bohemian and Hungarian Chancelleries from the old
Aulic Chancellery of the Reich was now a fully accomplished fact.

In the international sphere the rivalry of France and Spain was
replaced by the still more acute rivalry between France and Austria,
between Bourbon and Habsburg. The period of religious wars is ended ;
the fluctuations that characterized the long interval from 1555 to 1648
are no longer possible, and gains and losses are stabilized. Bohemia is
left on the wrong side of the line of division. Finally, it is significant that
the Pope should fail to assert his position as a mediator in European
affairs, and should be left impotently protesting. The age of the great
Cardinal statesmen is already passing, and henceforth the lay element
is more and more predominant in diplomacy. With all its faults and
blunders, it was the first attempt on a grand scale to establish European
peace by negotiation and thus, from the international aspect, it opens
a new era, culminating in the three great Congresses of the nineteenth
century and the Peace Conference of 1919.

Comenius

To those who still preserved the hope of Bohemian independence, and
above all to the Czech exiles, the abandonment of Bohemia to her fate
was a cruel blow, and to none more cruel than to Comenius, whose name
will always be linked with this most tragic period of her history. As
events stood in 1648, the most that could be hoped was that the Palatinate
should be restored to Frederick's grandson and erected into an eighth
Electorate, by the side of Bavaria, while the House of Habsburg remained

in unchallenged possession of Bohemia. But Ferdinand III had threatened to continue the war rather than consent to the return of a single non-Catholic exile to his native soil. 'They have sacrificed us at the Treaties . . .' wrote Comenius. 'I conjure you by the wounds of Christ that you do not forsake us, who are persecuted for the sake of Christ.'

John Amos Komenský was born in 1592 at Uherská Brod, in Eastern Moravia, was educated at the Latin school of the Brethren in Přeov, studied at the Universities of Herborn and Heidelberg, and in 1616 was ordained a priest of the Brethren. In the year following the White Mountain, his house and library at Fulnek were set on fire by Spanish mercenaries, and for some years—despite the protection offered him by Charles of Žerotín—he lived a precarious life, changing his abode several times, until after the promulgation of the Renewed Ordinance in 1627 it became obvious that Moravia was no longer safe for the Brethren, and early in 1628 he and many hundreds of others settled at Leszno in Poland, where religious tolerance was not yet a thing of the past. Here he published, in 1631, the first of the learned works to which he owed his fame, *Janua Linguarum Reserata*, a mixture of grammar and compendium of useful knowledge, which had an enormous circulation for those days. Here, too, in 1632 he was consecrated Bishop of the Brethren, and here the headquarters of that exiled community remained, until the sack of Leszno in 1656, during the war between Poland and Sweden, wiped out the all too slender accumulations of thirty years. During this period his learning, backed by simple faith, charm of character and fervent patriotism, won him an altogether unique reputation in the educational field, and it is instructive to contrast his methods and his general outlook with those of his redoubtable Jesuit contemporaries. He received periodical invitations from various centres of Protestant Europe. The first, in 1638 from Sweden, he refused ; but when invited to England in 1641 he finally accepted, after much hesitation at the perils of a sea voyage—hesitation which was in due course justified by a narrow escape from shipwreck. The original invitation was conveyed by Samuel Hartlib, a Baltic merchant of German birth, who seems to have aspired to act as mediator between English and Continental scholars ; but on reaching London Comenius found that (in his own words) he had been 'summoned by command of Parliament.' The nine months of his stay in this island brought him into contact with such men as Bishop Williams of Lincoln, Archbishop Ussher of Armagh, John Pym and John Selden. But he had left a Bohemia and a Germany convulsed by the horrors of a long war, only to find England on the very eve of civil dissensions no less profound ; and his various plans for a 'Baconian College,' dedicated to collective scientific research, to be combined with a general reform of schools and established on truly international lines, never assumed really concrete form, even though there are grounds for regarding him as a forerunner of the Royal Society, which was founded in 1662. He got the length of considering whether the best site for the Academy, or 'College of Light,' would be the Savoy, Winchester or Chelsea.[1] Indeed, when he published his belated *Via Lucis* in 1668, he dedicated it 'To the torchbearers of this

[1] Much interesting information will be found in Dr. R. F. Young's learned publication, *Comenius in England* (Oxford, 1932), in his pamphlet, *Comenius and the Indians of New England* (1929), and in Dr. Odložilík's admirable essay on *Jan Amos Komenský*, published by the Czecho-slovak National Council of America on Comenius' 350th birthday. (Chicago, 1942.)

enlightened age, members of the Royal Society of London, now bringing
real philosophy to a happy birth.' . . . 'Throughout the world the news
will be trumpeted that you are engaged in labours the purpose of which
is to secure that human knowledge and the empire of the human mind
over matter shall not for ever continue to be a feeble and uncertain
thing.' It is pleasing to note that Milton, in response to Hartlib's appeal
for interest in the projected Academy, wrote of Comenius as 'a person
sent hither by some good Providence from a far country, to be the
occasion and incitement of great good to this island.' In London Comenius
met John Winthrop, the younger son of the Governor of Massachusetts,
and was sounded by him as to the possibility of his becoming Master of
the newly founded College of Harvard, where he could have 'combined
educational work with missionary activities among the Indians.'

'That incomparable Moravian,' as Cotton Mather called him in 1703,
did not become an American, because throughout his years of exile he
continued to work for the restoration of his ruined country, and the
propagation of his educational theories in Europe. From England he
went to Holland—meeting Descartes there—and then to Elbing, where
he lived for several years under Swedish protection, maintaining close
contacts with other Czech exiles and with the directors of Swedish policy
and operations. In his bitter disillusionment at Sweden's abandonment
of the Czech cause at the peace negotiations he accepted a fresh invitation
from an arch-enemy of the Habsburgs, George Rákóczy, who entrusted
him with the reform of schools. For four years he worked at this task at
the Protestant College of Sárospatak, but in 1654 he returned to Leszno,
only to suffer fresh disaster when war engulfed that town and all his
manuscripts and his precious library were annihilated. This time he
found a last haven of refuge in Holland, and died at Amsterdam at the
age of seventy-eight, after an old age spent in patient resignation and
unshaken faith. (January 15, 1670.)

It is not possible to deal here with the writings of Comenius, the best
known of which were *The Great Didactic*, *Janua Linguarum* (published in
English as early as 1631), *The Labyrinth of the World* (which for all its
contemporary popularity did not appear in English till Count Lützow
translated it in 1901), and *Orbis Pictus* (which appeared in English in
1659 and reached its twelfth edition in 1777). Two lesser works have
a special interest for British readers: *An Exhortation of the Churches of
Bohemia to the Church of England* (1661), which as an interpretation of
the persecuted Brethren met with a warm welcome in Restoration
England, little though they had in common with it, and *Primitive Church
Government in the Practice of the Reformed Churches in Bohemia*, which
appeared in English in 1703, this time, fittingly enough, in Edinburgh.
Pansophia, which he himself probably regarded as his crowning achievement, is too discursive and too visionary to appeal to any modern reader.
Even the *Labyrinth*, though it contains passages of great charm and
conveys an attractive impression of its author, cannot for a moment
stand up to the challenge which it inevitably suggests with Bunyan's
Pilgrim's Progress. It is less direct, it lacks Bunyan's vivid imagination
and powers of narrative, and it has nothing which can really be described
as a plot. In all that Comenius wrote there is vast erudition and a tinge of
mysticism that sometimes degenerates into credulity ; but there are also
lovable and essentially human qualities that gave impetus to his teachings
—a belief in the natural goodness of man, in the humanizing power of

education, in peace as an ideal, and a refusal to believe that the Bible and human reason are incompatible. 'Christianity,' he continued to declare after the disaster of 1656, 'is above all peace with God and with mankind.' He left no direct school behind him, but his ideas are the raw material which generations of educationalists have used and worked upon and recast, often without knowing to whom they owed the inspiration. To-day he stands as the acknowledged pioneer of modern pedagogy ; and the debt which the modern world owes him has been well summed-up by Dr. Odložilík in these words : 'The infant school of kindergarten, female education, the incorporation of history and geography in the curriculum, the value of drawing and manual training, the fundamental importance of self-training, the physical and the ethical elements in education, and finally that education is for all and not for a favoured few only, were all articles in the creed of Comenius.' 'Nature,' said Comenius, in strangely modern phrases, 'cannot be forced, but must be led willingly. All the senses must be called into play by the lesson ; and the later lessons should be the natural development of the earlier ones. Whatever is to be known should be taught : whatever is taught should be taught as a present thing of definite use.'

In an historical survey such as this due emphasis must be laid upon the Czech patriot in Comenius. He has placed it on record that he devoted the first few years of his stay at Leszno to studying 'the short-comings and defects of the method employed in schools, and to bethink myself of improving the same, so much so that certain goodly observations of mine began to grow together as a system of didactic art.' His aim is expressed in words which our generation should take to heart, confronted as we are with the task of re-educating a perverted world, as the sole hope of permanent peace. He had resolved, he tells us, that 'Should God, in His mercy towards us, restore us to our native land, supports might be in readiness, whereby the harm wrought to our schools and our youth might be more rapidly repaired.'

His devotion to the Czech cause reaches its loftiest expression in the *Bequest of the Dying Mother of the Unity of Brethren*, written in 1650 when the fate of Bohemia was sealed. It is only possible to quote the more outstanding passages of this poignant appeal, which in our own day was a daily inspiration to another Czech exile, Thomas Masaryk. But it is important to emphasize that while addressed very specially to his own people, the Czechs, it contains most affectionate messages to the Polish, German and Swiss Churches, and even to their mother 'who had become a stepmother,' the Church of Rome, but to whom he appeals in words that differentiate him from the bigots of the seventeenth century. Be it also noted in passing that he expressed regret at the practice among the English sectaries 'of ever searching for novelties and never attaining to stable convictions,' and besought them to 'learn to pray with David, "Let simplicity and uprightness preserve me".' And he goes on thus : 'To all Christian Churches together I bequeath lively desire for unanimity of opinion and for reconciliation among themselves, and for union in faith, and love of the unity of spirit.'[1]

Naturally, however, it is to the Czechs that he turns at the moment of final separation, reminding them that all through life he has had to repeat with the Apostles, 'Gold and silver have I none.' Like his Lord,

[1] The English version from which these extracts are drawn, is to be found appended to Professor C. H. Wright's admirable essay on Comenius (1941).

he had scarcely owned a place where to lay his head and had been dispossessed of such few worldly goods—church buildings, fields or small vineyards—as he ever possessed ; but in return for this he had been 'enriched with spiritual wealth,' which he now wished to distribute among his sons and friends.

'To thee, then, I turn especially, and make thee the chief claimant and heir of my treasures which the Lord hath entrusted me, following the example of many wealthy Roman citizens and tributary kings who, when dying, were wont to bequeath their possessions to the Roman commune, which ruled the ends of the earth. I trust God that after the passing of the storm of wrath which our sins brought down upon our heads, the rule of thine affairs shall again be restored to thee, O Czech people ! And because of this trust, I make thee an heir of all my ancestral inheritance, which I have preserved through difficult and trying times.

'And especially : First, a love of the pure truth which God revealed to us earlier than to other nations by the ministration of our own Master John Hus. . . . Thine is this inheritance, given thee earlier than to all other nations, my beloved native land ! Enter again upon thy possession as thy right, when the Lord, the compassionate, will show thee His mercy and will make way for His truth.

'Secondly, I command thee a zealous desire for an ever clearer understanding of the truth of God. And since our Lord commanded us to search the Scriptures, I leave thee for thy heirloom this book, the Holy Bible, which my sons translated into the Czech with the utmost diligence. . . . And though our enemies burned as many copies of this book as they could find, still believe and doubt not that God's Word shall be preserved. . . .

'Third, I commend a special inclination to my church polity, and to that loving discipline which should and must prevail among the children of God. . . . Use thy gifts according to Holy Writ or the example of the apostolic Church. . . .

'Fourth, I bequeath thee my zeal to serve the Lord and to serve Him in unity.

'Fifth, I bequeath thee an eagerness for the enrichment, purification and development of our beloved melodious mother-tongue. In this endeavour the zeal of my sons was known of old, when it was said by competent judges that no purer Czech existed than that in use among the Brethren and in their books. . . .

'Sixth, a better, more diligent and efficient education of children than that prevailing formerly. For I myself was at fault therein, having entrusted myself to foreigners, who corrupted and ruined my sons. . . . I beseech thee most earnestly that thou amend this fault. For even some of my sons have laboured at that task, and prepared a better method for the education of youth, without distinction of religion. But it belongs primarily to thee not to neglect thy inheritance which will be delivered to thee by my sons when the proper time comes.

'And what else shall I say ? It is time that I cease speaking and take leave of thee, my beloved land ! How shall I do it ? Even as patriarch Jacob did, when on his death-bed, taking leave of his sons, he gave them a blessing, or as Moses did, when he was leaving his people. From Moses' mouth shall I take my words and in a farewell to thee, my Czech people, I invoke upon thee the blessings of the Lord thy God, that thou mightest ever be and remain "a fruitful bough, a fruitful bough by a fountain, the branches whereof run over the wall. Although the archers have sorely grieved thee, and shot at thee and persecuted thee, still may thy bow abide in strength, and may thy arm be made strong by the hands of the Mighty One of Jacob, even by the God of thy fathers and by the Almighty, who shall bless thee with blessings of heaven above, blessings of the deep that spreads beneath, blessings of the breasts and of the womb. May the blessing be mightier than the blessings of my progenitors, unto the utmost bound of the everlasting hills."

'Live, O nation consecrated to God, and die not ! May thy men be without number ! '

As for himself, Comenius, with true modesty of mind, consoled himself for the failure of many daydreams with the thought that 'God's thoughts are other than ours, likewise His seasons and His agents. God disapproved not David's plan for the building of the Temple : but that the design should be brought into effect while David lived, and through David himself, He would not.'

Truly Ernest Denis was in no way exaggerating when he wrote that 'Comenius maintained the pure national tradition, and through him Dobrovský, the herald of the re-awakening, gives his hand to the martyr of Constance.' Michelet once called him 'the Galileo of Education.'

CHAPTER X

THE PERIOD OF TOTAL ECLIPSE (1648–1790)

O dark, dark, dark amid the blaze of morn,
Irrecoverably dark, total eclipse,
Without all hope of day . . .

But he, though blind of sight,
Despised and thought extinguished quite,
With inward eyes illuminated
His fiery virtue roused
From under ashes into sudden flame . . .
—Milton, *Samson Agonistes.*

The timeless, surly patience of the serf,
That moves the nearest to the naked earth,
And ploughs down palaces and thrones and towers.
—Roy Campbell.

After the Peace

IT would be hard to exaggerate the state of misery and prostration in which Bohemia found herself at the conclusion of peace. 'The mainspring of national life was broken—to all seeming, for ever.'[1] Historians such as Gindely and Huber have estimated that her population had fallen from three million to 800,000 ; another version is from $2\frac{1}{2}$ million to 700,000. In 1618 the number of landed peasant families in Bohemia was reckoned at 150,000 ; in 1645 the Estates reported to the Crown that their number was only 30,000. It has also been calculated that before the war there were 782 towns and 36,000 villages and manors, and that by 1648 these had fallen to 230 and 6,000 respectively. Although the ancient Czech nobility and gentry had been almost rooted out,[2] and replaced by crowds of foreign favourites and military adventurers, although the peasantry had sunk still further in the scale and lost the last semblance of liberty, and although all creeds save one had been strenuously rooted out, it is sometimes argued that the profoundest change of all was wrought in the towns. The ruin worked by expulsion, persecution, plunder, fire and plague is well illustrated by the fact that in Brno out of 1,356 houses 928 were in ruins, and 260 half-destroyed, in Königgrätz (Kralové Hradec) 495 in ruins and only 495 inhabited, in Komotau only 139 out of 545 inhabited. Olomouc, which had 30,000 inhabitants in 1630, only had 1,675 left in 1650.

Ferdinand III placed Bohemia under the special tutelage of the Virgin, and the Jesuits were more powerful and aggressive than ever, freely admitting that probably two-thirds of the population was still secretly attached to one or other of the proscribed heresies, and that until the lamentable dearth of trained clergy could be overcome, a complete remedy was not to be expected. With this in view, two new bishoprics

---

[1] Sir A. Ward.
[2] Among families of the first rank dating from before the catastrophe, may be mentioned those of Schwarzenberg, Lobkovicz, Harrach, Kolovrat, Kinsky.
    Several of the great Austrian houses—Liechtenstein, Dietrichstein, Windischgrätz —acquired wide estates in Bohemia also, and form a category by themselves.

were erected, at Litoměřice (Leitmeritz) and Königgrätz (Králové Hradec). Forced conversions on a large scale were supplemented by the wholesale destruction of books in the vernacular (but also of many German books, for the German districts of Bohemia had been quite as strongly infected by heresy as the Czech), and by the insidious institution of confession registers. But while the Jesuits had eager support from the fanatical Prior of Emmäus, Don Caramuel de Lobkovicz (a Spaniard born and bred, who took his mother's name), they for that very reason and many others came into conflict with Cardinal Harrach, the leader of the more moderate party, who more especially resented the Jesuit ambition to control education, and was intelligent enough to realize the paralysing, soulless effect of their teaching, of their attempt to banish history from the schools, and of their efforts to rope into their own order everyone who showed the slightest talent or originality. The thirty years of conflict between the Jesuits and the Archbishop, which had begun in 1621 when Ferdinand II handed over to them the Carolinum—the Utraquist University of Prague—and consented to its union with the Clementinum (their own foundation under Canisius in 1555)—were terminated in 1654, when Ferdinand III reconstituted the two as the 'Carolo-Ferdinandea' and left the Jesuits with a monopoly of the theological and philosophical faculties, which was in effect a stranglehold upon the whole University. This domination, and that of the short-lived sister University of Olomouc, lasted until the expulsion of the Jesuits in 1774. Their influence upon literature, exercised through the medium of an unrestricted censorship, is shown by the complete absence of anything that can be described as literature at all, even in German, and much more in Czech, which for a century and a half virtually dried up at the fountain-head. The one name placed by the Jesuits on the credit side of their account with the Czechs, in all that gloomy century, is that of Bohuslav Balbín, who wrote a monumental *Epitome Rerum Bohemicarum*, of no slight merit in an age at once bigoted and uncritical. But it is characteristic that almost a century passed before anyone could be found to publish his manuscript ; and even in his lifetime two other products of his pen, *Bohemia Docta* and an *Apologia for the Slav Language*— which will to all time occupy the modest niche of a pioneer in literary history and grammar—earned him strong disapproval from his superiors and something not unlike internment. As for the Czech language, it soon sank to a language of serfs, and there was a current prophecy that a Czech on the bridge of Prague would become as rare as a stag with golden antlers.

Meanwhile the civil administration of Bohemia had fallen into the hands of a small aristocratic clique, which devoted itself, without much success, to the accumulation of large estates and in some cases to the display of almost viceregal magnificence. Some of the great families, such as Dietrichstein and Liechtenstein, had large possessions in the hereditary lands also and therefore never came to feel a real identity of interests with Bohemia, and least of all with the Czechs as such. Foremost among the native nobility were the families of Lobkovic, Schwarzenberg, Czernin, Nostic and Kinsky. Wenceslas Eusebius Lobkovic was the all-powerful adviser of Leopold I during the first two decades of his reign, and became Chancellor and Prince ; Johann Adolf Schwarzenberg was for many years President of the Imperial Aulic Council, till his death in 1683 ; while Count Hermann Czernin was an early and most successful example of army contractor on a considerable scale. Bent upon wealth, titles and position, they allowed the Diet to become the merest farce and to show a growing subservience to the Court.

The exquisite Baroque palaces of the Malá Strana of Prague—in the streets and squares squeezed in between the River Vltava and the steep hill on which stand the Castle, the Cathedral and the Abbey of Strahov—still bear witness to the wealth then accumulated in relatively few hands, as also do the rococo country-houses and castles built during the eighteenth century in many parts of Bohemia and Moravia. In the history of art these condescending patrons occupy a unique place. The Sudeten historian Bretholz is fully entitled to stress the natural riches of Bohemia, and to quote the testimony of a contemporary that 'in all Europe Bohemia is second to none in fertility' even after all the ravages of war, and still produced the best and whitest bread, besides being rich in forests, pasture, game and fish. He quotes the saying of Prince Frederick Schwarzenberg : '*In Böhmen ist die Nutzbarkeit*'—in other words, 'Bohemia brings in most.' And indeed the central fact of Bohemian history in the seventeenth and eighteenth centuries is that the Czech lands were consistently bled white in order to finance the soaring ambitions of the House of Habsburg in every part of Europe. In 1682 the quota of relative contributions by Bohemia and Austria was as $11\frac{3}{4}$ to $6\frac{1}{4}$; and after the recovery of Hungary we shall see that she also did not pay her due share. So marked was the inequality that it caused considerable disaffection among the nobility, despite their relative political monopoly ; and upon the peasantry it weighed crushingly, all the more so when they burst into sporadic revolt in 1680, and thus gave the authorities an excuse for cancelling such rights as still remained to the serfs, and greatly extending the 'Robot' system of forced labour. "Robot," said the famous Court preacher of the day, Abraham de Sancta Clara, "what is this beast ? Ask that poor worker in the fields. Robot means that on Monday the peasant has to cultivate the land of his lord, on Tuesday to work in the vineyard of his lord, on Wednesday to cart wood to the castle, on Thursday to thresh corn or cut the straw, on Friday to fish in the pond or catch game for the table, on Saturday to do building work, on Sunday to serve as courier. Out of days make weeks, out of weeks months, out of months years, and you will understand the sort of Easter that the peasants have, and how it happens that they sometimes carry their bones and skin to market, for they really have nothing else."

Ferdinand III, like so many of his House, aged prematurely, and during the last decade of his reign devoted much effort to securing the succession. Only after somewhat protracted negotiations with the Electors was his son Ferdinand IV elected King of the Romans in 1653, and the weakened position of the Emperor inside Germany was further illustrated by the great difficulties which he encountered at the Diet of Regensburg, when he sought to make financial decisions adopted by a majority of the Electors binding upon all the rest. More and more the Habsburgs relied upon the resources of their own domains and added to the barriers that separated the one from the other. Hence the death of Ferdinand IV in 1654 during an attack of measles was a heavy blow to the Emperor and to Habsburg influence generally ; for his younger brother Leopold was only fourteen, and though amiable, distinctly mediocre in attainments. The boy was safely elected in Hungary in June, 1655, and received the Bohemian Crown in September, 1656 ; but the Electors were still boggling and bargaining over the Imperial succession when Ferdinand died on April 2, 1657. After a period of anxiety Leopold was unanimously elected Emperor in July, 1658 ; two factors especially contributed to this result—the revival of the Turkish menace, and the natural reaction against the intrigues of Mazarin and the French party, who seriously coveted the Imperial crown for Louis XIV.

Leopold succeeded at the age of eighteen and reigned for forty-eight years. At his christening his father had dedicated him to the Virgin and intended him for the Church ; his early education followed this direction and left indelible marks upon him. Religious sentiment was the dominant factor in his life, and he was as much a tool of the Jesuits, as devoted to the cause of Catholic militancy, as his father and grandfather ; at most it can be said that his was a milder nature, and that religious bigotry, though as monopolistic and uncompromising as ever, was during his reign slowly abandoning the more savage methods so generally accepted earlier in the century. Under the genial influence of his stepmother, Eleonora of Mantua, be became a model husband and father ; he had the traditional Habsburg love of music, was a voracious reader, showed literary and artistic tastes and had complete command of Latin, French, Italian and Spanish, as well as German, but he remained a pedant, with all the bureaucratic tendencies of his House, hesitant and ineffective. His frail physique, his irresolute nature, his reluctance to take great decisions, and also a certain trait of melancholy, seemed to reveal the decline of moral and physical faculties to which both the Austrian and Spanish branches of the House of Habsburg had reduced themselves by five generations of constant inter-marriage. By an irony of fate, this unadventurous mediocrity, entirely lacking in military capacity or ambitions, was to occupy the throne during two prolonged struggles that proved decisive for both Central and South-east Europe. 'The little Emperor in red stockings' was in no way equal to the occasion, though his Jesuit masters sang his praises in fulsome tones ; but he had a superb belief in the future of the House, which atoned for many faults and provided a dignified façade of authority, behind which the reviving forces of his dominions could be built up.

The Recovery of Hungary

At this point a short digression is necessary, in order to make clear the changes in the relative position of Bohemia and Austria, resulting from the recovery of Hungary from Turkish rule.

The Treaty of Zsitva Török in 1606 for the first time placed the Imperialists on a footing of equality with the Turks, and it may be supposed that but for the tremendous diversion of the Thirty Years' War a fresh attempt to expel the Turks might have been made before the middle of the century. But it is equally possible to argue that it was only the respite caused by a series of absorbing campaigns against Persia, diverting Turkey's main effort from west to east, that saved the Austrian dominions, perhaps even faction-ridden Germany herself, from a situation of extreme danger. In any case, both Austria and Turkey were engaged elsewhere, and there was something like a deadlock in Hungary, the main benefit being reaped by the Princes of Transylvania, notably Gabriel Bethlen and George Rákóczy I, who got nearer to a state of real independence than any of their predecessors or successors. The so-called 'Pacification of Linz' (1645), which brought the Court of Vienna, 'Habsburg

Hungary' and the Principality together in face of a common danger, was a prelude to megalomania on the part of George Rákóczy II, who succeeded his father in 1648, negotiated with the Swedes and played for the Polish Crown, seemingly in the idea that he had the resources to build up a new Great Power in the south-east, instead of continuing to balance precariously between Sultan, Emperor and King of Poland. Unfortunately for all concerned, this coincided with a marked revival of the Ottoman power and military discipline, under a series of great Viziers from the family of Küprülü. In 1660 the Turks turned their attention to Transylvania, and after defeating and killing George Rákóczy in battle, captured Grosswardein (Oradea Mare), one of the key fortresses of Eastern Hungary. It became their avowed aim to reduce Transylvania to a Pashaluk as helpless and subordinate as Wallachia and Moldavia, and to debar the Emperor from any further interference in its affairs. This prompted the Turkish invasion of 1663, which bore practical fruit in the capture of Neuhäusel (Galgocz, Hlohovec), the fortress commanding the lower Váh valley and its junction with the Danube. Its loss was a very serious menace to the whole of 'Habsburg Hungary,' and forced even the passive Leopold to action. The battle of St. Gotthard, on the Hungaro-Styrian border (August 1, 1664) was the first resounding victory of the Imperialist arms, and was hailed by contemporaries as the first obvious turn of the tide. But the victorious general, Montecuccoli, great both as a leader and as a student of strategy, was not allowed to exploit his victory. A twenty years' peace was concluded at Vasvár (Eisenburg) such as usually follows grave reverses, not brilliant success. Transylvania remained balanced between Emperor and Sultan, the fortresses of Grosswardein and Neuhäusel were left in Turkish hands, and Leopold was left to build a rival fortress for the defence of the Váh valley. There were very definite reasons behind this pusillanimous decision ; Leopold, pliant in the hands of his Jesuit advisers, was more afraid of strengthening constitutional and Protestant currents in Hungary than eager to eject the Turks. He had not realized the intense indignation which this would provoke among Catholics and Protestants alike—so intense that Vasvár is still regarded as nothing short of a betrayal, and one of the most shameful incidents in Hungarian history. It roused the guardians of national rights to further efforts, but it also prompted the conspiracy between the more adventurous of the Magyar and Croat nobility, which culminated in the execution of Zrinski, Frankopan and Nádasdy in 1671. It is impossible to discuss here the wide ramifications of this event, which included designs for Hungarian and Croat states, ostensibly independent, but inevitably vassals of the declining, but still formidable, Turkish power. The essential clue is provided by the Emperor's complete subordination to Jesuit designs for religious uniformity. The lengths to which this went are shown by his appointing a clerical commission[1] to decide whether he was bound to respect Hungarian liberties, or whether Hungary as a nation had forfeited these rights by rebellion and could therefore be subjected to a regime of autocracy and uniformity. It was his ambition to make of Hungary once more a *Regnum Marianum*'—a Kingdom of the Blessed Virgin—and to act on the principle ascribed to his grandfather Ferdinand II : *Faciam Hungariam captivam, postea mendicam, deinde catholicam.* In 1673, then, he set on foot wholesale persecution and expulsions of the

---

[1] Composed of 3 Jesuits, 1 Franciscan, 1 Capuchin, 1 Dominican and a secular priest.

Protestant clergy, who were deprived of 800 churches and all schools, and in many cases sent to man Neapolitan and Venetian galleys. In a word, the goal was to 'exterminate heresy' in Hungary on the same drastic lines as in Bohemia, both as an end in itself, but also as a step towards centralizing and fortifying the royal power.

During the early seventies Ahmed Küprülü pursued his great designs against Poland by land and Venice by sea—pushing his conquests deep into Podolia and the Ukraine (1672–6) and reducing Cyprus after a two years' siege (1669). But his successor Kara Mustafa looked in another direction, and from the moment of peace with Poland was already dreaming of Hungary and Austria as subject provinces of the Sultan. Vienna was this time alive to the danger and made an alliance with John Sobieski ; but, on the other hand, Louis XIV played openly with the Turks, and the Hungarian malcontents found a leader of some eminence in Count Emerich Tököly. Realizing the need for some concessions, Leopold in 1682 consented to abolish the special Tribunal in whose hands the repression of the Protestants had lain, to restore a limited number of churches, and to refrain from using foreign troops to garrison Hungary. It is sufficient to point out that as a result Hungary avoided the fate of her neighbour Bohemia, and preserved enough fragments of constitutional and religious liberties to survive into a more tolerant age and blossom anew.

It was in these circumstances that the Sultan and his ambitious Grand Vizier marshalled one of the most formidable armies which had ever invaded Central Europe, and in July, 1683, laid siege to Vienna. Leopold's preparations had been altogether inadequate, and at the critical moment he and his family, with a large part of the population, fled in panic in the direction of Linz. But for the steadfast courage and endurance of two men, Count Rüdiger Starhemberg and Count Kaspar Kaplíř[1], Vienna would have fallen before the armies of King John Sobieski, Duke Charles of Lorraine, the Electors of Saxony and Bavaria and a number of other German Princes could bring the necessary relief. There was acute friction between Sobieski, who thought he had done it all himself, and Leopold, who had simply run away, and now resented the King of Poland having entered the city in triumph without waiting for him. The preacher in St. Stephen's did not make things better by taking as his text : 'There was a man sent from God whose name was John.' 'The Germans,' wrote Sobieski to his wife, 'go so far as to regret that we helped the Emperor ; they could have wished that this proud race [the Habsburgs] had gone under, never to rise again.' Not long after he complained that the Emperor no longer bothered about what he said : 'they have gone back to their old arrogance, and seem even to have forgotten that there lives a God above them.'[2]

The breaking of this last great tidal wave was followed by a rapid ebb of Turkish power, and by an outburst of confidence in Christian victory, expressed in the contemporary tract of Hörnigk, 'Austria above all, if only she wills it' (*Oesterreich über Alles, wann es nur will*)—a phrase

[1] Descendant of the Starhemberg who led the Protestants in Upper Austria against Rudolf II, and grandson of the Kaplíř who died on the scaffold at Prague in 1621.

[2] I cannot resist quoting the remark of a later Slav monarch, Tsar Nicholas I, who in his anger at Austria refusing her help to Russia on the eve of the Crimean War, spoke of 'the two most foolish Kings of Poland—Sobieski and me !' The two, he of course meant, who had saved the Habsburgs from disaster in 1683 and in 1849

which a few of the more clear-sighted patriots were to repeat in varying tones to the very end, but with angry stress on the second half of the phrase. It may well be that Leopold would have sunk back into super-stitious lethargy, but this time Turkish defeat had become a point of honour for Germany, no less than Magyars or Roumanians or Southern Slavs, and there were several generals of the very front rank ready and eager to lead a counter-offensive. Late in 1683 the primatial city of Gran (Esztergom) was recovered, in 1685 Neuhäusel, and on September 2, 1686, the fortress of Ofen-Pest was taken by storm, after 145 years in Turkish hands ; in 1687 the Turks were defeated on the symbolic field of Mohács, and both Transylvania and Slavonia were swept clear of the Turkish forces. In 1688 the Elector of Bavaria took Belgrade by storm, in 1688 the Margrave of Baden won a series of victories in Serbia and Bosnia, and though in 1690 the Turks recovered Niš and Belgrade, the Grand Vizier was defeated and killed at the battle of Szalánkemen. The war then languished for eight years, not merely because of inferior generalship or lack of energy, but because the Imperialists were now engaged on the Rhine and in Italy as well as in the Balkans. Thus once again the double-headed eagle evoked complications in the West ; this time Louis XIV looked askance at the prospect of the Emperor altering the balance in Europe by the recovery of long-lost territories and the corresponding enfeeblement of the Ottoman Empire. The zealous appeals of Pope Innocent XI and the so-called 'Holy League' left him altogether indifferent. Another serious diversion was the active alliance of the recalcitrant Magyar patriots, under Tököli, with the Porte ; yet it is difficult to blame them too severely, when it is remembered that at the very height of the great campaign of emancipation in 1687, Leopold revealed his ill will and bad faith by entrusting Caraffa, another of his many foreign generals, with fresh dragonnades against the Hungarian Protestants. He only desisted when the Diet refused to discuss further war measures until the persecutions were called off.

It was in such an atmosphere that the Diet consented to the coronation of Leopold's eldest son, Joseph, as *hereditary* King of Hungary, and was induced to renounce the famous Article of the Golden Bull of 1222 which assured to the Hungarian nobility the legal right of armed resistance (*ius resistendi*) to any infringement of the constitution. The succession was now vested in the male line of the House of Habsburg, and the nation could only recover its right of free election after the extinction of both the Austrian and Spanish branches in the male line. Thus sixty seven years after Bohemia was robbed of the right of election, Hungary in her turn voluntarily renounced it ; the power of the Crown was greatly enhanced by the fact that hereditary right was now accepted throughout its dominions. The chances of Bohemia recovering her lost status were correspondingly diminished.

How utterly alien consitutional ideas were to Leopold and his advisers is shown by the project which they for a time quite seriously considered, for converting Hungary into an Electorate of the Empire. The pre-dominant theory was that Hungary had been regained by right of conquest (*iure belli*), and that rights dating from before the Turkish era were no longer valid. This attitude is best illustrated by the Imperial Diploma granted by Leopold in 1690 to the Serbian Patriarch and the many thousand Serbian families which followed him into exile and were settled in the fertile lands of Slavonia and Bačka, so recently recovered from

Turkish rule. The Serbs relied on the Emperor's solemn pledge of political and ecclesiastical autonomy ; but the Magyars from the very first challenged the legality of the transaction, on the ground that the territory assigned had always been an integral part of the Kingdom of Hungary, and could not be disposed of without the consent of the Diet.

This conflict of views, which was to influence so fatally the relations of Magyar and Serb, was due not so much to any intentional bad faith as to a mentality altogether incapable of taking constitutional right seriously. Absolutist ideas were more strongly rooted than ever, though in the coming century they slowly assumed a more secular and less fanatical form.

The long war ended almost with the century. The inferior generals of its middle period were replaced by a supreme military genius in Prince Eugene, whose crushing victory over the Turks at Senta in 1697 really decided the issue. The treaty of Karlowitz (Karlovci) in 1699, the most disastrous peace ever signed by Turkey until that of 1878, proclaimed to all the world its rapid decline. It restored to Habsburg rule the whole of Hungary save for the Banat of Temesvár, which was also recovered by the Treaty of 1718 ; Transylvania was re-incorporated, but it suited Vienna to maintain its autonomy. From the strictly Hungarian stand-point also the new situation was an obvious improvement, but it had grave drawbacks in the fact that the Crown could conclude it without even pretending to consult the Diet. This was resented on all sides as intensely as the similar procedure at the Treaty of Vasvár ; and, as then, it laid the foundations for unrest and even active rebellion.

Internationally, however, the position of the Habsburgs as a Great Power of the very first magnitude was now past all question ; and the desire to maintain it led to an ever-closer alliance between the bigoted *fainéant* Leopold and William of Orange, the defender of England and Holland against the soaring ambitions of Louis XIV. The two groups had obvious common political interests on sea and land, though intellectually they had next to nothing in common.

Bohemia and Hungary

It is scarcely necessary to add that though most of the events summarized above did not occur on Bohemian soil, they most vitally affected the evolution of Bohemia, which was now completely enmeshed—to-day we might say *gleichgeschaltet*—and thanks to her geographical position quite unable to escape from the net.

The contrast between Hungary and Bohemia as the century closed can hardly be exaggerated. While the old national nobility of Bohemia had been reduced to almost negligible proportions or replaced by families alien in language and in political or religious aims, Hungary retained a nobility strongly national in feeling, and in particular a 'gentry' class which gave to it the same powers of resistance which Bohemia had formerly owed to the knightly class, by this time virtually exterminated. Moreover, Hungary possessed a strong bulwark of liberty in the Comitat or County autonomy, controlled by local elective assemblies—an institution which Bohemia had never possessed ; and to this was due the fact that the Bohemian Estates failed to maintain their authority against the encroachments of the Crown, as did the Hungarian Diet. To the ruling class in Hungary the Magyar language was an instrument of liberty (even though Latin remained the official language of debate and of official business as late as 1840), whereas by the clique at the head of affairs in Bohemia a knowledge of the Czech language was either rejected out of hand or at most acquired as a convenience for dealing with domestics. Most important of all, the Jesuits and their colleagues in the task of proselytism had it all their own way in Bohemia, but could not push to the same extreme in Hungary, because the Central Plains under Turkish occupation were beyond their control, and still more because Transylvania was a model and an encouragement to the Magyars of 'Habsburg Hungary,' nay more, a refuge and an active support ; and this continued under other forms after the recovery, when it suited Habsburg designs to maintain Transylvania autonomous, and distinct from the rest of Hungary.

The Last Two Habsburgs : Joseph I and Charles VI

The Turkish wars and the long struggle in the West between Louis XIV and William III were scarcely at an end when Europe was again plunged into the whirlpool of war, this time as it were in two watertight compartments, the War of Spanish Succession in the West and the Northern War, in which Peter the Great and Charles XII were the two great protagonists, the Turks being meanwhile absorbed in a war of their own against Venice and only intervening against Russia after the overthrow of the Swedes at Poltava. Leopold I died on May 5, 1705, at the height of the struggle. He had never shown a gleam of greatness and had always been at the mercy of designing ministers, but fate had treated him more kindly than he deserved in granting him generals of supreme genius—Charles of Lorraine, Louis of Baden, and above all Eugene of Savoy—and at the same time the sense to employ them. It was entirely characteristic of Leopold in his later phase that he took the advice of the Jesuits as to whether he would be justified in allying himself with two heretic Powers against His most Christian Majesty of France, and that he received an affirmative answer when it accorded with obvious dynastic interests. It was policy, not any new-found tolerance, that led him to recognize the Elector of Brandenburg as King of Prussia and to grant to Hanover the electoral dignity.

Leopold's successor, Joseph I, offers so complete a contrast to his father, that a parallel has sometimes been drawn with that gay and cultured knight-errant, Maximilian, succeeding the phlegmatic and ineffective Frederick III. He was of strong physique, elegant and lively, a hard rider and much less blind to female charms than his immediate predecessors. There was not a trace of the Habsburg underlip ; and contemporaries must surely have ascribed this marked improvement in the race to Leopold's belated abandonment of the practice of in-breeding which had proved the ruin of his Spanish cousins, and was threatening his own family with extinction. Despite their ascendancy over Leopold, the Jesuits had not obtained control of Joseph's education, and the latter showed a very marked aversion from them. He was indeed impatient of all his father's counsellors, surrounded himself with 'new men,' and was zealous for reforms alike in the administrative, military and financial fields. The one veteran to whom he rightly clung, and for whom he had a boundless admiration, was the great Eugene. The death of Joseph on April 17, 1711, at the early age of thirty-one—the first Imperial victim of smallpox—before he had had time to make his influence fully felt, was probably a misfortune only less momentous than the premature deaths of Albert II and Leopold II at other critical moments in the history of the Habsburg Monarchy.

Joseph was succeeded by his brother Charles, who was as unmistakably a Habsburg as his brother was not—slow to move, inclined to melancholy, virtuous in domestic life, but haughty and pompous, with a passion for ceremonies and etiquette acquired during his years of Spanish adventure. Charles was already fighting a losing fight for the Spanish throne, and now his brother's death brought a complete transformation in the attitude of his allies in Europe and opened the way for a compromise with the French king. For the very foundation of their policy—the resolve that Spain and France should not be united under a single monarch, lest this should enable him to dominate Europe—was cut away at the root ; there was an almost similar objection to the union of Madrid, Milan and Naples with Vienna, Prague and Pest. 'Universal Monarchy' remained the bugbear. Thus the settlement of Utrecht left all the Austrian dominions in Charles' hands, while yielding Spain to Louis's grandson Philip of Anjou ; the status of the lesser Italian States as between Spain and the Empire was not finally regulated till later in the century. Despite his disappointment in Spain, Charles had greatly augmented the power of his House, but a recent historian is amply entitled to ask whether it was not a fatal legacy, since no inner forces bound together its widely scattered dominions.

In one other direction Joseph's brief reign is of no slight importance and in a manner that bore indirectly upon the fate of Bohemia. The discontent that had long smouldered in Hungary owing to Leopold's inveterate habit of deciding her fate without consulting her, burst into flame in 1703 under Francis Rákóczy, one of its most romantic leaders, heir to the Transylvanian princes of that name, and educated, ironically enough, by Bohemian Jesuits. The famous 'Kurucz' (crusading) movement had a semi-revolutionary peasant background and enjoyed the sympathy of the Protestants ; but Rákóczy, who himself was owner of vast estates, fell more and more into the hands of the great nobles and conceived of 'Libertas Hungariæ'—the motto on his coins—in terms of an oligarchy jealous of its privileges as the chief safeguard of the constitution. The Diet of Ónod in June, 1707, boldly deposed Joseph I and placed the vacant royal power in Rákóczy's hands. But the magnates were not united ; Rákóczy's foreign allies, in particular the French, used him as a means of diverting Imperialist troops from the Rhine ; his personal appeals to Poland and Tsar Peter for help met with but little response, and in 1711 the rebellious Hungarian Estates, in his absence, concluded a treaty of submission to the Emperor, actually signed a fortnight after Joseph's death. Rákóczy, an exile under Turkish supervision bitterly compared himself to 'an orange which is sucked dry, then thrown away.' This surrender ends a long epoch of sporadic rebellions and prepared the way for more normal and settled relations between Hungary and the Crown. The moral of these events for our present theme is that Bohemia, once reduced to slavery after 1620, lacked anything that might be compared with the Transylvanian tradition, and lacked any class capable of organized resistance in a cause labelled, however undeservedly, as that of liberty. We shall soon see the humiliating contrast in 1741. With the exile of Rákóczy, Bohemia is hemmed in more effectually than ever, and even in detailed histories its name only occurs at rare intervals and almost as an afterthought.

With the new century came a subtle change in political thought. The Absolutist creed is held as firmly as ever, but it begins to assume a more secular form. The Jesuits yield to lay counsellors. The spirit of enlightenment and of rationalism is at hand. Yet Charles VI is guilty of one last outburst of persecution. In 1725, becoming aware that the number of crypto-Utraquists in Bohemia was still surprisingly large, he issued an edict for the expulsion of all recalcitrant persons ; and during the next decade·many thousands were cruelly beaten, imprisoned or driven across the Prussian frontier, where a friendly asylum was at the same time being offered to the victims of a more famous *razzia* by the Archbishop of Salzburg. There was also a return to holocausts of books, it being the avowed aim of the Jesuits to wipe out all Czech religious publications prior to the year 1620. Father Koniaš, who claimed a record in destruction, was a mild and pious man, who argued very plausibly that it is a crime to leave accessible a pleasant dish that is known to contain poison.

A word in passing must be reserved for a valuable side-product of this persecution. A few last remnants of the Brethren found a hospitable refuge on the Saxon estates of Count Zinzendorf, a leader of the German Pietist movement in the early eighteenth century. Taking the name of Herrnhut (Protection of the Lord), in gratitude for this delivery, they made their new home the centre of the sorely-tried Unity of the Brethren ; and it was from Herrnhut that the famous 'Moravian' missionaries set forth on their work of conversion among the heathen. Here Jablonský, the grandson of Comenius, was consecrated Bishop in 1735 and two years later Zinzendorf himself.

It was in this concluding period of Jesuit domination that the Order took action that was to have far-reaching consequences. From the first they had felt the need for a substitute for John Hus in the sympathies of the nation, and the figure of St. Wenceslas seemed too distant and shadowy. Instead, the figure of John of Nepomuk, the insignificant victim of one of Wenceslas IV's rages, was exalted into a martyr of the faith, who died because of his steadfast refusal to betray the secrets of the confessional. In modern times this myth has been exploded ; it is as unreliable as the claim that when his coffin was opened in the late seventeenth century his tongue was found to be firm and red ! It was left to the learned Dobrovský, a century later—himself a pupil of the Jesuits on the eve of their dissolution—to tear to shreds the specious legend of Nepomuk ; but anti-clerical writers in the full tide of the Czech renaissance over-reached themselves and injured their own cause by claiming that the Saint had never existed ! Already in 1621 an altar had been erected in his honour in the Cathedral of St. Vitus ; in 1683 his statue was erected on the Charles Bridge, near the scene of his death, and rumours of miracles began to circulate. At last, as a supreme effort, the Jesuits persuaded Pope Benedict XIII in 1729 to pronounce his canonization ; and his sumptuous shrine, in the most flamboyant style of bronze and silver-gilt, still remains in the Cathedral as a solitary symbol of mawkish emotion at the height of Jesuit power, contrasting with the restrained and exquisite taste with which the Cathedral was restored under the free Republic. In this connection it is but fair to add that Bohemia, to a far greater degree than Vienna or the small provincial towns of Austria, is the home of Baroque and Rococo at their best ; nowhere have they survived in a more perfect and unalloyed form. As Ernest Denis has well said, this art has 'neither the adorable *naïveté* of the Middle Ages nor the smiling charm of the Renaissance'; but this does not mean that it has not a very definite charm of its own.

The Pragmatic Sanction

Joseph and Charles, realizing the need for refreshing the exhausted blood of the Habsburgs, married two Guelf princesses, daughters of the Dukes of Hanover and Brunswick; but in each case the only son died in infancy, leaving two sisters to survive to womanhood. It thus became the central preoccupation of Charles's reign to secure the peaceful succession of his eldest daughter Maria Theresa. He first concentrated his attention upon his own dominions, and between 1712 and 1724 obtained from the Estates in each of them solemn recognition of the female line, resting in the first instance upon a revision of the Habsburg 'House Law' as issued by his father Leopold in 1703. It is interesting to note that the first to accept the so-called 'Pragmatic Sanction' were the Estates of Croatia, which, declaring themselves to be 'freemen, not slaves' (liberi sumus, non mancipia), and without awaiting the decision of the Hungarian sister-nation, decided in favour of 'that Habsburg princess who, reigning at Vienna, shall also possess the duchies of Austria, Styria and Carniola.' The main problem for Charles centred round Hungary, and it was not until 1723 that the Hungarian Estates adopted their own Pragmatic Sanction, in return for the Crown's endorsement of all existing 'rights, liberties and privileges, immunities, prerogatives and recognized customs.' These included the pledge of triennial Parliaments, and the establishment of a Council of Lieutenancy in Pest, presided over by the Palatine, and the strict maintenance of county autonomy, which had proved itself to be the chief bulwark of Hungarian liberties. It is safe to assume that Charles and his advisers had learned the lesson of the Rákóczy rebellion and that this explained their patient forbearance during irksome and prolonged negotiation with the Estates. Once more the contrast was complete between Hungary and Bohemia, where the Estates made no real attempt to bargain, but deferred to the wishes of the Crown.

In Hungarian history the year 1723 is a decisive landmark, and in modern times was regarded by statesmen and lawyers as the real germ of that Dual System between Austria and Hungary which achieved its final form in 1867. The Hungarian Aulic Chancellery in Vienna, with the Council of Lieutenancy at Pest and Pressburg remained till 1848 the framework within which the county autonomy could rally from the periodic encroachments of the royal power. In Bohemia the development was in the opposite direction. Not that such autonomy as had survived Ferdinand II's absolutist innovations was literally abolished; but there was a certain shrivelling or shrinkage of Bohemian institutions, and Bohemia's identity was in danger of merging in that of the 'hereditary dominions.'

Having thus by 1723 assured himself, so far as was humanly possible, of the loyalty of his subjects, Charles VI devoted the rest of his reign to winning the endorsement of foreign Powers; and one after the other the monarchs and statesmen of Europe pledged themselves to respect the inheritance of Maria Theresa. Unfortunately, he not merely made the mistake of supposing others to have the same regard for the plighted word as he himself, he also threw away the advantages which had accrued to him in the relative period of peace that followed the victorious Peace with Turkey in 1718. In 1737, this time in alliance with Russia, he renewed the attack upon the Turks, with high hopes of ending their rule over the Balkans ; but instead of the great Eugene he now had generals of extreme incompetence and mediocrity, and at the Peace of 1739 had to surrender those portions of Serbia and Wallachia which he had acquired in 1718, including the key fortress of Belgrade itself. When he died some-what prematurely a year later, from a chill caught on a hunting expedition (October 20, 1740), he left behind him an army in decay, disordered finances and administration, widespread latent discontent, and secret enemies on all sides waiting for an easy prey. Looking back nearly twenty years later, Maria Theresa herself told the British envoy to Vienna that on her accession she found herself 'without money, troops or advice' ; yet she had a high spirit that no disasters could curb.

Bohemia and Maria Theresa

The sudden incursion of Frederick the Great into Silesia, in defiance of the plighted word given by his father, is one of the most famous incidents in modern history ; the contrast between this dark horse among the monarchs of Europe and the young and fascinating Queen of Hungary and Bohemia, seemingly doomed to irrevocable defeat, was heightened still further by the way in which the Hungarian Estates first drove the hardest of bargains with her, and then declared their readiness to rally and die for their 'King Maria Theresa.' It is, however, but right to point out that Frederick, cynical and unchivalrous as was his conduct, was not without certain historical titles to portions of Silesia, whereas most of his allies in the war thus provoked were playing a shameless game of grab, for which there could be no serious justification. It is too often forgotten that it was as Queen of Bohemia, and not as head of the Archducal House, that Maria Theresa was ruler of Silesia, but that simultaneously with Frederick's invasion of Silesia the Elector of Bavaria, Charles Albert, with French and Saxon help, overran Bohemia itself. Once more the strategic importance of Bohemia is strikingly shown, for it is against Prague rather than Vienna that the invader turns ; Frederick, it is true, blamed the Elector for not seizing the Austrian capital, believing that the Habsburg Monarchy would then have fallen apart, but here he had underestimated the support of the young Queen's subjects.

In November, 1741, the Bavarians and French stormed Prague after only trifling resistance, and next day Charles Albert attended a special Mass on the battlefield of the White Mountain, where his great-grandfather, Duke Maximilian, had won his resounding victory. On December 7 he was proclaimed King of Bohemia, and received the homage of the Estates, the Archbishop and over 400 members of the nobility, though many others held aloof. This success was followed in January, 1742, by Charles Albert's election as Emperor Charles VII—the first non-Habsburg to obtain the Crown since Sigismund died in 1437 ; it was unanimous, because the other Electors had taken it upon them to declare the Bohemian vote invalid. Charles Albert seemed to have attained his wildest ambitions, but fortune's wheel soon went full circle. The demand of six million florins as Bohemia's contribution to the intruder's expenses was received with stupefaction, and speedily alienated all sympathies. Two days after his coronation as Emperor, Austrian troops occupied his own capital of

Munich ; and it suited both Austria and Prussia to conclude peace with each other and to husband their resources for the next bout. For Frederick the retention of Silesia meant among other things the driving of a wedge between the Elector of Saxony and his none too secure Polish kingdom, and Augustus was left crying for the moon of Bohemian territory. The edict issued by Charles Albert, promising to all who helped him actively freedom from serfdom and two years' exemption from taxation, merely alienated his noble adherents without overcoming the distrust of the masses. It is perhaps characteristic of the transitional epoch in which she lived, that Maria Theresa was so shocked at the decree as to order it to be publicly burnt, but that she drew the line at the common hangman being employed on the occasion. And yet meanwhile the few villages which responded to the usurper's appeal were razed to the ground as thoroughly as Lidice and Kozláky in our own day. She often showed great clemency, but she never forgave.

In the summer of 1742 the French, rendered thoroughly unpopular by their reckless requisitioning, were besieged in Prague and in the end had some difficulty in effecting their retreat. Maria Theresa, who at an earlier stage had written to Count Kinsky : '*Il faut tout risquer et perdre pour soutenir la Bohême,*' had herself crowned at Prague in August, 1743, and showed remarkable restraint towards those who had paid allegiance to the Elector. There was not a single execution for treason, though a burgher of Prague was only reprieved as he knelt upon the scaffold. But it is legitimate to conclude that Bohemia's defection at her hour of need marked a decisive stage in the coldness between the dynasty and the nation. To her and her successors Bohemia remained permanently suspect, and in the first instance this undoubtedly strengthened the tendency towards centralist reforms.

Bohemia bore the brunt of the War of Austrian Succession, and suffered more than any other part of the Monarchy.

By the Treaty of Berlin (July 28, 1742) Frederick secured most of the booty at which he had originally aimed, and retained all Silesia save the three Duchies of Troppau, Teschen and Jägerndorf.[1] Maria Theresa signed with the utmost reluctance and dreamt all her life of Silesia's recovery ; both knew well enough that this was only the first round. Frederick excused himself to the French as having escaped from 'inevitable shipwreck' and barely made the harbour ; their Bavarian ally he dropped without a scruple. It is noteworthy that Frederick specially insisted that the Bohemian Diet should give its formal sanction to the transfer of territory which had hitherto belonged to the Crown of St. Wenceslas.

It was Frederick who opened the second Silesian war, suspecting, with pretty good reason, that her rapidly improving situation in the general European conflict, and in particular her success in overrunning the Bavarian Emperor's patrimony, might at any moment tempt her to seek her revenge against Prussia also. Yet again Bohemia's strategic position places her in the forefront of the struggle ; within a month of the reopening of hostilities the Prussians were in Prague and treating it with no less severity than the French two years earlier. Frederick found it necessary to evacuate Bohemia, but for the second time he held his gains, and the Treaty of Dresden (December 25, 1745) only confirmed the decisions laid down at Berlin in 1742. Meanwhile Charles VII died an exile, and the Imperial dignity fell to Maria Theresa's husband, Francis of Lorraine.

[1] Opava, Těšín and Krnov.

Silesia, it must be admitted, was rapidly assimilated under Frederick's efficient if unsympathetic rule.

Even more vitally important for Bohemia than the loss of Silesia were the internal reforms which were so marked a feature of Maria Theresa's reign, and in particular of the breathing-space of eight years between the double War of Austrian Succession (1740-1742, 1744-1748) and the Seven Years' War (1756-1763). To her, and to her 'Iron Chancellor,' Count Haugwitz, was due the origin of the modern bureaucratic system which replaced the outworn machinery of Maximilian I and Ferdinand I, and upon which 'Austria' was to rest for a century and a half. Under her we have passed from the period of purely personal and arbitrary government, inspired by the militant Counter-reformation, to the age of Enlightened Absolutism—prompted by the same motives of Reason and Humanity which react upon the Encyclopædists in France, and which in the next century prompt the utilitarian school of thought. But, of course, the motive force comes from above, not below, and the will of the sovereign is enforced by a trained body of devoted officials, placing the Crown above all other interests, essentially a-national, parental in their outlook and ready to interfere at every turn. The conception of *political* administration, so alien to the English mind, develops by leaps and bounds in this period. Maria Theresa inherited the absolutist tradition of her ancestors, and her reforms were prompted by expediency and necessity, not by inclination. Two quotations will suffice to show her haughty outlook. To the Estates of Moravia, she wrote on one occasion : 'I have no objection to the Diet continuing, but on the condition that what now exists is not even to be questioned.' And again to the Bohemian Estates : 'In discussions concerning the All-Highest commands, the Estates have not to debate the question "whether" (*ob*), but only the question "in what way" (*wie*).'

Though the substance of Bohemian liberties had been effectually crushed under Ferdinand II, a sort of phantom autonomy had survived —the shell of former realities, which under more favourable circumstances might assume new life. The administration had remained under the Bohemian Chancellor, who personified the State Rights of the Crown of St. Wenceslas, and under the Council of Lieutenancy in Prague, while the great offices of state were in the hands of the aristocracy—a narrow caste, out of touch with the old national tradition, but none the less still representing a certain barrier to complete assimilation. It is thoroughly characteristic of the changed outlook of the age that Maria Theresa, while neglecting no art of flattery, or entertainment that could attract and attach the great nobles to the Court, and thereby lead to eventual fusion, also set herself from an early date to reduce them so far as possible to a secondary, or at least individual, importance, and to surround herself by a bureaucracy, trained on new lines, entirely dependent upon the Crown for career and advancement. It was, moreover, her settled policy to reduce the Estates to insignificance, not by abolition but by building up other institutions at their side and never convoking them unless this proved absolutely necessary. The crudest example of this is the fact that in a reign of forty years she only allowed the Hungarian Estates to meet three times, and that Joseph II in the ten years that followed never summoned them at all.

The series of her great bureaucratic reforms opened in 1748, when Maria Theresa extracted from the Bohemian Diet the so-called 'Decennial

Financial Recess'; Bohemia was thus tied down to an annual quota fixed exorbitantly high. The phrase 'without prejudice to their well-founded rights' was far too vague to be of much practical use, and for the next thirty years there were renewals roughly every ten years, and in the intervening periods next to no control. It suited the Government in return to take over the care of the military forces and all matters of quartering and supply; it was the aim of Count Haugwitz, the real brain behind the reforms, to create a standing army of 108,000 men and to obtain an annual revenue of 14,000,000 gulden earmarked for that purpose. On this basis, in 1749, there was a distinct move towards Centralism. Both the Bohemian and Austrian Chancelleries and the office of Statthalter in Prague were abolished, and replaced by the 'United Bohemian-Austrian Chancellery,' which was to remain the central authority for both countries up to 1848. The higher administration was placed in the hands of a body bearing the clumsy title of '*Directorium in publicis et cameralibus*,' which in its turn was replaced in 1762, having been rendered superfluous by the creation of the new State Council (*Staatsrat*), 'completing the hierarchy of the new Centralizations.'[1] At the same time a Supreme Office of Justice (*Oberste Justizstelle*) was set up, combining roughly the functions of a Ministry of Justice and a Court of Appeal.

In 1751 the whole administrative system was re-arranged, each of the fourteen provinces of Austria[2] had its own 'Gubernium' and local government responsible to Vienna; and under each of these were established District Offices (*Kreisämter*), with a District Captain (*Kreishauptmann*, afterwards *Bezirkshauptmann*) at its head. Among their manifold duties were the control of the police, land registers, roads, weights and measures, the inquiry into complaints of peasants against their lords, and the supervision of clergy and teachers. There were sixteen of these districts in Bohemia, and the officials at their head were appointed by the Crown and virtually independent of the Estates. It was the constant aim of the sovereign to render the administration more uniform and to extend in every direction the methods of paternal interference that accorded so well with the prevailing spirit of Enlightened Absolutism. There was in particular a tendency to merge the individuality and national identity of Bohemia in that of the other provinces. In common official parlance the only distinction drawn is that between the 'Lands of the Holy Crown of St. Stephen' and the 'hereditary German Dominions,' of which Bohemia-Moravia-Silesia are now considered to form part.

The Seven Years' War

The new bureaucratic machine was only partially working when Austria, and with her, of course, Bohemia, again became involved in war with Prussia, as part of the first really world-wide conflagration. This began with one of the most sensational diplomatic revolutions of all time. Austria and France abandoned a quarrel that had lasted for two centuries, and became close allies, while Britain, for over two generations the ally of Austria, transferred her friendship to Prussia, and Russia, under the Empress Elizabeth, threw her weight into the Austrian scale against

---

[1] These reforms may be studied in detail in Professor R. J. Kerner's learned monograph, *Bohemia in the Eighteenth Century*.

[2] They were increased to 17 by the addition of Galicia (1772), Bukovina (1775), Dalmatia (1797) and Salzburg (1804).

Prussia. No man contributed more decisively towards this fundamental change in the European situation than Count Wenzel Kaunitz, whom Maria Theresa appointed as her State-Chancellor (or Foreign Minister) in 1753, and who, though belonging to one of the old Czech families of Bohemia, was, of course, essentially a-national in sentiment, though his origin and upbringing may be regarded as leading him to attach a capital importance to the recovery of Silesia. Once this was accepted as the keynote of Austrian policy, it followed that a predominantly maritime power like England would be a less effective ally for such a purpose than such military land-powers as France and Russia ; and his was the difficult task of preparing the reorientation of the Court of Versailles. Frederick, on the other hand, realized that 'the House of Habsburg, richer in men than Spain and Holland together, but weaker owing to its bad finances, is at a disadvantage because it has no navy.' The question whether Britain or Prussia gained most advantage by their alliance is likely to divide historians to the end of time : but all will allow that it was a union of heads rather than of hearts.

Kaunitz was to control Austrian foreign policy for nearly forty years, under Maria Theresa and her two sons, and came to be known as the 'Coachman of Europe' ; to his son-in-law, Metternich, he was destined to set a precedent of indispensability to the Crown. In domestic policy he did not interfere unduly, though he probably had greater influence than Metternich ; his aim, never too precisely defined, was the gradual welding of the Habsburg Monarchy into a unitary whole, roughly on French absolutist lines. Though essentially a *grand seigneur*, he does not seem to have ever seriously dissented from Maria Theresa's efforts to transfer the machine of State from the nobility to her new bureaucracy (including in it here and there individual nobles who played her game), and was never concerned to defend the interests of the Estates against the tumultuous impatience of Joseph II.

The Seven Years' War belongs to the history of Europe and of Austria, and cannot be told here. But it affected Bohemia no less fatally than the Thirty Years' War a century earlier, and many of its fiercest battles were again fought upon Bohemian soil, the laws of geography and strategy asserting themselves as inexorably as before. In May, 1757, the Prussians under Schwerin won a victory outside the walls of Prague, but were severely defeated at Kolín, and driven back into Silesia. The following winter saw two of Frederick's most memorable victories, at Rossbach over French and Austrians, at Leuthen over a greatly superior Austrian army under Daun ; and in the spring of 1758 he was laying siege to Olomouc, with the intention of pushing on to Vienna itself. From this plan he was forced to desist by Laudon, and his second retreat into Silesia is generally regarded as a masterpiece of strategy ; but even more decisive for the ultimate issue was Laudon's action, for henceforth the main field of operations lay outside Bohemia—in Brandenburg, Saxony, and Silesia, and on the Rhine—though Bohemia continued to be drained dry of recruits and to suffer from merciless requisitioning. The closing stages of the war were marked by two sensational diplomatic changes ; the fall of Pitt enabled George III and his incompetent favourite Bute to draw out of the war, regardless of their ally Frederick's fate, while another sudden turn of fortune, the replacement of Elizabeth on the Russian throne by Frederick's own devoted kinsman Peter III, led to the withdrawal of the Russian armies and saved Prussia from an almost desperate situation. By the summer of 1762 Frederick was again in possession of Silesia and planning a fresh assault on Prague. But both sides were by now near the end of their resistance, and peace was concluded at Hubertusburg (December 30, 1762) between Austria, Russia and Saxony, followed by the Peace of Paris (February 10, 1763) between the Eastern Powers. While the settlement of Paris changed the face of the overseas world, ended the French Empire in India, and secured to the English-speaking peoples predominance over the French in North America, in Central Europe the Prussian monarchy and state, after being nearly submerged altogether, emerged exhausted but unbroken, and maintained its conquests in Silesia and Glatz. There was thus a fresh political truce in the long rivalry between Austria and Prussia ; but for Bohemia the loss of Silesia was definitive, and henceforward with every decade the lost province became more Germanized. The process was facilitated by the superior administrative methods introduced by Frederick, by the prosperity which soon followed in their train, and by the Protestant sympathies of a considerable section of the population.

Professor Kerner has shown more clearly than earlier writers the extent of Bohemia's sufferings in this war. Summing up her financial history, he points out that 'Bohemia, of all the Lands, was most devastated by military expeditions, yet at the same time paid into the coffers of the Treasury the largest sums of any state belonging to the monarchy. Besides carrying between 32 and 49% of the ordinary public revenue of the Monarchy, Bohemia alone contributed four times as much as all the Hungarian lands, and if both the ordinary and extraordinary war revenues were counted, it contributed between 20 and 40% more than the Netherlands, the next richest source of revenue. Such facts are astounding. They also account perhaps for the famine and misery and commercial depression which came upon Bohemia after the war.'[1] Bohemia, it should be borne in mind, was then one-quarter the size of Hungary, with only one-third of the latter's population, and yet throughout the eighteenth and first half of the nineteenth century contributed infinitely more both in money and in recruits.

Maria Theresa and Joseph II

In 1765 Joseph II succeeded his indolent but by no means negligible father, Francis of Lorraine, not merely as Emperor, but above all as 'co-Regent' with Maria Theresa ; and this partnership, resting on the tenderest personal affection, and yet politically so altogether uneasy and unworkable, lasted for fifteen years. 'I could not play the rôle of my late father,' wrote Joseph to his mother in 1773 ; and two years later she on her side lamented ; 'It is a great misfortune that we cannot understand each other, even with the best will. You show too much antipathy for all old customs and for the whole clergy.' Two quotations will help to explain the riddle, as derived from Joseph's frantic and ungovernable impatience. 'Of all that I undertake,' he once wrote, 'I want to experience the effect. When I arranged the Prater and the Augarten, I did not take young saplings for posterity . . . no, I chose trees under whose shade I and my contemporaries can find pleasure and profit' ; in other words, he time and again flew in the face of Nature, and his attitude to *human* nature was every whit as unreasonable. Even more enlightening is the

[1] *Op. cit.*, p. 36.

comment of his rival Frederick after their first meeting : 'He (Joseph) was born at a bigoted court and has thrown off superstition ; he was brought up in pomp and has acquired simple manners, is nourished with incense and is modest, glows with love of fame and sacrifices his ambition to his duty as a child ; has had only pedants as tutors and yet has enough taste to read Voltaire and value his worth.'

Not the least fruitful source of disagreement between mother and son was their divergent ambition. Three wars had cured Maria Theresa of warlike ambitions. 'Never again will I be led astray into war,' she said ; and on another occasion : '*Je préfère une paix mince à une glorieuse guerre.*' This in no way corresponded to the views of her son and her advisers ; and indeed the real key to Joseph's perplexing career is the paradoxical fact that his high ideals in domestic policy, which entitle him to rank among the great sovereigns of all time, were balanced by a grasping cynicism in foreign policy that throws even his three contemporaries, Frederick, Catherine and Louis XV into the shade. *Non legibus sed armis regna acquiri*, was the motto upon which he acted.

The Polish Partition

The Seven Years' War was no sooner over than the Polish question began to take precedence over all others. Long dormant projects of partition began to revive, especially at the Courts of St. Petersburg and Berlin, which fanned the discord of rival Polish factions and agreed to prevent the restoration of hereditary monarchy and the abolition of the fatal *liberum veto*. The other Sick Man of Europe, Turkey, was the first to realize the danger, and when the leaders of the anti-Russian party in Poland were driven to take refuge on Turkish soil, the Porte in 1768 declared war on Russia in defence of Polish independence. Poland and Turkey had become twin pivots of one and the same situation, and behind all the elaborate negotiations and intrigues we find the three Great Powers hesitating between one or other of two partitions, and trying to calculate their own relative positions afterwards. If it had rested with Austria and Russia alone, there can be no doubt that the decision would have gone in favour of the partition of Turkey, but Frederick was, naturally enough, not interested in the aggrandizement of Russia and Austria in the south-east, and keenly interested in acquiring new territory on his own eastern border, and he therefore set himself to woo Joseph and Kaunitz and tempt them on in the direction of Poland. Austria was undoubtedly averse to the destruction of Poland and only gradually yielded to the seductions of 'compensation' ; but none the less the first breach in Poland's theoretical integrity came when Kaunitz, always hankering after the recovery of Silesia, proposed that Frederick should disgorge it in return for a free hand in Courland and Polish Russia. Moreover, while Prussia and Russia were still planning partition, Austria acted, and early in 1769 occupied the thirteen Zips towns of Slovakia, which Poland had held ever since Sigismund of Hungary had pawned them to her in 1412.[1]

Catherine's designs upon the Danubian Principalities and the activities of her agents in Greece, Montenegro, the Aegean, and even among the

---

[1]Frederick in his Memoirs says : '*Ce fut ce qui achemina le plus le traité de partage.*' There is a certain parallel between Kaunitz and Metternich, whose annexation of Cracow in 1846 precipitated events in Europe on the eve of the great Revolution.

Slav and Orthodox populations of Hungary, aroused resentment in Vienna ; but Frederick skilfully averted this by diverting Catherine's ambitions once more to Poland. Early in 1772 the Russo-Prussian scheme of partition was presented to the Court of Vienna as an accomplished fact, and Maria Theresa invited to become a third party, objected keenly to what she called '*agir à la prussienne*,' admitted that such things could only be done 'at the expense of honour, the great repute of the Monarchy, good faith and the religion of our ancestors,' but in the end yielded to the insistence of Joseph and Kaunitz. '*Elle pleurait, mais elle prenait toujours*,' was the cynical comment of Frederick, and when once she had taken the plunge she surprised even her companions in crime by her eagerness to draw the frontier as liberally as possible. "Permit me to say," said Frederick to the Austrian Ambassador, "that your mistress has a very good appetite."

While Russia snipped off the White Russian territory that lay between her and Poland proper, and Frederick secured West Prussia and territorial continuity with East Prussia (but without the Free City of Danzig), Austria acquired the whole of Galicia except the town and district of Cracow. The First Partition deserves its reputation as one of the blackest deeds in history and provides the key to much that was to follow. In the words of Lecky : 'It shook the political system, lowered the public morale and weakened the public law of Europe.' It laid the foundation of that conspiracy in crime between the three Conservative Powers of Eastern Europe which was to check its natural development and to poison their attitude towards other problems, right through the nineteenth century. From the special angle of Bohemia and the Czechs it had other scarcely less important results. Poland in its mangled and enfeebled form survived for twenty-three years, but the doom of yet another Slavonic state was already sealed ; Croatia, Bulgaria, Serbia, Bosnia, Bohemia had one by one vanished from the map, and Poland was now to follow. Russia alone remained, more powerful than any of the others, but involved up to the hilt in projects of aggrandizement, and committed by a long series of events culminating in the French Revolution, to co-operation with the Court of Vienna both in the east and in the west. The acquisition of Galicia by the Habsburgs (and three years later of Bukovina from the Turks) may be regarded as completing the encirclement and isolation of Bohemia and her exclusion from the list of Slav nations.

The Fall of the Jesuits

Two other outstanding events of Maria Theresa's reign—this time belonging to the domestic sphere—had a decisive, if not immediately apparent, effect upon the fate of Bohemia ; these were the downfall of the Jesuits and the laws regulating the status of the peasantry.

By the middle of the eighteenth century statecraft had been secularized even in the most Catholic of states, and the Jesuits, who had at times enjoyed almost a monopoly of royal confidence, now found themselves opposed by a number of zealous reforming ministers, and occupying an exposed post as the defenders of Ultramontane theory and rigid ortho-doxy. The first to expel them was Portugal, under her great statesman Pombal in 1759, this example was followed by France in 1764 and Spain in 1767, and a year later the Bourbon sovereigns made joint representations to the Pope in favour of the total abolition of the Order. The attitude of

Maria Theresa and the acute difference between it and that of Joseph
are characteristic of the intermediate position between the age of Religious
Wars and the age of the French Revolution ; and the fact that the
initiative against the Jesuits came, not from the Protestant North, but
from the monarchs of the most Catholic states in Europe, shows that long
before the Encyclopædists reached their prime, other factors were already
at work and producing a new school of philosophic and political
thought.   Joseph played an active part in the assault upon the Jesuits,
paying an incognito visit to Rome during the Conclave of 1769, and
turning the scale in favour of the election of Clement XIV, who was to
promulgate the Bull of Dissolution (July 21, 1773).   But while Joseph
greeted their misfortunes with open glee and even contributed to them,
his mother wrote to a friend that she was 'disconsolate and in despair' ;
having 'loved and honoured them all my life and never seen anything of
them but what was edifying,' she did what she could to delay the final
decision and give them a chance of transferring some of their property to
Protestant countries.

The overthrow of the Jesuits left a serious vacuum in educational
matters, but it also provided a solution, as part of its revenues were
applied to the endowment of schools.   Maria Theresa, for all her insistence
upon strictly Catholic principles, recognized the need for reform and
laid down the truly enlightened view that the prince and the landlord
could only profit by an extension of popular education.   She was intelligent
enough to see that 'the school is always a political affair' (*das Schulwesen
ist und bleibt allzeit ein politicum*).   Her penchant for the Jesuits did not
prevent her from giving steady support to their implacable rival Gerhard
van Swieten in his efforts to reform the University system, and in eventually wresting from the Order its control of censorship.   He did not live
to see the Bull of Suppression, but his labours had prepared the way for
gradual modernization.

Nowhere were the reactions more immediate than in Bohemia, since
nowhere in Europe had the Jesuits enjoyed such power and imposed
so rigid a strait-jacket.   According to the calculations of Bílek, the
Order at the time of its dissolution counted 1071 members in 20 colleges
and 12 houses in Bohemia alone, and its property amounted to 9,000,000
gulden.   The schools taken from the Jesuits were placed under state
control, and Latin came to be replaced more and more by the vernacular.
But in Bohemia it followed quite logically from this that German took
precedence everywhere over Czech ; and though it is quite true that
Joseph himself spoke Czech and sometimes reproached his officials for
not troubling to learn it, his standpoint was purely utilitarian.   Germanization was favoured not for its own sake, but as a prime instrument of
centralization and of bureaucratic efficiency ; Czech soon came to be
regarded as merely the language of the ignorant peasant.   Already in 1774
German was made the language of instruction.

It was only natural that the devout Empress should show a special
interest in Church affairs ; she put a check on priestly abuse by fixing
the fees for marriage and burial, restricting the right of asylum and the
abuse of processions as a money-making concern, and reduced the number
of feast days.   That she knew how to keep Rome within bounds is shown
by her rescript of 1768, declaring excommunication to be invalid until
sanctioned by the sovereign, and by a veto in 1771 upon the clergy
sending money across the frontiers, and again in 1773 upon communica-

tion by any of her subjects with the Curia, save through the medium of the Aulic Chancellory. Decisions which specially affected Bohemia were the erection of Olomouc into an archbishopric, the foundation of a new bishopric at Brno, and in 1771 the erection of a Uniate bishopric at Muka-čevo (Munkács) for the neglected Ruthenes of Northern Hungary. The reforms introduced in yet another direction deserve at least a passing allusion : torture, and such barbarous punishments as the wheel and the stake, the branding-iron and the pillory were abolished, and flogging at least greatly diminished.

One of the sharpest of the many conflicts of opinion between mother and son occurred in 1777, when it became known that about ten thousand Moravian Czechs had left the Catholic fold and acknowledged themselves as Protestants. Maria Theresa's remedy was to set up forty-nine new parishes and apply intensive methods of conversion, to which Joseph retorted : "Things cannot be done by halves. Either complete freedom of religion, or you must drive out of your lands everybody who does not believe as you do." The Empress's rejoinder rested on the view that 'nothing is so necessary and beneficial as religion. Would you permit everybody to act according to his fantasy ? If there were no fixed cult, no subjection to the Church, where should we be ?' She therefore went on her way with wholesale arrests and prohibitions, tearing the children away from their parents and entrusting them to Catholic hands. Joseph, when informed of this, was not content with declaring that 'whoever is responsible for this order is the most infamous of your servants, and a man who deserves only my contempt, for he is both a fool and short-sighted.' He actually threatened to withdraw from the Regency, and Kaunitz had to be brought in to mediate, and to secure the cessation of these persecutions, on the plea that true faith, being a gift of God, cannot be imposed by force. The Moravian Protestants were henceforth allowed to worship unostentatiously in their houses.

It is not too much to say that the combined efforts of Maria Theresa and Joseph, from their radically different standpoints, placed Austria in the vanguard of humane reforms during the century of Enlightenment ; but what happened after their death is a classic illustration of the futility of initiative from above unless it has solid and consistent backing from below.

The Problem of Serfdom

Meanwhile the cancer which gnawed at the vitals of the whole state, but in quite a special degree, of Bohemia, was the condition of the peasantry. A commission of inquiry set up in 1750 revealed appalling abuses of seignorial power and a grinding misery among the masses which sapped both the financial and military resources of the monarchy. Even the conservative Kaunitz, in a memorial addressed to Maria Theresa in 1763, admitted that 'the common man,' who is 'the true strength of the state,' is 'more oppressed in Bohemia than in other lands.' This verdict, from a Bohemian feudal noble, acquainted with the dreadful conditions prevalent in Hungary and Transylvania also, is a sufficiently grave indictment, but other memoranda have survived (such as that of Baron Unwerth in 1768) showing the impression made upon the mind of a con-scientious and humane official by the gross abuses of the landlords. At last in 1771 a military commission was apppointed to inquire fully into conditions, and as their report coincided with an outbreak of real famine in North Bohemia, due to complete harvest failure, Joseph decided to see things for himself and made a fairly comprehensive journey through Moravia and Bohemia. He returned to Vienna furious at the 'apoplectic debility' of the officials. "Petty reforms," he said, "will not do : the whole must be transformed." His anger was directed especially against the nobility : "Poor Bohemia is groaning, and all she gets for aid is words," but for all his anger his attempts at reform were successfully blocked by the Estates and the situation continued unchanged till 1775, when peasant outbreaks occurred in several parts of Bohemia. In that year the so-called 'Robot-Patent' was issued, restricting the corvée to one, two or three days in the week, according to a sliding scale of taxation, and also the number of daily hours of work, and encouraging landlords to convert their robot dues into money payments. Above all, the new Cataster, or land register, became an increasingly effective check upon abuses. But the Estates maintained a passive resistance to reform, and Joseph, after his mother's death, decided upon more drastic measures ; and though he did not achieve his full purpose, he made it finally impossible to revert to the old system.

The Reforms of Joseph II

Frederick the Great spoke the bare truth when he greeted the news of the death of his much-wronged rival Maria Theresa as 'the beginning of a new epoch.' Much had been accomplished in the way of modernization during the joint reign of mother and son ; but much had been omitted or abandoned owing to the profound differences of opinion and temperament between the two, leading with every year to more frequent disputes and trials of strength, in which—at any rate as far as domestic policy was concerned—the Empress almost invariably had the last word. Now the brake was suddenly removed and the carriage plunged forward along roads only intended for the most primitive traffic.

The reign of Joseph belongs to the history of Austria and of Europe and cannot be treated here in any detail ; yet the broad lines of his policy must be stated, since they affected the fortunes of Bohemia as vitally as, probably more vitally than, those of any other of his dominions. What he wrought by decree could be wiped out by another stroke of the pen, but the spiritual turmoil which his reforms evoked could never be undone, and spread like rings on the surface of a pond long after the stone flung into it had sunk to the bottom.

Joseph stands out as the foremost exponent of the Age of Enlightenment, of that specific brand which bears the German name of '*Aufklärung.*' But all his high ideals, impeccable standards and personal charm cannot obscure the fact that he was to the full as bigoted and intolerant in his philosophical and rationalist creed as ever Ferdinand II or Leopold I in their interpretation of Catholic doctrine. He was infected by that mania of his times, the search for a 'system,' which meant what we now mean by a 'panacea.' But unluckily he wanted everything as seemed best to himself ; he was at once too doctrinaire and too autocratic to allow for human nature ; and though he had an unrivalled knowledge of his dominions owing to his habit of constant travelling and his love for travelling incognito, he lacked the necessary tact in the handling of men, and indeed could not take the trouble to win them. 'He wanted to sow and to reap at the same time,' wrote a Magyar historian of the last century ; and worse still, in the words of Denis : 'He tried to accomplish a revolution without forming a revolutionary party.'

His reforms fall into two parts, civil and ecclesiastical, and it was with the latter that he began. There has always been considerable mis-apprehension concerning 'Josephinism.' Adam Wolff was quite right when he wrote : 'One might just as well call it Bourbonism or the system of the eighteenth century, for it flooded all Europe and had acquired impulse, strength and even results at the Bourbon Courts long before Joseph became active.' Secularist views of the state were spreading every-where, as a natural reaction from the age of religious persecution and wholesale interference ; and many favoured a restriction of the powers of the Roman Curia, who were not merely not anti-religious, but practising Catholics. Joseph himself was influenced by the ideas of Febronius, who saw a solution in strengthening the powers of the episcopate at the expense of the Pope. It was Joseph's aim to turn the Church in his dominions into a kind of provincial Church ; we must not say 'national,' for nationalism did not enter into his calculations, and indeed it was his exclusive atten-tion to the '*State*,' as opposed to the nations composing it, that proved to be in the long run the ruin of his hopes.

He began by extending the '*Placetum Regium*' ; bishops must hence-forth take oath to the Emperor as well as the Pope, and certain Bulls relating to such subjects as dispensations and censorship ('*In Cœna Domini*' and '*Unigenitus*'), were suppressed. Already in 1781 he launched his famous Edict of Toleration, which secured free exercise of their religion to Lutherans, Calvinists and Orthodox, and allowed the erection of churches for not less than one hundred families within a certain area. Non-Catholics became free to buy houses and lands and were admitted to offices and degrees from which they had been hitherto excluded. All at once the treatment of Catholics in Protestant England became a gross scandal by comparison with the treatment of Protestants in the most Catholic Austria, and the sensation filled all Europe. Mixed marriages were regulated on the basis, overthrown in our own century, that if the father were Catholic, all the children should follow him, but if non-Catholic, all the sons should follow him. As a result, many crypto-Protestants came into the open, and their numbers more than doubled within five years. At the end of the reign the number of Protestants in Bohemia was about 45,000, divided between thirty-five Calvinist and twelve Lutheran Churches.

The Jews were not included in this Edict, but the first pretence at political rights was given to them : they were admitted to Christian schools, and allowed to be artisans, merchants or agriculturists, and for the first time—momentous decision—they were free to settle in Vienna. It is thoroughly characteristic of Joseph's general outlook that he tried to turn the Jews to agriculture, in the hope, as he said, 'of regenerating this people, which hitherto has only concerned itself with usury and led a wandering life.' It was at this time that regular surnames were imposed upon the Jews by Austrian officials, and many of the names familiar in Austrian history, during the nineteenth century were taken from Moravian villages such as Trebitsch, Leipnik, Austerlitz and many others.

The names of colours, and flowers were often attached to some feature of the landscape, such as Rosental, Lilienbaum, Blumenfeld, Grünberg, Rothstein ; but when the local officials were in bad humour such grotesque names as Leibgeschwülst (abdominal ulcer) or Krautstoffl (cabbage stuff) were arbitrarily imposed. Nowhere, however, did the sharp turn away from clerical dominance to secular tendencies have more far-reaching effects than in the Czech lands, hitherto not so much priest-ridden as monk-ridden.

Church Reform

In 1782 came the decree for the dissolution of the Monastic Orders which was only applied gradually, but drastically enough. On the eve of this decision German Austria contained 2,163 monasteries with over 64,000 monks and nuns, and of these, by 1786, 738 houses had been dissolved, though 1324, with 27,000 inmates still remained. In Bohemia and Moravia the dissolution between 1782 and 1789 affected 61 and 33 monasteries and 13 and 7 nunneries respectively, with 1340 and 1073 inmates. Moreover, their property was sold and pooled in the so-called 'Religious Fund,' out of which needy parishes were endowed and new churches built ; by 1789 the sums realized amounted to 59 million gulden (about £5,000,000 in the values of, say, 1900). Considering that three-eights of the whole land in Austria had passed under the Dead Hand, it is unnecessary to emphasize the profound social and economic changes wrought by such a radical transfer of landed property. Reforms of such magnitude caused great alarm in Rome and moved Pius VI, while matters were still at their inception, to the almost unheard-of step of paying a personal visit to Vienna. But though treated with veneration by the masses on his route, and with profound respect by the Emperor and his Court—even by the anti-clerical Kaunitz—he was unable to secure any revocation of the reforms, or even to arrest their further progress.

Next year a fresh blow was administered, in the shape of civil marriage. Moreover, Joseph carried out a drastic redistribution of Austrian episcopal sees and parishes, he founded general seminaries in each province, under direct state control ; he interfered with processions and pilgrimages—many with time-honoured traditions, which had almost assumed the character of vested interests ; he reduced the number of feast days, and in everything showed a quite amazing disregard for popular susceptibilities or prejudices. Perhaps the crowning example of this were his prohibition of the use of coffins and the substitution of sacks, to be buried in quicklime, and again his insistence that Protestants, Jews, unbaptized children and suicides—a list which in itself supplies more than one clue to social conditions in his day—should be buried inside consecrated Catholic churchyards. For once in a way the popular outcry was so strong that he had to withdraw the edict.

Joseph and the Estates

Turning to the sphere of civil reform, we find Joseph, for all his love of levelling and neglect of ceremonies, an enemy of representative institutions ; a prime reason of this was his contempt for the Estates—which alone could claim to be in any sense representative—as narrow and oligarchic corporations, interested above all in upholding their own class privileges. In the hereditary lands he did not immediately abolish the Estates, but he took from them, one after another, their already restricted functions : he closed their permanent committees, he introduced fundamental reforms on taxation without even consulting them, and at last in 1788 he forbade them to meet except when it should please him.[1] This offered a curious contrast with France, where in this very decade the Assemblies of Notables were increasingly active.

Joseph and the Serf

Needless to say, the main source of this hostility was Joseph's sympathy for the peasantry and his knowledge that their ill-treatment not merely ran counter to all his humanitarian principles, but was sapping the very life-blood of the state. His most radical inroad upon aristocratic privilege was the celebrated series of decrees (issued at various dates in 1781 and 1782 for the different provinces), which may be summed up under the title of 'Abolition of Serfdom.' The ground, upon which he himself justified this veritable 'Revolution from Above,' was that 'the abolition of Serfdom and the introduction of a moderate hereditary villeinage (*Untertanenschaft*) will have a favourable effect upon the development of agriculture and trade, and common sense and love of mankind speak equally in favour of this innovation.' By it the peasant was no longer tied to the soil, but acquired the right to marry without his lord's permission, and to change his place of abode after paying all his dues, to choose his work without consulting his landlord, and to own property of his own. As a minor, but highly symbolic provision, it was most urgently laid down that the peasant must no longer kiss the hand of his landlord or agent, or bow to the ground before them. Such punishments as imprisonment in chains on a diet of bread and water, or almost unlimited flogging, were abolished, but it was laid down as 'a matter of course' that apart from the changes specifically decreed the peasants still 'owed obedience to their lord according to the existing laws'—in other words, the seignorial jurisdiction was only restricted, not abolished. Joseph himself set a personal example, not merely by fresh efforts to turn the Imperial domains into model economies, but also by hedging in the unrestricted right of hunting. Though himself a sportsman as passionate as any member of his House, he ordered his reluctant Master of the Hunt, Count Clary, to carry out a regular massacre of the wild boars who ravaged the peasants' crops. The Urbarial Decree of February, 1783, authorized the landlords and peasants to conclude contracts for the liquidation of the Robot and other feudal dues ; the details of the scheme followed those adopted by Hofrat Raab for the Imperial domains, but that enlightened administrator found himself faced by a dead weight of obstruction on the part of the landlords. Pursuing a stage further his 'physiocratic' theories, Joseph, in February, 1789, instituted a new land-tax, with the openly avowed aim of achieving 'equality' on a proportional basis, and thus 'enabling landlords to fulfil their obligations to the state without difficulty.' 'This aim can never be achieved so long as the lot of the serfs, burdened by too heavy demands, is not made easier.' The land was conceived as a central point round which the general system of taxation should revolve ; and indeed Joseph was forestalling Henry George when he laid down the principle that 'the land (*Grund und Boden*) is the sole source from which all comes and to which all returns, which serves for the maintenance of man.' New land registers and valuations were ordered, and the country was flooded with officials conducting inquiries and making experiments in commassation. Liability to taxation was imposed on all,

---

[1] Styria and Tirol were exceptions, for reasons which do not concern us here.

and profits from the soil were to be reckoned according to a ten years' average of crops. At the same time numerous medieval dues and tolls which had cramped the subject's freedom of movement and initiative, were abolished.

Needless to say, this reform satisfied no one ; it went too far for the nobles, and not far enough for the peasantry, among whom it produced a lively ferment of ideas, especially in Hungary and Transylvania ; and it had been only partially enforced when Joseph's death was followed by a temporary relapse into feudalism. None the less, his 'Patent' will remain one of the great landmarks in human liberty, like Tsar Alexander II's emancipation of the Russian serfs and the vast agrarian changes of 1917–19 in South-east Europe.

With such ideas on the land question it was only logical that in his trade policy Joseph should act on principles diametrically opposed to *laisser faire*. There was interference at every turn. Never before or since has the prohibitive system been carried so far, except in the economic blockades of Napoleon and of the two World Wars. In 1784 Joseph forbade the import of practically every kind of foreign goods, e.g. wool, timber, cloth and most metals—his idea being that the state should only employ its own resources and not place them at the disposal of foreigners. He disregarded the protests of the business world and ignored the rise in prices which his schemes produced. He not merely did all in his power to keep money from leaving the country, but discouraged his younger subjects from travelling, and doubled the taxes on subjects living abroad. The Customs line between Austria and Hungary was not interfered with, but he tried to prevent the rise of industry in Hungary and to keep it as an agricultural producing state ; to this end he ordered that Austrian products should be admitted into Hungary duty-free, and incidentally gave a certain impetus to the reviving Bohemian industries. He also waged war on the medieval guild system, throwing open the pursuit of handicrafts to all and sundry. Other measures, for the introduction of uniform weights and measures, the improvement of the postal service and the resumption by the state of the tobacco and lottery monopolies, were less open to criticism. His desperate efforts to increase the efficiency of the bureaucracy and to root out bribery and corruption also deserve high praise ; but he made the mistake of relying upon an inquisitorial secret police (which flourished luxuriantly under his nephew Francis), and his passion for cutting down salaries and pensions, though based on his own penurious habits, only aggravated the evil which he sought to eradicate. 'Let religion, nationality, or the difference of administrations arouse no rivalry among you'—so he wrote in a sort of 'pastoral' addressed to his officials in 1783. 'Regard yourselves as brothers and work in common for the general good.' 'That is my programme, and be convinced that I shall neglect nothing to follow it myself.'

Joseph and Hungary

A brief reference to his Hungarian policy is needed to complete the picture. As his chief aim was to weld all his dominions into a single unitary state, and to eliminate so far as possible racial or regional idiosyncrasies, he naturally found the foremost obstacle in Hungary, whose peculiar national traditions had resisted the centralizing efforts of his mother and were now more keenly awake than ever before. From the very first he never attempted to conceal his views. Realizing that he could never hope to win the Diet for his reform, he decided to dispense with it altogether ; in the forty years of Maria Theresa it had only been convoked thrice, in 1741, in 1751, and in 1764, and now it was to remain in abeyance throughout the ten years of Joseph II. He even declined to be crowned, because this would involve taking oath to a constitution which it was his firm resolve to overthrow ; and this was already a gross infringement of Hungarian constitutional theory, which regards the sovereign as not in full lawful exercise of his high office until he has become *rex coronatus*. The resulting discontent was increased tenfold by the symbolic act of removing the Holy Crown itself to the Hofburg in Vienna, whither it had been preceded, under Maria Theresa, by the regalia of St. Wenceslas.

Still more fatal was his next step—the introduction of German instead of Latin as the official language of Hungary and the setting of a limit of three years for all officials to learn it. This is the point at which to emphasize the fact that Joseph did not act from nationalist motives ; to him nation meant little or nothing, the state everything. In his own words : "I have no conception of 'love of fatherland' ; it seems to me at the highest a heroic weakness, with which I gladly dispense." He selected German as the most widely spoken language in his dominions, and therefore the one most likely to perform the function of *lingua franca* with a minimum of delay. In his autocratic way he assumed that he, as 'Emperor of the German Reich,' had a right to impose it, thereby giving a modern and secular form—*cuius regio, eius lingua*—to the famous motto so stubbornly upheld by his ancestors. 'Were Hungary the first and most important of my possessions,' he once wrote, 'I would make its language the language of my provinces ' ; and he once considered the claims of Czech, which he knew quite well, and only rejected it on purely utilitarian grounds.

Even before this he had transferred the Council of Lieutenancy (*Statthalterei*) from Pressburg to Pest, and revised the functions of the Hungarian Chancellory ; and soon finding that county autonomy was, as ever, the main bulwark of resistance to interference from without or from above, he abolished the whole framework of the Comitats and their elective assemblies, and cut up Hungary into ten districts, under Imperial Commissars. His introduction of a census was rightly interpreted, and disliked, by the ruling class, as a first step towards the taxation of the nobles and clergy. His overthrow of the Guild system and his curtailment of municipal rights were followed by a revision of the whole judicial system and by the imposition of the new Austrian civil and penal codes. Even more than in his hereditary dominions or in the Austrian Netherlands, he contrived to alienate all classes from him, even those who would in the end have benefited most obviously from his efforts. At the end of his reign he found himself almost alone.

Foreign Policy

What eventually proved Joseph's ruin was that, not content with raking out all the innumerable wasps' nests of a backward internal economy, he simultaneously pursued an aggressive, at times exceedingly rash and invariably unscrupulous foreign policy. His consuming desire in this sphere was the acquisition of fresh territory. Reduced to its essentials, Joseph's policy falls under five heads, in all but the first of which Austro-Prussian rivalry holds the first place and dictates his action.

(1) He dominated Italy ; Milan was his own, Tuscany belonged to his brother and heir Leopold, a third brother had married the heiress of Modena, while two sisters reigned at Naples and Parma. His designs upon Venice were premature, but were to be realized a generation later under Metternich.

(2) In Germany his main object was to erect barriers against Prussia, and but for Frederick in his old age, the design for exchanging the Austrian Netherlands (now Belgium) for Bavaria might have been realized. On a dynastic basis—the only one which was taken seriously by contemporaries—the scheme was not without certain merits, and it is interesting to speculate on what might have been the evolution of Europe if Austria and Bavaria had been consolidated in a single state and had rallied round them all Germany south of the Main.

(3) Of his Netherlands policy, after the exchange had definitely fallen through, it must suffice to point out that it rested on the apex rather than the base of the political pyramid, tearing up chartered rights and substituting arbitrary paper theories, till the nation broke into open rebellion. It is too often forgotten that the Belgian Revolution forestalled the French, and was already working itself out on sound liberal lines when the revolutionary flood from Paris overflowed the Belgian border.

(4) Towards Poland his attitude was mainly negative, being concentrated on preventing any further accession of territory to Prussia.

(5) It was no doubt all the more negative, because towards the end of his reign he became absorbed in designs for joint Austro-Russian aggression against Turkey. The extravagant claims pegged out by Joseph and Catherine rested on their belief—a belief shared by many of the leading statesmen of the day—that the Turks could this time be finally ejected from Europe, in which event Catherine's grandson would restore the Byzantine Empire, or at the least rule over a Dacian Kingdom, while Joseph would acquire Little Wallachia, Belgrade and Orsova and the whole Dalmatian coast, and Venice would be compensated in Morea and Crete.

The Turkish War of 1787–91 brought many keen disappointments to the allies ; Loudon stormed Belgrade by a brilliant operation, but failed to hold it permanently, and Joseph himself narrowly escaped capture after a severe defeat inflicted upon his troops by the Turks on Hungarian soil. Meanwhile Hungary was seething with discontent, and on the point of revolt, Prussia was massing her forces on the North Bohemian frontier, while the double revolution at Paris and at Brussels served, one as a signal to malcontents throughout the world, the other as a sign of Joseph's impotence. His health, already undermined by years of persistent overwork, broke down under the strain of the campaign against Turkey, and he crept home to die. In his disillusionment he exclaimed : "I have seen all my plans founder" ; and the farewell Rescript of January 28, 1790, contains this phrase of anguish : 'As we have convinced ourselves that you prefer the old forms of administration and find your happiness in them, we will not delay conforming with your wishes.' To his sister he had written six months earlier: 'It is hard to do good to the people against its conviction, for it is hard for a government or even the most enlightened minister to know better what suits a nation than the people itself and its representatives.' But this gleam of comprehension came too late; all his life he had neglected tactical necessities, and now found himself almost helpless and alone. His voluntary revocation of all his reforms, except the Edict of Toleration, and the Urbarium, created a certain revulsion of feeling in his favour, but on February 20 he was already dead. In one of his last letters to Leopold he calls himself 'the unhappiest among the living. You know what I may call my fanaticism for the good of the state, to which I have sacrificed all—such good fame as I possessed; the political prestige, which the Monarchy had acquired. All is gone. Grieve for me, dear brother, and may God preserve thee from a similar situation.'

Joseph II is one of the most tragic figures in history. He had found the Monarchy great and flourishing, and in ten years had brought it to the edge of the abyss. He could not tame the spirits whom he had summoned forth. He had awakened his peoples, but he found that they repudiated his remedies; yet his ideals were greater than his methods of applying them, and many of them are now accepted as the basis of every modern state. After him nothing could ever be quite the same again.

THE REBIRTH OF CZECH NATIONALITY (1790–1848)

As a nation, our life was almost gone. . . . This miserable generation had to be told the story of their great ancestors, who had feared neither the tyrannical worldly Popes, nor the land-hungry Emperor.

—Havlíček (1850).

JOSEPH'S brother and successor, Leopold II, who had ruled since 1765 as Grand Duke of Tuscany, and who stands in Italian history as the one really humane and enlightened ruler of his century, was the best of all the Habsburg Emperors ; and it was a supreme misfortune that he only reigned for two years. In that brief period he restored order to the state and showed tactical gifts that differentiate him radically from his brother. He lost no time in proposing peace to the Turks, and used the alarm caused to all monarchs by the events in Paris in order to reach an amicable accord with Frederick William II of Prussia. He was then free to reduce the Netherlands to obedience, while restoring the Charters which his brother had unwisely revoked. At home, as a disciple of Montesquieu and a believer in constitutional theory—whether he would have allowed it to pass into practice is a question that cannot be answered—he raised no objection to the immediate convocation of the Estates, and found it politic to let them vent their rage upon Joseph's now suspended reforms, from a narrow oligarchic angle. He was thus enabled gradually to concentrate his efforts upon the appeasement of Hungary, whose Diet now met at Buda for the first time since the Turkish Conquest. The opposition was allowed to blow off its fury, even in such open criticism of the Crown as the phrase : '*Nota infidelitatis rumpit filum successionis.*' But Leopold very cleverly conducted parallel negotiations with the Serbs of South Hungary and won from them, in return for permission to hold a National Congress at Temesvár, very considerable military concessions, which had a sobering effect upon the Hungarian Estates. Then, when the effervescence had subsided, Leopold was crowned with the Holy Apostolic Crown and sealed his reconciliation with the nation by ratifying a series of sixty-two enactments, vindicating the constitutional position and as it were bringing it up to date. Of these the most important was Article X, which declared that, while indissolubly united with the herediary dominions by the same rights of succession, Hungary is 'a free and independent kingdom—that is, subject to no other land or people, and in possession of its own state existence and its own constitution.' It was laid down that henceforth the Coronation must take place within six months of accession, and that the Diet must be summoned at least every three years. As a sign of the national revival it was proposed to make Magyar the official language of parliamentary discussion, side by side with Latin, but the Court managed to prevent this, and the only linguistic law was one for the endowment of chairs of Magyar language at the University and the principal gymnasia. Meanwhile, county autonomy was of course restored in its entirety.

Leopold and the Bohemian Estates

In the words of Professor Kerner : 'In 1789 Bohemia was totally in the hands of the bureaucrats ; it was officially German, tolerantly Catholic and wholly absolute in form of government.' Though events in Bohemia took a very different turn from those in Hungary, there can be little doubt that the latter's example had a certain electrifying effect in Prague. Leopold had very wisely met the discontent of the Bohemian nobles by immediately convoking the Estates and adopting a conciliatory attitude towards them ; but he was well aware that their aims were far less radical and dangerous than those of their Hungarian colleagues, and therefore dealt out concessions to them more sparingly. The special *desideria* of Bohemia were brought to Vienna by a delegation of the Estates ; first and foremost among them was the request that the former constitution should be restored, and Leopold be crowned in Prague. But while adroitly tolerating, and even encouraging, the interminable discussion of historic claims and grievances, Leopold firmly resisted the suggestion that Ferdinand II's 'Renewed Ordinance' of 1627 should be declared arbitrary and illegal, and that Bohemia should thereby revert to the constitutional position under the Letter of Majesty. He issued a decree on May 9 abolishing Joseph's new system of taxation, but he issued no repudiation of his brother, and though the fundamental measures of tolerance, emancipation and judicial reform remained incomplete and in suspense, they were in some sense like a potion circulating through the veins of the body politic, though as yet in inadequate doses. It is, however, broadly true that Leopold paid for the abandonment of constitutional claims by the Estates, by not pursuing further any inquiry into the treatment of the peasants by the nobles, and that under his nephew Francis all reform was ruthlessly thrown aside.

Leopold also declined to re-establish a separate Bohemian Chancellory, and thus Maria Theresa's bureaucratic machine survived in all its essentials. This was concealed from superficial view by the visit of King Leopold—elected as Emperor after a six months' interval, in September, 1790—and his coronation at St. Vitus's Cathedral with unusual pomp and ceremony (September 6, 1791), at which he swore to maintain the privileges of the Estates.

The first signs of national feeling among the Czechs were now stirring. Modern attempts to dismiss their national rebirth as due to the artificial devices of a handful of aristocrats, or again as a reaction against Joseph's Germanizing tendencies, are almost equally exaggerated. It would be more accurate to suggest that the spirit of nationality was in the air, and that it followed logically from those principles of 'Enlightenment' which Joseph professed, but which he covered up with the hard crust of paternal absolutism. A number of general causes contributed to the revival. The rise of a nationally conscious middle class in every European country reacted from the one to the other. The rationalist and philosophical movement of the eighteenth century in France, centring in the Encyclopædists, and the doctrine of the Rights of Man, all led logically to the assertion of national as well as individual rights. There was, too, the first faint moving of the waters in the Slavonic world—tendencies still very vague and undeveloped, whose importance it would be easy to exaggerate, but which contained immense latent possibilities. From Germany came the really great and inspiring influence of Herder's somewhat diffuse and sentimental, but highly infectious, philosophy ; and at home in the Czech lands there was the reviving study of the almost forgotten writings of Hus, Chelčický and Comenius.

A small group of men, influenced by Josephine ideas, were already asking themselves whether the pursuit of enlightened ideals was really more impossible in one language than in another. Count Francis Kinsky voiced this view by urging that children should be taught Czech sooner than Latin, and arguing that 'if French is the mother-tongue of the French and German of the Germans, the mother-tongue of a Bohemian ought to be Czech.' Another enlightened magnate, Count Kašpar Sternberg, protested mildly against the unmeasured abuse of the peasants by his noble colleagues in the Diet. These two men were among the first to look upon Czech as the proper medium for education, to reject the Germanizing theories of Josephine bureaucrats, and to realize the implications of Comenius's pedagogic teachings. The foundation of the Royal Bohemian Society of Sciences in 1784, far in advance of so many similar academies, was mainly their work, and it became the centre of intellectual life in the Czech lands. In 1775 the historian Peltzl was allowed by the Josephine censor—while the country was drawing its first breath after the suppression of the Jesuits—to publish the chronicles of the Jesuit Father Balbín, which had lain forgotten in manuscript for over a century ; his own Czech history, with most of the merits and demerits of a pioneer work, appeared in 1791, and a few years earlier the learned though uncritical Latin chronicles of the Piarist Gelasius Dobner.

From two other quarters came a plea for the Czech language—'this palladium of nationality,' in Kašpar Sternberg's words, which 'no people allows to be taken from it.' In 1784 Hanka, Custos of the Brno library, published in German and under Joseph's own patronage, 'a plea for the Czech language and literature,' bidding his 'degenerate compatriots' remember their patriotic duty. His appeal was specially addressed to officials in Bohemia, and reveals some understanding of the affinity of Czech with other Slav tongues ; he even treated it as the natural language of a monarchy in which the Slavs were the most numerous race. He hails the dawn and declares : 'We shall no longer have to fear the mockery of our neighbours and our political half-brothers, who in their insolence call Czech a language of thieves and please to button up their coats if a few words of Slav are spoken in front of them.' In the same year K. J. Tham, inferior in critical power, but with a certain rude vigour, also published a treatise entitled *Defence of the Bohemian language against its spiteful detractors*. Here he is not so much argumentative as lyrical, when he bids the nobility 'blush for shame, descendants of illustrious ancestors, whom you have so utterly forgotten.'

It is characteristic of the then situation that these effusions were as a rule written not in Czech, but in German, in which alone they had any chance of circulating. To this early stage of the Czech revival belongs the famous anecdote, so often dismissed as fictitious, but most certainly symbolic of the facts. A small group of patriotic *savants* was accustomed to foregather once a week at the *Stammtisch* of a Prague inn ; and one of its leaders, looking round the room, is alleged to have exclaimed : "If this ceiling were to fall, there would be an end to the national revival."

The restoration of the Crown of St. Wenceslas to Prague, invested with special ceremony and followed by the coronation of Leopold II and his consort, stirred historic memories. Some of the magnates began to affect

Czech once more ; and the Diet actually proposed the introduction of the language at certain gymnasia. Leopold himself founded a chair of Czech language and literature at the completely Germanized University of Prague, and Peltzl was its first holder. He also attended a special meeting of the Royal Bohemian Society, and listened to an address 'On the loyalty and attachment of the Slav peoples to the Arch-House of Austria'—containing very marked references to the Serbs and obviously intended as a counter-blast to the Magyars. Its author, a young priest named Joseph Dobrovský, thus made his début as a pioneer of Slav studies.

Francis II and Reaction

In two crowded years Leopold II restored normal conditions alike in domestic and foreign policy. He came to terms with a Hungary on the point of revolution, brought back to their allegiance and calmed down Bohemia and the other 'hereditary lands,' and slowed down the pace of reform in all directions without renouncing the possibility of a resumption in more favourable circumstances. At the same time he concluded peace with Turkey, even restoring Belgrade and reverting to the *status quo* save for the single fortress of Orsova ; while maintaining his brother's good relations with Russia, he concluded an alliance with Prussia and Saxony, and under the stress of events in Paris and of the dangers that threatened his sister and her husband, was already working for a coalition of conservative forces, planned on saner lines than those actually followed by his successor. His own preference was for moderate constitutional government, and if he had been spared longer, he might have built upon this foundation, in spite of the growing European crisis. His death on February 28, 1792, at the age of forty-five, was a major disaster for all his subjects and for the House of Habsburg. For whatever criticism may be levelled against the great Empress and her two sons, it is an incontestable fact that under them Austria was the centre of many political, social and cultural experiments, and was in many directions far ahead of any contemporary state, Britain not excluded. The accession of Francis II ushered in a period of stark reaction, which was to endure till 1848, and then, after a brief and stormy interlude, was prolonged for yet another decade. For two whole generations there was both political and intellectual atrophy ; and, long before the constitutional era dawned, Austria had lost the spiritual leadership of Germany, and the final issue of her long rivalry with Prussia was only a question of time.

There are few more striking instances in history of the extent to which a single man, of mediocre but stubborn character, can determine and deflect the development of a great state. Indeed, after himself ruling as an autocrat for forty-three years (1792–1835), the Emperor Francis left behind him an elaborate machine which continued to run almost of itself for another thirteen years under his weak-minded successor Ferdinand.

Francis is one of the least attractive of a family which has produced many highly attractive, but also many repellent, characters. It is worth quoting what his uncle Joseph said of him as a boy ; for it remained true throughout life : "He is of a slow, secretive and indifferent character, and therefore displays few pronounced passions. None the less he seems to possess energy and system. He has apparently worked diligently and acquired much knowledge. For his age he knows a great deal both of theory and practice. But it is all *machine* and *dictating* (*Diktandoschreiben*), no thoughts of his own, no style of his own either in writing or in talking.'' Or again : ''He is a spoilt darling . . . to whom the preservation of his own person alone seems endlessly important. Though backward physically, he possesses a boundless self-love, and with it sluggishness in action, indifference and indecision in what he thinks, does or leaves undone.'' ''Noble moral motives make not the slightest impression upon him . . . neither ambition, patriotism, honesty in the fulfilment of duties, nor even religious principles.''

His tutor, Count Franz Colloredo, lamented the difficulty of 'bringing him to anything reasonable' (*zu etwas räsonablem*), and when asked by Joseph for a list of the young man's qualities, produced the following verdict : 'Much self-love, secretiveness in action, distrust and suspicion, slow and laborious in comprehension.' It may have been partly that he shared his father's poor health. He never developed that passion for sport which has characterized so many of his House ; nor was he a keen soldier. He never tried to command the army in person, and during the long wars only went to the front for short periods. He neither danced nor rode.

His morals were good, he was an ideal family man, a kind father, and except in the time of his second wife, who seems to have encouraged him in frivolous amusements, he lived more like a good Viennese bourgeois, without pomp or ceremony, than like the master of one of the most ancient and exclusive courts in Europe. He was genial and accessible, had a certain dry humour and a good memory, used the broad Viennese dialect and joked with the market-wives and citizens ; and to this was very largely due the personal popularity which very seldom left him even to the end of his life. The words of the Imperial Hymn, immortalized by Haydn's music, were a true reflection of public opinion, and he remained '*Unser guter Kaiser Franz.*'

Above all, he was an egoist and a pedant, tireless and hard-working, but lacking all sense of proportion, unceasingly immersed in red tape and office routine, and reluctant to delegate even the most trifling matter. When he died, four thousand documents were in his study awaiting his decision or his signature ; with the best will in the world, he could not keep abreast and acted often enough, perforce, upon the principle crudely expressed by his brother Archduke Louis, 'Letting it lie is the best way of settling it (*Liegen lassen ist die beste Erledigung*)'. ''Believe me,'' said Metternich's colleague and rival, Count Kolovrat, in a moment of candour, ''he who has to serve for any time in the immediate entourage of the Emperor must become either a philosopher or an intriguer or an ox, in order to endure it.'' To which Baron Kübeck, perhaps the ablest and most efficient official of the Franciscan era, cynically rejoined : ''Of these three, most people hold to the *juste milieu*, namely intrigue.''

It may be thought that undue attention has been paid to the personalities of successive rulers, and especially to that of Francis, who was essentially a Viennese and completely out of touch with Bohemia, and looked with disfavour upon all nationalist movements among his subjects. Unhappily, in this era of 'Stability'—with this word the wooden-headed Francis got nearer to an idea than on any other occasion—everything centred round the throne ; stability meant a maximum of rigidity and a minimum of motion, and nothing could happen without his sanction or direct orders. Thus the monarch sets the tone and gives the clue. The lengths to which Francis carried his hatred of change or ideas are revealed in the terms in which he addressed the professors of Laibach gymnasium in 1821 : "Hold to the old, for it is good, and our ancestors found it to be good, so why should not we ? There are now new ideas going about, which I never can nor will approve. Avoid these, and keep to what is positive. For I need no savants, but worthy citizens. To form the youth into such citizens is your task. He who serves me must teach what I order. He who cannot do so, or who comes with new ideas, can go, or I shall remove him." On another occasion he replied thus to an address sent by one of the Hungarian county assemblies : "The whole world is going mad (*totus mundus stultizat*), and leaving its ancient laws is seeking for imaginary constitutions. You have a constitution received uninjured from your ancestors. Love it ; I too love it, and will preserve and hand it down to our heirs."

The impressions left on him in early life by the French Revolution, and above all the fate of his aunt, Marie Antoinette, dominated him throughout life, and if there was one thing which he viewed with ingrained suspicion, it was an intellectual or a writer. "Who *ordered* you to write them ?" was his frowning comment upon a collection of patriotic verse unwisely offered to him by its author. It is on record that he once apologized to a general for confusing him with the author of a treatise on strategy ! He had the traditional Habsburg love of music, and so Mozart, Haydn, Beethoven and Schubert could flourish in Vienna ; but German literature, beginning with Goethe and Schiller, was taboo, and Grillparzer, the greatest of Austrian dramatists, and himself an arch-conservative who wrote more than one eulogy of the Habsburgs, could place on record, after vegetating for many years as an Austrian official, that 'in the Austria of those days there was no place for a poet,' and that 'despotism has destroyed my literary life.'

Austria, then, throughout the long revolutionary and Napoleonic Wars, and in the period of political stagnation and high literary romanticism that followed, was the Police State *par excellence*, unsurpassed even by the Tsarist Empire for its all-pervading qualities, though seeming mild and benevolent to us who are the contemporaries of Hitler's Germany. Already in 1793 the police system, inaugurated by Joseph for very different motives, was greatly extended and spread with the rapidity of a fungus. Count Saurau, indeed, has been accused of manufacturing plots in order to allay the anxiety of Francis, and prove his own office to be indispensable ; and recent research[1] tends to suggest that the so-called Jacobin Trials in Vienna, and above all at Pest, were based upon gross exaggeration of practices which were in the main harmless, such as the planting of a tree of liberty or the signing of an indifferent national protest against the French War. Besides von Herbenstreit and Abbot Martinovics, allegedly arch-conspirators, one youth in his early twenties was sent to the scaffold, and a reprieve was refused by the Emperor on the specific ground that 'in view of the evil principles which they profess, there can be no hope of their improvement.'

It is significant of the more backward state of opinion in Bohemia and the relative lack of contacts with the outside world and with Hungary, that there were at this stage no such heresy hunts in Prague. The 'state atrophy' which characterized the reign was nowhere more marked than in the Czech lands, which were still subject to the triple influence of Centralization, Germanization and Catholicism. It expressed itself above all in a

[1] Especially Dr. Viktor Bibl's investigations in the Vienna Archives since 1919.

double censorship, civil and ecclesiastical, of the most stringent and far-reaching kind, extending not only to books and other publications, but even to such trifles as fans and snuff-boxes, and in a police system which had secret societies on the brain, and consistently discouraged the foundation of *any* society whatever, even of the most abstruse and scientific character, and interfered in the most intimate affairs of the citizen by its methods of espionage, denunciation and control of correspondence. It should at once be added that censorship and police weighed equally upon Germans and Slavs, and devoted much effort to isolating Austria from the great movements of German culture in every sphere, throughout the first half of the nineteenth century. It is also true that the Czechs were, in one sense, less severely treated, seeing that the Royal Society of Sciences, set up in 1784, was allowed to survive, and in 1818 the Society of the Bohemian Museum was founded. The general situation at the turn of the century may be summed up in the words of Ernest Denis, 'Bohemia remained what two centuries of State Religion and of Jesuit domination had made it—a country of profound indifference, veiled by superstitious practices.' In Hungary, too, the effervescence of 1790–92, followed by the Jacobin Trials, died down more rapidly than could have been expected, and the excesses of the French Revolution drove the classes as yet politically vocal, into a timid and unreasoning conservatism. The Bohemian Estates fell quickly into the background and only began to emerge again from their obscurity in the forties. In Hungary Francis found it necessary to summon Parliament in 1811, but after that date was able to dispense with it altogether until 1825, and with the Transylvanian Estates right on till 1834.

It would lead too far to consider the changes made by Francis in the central administration—notably the abolition of the old Staatsrat in 1801 and the creation of a body with the clumsy name of 'Staats-und Konferenz-Ministerium,' with terms of reference so unworkable that it had to be wound up some years later. It is only in our own day, as a result of the opening of the Vienna Archives, that the full gravity of the situation created by Francis's incompetence has become obvious.

In 1802 the ablest of the Emperor's six brothers, the Archduke Charles, presented to him a long memorandum entitled 'Serious Reflections upon the present position of the Austrian Monarchy, in Comparison with France before the Outbreak of the Revolution.' In this he went so far as to say that 'Austria has among all her enemies none more dangerous than her own Government,' and that she had gone back a full half-century as compared with her neighbours. There was no clear system, 'no concentration of the most important affairs in a single point' ; the Supreme Council, instead of dealing with high politics and holding together the threads, became involved in petty details such as the appointment of a clerk or a concierge. Charles poured out contempt on the Ministers ; what could be expected, he asked, when men are appointed 'who openly boast of not having read a book or a paper in thirty years.' Half-measures were useless, there must be radical changes, for 'Austria stands on the last step to utter ruin,' and her fall would affect all Europe. There was much more on the finances, in which Charles was highly competent. But Francis disregarded Charles's advice, the only brother to whom he ever listened was Ludwig, the most mediocre and negative of them all ; and the cancer continued to eat into the vitals of Austria.

Austria and the French Revolution

During the long struggle with the French Revolution and the Napoleonic Empire, Bohemia's identity seems to be more than ever submerged in the wider Austrian unit ; the story cannot be told here. It must suffice to emphasize the remarkable and unexpected powers of resistance displayed by the Habsburg Monarchy under its unimaginative and unresourceful monarch. Four times was Austria compelled to conclude an unfavourable peace—at Campoformio in 1797, at Lunéville in 1801, at Pressburg in 1805, at Schönbrunn in 1809. The terms imposed were progressively severe, and on the last two occasions they followed an occupation of Vienna by the conqueror. Yet in 1813 Austria was the soul of the final coalition against Napoleon, though the historians have been on Prussia's side, very largely because the Austrian censorship prevented the emergence of a school of Austrian historians.

The soaring ambition of the First Consul led him in May, 1804, to assume the Imperial title, and this had important consequences for Austria and for Bohemia. The upstart monarch was naturally eager to secure recognition from the genuine article, and Francis, although playing for delay, did not think it politic to refuse. But it raised in Vienna the fear lest, if Napoleon obtained a hereditary empire, the successors of Francis, as *elected* Holy Roman Emperor, might find themselves merely Kings of Hungary and Bohemia, ranking lower than the sovereign of France. There thus ripened in the mind of Francis and his advisers the plan of a 'hereditary Habsburg Empire,' side by side with the old elective dignity. At first he hesitated between 'Emperor of Germany' and 'Emperor of Austria,' but finally decided for the latter, since it was obviously impossible for anyone to challenge a title derived from his own hereditary provinces. As the French envoy sarcastically reported to Napoleon : "This accumulation of two Empires upon a single head does not frighten a sovereign who is already accustomed to wear three crowns." Napoleon raised no objection, but insisted that his own empire must be proclaimed first : and thus it came about that it was not until August 11 of the same year that Francis II, Holy Roman Emperor, also became Francis I, hereditary Emperor of Austria. His jealousy of Napoleon is openly expressed in the manifesto, which speaks of 'maintaining full equality of title and dignity with the foremost European rulers.' In passing it should be noted that the new dignity continued to bear the marks of its improvised and so to speak *ad hoc* origin ; for neither Francis nor his three successors as Emperors of Austria ever went through a coronation ceremony, though they were crowned Kings of Hungary with all the traditional pomp. Ferdinand V was even crowned as King of Bohemia, but Francis Joseph twice promised and then broke his pledge, while Charles had perhaps some excuse for postponing the ceremony at Prague until it was too late.

Francis's decision was received with great suspicion in Hungary, as an attempt to swallow up the identity of the Holy Crown of St. Stephen in a new and loftier dignity. Francis gave the assurance that the title had only been chosen because it coincided with that of the ruling House, and was not intended to affect the constitutional position ; he thus averted a formal protest, but the suspicion remained latent and was certainly not unfounded. Bohemia reacted less strongly, and was unable to prevent a decline in precedence ; it now came to be treated as an integral part of the Austrian Empire, and the phrase 'hereditary dominions' fell into disuse. Bohemia took its place in more than one of the phantasies that floated before the eyes of Napoleon or his contemporaries. In one of them there was to be an 'Empire of Bohemia,' Austria proper being detached from Bohemia and united, by way of compensation, with Hungary. At another time the separation of the three Crowns of Bohemia, Hungary and Austria was under consideration. In 1808 Tsar Alexander I offered Napoleon a free hand in Bohemia, and in 1809 there was an idea of uniting Bohemia with Bavaria or with Saxony, as part of a further regrouping of political forces in Germany. But geographical facts again asserted themselves, and the Bohemian bastion survived, to all seeming as an integral part of the reconstructed Habsburg state. In the initial stages of the long European struggle Bohemia escaped the ravages which had been her lot in the seventeenth and eighteenth centuries; Italy, the Low Countries, Germany, had been the main theatres of war. But in the campaign of 1805 the decisive battle was fought between the French invaders and the combined forces of Russia and Austria on the soil of Moravia, in admirably prepared positions between Brno (Brünn) and Austerlitz (Slavkov). What is sometimes called the Moravian gap was successfully defended against the Russian advance from the north-east; Bohemia this time was left on one side. Napoleon's victory enabled him to drive a wedge between the allied armies, and to dictate peace at Pressburg, under threat of invading Hungary and perhaps alienating it from the Habsburg cause. By the Treaty of December 26, 1805, Austria had to disgorge Venetia and all the Adriatic territories which had come to her on the downfall of Venice two years before, and an even greater blow to her prestige was the cession of Tirol, that most typically Austrian of provinces, to Bavaria. The recognition of Bavaria and Württemberg as Kingdoms and of Baden as a Grand Duchy was the logical prelude to the liquidation of the Holy Roman Empire, which had by now amply justified the old gibe of Voltaire that it was neither Holy nor Roman nor an Empire. None the less, no little pressure from the victor was required in order to induce Francis to renounce the proudest crown of Europe, after it had been associated with his House for over four centuries; but, of course, externally there was every show of a spontaneous and well-considered act. By many Germans it was greeted as an act of betrayal and humiliating; to the Czechs (and in this case even to their nobility) it was a matter of complete indifference.

Within less than three years Napoleon delivered another frontal attack upon Austria, but this time the decision fell at Wagram, in Lower Austria, and the Czech lands were spared invasion. Playing with the idea of a national awakening, he issued a grandiloquent manifesto to the Magyars, inviting them to co-operate with him for the recovery of their independence; all Europe had its eyes upon them, he declared, adding that he could not believe that they would prefer the rule of 'feeble princes, the slaves of ministers corrupted and sold to England, that enemy of the Continent whose prosperity is based on monopoly and our divisions.' But the appeal fell entirely flat; and even more hopeless would have been overtures to Bohemia, where a knowledge of his designs of partition had been allowed to penetrate. In the culminating stages of the war Napoleon found himself taken from the rear at the great battle of Leipzig, because he had failed to assure to himself the necessary control of the Bohemian salient. Thus in the Napoleonic wars the strategic importance of the Czech lands was again demonstrated as strikingly as ever.

The Metternich Regime

The Congress of Vienna, following upon the overthrow of Napoleon and the occupation of France by the allied armies, placed Austria once more at the very height of her prestige. Francis, rigid and unconstructive as he was, had the supreme good fortune to possess in Metternich a Foreign Minister of the very front rank, and enough intelligence to give him due scope and retain him in office. Metternich, whatever may have been his defects, was entirely loyal to his master, but was careful to insist on more than one occasion that the real power always lay in the Emperor's hands : and though it was good tactics to say so, it was also but the bare truth. "If he heaps favours on me and trusts me," he once told a general in the suite of Tsar Nicholas, "it is because I go the way which he prescribes to me ; and had I the misfortune to stray from it, Prince Metternich would not remain twenty-four hours Foreign Minister." His famous phrase : "I have sometimes governed Europe, but Austria —never," is two-edged. In the period of reaction that followed the Treaty of Vienna, Metternich on the one hand controlled the policy of the German Confederation, imposing his anti-democratic views upon most of the lesser courts and stifling all progress in the academic sphere ; and at the same time he completely dominated Italy—Lombardy and Venetia by direct rule, Tuscany, Parma and Modena through well-drilled cadets of the House of Habsburg, and the Papal States and Naples by sheer necessity. But even at the height of his influence upon foreign policy— which began to decline after the death of Castlereagh in 1822, was under eclipse during the first five years of Tsar Nicholas I, but took a new lease of life, after the Revolution of 1830 and, though henceforth subject to fluctuations, remained formidable right up to the collapse in 1848— Metternich was never able to assert his authority in domestic affairs, and found his advice and warnings constantly disregarded. Abroad the doctrine of Stability allied itself with Balance and Legitimacy against the corroding forces of Constitutionalism and Nationalism ; at home Stability became absolute rigidity, and the frontiers were in an intellectual sense a Chinese Wall designed to keep out all new ideas as far as possible.

The disasters of the year 1809 seem to have roused Francis from a certain lethargy and triviality which marked the first two decades of his reign ; henceforth he not merely became more autocratic, but devoted a much closer attention to public affairs. Under him the real power lay with the Chief of Police, Count Saurau, and after 1817 the all-pervasive Count Sedlnitzky, who had no superior—not even his more famous contemporary Fouché—in the arts of espionage, censorship, denunciation and interception. Saurau's attitude to education, presumably endorsed by Francis and clearly reflecting his mind, was defined as follows in 1817 : 'The State pays public teachers in order that they may teach those principles which are approved by the Church and by the State administration, and it is a dangerous error if a professor believes that he may teach the youth entrusted to him according to the tendency of his individual conviction or according to his peculiar views.' After the July Revolution Sedlnitzky put a veto upon students visiting Paris or other foreign cities, and in a minute to Metternich justified his attitude by giving a list of the false doctrines from which he desired to keep them immune—'philosophical materialism, religious rationalism or mysticism, so-called liberalism, the revolutionary principle, and the corporative spirit.' The official attitude to the press has been defined by the most authoritative of Metternich's biographers, H. v. Srbik, who not merely argues that Metternich's whole system rested on 'the principle that press freedom leads to the destruction of the foundation of the state and of society,' but quite openly endorses the view !

It would, however, be a grave error to accept the conventional view of Metternich as an opponent of all progress. On the contrary, he believed in the necessity of political reforms, though of a moderate character, perhaps half-way between the British and Hungarian models, and above all intended to nip more radical tendencies in the bud. Already in 1811 he laid before the Emperor proposals for the revival, in a modified form, of the State Council of Kaunitz's day ; and after 1814 some of his suggestions were adopted. The establishment of a Ministry of Finance in 1816 was the result of his initiative. Encouraged by this, he put forward in 1817 a plan for the reorganization of the central authority, the main feature being the creation of a Supreme Chancellor (*Oberster Kanzler*), with four subordinate Chancellors under him, for (*a*) Bohemia-Moravia-Galicia, (*b*) Austria, (*c*) Illyria (with Dalmatia), and (*d*) Italy. The Hungarian and Transylvanian Chancellories remained untouched, on parallel lines. His insistence that the scheme 'contains nothing harsh, nothing subversive, no single daring principle' reveals the sort of reaction which he expected from his master, and in fact it remained stillborn. During the next ten years he did what he could to encourage the setting up of provincial Diets, drawing a very strong distinction between the system of Estates and the parliamentary or representative system, to the latter of which he was opposed.

In 1826, after a severe illness, Francis promised Metternich that he would seriously take up his suggestions for reform ; but nothing had yet come of these good intentions by 1830, and after the July Revolution the very name of reform stank in the old man's nostrils. In June, 1831, he said to Pillersdorff : "I won't have any innovations. Let the laws be justly applied : our laws are good and adequate. This is no time for reforms. The peoples are, as it were, badly wounded. One must avoid irritating these wounds by touching them." At the New Year of 1835 the Emperor met his Chancellor's good wishes with the words : "I stand once more like a penitent sinner before you, but the year 1835 shall not pass without my debt being paid." But two months later Francis died, and the strange and abnormal situation which arose under his successor put an end, as we shall see, to all hope of reform.

The Forerunners of the Czech Revival

It is against this background that the first champions of Czech national feeling stand out. The obstacles to free thought, and indeed any kind of intellectual effort, were not confined to the Czechs. The contrast between the enforced stagnation in Vienna (partially obscured by glorious exceptions in the world of music) and the luxuriant blossoming of German literature and of scientific research in every sphere, and in particular in history and criticism, can hardly be exaggerated. Meanwhile the rich literary output of the Hungarian renaissance was also driven into the background ; there was complete political stagnation, and Francis continued to avoid summoning Parliament from 1811 till 1825. If this was possible in a country where national consciousness was as strong as in Hungary and where the county assemblies and administration, for centuries the bulwark of the national cause, were still in being, it is not surprising that the revival in the Czech lands, and still more among the Slovaks, should have followed very modest lines.

Reflection, will however, show that it was no mere accident that the Czech revival owed its inception and directive above all to the scholar and thinker, to men of whose very existence the political authorities of their day were almost unconscious. For this is a current running right through the history of the Czechs, from Hus the '*poor persone*' and University professor, Comenius, the educational pioneer, Dobrovský, the pure savant Palacký the historian, and in our own day that triumvirate of scholars, Masaryk, Beneš and Štefánik, who achieved Czechoslovak independence. For the period of Metternich, then, it will be well for us to concentrate upon five or six truly representative figures who laid the foundations of a new age.

Five Pioneers : (1) *Joseph Dobrovský*

First in order stands Joseph Dobrovský (1753–1829), who was born of Czech parents in Hungary and was preparing himself for the Jesuit Order when it was abolished. His whole career is in itself an illustration of the changed circumstances of his day ; the new movement is no longer even primarily in the religious sphere, though the Hussite tradition is of course always a contributing factor. It is above all intellectual, with a strongly ethical basis. Dobrovský, the pupil of the Jesuits, retains his orders but never holds any priestly office ; he is not merely imbued with rationalist and philosophic ideas, but he becomes a Freemason. As a young man he spent eleven years as tutor to the family of Count Nostic, and indeed to their generous patronage, and to that of the Sternbergs in particular, he owed the possibility of a life of quiet and fruitful research and of occasional pilgrimages to the libraries and museums of Europe. He soon became one of the chief ornaments of the Royal Bohemian Society and of the Bohemian Museum Society, which was founded in 1818 and after a short-lived interval founded the first scientific Czech periodical, the *Časopis Musea*. Though he himself wrote mainly in German and Latin, he did priceless service to the cause of Czech linguistic purity, for just at the most crucial period of the reshaping and modernizing of a language suffering from centuries of misuse and neglect, he set stringent standards and rejected the reckless and amateur methods which some of his contemporaries were only too ready to accept. His detailed Czech Grammar (*Ausführliches Lehrgebäude*) and his *History of the Czech Language* (*Geschichte der böhmischen Sprache und aeltern Literatur*)[1] were pioneer works of the utmost importance, while his *Institutiones Linguæ Slavicæ Veteris* entitle him to be regarded as the real founder of Slavonic philological studies, with all their implications, political no less than scientific and ecclesiastical, for all Slav countries, not excluding Russia. A specially qualified centenary writer, Miloš Weingart, has said of the *Institutiones* : 'This is not merely a grammar of Church Slavonic, as is sometimes asserted. The age of Cyril and Methodius, the glorious dawn of Slavonic civilization, had been his favourite study from his earliest years. . . .

[1] First published in 1792, and in a completely revised form in 1818.

He was concerned with working out the whole of the linguistic facts of literary Church Slavonic, as used from the ninth to the eighteenth centuries by the Russians, Serbs, Bulgars, Glagolitic Dalmatians and later the Uniates, and regarded the language as a mark of civilization common to the great majority of all the Slavs.' His was an eminently sober and critical spirit, and he refused to be led away, like some of his colleagues and pupils, by legendary fancies or even bogus documents. Before Palacký had even begun to write, and while the spirit of the Counter-Reformation was still predominant, this free-thinking ex-Jesuit had coined the phrase : 'We must blush at a past in which there was such misuse of religion.' It is not surprising that his reputation stood higher a century later than in his own lifetime, and he left worthy pupils behind him—not least of all the young Slovene scholar Kopitar, whose learned studies lie at the root of the Slovene national revival.

(2) *Joseph Jungmann*

Scarcely less vital in the early stages of the revival was Joseph Jungmann (1773-1847), who first made a certain name for himself by a long series of translations into Czech. The very fact that as early as 1811 he had translated Milton's *Paradise Lost* is a sign that the dry bones were moving. He also translated Gray's *Elegy*, many poems of Goethe and Schiller, and Chateaubriand's *Atala*. But what has given him a permanent place in the affections of every Czech patriot are his *History of Czech Literature*, published in 1825 in Czech—not in German, like Dobrovský's —and his Czech Dictionary, great as an achievement and still greater in bulk. Of these two the former was in some respects more of an encyclopædia than a history ; it was diffuse and none too critical, making inclusion rather than selection the almost invariable rule. But a century later it is still regarded as an indispensable handbook by all serious students of Czech origins. The application of the inclusive method was, of course, not open to the same criticism in the case of the Dictionary, which appeared in five large volumes of 4,500 pages in all, between 1835 and 1839, after labours of almost forty years. When it is realized that much of the material on which he relied was only available in manuscript, or difficult of access in uncatalogued and neglected libraries, his achievement is little less than marvellous, the more so since he was continually subject to interference from the censorship. 'We must touch neither Eros nor politics ; such are the orders and commands of the Censor,' he wrote to Kollár, when the latter asked for help to publish his poetry. 'They treat even the word "Slav" with the greatest suspicion at the censorship, and Palacký has made it a rule to mention the Slavs as little as possible in the Journal of the Museum. . . . They only gave permission to print an ancient Czech chronicle on condition that it should be printed in Latin characters and published at a high price, so that it may come into few hands. . . .' With all his necessary caution, Jungmann was an ardent patriot, and more prone to daydreams than the sober Dobrovský. He was even ready to accept a common Slav language, engulfing Czech and, possessed of a common orthography. The forgotten writings of Križanić, the Dalmatian Croat priest who visited the Court of Tsar Alexis in the seventeenth century, and pleaded the cause of a common Slav language, had just been resuscitated in Russia, and were engaging literary opinion. 'Why should community of language,' wrote Jungmann on this theme, 'which does not involve the political unity of the Germans, involve that of the Slavs?' Panslavism, before whose apparition they tremble, or pretend to tremble, is the invention of a blind hate which takes pride in its Pangermanism. . . . They want to keep us isolated, in order to weigh us down under an eternal slavery.'

Jungmann, says Ernest Denis, provided future Czech writers with 'the elements of their success.' First had come the regenerators of the language, bearing the instruments for its use ; there soon followed the men capable of employing them with full effect. After philology came literature, and in particular Kollár, Šafařik and Palacký, whom Jungmann in 1821 had called 'my most beloved Trinity.'

(3) Jan Kollár

Jan Kollár (1793–1852) was the first poet of any real eminence whom the Czech revival had produced, and though a Slovak, wrote in Czech. He was a student at Jena at the moment when that University was in the forefront of the German patriotic movement, and was afterwards for thirty years pastor of the Slovak Lutheran Church in Budapest. As early as 1824 he electrified the whole Slav world by his publication of the first three cantos of *Slavy Dcera* (The Daughter of Slava), containing 150 sonnets, to which were added in 1832 two more cantos, bringing the whole poem up to a total of 622 sonnets. The daughter of Slava is a maiden whom the poet meets on the banks of that once Slav stream, the Thuringian Saale (Zala), and to whom he dedicates his heart. Severed from her by cruel fate, he wanders disconsolately through the regions of the Elbe (Labe), the Rhine and the Moldau (Vltava), and at length, beside the Danube, he learns of her death. This very slender erotic thread is very skilfully used to link up the great memories and departed glories of the Slav race ; and the two additional cantos are a crude attempt to create, on the banks of the mythical Lethe and Acheron, a Slav Valhalla and a Slav Hades, where the heroes of the Slav race, and their foremost friends and enemies, received the reward or punishment of their respective attitudes towards the cause of Slavdom. There is a certain incongruity in the fact that the real heroine who inspired his lay was a certain Wilhelmina (Mina) Schmidt, the daughter of a German Lutheran pastor near Jena, whose family (or so Kollár at least persuaded himself) came from the once purely Slav, but now very largely Germanized, province of Lusatia, and whom he made his wife after waiting a good deal longer than Jacob did for Rachel.

The poem is an ecstatic address to Liberty. 'The despot is endured until the feeling for freedom becomes general ; but then the slave breaks his chains and the despot must fall.' In Hungary, the Slav is bidden to bury his language, but 'who forged this law ? Men : and shall they weigh more than God ?' 'Concord and culture' alone are lacking to the Slavs ; with them 'we should excel all the peoples of the past. Twixt Greek and Briton our name too would shine and lighten all the firmament.' 'Scattered Slavs,' he cries, 'let us be a united whole, and no longer mere fragments. Let us be all or naught !' Were the disunited Slavs but precious metals, he would mould them into a mighty statue : Russia would form the head, the Poles should be the body, the Czechs the arms, and hands, the Serbs the legs and feet ; of the smaller races he would forge armour and weapons. 'All Europe would kneel before this idol, whose head would tower above the clouds, and whose feet would shake the earth.' For a hundred years hence what would be the fate of the Slavs, and what the fate of Europe ? 'Everywhere Slavdom like a flood extends its boundaries ; and the language which the false ideas of the Germans held for a mere speech of slaves, shall resound in palaces and even in the mouths of its rivals. In Slav channels the sciences shall flow, our people's dress, their manners and their song shall be in vogue on the Seine and on the Elbe. O that I was not born in that great age of Slav dominion, or that I may not arise from the grave to witness it !'

The later cantos are markedly inferior. In Valhalla the goddess Slava on her golden throne welcomes Slav champions and noted foreign friends of the Slavs—notably Herder, Grimm, Goethe and Sir John Bowring (the indefatigable but wooden translator of Slavonic verse). But in Hades one crudity follows the other. Henry the Lion, Charles the Great, Arpad and other medieval opponents of the Slavs are seen swimming in a sea of burning pitch. Koniaš, the Jesuit destroyer of Hussite books, is himself roasted on a pile of books. Basil 'Slayer of the Bulgars' has to do penance by beating his head against the rocks. Dugonics, a zealous advocate of Magyarization, and himself a renegade Slav, is plagued by swarms of hornets, flies and lice. The inventor of the Magyar proverb, 'The Slovak is no man' (tót nem ember) is impaled, though Kollár has the grace to beg for his release. And as the poet and his divine guide leave Hades they meet a group of writers tilting at the Panslav windmill —John Paget (the author of an admirable book of Hungarian travel) as Don Quixote on Rosinante, and the long since forgotten Julia Purdoe, covered with gold and snuffing tobacco. The whole poem ends with a phrase : 'From the Tatra to the Black Mountain, from the Giant Mountains to the Urals, resound the words, "Hell for the traitors, Heaven for the true Slavs !" '

The 'Daughter of Slava' had been one of the major literary sensations of its day ; scarcely less sensation was caused by a small book entitled *Concerning Literary Reciprocity between the various races and dialects of the Slav Nation.* Written with all the preacher's accustomed fire, it became a focus of violent controversy, especially in Hungary, and received far more attention than it deserved. The Slav nation, he argues, 'is striving to return to its original unity,' and a common bond of a 'literary and intellectual character' is needed. Literary reciprocity does not involve demagogy or revolution ; it is possible even when a nation is divided under different states and monarchs, and where there are differences of religion, script or customs. It is not, however, enough to speak only one's own tongue ; every Slav ought to know the kindred Slav languages and take an interest in everything Slavonic. 'The Slavs have gradually come to realize that after all they are but one nation and have but one language ; they have counted their numbers, and so discovered that they are the most numerous in Europe.' In passing he makes the apposite point that the Slovaks, forming 'the central point of all Slav dialects . . . had hitherto almost nothing of their own in literature, and therefore were the first to stretch out their hands to embrace all Slavs.' 'It is not only a natural instinct and natural right, but also a duty of reason for every nation, that it should seek to maintain its existence in a just manner, to develop its innate forces according to its position among mankind, to give public expression to its manner of life.' Here speaks the Slovak who sees his nationality threatened by Magyarization.

Slav literature, however, in its regenerated form, will not blot out other literatures, or Slavize them, but will infuse their romanticism with humanitarian elements. The long sleep of the Slavs does not affect the question. 'It is true that we came somewhat late, but so much the younger are we.' This brings Kollár to definite proposals for a common alphabet for all Slavs, and the advantages and drawbacks of such an idea. He suggests dividing Slavonic into seven branches : (1) Old Slavonic (the liturgical language) ; (2) Ancient fragments ; (3) Russian ; (4) Illyrian ; (5) Polish ; (6) Czech ; (7) Folksongs, tales, proverbs, etc. 'Whatever is Slav is ours, wherever it may be.' The political result would be that Slav risings and revolts against rulers who belong to other peoples will come to an end ; for with this reciprocity the longing for union with other Slavs will cease, or at any rate be greatly weakened. 'They will have no reason for breaking away, and everyone will remain at home, because he will have at home the same as he would receive at his neighbour's house. Indeed, the weaker Slav races find under foreign non-Slav rulers, if only these latter are tolerant, more guarantees of security for their special position and the survival of their dialect, which under the rule of another more powerful dialect might, according to the laws of attraction, be completely swallowed up, or at least might be fused in it and so disappear. Even the Governments which are concerned with the culture of their peoples will not merely not block and repress this innocent and beneficent reciprocity, but will far rather give it wise encouragement and fatherly support.'

Kollár held grimly to his exposed post in Budapest, amid the growing vituperation of all Magyar circles ; in the Revolution of 1848 his life was in danger, and he took refuge not in Russia, but in Vienna, to which his colleagues, Štúr, Hurban and Hodža, also turned in their distress (see p. 187). In 1849 he was appointed—as a reward for Slovak loyalty to the dynasty—Professor of Slavonic Archæology at Vienna University, but died only two years later. He was entirely unsuited to such a post, and would not have increased his fame if he had lived longer. The acid Havlíček somewhat cruelly remarked of Kollár that he was a philologist or archæologist in his poems, and a poet in his philology and archæology ! But his poetry was in these early stages of the revival little less than a Bible for all the submerged Slavonic nations, and his insistence on the essential affinity of Czech and Slovak was one of the decisive facts in the movement for Czechoslovak Unity.

(4) *Šafařik*

Another Slovak, Paul Joseph Šafařik (1795–1861), also belongs to the innermost group of forerunners. Born as the son of a Slovak Lutheran pastor, he too studied at Jena University, and on his return became tutor to a noble family at Bratislava. The friendship which he here formed with the youthful Palacký was one of the decisive influences of his life. In 1819 he was appointed director of the new Serb Orthodox Gymnasium of Novi Sad (Újvidék, Neusatz), the centre of Serbian culture in the Bačka, the rich province of Southern Hungary then still bordering upon the Ottoman Empire. He first attracted attention by his German *Geschichte der slavischen Sprache und Literatur*—published in Ofen-Pest in 1826—which starts from the same premises as those of Kollár and assumes the essential unity of all the Slav tongues. It is characteristic of the primitive state of such studies only a century ago that this book should altogether omit Bulgarian from the ranks of Slavonic languages, though including two distinct dialects of Lusatian Sorb.

Šafařik was not happy in Novi Sad, between the growing chauvinism of the Magyars and the none too tolerant attitude of the Serbs, who removed him from the Directorship because he was a Protestant ; and in 1832, with the more than modest help of Czech sympathizers, he was able to transfer himself to Prague, where despite chronic financial difficulties, he found a congenial field for his archæological and other studies. His great achievement, on which his chief claim to fame rests, was a book entitled *Slav Antiquities* (published in Czech in 1837, in a revised German form in 1843). It has, of course, been superseded or supplemented in many directions, for it resembled an ancestral plough applied to virgin soil, and was the first to lay bare hitherto unsuspected strata. But it had an almost revolutionary effect in its day, stimulating the dawning interest in the racial origins, the early history and culture of the Slav peoples. In Russia in particular, Šafařik may be regarded as the founder of a whole school of scientific writers, whose work had a very direct political bearing upon the whole development of the Slav world. His special acquaintance with the Southern Slavs was an important contributory factor to the close friendship which grew up between them and Prague. He was too much of a pure savant to play an active part in politics, but his influence in the background was deep and permanent. His attitude may be summed up in one phrase of a letter to Palacký : 'If we die, like our fathers, without gaining anything, we shall have died for an idea, and it is the glorious mark of Man that he knows how to die for an idea.'

(5) *Palacký*

The fifth and greatest of the men whose names are generally accepted as the forerunners of a new age was František Palacký (1798-1876), not merely the first really great historian whom the Czechs had produced, but one who restored to the nation its buried past and sounded a veritable clarion call for the future. It was hardly an accident that Palacký was born in a Moravian village near Přerov, where the traditions of the Brethren had never wholly died out and of one of those families which had pursued its Hussite faith in secret through the long period of persecution. His parents were among those who availed themselves of Joseph's Edict of Tolerance in 1784. In 1812 he was sent to the Protestant Lycée at Pressburg (Bratislava), and the years which he spent there were a further formative influence upon him and left him with a deep sympathy for the oppressed Slovaks and a knowledge of their conditions not shared by many contemporary Czechs.

It is generally assumed that his inspiration as a historian came from Germany and from the little band of Czech and Slovak scholars who had studied in Jena ; but it has been quite clearly established that William Robertson, Gibbon, Bolingbroke's Essays and Blair's once famous *Lectures on Rhetoric* were among his special favourites. After some years of tutoring the budding historian went to Prague, attracted the attention of Dobrovský, was introduced by him to Count Francis Sternberg, and was entrusted with the charge of his family archives. Thanks to Francis Sternberg and his brother Kašpar he made the acquaintance of the small group of enlightened Bohemian aristocrats who were responsible for the foundation of the Bohemian Museum, and his association with them spelt leisure for historic research, access to all-important private libraries, and immunity from the attentions of the Censor. In 1827 he was made editor of the Czech edition of the *Museum Journal*, which for many decades was to remain the intellectual focus of the reviving nation. Two years later the Diet conferred upon him the honorary title of 'Historian of the Bohemian Estates,' and he was enabled to extend his studies by visits to foreign archives. For twenty years he worked at his great *History of Bohemia*, the first volume of which appeared in 1836 and three more before 1848. The tenth and final volume was not published until 1865, by which time he had decided not to bring the narrative beyond the accession of the House of Habsburg in 1526. He had never intended to go beyond the fall of independence in 1620 ; knowing well the obstacles opposed to his researches in the Hussite period, he had assumed that a guilty conscience on the part of the authorities would hedge off from him the documents of the absolutist period. He lived to see Austria transformed and modernized and to contribute materially to the process ; but by that time he was too much absorbed in public affairs to attempt a continuation.

The *History of Bohemia* was Palacký's real life-work and made him the father of his people ; it was this achievement, whose full value can only be realized in the setting of an enslaved nation, a long-neglected language, a hostile Church and a denationalized middle class, that thrust upon him, with that suddenness which revolutions evoke, the political leadership of a new epoch. But this final stage of his career belongs to a later chapter.

To a foreign reader, especially at the distance of a century, there is nothing very thrilling about Palacký's writings. Denis is fully entitled to contrast his absence of rhetoric with the prophecies of Michelet, the picturesque anecdotes of Thierry or the philosophic comments of Guizot. 'His clear and ample narrative unfolds itself with attractive simplicity ; the reader, steeped in an atmosphere of moral probity and serene confidence, is gradually transported to a region inaccessible to storms and overcome by a mysterious calm, made up of reverence for the dead, disdain for injustice, confidence in the future.' The tone is perhaps pitched too high, but it must never be forgotten that what Palacký did for the Czechs was little short of a revolution. He brought them back to life, gave them courage and belief in a forgotten or despised past, and proved to them that they had achievements in the moral and intellectual sphere of which any nation might be proud, and the restraint with which he wrote only served to heighten the effect upon his contemporaries. Built up without much controversial argument, and seeming to pursue Ranke's object of discovering 'how it really was,' Palacký's *History* creates step by step in its reader a philosophy of Czech history and never lets him stray far from the ideals to which he himself pinned his faith as a historian. The two guiding threads—the racial conflict between Czech and German, the spiritual conflict between Rome and the Reformation—are shown at every stage to be closely interwoven. In the words of Dr. Werstadt : 'Palacký wrote his *History* and conceived his philosophy of it as an adherent of a well-defined national religious, philosophical and political faith. Czech nationalism, enriched and hallowed by the ideals of humanity, justice and rectitude, wholly engrossed the great historian's reflections on the history of his country.' And it may be added that the real measure of his greatness is to compare the state of historical study in Bohemia when he found it, and when he left it, and to note the extent to which he kindled criticism and patriotism together, never allowing the latter to obscure the former.

Thus the philologist, the grammarian, the poet, the archæologist and the historian combined to lay the foundations upon which the Czecho-slovak Republic was to rest, and completion of which was to be the work of a philosopher, a political economist and an astronomer.

Lesser Lights

We have already noted the importance of the Royal Bohemian Society and of the Museum Society in the early days of the revival. In 1831 a third institution was set up which catered for a wider public than the other two, but to which Jungmann, Palacký, and Šafařik after they had brought him to Prague, supplied the driving force. This was the Matice Česká, modelled upon the modest Matica Srpska which had come to birth at Novi Sad in 1826, and devoted to the publication of Czech classics long inaccessible to the Czech public, of standard translations and of new works of merit for which a subsidy was needed.

If Kollár was the Czech poet *par excellence* of the high romantic period, he none the less did not stand alone, and it would be unpardonable to omit the names of F. L. Čelakovsky, (1799–1852), that indefatigable translator of folk-songs from every Slav tongue, and imitator of Russian and Czech romantic poetry, and of K. H. Macha (1810–1836), whose tragic muse, cut off at the early age of twenty-six, is more highly appreciated now than in his own day. Macha's poem, *May*, is not without a certain morbid quality, and has earned him the all too obvious comparisons with Byron or Lermontov; but critics are generally agreed as to its high originality of *timbre* and *motif*.

There is another name which was generally added by contemporaries to the list of forerunners, but which now stands deservedly under a cloud. Wenceslas Hanka (1791–1861) was a zealous collector of Czech popular poetry, and author of numerous translations of poetry. Though essentially hostile to everything German and an almost slavish adulator of Russia (he actually wanted to introduce the Cyrillic alphabet among the Western Slavs), he drew his first inspiration from Herder's *Lieder der Völker*, and so perhaps in turn from Herder's master in this field, Bishop Percy. He was, moreover, most active at the very moment when Brentano and Grimm were making their unique contributions to folk-lore, and when the greatest of all such explorers, Vuk Karadžić, was digging in the rich soil of Serbian songs and ballads. In 1817 Hanka made known a MS. of ancient Czech poems, which he claimed to have discovered in a church tower of Kralové Dvůr (Königinhof) in Northern Bohemia. Only when he had convinced the sceptical Dobrovský of its authenticity did he give it to the world, and this contributed to the profound sensation which it aroused and led to its complete acceptance by such men as Palacký and Šafařik. Encouraged by his initial success, Hanka and one of his friends unearthed a second MS., this time at the castle of Zelená Hora (Grünberg) in Southern Bohemia. This time Dobrovský was suspicious, and controversy soon began to rage. But for the greater part of the nineteenth century belief in the authenticity of both manuscripts became an article of faith for many Czech patriots. Some excuse for the tenacity with which this belief was upheld may perhaps be found in the importance of the issues involved; for Czech would then have been seen to possess some o the earliest epics and lyrics in all European literature, and the whole focus of Czech literary history would have been altered. The quarrel lasted till well into this century, and indeed there was a certain relapse among a group of chauvinists under the Republic. But in the end overwhelming proofs of forgery were produced by the second generation of Palacký's historical students, and in particular Goll, Gebauer and Masaryk. It was not the least enormity of Masaryk the idealist, in the early stages of his career, that he should have preferred to destroy an accepted legend rather than base national recovery upon a lie.

One name must still be added to this brief sketch—Bernhard Bolzano (1781–1848), a Catholic priest and professor of religious philosophy at the University of Prague in the second decade of the nineteenth century. He was a close friend, and in some degree pupil, of Dobrovský, inheriting from him the rationalist tradition of Leibniz, exercising a remarkable influence upon the younger generation, and always bent upon proving a complete harmony between reason and Catholic theology. This did not suit the Papacy in the Restoration period, and in 1820 Bolzano was expelled from his Chair, suspended by Rome, and left to twenty years of obscure and patient literary studies. Writing only German himself, he urged Czechs and Germans in his native Bohemia to learn each other's language and thus establish a united people on a basis of equality and mutual esteem. His direct influence is difficult to gauge, but when he died in the year of Revolution no other than Havlíček declared that 'the Liberal movement in Bohemia is in great part the fruit of the seed which he scattered.'

Metternich and Kolovrat

Not content with blocking all progress during a reign of forty-six years, Francis committed the supreme blunder of leaving the Crown to his weak-minded and epileptic son Ferdinand—'Dottled Ferdy' (Nandl der Trottel) as he was familiarly nicknamed in Vienna. Francis deliber-ately passed over his three really brilliant and enlightened brothers, Charles, John and Joseph, and selected the one who had the least energy and fewest ideas. The supreme control was thus vested in an ill-assorted triumvirate, the Archduke Louis, Prince Metternich and Count Kolovrat. In practice, Louis could only maintain himself by playing off Kolovrat and Metternich against each other, and as neither was strong enough to gain the upper hand there was a complete deadlock, and all initiative became impossible. Metternich himself accurately diagnosed the disease of which Austria was dying, as a 'failure to govern on the part of those called to govern,' and the ablest of all her bureaucrats, Baron Kübeck, put on record after his first audience with the new Emperor : 'We now have an absolute monarchy without a monarch. The principle of Legi-timacy could not have been more terribly attacked than by this foolish adaptation of it.' Metternich continued at intervals to press for reform ; in 1843 his wife records in her diary : 'Clement plays the role of Jeremiah, and no one listens to him.' But he was not prepared to push matters to the length of resignation, being naturally enough reluctant to relax his hold upon European policy after so many years ; and so the internal situation steadily deteriorated.

In 1851, after the great upheaval was over, the young Francis Joseph's mother, Archduchess Sophie, in conversation with Princess Metternich, openly reproached her husband for 'willing an impossibility'

—to conduct the Monarchy without an emperor, and with an idiot (Trottel) as representative of the Crown.' Melanie in her biting way retorted with the inquiry, what possible substitute there had been—thereby implying that Sophie's own husband, Francis Charles, was little better than his brother Ferdinand.[1]

It would be easy to multiply such anecdotes in order to show that the 'state atrophy' already apparent during the Napoleonic wars had in the 'forties assumed proportions such as filled even the most responsible of Austria's rulers with grave alarm. Specially remarkable symptoms of this attitude are to be found in the diaries of Baron Kübeck, which only saw the light in 1909, the autobiographical fragments of the poet Grillparzer, and the essay which Metternich's friend Count Hartig published shortly after the event, on 'The Genesis of the Austrian Revolution.' The disquietude prevailing at the time was voiced in an anonymous book entitled *Austria and her Future*, published at Hamburg in 1840, but soon discussed in every *salon* of Vienna. Its author, Baron Andrian, an aristocrat of liberal leanings and actually an official of the *Hofkanzlei*, continued to keep the secret of its authorship for a very long time. It was a grave and detailed indictment of the whole bureaucratic machine, and of centralization as 'the pest of the century.' He only wrote what everyone was saying, and did not hesitate to treat Austria as surrounded by a Chinese Wall or to compare it to a corpse buried in the ashes of Pompei, unable to bear the slightest contact with sun or wind or air. The choice before Austria, he argued, was peaceful and gradual change, or an abrupt revolution.

The most ominous symptom of disease in the body politic was the growth of an opposition in the 'forties in what had hitherto, quite rightly, been regarded as two strongholds of Toryism and reaction—the Estates of Lower Austria and Bohemia. For two centuries the latter, in particular, had been deprived of all real power ; for a brief moment in 1791 it had woken from its slumbers and then had gone to sleep again for four decades. In 1842 it began to press for a reform of taxation, and sent a deputation to Vienna, which saw the shadow Emperor and was received somewhat cavalierly by Metternich. A committee was appointed to discuss matters with them, but anything in the nature of *desideria* was rejected. Count Joseph Thun handed in a memorial on the constitutional rights of Bohemia, which was very long-winded, and was laid aside, but which at least marked the beginning of a new stage in the relation of Crown and Estates. On the return of the delegation to Prague, a committee was even formed for the assertion of the rights of the Estates ; it enjoyed little sympathy among the general public, whether Czech or German, but it was a sign that the whole bog was beginning to move.

Metternich's attitude was doubtless partly determined by his rivalry with Kolovrat, who regarded himself as a Czech and always showed a soft side for Czech petitions or interests, and was familiarly known as '*der Böhm' der Böhmen*' (the super-Czech). With him, to quote Viktor Bibl : 'the aristocratic Czech Fronde gained entrance even to the Imperial Court.' Kolovrat has left on record his sense of 'the intolerable vanity' of Metternich, 'who in all his life has never been wrong, has foreseen

---

[1] It may amuse the reader to have the comment of Metternich upon the Czech revival. "Czechism," he once said, "is a tendency which, if things take their ordinary course, only lead to small aberrations, but in an epoch of general excitement works like bean-salad in a cholera epidemic." (1843.)

everything and still foresees everything that happened and didn't happen. In a word, I can't get on with him.' And Metternich returned the compliment by writing of Kolovrat as one of 'those people who think they are leading when they are led' and are 'born to be the instrument, but not the hand.' Francis once confided to Metternich the view that if he only had such servants as Count Kolovrat, he would presumably not be in a position to preserve the Austrian State. But none the less he kept him in office and left him as a fatal brake upon Metternich after he himself was gone.

The Influence of Hungary

The ferment in the Estates was unquestionably stimulated by the events of 1846 in Galicia, in many districts of which the peasantry rose against its lords and caused a temporary panic, which was increased by the suspicion that Vienna was backing the Ruthenes against the Poles. But there was another far stronger influence which cannot be ignored, if the background of the Bohemian picture before 1848 is to be understood. For over twenty years Hungary had been in constantly growing fermentation. Francis had managed to dispense with the parliamentary regime from 1811 to 1825 ; but from this latter date the constitutional movement became irresistible, the more so as it ran parallel with a strong literary revival, led by a whole galaxy of brilliant poets and dramatists, outshining all the neighbouring races. The year 1830 saw the establishment of the Hungarian Academy of Sciences, its lack of funds having been overcome in dramatic fashion when Count Stephen Széchényi ('the greatest Magyar,' as his admiring compatriots still call him) rose from his seat in the Diet and offered for this cause his whole income for the year, and when his example was immediately followed by a number of other magnates. In the same year a knowledge of Magyar was made obligatory for all persons holding any public office or an advocate's diploma. In 1835 its use was extended to the law courts, though still as an alternative to Latin, while Magyar was made an optional language for all official documents and obligatory for the register in all parishes where Magyar services were held. In 1839 the Addresses to the Throne were for the first time drawn up in the Magyar language, and in the following year a law was passed by which Magyar superseded Latin as the official language of the Government and of Parliament. Its knowledge was enjoined upon the clergy of all denominations, while all registers were to become exclusively Magyar after a lapse of three more years. Finally, in 1843, Magyar was proclaimed as the exclusive language of the legislature, the Government and official business, and also of public instruction, though this latter innovation was left to be dealt with by a special law. By this time, under the demagogic leadership of Louis Kossuth, the Magyar national movement had kindled the alarm and opposition of all the non-Magyar nationalities, and the constitutional issue had been fatally confused with designs of wholesale and speedy Magyarization. This aspect will have to be treated in greater detail in the chapter relating to the Slovaks ; for the moment it will suffice to indicate that the gathering impetus of the Magyar movement and its increasingly hostile attitude to the Slovaks served as a double incentive to the Czechs.

In this connection reference may most suitably be made to two polemical works by a man who was destined to play a leading role in the reactionary regime of the late forties and the fifties, Count Leo Thun.

The first, entitled 'On the present state of Bohemian Literature and its Importance,' began with a sympathetic survey of the Czech revival, laying special stress on the merits of Dobrovský and Jungmann, and claiming that the new literature 'is winning year by year more practical validity.' He went on to challenge the various arguments in favour of the Germanization of Bohemia, claiming that if the language had survived two centuries of the most unfavourable circumstances imaginable, it would be utterly impossible to suppress it under the greatly altered circumstances of the day. He referred to the influence of the Czech revival upon the Illyrian movement under Gaj ; but declined to take seriously the myth of a 'Slav Universal Monarchy' or the danger of Russian domination of the Western Slav nations. 'The power of a state rests upon the development of the spiritual forces of its peoples; for the spiritual development of the Bohemian people a Slav national feeling and the revival of the Czech language is a necessary, indispensable means ; and this is why we believe that this event (sic), so far from endangering the Austrian Monarchy, would increase its strength.' The letter ended with an appeal to all his fellow-citizens to discard their suspicions or contempt for the Czech language, and thus to contribute towards a strengthening of the Monarchy and 'even the solution of European problems.'

Count Thun sent a copy of his book to the Magyar publicist, Francis Pulszky, who afterwards became Kossuth's secretary in exile, and from this there resulted a polemical exchange of letters, which in 1843 was published in pamphlet form, in German and Czech. From the first word Pulszky struck an aggressive note. 'The Czech language,' he wrote, 'has in Hungary no future, and much as I value the talent of a Kollár, I still think that if in a Slav of Hungary the feeling of his Czech origin awakes and develops into hostility towards the Hungarian language, then there is nothing left for him but to emigrate with Palacký and Šafařik to a place where his aspirations are recognized, and his spiritual activity finds a wider and less unfruitful field than in Hungary.'

Thun hereupon put the fundamental question, whether Pulszky would allow the Slavs of Hungary to feel as Slavs, and to be imbued with this feeling in their moral and cultural development, 'just like the Magyars.' He denied the Russian orientation of the Slovaks, and even accepted the idea of Magyar as the 'common language' of Hungary, but not, of course, the view so widely upheld at this time, of Magyar as the 'national language' par excellence. The Czechs, he argued, could not abandon the Slovaks ; 'the national contact with the Slovaks contributes to promoting our own intellectual life. . . . We need them just as much as they need us.'

But Pulszky was by now quite uncompromising ; he retorts as 'patriot, not cosmopolite' : 'Hungary, which is certain of a great future, would, if peopled by some other race than the Magyars, be of complete indifference to me.' Hungary was not likely to confer political rights on 'enemies of the Hungarian name, since hollow philanthropic phrases will hardly let us forget our weak and isolated position in Europe.' 'We do not ask more from the Slavs than the English from the Celtic inhabitants of Wales and Scotland, or the French from Brittany and Alsace. We wish all public documents in Hungary . . . to be in Magyar, and the language of instruction to be Magyar—in a word, that Magyar should in every respect step into the rights of Latin, while the Slav language may content itself with such rights as it formerly possessed. But into the household circle the Magyar language will never *forcibly* enter. But that this too will gradually be Magyarized as culture spreads is natural enough . . . and Magyar will find its way without any compulsion into every family.' The crudity of Pulszky's attitude rendered a rejoinder wellnigh superfluous, but Thun, after exhorting the Slovaks to moderation and a purely defensive line, and denouncing the hypocrisy of the Magyars in refusing permission for a Slovak newspaper at Pressburg and in the same breath scoffing at the Slovaks for their lack of journals, ended with the blunt warning that 'the language quarrel in Hungary is not merely a Hungarian affair.' With this brief duel, whose clash echoed through the whole Slav world and was not without its reactions in Germany, the relations of Czech and Slovak may be said to have entered their modern phase.

Karel Havlíček

On the eve of the great upheaval of 1848 a sixth figure must be added to the small gallery of Czech forerunners. Karel Havlíček (1820–1856) stands in perspective as the true founder of Czech democracy; but like his spiritual disciple, Thomas Masaryk, a generation later, he had a hatred for demagogic methods and a firm belief in political realism—the need for shaping political programmes and aims according to the practical possibilities of the moment. As a youth he paid a pilgrimage to Russia, with his head crammed full of Slav romanticism, but a residence of two years cured him effectually of any such ideas. But he found it difficult to breathe in the 'political limbo' of Austria, and his soul revolted against the censorship and its accomplice the Roman hierarchy. His satirical talent found vent in *The Baptism of St. Vladimir*, but his chief work was in the field of journalism. He hit upon the ingenious device of utilizing the Irish question as a subject of articles and information, leaving his public to read between the lines and to translate the lessons of Ireland and Repeal and O'Connell into terms of Bohemia and national recovery and Liberal reforms. When the censorship was removed in 1848 he at once founded his own paper, *Národné Noviný*, which ran till January, 1850; his last vent-hole was removed with the suppression of *Slovan* in August, 1851. He was deported to Innsbruck, was not allowed to return home to see his dying wife, and was only released when himself at the point of death. His *Epistles from Kutná Hora*, so called from the scene of his trial, were rigorously suppressed, and the taboo upon them was not lifted for forty years.[1] But the leaven worked unseen, and his name and teaching remained an inspiration to a new generation of torch-bearers.

A sure instinct made Havlíček lay his main emphasis upon education, and self-help; 'One cannot,' he said, 'repair in two or three years the evil of several centuries.' But above all he was a Realist; he realized that the Czechs could not as yet hope to stand alone, and that all-too-radical theories might drive them to utter ruin; he was therefore ready to accept Austria, if she could only be reconstructed on federal and liberal lines. He never could accept the posture of passive adoration before Moscow, as adopted by some later Slavophiles of his nation. 'In our desire to be good Slavs,' he said, 'we must first and foremost seek the good of our own nation. Without doubt we are free to wait patiently

---

[1] Masaryk wrote a short critical essay on Havlíček in 1896, and Herben, editor of Masaryk's daily, *Čas*, published an edition of the *Epistles*.

till at a given moment Russia snatches us from our enemies ; it is very convenient, and moderately honourable.   But we can also work for ourselves to develop our nationality, and in thus serving the idea of liberty which Russia does not know, exercise a good influence upon her. . . . I do not contest the reality of Slavia, but it rests on the reality of the various Slav groups.' And again : 'The Slav spirit will only flourish when its individual representatives, notably the Czechs, the Slovaks, the Jugoslavs, the Poles and the Russians, exert themselves separately and with each other in friendly assistance.'

There were, however, times when even the disillusioned Havlíček burst out with the reminder that 'the Slavs of Austria, though only poor flute-players, had a rich cousin who plays the bassoon and who serves as the base of the music of all Europe. . . . We do not deny that light came to us from Germany, especially the torch which set a light to the stake of Hus, and such was the glow of this torch that it sufficed for Žižka to drive across the frontiers a terrible army of the Holy Roman Empire. Then it was the Jesuits' turn to enlighten us, when they burned our books, doubtless in order that from these fruitful ashes Germanic civilization should sprout.'

One further famous passage from Havlíček deserves quotation here : 'Austria will be what we want her to be, or she will cease to be. The bayonets beyond which you hide' (he turned half-consciously to rebuke his masters to their face) 'they are *we*, our people. They do not know it to-day, but to-morrow, in a year, in a few years, they *will* know. Our partisans counted yesterday by hundreds, now they count by thousands, soon they will be millions.' There is a striking resemblance to the words addressed a few years earlier to the Magyars by Ljudevit Gaj, the Croat leader : 'To-day you are in the majority, but the child as it is born is mine !' And events were to reveal both Gaj and Havlíček as true national prophets. Commenting on Havlíček's all too brief career, Ernest Denis wrote : 'The Czechs never despaired of Austria ; on the day when it disappeared, and they were face to face with Germany, they would have as last resource the fate of that mass of Eastern Slavs, which, insensible and sluggish as they may appear, recover and impose their will at decisive moments of history.'

CHAPTER XI

THE REVOLUTION OF 1848

The denial of nationality implies the denial of political liberty.
—Lord Acton.

THE Habsburg Monarchy was already an obvious target for the incendiarist, when the sparks kindled from the February Revolution in Paris caused a series of explosions all over Europe—in Germany and Italy no less than Austria and Hungary. The sceptic and the cynic have always found considerable food for reflection in the fact that reactionary Russia and constitutional Britain were the only two major states which entirely escaped revolution. 1648 had marked the lowest depth, 1848 a noticeable recovery.

To the student of the Czech revival a still more interesting fact is that the outburst came in Prague four days earlier than in Vienna itself, though it also exhausted itself much more quickly. The 'aristocratic Fronde' of the Estates fell speedily into the background. In Prague the little group of radical doctrinaires in the 'Repeal' Club at once took the lead and proclaimed their aims at a meeting in the Wenceslas Baths—freedom of assembly, abolition of the censorship, emancipation of the peasantry, equality of Czech and German before the law, and a number of social reforms. The demand for the restoration of Bohemian autonomy was not as yet formulated quite clearly, though it was proposed that the new Diet for all the lands of St. Wenceslas should meet alternately at Prague and Brno.

A deputation was appointed to present these demands to the Emperor, but before it could do so the situation was completely transformed by the Revolution in Vienna, the fall of Metternich (who had brought upon himself, without entirely meriting it, the role of scapegoat), the promulgation of a new Austrian Constitution and the adoption at Pest of the so-called 'March Laws' which, on paper, changed Hungary overnight from a feudal oligarchy into a parliamentary limited monarchy. Events moved too rapidly to permit proper consultation between Vienna and Prague, and the pace was still further hastened by the action of the German Federal Parliament in Frankfurt, which assumed all Austria to fall within its sphere and launched the catchword, 'Either Austria will be German or she will cease to be.' Side by side with a body whose representative character as regards Germany no one could challenge, the old provincial Estates were obviously inadequate, and fell into instant disrepute ; and the new Premier, Baron Pillersdorff, hastened to promulgate a new Austrian Constitution on April 25, in the fear lest an impatient mob might plunge into Pan-German tendencies. This hurriedly composed document was strongly weighted in a centralist sense, and was in clear conflict with the promises made on April 8, to a second Czech delegation, led this time by Ladislav Rieger, already one of the chief spokesmen of the rising generation. They had been promised that a reformed Diet, with full legislative powers, should meet in Prague, that the Robot should be abolished, and that Czech and German should be placed on an equal footing. A curious situation was already developing, in which the Court, almost equally disquieted by events in Frankfurt and in Budapest, both of which were, from its own point of view, separatist, was inclined to lean on the Slav elements in Austria, and not least on the Czechs. The Government actually invited Palacký to become Minister of Education, but he refused, not so much because of the open hostility of revolutionary Vienna to him and the Czechs generally, as because he was more than ever tied to Prague. For events had brought Palacký at a bound to a position of unquestioned leadership among the Czechs ; and it fell to him to answer the invitation addressed by Frankfurt (the so-called Vor-Parliament, or Preliminary Parliament) to the representatives of Bohemia. His refusal, in courteous but unmistakable terms, is one of the landmarks of Czech history ; Czechs and Germans fell rapidly apart, and in place of the cordial relations of the 'forties, in which writers like Meissner or Hartmann celebrated Žižka or Hus, there is soon open hostility, based on the desire of the Germans to retain the artificial majority which they owed to a narrow franchise, and of the Czechs to regain all the ground lost in two centuries of subjection, and if possible augment it still further. It was a situation such as lent itself to friction, and there was never any lack of agitators on both sides to aggravate the quarrel.

Palacký's reply deserves to be quoted in full, but it must suffice to give the most salient passages. 'I am a Czech of Slav race,' he wrote, 'and with the little that I have and can do, have given myself wholly and for ever to the service of my nation. . . . Its rulers have for centuries had relations with German princes, but it has never regarded itself as German. All the links of Bohemia with the German Empire, and afterwards with the German Bund, were purely dynastic. All the world knows that the German Emperors *as such* had hardly any dealings with the Czech nation, that in Bohemia they possessed neither power nor right to make laws or pass sentences, that they had no right to send armies into the country, and that Bohemia and her lands never counted themselves as one of the ten German Kreise.' Of Austria he wrote that she had misread the true basis of her existence, namely the principle of equal rights for all her peoples. Nature, he argued, knows no ruling and no serving nations ; Metternich fell as the enemy of liberty, but also as the enemy of Slav nationality. At the same time he made abundantly clear his opposition to Russian absolutism and designs of universal monarchy. Austria had a mission equally against Pan-Germanism, Magyarization and Pan-Russianism. 'And if Hungary, following her inclinations, breaks away from the Monarchy, or what is nearly the same thing, becomes the centre of gravity of the Monarchy, will Hungary, who refuses to hear of national equality of rights within her own borders, be able to maintain herself permanently free and strong ? Only the just man is truly free and strong. But there can be no question of a voluntary union, still less of compulsory union, on the part of the Danubian Slavs and Wallachs, or even of the Poles, with a state which lays down the principle that before all one must be a Magyar, and a man only as a secondary consideration.'

The culmination of his whole argument lies in two phrases : 'Vienna is the centre which is competent, and called upon to assure and protect the peace, freedom and right of my people,' and again : 'If Austria did not exist, it would be necessary to create her, in the interests of humanity itself.' Few phrases have been interpreted in so superficial or misleading a sense as this ; we shall soon see that it was a genuine expression of faith in a strong Monarchy and lay at the root of his federalist programme. It was only towards the close of his life, when shaken by many disappointments, that he coined that other prophetic phrase : 'Before Austria was, we were, and when Austria no longer is, we still shall be.'

Meanwhile Vienna was again in ferment ; on May 17, the Emperor and the court fled to Innsbruck, and nine days later there were barricades in the streets, and the weak Pillersdorff Cabinet swayed to and fro at the dictates of the new Committee of Public Security, until early in July it fell with a crash. By this time the Czechs stood quite aloof, and for the moment found common ground with the more conservative groups ; the radical intellectuals were like a quick-growing weed that shrivels at the first test. From the first there was open hostility between the Czechs and the Magyars, and no basis for co-operation when the latter openly linked up with the Viennese revolutionaries against the Court, the Army and the Croats. Count Leo Thun, as Governor of Bohemia, on May 17 issued a decree convoking the Diet of Bohemia as a rival bent on forestalling the central Parliament in Vienna ; and yet another deputation, consisting of Count Nostic and Rieger, was sent to the Emperor, this time urging that Archduke Francis Joseph should be made Governor and set up a government in Prague. On May 29 Thun, arguing that the Government in Vienna was no longer a free agent against mob violence, announced his intention of setting up a Provisional Government for Bohemia. But in putting its veto upon this, Vienna had the backing of the Court in Innsbruck, and the proposed government was stillborn and was never properly constituted.

The Slav Congress in Prague

Palacký and his friends meanwhile devised an impressive counterblast to Frankfurt by convoking in Prague a Congress of all the Slav races of the Monarchy, and inviting guests from the other Slav countries also. From the very outset a whole series of delicate questions arose. A very special effort was made to attract the Poles, with whom its organizers had close relations ; but this offended official Russia, and in the end the revolutionary exile Bakunin was the chief Russian representative, contributing to the liveliness of the discussions, but offending at one blow St. Petersburg and Vienna. Moreover, the Magyars, who were soon to be led against Russia by two noted Polish generals, Dembinski and Bem, were already straining every nerve to embroil the Czechs and Poles and to persuade the latter to hold aloof from the Congress. On the other hand, a strongly Magyarophobe atmosphere was created by the Slovaks and Croats ; Štúr, Hurban and Hodža, the three Slovak leaders, played a very prominent part throughout the Congress, and Stanko Vraz, the Slovene poet, was made Vice-President. The Poles who did actually attend were Princes Lubomirski and Sapieha, the historian Moraczewski and the Radical deputy Libelt, who of all the delegates was nearest to Bakunin. The Vladika Peter of Montenegro, to-day recognized by the Serbs as their greatest poet, and always keenly alive to the cause of Slav unity and concord, would have liked to attend, but hesitated to offend Tsar Nicholas ; while Miloš Obrenović, the exiled Prince of Serbia, invited by Hanka, only decided at the last moment to stay away. In his fortunate absence, the Serbian delegation provided the chief ornament of the Congress in Vuk Karadžić, whose rich collections of ballad poetry and folk-lore have established his fame to all time. He was accompanied by Daničić, his colleague in the translation of the Bible, and by Marinović, afterwards the most Russophile and conservative of Serbian Premiers. The Croats were too busy at home organizing resistance against Hungary to spare their most active leaders, but the Croatian Sabor nominated delegates to the Bohemian Diet as a sign of future solidarity, and Topalović went further than anyone else present in emphasizing the refusal to accept orders either from Vienna or Budapest.

The greatest reception was given to the opening speech of Šafařik, who claimed that in declining to become Germans, Italians or Magyars, the Slavs were not acting as barbarians, but simply refusing to betray their country or the cause of liberty. "The Slavs ask nothing but justice ; they rest upon moral force only. . . . It is only by struggle that we pass from slavery to liberty. Let us therefore be victors, and we shall be free in a free nation, or let us die with honour, and glory will follow us to the grave." 'Our Apostle Paul Joseph,' as he was called, created a highly emotional atmosphere, which was heightened by a procession through the streets to one of the churches of Prague. But the discussions had from the first an air of unreality, before ever external events brought them to an abrupt conclusion. The only concrete result of the Congress was a grandiloquent manifesto addressed to the peoples of Europe, and recommending a general Congress of European free *Peoples*, as being 'more likely to understand each other than salaried diplomats.' As the Congress proceeded, a strong conflict developed between its president, Palacký, who continued to favour a federalized Austria, and Bakunin, who advocated its complete dissolution, as the first indispensable step towards universal revolution, the break-up of Russia and a drastic re-drawing of the map of Europe. Between the two stood Havlíček, who had no illusions about either Russia or Austria, but set his real hopes upon constitutional development of a radical Western type. It is not improbable that if the Congress had continued, he and Štúr, who met on the narrower field of Czecho-Slovak co-operation, might have rallied round the more conservative Palacký against Bakunin and Libelt. Leo Thun was ready to summon a Constituent Assembly to Prague and to adopt as his programme the restoration of Bohemian State Rights ; but though a sincere patriot, he was debarred by his clerical and reactionary views from meeting the recognized Czech leaders on common ground.

The effervescence in Prague to which the Congress had so notably contributed reached its height on Whit Monday, June 12. Soon there were barricades and martial law, and Prince Alfred Windischgrätz— commander of the Austrian forces in Bohemia, an aristocrat of integrity, and not devoid of military talent, but a reactionary to his finger-tips, and commonly credited with the much-quoted phrase, 'Man begins with Baron' (*der Mensch fängt mit Baron an*)—was only too glad of an excuse for drastic action against the mob. As a man, he was milder than his brother-in-law and future colleague, Prince Schwarzenberg ; but the accidental death of his wife from a stray bullet did not diminish his desire to crush the Revolution once and for all. On June 17, after an unnecessary bombardment followed by panic and ineffective resistance, Prague was at his feet, and the first active step in the Counter-Revolution had been taken. Long afterwards it transpired that one special cause of Windischgrätz's alarm was a secret memorandum of a certain Slovak spy in Magyar pay, named Turanski, whose function it was to convince the authorities that a plot was on foot for the establishment of a Western Slav Empire, at Hungary's expense, by the joint efforts of the Poles, Czechs, Croats and Slovaks.

The Constitution of April 25 and the Peasants

The Doblhoff Cabinet, which took over from Pillersdorff early in July, enjoyed a scarcely less precarious existence, but it was able to convoke Parliament in Vienna, and Archduke John came from Frankfurt to open it, at a time when the fall of Milan before Radetzky's armies seemed to close the second act of the growing reaction. Its chief features were its unexpected Slav majority (190 Slavs to 160 Germans), the large proportion of peasants elected, and the almost complete absence of the aristocracy. The Right was held by the Czechs, led by Palacký and Rieger, reinforced by their faithful adherents the Ruthene peasants, while the Left was doctrinaire, anti-Slav, and looked towards Frankfurt and 'the great task of regenerating the fatherland'; the Centre was especially strong in Tirol, had an essentially Habsburg outlook, and voted in political questions with the former and in national questions with the latter. 'First Germany, then Austria,' was the cry.

Almost from the first the main interest of this Parliament was the question of Serfdom, and for all its divergences of opinion it held steadily to the purpose of emancipating the peasantry. From July 26, when Hans Kudlich first tabled his motion for 'the abolition of serfdom, with all rights and duties arising from it,' and it was accepted by acclamation as the subject of immediate debate, until September 7, when this great reform was adopted, there was never any hesitation, save on the delicate question of compensation. Alexander Bach, the revolutionary now already in process of turning reactionary, and already the only man of outstanding merit in the new Cabinet, stubbornly upheld the principle of compensation by the state, but never even attempted to challenge the fundamental reform. This time emancipation of the serfs and abolition of all feudal dues and obligations had come to stay, and though at almost every other point feudal reaction reasserted itself, in this respect no such reversion as that of 1790 was even attempted. And this although the more far-sighted among the nobility saw that (in the words of Louis Eisenmann) 'the two points upon which the old Austria rested—absolutism and feudalism—had suffered an equal blow, from which they could not recover, because the two were bound one to the other.' This reform changed the whole face of Austria : 'it was thanks to it that the struggle of nationalities became a war of the masses, instead of a duel between privileged persons.' Moreover, Eisenmann in no way exaggerates when he affirms that though all the nationalities profited by the Revolution, none profited to the same extent as the Czechs ; for 'through it, in the countries where they had formerly been masters, and where since their defeat the bourgeoisie was in great majority German and the nobility indifferent, they succeeded in resuming the front rank. It was only emancipation that enabled them to sustain the effort by which they resuscitated their nation—seemingly dead since the White Mountain.' This penetrating interpretation of the French historian is completed by his remark that the events of 1848–1849 proved 'how indissoluble is the link that unites the ideas of nationality and liberty.' This is, if possible, even truer in 1943 than in 1848 or in 1904, when Eisenmann wrote his book—one of the few really great books of political analysis published since Albert Sorel.

The Breach with Hungary

The adoption of a new peasant order was the one concrete achievement of the Parliament of 1848 ; the peasant deputies showed little interest in, or grasp of, the other problems, the Slavs were increasingly reserved, while the Radical Left became increasingly vocal in a 'Great German' sense, submitted to dictation from street demagogues, and flirted openly with the Magyar nationalists, mainly because the latter were Slavophobe, and at the very moment when a breach between Hungary and the Crown seemed almost inevitable. The Court returned to Vienna from Innsbruck early in August, but the so-called 'Camarilla' grew if anything stronger rather than weaker as a result ; the alliance between Windischgrätz, Schwarzenberg and Bach, the Croat Ban Jelačić and the masterful Archduchess Sophie, wife and mother of the next two heirs to the throne, was the decisive factor behind the scenes. On September 11 Jelačić, at the head of a considerable army, but also as the unchallenged leader of the Croat nation, crossed the Drave and marched against Budapest. In the week following Parliament declined—mainly owing to open Czech hostility—to receive a Magyar deputation, but the democrats of Vienna organized a torchlight procession in their honour, cheered to the echo Wesselényi's speech and thundered against a 'Hyena Ministry' and a 'miserable Reichstag.' The moderate elements in Hungary fell into the background, Széchényi lost his reason and flung himself into the Danube, Eötvös fled to Germany, Deák was reduced to silence by the demagogic oratory of Kossuth, who now summoned the nation to arms and committed the supreme folly of driving all the non-Magyar races into the arms of reaction. On September 28 Count Lamberg, the Emperor's special commissioner to Hungary, was murdered on the Suspension Bridge between Pest and Buda by an armed rabble, and only a week later the chronic disturbance of which Vienna had become the scene culminated in the murder of the War Minister, Count Latour, the mob hanging his mutilated body on a lamp-post.

This gave Windischgrätz and the reactionaries the chance for which they had been waiting. The phantom Emperor and his entourage fled a second time from Vienna, and this time were installed in the little Moravian cathedral town of Olomouc, while Windischgrätz marshalled his military forces for the capture of Vienna and the conquest of rebel Hungary. The Parliament in Vienna, already in process of becoming a Rump—now passed a resolution to the effect that as Constituent Assembly it could not be dissolved and could under no circumstances disperse, and summoned all absentee deputies to return to its fold within a fortnight. To this the Czechs retorted by a protest against its continuance in Vienna, on the ground that it was sinking to the mere level of a local Committee of Safety, and was even conniving in the outrage upon Latour. So long as such anarchy prevailed, they would not take their seats or regard its decisions as valid. The whole weight of the Czech movement was being deliberately thrown into the dynastic scale, in the hope that the constitutional problem would be solved on federal rather than centralist or 'Great German' lines.

For the time being Windischgrätz was all-powerful, and was nominated Commander-in-Chief of Austria's entire forces save those of Radetzky in Italy; Jelačić was thus thrown aside with rather scant courtesy. While Kossuth gained the upper hand in Hungary and presided over a Committee of Public Safety which soon became the real Government, there was enough sanity left in Vienna to send a parliamentary deputation to the Court; but behind the shifty evasion which it met with at Olomouc was the uncompromising reality of Windischgrätz: 'With rebels I shall not negotiate.' His manifesto to Vienna went still further; he had come to free them from the power of 'a handful of criminals,' and he demanded the surrender of the Polish and Magyar volunteers in their ranks, and above all of the murderers of Latour. After a week's siege Vienna shared the fate of Prague and Milan; and by way of answer to the interference of Frankfurt in Austrian lands, the victor ordered Robert Blum, one of the four deputies of the German Left who had come to Vienna counting upon their immunity, to be put against a wall and shot. After this defiant warning to revolutionary Germany—which naturally contributed to the decline of influence of the Federal Diet and the whole constitutional movement in the Reich—Windischgrätz concentrated his whole efforts upon the subjugation of Hungary and soon found it to be beyond his own unaided powers.

Kroměříž

Windischgrätz would undoubtedly, if he had had his way, have abolished Parliament out of hand and reverted to absolute rule under the system of provincial Estates; but other less crude influences prevailed. Largely on the advice of Palacký, Parliament was not dismissed, but summoned to the quiet little country town of Kroměříž (Kremsier) in Moravia, where it would be within easy reach, and under the control, of Oloumouc, and would enjoy the necessary calm for the delicate task of drafting a new and workable constitution. On November 27 the Government was reconstituted under the Premiership of the cynical, but able and very energetic Prince Felix Schwarzenberg; his two most influential colleagues being Count Francis Stadion, who was a genuine believer in constitutional government, but whose mind broke down at the decisive moment of completing the new draft, and Alexander Bach, the time-serving, supple ex-revolutionary, who was already indispensable to the colleagues who distrusted and disliked him. Prompted by them and by the Army, the poor dazed Emperor was induced to abdicate, in favour of his eighteen-year-old nephew Francis Joseph, in whose name a grandiloquent manifesto declared that 'firmly resolved to maintain untarnished the glory of the Crown, but ready to share Our rights with the representatives of Our people, We trust that We shall succeed . . . in uniting all the lands and races of the Monarchy in one great organism' (Staatskörper). Francis Joseph, so the Camarilla calculated, was not bound by the word of his predecessor and could therefore fling the Constitution of April 25 into the limbo of inconvenient state documents, whenever it had served its temporary purpose. For the moment it was left undisturbed, both because it was so much more docile at Kroměříž than in the capital, and because all thoughts were concentrated upon the defeat of Hungary. Windischgrätz occupied Budapest on January 5, 1849, but found that he was almost as far as ever from reducing the country to submission.

A respite of three months was thus afforded to the Constitutional Committee, composed of thirty members—three for each of the then provinces of Austria ; its first meeting was on January 13, and working almost daily under the growing menace of reaction, it was able on March 4 to pass in third reading, for submission to Parliament in full session, the agreed draft of a new Constitution. Though it never took effect, it will always remain one of the most remarkable political documents of the century, proving, as it does, that with adequate good will and in a congenial atmosphere rival nationalities, with very divergent and strongly-held views, are yet capable of reaching a compromise on fundamentals. As Anton Springer, the Austrian liberal historian who himself passed from the Czech federalist to the German centralist camp, has quite justly remarked, the contemporary gibe that the Committee had produced a 'centralist-federalist' constitution was not really so very far from the mark. Its principal members deserve special mention—Palacký and Rieger, 'the head and mouth' of the Czech party, and their two lawyer-colleagues, Pinkas and Strobach ; Dr. Fischhof, the German-Jewish liberal doctor whose writings on 'equality of national rights' (*Gleich-berechtigung*) occupy a special place in Austrian history ; Lasser, Gold-mark and Violand for Lower Austria ; Aloys Fischer for Salzburg and Cajetan Meyer for Moravia ; the Slavist Miklošić for Styria ; two distinguished Polish lawyers, Smolka and Ziemialkowsky, and the Ruthene Uniate Bishop Jachimović for Galicia.

The draft is generally regarded as inspired by the model of the Belgian Constitution and influenced by various liberal constitutional theories from the West, but the main constructive effort is undoubtedly to be credited to Palacký, whose unrivalled knowledge of all the rival State Rights of the Habsburg dominions stood him in good stead. Palacký had originally contemplated the division of the *Gesammtstaat* (in this case Austria, to the exclusion of Hungary) into four groups, a German-Austrian, a Polish, a Bohemian and an Illyrian—each of the four having a special *Landesminister* at the head of its local government, but sending delegates to a central Reichsrat. He would have been ready to accept the severance of 'German-Bohemia' from the Czech districts, on condition of Slovakia being united with the latter. Early in the Committee's debates he propounded a more thorough-going scheme, which started quite logically from the view that the reorganization of Hungary was a question of life or death for the nationalities, and again, that Austria —this time the real *Gesammtstaat*, the state as a whole—must be so constructed that her various peoples are glad to live there. He therefore favoured the formation of eight federal groups : (1) German-Austria, including the Sudetian districts ; (2) the Czech lands (Bohemia, Moravia, Silesia, together with Slovakia) ; (3) Poland, including Bukovina and the Ruthene districts of Hungary ; (4) Illyria (consisting of the Slovene districts) ; (5) Italian Tirol, with Lombardy-Venetia ; (6) the Southern Slav districts (Croatia-Slavonia-Dalmatia, with the Voivodina) ; (7) the Magyar districts of Hungary ; (8) the Roumanian districts. He repeated his readiness to separate the German and Czech portions of Bohemia from each other, if it could be done ; 'but Bohemia is a basin (*Kesselland*), and a basin cannot be divided up without destroying it.' It will be noted that these proposals in effect amounted only to seven, not eight, provinces, for the fourth and sixth would fall automatically into their place as a single Southern Slav unit, if the other difficulties were once overcome. Finding that he could not carry the Committee for a full federalist programme, Palacký wavered between what might be called the nationalist and the historical solution, a return to 'State Rights' being for the Czechs the most obvious alternative to federalism. But he was the first to raise the federal issue clearly, and the Czechs were more particularly identified with it right on to the collapse of the Habsburg monarchy. What neither he nor any other member of the Committee succeeded in defining was the relationship that was to exist between the Austrian lands and the lands of the Crown of St. Stephen.

His more moderate colleague Pinkas was also responsible for propounding a new form of constitutional compromise, which was put forward periodically as a practical solution for equable national representation in mixed districts, and which was the instrument that imparted to the first Reichsrat of Universal Suffrage, in 1907, its first fine careless rapture. This was the national *Curia* (or Kurie) which enabled the various nationalities to vote separately according to an exact proportional scale, with the result that inter-racial conflicts at the polls were avoided, as also all danger of votes being wasted or assigned to the rival nationality, as was deliberately done at the Hungarian elections. It naturally did not, and could not, put an end to rivalry in the higher spheres of the state, but it assured the struggle being conducted on a basis of justice and equality. What gave to the Kroměříž Committee its harmonious character was the fact that all its members, Germans and Slavs alike, accepted *Gleich-berechtigung* as a basic principle. The essential problem that confronted them (as Joseph Redlich has very clearly put it) was that of transforming an absolutist state of the eighteenth-century type into a modern liberal constitutional state. With this was linked up the lesser, but no less vital and still more practical problem of solving the relations of the central and local powers. It may be that Redlich goes too far in arguing that the adoption of Palacký's ideas would have cut the ground from under the feet of the dynasty, destroyed the German character of the army, and doomed the non-German peoples to decay. What is certain is that the deputies of Kroměříž, so far from failing, reached agreement on fundamentals by their own unaided efforts, but that it did not suit the various interests hitherto supreme in the state to give them the chance of putting their theories into practice—the aristocracy, whose abolition they were unwise enough to advocate, the Church, which disliked their Josephine outlook, the Army, which was driven to take a centralist view by its conflict with the Magyars.

The draft was adopted by the Committee on March 4, and already on the 7th the Parliament of 1848 was unceremoniously dissolved, against the advice of Count Stadion himself. At the same time the so-called 'Decreed Constitution' (*oktroyierte Verfassung*) of March 4, 1849, valid no longer for Austria only, but for the whole Monarchy, was, as it were, flung by the Crown at the heads of its motley peoples. The special constitutions of Hungary, Croatia and Transylvania were not actually revoked, but were subordinated to the superior jurisdiction of the new central Parliament and Government. In the same way the provincial Diets of Austria, and among them the Bohemian, were allowed to survive, subject to the Cabinet enjoying special powers of suspending their decisions. A solemn Imperial Coronation was envisaged, but the Crowns of St. Wenceslas and St. Stephen were passed over in silence. Of great practical significance was the abolition of all internal tolls or tariffs, and the creation of a single Customs and trade unit.

As this Constitution in its turn proved a complete abortion, it is superfluous for our present purpose to dwell upon further details. In essence it was an attempt to create an unitary and highly centralized Austrian state, fortified by a number of economic measures, and entrenched against any rival theory resting upon Greater German Unity.

It was a lame enough compromise between the rival conceptions of Stadion and Schwarzenberg. The former was its author, and what he aimed at was the 'liberal unitary state,' in reality a blend of constitutional monarchy with a strongly conservative bureaucratic machine ; and, as Friedjung truly says, this idea 'lived and fell with him,' when illness removed him from the political scene that very summer. Schwarzenberg, in his cruder and highly amateur way, believed in a '70-million German Empire,' which Austria would enter at the head of all her secondary peoples, and in which she would outvote and overbear her Prussian rival with the help of their numbers. This simply showed that Schwarzenberg had never thought out the problem of modernizing the Habsburg Monarchy to its logical conclusion, and was above all concerned with restoring its endangered position as a Great Power. By recalling the clerical deputies from the Frankfurt Federal Diet on April 5 he dealt one of the final blows to its tottering structure ; little as they loved each other, Austria and Russia were now competing for the destruction of the constitutional movement in Germany.

The most serious opposition to the 'Octroi' came from Hungary, where Kossuth, encouraged by a series of minor military successes at the expense of the Imperialists, and against both Windischgrätz and Jelačić, committed the folly of solemnly deposing the House of Habsburg and proclaiming himself as Governor of an independent Hungary (April 14). It was then that the Vienna Cabinet reluctantly decided to appeal to Tsar Nicholas for help, and that the latter, mindful of his earlier promises to the Emperor Francis, poured an army of 180,000 men across the Carpathians, with the purpose of suppressing the Revolution in its last refuge. Hungary was completely isolated, nowhere was there any prospect of military help. The other races of the Monarchy had already been reduced to passivity, and most of them were in any case hostile. The final stages of the tragedy were the capitulation of Görgei's army at Világos (August 13, 1849) and the execution of the first constitutional Premier of the new era, Count Louis Batthyány, and of the thirteen generals known in Hungarian history as 'the Martyrs of Arad.' Venice meanwhile had been forced to surrender to Radetzky, and Italian resistance to Austria was once more overcome. Kossuth fled to England, and for a whole generation of exile filled the world with his denunciations of Austria and the Habsburgs. His persuasive eloquence, distorted by the prevalent romanticism and the genuine tragedy of events, blinded his contemporaries to the real issues at stake. The Magyars were unquestionably the torchbearers of constitutional liberties and had behind them in this respect a tradition such as no people of Danubian Europe could boast ; but unhappily they also stood for racial monopoly of the harshest kind, denying to the non-Magyar races the rights which they claimed for themselves. In the words of a famous Slav brochure of the 'thirties' ;[1] 'What they regard as their own

---

[1] *Sollen wir Magyaren werden?* p. 10.

greatest virtue, namely love for their own people, is condemned in our case and regarded as a great sin.' Thus, by a cruel irony of fate, the champions of nationality were driven to support a reactionary dynasty and the organizers of absolutism, while the champions of constitutional and political reform were pushing a policy of forcible assimilation against all the other races. In such a situation failure was inevitable for both the contending parties ; reaction was the *tertius gaudens*.

CHAPTER XII

THE ERA OF CONSTITUTIONAL EXPERIMENT (1849–1867)

*La grande difficulté dans la Monarchie austro-hongroise, est de concilier
le droit historique de certaines nationalités avec le droit naturel des autres.*
—Louis Eisenmann.

Schwarzenberg and Bach

ONCE again Bohemia found herself condemned to a passive role, in the
face of major events in Austria and in Europe. Altogether symbolical
of this helplessness was the fate of Palacký, who, after entering a protest
against the suppression of the Kroměříž Parliament, withdrew into
private life and was for the time being absorbed in the later volumes of
his great History of Bohemia, and again of Havlíček, who, after being
unanimously acquitted of offences against the Press Law, was rearrested
and transported to Brixen in Tirol, whence he was only allowed to return
when already at the point of death. The suggestion of trying Palacký by
court martial was for a time seriously considered, and he found himself
in the position of a pariah : the nobles who had given him their friendship
held aloof from the national cause, and the Museum Society and the
Matice Česká were in imminent danger of dissolution, the latter even
hesitating to publish a Czech Grammar !

No attempt was made on the part of those in power to distinguish
between the Magyars, who were guilty of open rebellion, and the Czechs,
who had shown marked leanings towards the cause of the dynasty and of
of the *Gesammtstaat*. Centralist tendencies were now triumphant, and
they went hand in hand with Germanization of the whole administration.
Representative principles were at a discount, and the Octroi of March
1849, remained permanently on paper. At last, in August, 1851, the
Emperor appointed a commission to consider whether or not the constitution was workable, thus indirectly casting considerable doubt upon the
good faith or intelligence of its original framers, and at the same time
he suspended ministerial responsibility. Finally, on December 31, 1851,
the constitution was abrogated by Imperial decree.

Whatever may be thought of its political outlook, it cannot be denied
that the new regime had at its head a group of men of quite exceptional
ability. Schwarzenberg himself died prematurely early in 1852, after
inflicting a resounding diplomatic defeat upon Prussia at Olmütz (Olomouc) in November, 1850, but without carrying into effect his ill-conceived
designs for Austrian hegemony in Germany. Anton von Schmerling, one
of the foremost Austrian delegates at Frankfurt, had been attracted by
Schwarzenberg's 'Great German' leanings, but preferred to leave the
Cabinet and bide his time until in the radically altered situation of the
'sixties he himself was given the task of realizing 'the 70-million Empire,'
and found this to be beyond his powers. Baron Bruck, as the originator
of the Southern Railway, the Semmering tunnels and the Austrian Lloyd,
and as the advocate of an Austro-German Customs Union, canalized
Austrian commercial and industrial development in certain directions at
the most critical moment of the new Railway Era. Count Leo Thun, as

Minister of Education, a man of devout character and sincere patriotism, set himself the impossible task of squaring the circle of clericalism and tolerance. But there was another figure that more and more dominated the scene. Alexander Bach had long since moved full circle from the ideas which brought him into prominence in 1848 ; and it was not without reason that, as Stadion and Bruck and Schmerling dropped into the background, the period of the fifties acquired the nickname of 'the Bach regime,' and that the able and incorruptible bureaucrats whose business it was to make Hungary toe the line in the new centralized and Germanized state, were contemptuously known as 'Bach Hussars.'

The Bach regime, it has been caustically remarked, rested upon four supports : 'the soldiers upright, the bureaucrats seated, the priests kneeling, the spies rampant.' Its most concrete achievements were the Press Law of 1852, the Penal Code of 1853 and the Concordat of 1855—three of the most consciously reactionary documents promulgated by any modern state. Under the auspices of Cardinal Rauscher, once a tutor of the youthful Francis Joseph, the Catholic clergy, themselves subjected to a greatly augmented episcopal control, imposed upon the state the provisions of the Canon Law in matters of marriage and divorce, and acquired almost unrestricted control of education. The lack of restraint thus shown by the Clerical party and by the Crown inevitably rallied all progressive forces against the Concordat, and contributed towards that unnatural and regrettable gulf of opinion which came to separate the Church from the bulk of the intellectual and academic class, thereby creating a lack of balance and a bitterness that reacted upon all current questions and especially upon the question of nationalities. Hand in hand with clerical interference went the German language as the exclusive language of the Universities and the higher secondary schools (the mother tongue being graciously permitted in the lowest classes).

In two other directions Bach gravely miscalculated, and was let down by his closest allies. The Foreign Minister, Count Buol, by his clumsy and inept policy during the Crimean War, isolated Austria in Europe, and exposed her to a double rebuff at the Congress of Paris on the Italian and Roumanian questions. Untaught by experience, and still confronted by the genius of Cavour, he persisted on a course which rendered war in Italy inevitable, while assuring to his much weaker opponent the active support of the French Empire, while Russia, Prussia and Britain for a number of different reasons, stood aside and left Austria to her fate. The dangers of the situation were augmented by the mediocrity of her military leaders, and by the progressively decrepit state of the finances. But the crowning folly of the regime was that though owing its victory over the Magyars—under God and the Tsar !—to the support freely offered by the other nationalities, it did nothing whatsoever to propitiate them or to strengthen their powers of resistance. The witty Francis Pulszky, Kossuth's secretary in exile, was merely parodying the undoubted facts of the case when he reminded the Croats and Slovaks that they had received from Vienna as a reward what the Magyars had received as a punishment.

The Emperor plays at Constitution-making

After Austria's resounding defeat at Solferino in 1859 the Bach regime was bankrupt, alike financially and morally, and fell like a stone. Francis Joseph found himself confusedly groping in a twilight of conflicting constitutional programmes, offering many *nuances* between the extremes of centralism and federation. On August 22, 1859, as a first step, after fruitlessly sounding among the high Magyar aristocracy, he replaced Bach by Count Agenor Goluchowski, the Governor of Galicia— 'a Polish aristocrat, but also an Austrian official, very dynastic, and advocate of a moderate centralism' (Eisenmann). His was above all the function of the stop-gap ; the 'Augmented Council' (*verstärkte Reichsrat*) convoked under his auspices, and patched together according to no obvious principles, satisfied no one and was without form and void. 'All that is a roof, with nothing beneath it, neither foundations nor building,' commented the Magyar conservative Szögyény in his Diary ; and in any case, Francis Joseph, with that blend of impatience, hesitation and opportunism which never left him, did not allow his new creation the time to function. It had not got beyond the stage of exploratory discussions of the vaguest kind, when it was thrown on to the rubbish heap, to make way for the 'October Diploma' of October 20, 1860. Behind the scenes the constructive proposals of the Magyar conservative Count Emil Desewffy were botched and tinkered at until they were scarcely recognizable ; and the Diploma, though marking a definite breach with the centralist absolutism of Bach and a tardy enough recognition of those historic units to which the Monarchy—the *Gesammtstaat*—traced its origin, did not make the necessary concessions to Hungary, who held the key position and had in Francis Deák a leader at once urbane, logical and adamant in his powers of resistance and definition. The Diploma was at one and the same time a manifesto of the Emperor to his peoples, and a draft constitution, presented with a view to forestalling their proposals ; in actual fact it was neither fish nor flesh nor good red-herring. It did not go far enough for any section of Magyar opinion, it offended the German centralists, and yet it virtually ignored the Slavs, or, worse still, sought to drive a wedge between the Czechs and Poles. But the storm of indignation which it aroused in every section of Hungarian opinion took the Emperor by surprise, and tempted him to yet another change of tactics.

The role played by Count Clam-Martinic in these abortive negotiations brought out more clearly than before the essential difference between the two nobilities of Hungary and Bohemia, as a vital factor in the whole political development of the Habsburg monarchy. No one has done more to elucidate this than Louis Eisenmann.[1] As he points out, the political individuality of Hungary is incarnated in the Hungarian nobility, which is identical with the Magyar nation and draws its own advantage from the Magyar hegemony, whereas 'in Austria there is no *national* nobility ; that of the German lands is solely Catholic and dynastic, while the feudal nobility of Bohemia is regional (*provincialiste*). When it allies itself with the Czechs, it is from calculation and not sentiment ; its dream is to exercise between the two nationalities of the country, Czech and German, a fruitful mediation. Even its conception of the historical individuality of Bohemia is not national. For the Czechs this individuality is that of the Bohemian state, formed out of the three lands of the Crown of St. Wenceslas—Bohemia, Moravia and Silesia. It is thus they conceived it in 1848 ; it conforms with history and with their interest. For the Bohemian state, thus reformed, would include the richest provinces of Austria, and they would be in the majority there because of their numbers.

[1] See *Le Compromis austro-hongrois*, especially pp. 225–226, and the chapters on the period of constitutional experiments.

. . . .They only have the choice . . . between this strictly historical programme or a purely ethnic programme—to abandon the German districts of their three Lands, while uniting with the Slovaks of Hungary, that powerful reserve of their nationality, to form an ethnic group of eight millions.' It was between these two alternatives that Palacký and his successors inevitably wavered. Clam's suggestion of limiting the programme to Bohemia in the narrow sense (to the exclusion of Moravia and Silesia and still more of Slovakia) was one which no Czech could take at all seriously.

Schmerling's Centralism and the Czechs

Only seven weeks after the promulgation of the October Diploma Goluchowski was dropped with all the callousness habitual to Francis Joseph, and his place was taken by Anton von Schmerling, a man of high integrity, but inelastic, often obtuse in his judgment of men or situations, handicapped by a bitter tongue and provocative manner, and almost fantastically vain. After a further interval of two months the Presidency of the new Cabinet was assigned to the Emperor's cousin, Archduke Rainer, as though to give a dynastic hallmark to the 'Great German' Schmerling, who of course remained the indispensable moving spirit.

The February Patent (February 26, 1861) was an abrupt reversion to centralist ideas, entered upon before the decentralizing possibilities of the Diploma had been tested out or their implications seriously considered. The shadowy Reichsrat of 1860 was now transformed into a central Parliament of 343 members[1]—not deputies elected at a popular poll, but delegates elected in the reconstituted provincial Diets. The powers of these Diets were very carefully restricted, and their respective franchises doctored in such a way as to give to the Germans, and incidentally to the towns, with their German or semi-German culture and outlook, an altogether undue representation. For instance, in the Bohemian Diet, out of a total of 241 the towns had 72, the country districts 79, seats, while the great landlords (*Grossgrundbesitz*) whose sympathies were predominantly German, had 70 seats ; in the Czech districts there was one seat to every 53,000 voters, in the German one to every 40,000. Electoral geometry was for a generation to come to be one of Austria's leading industries. To overcome the many obscurities of the new constitution, the Government was provided with that dangerous political boomerang, the 'Emergency Paragraph' (*Notverordnungsparagraph*), which legalized the execution of urgent measures without reference to Parliament, and even dispensed it from reporting upon them retrospectively. All this, combined with the lack of ministerial responsibility, the absence of a clearly defined immunity for the deputies, and the maintenance of the reactionary Press Law and of the Concordat in their original form, and the very limited control exercised over foreign and military affairs, made it impossible for the advocates of constitutional liberties to view the February Constitution with anything but distrust.

Moreover, it soon became obvious that even Schmerling himself had no clear idea of the distinction between the 'full' and 'restricted' sessions of the central Parliament—i.e. when the whole Monarchy, or only the Austrian dominions, were represented. This at once assumed capital

---

[1] Of these 120 were assigned to Hungary, of which 26 went to Transylvania and 9 to Croatia. The Lands of St. Wenceslas had 92 (54 Bohemia, 22 Moravia, 6 Silesia).

importance, for the Italians, Magyars and Croats refused to sit and adhered to a policy of rigid abstention. The Czechs, led by Rieger, Brauner and Gregr (Palacký was in the Upper House, an isolated and discontented figure), played their cards very badly, completing the alienation of the none too friendly Magyars, yet winning no concessions from Vienna for their distinctly ungracious complaisance. On the eve of Parliament opening, a delegation was sent by the Diet of Bohemia, on the initiative of the Archbishop of Prague, inviting Francis Joseph to be crowned King of Bohemia like his ancestors ; the Emperor graciously consented, but broke his promise, not for the last time. This turned the scale in favour of attendance, but there was friction from the very first, the German majority being in a refractory and aggressive mood, venting upon the present Slavs its ill-humour against the absent Magyars. Already in June, 1861, Poles and Czechs marked their displeasure by a demonstrative withdrawal ; and Rieger declaimed, in one of his most eloquent speeches : "We are legal sons of the House, just as much as the Germans, and we demand to be treated as such." Some of the most rabid German centralists came from Bohemia and Moravia, and Herbst and Giskra in particular made violent attacks upon the whole idea of the Crown of St. Wenceslas and Bohemian State Rights.

It is not quite clear whether the Czechs, in attending, had calculated that their example would lead the Magyars to follow suit, and that then between them they would form a majority and be masters of the situation. If so, they radically misjudged the Magyars, who under the calm but unbending leadership of Deák went their own way. The Diet convoked at Budapest in May, 1861, was envisaged by Schmerling and Francis Joseph as on a par with the new Diets of the Austrian provinces, but to every Magyar it was the lawful Parliament of Hungary, and acted accordingly, reaffirming in its Address to the Throne the constitution 'consecrated by long centuries,' and declining to negotiate except upon the basis of its recognition. This was answered by dissolution and a state of siege, and for the next four years, while in Austria Schmerling governed on bureaucratic lines, with a Parliament lacking from the first in prestige and stage by stage reduced to the merest Rump, as one nationality after another withdrew, Hungary stubbornly maintained her passive resistance to the revived militarist and absolutist regime imposed upon her. This hybrid regime, known as the 'Provisorium,' really lasted till 1867, though in 1865 and 1866 Francis Joseph made two more abortive attempts to find an exit from the impasse. In short, the February Constitution had, within the brief space of a year, led quite logically to a revival of absolutism in Hungary and to a situation in Austria that rested on compromise and camouflage. But it should be added that the fundamental reason for Schmerling's obstinacy lay in foreign policy—in his dream of the '70-million Reich,' which was equally unacceptable to Russia, to Hungary, and to the Slavs.

Palacký and Rieger

Under such a regime little that was constructive could be achieved, and parliamentary government tended to be a pretentious sham. Schmerling, like Bach before him, was in Eisenmann's phrase 'prisoner of the liberal illusion, unable to bridge the yawning gulf between Liberalism and Nationalism.' Whatever may have been his hopes at the outset, it very soon became for him a political necessity that the Magyars and Croats, and preferably others also, should not attend and swamp his artificial German majority. It suited him fairly well that in June, 1863, the Czechs should have lost patience altogether and withdrawn from the Reichsrat in a body, to initiate a period of sixteen years of barren abstention, which their enemies described more bluntly as sulking in a corner. The moment of their entrance into Parliament had been ill-chosen, though it is but fair to add that it was determined by the alliance recently concluded between Rieger and a section of the Bohemian feudal nobility, against the better judgment of Palacký. The moment of their exit was almost equally ill-chosen, and the grounds which they adduced and their excessive insistence upon Bohemian State Rights, while naturally welcomed at home in Prague, narrowed the field of their supporters at the very moment when it might have been extended to include the Poles, the Southern Slavs and at least a section of the German Clericals and Conservatives. Moreover, Palacký and Rieger committed the grave political blunder—to say nothing of its moral aspect—of condoning the action of Russia in her savage repression of the Second Polish Insurrection. This caused a split among the Czech ranks, and marks the first beginnings of the 'Young Czech' party which (in contrast to the 'Old Czech' Conservatives) was ere long to dominate Czech politics.

There was in Rieger and Gregr, and even in Palacký for all his intellectual and moral greatness, a certain tactical crudity, an imperfect sense of values, that markedly differentiated them from Deák, Andrássy and Eötvös, the three great Magyar leaders who steered their ship of state into the harbour of Dualism. After two and a half centuries of utter suppression a political tradition among the Czechs could not be stamped out of the ground in an instant of time. Another generation was still required for the organization of political parties capable of holding their ground ; and yet another generation had to elapse before those parties had learned to reconcile their aspirations with the practical requirements of the moment—in other words, to adopt a policy of true realism. In 1861–1863 they were in a far less favourable position than the Magyars ; while the latter were led by their own powerful nobility, the Czechs had the support of only a small fragment of theirs and the active hostility of the majority. Both nations were weak in a middle class, but the Magyars more than made good this deficiency by their control of the county autonomy, while the Czechs were handicapped by the active hostility of the German middle class. When the Magyars abstained from the Reichsrat, Hungary was unrepresented in that body ; when the Czechs withdrew, a majority of Bohemian votes—those of the German-Bohemians and of the feudal landlords—remained behind. If the Czechs had added to their folly by boycotting the Diet of Prague (they did so at a later date and thus tested its folly) the only result would have been that it would have sat with 150 members instead of 240, and that the sittings would have been much quieter. Meanwhile Schmerling found himself in an altogether false position towards the other nationalities, upon whom Bach's bureaucratic absolutism had acted as a cold douche. He could not hope to centralize Austria against the Slavs and propound schemes to the non-Magyars of Hungary for the federalization of Hungary. For the moment indeed the Serbs of the Voivodina, no less than the Croat autonomists and the Roumanians of Transylvania, looked to Budapest rather than Vienna, and were reassured by the statesmanship of Deák and the liberal views of Eötvös. Schmerling tried to clothe the old absolutist centralism of the 'fifties in a mantle of Liberal phrases, and was therefore of all the statesmen of the Liberal era the most barren.

Schmerling's Downfall : The Era of 'Suspension'

In the end Schmerling's fall was above all due to the failure of his and Rechberg's foreign policy ; but probably no one was taken more completely by surprise than he himself when on July 27, 1865, he was replaced by Count Richard Belcredi ; and what was commonly known as 'the Ministry of the Three Counts.' In the so-called 'Period of Suspension' (*Sistierung*), when Francis Joseph in his abrupt and amateur way again annulled one of his own political creations, all else was overshadowed by the growing friction with Prussia ; Rechberg, who had been outclassed by Bismarck at Frankfurt when they represented their respective Governments at Federal Headquarters, was still less able to stand up to him when they became Foreign Ministers in Vienna and Berlin. Austria's isolation and clumsy manœuvring, accentuated by bad finance, was obviously leading to war ; and there was no little irony in a situation that pitted the foremost spokesman of the Great German idea against the greatest statesman whom Prussia had produced. But in proportion as friction grew, Francis Joseph sought to hasten the pace of an agreement with Hungary, and here Schmerling was not merely inadequate, but a positive obstacle. In December, 1865, Francis Joseph opened the Hungarian Parliament in person, recognizing the legal continuity of the constitution and the all-important Laws of 1848 ; and nothing throws such light on the true situation as the fact that he did not even think it necessary to consult the Czechs, much less negotiate with them, as he did with the Magyars. Parliament sat on at Pest till the rupture with Prussia in June, 1866, and was then prorogued ; Deák was playing a masterly game with most of the cards in his hands.

It was while goaded by this contrast in the attitude of the Crown towards Pest and towards Prague, that Palacký published his remarkable little book, *The Idea of the Austrian State*, the main argument of which was the absurdity of pretending that the resources of a great Empire were exclusively at the service of two chosen peoples while the others were their servants. There could be no durable reconcilation on the basis of non-German inferiority. The Slavs desired the survival of the Monarchy, but only if it guaranteed their existence within it ; Dualism would be the first step towards its dissolution. It is here that Palacký coined his famous phrase : 'Before Austria was, we were, and when Austria no longer is, we still shall be.' This, be it remembered, was almost on the eve of events which once more proved Bohemia's position as one of the main strategic bastions of Europe, whose capture assured to Prussia the hegemony of Germany.

Belcredi had been Governor of Bohemia and was quite ready to allow for Czech susceptibilities, but though he played with a project of dividing the whole Monarchy into five federal states, his main idea seems to have been a return to the pre-1848 system of Estates, now as dead as a doornail. He would have dearly liked to show the Germans of the Monarchy, and especially of Bohemia, that they were not as indispensable as they themselves thought ; but tactically he was handicapped by the impossibility of alienating them from the state at the very moment when war with the rival German state was imminent. The extent to which

Francis Joseph was still vacillating between rival policies was shown not only in the selection of Belcredi, but also in the cordial answer sent to the Bohemian Diet's appeal to him to be crowned at Prague. 'I salute in advance the moment when the success of great designs will permit me to make my entry into my illustrious city of Prague, to accomplish amid my faithful Czechs, and in conformity with right and sacred usage, the act of coronation.'

The War with Prussia

Once more Bohemia was the strategic centre of the picture, and the invading Prussian armies inflicted so decisive a defeat upon Benedek at Königgrätz-Sadowa (July 3, 1866), as utterly to outweigh the victory over the Italians at Custozza and the still more complete naval victory of Tegetthoff off Lissa. With Prague in Prussian occupation, Bismarck had no such scruples or hesitations as Belcredi. Simultaneously with plans for a Magyar Legion under General Klapka, and overtures to Serbia and to the Croat malcontents, he sent as an emissary to Gregr and Sladkovský, the leaders of the extreme Czech wing, that romantic adventurer Frič, who had already atoned for his wild-cat schemes with many years of prison. During the invasion Bismarck circulated a manifesto in Czech, declaring that a Prussian victory would enable the Czechs 'to realize their national wishes, like the Hungarians.' Nothing came of this, for the simple reason that the war was over in seven weeks, and Bismarck was already sailing on the opposite tack, anxious to deter his victorious master, King William, from exacting vindictive terms from the suppliant Francis Joseph. Bismarck was at his greatest when he fought tooth and nail against the Crown and the General Staff for a treaty such as would not be an obstacle to reconciliation between the two German rivals ; and it is tempting to speculate as to what Europe might have avoided if he had treated France in 1871 with the same forbearance. At the same time his whole attitude provides useful clues to the relative strength and political judgment of the various peoples of the Monarchy at that date. Austria was to be excluded altogether both from Germany and Italy ; but having once submitted to this drastic operation, was to be maintained as a centralized and predominantly German state. The Slavs were to be kept in their place, and the Magyars, being too strong to be swallowed whole or altogether sidetracked, were to acquire a special privileged position, side by side with the Germans. If the Habsburgs could be encouraged to transfer their centre of gravity to Pest and to rely more than ever upon the Magyars, this would suit Bismarck very well indeed.

Effects of Königgrätz

Königgrätz brought to an abrupt close two policies which had inspired and dominated Habsburg ambition for centuries past. Austria's expulsion from the German Confederacy spelt the triumph of Prussia's 'Little German' policy, and the final abandonment of such dreams as those of Schwarzenberg and Schmerling, while her loss of Venetia meant the emancipation of Italy from that Austrian interference which had been chronic since the days of Joseph II, and indeed much earlier. The whole orientation of Austria was suddenly and violently altered, and the shock to the political system could not fail to be serious. But her recovery— only one in a series of such recoveries in the course of two centuries, though this time it proved to be the very last—was so remarkable as to explain and excuse the very widespread belief that politically she bore a charmed life and had become a European necessity.

Henceforth everything in Austria may be said to revolve round the problem of finding a new basis for the state, under the altered circumstances of the modern world. The motive of common defence had rallied many divergent peoples and provinces under the rule of a single dynasty, and had led them to bear with the curtailment of their liberties by a central Government. When the Turkish danger was at an end, the real mission of the Habsburgs was also at an end, and a new *raison d'être* had to be found, in a period when the most disintegrating force of modern times, nationality, was working like a strong poison among the ten chief races and endless racial fragments of the Habsburg dominions. The essential question, then, was whether the dynasty could provide satisfactory institutions to counter the centrifugal tendencies which reasserted themselves now that the enemy was no longer at the gates, or, stated in another form, whether that which was good enough for the privileged classes could be made good enough for the peoples—above all for the submerged nations now slowly rising to the surface again—'The Unhistoric Nations,' as Dr. Renner has aptly called them. The answer to these questions lies not in the impossibility of the task, but in the careless diagnosis and quack remedies applied. Prussia's victory made it impossible to go on tinkering with one 'Provisorium' after another, followed by haggling in half a dozen directions. But this time, though drastic decisions were taken, they were fatally distorted by the promptings of revenge, and not based in any way upon an impartial weighing of the facts. Francis Joseph and his cousin Albert, the victor of Custozza, subordinated the internal policy of the Monarchy to the belief that in a new war, this time in alliance with the Second Empire, Prussia could be overthrown.

Beust as Chancellor

This underlying motive explains the fatal choice, as successor to Belcredi, whose federal day-dreams had become an embarrassment, of Baron (later Count) Beust, whom King Albert of Saxony had been forced to dismiss from the position of Saxon Premier, owing to his unstinted hostility to Bismarck and the 'Little German' party. In the first instance Beust replaced Mensdorff as Foreign Minister (October 30, 1866), resuming the title of Chancellor, dormant since Metternich ; it was only a matter of time for him to replace Belcredi himself as Premier (February 7, 1867). Though versatile and energetic, the new Minister was not a statesman of the first calibre ; he was swayed by personal sentiment and resentment, and above all was handicapped by a colossal vanity which made him imagine himself to be more than a match for Bismarck. On the other hand, as a foreigner, a German of the Reich and a Protestant, he failed to grasp the peculiar Austrian mentality, did not understand the complex internal politics and, worse still, was quite blissfully unaware of his own ignorance. No other than the German Liberal leader, Kaiserfeld, has left on record his view of Beust as 'a complete ignoramus in our affairs,' and therefore likely to 'do more harm than good' in a question 'which is decisive for the fate of Austria.' A spiteful saying preceded him to Vienna : 'He has buried Saxony, he has buried the Confederation, now he is going to bury Austria.'

One thing Beust grasped clearly—that until the Magyars were placated there was no possibility of Austria resuming an active foreign policy, and as this activity was essential to his plans for Germany, placated they must be at all costs. In this he found a valuable ally in 'Hungary's fair Providence,' the Empress Elizabeth, who had a sentimental attachment for the Magyar cause, entirely devoid of any political knowledge. But the decisive factor which turned the scales was undoubtedly the statesmanship of the Magyar leaders, and the tactical inadequacy of their Czech rivals. As early as July, 1866, within a fortnight of Prussia's victory, Deák had given to Francis Joseph his memorable reply: 'Hungary asks nothing more after Königgrätz than she asked before it.' Only the biggest men are capable of an attitude so magnanimous, though of course defeat had automatically—without his lifting a finger—changed Hungary's maximum into Hungary's minimum, the prospect of attainment being now so infinitely greater. It is the measure of the difference of stature between Deák and Francis Joseph that the former realized this to the full at the time, and the latter seemingly not. When asked at a later date to explain the phrase, Deák simply replied: "Because it was not a question of asking all we could get but of not asking more than we were sure of being able to keep." Deák, with his unequalled knowledge of Hungarian constitutional law, his contempt for honours or even office on the one hand and for demagogic tactics on the other, had at his side Count Julius Andrássy, the magnate with his social prestige, his diplomatic experience and his knowledge of Europe, and Baron Joseph Eötvös, the most truly Liberal of all his contemporaries, adding to his literary gifts a thorough grasp of political science and theory.

Of Francis Joseph, Joseph Redlich has well said that 'he never possessed a sufficiently clear grasp of the actual balance of forces to make a sacrifice at the right moment, but was always to have sacrifices forced upon him by defeat in the field.' The making of the Ausgleich provides the classic example.

The Ausgleich of 1867

The details of the final negotiations for the momentous Ausgleich or Compromise need not concern us here. The seventeen Diets of Austria were convoked for February 18, 1867, on a basis of direct election in place of the delegated authority of the original Reichsrat ; this change was due to Belcredi, and caused grave misgivings to the Germans, who had relied upon elaborately doctored franchises in the provinces to retain much more than their due share of power. But when the Diets met, it was only to be informed that the Emperor had found it necessary to come to terms with Hungary without delay, and that the projected 'Extraordinary Reichsrat' was now superfluous. On February 7 Beust replaced Belcredi, on the 17th, Andrássy became the first Premier of the new constitutional regime, Deák preferring to remain a private member ; and the rescript of February 27, formally restoring the Hungarian Constitution, showed that Francis Joseph had this time burnt his boats behind him. During March Parliament debated and adopted Law XII, regulating the new Dualist position between Hungary and Austria : all the illegalities of the past were recapitulated and legalized, and on June 8, Francis Joseph was crowned Apostolic King with all the traditional pomp.

For the purposes of this book it will suffice to summarize quite briefly the salient features of the famous Ausgleich. By it the old 'Austria' of

Francis I, which had been deliberately designed as an imperial super-structure to include Hungary, was divided, in theory and in practice, into two entirely distinct and equal parts—the Empire of Austria with its central Reichsrat and its seventeen provincial Diets, and the Apostolic Kingdom of Hungary henceforth incorporating Transylvania, and possessing only the central legislature in Budapest and the subordinate autonomous Sabor of Croatia-Slavonia in Zagreb. There was no common Parliament, and § 28 of the Hungarian Law xii of 1867 expressly declared any form of central Parliament whatsoever to be unacceptable to Hungary. Thus the two Premiers and Cabinets were responsible to their respective Parliaments only, though at times the Premiers met at Crown Councils presided over by the sovereign.

'Joint Affairs' were in the hands not of the Premiers and Cabinets, but of the three Joint Ministries of Foreign Affairs, War and Finance. Their heads were appointed by the Crown, and by a kind of unwritten understanding the post of Foreign Minister was supposed to be filled alternately by an Austrian and a Hungarian subject. In practice, of the seven holders of Foreign Affairs the two Andrássys and Burián were Magyars, Haymerle and Aehrenthal Austrians, while Kálnoky and Berchtold had almost equal ties of blood and property with both halves of the Monarchy. The Finance Ministry was occupied almost throughout the Dualist period by Hungarians—Lónyay, Kállay (1882-1903) and Burián. The Magyars came to occupy an altogether disproportionate share of diplomatic appointments : in 1914 they held the Embassies of Berlin, Rome, Paris, St. Petersburg and Constantinople.

The unique feature of the Dual system was the institution of the two Delegations, to which the three Joint Ministers were responsible. These were two parallel bodies of sixty members each—forty from the Lower, twenty from the Upper House of each Parliament, and in each case selected for one year only, from inside these respective bodies. Just as the two Parliaments never communicated direct, but only through the Joint Ministry within whose sphere the particular question at issue might fall ; so even the two Delegations were kept scrupulously apart, by care-fully contrived machinery (so anxious were Deák and his friends to avoid even the semblance of a unitary assembly). The two bodies met alter-nately in Vienna and in Budapest. They deliberated apart, and communi-cated with each other by writing—the so-called 'nuntium.' In the case of a difference of opinion between the two, and if after three exchanges of written views agreement was not reached, either body had the right to propose a joint vote. But though for this purpose they were to meet, discussion of any kind was ruled out : they were simply to vote and at once separate again. In practice, Hungarian opinion from the first set itself against even this faint reflection of unified action.

Their chief function was to control and pass the Joint Budget which, once adopted by them, was binding on the two Parliaments and Govern-ments ; and this power naturally carried with it the power to criticize policy. They also had the right to impeach a Joint Minister and to appoint a special *ad hoc* Tribunal to try him. But in practice this right was never exercised during the half century of Dualism.

There were thus three Budgets—an Austrian, a Hungarian, and an Austro-Hungarian, the third being reckoned on the basis of the so-called Quota—originally a proportion of 70-30 as between Austria and Hungary. This is the most striking example of that absolute parity between two sovereign states, with which Hungary made so much play. As soon as it came to paying, Hungary insisted on population as a fair basis, and even on this footing a deduction was made, for the proportion originally fixed was 57–42 of the total population. It is true that the Quota was modified on two subsequent occasions and finally stood at 65.6–34.4.[1]

As regards the State Debt, Hungary in the Ausgleich document specially repudiates all liability for any debts contracted 'without legal sanction' (i.e., without Parliament), but declares itself ready to take over its share of the burden, as the result of negotiations with Austria, 'as one free nation with another.' The basis of future finance was reached by the conversion in 1878 of the old National Bank in Vienna into the joint Austro-Hungarian Bank, in which Hungary step by step afterwards acquired a fuller share of control.

In its essence the Ausgleich was a permanent *political* accord, combined with a temporary *commercial* accord. The decennial economic renewals loosened the whole system, owing to the fatal blunder of fixing a date at which each accord expired, instead of its being automatically valid until its revision had been negotiated. The result of this was often enough to transfer the crisis from one half of the Monarchy to the other, in the desperate search for concessions here, there, and everywhere ; and eventually it was found that the Ausgleich could only be maintained by illegal means, above all by the notorious Paragraph Fourteen, which figures so prominently in the inner history of Austria under the Dual System. On a good many points, such as the postal service, coinage, weights, patents, monopolies, maritime law, uniformity had been imposed from the first. But there remained endless subjects of economic disagreement, and as the renewals had to be negotiated, *not* by the Delegations, but by two special Parliamentary Committees, while commercial Treaties had to be drafted by the Joint Foreign Office in agreement with the two Ministries of Commerce, the whole question of economic relations was dragged into the vortex of political and party intrigue. The sound German example had been ignored, and instead of a *Zollverein* leading to political union, economic relations were so fixed as to become a cause of permanent friction.

It cannot be too strongly emphasized that the Ausgleich was not what it pretended to be—namely, an agreement between Austria, Hungary and the Crown, the three parties affected—but simply an agreement between Hungary and the Crown over the head of Austria. Law XII of the Hungarian Parliament was in every way constitutional, the work of Crown and nation in unison ; the corresponding Law of the Austrian Reichsrat, of December 21, 1867, was, as regards its origin though not as regards its future effects, a mere 'blind,' to cover already accomplished facts. In other words, if the constitution of Hungary merely resumed, after many centuries of infringement and illegality, its ancient legal position, subject to certain restrictions voluntarily assumed in respect of its association with Austria, the constitution of Austria, on the other hand, had virtually no traditions behind it, and could almost without exaggeration be described as a free grant of the Crown.

A significant expression of this difference lies in the fact that while

[1] An instructive commentary on parity is to be found in a speech of Count Andrássy as Premier (January 16, 1869) : 'If anyone says that the conditions are unfavourable to us, I answer him thus : we contribute at present 30 per cent to the joint expenses, and enjoy just as many rights as those who contribute 70 per cent.'

in Hungary only the *rex coronatus*—the king crowned within a stated period, after a solemn oath to the Constitution—is legally entitled to sign decrees and exercise certain other royal functions, in Austria, on the other hand, there are no legal penalties for infringement of the constitution, no fixed term within which the Crown is bound to conform with its provisions, no apparent guarantee, except in the political circumstances of the moment, against the Crown resuming powers which it had voluntarily conceded. This is what the Crown actually did with the two constitutions of 1848 and 1849, and again with the October Diploma of 1860 and the February Patent of 1861 ; and there can be little doubt that Francis Joseph, when he signed the Ausgleich in 1867, by no means regarded it as a law of the Medes and Persians that cannot be altered, but was perfectly prepared for the possibility of a further *octroi* from above. This is amply proved by the events of 1871.

That the Reichsrat submitted to such vital decisions being taken over its head is to be explained by the fact that it was as yet a predominantly German body, and that the Ausgleich was, in the hard terms of domestic politics, an unholy compact between the two strongest races of the Monarchy, the Germans and the Magyars, with the connivance of the Crown. In effect, they divided the Monarchy between them ; each was to exercise hegemony in its own half, and, incidentally, each was to enlist the service of the two next strongest races—the Poles and the Croats—as accomplices in holding down the rest, by the grant of fairly wide autonomy to Galicia and Croatia.

From the standpoint of the Germans, the Ausgleich was an illustration of the proverb, *reculer pour mieux sauter*. It was by now abundantly clear that any attempt to squeeze Hungary into the strait-jacket of centralism was foredoomed to failure and might wreck the Monarchy in the process. By dropping the Hungarian ballast, and leaving the Magyars a free hand against the non-Magyars, they might hope to maintain Austria on centralist lines, and to keep the obstreperous Czechs in their place. And indeed the history of Austria for the next fifty years centres round the struggle of Germans and Czechs, personifying in one formula after another the rival principles of centralism and federalism.

In one respect the seeming complaisance of the Austrian Germans was in reality the price paid by them for an enormous prize. After the experiences of the previous nineteen years they might be excused for doubts as to whether the constitutional regime now about to be introduced in Austria would be any more permanent than its predecessors. Throughout the negotiations between Hungary and the Crown Andrássy in particular had insisted that 'the monarchy can only be strong if its two halves are free and constitutional, each in its own way, but both equally.' Now the result of his insistence was that the Ausgleich laid down as two absolutely 'fundamental conditions,' on the one hand 'the maintenance of the Hungarian Constitution' and on the other 'full constitutionalism' *in Austria*, because 'Hungary can only enter into contact with the constitutional representatives of Austria in the matter of common relations.' This amounted to a mutual guarantee of constitutionalism between Hungary and Austria, and the fact that in each case this was automatically bound up with racial hegemony made the bargain all the more attractive. In effect it gave Hungary a certain right of interference in Austrian internal affairs ; the most notable example was in 1871, when Andrássy turned the scale against the federalist experiment of Hohenwart, and justified his action quite openly on the ground that it was no mere internal question, but affected the whole Monarchy, if Hungary were to be confronted with a series of small federal Diets in place of the central Reichsrat.

More than this, the so-called 'December Constitution,' which represented Austria's side of the bargain, consisted of a series of really liberal fundamental laws, assuring full equality before the law, inviolability of property, free expression of opinion, liberty of conscience and teaching, freedom of assembly and association and the right of petition. No less remarkable, though less easy to realize, were the two articles assuring to every race (*Volksstamm*) 'an inviolable right to the maintenance and use of its nationality and language,' and 'equal rights' (*Gleichberechtigung*) of all languages in common use, 'in school, office and public life.' This placed Austria at one stroke far ahead of Hungary, where liberty of assembly and association was withheld, and where the famous Law of Nationalities passed in 1868 remained from the first entirely on paper.

The Czechs and the Ausgleich

It is necessary to add that the Czech leaders were in no way equal to the occasion. Palacký, Rieger and Brauner were, like Deák, received by the Emperor a few weeks after Königgrätz, but they made a far less favourable impression upon him and alienated him by their doctrinaire over-insistence on 'State Rights.' In theory Bohemia and Hungary were, of course on the same level as ancient independent states, but when Rieger tried to draw a parallel between the surrender of Világos in 1849 and the capitulation after the White Mountain, in 1620, he was shutting his eyes to the reality of two whole centuries and to the many factors in the domestic and foreign constellation that favoured the Magyars rather than the Czechs. It was just nonsense to argue that if the 'Laws of 1848' were Hungary's historic right, so the Imperial rescript of April 6, 1848, was Bohemia's historic right, guaranteeing the restoration of her independence. He was on stronger ground when insisting on the solidarity of all the Slav nations of Austria ; for he had repeatedly conferred with the Croat Bishop Strossmayer and—more important from the point of view of winning over the Crown—with Count Goluchowski. But he did not help the Czech cause by declaring that Austria would only 'exist so long as her Slav peoples wished it,' and that 'if they once really ceased to wish it, God Himself could not preserve it.' It may well be that the cautious tactics of his allies among the feudal nobility were partly due to indiscretions of this kind ; certainly their reserve contributed materially to the failure of the Czech leaders and to their lack of any real contact with the Crown at the very moment of its decisive negotiations with Deák and Andrássy. By comparison with this, the overtures made by Adolf Fischhof for direct discussions between Germans and Slavs hardly weighed at all in the balance, and did not win the support which they deserved. Fischhof, a Jewish advocate of character and vision, who had played his part at Kroměříž, may be called the Cassandra of the German Liberals. His book on *Austria and the Guarantees of her Existence* showed what might have been if sanity and tolerance had prevailed on all sides. In actual fact his watchword of a 'monarchical Switzerland' was constantly quoted, but no serious attempt was ever made to put it into practice.

In October, 1866, Francis Joseph paid his first visit to Prague after peace had been signed with Prussia in that city, and under the impression of Prussia's failure to kindle any response among the Czech masses. He was greeted by the Mayor Bělský with pointed hopes for a speedy coronation. In December the Address of the Bohemian Diet, presented to the Emperor by Count Leo Thun, again broached the question of coronation and hoped that 'the Lands of the Bohemian Crown will not be included in any new form of State Rights without the consent of their legal representatives.' In the Diet Rieger insisted that the Czech nation demanded equality with Hungary, and that Dualism would involve the ruin of Austria. Austria, he said, "will only survive so long as the Slav peoples hold to Austria."

Already the Bohemian Diet, now with a Czech majority as the result of Belcredi's policy of direct elections, had adopted an Address, challenging the powers of the Reichsrat, affirming the equal rights of Bohemia and Hungary, and even declaring that 'the legitimacy of dynasties and that of peoples, have common, intertwined roots; tear the latter from the soil and the former will no longer be solid.' But the Emperor had taken the plunge and could not turn back; he sent his brother to Prague, to warn the aristocracy to leave the sinking Czech ship, and at the elections of April the Germans recaptured their lost majority at the Diets of Prague and Brno. Rieger, summoning all his rousing eloquence, warned a hostile House that injustice to the Czechs would weigh heavily upon the Monarchy; he even quoted St. René Taillandier's view that their treatment was supplying Russian propaganda with an effective weapon. His protests were treated with open contempt by the German deputies, and the Reichsrat, which met in May, 1867, was entirely subservient to Beust and accepted the accomplished fact.

The crowning blunder of the Czechs was the visit of Palacký, Rieger and Gregr to the Moscow Exhibition in the summer of 1867. Rieger's eloquence at a banquet led him to declare that though the Slavs were the youngest nation and had come rather late, their turn had now come for the Age of Slav Enlightenment. The main task was Russia's; if she fulfilled it, then all Slavs would bow before her. Prague and Moscow were of equal fame : "Prague is preparing the Slav idea of the future, and we, her children, bring this idea from Prague to the mother city of Moscow." This demonstration had the double disadvantage of greatly annoying Francis Joseph and his entourage, and of offending the Poles at a moment when memories of Russian repression in 1863 were still at white heat, and thus of facilitating the efforts of Vienna to win over the Austrian Poles by an extension of Galician autonomy, and to separate them from the Czechs. It was entirely barren, as the Government of the Tsar had no intention of quarrelling with Vienna for the sake of the politically powerless Czechs ; and it only produced, on both friend and foe, the impression of pique, combined with perplexity. By adhering to their policy of parliamentary abstention in Vienna, they played straight into the hands of the Germans, who were left in an unassailable position.

CHAPTER XIII

CZECHS AND GERMANS UNDER THE DUAL SYSTEM
(1867–1914)

L'Autriche n'était point un état, mais une juxtaposition incohérente de domaines en friche, un assemblage bizarre de chancelleries et de conférences.

—Emile Bourgeois.

L'Autriche n'est pas une nation, pas même un état, mais uniquement un gouvernement.

—Prince Gortchakov.

How false was the impression thus created may be gathered from a minor incident of this period. In July, 1869, Rieger paid a visit to Paris, where he had a secret audience with Napoleon III and handed him a memorandum which was soon afterwards, by an indiscretion, published in a garbled form in the Vienna press. This incident naturally earned him the denunciation of the German Nationalists and was embarrassing to the Court of Vienna ; but Rieger's underlying motive was to secure Napoleon as intermediary between Russia and Austria in the cause of the Austrian Slavs. It coincided with secret negotiations between Vienna and Paris for an alliance against Berlin, in which St. Petersburg's sympathies were to be enlisted on the Franco-Austrian side. The whole affair is an illustration of the fluid state in which the main problems of the Habsburg Monarchy still were, and of the extent to which they were bound up with major European policy.

There was clearly much spade work to be done before the Czechs could acquire the necessary political experience and successfully attempt a forward policy. They lacked the long political tradition of the Magyars. They lacked the support of all save a fraction of the aristocracy. They had no such national entrenchments as were possessed by the Magyars in the county assemblies and administration, and they had against them not only the Germans, with their older and better organized social system, and the bureaucracy with its definitely *anti*-national, centralist and dynastic tradition, but also the obstructive influence of the Church. For by a great misfortune the hierarchy had become the tool of the Habsburg dynasty, and this fact, together of course with the Hussite memories of Bohemian history, gave a certain anti-clerical tinge to the national movement. It is quite true that the parochial clergy—recruited in the main from the peasantry—was genuinely patriotic in sentiment and deserved well of the nation. But on the whole it is true to say that among the Czechs, as indeed throughout the greater part of the Austrian Empire,[1] there was a divorce between intellect and the Church. The bourgeoisie, and above all the academic class, tended to be free-thinking or indifferent.

A New Stage in the Czech Revival

By the early 'sixties the tide of national revival was running fast in Prague. Eminent scientists like Purkyně and Presl were no longer

[1] Here, as so often, Galicia must be carefully excluded from any such generalization.

compelled to write in German for lack of an adequate Czech terminology. Kaloušek had laid the foundations of a constitutional history of Bohemia, at the moment when, it must be admitted, 'State Rights' almost performed the functions of a fetish. Tomek, the historian of Prague, paid the price for writing in Czech only by forfeiting his place among his continental fellows. Meanwhile a new school of writers was coming to the front ; notable among them were the peasant tales of Božena Nemcova, faintly reminiscent of George Sand, and the short stories of Neruda, drawn from the life of the *petite bourgeoisie* of the 'Malá Strana' of Prague. Above all, the first portents of modern Czech music made themselves known ; Smetana's first opera, *The Brandenburgers in Bohemia*, and the incomparable *Bartered Bride*, were performed in 1863 with considerable success, in the city which had witnessed the first triumphs of Gluck and Mozart's glorious but alien art, and was now to develop its own rich native talent. In 1868 the first stone of the Czech National Theatre was laid. Everywhere the buds were breaking after the frosts of a prolonged winter.

Special mention must be made of the foundation of the *Národni Listý* in 1861, the first big Czech political daily. Its first editor was Rieger, and the main plank of its programme was 'complete and equal rights' for all races, including the Jews. 'The problem of national freedom at this time is the crucial issue in the state . . . our claim is for equal rights,' as in 1848. 'But let no one imagine that we can be assuaged with an empty and barren recognition in principle of our demands. Not words, but deeds— we must see 'our equality acknowledged in all walks of public life, even to the state agencies and the schools.' Moreover, the less numerous a nation is, the greater must be its activity in self-affirmation, the greater its care for a healthy and well-ordered development ; for stagnation and corruption set in most easily among small nations.

Havlíček's zeal for the coming generation inspired another movement, more remarkable than anything of its kind which Europe was to know until the days of Baden-Powell and the Boy Scouts, and even more decisive in its influence upon the mind of the Czech nation. What the Czechs are to-day they owe in very large measure to the Sokols,[1] the gymnastic society founded in 1862 by Fugner and Tyrš. Modelled on the German *Turnvereine* which played so great a part in the student movement of Germany, and hence in German politics, after the War of Liberation, it was very far from being imitative. Physical drill and gymnastics were the most striking external feature, and the vast assemblies of 15,000 men and women drilling in union at the 'Slet' (or Assembly of all the Sokols) soon became one of the memorable things in modern Prague. But this was merely external and preparatory. The goal set by Tyrš is revealed in the Society's statutes—'By the education of body and spirit, by physical energy, by art and science, by all moral means, to revive the fatherland.' "Let us learn to serve our nation," he said, "it is the noblest aim to offer to our efforts." Every nation, however small, had in his view a right to exist, but only if it showed itself capable of asserting this right. "It is not the past, even the most flourishing, that can guarantee the existence of a nation, but its activity and health in the living present."

The motto of the Sokols should be 'eternal evolution,' or indeed 'eternal discontent.' The whole nation should help in developing 'its strength, its valour, its pugnacity. . . . It is only when we have reached such a degree of perfection as to fear no comparison with the foreigner

[1] Sokol means Falcon.

that we shall have fulfilled our duty towards our own selves. Whoever is content with less, it is as though he wished nothing. . . . We must march freely with head held high. Perish on the way or be first to reach the goal. All or nothing. There are mottoes for you.' 'Tyrš was not content to introduce an almost scientific system into gymnastics ; he tried to give them a philosophic basis in the evolutionism of Darwin, then at the height of its vogue. His æsthetic side is shown at its most original in the mass exercises in which the Sokol Congresses of recent decades culminated, and which in our own day evoked a special kind of musical accompaniment—a living and rhythmic symphony. In a word, gymnastics as conceived by the Sokols are of a higher order ; they are a factor in our outlook on life, an artistic and moral expression of the human soul, a joyous cry of mass enthusiasm. The Sokol movement created something entirely new out of materials which were merely the raw mass of the older gymnastic serving purely physical ends.'[1]

It should be added that Tyrš had fully grasped the lesson which is to us a commonplace of modern warfare, but was by no means so universally obvious in the 'sixties. His idea was that soldiers can be taught the use of arms fairly rapidly, but that what takes so much time is to give them what he calls 'the indispensable combative qualities' ; this needs 'long years of repeated exercises.' In other words, he had studied the 'philosophy of discipline' and his teaching involved not merely physical drill, but intellectual drill in the ethics of citizenship.

Perhaps even more fundamental was the fact that the Sokol movement rested on essentially democratic principles, without any distinctions of rank or class. It, as indeed the whole Czech revival, was essentially a middle-class movement. With trifling exceptions the aristocracy stood aside, and the intellectual leaders were drawn from the ranks of the bourgeoisie and peasantry.

Some idea of the resentment felt by the Czechs at the attitude of the Crown may be gathered from incidents that followed the transfer of the Bohemian regalia from Vienna to Prague and a visit of the Emperor to open a new bridge. When it was recalled that the day selected was the anniversary of the execution of Czech patriots in 1621, broadsheets were put about denouncing all who attended the ceremony as traitors to the nation, and there was an exodus of thousands from the city for the day. Things were not improved by the remark officially put in the Emperor's mouth : 'Prague makes an entirely German impression.'

The 'Bourgeois Ministry'

There can be no doubt that the new constitutional era in Austria, known as the 'December Constitution,' began as yet another 'Provisorium,' in the minds both of those who made it and those who had to work it. The fateful decision of the Czechs to uphold their policy of abstention under the so-called 'Bourgeois Ministry' of Prince Carlos Auersperg (December 31, 1867--April 4, 1870) and under his immediate successors in office, gave to the whole regime a very definite impetus in one direction. The period from 1867 to 1879, with one significant interlude, was the golden era of the German Liberals in Austria. Though often doctrinaire in views, and certainly narrow in their racial outlook, its leaders —men such as Herbst, Giskra, Plener, Hasner, Berger, Kaiserfeld—

[1] Macháček, 'The Sokol Movement' (*Slavonic Review*, No. 49, July, 1932).

genuinely stood, according to their lights, for Liberal principles, and were responsible for the legislation which, after two generations had been wasted, was to bring Austria more or less into line with Germany and the West. The fundamental laws of 1867 were followed by a new Penal Code, by the introduction of juries for press offences, by financial measures to check the chronic deficit by a reorganization of the administration (notably the system of political districts, *Bezirkshauptmannschaften* dependent on the Ministry of the Interior). Moreover, the Crown by its alliance with the German Liberals found itself reluctantly driven to renounce the Concordat, and to accept a series of laws which knocked the bottom out of the old Clerical-absolutist regime. The most notable of these, which had results no less profound among the Czechs than elsewhere in Austria, were the Marriage Law, which established the jurisdiction of the civil courts and removed the decision from the hands of the clergy, though leaving undisturbed the provisions of the Roman Canon Law in matters of marriage and divorce, and the Education Law, which transferred the control from the clergy to state officials, though clerical influence, direct and indirect, still remained immensely strong.

The Czechs and the German Liberal Regime

Francis Joseph, to whom close dealings with bourgeois ministers were antipathetic, had at first hoped to impose a check upon them by adding such *grands seigneurs* as Auersperg, Count Taaffe, and Count Potocki, whose special task it was to win over the Poles by wide autonomy in Galicia. But though the hostile, and indeed openly oppressive, attitude adopted towards the Czechs in 1868, in response to their 'Declaration' of the grounds determining their abstention from the Bohemian Diet as well as the Reichsrat, was now definitely dropped by Alfred Potocki. The Old Czechs under Rieger, prompted by their allies among the feudal nobility (notably Thun, Karl Schwarzenberg and Clam), were deaf to official overtures and followed an 'all or nothing' line which did not correspond to the real facts. The German Liberal leaders invited Rieger and Slavkovsky to confer with them in Vienna, but Old and Young Czechs sent a joint refusal. The Poles also decided to absent themselves from the Reichsrat, to be followed by Roumanians, Slovenes and Italians, and finally even a trickle of German Clericals, until finally only 129 deputies (ninety German Bohemians forming the backbone) still attended its sittings. The Poles did not hesitate to declare that the system was bound to lead, not to peace and understanding, but to fresh conflicts, ending in either despotism or paralysis. On the Austrian side the whole Dual System seemed to be crumbling, while clouds rapidly gathered in the sky of Europe. The July elections produced a federalist majority in the Diet of Bohemia, which provisionally recognized the Ausgleich with Hungary, subject to the Crown promising to the Lands of the Bohemian Crown equal independence and legal status. To Herbst's denunciations of federalism Rieger flat-footedly retorted : "The Germans want to make our king the vassal of King William of Prussia ; they believe in blue blood among the nations, in a privilege of the Germans as against the Slavs," whereas all the Czechs asked was 'self-determination, for the honour, power and liberty of Austria.' On September 29 came an Imperial Rescript in answer, paying high tribute to the prestige of the Bohemian Crown and treating coronation at Prague as a symbol of 'inward union

with the Czech people of Bohemia.' It even expressed a readiness to
revise the relations between Bohemia and the monarchy as a whole, but it
insisted that the first and most urgent need of the situation was that the
representatives of Bohemia should take their seats in the Reichsrat
without delay. It met with a flat refusal, all the more sensational because
its spokesman was no other than Count Leo Thun.

France and the Czechs

Meanwhile the Franco-German War had broken out, and took from
the first so decisive a turn that Austria-Hungary, on the very eve of
binding arrangements with France, withdrew into a neutrality all the
more embarrassed because the Tsar took Bismarck's side and was able,
as the price of his benevolence, to tear up the Black Sea restrictions
imposed upon him in 1856. For the Czechs the situation was tragic ;
France was in distress, Austria held aloof, Russia was virtually in the
Prussian camp. Undeterred by all considerations of expediency, Rieger
and his colleagues in the Diet, on December 8, 1870, drew up a memorial
expressing sympathy for 'the noble and glorious French people, which
has rendered such services to civilization, progress and liberty,' and
protesting against Prussia's designs upon Alsace-Lorraine as bound to be
'a source of new wars.' It went on to greet the emancipation of the
Balkan nations, to hope for the future union of all the Balkan Slavs, and
to define Austria's historic mission as 'a free association of peoples bent
upon common defence and enjoying wide autonomy and equal rights.'
At a party organized in honour of the French Consul, Palacký himself
declared that 'all Slavs love France, because they are democrats by nature
and consequently demand right and liberty for all, whereas the Germans
and Magyars aspire to dominion over subject peoples.' When all Europe
was silent, and France was on the verge of ruin, the Czechs took their
stand openly and remained true to type.

Shortly before the war Rieger had addressed a Memorandum to the
Duke of Gramont, then French Ambassador in Vienna, expounding the
importance of a Czech state in Europe, and reminding him that 'Bohemian
territory in the pass of Taus (Domažlice) is not so far from the Prussian
frontier as is Saarbrücken from Paris. A French army could therefore
be thrown more quickly into Bohemia than a Prussian army advancing
from Berlin could reach Frankfurt.' It is not surprising that the vain
and superficial Beust should have regarded Rieger's attitude as nothing
less than treasonable.

The Hohenwart Interlude

Francis Joseph, torn between his lack of sympathy for the Czechs
and his detestation of the German Liberals, especially after their onslaught
on the Concordat, began to waver once more on major constitutional
issues. In face of a victorious Prussia it was more than ever urgent for
him to establish in Austria a regime that was capable of smooth working.
In February, 1871, then Potocki was replaced by Count Carl Hohenwart,
with Dr. Albert Schäffle, a Württemberg economist of some note, who had
become Professor in Vienna and was a convert to federal ideas, as his
alter ego. For the first time a Czech was made Minister of Education, in
the person of the distinguished historian Joseph Jireček, the son-in-law
of Šafařik. These appointments were greeted with scorn and abuse in

German liberal circles—in the phrase of the *Neue Freie Presse* : 'the Sedan of the German spirit in Austria' ; but when they laughed at his 'Carnival Cabinet' (*Faschingsministerium*) there came the reminder that the Czechs had buried, one after another, the Cabinets that had shown themselves more rigid than Hohenwart. Schäffle, however, had won over the Emperor to the view that the artificial Austrian franchise and indirect elections were 'a great constitutional lie' which was to blame for the whole situation. The Imperial rescript of appointment described the new Cabinet as 'a truly Austrian Government, standing above the parties.'

The summer passed in a marshalling and redistribution of forces in the seventeen Diets ; but on September 10, 1871, an Imperial Rescript was issued, recognizing the rights of the Bohemian kingdom and the monarch's readiness 'to renew this recognition by our coronation oath.' At the same time the draft of a new Law of Nationalities was laid before the Bohemian Diet. Its main clauses assured equal linguistic and other rights to Czechs and Germans, insisted on a knowledge of both languages in speech and writing as a condition of appointment as an official or judge, and divided the Diet into distinct national Curiæ, in each of which a two-thirds majority would suffice to block any bill. The Germans, whose main concern was not to achieve equality but to maintain their own tottering supremacy, withdrew in a fury from the Diet, arguing that the Rescript had the effect of removing Bohemia from the framework of the Constitution. The combined Czech and feudal majority was left in possession of the field, and submitted to Francis Joseph, together with its address of homage, eighteen 'Fundamental Articles,' negotiated between Schäffle and the Czech leaders. In them the Czechs recognize the Ausgleich with Hungary, but all matters not expressly defined as 'common affairs' of Austria-Hungary (i.e. all except foreign affairs, military affairs and finance) fall within the province of the Bohemian Diet, which will henceforward elect direct to the Delegations. The office of Bohemian Aulic Chancellor is revived, and a special Bohemian Cabinet is to be formed under him. Bohemia's quota to general Austrian finances is to be arrived at by negotiation with delegates from the other provinces.

As nothing came of all this, it is unnecessary to dwell on further details. It is, however, to be noted that the new federal project was never put to the test, but violently denounced from the first day. Even so moderate a writer as Richard Charmatz takes it for granted that its application would have caused 'a chaos of rights and duties, representative bodies and responsible officials,' and would have ended, not in peace, but in 'war *en permanence*.' The whole incident is the crowning example of that blend of uncertainty, haughty disdain and perfidy which lay at the root of Francis Joseph's character, far deeper than his undoubted good intentions and powers of application. He had told Hohenwart when he appointed him, that there could be no more turning back (*es giebt kein rückwärts mehr*). Yet within a month of the Fundamental Articles he had, for the sixth time in his reign, reversed the machine of state and reverted from one constitutional experiment to another of an entirely different character. This time there was a desperate storm upon him from many quarters. The German Liberals threatened to leave the Reichsrat, in view of the new clerical-feudal-federalist majority that was forming there. Count Andrássy took alarm at the probable bearing upon the whole Ausgleich settlement, and left no stone unturned at the Court. He based his action on the view that the proposed innovations could not possibly be regarded as a mere internal affair of Austria, but intruded a new and unauthorized factor into the constitutional position. Beust, in his turn, saw the rival nationalities in Austria growing beyond his control and comprehension ; and by an irony of fate he found himself giving to Francis Joseph the same advice that came from Bismarck and William I. Beust's former master, King Albert of Saxony, came to Vienna specially to urge his view upon his friend and kinsman the Emperor. The Poles began to hesitate, and the feudal nobility seem not to have played their cards well with the Emperor. In the Cabinet Hohenwart found himself in a minority on October 20, and a week later he was dismissed from office. After a short interlude of uncertainty Prince Adolf Auersperg, a younger brother of the late Premier, took office with a cabinet of German Liberals and officials.

The abandonment of the Hohenwart experiment had a disastrous effect upon the Czechs ; Francis Joseph broke his plighted word for the third time, and neither was forgiven nor himself forgave. Rieger, when he returned to Prague after Hohenwart's fall, openly told the crowd : "The Czech people has suffered a severe blow. We have lost the battle, but kept our honour unimpaired. Strangers have pressed in between us and the Crown, people who have no heart and no understanding for the state, and they have won. But we shall hold out on the path of right until a better view prevails where the decision lies. . . . We are driven back, but not conquered ; and we appeal from the monarch badly informed to the monarch better informed, with whom we shall be reconciled once more." He was wrong. This time Francis Joseph never turned back again, but clung, for good or for ill, to that Dual System of which he was proud to be one of the creators, and whose fatal influence upon the development of the Monarchy he never fully grasped.[1]

It was characteristic of the Emperor that he used this opportunity for also dropping Beust, who was replaced as Foreign Minister by Count Andrássy, the first Premier of the revived parliamentary Hungary. The evil that Beust had done lived after him, and the far abler Andrássy, quite logically from the standpoint of Transleithania, may be said to have acted as gaoler in two directions—to guard the Emperor from the temptation of further lapses into federalism, to preserve inviolate the Ausgleich settlement, and also to remove obstacles from the path that led to an alliance between the former rivals, Austria and Prussia. Once more Francis Joseph acted on the principle : 'The Moor has done his duty, the Moor can go.' His ingratitude towards his military and political advisers, already shown towards Bach, Bruck, Benedek and Tegetthoff, and now applied to Beust, was to remain proverbial throughout his long reign, and Andrássy himself was to experience it eight years later.

It is perhaps worth quoting the verdict of an unusually well-informed German Liberal writer, writing a whole generation after the event ; if he could write thus in 1903, it may be imagined what the still dominant Germans in Vienna and Prague felt in 1871. 'The eleven months of the Hohenwart era,' writes Gustav Kolmer, 'had shaken Austria to her foundations, increased the appetite of the nationalities, discredited Liberalism and the Liberal party, strengthened the general distrust

---

[1] Schäffle has left on record his appreciation of the way in which Francis Joseph's mind worked : 'to live from hand to mouth, to accept what every day brings, and when this does not work, to experiment, and soon to give way again, after the first impatient grasp.'

towards any serious resolve of the Government to restore internal peace, dragged the Crown into the strife of parties, and caused such general confusion that all hope of removing existing differences between the Kingdoms and Lands seemed at an end. What still remained of the old Austria was henceforth destroyed by the jealousy of contending parties and nationalities ; official authority was undermined.'[1]

Czech Abstention

The policy of boycotting the central Parliament in Vienna was now resumed, and for the next eight years the Czechs sulked in their corner, while the new Government, anxious to prove its Germanism to its perturbed followers, proceeded to try intimidation—sending General Koller back to Prague as Military Governor. The Press was muzzled, and the cases of Czech journalists were tried before German juries. The right of assembly was rigidly curtailed. Members of the Royal Society of Science were deprived of the right to lecture at the University. Nothing illustrates more crudely the impasse which had been reached than the imposition of fines upon those who placarded the Imperial Manifesto of September 12, 1871 ; for it was impossible to read its text without realizing that Francis Joseph had once more broken his word to the nation. The intensity of feeling on the Czech side is no less clearly reflected in the 'political testament' which the veteran Palacký addressed to the nation in 1872. In it he deliberately revoked his much-quoted phrase : 'If Austria did not exist, it would be necessary to create her.' He had originally coined it in reliance upon the sense of justice of the German nation ; now that that nation was trampling Czech rights underfoot and building a new state edifice upon contradictions and lies, the phrase had lost its validity. This was Palacký's last public utterance ; in 1876 he died full of years and enshrined in the heart of the Czech people, leaving the leadership of the now increasingly Conservative 'Old Czech' party to his son-in-law Rieger, in close alliance with Count Henry Clam Martinic and Prince George Lobkovicz.

Rieger, with his watchword, 'We won't give in,' and his friends among the feudal nobility, had led the Czechs into a blind alley ; and they pushed their logic to the length of boycotting not only the Reichsrat, but the Diets of Prague and Brno. The result was to leave the German Liberals supreme in all three bodies, and to renounce for themselves every trace of control over foreign or domestic policy. This barren policy of abstention led inevitably to political schism ; the Young Czechs, whose seven deputies in the Diet defied the boycott imposed by the Old Czechs, kept themselves increasingly in evidence by their lively agitation, though the quarrel at first took an unedifying form owing to the revelations of the police spy Sabina, originally one of their foremost demagogues.

From 1871 to 1879 the German Liberals still ruled Austria, but they were less firm in the saddle, they no longer enjoyed the same moral force and their ranks were torn by dissensions. Their power rested simply on a bargain with the Crown ; it would govern constitutionally if they in return would vote all military credits and so leave untouched the Crown's prerogative and the country's prestige abroad. Court circles were not friendly, but in Charmatz's phrase : 'They held the responsible ministers to their posts, because they saw that with the Government a system which

<hr />

[1] *Parlament und Verfassung in Oesterreich*, ii, p. 202.

was repellent to them was also in its death throes.' They checked the dry rot that was already noticeable by the partial electoral reform of 1873, which introduced direct elections and increased the number of seats from 202 to 353 ; but this was set off by a complicated system of Curiæ, or Electoral Colleges, setting up quite arbitrary distinctions between town and country districts, assigning eighty-five seats to the landed interest (*Grossgrundbesitz*) and maintaining an objectionable 'electoral geometry.'

The regime was weakened by the financial 'Krach' of 1873 and the ensuing scandals in Parliament, which revealed the lax manner in which some parliamentarians had interpreted the incompatibility of mandates and office with directorships and other profitable business propositions. Herbst and Giskra in particular, were lacking in tact, and their anti-clerical leanings were much resented in high quarters. To the Crown they were mere tools, to be discarded at the first occasion, while the other strongest forces in Austria—the high aristocracy, the Church, the bureaucracy, the Army, were all frankly hostile to the regime. The German Liberal leaders were too obtuse, or too cocksure, to realize that they held office only on sufferance ; that there were two fields in which the Crown would under no circumstances tolerate interference—namely, military affairs and foreign policy ; and that they would interfere at their peril. Already distrusted because of their campaign against the Church, they gradually allowed themselves to be led into opposition to military credits, which to Francis Joseph seemed a breach of contract and little short of a declaration of war. But their attitude during the Eastern Crisis of 1875–1878 added fuel to the flames, at a period of prolonged tension and uncertainty. They were violently anti-Slav—thereby provoking the Czechs and Southern Slavs to demonstrate in favour of Serbia and Russia —and at the final crisis opposed the occupation of Bosnia by Austria-Hungary mainly on the ground that it would increase the Slav population of the Monarchy by about two millions. The scandal reached its height when Herbst and most of his colleagues voted against the credits which Andrássy asked from the Delegations as a backing for his policy at the Congress of Berlin, and openly opposed occupation, still more annexation. Andrássy's secretive tactics were partly to blame, but Prince Auersperg, having denied any design of military action, found himself in an impossible position when the Congress assigned the mandate to Francis Joseph in July, and the army of General Filipović crossed the frontier a fortnight later. The 115 recalcitrants of the Left were constantly voicing their protests, and Herbst, in demanding that the Reichsrat, and not merely the Delegation, should speak 'a free word,' roused the Emperor's anger still further.

Auersperg resigned on July 5, 1878, but remained *in statu demissionis* for many months, while Francis Joseph looked around him. The last straw in alienating him from the German Liberals seems to have been the attitude of Herbst, who recommended Baron Depretis as the suitable candidate for the Premiership and then withheld all backing from him, thereby making his failure a foregone conclusion. Francis Joseph never forgave this ; a phrase which he let drop in conversation probably supplies the clue : 'You are always talking of Andrássy's policy ; don't forget, that is *my* policy !' After several abortive attempts to form a Cabinet on the old basis, he decided to transfer his support from the Liberals and, not without hesitation, to look elsewhere for a majority. This meant the abandonment of the German monopoly in parliamentary life, and a reorientation, not whole-hearted, but still sufficiently pronounced, in the direction of the Slavs.

In February, 1879, Auersperg gave place to a provisional and colourless Cabinet under the former Minister of Education, Dr. von Stremayr ; in June elections were held, at which the German Liberals lost their majority ; and in August Count Edward Taaffe became Premier, with a Cabinet composed according to methods hitherto unknown in Austria. The majority by which Taaffe governed from 1879 to 1893—the so-called 'Iron Ring'—was made up of three main sections, the Poles, the Czechs and the 'Hohenwart Club' (or Right Centre, which might perhaps be described as Conservative rather than Tory). The first and third of these numbered 57 each, the second 54, making a total of 168 ; and the German Liberals and Progressives, whose combined strength was 145, thus found themselves in a clear minority.

A few words are needed to explain the changed attitude of the Czechs. As late as 1875 Rieger and Prince Lobkovicz had sent a categorical refusal to enter the Reichsrat ; and again in November, 1877, thirty-two Czech deputies had sent a more than usually long-winded exposé of their historic claim, refusing to enter an assembly which demanded their 'unconditional submission' to what they regarded as illegal. But already in 1876 Edward Gregr had published a pamphlet in favour of a return to the Reichsrat, arguing quite bluntly that State Rights, in their present undefined form, were not worth one pipe of tobacco. The tide was running strongly against Rieger, who found it expedient in October, 1878, to confer with the veteran Liberal Fischhof, and Etienne and Scharf, then editors of the *Neue Freie Presse*, and the *Sonn-und-Montagsblatt*. Four points were accepted as a basis for a national peace—the drafting of an Austrian 'Law of Nationalities,' electoral reform, provincial self-government, and the return of the Czechs to Parliament in defence of the principle of liberty. But Herbst was hostile and deliberately wrecked a most promising line of advance ; and Etienne, who was furious at his whole attitude, died during 1879, leaving the control of the *Neue Freie Presse* to fall into the hands of Moritz Benedikt, one of the most brilliant, most mischievous and most influential of the great Jewish journalists of the Dualist era. In view of Hitler's naïve assertion[1] that the Jewish Press of Vienna was hostile to the German cause, it is necessary to insist very strongly that, on the contrary, its chief organs stood quite openly in the service of Berlin and the Triple Alliance, and consistently threw their whole weight into the scale for the Magyars and against the Slavs, alike in Bohemia, among the Southern Slavs and in Hungary. How little he knew of the land of his birth is further illustrated by the ludicrous accusation levelled against Francis Ferdinand, that he was working in the interests of the Czechs.

Taaffe and the Iron Ring

Taaffe was neither a man of keen convictions nor of profound intellect ; and indeed, if he had been, he would hardly have been acceptable to Francis Joseph, who both preferred and found it more convenient to surround himself with political mediocrities. He was accustomed to Taaffe as an old school comrade and Taaffe, who had the sort of jovial wit which corresponded to the Emperor's own moods, set himself to be

[1] *Mein Kampf*, pp. 57–9,.

the 'Kaiserminister' *par excellence* and to deserve the title of a famous play of Grillparzer, *Ein treuer Diener seines Herren*. His advent thus meant a great accession in the power of the Crown.

He was not long in formulating two novel principles of government : 'None of the various nationalities in Cisleithania is to obtain decisive predominance. In Austria no one may be squeezed against the wall' (*In Oesterreich darf Niemand an die Wand gedrückt werden*). And again : 'A party government is in contradiction to the principles on which the Monarchy rests.' Both these phrases represented a complete reversal of the system which had hitherto prevailed under Dualism, and the second was unique in the annals of parliamentary government, if not necessarily a denial of its *raison d'être*. They meant that Taaffe stood for a programme of reconciliation, and relied for its achievement upon a coalition of different elements.

Taaffe started with one great achievement—the abandonment of abstention by the Czechs and their entry into the active current of affairs in the Reichsrat. This time everything was made easy for them ; they handed in a fresh statement of their historic claims, and the Speech from the Throne (October 8, 1879) welcomed their return 'in response to My call, without detriment to their legal convictions, and without regard to their difference of view.'

Czech support was purchased in three main directions.

(1) The first of a series of Language Decrees for Bohemia was issued in 1880, enjoining the political, administrative and judicial authorities to use in each case the language employed by the parties concerned. This was intensely resented by the Germans of Bohemia, who always took the view that an inroad upon their hegemony was almost in the nature of persecution. "Germans we are," said Schmeykal, one of their leaders, "and Germans we wish to remain. As such we want to be not merely counted, but weighed and esteemed" (*nicht bloss gezählt, sondern auch gewogen und geachtet*).

(2) A new franchise was introduced for the Bohemian Diet, with the result that in the powerful party of the '*Grossgrundbesitz*,' or large landed proprietors, the Czechs secured a considerable share of control, and that several of the leading Chambers of Commerce, notably Prague, Pilsen and Budějovice (Budweis), sent only Czechs as their representatives.

(3) By Imperial Decree of April 4, 1881, the University of Prague was divided into two entirely distinct Universities, a Czech and a German. It will be remembered that Ferdinand I in 1555 set up a second Catholic and Jesuit University at the side of the old Utraquist institution originally founded by Charles IV in 1348 ; that in 1654 Ferdinand III united the two into the Carolo-Ferdinandea ; and that its unity was not interfered with when the Jesuits were evicted in 1773. Throughout this period its main language had been Latin, but it became Germanized under Joseph II, though Czech made its first modest entry in 1784. From 1848 onwards there were constant demands that the two languages should be placed on an equal footing, and more than ever after Taaffe's decision both Czech and German continued to claim continuity with the original Caroline University, each to the exclusion of the other. Much more important was the fact that at last the Czechs recovered their lost control of higher education, and that the new University from the first day acquired a capital importance in the life of the nation. At the same time there was a steady growth of the Czech middle school system, which during the next

thirty years was to be so thoroughly developed that, when the Great War came, illiteracy was as little known among the Czechs as among the Germans.

Undoubtedly one of the factors which most contributed to this was the frantic rivalry of the two races in the educational field—the Germans resisting the Czech demands for schools step by step, and the Czechs in their turn never wasting an opportunity for aggressive action. The amount of energy squandered on utterly barren strife of this kind is almost incredible, and its annals are indeed depressing reading for the foreign student. Yet it is characteristic of the success which slowly but surely crowned the Czech efforts that while the Germans of the mid-eighties launched the famous cry : '*Lieber deutsch sterben als tschechisch verderben*' (Better die as Germans than decay as Czechs), the next generation of Germans on the eve of the war was increasingly disposed to listen to the catchword proclaimed by some of the more clear-sighted among them : '*Deutsche, lernt tschechisch !*' (Germans, learn Czech !).

The 'eighties, then, are a period of furious racial strife. The German bourgeois parties, embittered at their fall from power, cannot reconcile themselves to the new position, and contest at every point the advance of the Czechs (as also of the Slovenes in the south)—village by village, house by house, street sign by street sign. The address on a post-bag, the letter of a school-teacher, the directions to foot passengers or the inscription over a shop or even a lavatory, form the subject of endless wrangling and threaten the life of Cabinets. A special bone of contention is, of course, the school, and the rival activities of the German *Schulverein* and the Czech *Matice Školská* do much to embitter feeling still further and to prevent any return of calm or political sanity.

In all this it is impossible to assign the entire blame to one side ; and indeed any verdict whatever tends inevitably to assume colour from individual sympathies. In one sense it is obvious that the Czechs were the aggressors ; for they were fighting for equality, to make good the losses of three centuries, and, if it might be, to improve still further upon their original position, in the light of modern progress. While it is impossible to deny their full right to adopt such a policy, it must be admitted that their whole tone was increasingly aggressive and blunt. Their leaders were, of course, drawn almost entirely from classes which are less remarkable for external polish than for sterling merit. Moreover, they were experiencing the same truth which Parnell was bent upon bringing home to the Irish after a generation of Isaac Butt's leadership—that equality cannot be won by kid-glove methods and polite phrases, since an Ascendency class treats them as signs of weakness and only yields to the challenge of brute force and ruthless determination.

Meanwhile Czech literature was gathering in volume. Svatopluk Čech's *Songs of a Slave*, Vrhlický's poetic travel pictures, the historical romanticism of Julius Zeyer and the more materialist and challenging epics of Machar—notably *Confiteor* and *Tristium Vindobona* (Vienna of the Griefs), could not compare with the contemporary masterpieces of Poland or Hungary, but were of a high originality and of great promise for the future. On the other hand, Czech art soon put out rich blossoms, under the inspiration of Joseph Manes (1820–1871), who was not merely a draughtsman of extreme delicacy, but inspired a whole school of younger artists, though the isolation of Prague delayed the wider European recognition which it deserved. Above all, the musical talent of this most naturally musical of peoples found expression in three composers whose genius stands higher in the world to-day than their contemporaries could have dreamed. In the 'eighties Dvořák won recognition by his *Stabat Mater* and his Slavonic Dances ; it was not till later that his New World Symphony struck home, and became, as it were, a symbol of Czech aspirations towards democracy and freedom. Perhaps still more characteristic of his nation was the retiring figure of Smetana, whose operas, with the exception of the *Bartered Bride,* have rarely crossed the frontiers of Bohemia. Of Fibich, Ernest Denis has written as being 'more preoccupied by æsthetic considerations, more refined and more tormented. Like Wagner, of whom he was from the first the enthusiastic apostle, he takes by storm and would fain annex to music the whole world of thought.'

A word must be reserved for the National Theatre of Prague, which was built by popular subscription, without much support from the wealthier classes, who still looked elsewhere for their art and their drama, even when their national conscience had fully revived. It was burnt to the ground only a few weeks after its first opening, but its promoters, nothing daunted, gathered fresh subscriptions ; and when it reopened in 1881, it was enshrined in the hearts of the nation, and soon justified itself equally in the sphere of opera and of drama.

Taaffe in Decline

Taaffe's success in bringing in the Czechs gave him at first a very considerable prestige, especially with the Emperor, and no less an authority than Baron Ernest Plener, the leader of the German irreconcilables during most of the Taaffe regime, gives it as his very definite opinion, in the memoirs which he published as an old man, that Taaffe, if he had had a real plan for settling the racial and linguistic dispute, could have carried it through during his first year, however distasteful it might have been to the Germans.

But ere long it became clear that he had no plan, and no constructive ability whatever ; and he has left us his own monument in the famous but untranslatable word '*Fortwursteln,*' which he himself used to describe his method of jogging along, of managing by hook or by crook, of 'muddling through,' somehow or anyhow. It is true that he was less narrow than his Liberal predecessors, that he saw the need of moving with the times, both in racial and in social questions, and made himself the instrument by which the new nations and new classes steadily made their way towards political expression. But a high official who served under him has put on record that Taaffe 'was neither Clerical nor national in feeling, and only turned in this direction because it helped him to combat Liberalism.' He did not at first wish an open breach with the Liberals and aimed at a Middle or Centre Party. But he soon became dependent upon the Bohemian Grandees' and generally speaking the party of the *Grossgrundbesitz.* The unseen power at his elbow was always Hohenwart, 'a pastmaster of parliamentary strategy and diplomacy' ; when eventually Hohenwart withdrew his support, Taaffe fell.

For fourteen years Taaffe governed from hand to mouth—'*von Fall zu Fall*'—never originating anything, but merely showing skill 'in cutting down at the last moment' the concessions wrenched from him, 'in order that he might still have something to bargain with next time.' In a nutshell, his regime centres in the paradox of moving steadily to the Right politically, yet at the same time to the Left nationally. It suited the Crown admirably, because recruits for the army were assured and there was no interference with foreign policy—the Czechs and Poles who composed the majority thus making possible the German Alliance. But the Crown was as usual short-sighted; for it is impossible to deny the justice of Plener's criticism that the Taaffe regime undermined the unity of the state and especially 'broke up the unity of the bureaucracy as an instrument of government.' After 1879 the majority belonged to those who desired the revision, not the maintenance, of the constitution. But in the first place they lacked the necessary two-thirds majority; secondly, though the various groups agreed in favour of revision, they could not agree as to what form of government should be substituted; and thirdly the consent of the Crown was unattainable, and could be withheld without difficulty so long as no agreement was reached on so cardinal a point. But the general result was a policy of negation, and the complete absence of any constructive programme.

The 'eighties, then, were a period of disorientation, preparing the way for the disintegration of the 'nineties. The barren records of nationalist agitation, the mutual abuse of rival demagogues outbidding each other cannot detain us here. We must limit ourselves to tendencies among the contending parties and races; but it may perhaps serve to bring home to the reader the lamentable state to which Austrian parliamentary government had been reduced, if we give a few short extracts from outstanding speeches in one of the many debates devoted to the vexed 'Question of Nationalities.' During the debate on the Address on October 17, 1885 Rieger himself, now driven on to the defensive by his Young Czech critics opened the discussion by denying the charge that the Czech federalist programme aimed at the break-up of the Monarchy, and went on to argue that the real wreckers were those who wished to split Bohemia into two and to give Galicia and Dalmatia a separate status. "What does this German Bohemian question amount to after all?" he asked. "It simply resolves itself into the fact that about one hundred young men who enter the state service every year refuse to learn the second language of the country, though they need it for their work." The 'German State Idea in Austria he dismissed as a mere phrase, and argued that Austria must "make peace with the idea of the nationalities, which is the dominant idea of our time and the really constructive (*staatsbildend*) idea. . . . Austria if she allies herself with this idea, will find in it a powerful helper; for the protection of all the nationalities united under the sceptre of our Empire must make her strong and powerful." He was followed by his Young Czech colleague, Dr. Gregr, who set the ideal of 'Equal Rights for All' against that of 'German Leadership' (*deutsche Führung*). In return Baron Schar schmid denounced the Czech creed of 'constitutional loyalty with notice to quit' (*auf Kündigung*), and Knotz recounted a long array of Czech excesses —how, for instance, they gave to their dogs the names of Knotz and Herbst and other German leaders. It was left to Swoboda, a Germanized Czech, to underline the German attitude still further. "The difference between Germanization and Czechization," he said, "is in its essence as follows. If the Czechs in Bohemia are made into Germans, that is in my view no deadly sin, for they rise from a lower step to the sunny height of a highly civilized nation. But to seek to Czechize the Germans in Bohemia is quite another thing; that would be a disgrace unheard-of in the pages of world history. That is the difference, Dr. Rieger, between Germanization and Czechization !'

At a later stage in the debate Ernst von Plener denounced what he called the 'Czech invasion' of German territory, compared the idea of a Bohemian state to the *fata morgana* of the Hungarian state, and said that it might come to a Coronation in Prague, but that the Germans of Bohemia would not be present at it. "If the Czechs were to adopt the standpoint of absolute, radical equality of rights . . . they would make all state order in so complex an organism as Austria impossible. In its extreme consequences it must lead to a war of all against all, or to the polyglot administration of the state, which would be a ludicrous absurdity." Finally the Pan-German extremist Türk roundly predicted that the "national struggle will not be settled on parliamentary ground, but some day in quite another field and with other weapons, namely, with blood and iron." This long array of utterly conflicting views advanced in the course of a single debate—prolonged, it is true, over some days—gives a better insight into the rival forces at issue than many isolated incidents in the conflict.

Rival German Parties

In the 'eighties the German Liberals, so recently the ruling class, found themselves in frank opposition to the regime, and many disintegrating forces were at work among them. Their weakness was resented by their kinsmen in the Reich, and Bismarck himself voiced this feeling in 1882, when in the Reichstag he openly attacked the Austrian Liberals, twisting their leader Herbst's name into the nickname of '*Herbstzeitlosen*' (Autumn Laggards), because they never did anything at the right time. By their excessive doctrinairism, he argued, they were forcing the dynasty to turn in self-preservation to other factors in the state.

Faced by the Iron Ring majority, the Germans of Austria were for the first time driven on to the defensive, and with every decade there was, for all their efforts, a fresh crumbling of their predominance, as fresh positions were gained by the oncoming Slavs. But they clung stubbornly to the view that German must be the medium of the Austrian State Idea. As the most distinguished of their leaders, Ernst von Plener, publicly declared : "It was our fortune and our merit that Germanism and Austria coincided, and it would be criminal to produce a conflict between the two things."

A whole series of fissures were appearing in the German ranks. The unusually outspoken attitude of the Crown in the winter of 1881, in denouncing the Opposition as 'factious,' injured it in the eyes of moderate men and of the rural population. The growth of capitalists, and therefore of Jewish influence, in the Liberal party was widely resented, and attempts to check it came too late, very largely owing to the hold which the Jews had already acquired over the Press. Moreover, their economic policy, compounded of Manchester principles and *laisser aller*, aroused the hostility of the 'small man' (*der kleine Mann*)—the small trading class especially in Vienna ; while their efforts to win the peasantry by special pledges were increasingly unsuccessful. The peasants, as soon as they became politically articulate, were suspicious of the towns, of middle-class business men, of the Jews and the emancipated academic class, and began to go over in masses to the Clerical groups. It was an era of rapid social transformation. Whole classes and nationalities which had slumbered till now became keenly conscious of new needs and wishes, and also of their latent political power. The worst indictment of the German Liberals is that they failed to recognize these signs of the times till their rule was over, while the secret of Taaffe's long success was just the contrary. Though superficial and unconstructive, he saw a little farther than most of his mediocre rivals, and was for a time able to exploit the new forces of clericalism and nationalism, though in the long run he was quite unable to ride the whirlwind.

The Linz Programme

Though the official leaders were blind and incapable of escape from the old grooves, there were younger men who saw the need for a revision of party aims and drew up what came to be known as the Linz Programme. It was the combined work of men who now came rapidly to the front—Engelbert Pernerstorfer and Viktor Adler—two of the foremost leaders of Social Democracy after 1906, and the latter, for a short week before his death, first Foreign Minister of the young Austrian Republic ; Heinrich Friedjung, the historian of Austria's struggle against Prussia, and Georg von Schönerer, who came last and virtually captured the Programme for his own ends.

The Linz Programme only served to complete the scission of the Germans into the three rival groups of Liberals, Radicals and Clericals. To the Liberals it was inacceptable as creating an impression of being unduly on the defensive, but in reality because it tried to throw certain ballast overboard and to look facts in the face in a way that the true Austrian Liberal was incapable of imitating. To the Clericals it was inacceptable because its social and educational programme was too advanced, and because in international questions it was apt to emphasize the German, at the expense of the Austrian, point of view. In this connection it is important to note that, with a view to rendering the centralist position more unassailable, it advocated the Personal Union with Hungary, the transference of Dalmatia from Austrian, and of Bosnia from joint Austro-Hungarian rule to purely Hungarian rule, and finally the separation of Galicia and Bukovina from the rest of Austria, and either their administration on lines similar to Croatia under Hungary, or, if necessary, their actual transfer to Hungary. The purpose of these changes was sufficiently obvious. It would remove the two main excrescences from the body politic of Austria, and restore to it some pretence at geographical unity by leaving only the two original groups, namely the hereditary Alpine provinces and the Lands of the Bohemian Crown. Still more, it would rid Austria of eight or nine millions of Slavs, and thereby consolidate her as a predominantly German state, in which the Czechs and Slovenes would be in a clear and irrevocable minority and would have to toe the line. A centralist regime and the introduction of German as the language of state would thus at once become matters of practical politics. That such a scheme would transfer the numerical superiority from Austria to Hungary, did not disturb its advocates, partly because they regarded the consolidation of a smaller state as more desirable, and a source of greater strength, than the continuance of existing conditions, and partly, no doubt, because of an *arrière pensée* that Hungary on her side would not really be strengthened, but actually weakened, by the addition of so many Slav subjects, and so would become a less dangerous rival to Austria. That it was especially distasteful to the Czechs is not surprising, for it meant their ruin and the fruitlessness of all their dreams of a national rebirth ; and it confirmed the wisdom of becoming members of a majority in Vienna, sufficiently powerful to prevent it from being put into practice.

Schönerer and the Pan-Germans

In many ways the most remarkable figure of these days was Georg von Schönerer—'Ritter Georg,' as he was nicknamed on the utterly unsuitable analogy of Luther on the Wartburg—who set himself to radicalize public life and to unchain passion and unreason by simultaneous anti-Semitic and anti-Clerical movements. Early in 1882 he attacked a colleague who had declared that the party gravitated to Vienna, in these uncompromising words : "That, of course, means the Hofburg in Vienna, and that proves the party to be Black and Yellow.[1] Now I and my colleagues do not gravitate towards Vienna, but to wherever there are Germans." The influx of 'East Jews' was at this time very noticeable in Vienna, and was linked up in the popular mind with the reckless speculation and profiteering which both provoked and followed the great Krach of 1873. Schönerer, skilfully combining tactics and demagogy, gave a strongly anti-Semite turn to his agitation, with the ironic result that men like Adler and Friedjung, who had had a decisive influence in the formative stages, found themselves excluded from the newly constituted 'German National Union,' by the addition of an extra clause (the so-called *Judenpunkt*) limiting membership to those of Aryan descent. His two chief watchwords at this early stage were '*Durch Reinheit zur Einheit*' (Through Purity [of Austria, not of morals !] to Unity), and 'For unadulterated Germanism (*unverfälschtes Deutschtum*) and for social reform.' In foreign policy he preached 'a united Great-Germany under the leadership of Prussia.' 'Ritter Georg' should have been born three centuries earlier, as comrade-in-arms of Götz von Berlichingen and Franz von Sickingen ; but behind all his impudence and overflowing spirits there was enough character to command a hearing, despite his almost ranting fanaticism. An ardent exponent of the Great-Austrian idea, Theodor von Sosnosky earned himself the charge of partiality in those far-distant days of free speech in Austria, by defining Schönerer's creed as 'There is One God, Bismarck, and I, Schönerer, am his Prophet,' and his three aims as (a) the Germanization of Austria and its union with Germany ; (b) Down with the Jews, and (c) Down with the Catholic clergy. With our present perspective we can see that Sosnosky was right ; for Hitler and his satellites glorify Schönerer as their forerunner just because of the extravagance of his creed. His agitation took a specially dangerous direction in 1885, when he denounced the deal concluded between the Taaffe Government and the shareholders of the Northern Railway, the so-called 'Rothschild Group' ; if fresh concessions were made, instead of nationalization on reasonable terms, there would, he declared, be consequences which even he could not view without alarm, and the masses would certainly regard those responsible as 'consciously or unconsciously traitors to the state and nation.' The anti-Semitic features of the agitation he exploited to the full.

As he is the real originator of the theory of pure Aryan race, afterwards embroidered by Chamberlain and Gobineau and applied with perverted devilry by Hitler, it is important to note that already in 1887 he was

[1] The colours of the Imperial Austrian flag.

confronted with proof that his own wife, to all seeming the type of a true Nordic blonde, had a Jewish great-grandfather and thus made nonsense of his tub-thumping anti-Semitic theories.

In 1888 he had a serious setback ; the *Neues Wiener Tagblatt*, one of the two great Jewish Liberal dailies of Vienna, published a premature report of the death of the Emperor William I (then actually lying in coma, at the age of ninety), and Schönerer, with a band of young roughs, invaded the offices of the paper and assaulted one of the editors. For this, and his public toasting of William II as 'our glorious Emperor,' he was sent to prison for four months, and lost both his title and his parliamentary mandate. But nothing could silence him, and he continued to play a part beside which that of Paul Deroulède and his fellow-Chauvinists in France seems almost mild. Certainly he had been one of those most responsible for making irrevocable the growing rift in the German ranks ; from 1887 onwards the more radical 'German National Union' stood opposed to the 'United German Left'—the broken fragments of the *'Herbstzeitlosen.'*

Rival Propaganda

The concessions to the Slavs—the Slovenes and Croats kept pace with the Czechs—were publicly welcomed by Rieger as a proof of the 'loyal and good Austrian attitude of the Right,' which demanded a response from their side. 'Give the Slavs equality of rights,' he argued, 'and you have nothing to fear from Panslavism—Austria least of all.' But the Germans, enraged at the curtailment of their unfair predominance, continued to inveigh against the Panslav bogy. The Czechs acquired a majority in the Diet of Bohemia—167 Czechs to 75 Germans ; and Rieger chose this moment to offer negotiations, but received a flat refusal from the German leader Schmeykal, while Herbst, now in a really autumnal mood, concentrated upon the demand for the *Zweiteilung* of Bohemia into two distinct provinces, one Czech and one German.

On both sides there were determined attempts to expedite or impede the progress made by the non-German nationalities towards equality. In particular, the Deutsche Schulverein was founded in 1880, and with the ardent support of the German Universities and various student unions, set itself to assist or subvention threatened schools in the mixed areas, to supply equipment, to watch the interests of the teachers and to publish school-books of unexceptionable national sentiments. Within ten years it had 1,029 local groups and continued to develop steadily. But two can play at such a game, and the 'eighties also witnessed the foundation of a whole series of rival institutions—the Matice Školská by the Czechs, the Slovenska Matica by the Slovenes, the Society of Saints Cyril and Methodius by the Croats, and the Lega Nazionale and the Dante Alighieri Society by the Italians. There also arose a network of so-called defensive leagues (*Schutzvereine*) which were often anything but defensive in tactics or in intention, and indeed lived by racial ill-will. The three most notable were the Bohemian Forest League (*Böhmerwaldbund*, 1884), the North Moravian League (*Nordmährerbund*, 1884) and the South Mark (*Südmark*, 1889).

No one could outbid the Czechs in intensity of national effort. Their increasingly radical sentiments were due to a number of causes. In the first place, industrial and social changes were bringing new classes into being, and providing them with new educational facilities, which rendered them politically vocal for the first time. One social aspect of this was the desperate competition for bureaucratic posts, especially those innumerable minor posts on the railways and in the postal and telegraphic services, which had hitherto been very largely a German monopoly, but to which the Slavs now laid increasing claim, as the struggle for life grew keener. Secondly, violence came as a natural reaction against the violence of the Germans, cause and effect being hopelessly intermingled, as in all such movements. The Young Czechs were by now rapidly outdistancing their Old Czech progenitors, being able to show practical results from their abandonment of passivity ; but already the Czech Radicals and Czech Agrarians were treading on their heels, urging the need for still more demagogic and aggressive tactics, as the only possible answer to the mud-slinging of Schönerer and his Pan-Germans. In 1889 the Young Czechs won 37 seats in the Diet, and in 1891 their number rose to 51, against 37 Old Czechs. The Germans now changed places with the Czechs by sulking in the opposite corner.

It was under these circumstances that in January, 1890, direct negotiations were set on foot between Taaffe's Government and the Old Czechs, and led to the signature of a kind of German-Czech Compromise. Its main provisions were for the duplication of administrative machinery in Bohemia in both languages, and for the rights of minorities in the schools. But the Old Czechs had committed a fatal blunder in excluding their rivals from the negotiations, at the very moment when the latter were gaining strength in the country districts. In this they doubtless yielded to pressure from Francis Joseph himself, who, abandoning for once his habitual caution in the expression of any sort of political view, openly referred to the Young Czech victory as a certificate of lack of intelligence on the part of the peasants, and an indication of revolutionary aims on the part of the leaders. This did not prevent the great majority of the nation from transferring their allegiance to the Young Czechs, who in the first flush of victory repudiated the new Compromise. Rieger and Schmeykal, Plener and Zeithammer were, as it were, left at the same table, looking supremely ridiculous because they could not deliver the goods, and new and less conciliatory men came to the front.

This was the parting of the ways. The Crown finally gave up the idea of reconciliation with Bohemia and may be said to have remained at least latently anti-Czech for the remainder of the reign. The Young Czechs on their side denounced the Compromise as nothing less than the partition of Bohemia, and Rieger in his old age was accused of treachery. The Prague Ethnographic Exhibition of 1891 was made the occasion of Francophil demonstrations, reviving the memories of 1871, when the Czech parliamentarians, alone in Europe, protested against Germany's annexation of Alsace-Lorraine. The growth of Czech sympathies for France was emphasized by a return visit of the Sokols to Nancy in 1893 ; and this not unnaturally led to further friction with Vienna and was keenly resented at the Hofburg.

In the same year (1893) there were anti-dynastic demonstrations in Prague, always noted for its turbulent mob ; and their sequel was the famous Omladina Treason Trial, in which seventy-seven youths between the ages of seventeen and twenty-two were implicated on revolutionary charges, and sentences amounting to a total of over ninety years were distributed among all save eight of them. One of the ringleaders was Dr. Alois Rašín, who twenty-two years later, during the World War, was tried and condemned for high treason together with his friend Dr. Kramář, but who lived to become first Finance Minister of the Czechoslovak Republic and the saviour of the Central European financial situation. Here, yet again, it is necessary to remember that what passed as extreme severity in the relatively free Austria of 1890 is a mere trifle beside the savage executions and tortures of the enslaved and enslaving Reich of Hitler.

Electoral Reform

In 1882 Taaffe introduced a partial reform of the franchise, which made the vote in the rural and urban *curiæ* dependent on a minimum of five gulden (8s.) paid in direct taxation. In practice this meant the transfer of predominance from the *grande* to the *petite bourgeoisie* and an increase of strength to the Clericals. This is another way of saying that the Slavs, being as yet more backward in their social development, though making very rapid strides forward, were on the whole more Clerical than the Germans, and that 'the small man' (*kleine Mann*), who has long played so important a part in Austria between the upper middle class and Labour, was also keenly Clerical. His admission to political life was soon followed by the appearance of the Christian Socialist Party, which came into being in the same year (1887), which saw the open breach between the Liberals and Radicals. This was a form of demagogic Clericalism, which was better adapted to the new conditions than the more aristocratic and conservative Clericalism of the 'sixties and 'seventies. It was a natural reaction against the cynicism and corruption of the Liberal capitalist system, and therefore inevitably took on an anti-Semitic tinge, since the Jews, pressing into the capital in alarming numbers from Galicia and still further East, had secured an altogether excessive influence over the Liberal party machine, the German Liberal press, and the big Viennese banks. It certainly represented a movement of self-defence on the part of the small trader against the ruthless commercial policy of Jewish high finance. By the turn of the century it had another formidable competitor from the opposite flank, the rising power of Social Democracy.

Early in the 'nineties Taaffe, seeing his majority slipping from him, tried to save himself by another Electoral Reform, but here he had miscalculated. His scheme was opposed not only by the German Liberals (the gilt had by now worn off the liberalism) for national reasons, but by most other parties. Some felt it as a blow against the German *bourgeoisie*. Hohenwart and the Conservatives objected to it as 'the transfer of the political balance from the propertied to the unpropertied classes.' Kálnoky, the Foreign Minister, and behind him his Magyar allies, opposed it from a mixture of reasons, as likely to loosen the Dual System. Only the Radicals and the Czechs supported him.

In 1893, then, he was abandoned by his majority, the Reform Bill fell with him, and the two Cabinets which succeeded him simply marked time through two years of uncertainty. But so unreal and unsatisfactory was the existing franchise and so confused had the parliamentary situation become, that some kind of reform was found to be inevitable, and indeed the only obvious exit from an *impasse*. But as the Conservatives were strong enough to prevent a really logical solution, and as the voice of the working class was already too audible to be ignored, a typically Austrian form of compromise was devised. The Reform Bill of 1896 reduced the taxation qualification from ten to eight gulden and, while preserving the artificial Curial system and the old privileges of the *Grossgrundbesitz* with its eighty-five seats, added a fifth Curia of seventy-two seats to be filled by Universal Suffrage. This was the thin end of the wedge ; the democratic forces had not merely made their entry, but their opponents had now an utterly indefensible and illogical system to defend. The fall of the Curial system could in effect only be delayed for another ten years.

Badeni and Lueger

The Premier who steered this reform through Parliament was Count Casimir Badeni, a Polish magnate who, like Taaffe, enjoyed the complete personal confidence of Francis Joseph and had for some time past been regarded as the 'coming man.' Appointed in August, 1895, he found growing chaos in the political situation, and a whole series of problems which had been allowed to slide, and of which electoral reform was only the most notable. In particular he saw the urgent need for conciliating the Czechs, who had reverted to opposition since the fall of Taaffe. He therefore revoked the state of siege which had prevailed in Prague for over two years, released some of the Omladina prisoners, and removed the repressive Governor of Bohemia, Count Francis Thun.

Badeni was further embarrassed by an acute quarrel which raged in the municipality of Vienna, over the election of Dr. Karl Lueger as Burgomaster. In him the Christian Socialist Party had found a leader of ability bordering on real genius, a born demagogue who swayed the masses by his rough humour and his appeals to their passions ; but being also a hard hitter who was not very choice either in his language or in his methods, he had roused up a host of enemies who poisoned the ear of the Crown against him. In Mr. Steed's words : 'he represented the instinctive revolt of the average man against . . . the crushing force of an agglomeration of capital.' He set himself to protect the interests of the 'small man' and entrench him against the big capitalist, while at the same time propounding a policy of state and municipal socialism—checking monopolies, regulating wages and competition, and trying 'to individualize the worker and personalize his work.' In 1895 his influence asserted itself triumphantly against the Liberals in the elections for the Vienna Town Council ; three times he was elected Mayor, and three times the authorities, hoping to conciliate Liberal opinion, annulled the election ; but the Christian Socialists stood solidly behind him, and when he was elected yet a fourth time the only way out of the deadlock was for the Emperor to ask him, as a personal favour, to stand aside until passions calmed down. Lueger knew how to wait, and when in 1897 his fifth election was confirmed, he entered upon office almost as the uncrowned King of Vienna, and his authority and popularity grew side by side until his death in 1910.

Throughout this period he and his party became more and more identified with the so-called Great-Austrian programme. They were strongly anti-Magyar, both because they resented the ill-treatment of the non-Magyars in Hungary and the reactions of that policy upon racial disputes in Austria, and also because they considered that Hungary possessed undue influence in foreign policy, and in the neighbourhood of the throne. They were hostile to the Czechs, for the simple reason that in the period following 1895 no German party could be pro-Czech, and also because the Czechs had so strong an anti-Clerical tinge ; but their active sympathy for the Slovaks was water to the Czech mill. Lueger, however, knew how to manage the growing Czech minority in Vienna itself; one of his most ardent followers was the once Czech alderman Bielohlavek, and Lueger once coined the untranslatable phrase, so full of political innuendo : 'Lasst 'mir meine Böhm' in Ruh !' (Don't touch my Czechs !). Lueger's own particular preference was for the Roumanians, and certainly anti-Semitism provided a common bond of union ; when he visited Bucarest he demonstratively avoided travelling across Hungarian territory, and received an ovation usually reserved for monarchs.

Badeni and the Beargarden

The rise of the Young Czechs, who had been short-sightedly excluded from the negotiations of 1890, knocked the bottom out of Taaffe's last plan for a Bohemian settlement. After his fall in 1893 Francis Joseph governed for some years from hand to mouth, appointing a series of grands seigneurs, interlarded by high bureaucrats, to the Premiership— Prince Alfred Windischgrätz (November, 1893), Count Kielmansegg (June, 1895), Count Casimir Badeni (October, 1895), Baron Gautsch (November, 1897), Count Francis Thun (March, 1898), Count Clary (October, 1899), Dr. Wittek (December, 1899). More and more the whole Austrian problem, and even that of the survival of the Dual Monarchy as a Great Power, came to centre round the German-Czech quarrel, and as the Emperor lacked the necessary goodwill and confidence, there was no one possessing the prestige and energy to steer safely into harbour the many forces of reason that still survived.

On the contrary, Count Badeni, by his Language Ordinances (Sprachenverordnungen) of April, 1897, for both Bohemia and Moravia, unloosed the greatest storm in modern Austrian politics. They centred round the provision binding the civil authorities to use in their intercourse with each individual applicant the language in which the first application was made, and making the language in which the applicant made his first verbal statement the official language throughout the conduct of the case. It followed logically from this that all officials appointed after July 1, 1901, must show a knowledge of both Czech and German in speech and writing. The Ordinances certainly did not go to the root of things, but merely attempted to clarify points of immediate detail, but they did not deserve the violent abuse levelled against them from both sides. For the Czechs in their new combative mood they were not enough, and Kaizl, the most conciliatory of the Young Czechs, whose premature death some years later was a serious loss to the cause of sanity, went back upon his original concessions under popular clamour. For the Germans any concession was objectionable, and this particularly so, because it altogether ignored their insistent demand for 'Zweiteilung.' The fundamental difficulty, insuperable unless there was a reasonable amount of goodwill on both sides, was that the Germans were not prepared to learn Czech, calculating quite rightly that as German was a world-language the Czechs would in any case be forced to learn it. This was an unfair advantage which they were not willing to forego and which lay in the nature of things. Still more untenable on any legal or logical basis was the German anger at Badeni launching these decisions by administrative decree rather than by legislation. They could not escape from the argument that linguistic equality had already been laid down by the famous Article XIX of the Austrian

Fundamental Law of December, 1867, and that it only remained to ensure its much-belated enforcement.

The result was frantic and organized obstruction in the Reichsrat and a demand for the impeachment of the Cabinet. Racial friction degenerated into fisticuffs on the floor of the House, and there was keen competition in cat-calls and inkpot-throwing. Even the Socialists, a small group of whom had found its way into Parliament thanks to the new fifth Curia, joined in the horseplay, and on one notorious occasion stormed the President's tribunal and tore up his papers. Badeni was suddenly dismissed in November, 1897, and the objectionable Language Ordinances were withdrawn, but the provisional Ordinances substituted for them by Baron Gautsch in March, 1898, satisfied no one, and in the place of German obstruction there came a no less strenuous Czech obstruction which paralysed the whole proceedings of Parliament. The Gautsch Ordinances in their turn were withdrawn in October, 1899, by the Clary Cabinet, but this, of course, only stiffened Czech obstruction, and the growing excitement among the Czech population found vent in unfriendly manifestations against the Army and anti-military tendencies, which had an instant reaction upon the Crown's attitude towards the Czechs.

The two years 1898 to 1900 represent the nadir of Austrian parliamentarism. All serious business had become impossible, manners were incredibly rough (or rather non-existent), and government could only be continued by the constant use of Paragraph Fourteen. The extent of the breakdown is shown by the fact that this was used not only for the Budget, but for the renewal of the Commercial Ausgleich with Hungary (the old one had been prolonged for one year from 1897), for the extension of the Charter of the Joint Bank and even for the introduction of new taxation !

The Reichsrat had so completely lost all prestige that Francis Joseph, whose public utterances throughout his reign were always deliberately couched in the most banal terms, in 1900 allowed himself to address a Czech deputy with the pointed phrase : "We have become the laughing-stock of the whole world." Worst of all, public opinion showed alarming indifference, which was natural enough in view of the extent to which the masses were excluded from representation. Yet the Czechs, sinned against, but also sinning, went their own way and resorted more than ever to their predilection for rousing demonstrations. Two especially notable ones occurred in 1898, the unveiling of the Palacký monument, at which a Russian general made a most tactless anti-German speech, and the centenary of Mickiewicz, which provided an excuse for Czecho-Polish fraternization. Meanwhile the Germans kept up a permanent provocation by the so-called 'Student Bummel' on the Příkop (or Graben), parading in serried ranks, wearing their corps colours and singing their most aggressive songs—in fact, trailing the tails of their coats before the Czech students and bidding them go and do likewise ! And the Government's feeble attempts to stop the tomfoolery were greeted with howls of rage.

By this time Rieger was over eighty and living in retirement ; but though the younger generation had far outstripped him and left him breathless, it is but bare justice, as we take leave of him, to quote his farewell testament to the Czech people. "It is my most profound wish that my nation may never allow itself to fall into despair nor ever become conceited in its pride. I should be very glad to see it defend its rights, which have been clearly and objectively formulated ; but let it never be betrayed by passion into wronging anyone else. I wish that it may give heed only to the advice of men who are in all things honourable, whose integrity has been proved by their patriotic deeds ; but let it close its heart against the loud words and empty slogans, the flatteries playing upon self-conceit, which are often uttered by people who may be immature, self-seeking or of dubious honour. I counsel it to put supreme confidence in its own strength. For this, it must first appraise its strength without over-estimating it. Armed with self-knowledge, let it never plunge into any foolish adventures which, irrespective even of success or failure, are dangerous to the nation. Let it rather remember always that only by honest, patient effort in the realms of the spiritual and the material will it lay the secure foundations for a brighter future. Furthermore, I trust that my nation may never abandon its ideal and Christian endeavour, exemplifying the eternal principles of honour, justice and humanity. I wish above all that it may never turn its back upon the claims of justice or resort to force, in spite of the fact that a brief violation of justice may promise some immediate success. Bear in mind that universal, international respect for justice provides the one bulwark for nations, especially for small nations. For them, it is particularly dangerous to desert this bastion and to tread upon the quagmire of 'might makes right'."

Pan-Germanism and 'Los von Rom'

Foremost in the conscious effort to destroy Austrian Parliamentarism was the Pan-German group, led by Schönerer at the height of his frenzy. His renewed activity coincided with the agitation of the Pan-German League in Germany. In 1897 it held meetings in Dresden and Leipzig, protesting against the Badeni decrees as 'a humiliation for the whole German people,' and announcing a campaign against Slavization. In the same year the historian Mommsen published a famous letter against the Slavs in the *Neue Freie Presse* of Vienna, affirming that ' just as the Germans of Austria look towards Germany, so do the Germans of the Empire look towards Austria.' Bidding them stand firm and united, he declared : 'The brain of the Czechs does not understand reason, but it understands blows. This is a struggle of life and death.' Eight hundred German Professors of the Reich, led by Heidelberg, sent an address of encouragement to the German University of Prague, in its struggle against the Czechs ; and there was a deputation of students from the Reich to Vienna which placed the East Mark and Strasburg together as common objects of defence. Quite a number of societies—national, political, economic, religious, educational—in Germany began to devote their attention to Austrian questions, and to spend money on propaganda in Austria—the Odin-Verein, Gustav-Adolf Verein, Evangelischer Verein, Allgemeine Deutsche Schulverein, Verein zur Erhaltung des Deutschtums im Ausland.

Most significant of all Schönerer's patriotic 'stunts' was the 'Los von Rom' movement. In it religious motives were not entirely lacking, but its driving force was the knowledge that Protestant North Germany had considerable misgivings about welcoming to its arms eight to ten million German Catholics, and thus turning the political balance in the Empire in favour of Catholicism and the Centre party. These misgivings, and with them the main obstacle to union with Germany, were to be removed by wholesale proselytizing. As Protestants, it was argued, they could not be refused by their kinsmen. But though much advertised, the movement proved a failure, the number of converts never exceeding 30,000. It, of course, found itself up against the combined might of the Roman Church and the civil administration. The Heir Apparent, Francis Ferdinand, in particular, put himself at the head of a newly founded Katholische Schulverein für Oesterreich, and publicly expressed the view that 'Away from Rome means Away from Austria.' There was indeed little prospect of winning the Austrian intellectual class, since the form assumed by Protestantism in the materialistic Germany of William II hardly offered a counter-attraction to those who had already thrown off Catholicism and emancipated themselves from all religious influences. Moreover, many of them were led to pause by the very reasonable fear of increasing still further the gulf which already separated them from the still very devout peasantry.

The Pan-Germans, finding their inadequate religious camouflage torn aside, resorted to frantic violence in expounding their political creed. Streets were named after Emperor William in the North Bohemian towns, monuments were erected to Bismarck. An Eger deputy, bearing the once Habsburg name of Hofer, saluted 'One God, one Emperor, one Empire' (*ein Gott, ein Kaiser, ein Reich*), while another coined the impudent phrase : 'Königgrätz was the first act, Sedan the second, we await the third with ardent longing.' In 1901 the little Pan-German group ostentatiously left the House when its President called for three cheers for Francis Joseph, and a year later they eclipsed all previous records by yelling '*Hoch und Heil den Hohenzollern,*' amid the lively protests of all other parties. Even Schönerer himself was outdone by Karl Hermann Wolf, who, before he was removed by the police, kicking and cursing, had been the first to proclaim the ideals of 'Germania Irredenta,' and to sing the song of challenge :

> "*Wir schielen nicht, wir schauen*
> *Wir schauen unverwandt,*
> *Wir schauen mit Vertrauen*
> *Ins deutsche Vaterland.*"

> (No sidelong glance, but face to face
> We take our fearless stand,
> We hail with firm assurance
> Our German Fatherland).

Schönerer in his turn coined the doggerel cry : '*Ohne Juden, ohne Rom, wird erbaut Germania's Dom*' (We need no Jews, we need no Rome, to build our stately German home) ; and Türk declared that 'Germans must look outside Austria, if justice is not done to them inside.' Such were the men from whom Hitler first learned the doctrine of the Herrenvolk and its rights over inferior races. And foremost in their political creed was the consciousness that a reconciliation between Czech and German was the pivot upon which Austria's survival turned, and that it must therefore be prevented at all costs, in the interests of Greater Germany.

The Jews and the Press

In this situation the three main trends of German-Austrian opinion were very neatly defined by the labels : 'Only Austria' (*Nur Oesterreicher*),

'Germany too' (*Auch Deutsche*—Germans as well as Austrians, but as an afterthought), and 'Only German' (*Nur deutsch*—the opposite of the second label). Curiously enough, many Jews, while naturally resenting the foul anti-Semitic campaign and claiming the right to pass as Austrians no less than the purest Alpine Germans, showed a tendency to be more Prussian than Austrian in their international policy, and so indirectly to play a Pan-German game which did but increase the hostility of the Clericals towards them. This was, above all, true of the Liberal journals of Vienna, *Neue Freie Presse* and *Neues Wiener Tagblatt*. The former, one of the most brilliantly edited papers in all Europe and justly proud of its international reputation, was the foremost organ of the assimilationist theory or crypto-Judaism, as it was sometimes called. Its power was enormous, and the harm which it did incalculable. It certainly frustrated a German-Czech understanding on more than one occasion, and it had unique methods of unscrupulous attack, or alternately of 'killing by silence' (*Totschweigen*). Mr. Steed stated the bare truth when he wrote in 1913 that 'to be attacked by the *Neue Freie Presse* is a certificate of political uprightness, but politicians and officials nevertheless fear it.' It was equally feared and hated, and was unquestionably one of the chief breeding-grounds of that anti-Semitic feeling which it resented so keenly. The disproportionate influence of the Jews in the press of Vienna, though due in part to the emergence of a number of really brilliant Jewish pen-men, was one of the most important social factors in the Dualist era. Curiously enough, while this was even more true of the Budapest press (which in the first decade of the twentieth century had no less than forty dailies, the great majority edited and staffed by Jews), it was not at all true of Prague, where from the *Národní Listý* downwards, and including the Old Czech organ in German (*Union*, afterwards *Politik*), the Czech press was almost exclusively in the hands of Czech nationals.

Social Democracy

The last decade of the century saw yet another division among the German ranks in Austria, as a result of rapid industrialization and the rise of a self-conscious working class and proletariat. The Labour movement in Austria really begins with the foundation of the Arbeiterbildungsverein in 1867 in Vienna, and of branches in other towns : it acquired its first party organ in 1869 in the *Volksstimme* (afterwards *Volkswille*) ; but it had at first an uphill fight, owing to the narrow franchise which virtually excluded the working-class voter, and also owing to the restrictions upon the rights of association and assembly and of press freedom maintained by the bourgeois 'Liberal' regime of the 'seventies, and more fitfully by the clerical regime of the 'eighties. The neglect of social conditions— 'social welfare' was as yet hardly dreamt of—was very great, and the prevailing infant mortality hit the Germans even more than the Slavs. In the mid-eighties there was a tendency on the part of the authorities to treat Socialism and Anarchism as identical, and to repress both by measures against the press and by suspending the jury system for all offences directed against the existing social order. But these measures roused many protests from the bourgeois parties, and from 1891 onwards were much relaxed ; the proposed 'Anarchist Law' had to be abandoned.

Meanwhile in 1889 the rival Socialist groups, thanks largely to the tact and energy of Viktor Adler, managed to reach a common basis at the party congress of Hainfeld, and from this dates the steady rise of Social Democratic influence in Austria. They proclaimed themselves an international party, opposed to all privileges of nations, no less than of birth and property. While describing parliamentarism as 'a form of modern class rule,' they none the less placed Universal Suffrage in the forefront of their programme, and followed it by the demand for universal free education, released from Church control, and for the separation of Church and State. For the next fifteen years the Social Democrats fought the Christian Socialists steadily for the possession of Vienna and the big towns. They were not merely negative, and in the burning question of language and nationality pronounced in favour of national autonomy—especially the idea that the nationalities should vote in separate electoral colleges, according to a key of population, and thus reduce conflicts to a minimum. This question forced them to be on the whole less extreme than their comrades in other countries, for it cut right across their organization, and they had to be content with a general Austrian Social Democratic party, divided into national subsections. The partial franchise reform of 1896 brought them for the first time into Parliament, and enabled them to extend and strengthen their organization, so that with the coming of Universal Suffrage a decade later, they became at one bound one of the recognized forces in the land.

Francis Joseph's Attitude to Parliament

In these closing years of the century Francis Joseph still followed that policy of half-measures which had become a second nature to him —both as regards Electoral Reform, each fresh instalment of which failed because it did not cut deep enough, and also as regards the still more fundamental Question of Nationalities, a radical solution of which was really blocked by the position of Hungary under the Dual System. That Francis Joseph tolerated this was no doubt very largely due to the fact that Dualism had become an impasse, but above all to the fact that the impotence of the Austrian Reichsrat left the real power in the hands of the Crown and its nominees.

In the twenty-one years that separated the fall of Taaffe from the Great War (1893–1914) there were thirteen Austrian Cabinets—or fifteen, if Bienerth's three successive Cabinets be counted separately ; and not one of them was parliamentary in the western sense. The Premier was invariably a direct nominee of the Crown—in four cases a *Grand Seigneur* who was *persona grata* at the Hofburg, in other cases a high official who was almost invariably colourless and lacking in initiative, and who devoted his energies to patchwork solutions designed to make the wheels go round. And under such a system the wheels tended inevitably to go slower and slower. As M. Eisenmann has pointed out, despite the ultimate danger to the state from such conditions, neither Crown nor bureaucracy had any pressing interest in achieving that understanding between the various nationalities which alone could check the paralysis. This was due to the simple reason that the first immediate consequences of such an understanding would have been the advent of a Liberal regime, and a speedy end to the joint domination of the Crown and the bureaucracy. The Crown hesitated for the additional reason that it would have meant a strengthening of Austria as against Hungary, and by 1900 Francis Joseph had not only got accustomed to Hungarian predominance in joint affairs, but also realized that Austria's revival would dislocate the whole Dual System, which was only workable when one scale or the other was high in the air. He preferred, therefore, not to fly to evils that he knew not of.

With the turn of the century, however, political life in Hungary became increasingly stormy, and the Crown took alarm, while the Christian Socialists and the Heir Apparent, whose Clerical leanings identified him to some extent with their party, favoured as the true dynastic policy the forcing-up of the Hungarian scale and the transfer of the crisis from Austria to Hungary. But Francis Joseph disliked this idea. He was sceptical of Austria's capacity for the dominant rôle, he clung to Dualism as his own creation, and he had come to trust and like the Hungarian parliamentary system, believing that he had its ruling party well under control, thanks to his method of periodical changes in the position of the Liberal leader.

Between 1900 and 1905, however, there was a distinct recovery in Austria, under Dr. Ernst von Körber, the most remarkable of Austria's modern Premiers, indeed almost the only one of outstanding merit. He, too, was an official, but he had an amazing energy and capacity for work ; he was very precise, very efficient, very exacting, and he surrounded himself with other first-class officials ; best of all, he was open to modern ideas and had a definite social programme. His aim was to make the parliamentary machine work once more, and this was to be attained by placing economic, social and educational problems in the foreground, in place of purely national questions. This logically involved a new note of friendliness towards Labour. Körber's most notable achievements in this direction were the scheme of Old Age and Sickness Insurance and a very real relaxation of press restrictions. The Socialists only held ten seats in Parliament as yet, but they were already a force to be reckoned with and their rise only served to promote still further the disintegration of the German parties, whose unity was thus threatened both from Left and from Right.

Körber, it is true, failed in his repeated attempts to produce a settlement of the German-Czech dispute, and in his case the failure was very largely due to the sterile intransigeance of the Czechs, who found themselves isolated in consequence. But he did succeed in securing parliamentary sanction for the Budget and other vital laws, dispensing with Paragraph Fourteen and passing important railway and canal legislation ; he also, literally at the eleventh hour (at 11 p.m. on December 31, 1902), concluded the new Commercial Ausgleich with Hungary, which his predecessors had failed to pilot through interminable crises. Two notable innovations were the so-called 'autonomous Customs Tariff'—a concession more to the letter than to the spirit of Hungary's claims to independence—and high protectionist duties on cattle and grain, which were to exercise very great political influence in the ensuing decade, especially in Hungary. In this case the interest of the Magyar and the Polish high aristocracy combined in favour of an arrangement for which the poorer classes paid the bill.

As has already been hinted, it was hardly an accident that the revival in Austria coincided with a decline in Hungary. In 1902 begins 'the revolt of the Hungarian Parliament against the Crown,' the attack upon the Joint Army, and a period of fierce obstruction and 'Ex-lex' (the Hungarian equivalent of Paragraph Fourteen), which ended with the downfall of the Liberal Party at the Hungarian elections of January, 1905. This agitation against the unity of the Army and in favour of Personal Union (that is, the Crown as sole link between Hungary and Austria) was keenly resented in Austria and strained the relations between Vienna and Budapest, which were also year by year embittered by national discords and especially by the growing resentment of more than one nationality in Austria at the ill-treatment of their kinsmen in Hungary. A landmark in the controversy was the famous Army Order of Chlopy (September 13, 1903), which culminated in the phrase: 'I wish my Army to know that I shall never part with the rights and control which are guaranteed to its supreme war lords. My Army must remain what it is, Joint and unitary— a strong power which shall defend the Austro-Hungarian Monarchy against every enemy.' This uncompromising demonstration on the part of the Crown was followed up in December by Körber, who denounced the idea of separating the Army into two as a crime against the Monarchy as a whole. A resolution was even introduced in all seriousness in the Reichsrat, though not actually carried, in favour of an express affirmation of the sovereign's sole power to decide matters of army organization, without any influence of the two Parliaments. Needless to say, this revelation of tendencies did not ease the situation in Budapest.

Körber fell on the last day of 1904, the victim of fierce party attacks, but 'also of his own method.' For by retaining the portfolios of Justice and the Interior in his own hands, he was simply attempting the impossible, while his predilection for constant bargaining only served to whet the appetite of the various parties. That discreet opportunist, Baron Gautsch, thus became Austrian Premier for the second time, at a moment when the Hungarian crisis was entering upon an acute stage, and when the Crown, alarmed for its precious military prerogative, allowed the unconstitutional government of Baron Fejérváry to launch the momentous watchword of Universal Suffrage and so to threaten at the roots the whole structure of Magyar racial and class hegemony. If Francis Joseph's motive was almost certainly opportunist and intended to bring the Magyars to heel, Francis Ferdinand as definitely advocated reform, not, of course, because he was radical or unautocratic in outlook, but because he saw in it the chance of overthrowing an impossible regime, and believed this to be in the interests of the dynasty and of state unity.

Universal Suffrage

The movement for, or rather against, a proper franchise reform, was to dominate Hungarian politics for many years to come. But its most immediate effects were in Austria, where the agitation for Universal Suffrage, launched in September, 1905, by the Social Democrats, was promptly transferred to Parliament itself. Already in October a motion in its favour was carried by 155 to 114, and though this fell short of the necessary two-thirds, it was obvious that no party would risk the unpopularity which unreserved hostility would earn it. The news of the Russian Revolution and the institution of the Duma rendered the atmosphere in Vienna still more electric, and gave an irresistible impetus to the cause of reform. On November 28, the Labour organizations of Vienna organized a monster demonstration of 250,000 persons outside the Reichsrat buildings on the Ringstrasse; and as the Crown raised no objection, serious opposition was only possible behind the scenes. The indefensible parliamentary franchise crumbled almost in a day. What is sometimes known as the Moravian Compromise, reached in November, 1905, paved the way for the wider reform ; by it the proportions of Czech and German representation in the Diet of Brno were fixed in a ratio of 39 to 14 in the country-side curia, 14 to 6 in the general curia, and 20 each in the town curia. Voters were registered according to their nationality and minorities of over 20% had a right to be attended to in their own language.

In February, 1906, Gautsch introduced a Bill abolishing the Curial system and establishing Universal Suffrage, with various guarantees of electoral freedom and immunity of deputies. The long debates were mainly appeals 'through the window' (as the German phrase goes) ; the real struggle centred round the proportion of seats to be allotted to the various nationalities. The Poles in particular, who already possessed 78 seats, and were now assigned 88, demanded 118. Their blocking action led Gautsch to resign in April. But the Crown assumed an attitude of marked favour to the Reform, first by appointing as Premier Prince Conrad Hohenlohe, whose democratic leanings had earned him the nickname of 'the Red Prince,' and then a month later (when Hohenlohe resigned owing to friction with the new Hungarian Coalition Cabinet), by selecting as his successor Baron Beck, yet another high official without any party ties, but known to enjoy the confidence of the Heir Apparent, who stood behind the reform movement.

Beck's diplomatic skill evaded the rock of plural voting and steered the Reform Bill through the House by December, 1906. The franchise was assigned to all male citizens of twenty-four, subject to one year's domicile ; and what was no less important, the number of seats was increased from 425 to 516, and the constituencies were divided up according to nationality (the so-called *nationale Abgrenzung*). This had the double advantage of ensuring just proportional representation and of keeping the rival races from each other's throats at the polls. The one serious flaw was in Galicia. The Poles were in a position to obstruct the Bill almost indefinitely, and in the end it was found necessary to assign to them twenty seats in excess of their due share, at the expense of the unfortunate Ruthenes. But this, of course, only affected one Slav group as against another. All hope of a German majority had finally vanished, and the new House contained only 233 Germans as against 283 non-Germans.

The elections of 1907 naturally transformed the Lower House. The party of large landowners (*feudaler Grossgrundbesitz*) disappeared altogether from the list of parties. The German National Union now stood only fourth numerically with 80 deputies, as against 83 deputies of the Czech Club. The chief gains went to the Christian Socialists, who now absorbed the old Clerical group and became a solid party with 94 seats, and to the Social Democrats, who sprang suddenly from 10 to 87. The rest of the House was composed of parties resting on a national basis. In this new situation Baron Beck governed by a Cabinet of Coalition, or 'Concentration for hard work,' as he preferred to call it. The Ministers were no longer chiefs of departments, but representatives of the chief parties and nationalities.

At first the new Parliament seemed to work well. Paragraph Fourteen was happily banished, the necessary legislation duly found its way through Parliament, the Budget of 1907 showed a financial surplus of

146,000,000 kronen (over £6,000,000 of pre-war value), and the new Commercial Ausgleich with Hungary, though it secured to Hungary the technical triumph of substituting a Customs and Commercial treaty for a Customs Alliance (*Vertrag* instead of *Bündnis*), left to Austria the real success, since Hungary's quota, or relative contribution to the joint expenses of the Dual Monarchy, was raised to 36·4%.

Needless to say, the advent of a compact body of eighty-six Socialists, under such able leaders as Adler and Pernerstorffer helped for a time to divert attention from national to social lines of cleavage. But the main result of their rise to power was to complete the chaos in German party life. Universal Suffrage had placed the Germans in Austria in a permanent minority, and now there was added a permanent disunion among the Germans themselves, whereas the Czechs or Poles or Jugoslavs or Ruthenes were always able to put national issues higher than social or purely political. The great merit of the Socialists was that they saw more clearly than the narrowly bourgeois parties the absolute need for a new attitude on the part of the state towards national questions, but this very fact made a united front all the more unattainable. The Liberals of the Plener type had to fight simultaneously on two fronts—against the Slavs and against the extreme Pan-Germans and German Clericals. The Clericals, reproached by the German Nationalists for alliance with the Slavs, were yet at one with them regarding the national character of Vienna, and never realized how great a tactical value would reside in making all the nationalities of the Monarchy feel at home in so beautiful a capital. Lueger understood this and made more than one bid for the allegiance of the other races ; but his successors, by closing the Komenský schools which the 130,000 Czechs of Vienna had built by their own unaided efforts, contributed immensely to the final alienation of the Czech nation.

The transformation wrought in Austria during the last thirty years of its existence was very ably summed up by Austerlitz, then editor of the *Arbeiterzeitung*, in an outspoken article in July, 1918, on the eve of the final collapse. 'The Germans,' he said, 'were once in Austria those who fought for freedom, while the Slavs opposed to them the resistance of the dead mass. To-day, on the contrary, all Slav nations are democratic, while the German bourgeoisie is obstinately opposed to democratic progress. . . . The Czechs have simply ejected the nobility from their nation, and their highest ambition is to rally the whole nation—the working class at its head—beneath the democratic banner ; for the Germans the Socialist workman is an outcast, and the "alliance" with the nobility of the Herrenhaus is their pride. . . . The national policy of the Czechs involves democracy, whereas that of the Germans involves privilege.' This is the real key to the crisis of the Great War, when all the races save the Germans and Magyars were faced by an actual conflict between loyalty to their nationality and patriotism to the state.

Revival of Confidence

The surprising ease and speed with which Universal Suffrage surmounted so many obstacles, and the great prosperity which marked the first decade of this century, led to a striking revival in public confidence ; many even of those who did not subscribe to the Christian Socialist programme threw off for a brief space of time their old pessimism as to the future of the Habsburg Monarchy. Intellectual life flourished, and the novelists and dramatists of Austria—men like Hofmannsthal, Schnitzler, Bartsch, Rilke, Hermann Bahr, Rosegger, Müller-Gutten-brunn, Karl Kraus—were among the most talented of any writing in German. Vienna maintained its lead in music and in medical science. In the political field three books of high originality appeared within a few months of each other and served as a stimulant to public opinion. *The United States of Great Austria*, by Aurel Popovici, a Roumanian who had been forced to escape from Hungary and as an exile gravitated towards Christian Socialism and established valuable contacts with Brosch and Bardolff, the heads of Francis Ferdinand's Militär-Kanzlei, was a more conservative (and less practical) edition of Palacký's federalist ideas ; starting from the thesis that Dualism was *mater discordiæ*, he concentrated his criticism upon the 'Magyar national state' as a sham and a monstrosity. Carl Renner, under the pseudonym of 'Rudolf Springer,' published *Foundations and Aims of the Habsburg Monarchy*, setting himself to prove, with less passion and superior knowledge, the slight value of historical tradition, the inroads of the 'Unhistoric Nations' upon the artificial (and in his view, played-out) Dual System, and finally, the folly of submitting to Magyar megalomania, when all the time Austria only had to give the word and Hungary would be obliged to follow suit. Austria, he argued, had escaped with an effort from the errors of the Bach regime, the Concordat, the October Diploma and the experi-ments of Schmerling and Beust, and had suffered much, but learned still more. 'Our strength is steeled, our will disciplined, our eye is clear. We see a goal before us, and will follow the path to it.' The book may be described as a Socialist version of the famous lines of Grillparzer, *'Wann steigt der Kaiser zu Pferde?'* (When will the Emperor mount his horse ?) so often on the lips of Austrian patriots of every party in those days, or of the much older watchword : 'Austria above all, if only it wills it.'

A third book, *The Question of Nationalities and Social-Democracy*, came from Renner's colleague, the Socialist deputy Otto Bauer ; much more diffuse and often lapsing into Marxist jargon, it was nevertheless an eloquent plea for passing from the 'all against all' brawlings of unsatisfied nationalism to the higher unity to which Socialism seemed to him to offer the key. 'We fulfil our actions best by leading the proletariat to a struggle against the Class-state and Class-society. . . . We must unite the proletarians of all nations in a powerful body, inspired by a single will, in order to make the treasures of our national culture the possession of the whole nation, and to win for our nation unity and liberty.' In this, the culmination of his argument, we see another confusion as to who and what a 'nation' is. Of the three, Renner was certainly the least doctrin-aire, and attracted wide attention; but no stone was left unturned from the Hungarian side to prejudice those in authority against them all, and to counteract the relationship established between Popovici and the anti-Magyar Heir Apparent. These books were yet another proof that men did exist in Austria with the requisite knowledge, ideas and breadth of vision to solve the vexed 'Question of Nationalities' ; it was in the Hofburg itself that the goodwill and constructive ideas were lacking, and the old Emperor was surrounded by a tiny clique—Montenuovo, Paar and others—utterly destitute of ideas and ready to commend the exact opposite of anything that the impatient, and even violent, but far-sighted Francis Ferdinand might suggest.

Bosnia and the Relapse

The high-water mark of the short-lived revival of confidence that followed the reform of the Reichsrat was the annexation of Bosnia in 1908, which was very widely welcomed as the herald of a new era. Even those who admitted that the manner of its execution had been aggressive and maladroit, hailed it as at least a proof of virility and a much-needed reminder to Europe that Austria-Hungary still ranked among the Great Powers. There was even a current of opinion which looked upon a foreign war as the best means of rallying conflicting races and parties around the dynasty, and also a step to be followed by a modification of the Dual System in a more centralist sense. It is but fair to add that neither the Emperor nor his heir, from their very different angles of vision, desired war, but far rather looked forward to the re-establishment of a system such as the Three Emperors' Leagues of the 'seventies, as the surest guarantee of stability and dynastic principles in Eastern Europe. But instead of increasing the Monarchy's prestige, the gross scandals connected with the Zagreb Treason Trial, and with the libel action brought by the Serbo-Croat Coalition against the historian Friedjung, shook the Monarchy to its core, finally destroyed all hope of a Serbo-Austrian understanding and reacted upon the Croatian and Roumanian questions also. The whole world learned that Baron Aehrenthal had based his preparations for annexation upon police espionage and forgery, the incriminating documents having actually been prepared in the Austro-Hungarian Legation at Belgrade, with the knowledge of the Minister, Count Forgács. The result was that with most right-thinking men the brief rally of optimism was followed by a relapse into the deepest gloom.

There were, moreover, other ominous signs in the situation, before ever the Bosnian crisis had been launched on an unprepared world. The assassination of the Governor of Galicia, Count Adam Potocki, the monster-trial and hunger strike of Ruthene students at Lwow (Lemberg), testified to the unrest throughout the province and the acute friction between Poles and Ukrainians. Meanwhile the feud between Germans and Italians in Tirol, which centred round the latter's demand for a university or high school of their own, led to bloodshed at Innsbruck. In Carniola and Styria there was constant friction of a minor kind between Germans and Slovenes. Moreover, the Slav Congress convoked by Dr. Kramář at Prague during the summer of 1908, in pursuance of his 'Neo-Slav' theories (and attended by every branch of the Slav race except the Ukrainians, whom the Russians and Poles united to exclude), was regarded by the German extremists as a deliberate challenge, and certainly exacerbated still further the German-Czech quarrel. As a result, the 60th anniversary of Francis Joseph's accession was celebrated in Prague by the proclamation of a state of siege. The Czechs, when the Bosnian crisis broke out without, of course, their having had any say in the policy which decided it, could not fail to view with misgivings a situation in which the Slavs of Austria might at any moment find themselves involved in an European conflict, with their Slav kinsmen outside the monarchy ranged in the enemy's ranks. Such considerations were a determining factor in the formation of the so-called 'Slav Union' in the Reichsrat, which brought the Czechs, Slovenes and Croats definitely into alliance. As, however, the Ruthenes also gravitated towards it, the Poles held aloof and, it must be added, by their continuance of support to Vienna made the survival of the Triple Alliance possible. This was of course the direct result of Russia's repressive attitude towards her own Poles, which outweighed even the grievances of the Poles in Prussian Posnania. None the less there was, on the eve of the catastrophe, a noticeable tendency for the 'All-Poles' in Galicia to pursue a Russophil policy, and therefore to link up with the Russophil Young Czechs.

On November 18, 1908, Baron Beck resigned office, and under his successors—Baron Bienerth, the grandson of Schmerling, Baron Gautsch and Count Stürgkh—there was a reversion to the old practice of forming purely bureaucratic cabinets, in which the chief portfolios were assigned to permanent officials in the various ministries—the sole exception being two or three so-called 'Landsmann-Minister,' who were watchdogs for their respective nationalities. Thus even the notable reform of 1906, on which so many hopes had been set, had failed to arrest the process of decay. Reform had come too late, and now it became increasingly obvious to all that the real canker which threatened the state was no other than the Dual System itself.

New Leaders : Kaizl, Kramář, Masaryk

It is only against this confused and shifting background of Austrian politics that the progress of Czech nationalism in the first decade of the twentieth century acquires either shape or perspective. It would be quite unprofitable to pass in review the abortive efforts of successive Governments to solve the linguistic quarrel in Bohemia, after the outstanding failure of Badeni. One after the other various schemes were withdrawn, though Körber's project of *triple* partition, into a German, a Czech and a mixed province, continued to hold the field, if only for lack of any feasible alternative. Unhappily the whole trend of affairs, coupled with the Emperor's personal mood, was now increasingly unfavourable to the emergence of a great statesman capable of rising above these strictly national issues. On the contrary, every man in public life tended to be judged according to his racial affinities, rather than on his own merits.

During the late 'nineties the Old Czechs had been driven finally into the background, at the very moment when they were trying to replace their fatal policy of passivity by something less conservatively negative. Under Badeni the Young Czechs, with new and more obstreperous leaders, showed that they could equal the German obstructionists at their own game ; but there was this great difference, that the Germans could act on the motto : '*J'y suis, j'y reste,*' whereas the Czechs had to regain piecemeal, and by bitter struggle, what had long since passed out of their control.

In this new period, while Rieger died without leaving successors, and the two Gregr brothers were little better than able demagogues, the leadership of the nation passed to three men for whom widely different fates were reserved. Already in the 'eighties Kaizl, Kramář and Masaryk had formed a small political group, based upon those principles of realism which lay at the root of Masaryk's whole philosophy and were the secret of his great and growing influence among the youth of the nation. Their political partnership was not of long duration, and while the other two joined the Young Czech party, Masaryk returned to the University, and became the first exponent of Locke, Hume and Mill among his compatriots. In his own words : "I overcame the Slav anarchy in myself by the help of the British empiricists." Meanwhile Kaizl became the link between the Young Czechs and Vienna, and in 1897 entered Count Thun's Cabinet as Finance Minister ; his premature death in 1903 removed one of the very few who might have achieved a compromise in the perennial German-Czech brawl, and his biography, published shortly before the Great War, revealed how varied and complex were the political threads which he had come to manipulate. Karel Kramář, who came all the more rapidly to the front after Kaizl's death, was a man of ebullient nature, but wide culture, the son of a wealthy industrialist, educated at Prague, Strasburg, Berlin and Paris, steeped in wider Slav feeling and married to the daughter of a rich Moscow manufacturer, and incidentally the owner of a villa in the Crimea. He thus possessed an outlook upon international affairs such as none of his political colleagues could equal ; already in the late 'nineties an article of his in the *Revue de Paris* had reverberated through Europe and caused an exchange of views between Francis Joseph and William II ; and he soon came to be regarded as one of the indispensable critics of foreign policy at the Delegations, and as the man best qualified to interpret the Czech problem in its wider Austrian and European setting. While accepting the *status quo* and desiring Austria's survival as a Great Power, he looked upon the Dual System as a passing aberration which unduly elevated Hungary at the expense of Bohemia, and clung, to a very late date, to his belief in the possibility of reconstituting the monarchy as a predominantly Slav state. This aim, he recognized, could not be attained without a reversal of the alliance between Vienna and Berlin ; and it followed logically that he desired to substitute an Austro-Russian alliance, no longer on the old basis of parallel action in the Balkans and in defence of Conservative principles in Europe, but on the basis of a Slavdom emancipated from German control or influence. From the domestic angle he argued that 'any weakening of Austria means, *rebus sic stantibus*, a strengthening of Germany, but for our people (i.e. the Czechs) a weakening of its importance and a strengthening of those who dream of nothing else save how to subject us to a ruthless regime of Germanization.' In a much commented book on *Czech Policy*, published in 1906, he argued that 'the Czech people has already done Slavdom a priceless service, simply by being there, forming a living wedge in the German body. It is its prime Slav duty to be so strong and healthy that there can never be the slightest fear of its yielding to German pressure. . . . Every strengthening of the Czech people is also a success for Slavdom.' When the famous Berlin economist, Adolf Wagner, gave an address in Vienna, in which he treated Austria as a 'second German state,' Kramář publicly retorted that there was a Slav majority in Austria, which had no intention of watching either on Rhine or on Danube.

In 1900 Masaryk could no longer resist the call of politics, and founded a party of his own, the so-called Realists ; he already had a political review, *Naše Doba*, since 1893, and he now found the necessity for a progressive daily, the *Čas*. But though he had a great following among the cream of the Czech intelligentsia, and an influence far beyond the borders of Bohemia, his group never secured more than three seats in Parliament : the big battalions followed the all too vocal demagogues of the recently founded National Socialist and Agrarian parties (led by Klofáč, Choc and Švehla). His Spartan outlook upon life gradually permeated his disciples, linked him with the Hussites and the Brethren and placed him in the line of succession from Palacký (the historian, but not so much the politician) and still more from Havlíček as the teacher of youth. Keenly alive to social evils, he wrote a challenging book on *Suicide as a Social Mass-Phenomenon*, and in *The Foundations of Marxist Theory* showed how far Marx was from deserving his reputation as an infallible prophet. Masaryk held earnestly to the Hussite motto : 'The Truth prevails' (*Pravda vítězí*), and in his zeal for reality often found himself acting upon the words of Russell Lowell : 'They are slaves who dare not be, In the right with two or three'—now abused as an atheist or perverter of morals, now as a traitor to the national cause. The first and perhaps the most revealing of these conflicts came when he joined Gebauer and Goll in exposing as no better than an impudent forgery the manuscripts produced by Hanka as proof that Czech was one of the first European languages to develop an original ballad poetry comparable to Beowulf or the Chanson de Roland. Masaryk not merely proved his case overwhelmingly, but in the teeth of much obloquy rubbed in the lesson that forgery is a radically unsound basis for a national revival.

A second example of Masaryk's methods was his bold protest against the shameful Ritual Murder myth and the wild anti-Semite agitation which raged around the trial of a Jewish butcher named Leopold Hilsner in 1889. The public attitude to this disgusting story, he declared, 'wounded him to the heart,' since it betrayed 'so much lack of judgment or ideas, such passionate over-haste and inhuman cruelty.' He was hooted down and forced for a time to discontinue his lectures ; but in the end his enemies were reduced to a shamed silence, though this has not, of course, prevented the criminal perverts who surround Hitler from reviving the myth in a still cruder form.

A third example is the case of Professor Wahrmund—the unsympathetic and tactless German professor who was rash enough to publish a free-thinking pamphlet in the ardently Clerical milieu of Innsbruck University, and came near to ruining his career in consequence. Masaryk, without sharing many of his views, published a pamphlet in defence of freedom of opinion, and made this the occasion of a speech in the Reichsrat which culminated in something very like his own religious confession of faith.

There was yet another case in which Masaryk's views on political liberty almost inevitably forced him to intervene in the foreign policy of the Dual Monarchy, and made of a Czech professor the foremost champion of the Croats in their struggle against Magyar oppression, and of Serbia in her unequal resistance to Vienna and Budapest combined. His speech in the Reichsrat, in 1909, on the gross scandals of the Zagreb Treason Trial, was all the more resounding because such a subject really belonged to the sphere of the Delegations rather than the two Parliaments, and because he was thus asserting a claim on behalf of the Austrian Parliament which the Hungarian had always acted upon with impunity. The Zagreb Trial had its sequel in a libel action, brought before a Vienna Court by the deputies of the Serbo-Croat Coalition in Croatia, against the historian Friedjung and Funder, the editor of the official Clerical daily, *Reichspost*. The allegation of the defendants that the leaders of the Serbo-Croat movement inside the Monarchy were mere agents in the pay of the Serbian Government, was proved to rest upon a long series of forged documents concocted in the Austro-Hungarian Legation at Belgrade, passed on as authentic to the Ballplatz, and finally supplied to Friedjung and Funder as the basis of a press campaign timed to coincide with an Austrian invasion of Serbia, and to cut at the roots of foreign sympathy for the Southern Slavs. This time Masaryk, after visiting Zagreb and Belgrade and collecting a dossier of damning original documents, made a frontal attack upon Aehrenthal himself in the Austrian Delegation, and reduced him to silence by his slashing comparison of Count Forgács with Azev—the notorious Russian police spy who in 1905 betrayed the police to the revolutionaries and the revolutionaries to the police. For many years the cream of Croat and Serb students had been disciples of Masaryk at Prague University, and this was how, in his Reichsrat speech, he came to say : "For Supilo, Pribičević and Lukinić I would lay both my hands in the fire." His little book on the forgeries, with its utterly damning facsimiles, remained unanswered, because it was unanswerable, and the Austro-Magyar plot leading up to the Bosnian annexation stood exposed before Europe, in all its perfidy. Thus in the years preceding the Great War co-operation was growing ever closer between Prague, Belgrade and Zagreb, and leading inexorably to the partnership of the World War.

In this final period Kramář pursued his 'Neo-Slav' ideals, following up the Slav Congress of Prague in 1908 by those of St. Petersburg and Sofia in 1909 and 1910. It would be quite unjust to suppose him blind to the dangers of the international situation ; but he was on the horns of a dilemma. Although spokesman of a democratic party and nation, he found himself inevitably relying for the achievement of his programme upon the might of Tsarist Russia and frowning upon both Poles and Ukrainians as traitors to the Slav cause, because their utter repression by Russia rendered them disinclined to attend congresses side by side with such rabid reactionaries as Count Bobrinski or General Spiridovič. Masaryk, on the other hand, devoted much of his time to a book on *Russia and Europe*,[1] which contains the most searching interpretation of Russian psychology and political thought that has yet appeared in any language. A third volume, on Dostoevsky as the key to all that is most ideal and most unbalanced, noblest and most destructive, in the Russian character, has remained in manuscript, and may well have perished in some Nazi holocaust.

It will be seen from this short survey that Kramář and Masaryk in their widely different approach to the Russian enigma, presented to their Czech compatriots two clearly cut alternatives, between which, when war came, they could no longer avoid choosing. On that choice was to depend their fate as a nation and their power to contribute to a new world as yet unsuspected.

The Eve of War in Austria

The three Cabinets of Baron Bienerth (1908–1912) governed from hand to mouth, equally unable to overcome German obstruction in the Bohemian Diet and Czech obstruction in the Reichsrat. On one occasion the Czech Agrarian deputies introduced thirty-seven urgency motions, and it came to a permanent sitting of over forty-eight hours, at the end of which a reform of the Standing Orders of the House was pushed through, and the extremer forms of obstruction were rendered impossible. But the unsolved racial issue, above all between Czechs and Germans, paralysed the whole life of Parliament, and even infected the Socialists, who had

---

[1] Published in English in 1918, under the title of *The Spirit of Russia*.

for a time subordinated national to social interests. Finally, the general elections of 1911 brought a severe defeat of the Christian Socialists in Vienna and the Alpine Lands, and the confusion that resulted inside the Government majority brought the unresourceful Bienerth to the end of his tether. Gautsch became Premier for the third time, but after five months it was obvious that his usefulness had been finally exhausted, and his place was filled by Count Stürgkh, a well-meaning but hide-bound and long-winded bureaucrat of aristocratic leanings, equally devoid of drive and of imagination. He included two Czechs in his Cabinet, which otherwise consisted of high officials. He professed great zeal for a German-Czech Ausgleich ; but neither he nor Prince Francis Thun (the former Premier), whom he appointed Governor of Bohemia with this object, proved capable of bringing the never-ending negotiations to any conclusion. Moreover, the Young Czechs in their turn were now handicapped by the violence of their Radical and Agrarian rivals, who in October, 1912, evolved new ingenuities of obstruction ; Fresl eclipsed all previous records by speaking for sixteen hours on end, and he and his friends found a welcome support among the Ruthenes, now in a positively revolutionary mood.

Needless to say, the task of Stürgkh and Thun was greatly complicated by the Balkan Wars of 1912–13, in which the Czechs more than ever sympathized with the Croats after the Magyar suspension of their constitution and the establishment of the first of a long series of dictators in the person of Baron Cuvaj. They also shared, in no small measure, the delirious joy that swept through all sections of the Southern Slavs at the news of the Balkan victories over the Turks ; they intensely resented Austria-Hungary's hostile attitude towards Serbia and her deliberate incitement of Bulgaria to a fratricidal war. They were only too conscious that at any moment the growing gulf between the Triple Alliance and the Triple Entente might cause a European explosion, and that they themselves, without ever being consulted (or considered, save as providers of so much cannon fodder), might find themselves involved in what might be for Bethmann Hollweg a conflict between Slav and Teuton, but for them would be a civil war against their Russian, Polish and Jugoslav bloodbrothers. Small wonder if there was little inclination to be conciliatory in the domestic quarrel which kept pace in Bohemia with the international crisis, and if, even among the more clear-sighted and genuinely conciliatory Germans of Austria, there grew up a psychology which accepted war or a *coup d'état* as the only possible exit from a blind alley.

By the summer of 1913 the Bohemian Diet had ceased to work, there was a financial crisis so acute that the banks withheld credit and overdue increases of salary had to be postponed. Stürgkh allowed himself to be driven further along the path of illegality, and on July 26 the constitutional regime in Bohemia was suspended, and an Administrative Commission (*Landesverwaltungskomission*) was appointed by Imperial decree to carry out its functions. Paragraph Fourteen was employed more unashamedly than ever before ; the renewed German-Czech negotiations under Stürgkh's own auspices failed miserably after a few days. But the Reichsrat was sent about its business in March after a last flagrant exhibition of Ruthene obstruction, and though the Delegations met in April neither they nor the Reichsrat were again summoned when the supreme crisis came after the Archduke's murder on June 28, 1914.

The history of the forty-seven years preceding the Great War is the history of the slow crumbling and collapse of the Dual System. If proper machinery had existed, timely steps might perhaps have been taken to strengthen the edifice, even in spite of the negative and unconstructive outlook of its chief creator, Francis Joseph. But in actual fact there were never more than patchwork and provisional repairs, such as are undertaken to bring a badly running car to the shelter of the nearest garage, but never any attempt at a thorough overhaul. In the end, as we shall see, the Dual System was not broken up from outside ; it broke down from within, by its own innate rottenness.

CHAPTER XIV

THE SLOVAKS UNDER HUNGARIAN RULE

'*Wer mir meine Sprache verdrängt, will mir meine Vernunft und Lebensweise, die Ehre und die Rechte meines Volkes rauben.*'
—Herder.

It is inevitable that Slovak history should be treated on somewhat different lines from that of Bohemia, for the simple reason that for one thousand years Slovakia had no separate history of her own, but formed a mere annexe to that of Hungary, thus compelling us to concentrate upon a series of episodes and tendencies in place of any consecutive narrative.

Czech and Slovak

No attempt will be made to discuss the obscure origins of the two nations and their languages. The date of their settlement in their present homes, their mutual relations in the migratory period and in the first formative years of their new life, are matters of theory and bold conjecture, and will always remain so for lack of positive evidence. With those who contest the view that the Czechs and Slovaks are the most closely related of all the Slavonic stocks it would be futile to argue, just as little or no purpose is served by learned arguments to prove that Czech and Slovak are two separate languages, or that one is a dialect of the other. The mere fact that it is possible to take sides in such an argument is the best proof of their essential kinship. Czambel, a learned Slovak in the service of the Magyars at the close of last century, tried to demonstrate that the Slovaks came, not from the north-east like the Czechs, but from the south, and therefore belong to the Southern Slav branch ; but he failed to produce any conclusive evidence, save the generally admitted fact that in the century preceding the coming of the Magyars to Central Europe the Slavs on both banks of the Danube between the original Vindobona and Aquincum (Vienna and Budapest) were in closest contact and at times subjects of the same state. Czambel's theory pursued the very obvious political aim of separating the Slovaks from their Czech brethren, and was only a few degrees less tendencious than the fantastic claim of Professor Šegvić that the Croats are not of Slav, but of Gothic, origin (and therefore should become the obedient vassals of Adolf Hitler, who is himself not of a very obvious Teutonic type). There is not a single modern writer of authority who accepts Czambel—least of all Lubor Niederle, the foremost authority upon Slavonic antiquities whom this century has yet known. On the contrary, contemporary philologists have provided their quota of circumstantial evidence in favour of the essential kinship of Czech and Slovak.

Brief reference has already been made to the short-lived and somewhat shadowy 'Moravian Empire' of the ninth century, and to the apostolate of Saints Cyril and Methodius, so epoch-making in the history of all Slavonic peoples, languages, and creeds (p. 13). Nitra, in Western Slovakia, was probably the capital of Rostislav and Svatopluk,[1] and

---

[1] Some authorities believe that Velehrád-Devín was the capital.

certainly the metropolitan see of St. Methodius ; but few details have survived, apart from the vicissitudes of German-Slav ecclesiastical rivalry in Rome, and in the last century even this has been embroidered over with legendary lore and political imagination. Svatopluk, as portrayed by the Slovak romantic writers of the last century, is certainly very different from the real man, who played his own game with German kings and Germanizing bishops. But Methodius represents a great unifying tradition which nothing can erase from the pages of history.

The Magyar Conquest

The coming of the Magyars, and their speedy destruction of the Moravian state, at an indeterminate date between 896 and 906, ended the first brief experiment of Czecho-Slovak Unity. This was a decisive factor in the shaping of Central Europe—decisive because it drove a wedge that was to become permanent between the two main groups of Slavs, and also because it ensured the relative isolation of the Slovaks until quite recent times. The geographical factors which furthered this isolation, while at the same time pushing the Czechs westwards into the main currents of European life, are abundantly clear to any careful student of the physical map of the Continent. Bohemia is a lozenge-shaped territory, with strongly defined mountain barriers on almost every side, forming a Slav bastion in the German heart of the Continent, brought into touch with Bavaria, Saxony, Poland by many important routes of trade and communication leading to the Main and Rhine, to the Elbe and to the Oder and Vistula. Slovakia, on the other hand, is cut off from her neighbours to the north by the High Tatra Mountains (open, it is true, at each end, along the valleys of the Orava and Poprad), and finding her most natural means of expansion towards the south (and especially towards the Danube), where her ethnographic boundary has always been fluid and ill-defined. Speaking in very broad terms, the Slovaks and Magyars, to-day as in previous centuries, blend almost imperceptibly near the point at which the last foothills taper off into the great plain of the Danube and Tisza. Restated politically, this means that Slovakia has on the whole not been much affected by Poland, even though the district of the Zips towns provided the necessary contact between Poland and Hungary right on until the modern railway era. Farther to the east the Carpathians formed a very real barrier, while westwards, as will become obvious from our brief survey, there were periodical contacts of an intimate kind, ending in long periods of isolation due as a rule to the changing political fortunes of the Bohemian state.

After another half-century of semi-nomadic habits, the Magyars were decisively defeated on the Lechfeld, near Augsburg, by Otto the Great, and the Bohemian Duke Boleslav I, as a reward for his military support, acquired a considerable portion of what we now know as Slovakia. So far as can be judged, the mountainous districts of the north were till much later very thinly populated, and large tracts in the Matra and still more in the future 'Carpathian Ruthenia' were kept almost empty, as royal hunting grounds. It is interesting to note that Slovakia became Christian sooner than the central Magyar plains ; the connection with Duke Boleslav resulted in its falling at first under the jurisdiction of the newly created Bishopric of Prague (976), and in the work of the Czech missionary St. Adalbert (or Vojtěch), in Christianizing Hungary and baptizing the future Saint Stephen, who in the year 1000 received from Pope Sylvester II the gift of the Holy Apostolic Crown. Under Stephen the new kingdom consolidated more rapidly than Bohemia, and easily resisted Czech attempts to reassert their transitory hold upon Western Slovakia, which now fell under the jurisdiction of Esztergom (Gran), the future primatial see of Hungary. From the first the great king looked to Rome rather than Byzantium, and in a memorable letter to his son and heir—so often used as a blind for quite other sentiments—he advised that the new settlers whom it was his policy to welcome should be 'held in honour, for they bring fresh knowledge and arms ; they are an ornament and support of the throne, for a country where only one language and one custom prevails, is weak and fragile' (*Regnum unius linguæ uniusque moris imbecille et fragile est*). The manner in which this good advice was acted upon distinguished Hungary from many other countries until the nineteenth century, when by some strange mental aberration the directly opposite policy of unreasoning assimilation to a single type gained the ascendant and, by driving all the neighbouring nationalities into opposition, rendered inevitable the final partition of the old Hungary.

It belongs to the philologist rather than to the historian to demonstrate the very considerable Slav influences upon the Magyar language, which cannot surprise us when we reflect that Pannonia, when the Magyars reached it, was mainly inhabited by Slav tribes. It is, however, interesting to note in passing that the Magyars took over from the Slavs the names for their king (*Király*), for their county unit the Comitat (*megye, medza*), and for their chief administrative officer, the Ispán (*Župan*).

The German Colonists in Hungary

It was the policy of the Árpád dynasty, like that of their neighbours and rivals the Přemyslides, to encourage German colonization in their dominions ; but while in the latter case the principal motive was to create a wealthy class and certain centres of industry, and thus to free the monarch to some extent from dependence on the nobility, in the former the main consideration was defence of the frontier against invasions from the still nomadic tribes of Eastern Europe. The towns in Hungary were never allowed to play a political role ; they were given royal charters and held direct from the Crown, living their own life and retaining to a surprisingly late date the power to exclude the nobility from influence within the circuit of their walls. The movement had already begun in the middle of the twelfth century, and early in the thirteenth the newly founded Teutonic Order, under Hermann von Salza, settled in what was coming to be known as Transylvania, though they soon moved further afield to the still heathen Baltic coast. The Mongol invasion of 1241, which for a time submerged Hungary and drove King Béla IV into exile, served as a stimulant for further settlers, and while the Saxons were consolidating themselves in southern Transylvania (their 'Golden Bull,' providing a special autonomy for their two Districts and nine Towns in 'Siebenbürgen,' already dates from 1224), the older colonies of the Zips, on the north-east Polish-Slovak border, were strengthened in the three following decades. In 1261 special rights were conferred on the king's 'German guests' in Kaschau (Košice) ; and in 1271 a charter was granted to the 'totality (*Gesammtheit*) of the twenty-four Zips Towns,' with Leutschau (Levoča) as their little '*civitas provinciæ capitalis.*' Farther west, in the central Slovak districts, an even more important part was played by the so-called 'Mining towns' (Bergstädte) of Altsohl (Banská Bystrica, 1254), Neusohl (Zvolen, 1258), Schemnitz (Stiavnica) and Kremnitz (Kremnica)—which later became the seat of the Hungarian Mint. The settlers in these and other towns brought their German code with them—generally the *Magdeburger Recht*; and the extent to which their privileges went may be gathered from the fact that under the charter of Neusohl only Germans might own property in the towns, while even in that of Pest no house or land could be sold to a 'stranger' (which meant, a non-German). In the fourteenth century the position of the Germans was still stronger, and in 1328 the king confirmed the privileges of the Zips towns 'forever' in the German language ; the long list of fresh privileges conferred upon the German towns under Louis the Great includes the names of Eperjes (Prešov), Bartfeld (Bardiov), Sillein (Žilina), Skalica, and even Debreczen was partly German. The first serious blow to this flourishing and independent community was the pawning of thirteen of the twenty-four Spiš (Zips) towns to Poland by King Sigismund, to pay the expenses of his many European adventures, culminating in his quarrel with the Hussites ; nor were they restored to Hungary till the days of Maria Theresa, as a foretaste of the Polish Partition. The Mining Towns successfully survived the troubles of the Hussite Wars, and Buda (Ofen) was so overwhelmingly German that it developed its own special code—'*Ofener Recht*,' being an adaptation of Magdeburger Recht—and gave this to numerous other towns, including Pressburg (Bratislava, Pozsony), Klausenburg (Cluj, Kolozsvár), Kaschau (Košice) and Kronstadt (Brașov). With the Turkish conquest of 1541 disaster came upon it and the German cities of the Hungarian plain ; yet after the expulsion of the Turks Ofen again became a German town and only lost that character in the second half of the nineteenth century, thanks on the one hand to the phenomenal expansion of Pest, across the river from Ofen, and simultaneously to a policy of intensive Magyarization. It may be added that the chief historians of the Germans in Hungary have calculated that at their height they amounted to about one-sixth of the total population of Hungary, and one-fourth of the total Magyar population.

It is hardly too much to say that under the Angevin dynasty, and even later, it was the Germans who played the chief part in Slovakia, rather than either Magyars or Slovaks. But special conditions favoured the growth of powerful noble families, and the ruined castles perched upon key positions along the River Váh still show us the sources of their power. It would, however, be a mistake to attach undue importance to the episode of Matthias Csák of Trenčín, sometimes called '*dominus Vagi et Tatræ*,' a feudal baron who defied Charles Robert and assumed a semi-royal magnificence, but was finally overthrown in battle in 1321. Writers of the romantic revival sought to make of him a national hero, aiming at Slovak independence, but this may be dismissed as entirely mythical. The truth is that the Slovak population was not numerous, found itself at the mercy of the rising feudal tyranny, and did not produce leaders of its own.

The Hussites in Slovakia

The death of Louis the Great without male heirs brought the Crown of Hungary to Sigismund of Luxemburg, who, as we have seen, was at once the heir of his childless brother, Wenceslas of Bohemia, and the

champion of orthodoxy against Bohemian heresy; and indeed without
the resources of his Hungarian kingdom he could not possibly have played
so great a role in Europe. It is not necessary to revert here to the Hussite
struggle, except to point out that Hussite ideas and Hussite arms penetrated at an early date into Slovakia. In 1423 Žižka advanced as far as
the River Hron (Gran), in 1437 Prokop overran the western Slovak
districts, and in 1429 it was at Pressburg that he and his colleagues met
and negotiated with Sigismund. The final reconciliation with Prague,
though only achieved in the year preceding his death, meant the Personal
Union between Hungary and Bohemia and thus brought the Czechs and
Slovaks nearer together. But there were many setbacks to the idea.
Albert II, who seemed destined to weld Danubian Europe together, only
lived two years, and Hungary sought union with Poland rather than
Bohemia and Austria; under the child-King Ladislas Posthumus union
was little more than skin-deep. After his death, the two neighbours not
merely elected national kings of their own, but fought each other fiercely
for years, and it was not until 1490 that Personal Union was restored
under the feeble Jagellon Kings, and the two continued to go very much
their own ways.

There was, however, a brief interlude in the years immediately
following Albert's death. Jiskra of Brandys, a Czech noble who had
taken service under the widowed Queen Elizabeth, established himself at
Zvolen and Košice, with the title of 'Supreme Captain,' and for close upon
twenty years (1438–1457), with the help of another noble Czech adventurer,
Peter Aksamit, governed most of Slovakia from Nitra to Košice and
Prešov, as a sort of autonomous domain, fortified against the south by
a chain of castles and fortresses along the foothills. Within this area
Hussite doctrine had time to strike root. But by 1459 John Hunyady
was sufficiently strong as 'Gubernator' of Hungary to issue a challenge to
the Czech intruder; on September 7 of that year, Jiskra, though gravely
outnumbered, defeated the Hungarian army at Lučenec (Losonc), and
signed peace on the basis of the *status quo*. In 1453, however, young
Ladislas, on reaching his majority, threw over Jiskra, who had always
acted as his deputy; after many losing and delaying actions first Jiskra
and finally Aksamit, had to evacuate Slovakia, leaving behind them, however, a considerable number of Czech settlers and through them both
linguistic and religious influences. Though Alois Jirášek has made the
episode of Jiskra the subject of one of his most famous historical novels,
there is only very scanty documentary evidence as to internal conditions
in Slovakia in the following hundred years.

Lutheranism and the Slovaks

One thing is certain, that though Jiskra's failure led to a further
strengthening of aristocratic, at the expense of democratic, currents, none
the less the Reformation, when it began to infiltrate, found the ground
already prepared by Hussite undercurrents. In this respect it was
naturally enough the German towns that played a decisive part in the
spread of reformed doctrines, which followed the trade routes from
Leipzig, and therefore from Wittenberg, along the Carpathians into
Transylvania and on to the Black Sea. The Germans adopted Lutheranism, whereas the Magyars definitely turned to Geneva in 1563, so that
the Calvinistic faith came to be known as '*a magyar hit*' (the Magyar faith)

par excellence, and Debreczen the Magyar Geneva. But the Slovaks, in so far as they became Protestant, threw in their lot with the Lutherans. Between the years 1522 and 1564 over two hundred Slovaks and Germans from Hungary are on record as having studied at Wittenberg, which shows the rapidity with which Protestant tenets took hold. Already in 1549 the five Royal free cities of North Hungary drew up a Confession of Faith, modelled on that of Augsburg, and known as 'Confessio Penta-politana' ; a modified version, known as the 'Confessio Montana' (that of the seven Mountain or Mining Towns, led by Kremnica) appeared in 1558, and it was not till 1575 that the 'Confessio Bohemica' was drawn up in Bohemia, as an attempt at compromise between Lutherans and Utraquists (see p. 96). In this period, however, a large proportion of the great families of the north—notably those of Thurzo, Illesházy, Nádasdy and Révay—adopted the Lutheran creed.

An altogether new situation for the Slovaks resulted from the Turkish conquest of Hungary. The real Magyar kernel of the country having been completely overrun, while Transylvania was isolated in the bend of the Carpathians and developed a peculiar life of its own, especially from the constitutional and ecclesiastical point of view, the northern districts became the rallying point of all who remained loyal to the House of Habsburg, and the centre of organized resistance to the Turks. The Diet now met in one or other of the northern towns, especially Kaschau and Pressburg, which gradually acquired the position of the coronation city and retained it even after the recovery of Buda. It is interesting to note in passing that the new southern frontier, that of Slovakia (or 'Habsburg Hungary') during 160 years (1541–1699), though it fluctuated somewhat according to military vicissitudes, bore a sufficient resemblance to the frontier of 1918 to 1938 between Czechoslovakia and Hungary, to suggest that this latter was not so destitute of geographical merit as its critics suggest.

The Nobles and the Towns

The result of partition was to concentrate a great part of the political, ecclesiastical and cultural life of Hungary in the northern districts. It gave fresh impetus to the onslaughts of the nobles upon the monopolistic rights of the Towns ; already as early as 1553 the towns were compelled to admit fugitive nobles from Turkish territory and to allow them to buy house property, though as yet without thereby acquiring rights of citizenship. At last in 1608 this concession was extended to include equal rights with the burghers. Moreover, the Germans were now obliged to admit both Magyars and Slovaks to municipal office, and refractory towns were heavily fined. In 1647 it was laid down that all legal disputes should be decided no longer by town-law, but by the general laws of the country. This opened the flood-gates, and the privileged position of the Germans was rapidly undermined in all directions. To take but a single instance, at Karpfen (Krapina), which admitted the first Magyar and Slovak in 1611 and 1612 respectively, the German language had almost disappeared in the eighteenth century.

Cardinal Pázmány and the Counter-Reformation

The onslaught of the nobles on the towns corresponded with the revival of religious persecution, and was used by the central authorities as a means towards the extirpation of heresy. The inroads made upon

German monopoly seemed at first to bring advantage to the Slovaks, but in the end left the road wide open for Magyarization. In the opening period of the Thirty Years' War the Prince of Transylvania, Gabriel Bethlen, made himself the champion of Protestantism and was able not merely to keep the Counter-Reformation at arms' length in his own realm, but to intervene constantly in Habsburg Hungary. But neither he nor men like the Palatine Thurzo, a no less ardent Protestant, were able to hold their own against the triumphant aggression of the redoubtable Cardinal Peter Pázmány, who set himself with great success to reclaim Hungary for the Catholic Church. He began with the great families, notably the Esterházys, the Pálffys and the Zrinskis. An ardent pupil of the Jesuits, he shared their zeal for education, and his principal controversial book (*Kalauz*, or Guide) had the rare distinction of also possessing great literary merit and therefore influencing the revival of the Magyar language. He was instrumental in depriving the Protestants of three hundred churches—they had already been expelled from the Cathedral of Košice in 1604. His efforts to accomplish the reunion of Transylvania with the 'Felvidék,' or northern districts, were a blend of most genuine patriotism, since union would obviously increase the prospects of at last expelling the Turks, and of a design for complete re-Catholicization. In this he failed, but his princely foundations, the seminaries for young priests established at Vienna (and ever since known as the Pazmaneum), and at Trnava (NagySzombat) in 1635, and his new Jesuit university at the latter town, on Slovak soil thirty miles east of Pressburg, were largely instrumental in turning the religious balance in Hungary very definitely in favour of Rome.

Bohemia and Austria having been successfully re-Catholicized under Ferdinand II, it was left for Leopold I to attempt, with far greater success, similar drastic measures against them. By the Treaty of Linz in 1645, the Protestants had been guaranteed full freedom, and ninety churches were restored to them. But during the 'seventies and 'eighties there was a wave of persecution, many of the Protestant clergy being deported and sent to the Neapolitan galleys (whence some of them were rescued by the Dutch Admiral van Tromp) ; the Protestants were deprived of eight hundred churches and of all their schools, and a bloodthirsty Italian General, Count Caraffa, instituted the so-called 'Blood Tribunal' of Prešov (Eperjes) at which a number of leading Lutherans were executed. It seems almost incredible that such proceedings should have coincided with the series of brilliant campaigns by which the Imperialists were at last driving the Turks out of Hungary. The Hungarian Parliament, when it met in 1687, refused to discuss even such news as the recovery of Buda, until orders had been issued to put an end to the terror, and this was never resumed. But the Protestants never recovered their lost position ; for the next century they were a dwindling minority, and in 1781, when Joseph II issued his Edict of Tolerance, only two hundred and five Lutheran parishes still remained. By 1790, when a special Protestant Law was adopted, the number had already risen to four hundred and thirty-five and two hundred entirely new parishe could be added. At this stage the Lutheran Church was divided into fou Districts or Synods, each with a bishop and a lay inspector, as a rule a Magyar noble who could thus represent his co-religionists at the Diet, and an inspector-general, who already had a dangerous degree of influenc over the policy of the whole Church. In it the Slovaks already out numbered the Germans and Magyars combined, and though they were only a minority of their nation, possessed a cultural importance out of all proportion to those numbers, for reasons that became more apparent in the nineteenth century. Intercourse with the tiny remnant of Czech Protestants was hardly possible during the long period of oppression which has been described earlier in this book ; but there were certain spiritual links which nothing could ever destroy—the Kralice Bible and the Hymn-book of Tranoscius (George Tranovský, pastor of Liptovsky Sv. Mikuláš, but a native of Silesia, whose third centenary was celebrated in 1935 with affectionate and devout rejoicing). It was due to their literary pre-eminence that Czech remained the language of the Slovak Protestant liturgy until modern times.

The Eighteenth Century

Though Slovakia was more fortunate than Central Hungary in escaping the ravages of Turkish occupation, and benefited in certain respects by the concentration of political and cultural life within its boundaries, this was offset by the fact that 53% of the whole privileged class of Hungary took shelter there, and while enjoying exemption from taxation put the main burden of taxation on to the shoulders of the peasantry. 'During the Turkish occupation only Slovakia paid taxes into the treasury. After the expulsion of the Turks the arable land was without owners, and was administered by military authorities. The population lived almost like nomads and was not subject to any official control or to the obligation to pay taxes.' This, of course, gradually readjusted itself, but it remains true that Slovakia continued relatively to be more heavily taxed than the other districts of Hungary. At the same time it is to be borne in mind that Hungary, especially after the exemptions granted to the nobility by Maria Theresa at the celebrated Diet of 1741, evaded her proper share of the taxation of the Habsburg Monarchy, and indeed actually paid less in taxes than Styria, and only a third of Bohemia's contribution.[1]

Many of the foremost families of modern Hungary are of Slav or Roumanian origin, but long since Magyarized by a process which was both natural and inevitable ; in the lower nobility there were very large non-Magyar elements owing to the generous, sometimes wholesale, manner in which groups of men or even whole villages were ennobled for services rendered in the wars against the Turks. The attempt of Joseph II to introduce German throughout his dominions as an instrument of centralization, was the first stage in the modern struggle of rival races and languages. It was resisted for its own sake, but still more because it involved the intrusion of German-speaking officials in every direction, and thus was a challenge to all vested interests. Moreover, it involved the pegging out of a rival claim. German, by which Joseph had wished to supersede Latin in Hungary, was not to be tolerated; but Latin was to give way to Magyar, as 'the national language'—nemzeti nyelv, as it now came to be called more and more. This in its turn led in 1790 to the advancing of demands by the Serbs for the restoration of their suppressed autonomy and national rights, by the Roumanians for their admission to the Diet of Transylvania as a fourth nation beside the three privileged nations (the Magyars, Saxons and Szekelys), and even by the Slovaks and

[1] Dr. S. Janšák, 'The Land Question in Slovakia' (*Slovakia Then and Now*).

R/HCS

Ruthenes for the use of their language in the schools. Henceforth the mother tongue plays the foremost part in all nationalist claims.

The Literary Revival

It is important to bear in mind that the revival of national sentiment and literary effort was not the monopoly of any one race in Hungary, but a very general phenomenon, stirring the Croats, Serbs and Slovaks quite as early as the Magyars. The first Magyar newspaper, *Magyar Hirmondó*, appeared in Pressburg in 1780, and was followed in 1783 by the first Slovak newspaper, *Prešpurské Noviny*, which, it is true, only lived for three years ; at this moment there were more German than Magyar papers in Hungary. In 1783 also a first attempt was made to use Slovak as a literary language ; this was an insipid novel entitled *The Adventures of the Young Man René*, by a Catholic priest, Joseph Bajza, who wrote on the model of Fénelon. In 1803 a promising institute of Slav language and literature was established at the Lutheran Lycée of Pressburg, while Slovak book stores and literary societies were established about the same time in several of the North Hungarian towns, under the patronage of Cardinal Rudnay, who recognized himself to be a Slav.[1] The Magyars, however, though they had no great start, very rapidly outdistanced the other races. They had immense advantages in their central position, their control not only of the central, but still more of the local, administration, the strength of their social position and resources ; moreover, in the first half of the nineteenth century they produced a rich crop of poets, dramatists and other writers, who would have been an ornament to any language and threw the Slovaks, Serbs or Roumanians completely into the shade. Politically, even the Magyar movement languished during the decade following the Napoleonic Wars, when the reactionary views of Francis reigned supreme. From 1812 to 1825 the Hungarian Parliament was not allowed to meet, but in the latter year even Francis found it expedient to yield and from 1825 to 1848 the movement for political reform gained every year in volume. This movement had a double side, a constitutional and a national. The first, which sought to vindicate Hungary's ancient and often violated constitutional rights and to adapt them to the requirements of a new and more democratic age, won for the Magyars the sympathy of liberal reformers in the West. Unhappily, while steadily raising their own demands, they showed increasing intolerance towards all the other races, and insisted upon identifying the two essentially different conceptions of 'Hungarian' and 'Magyar.'

Bernolák and Hollý

There is no little irony in the fact that the first incentive to Slovak literary expression should have come from the Jesuits, who were so largely responsible for the decline of Czech. But the explanation is simple enough ; they wished to erect a barrier between the two kinsmen. In 1718 a Paulinian monk named Macsay published a collection of sermons written in the western Slovak dialect, and the Jesuits of Trnava followed this up by various books of devotion written in a mixture of Czech and Slovak. In 1746 Matthew Bel, Hungary's foremost scholar in that age and a leader of the Pietist movement, wrote a preface to a 'Slavo-Bohemian Grammar,' expressing pride in his own Slovak nationality and

[1] *"Slavus sum,"* he said, *"et si in cathedra Petri forem, Slavus ero."*

the zeal with which it was then being cultivated by the magnates and gentry of Slovakia.

The Slovak revival took a fresh step forward in the first decade of the nineteenth century. Its leader, a Catholic priest named Anton Bernolák (1762–1813), published in 1787 an essay on Slavonic philology and the first Slovak Grammar, and in 1792 founded a Slovak Literary Society at Trnava, in which the Western Slovak dialect was put forward as a substitute for Czech, as the Slovak literary tongue. His elaborate lexicon in five languages (Czech, Latin, German, Magyar and Slovak) and in six volumes was not published till a decade after his death. Bernolák left behind him a pupil of no small merit, in another Catholic priest, Jan Hollý (1785–1849), who first translated into Slovak some of the great classics—Homer, Virgil, Horace and Theocritus—and followed them up by long and meritorious, if not inspired, epics of his own, on such topics as Svatopluk and Saints Cyril and Methodius, casting their distant light upon a reviving Slovakia. Though departing from Kollár's practice of writing in Czech, Hollý was in all essentials of the same mind as his Protestant contemporary, being equally infected by vague Panslavic doctrines.

Meanwhile the Protestants, while avoiding any quarrel, preferred to hold aloof from the zealously Catholic centre of Trnava and grouped themselves round the Lutheran Lycée of Bratislava (Pressburg), where George Palkovič filled the first chair of Slavonic at the new Slav Institute, until his place was taken by Ludevit Štúr, destined to be the Slovak leader in 1848 and the regenerator of the language. There was, however, a third but parallel line of endeavour ; Kollár and Safařík, the two most distinguished Slovaks of their day, belong to the Czech revival, owing to their persistent use of Czech rather than Slovak. Strangely enough, when the great moment of decision came, it was Štúr who chose intimate co-operation with the Czechs, while Kollár held back and, when Budapest became too hot for him, went to Vienna rather than Prague. Needless to say, however, their writings were of capital importance in the whole Slav revival of last century, and form a strange sentimental link between the Western romantic school and the extravagances of Panslavism.

Petöfi and Kossuth

This is the moment at which to point out the Slovak origin of two of Hungary's most famous sons. Alexander Petöfi, the inspired poet of the Magyar Revolution, who is sometimes called the Magyar Burns and fell like Theodor von Körner on the battlefield, was the son of purely Slav parents, and only Magyarized his original name of Petrovič when he was a student. Louis Kossuth came from good lesser 'gentry' stock in Košuty, near St. Martin, the very heart of Slovakia, ar 1 his uncle George was a minor poet who wrote in Slovak. The evolution of these two men illustrates the grave handicap under which the Slovaks lay, still isolated in their mountains, and with the axe already striking at the roots of education for the next generation.

Magyarization

During the 'forties a wave of Magyarizing frenzy swept Hungary. Already in 1830 Parliament had passed the first of a series of laws extending the sphere of the Magyar language ; and Count Stephen Széchényi had won a unique position by his sensational offer of a year's income as preliminary endowment of a Hungarian Academy. In the same year Magyar was made obligatory for all advocates or holders of public office. In 1836 it was made, jointly with Latin, the language of the laws, and became optional for all official documents, and in courts of second instance. In 1839–1840 it became the official language of the Government and the exclusive language of all registers and its knowledge was made obligatory for clergy of all denominations. At last, in 1843, it was declared the exclusive language of legislation, of the Government and of official business, and it was declared in principle to be also the exclusive language of public instruction, though the details of this were left to a future parliament. Meanwhile, in many of the county assemblies much more extreme projects were aired for the complete Magyarization of all the other races ; and this aim was preached year in year out by a number of newly founded Magyar newspapers. The controversy roused a considerable echo in Austria and even in Germany, where numerous polemical pamphlets began to appear, voicing on the one hand Magyar ambitions and on the other the protests and alarm of the Slavs and Roumanians of Hungary. Most sensational of all was the exchange of shots between Pulszky and Leo Thun, to which allusion has already been made (p. 182).

In 1840 an open assault upon the Slovaks was made at the General Assembly of the Lutheran Church. Count Charles Zay, speaking as Inspector-General of the entire Church—in other words, its leading layman—proclaimed the doctrine of racial apostasy as a duty which the Slav Lutherans owed to their fatherland and their religion. Since 'the Magyar language is the truest guardian and protector of the liberty of our country, of Europe and of the Protestant cause,' it follows that Magyarization is 'the duty of every eager champion of freedom and intelligence' ; its triumph 'is the victory of reason, liberty and intelligence.' Following closely, by preconcerted plan, came a series of attempts to eject the Slovak language from the Lutheran synods and presbyteries, and Kossuth himself, as an elder of the Church, spoke publicly in favour of the abolition of all existing Slav societies in Lutheran schools. Such a society at Levoča (Leutschau) had already been suppressed, as a breeding-ground of 'Panslavism,' its library being broken up and its president losing his post at the gymnasium. In 1842 a petition signed by two hundred Slovak clergy, recounting the various forms of persecution to which both clergy and laity were subjected, was addressed to the Emperor in Vienna ; but the only result was that at the next General Assembly the Superintendent Jozefi and his colleague Hodža were accused by Kossuth himself of betraying the Magyar cause and the Protestant religion, and were howled down by the public. Amid the orgy of Chauvinism two voices were raised in defence of the Slovaks—Count John Mailáth, the well-known Catholic historian of Hungary, and Count Stephen Széchényi who, in a famous address to the Academy which he had founded, admitted that he hardly knew of a Magyar who 'is not transformed into a madman and even more or less deaf to the laws of fairness and justice, whenever the question of our language and nationality is raised,' and begged his compatriots to follow the precept 'do as you would be done by.' But from the day on which 'the greatest Magyar' and his fellow-magnate entered these protests, their once great popularity began to fail ; the fine frenzy of Kossuth, voiced in his brilliant and aggressive organ, *Pesti Hirlap*, carried all before it. Already in 1842 he declared in one of its leaders : 'Verily, verily I say unto you, that a Slovak nation has never existed even in a dream' ; and in 1843, in a controversy with the Augsburg *Allgemeine Zeitung* (then the leading South German newspaper, with a wide circulation in the Habsburg dominions), he boasted of his glowing love for his own nation as 'the only nation in Hungary which has any future based upon history, politics, or law.' The argument of the German *Herrenvolk* : 'We must be masters in our own house,' was already being applied in the 'forties by the Magyars to the 'foreign inhabitants ' (*idegen ajkuak*) of Hungary.

Štúr, Hurban and Hodža

In this dangerous situation the Slovaks found three leaders, weak by comparison with those whom the more favourably situated Czechs or Croats had produced, but none the less full of courage and self-sacrifice. Ludevit Štúr (1815–1856) had, like Kollár, studied at Halle, and had already in 1837 acted as deputy for Palkovič in the chair of Slav language and literature at Bratislava ; he himself was the son of a Protestant teacher while his two close colleagues, Joseph Miloslav Hurban (1827–1888) and Michael Miloslav Hodža (1811–1870), were both Lutheran pastors. In 1844 Štúr was dismissed from his post, owing to his resistance to Count Zay's plans of Magyarization through the school, and he then became editor of a Slovak newspaper entitled *Slovenskje Národnje Novini* (Slovak National News), with *Orol Tatranski* (The Eagle of the Tatra) as a fortnightly literary supplement. Hurban, who edited this latter, also published an almanack called *Nitra*, the first volume in Czech in 1842, the second in Slovak in 1844.

We thus find the curious contradiction that the literary breach between Slovak and Czech and the decision in favour of the central, rather than the western, dialect as the Slovak literary norm, was the work of ardent Czechophils, who as Protestants defended the Czech liturgy and the Kralice tradition, whereas the foremost Catholics of the revival clung to the western dialect, despite its Czechophil orientation. Convinced that the Bernolák dialect was inadequate, but also that it was impossible to maintain Czech as the language of Slovak culture, Štúr, Hurban and Hodža took their decision in favour of the central dialect, for essentially political reasons. They believed that it would strengthen the position of the Slovaks in their struggle against the Magyars, and they could not fail to see that the Czechs were not as yet in a position to give very effective political support. A learned controversy ensued, brought to a head by Štúr's book on *Slovak Dialects* (*Nárečja Slovenskuo*) ; and while Šafařik, Palacký and Havlíček all joined battle with Štúr, Kollár plunged into vehement attacks upon the central dialect and would not hear of its primitive purity and ancient lineage, as argued by its adherents. In 1847 the three groups met and discussed their rival views, and it was agreed to refer to the arbitration of Martin Hattala, a young Slovak philologist in Prague ; after the Revolution of 1848 he was able to publish his results, which may be said to have canalized the literary development and imposed restraints upon what threatened to become a frankly separatist movement.

In 1847 Štúr was elected to the Hungarian Parliament as deputy for the town of Zvolen, but as the only Slovak in the House could do little or nothing. But with the outbreak of the March Revolution of 1848 events moved as rapidly for the Slovaks as for the other races. Štúr transferred himself to Vienna and there came into contact with other Slav representatives—notably the Croat Kukuljević and the Slovene poet Vraz—and, still more important, with the Ban Jelačić and the Serbian Patriarch Rajačić, who were working hand in hand and paid a joint visit to the Imperial Court. At this early stage he received an invitation from the students of Prague, played a decisive part in the preparations for a Slav Congress, and on April 30 made an impassioned appeal in favour of common action between Slovak and Czech. The disagreements of previous years vanished, Kollár sent his blessing from Pest, and Havlíček, in whose paper Štúr expounded his motives in cultivating a special Slovak literary language, speedily established terms of cordial intimacy with the Slovak leader. Hurban had at first remained at home in order to preside over a 'National Assembly' at Teplice; and here on May 10 a programme was issued in the name of the Slovaks as the original occupants of the soil, addressed simultaneously to the Crown and to the newly-formed National Government at Pest. Its main demands were 'the summons of a general Parliament for the brother nations of Hungary,' special provincial assemblies on a racial basis, the right to use the mother tongue in all public deliberations and in courts of law, Slovak schools and a university, a Slovak National Guard, Universal Suffrage and complete freedom of assembly, association and press. Any further movement was promptly scotched by the Magyar authorities, and Kossuth thundered in Parliament against the 'Panslavs.' Hurban and several other Slovak stalwarts only just fled in time, joined Štúr in the attempt to rouse Bohemia, Moravia and Slovakia to common action, and acclaimed Prague as the heart of the Slav world. Meanwhile his colleague Hodža issued a small book in German on the Slovaks which answered Count Zay's summons to choose between Magyarism and the Russian knout, in the fiery phrase : 'Rather the Russian knout than Magyar domination, for the one could only enslave our bodies, while the other threatens us with moral ruin and death.'

The Slovaks and Prague

It thus came about that at the Slav Congress the four Slovaks, Šafařik, Štúr, Hurban and Hodža, played a part second to none save Palacký himself ; and it was their avowed aim to bring Slovakia into line with Bohemia and Moravia, no longer as an integral part of Hungary, but as part of a 'Czechoslav' federal unit such as Palacký contemplated. Štúr, however, made it clear that his aim was not to preserve Austria, under whom the Slavs had hitherto 'rotted,' but to preserve his own people ; Austria, he added, was decrepit and lay under a curse. Hurban's views fell short of absolute separation from Austria, though his whole reckoning rested on the closest co-operation with the Czechs, while Hodža, unable to shut his eyes to signs of Slav dissension inside Austria, was anxious not to quarrel with Vienna or the Germans, and would have been content with a local Slovak Diet subordinate to the Hungarian Parliament. There was a special point of contact between Štúr and Havlíček, both of whom set great store upon close accord between the Czechs, Slovaks and Southern Slavs ; but this tended to bring them back to the Austrian fold, since the Croat leader Jelačić commanded the Habsburg army in its first action against the Hungarian Revolution. Eventually the address submitted by the Slav Congress to the Emperor included the demand that the Slovaks—and now, for the first time, the Ruthenes of Hungary are expressly added—shall be acknowledged as a nation, with their own Diet, schools, university and equality of rights with the Magyars.

Windischgrätz's high-handed measures of repression in Prague (see p. 190) brought the Slav Congress to a hurried conclusion, and were, of course, conceived by him as the first step towards quelling the still more formidable Magyar movement. Štúr and Hurban at once went to Zagreb to confer with the Croats, and it is highly interesting to find that in August Štúr had a meeting at the little watering-place of Roháč with the exiled Prince Michael Obrenović of Serbia, who placed a considerable sum of money at his disposal. When Jelačić marched against Pest in September, 1848, the Slovaks also found themselves inevitably on the side of Austria, and Hurban returned to Zagreb to organize joint action with the Croats. Then, suddenly letting himself go, he issued a manifesto bidding the Slovaks, throttled for so many centuries, to rise against the Magyar 'hordes'; and broadsheets were posted up in the towns of Western Slovakia in favour of a fight for liberty. It is perhaps hardly surprising that the Pest Government as early as October 17 outlawed the three ringleaders and set a price upon their heads. Small detachments of Slovak volunteers crossed over from Moravia, but the expected general rising did not take place, partly because of the drastic enforcement of martial law by the Magyars. 'Kossuth Gallows,' as they were nicknamed by the great Slovak renegade's aggrieved compatriots, were erected in many villages along the Váh valley; and they bore liberal fruit under orders from Baron Jeszenák, who afterwards himself fell a victim to the butcher Haynau. Slovak sentiment attached itself with special fervour to the memory of two students, Holuby and Šulek, who were offered the choice between death upon the gallows and abjuration of their Slav feelings,[1] and preferred death. At Ružomberok, a young Moravian volunteer named Hrobářik cried from the foot of the gallows : "Just wait, hangman ; I am the last from Moravia whom you will hang guiltlessly. Then it will be your turn."

The Slovaks, the Habsburgs and Pan-Slavism

The Hungarian Revolution was unhappily a war on two fronts— against Vienna on the one side, against the non-Magyar races on the other. To the former Kossuth offered armed resistance in the hope of asserting the very claims which he denied to the latter on the ground of historic rights. It was no idle phrase of Széchényi when he accused Kossuth of 'goading into madness against the Magyar nation' all the other races of the Crown of St. Stephen. This is not the place to dwell upon its wider aspects ; but it must be borne in mind that, parallel with the unsuccessful Slovak rising, there was a large-scale Croat military campaign against Hungary, a furious racial war between Magyars and Serbs (the latter helped by volunteers from Serbia proper) and mutual excesses between Roumanians and Magyars in Transylvania.

During the later phases of the war the Slovak leaders not only exploded the charge of Panslavism levelled against them, but looked increasingly to Vienna. First in March, 1849, at Olomouc, and then in September at Vienna, Slovak deputations presented loyal petitions to

[1] The present writer had the honour of attending, and speaking, at a ceremony early in May, 1919, at the scene of their execution near Hlohovec, where members of a free Czechoslovak Government erected a wooden cross.

Francis Joseph. But their appeal for recognition of the 'three million Slovaks' as a distinct political nation, met with polite evasion : they were assured of his desire to do all in his power for their welfare, but in actual fact nothing whatever happened. The all-powerful minister Bach found in Germanization one of the prime instruments of his regime, and the Slovaks, perhaps even more than the Croats or Roumanians, learned the truth of Pulszky's gibe that the non-Magyars were receiving from Vienna as a reward what the Magyars were receiving as a punishment. Just as the disillusioned Jelačić sulked in his tents at Zagreb, but felt bound by the obligations which a high officer owed to the Habsburg dynasty, so in a more modest sphere Štúr withdrew into the background, and after writing a small book of poetry and a not uninteresting little book entitled *The Slav World and the World of the Future*, died prematurely in 1856, as the result of a gun accident. Viewing the world from the peculiar perspective of a tiny Slovak town, Modra, he condemned the Western nations without exception ; to him Catholicism was a spent force, and Protestantism was growing feebler, while constitutional forms lacked any real basis of principle. Among the Slavs, on the other hand, Christianity was a living force—in Russia especially holding Church, State and people together. The Slavs have a choice of three alternatives : they can form federal states, they can make of Austria a Slav state, including all the Southern and Western Slavs, or they can all unite with Russia. The first is impracticable, since the federal groups would lack a common religion or culture, and would not suit Russia ; the second equally so, because Austria has always tried to Germanize, and has now missed her opportunity. There thus remains only union with Russia, who has always defended the small Slav peoples. As the revival of the latter has attracted Russia's support, why struggle against her ?—all the more so as Western ideas are leading the world to perdition. Of all the Slav peoples there is but one, the Polish, which could object to Russia's predominance ; but then a people which has governed itself as badly as the Poles cannot have the mission of creating new forms or leading other peoples. The first duty of the Slavs is to turn their eyes to the Orthodox Church, as superior both to the Catholic and the Protestant ; and in the same way the Russian language is best suited to be the common Slav literary tongue, being sonorous and full of power. This crude production is quoted as a curiosity rather than on its own merits, and there are not lacking grounds for the suspicion that the Russian edition in which it was first published has been tampered with for political purposes. It is useless to speculate as to the lines on which Štúr's thought would have developed if he had lived to a full age ; but his high romantic, and somewhat unreasoning, attachment to Russia is fully in line with Kollár before him and with Svetozar Hurban after him.

Leo Thun and the Slovak Protestant Church

The ten years of the Bach regime were in the main uneventful for Slovakia, though the employment of Czechs in many official posts not merely eased the language difficulty, but undoubtedly brought higher standards of efficiency and integrity. In one direction there was still more direct improvement. Haynau, as the head of the military administration of Hungary, issued by arbitrary decree in 1850 a new constitution for the Lutheran Church ; the main change was the appointment of new superintendents, with officials nominated by the Government at their side, and the power of the lay element was curtailed. Haynau, in his new role of Hungarian dictator under the Crown, had speedily lived down his evil reputation as the 'Butcher of Brescia,' and his action, though not recognized as legal, did not arouse violent Magyar opposition. But when in 1856 Count Leo Thun, as Minister of Education in the Bach Government, summoned representatives of both the Lutheran and Calvinist Churches to Vienna to discuss the draft of a new Church Constitution, the answer was passive resistance, which soon led to chaotic conditions. On the other hand, the so-called 'Protestant Patent' issued by Thun on September 1, 1859, was a really enlightened document which won the support of a majority among the Slovak Lutherans, but was vitiated by the arbitrary manner of its promulgation. It was violently denounced by the Magyars, to whom Thun had been suspect ever since his controversy with Pulszky (see p. 182), and was accepted by the Slovaks merely because they preferred an imperfect Church organization to the far greater danger of Magyarization and national extinction. It was in any case stillborn, as it only appeared on the very eve of Bach's fall ; and the Slovaks who had favoured it had to bear the brunt of Magyar anger in the synods and presbyteries of the Church.

The Slovaks under the 'Provisorium'

During the 'Provisional Era' of the 'sixties the Slovaks, like the other non-Magyars, naturally favoured federalist tendencies, but in their northern backwater they were scarcely able to affect the main course of events. The resistance of the Hungarian Parliament, under Deák's sure hand, first to the abortive October Diploma of 1860, and then to the still more objectionable February Patent introduced under the auspices of Schmerling, was in many ways the most dignified and impressive episode in the whole modern history of Hungary ; incidentally, the stress which it laid upon constitutional rights and historical development produced a corresponding ferment among the 'unhistoric nations,' some vigorously denying that status, and others eager to escape from it. On June 6, 1861, a large gathering of prominent Slovaks—including on the one hand Hurban, the poet Pauliny-Tot, and a number of priests and pastors, and on the other representatives of such families as Szentiványi, Révay, Justh, who afterwards submitted to being Magyarized—met at Turčiansky Sv. Martin and drew up a memorandum for submission to Parliament. Starting with a somewhat idealized picture of the brotherly accord that had prevailed for centuries in Hungary, so long as common defence against invasion was the main issue, and affirming that 'it never occurred to any one of them to despise or hate the language of another, or to aggrandize itself by exterminating the other,' it went on to claim that the Slovaks were 'as much a nation as the Magyars or any other nation in the country' and were entitled to equal rights. It then proceeded to demand the recognition of their 'national individuality,' the formation of a 'North Hungarian Slovak District ' (Hornouhorské Slovenské Okolie), the establishment of Slovak as the official language of this territory, and the creation of a Slovak Academy of Law and a Chair of Slavonic at Pest (not this time a Slovak University, as in 1849). In return for this Magyar would be recognized as the diplomatic and official language of the central authorities.

Parliament declined to receive the Memorandum, and a violent campaign was worked up against it in the county assemblies ; but on the eve of its own dissolution, on orders from Vienna, an *ad hoc* Committee presided over by the great Liberal statesman, Baron Eötvös, presented a Report laying down the broad principles for the solution of the racial question. It is not too much to say that if this document had been put into practice, the evolution of Hungary might have followed altogether different lines and many disasters would have been averted. It rested upon Eötvös's own writings on political philosophy,[1] which have never received the attention which they deserve—some would say, because they attempt to square the circle. He recognized that absolute equality of all languages in a polyglot state is incompatible with constitutional development and leads inevitably to absolutism ; but he also realized that the principle of the majority cannot justly be enforced in racial questions and that the worst evils of the French Revolution were due, not to democracy, but to the despotic power of a numerical majority. But he also disliked federation and sought a *via media*, based on a recognition of 'the individual nationalities as corporations.' On this abstract basis the Report of 1861 tried to dovetail into each other two opposite tendencies; all citizens of Hungary are declared to 'form politically only one nation, the unitary and indivisible Hungarian nation,' while 'all peoples dwelling in this country, Magyars, Slovaks, Roumanians, Germans, Serbs, Ruthenes, etc., are to be regarded as nationalities possessing equal rights, who are free to promote their special national claims within the limits of the political unity of the country, on a basis of freedom of the person and of association, without any further restriction.' The linguistic provisions that were added were of a really liberal and far-reaching character, but as they were never pursued further, they need not be discussed here. The whole trend of opinion was already moving in an anti-liberal direction.

Even under the 'Provisorium' of Schmerling the local Magyar authorities were strong enough to defy the instructions sent to them from Vienna to respect the Slovak language in their reorganization of Catholic gymnasia: and this led Mgr Stephen Moyses, Bishop of Banská Bystrica, to head a Slovak deputation to the Emperor. They were received in the Hofburg in December, 1861, and reaffirmed the claims of the June Memorandum, protesting against the Magyar design of 'cutting off from the Slovaks every road to culture and thus leaving them to languish in a condition of moral and social atrophy, as the prey of a future Magyarizing policy.' They were, however, careful to insist that the Slovak 'Okolie' would form 'an integral part of Hungary.'[2]

For some years to come help from Vienna enabled the Slovaks to breathe rather more freely. In 1862 the Lutherans were able to found two Protestant gymnasia at Revúca and Turčiansky Sv. Martin, and in 1867 the Catholics set up a third Slovak gymnasium at Kláštor pod Zniovom ; but from the first day their position was precarious, and they were vehemently denounced as 'nests of Panslavism,' in other words, of Slovak patriotism. Equally important with the schools was the foundation, with official sanction and even with a handsome donation from Francis Joseph, of a Slovak Academy at Sv. Martin, christened the Slovenská Matica. When Bishop Moyses attended the opening ceremony

---

[1] *Ueber die Gleichberechtigung der Nationalitäten in Oesterreich.*

[2] The Bishop's own memorial is printed in Appendix II of my *Racial Problems in Hungary*, the Committee's Report of 1861 and the Law of Nationalities of 1868 being also translated in full in Appendices I and III.

he was greeted as 'father of the people' by crowds in every village on his route, and welcomed by the Lutheran Superintendent Kuzmány. During its eleven years of existence it displayed great literary activity, published historical material, collections of folklore and popular poetry (in which the Slovaks are more than usually rich), began work on a new dictionary, opened village reading-rooms and helped the studies of poor students.

The Law of Nationalities

Schmerling's centralizing experiment was already breaking down in the face of organized Magyar resistance, even before the war with Prussia shook the whole edifice from the outside. The Ausgleich of 1867 opens a new era for all the non-Magyar nationalities, who were handed over to the unrestricted political control of the now dominant Magyars. Already in 1860 the so-called 'Serbian Voivodina' had been re-incorporated, and now in 1867 Transylvania shared the same fate, while Croatia was allowed to retain a partial autonomy which had its distinct advantages, but at first isolated her from the other non-Magyars. In the new Dualist Hungary the status of the non-Magyars was regulated by the 'Law of Equal Rights of the Nationalities' (XLIV, 1868), which was above all the work of Deák and Eötvös, and intended by them to be carried out. They were entirely at one with their chauvinist successor Koloman Tisza in regarding assimilation as the ideal solution of the racial problem ; but they differed from him radically in their choice of methods. They held that a policy of mildness and concession would prove more efficacious than restrictive methods, and that Magyar culture, if it was to prove equal to the task of assimilation, could only conquer in virtue of its innate superiority and moral force. On these grounds they refused to recognize the nationalities as separate entities within the state, but designed a law which should make it possible for every race to develop its own language and culture without let or hindrance.

For the next two generations this Law was held up to the outside world as a model of tolerance in theory and a proof of tolerance in practice : but in reality it remained a dead letter from the first day. It laid the greatest stress upon 'the political unity of the Magyar nation' ; and the fact that no distinction could be drawn in the Magyar language between the conceptions of 'Magyar' or 'Hungarian' opened the door for fundamentally conflicting interpretations all along the line. Magyar was of course reaffirmed as the official language of the State, of Parliament, Government and administration, of the county assemblies and their officials, of the law courts and of Budapest (then the only) university. These provisions in favour of the 'national language' were scrupulously observed, but in one way or another, the remainder of the law was suspended or evaded. For instance, it was laid down that the county and communal assemblies had the right to conduct their proceedings in the mother-tongue as well as in Magyar : but this was rendered nugatory by the peculiar franchise, half-virilist and only half-elective, which continued to prevail throughout the Dualist period. The virilists (or principal taxpayers) who were overwhelmingly Magyar and the numerous officials who sat in the assemblies *ex officio*, were always able to turn the scale decisively against the non-Magyars, and there was not a single instance in the whole period under review of a non-Magyar majority in any of the sixty-three counties. Another clause enjoined upon the local officials a knowledge of the other languages of their district as well as of Magyar ; this was only very imperfectly enforced, and as late as December, 1907, Count Andrássy, as Minister of the Interior, issued general instructions to the county officials which were meaningless except on the assumption that most of them were unable to converse with the non-Magyar inhabitants or 'make their own orders comprehensible to them.' Another clause guaranteed every citizen's right to present petitions or applications in his mother-tongue ; but the best commentary upon this is the fact that in June, 1906, Dr. Wekerle, speaking in Parliament as Premier of the new Coalition Government, flatly declared that he was 'not in a position' to fulfil the clause.

In the law courts very concrete linguistic rights were assured to the non-Magyars. But in 1868 the whole judicial system of Hungary was already under consideration, and two years later was completely revised by a new law, from which all the rights laid down in the Law of Nationalities were bodily omitted, in utter defiance of non-Magyar protests. Henceforward the proceedings of all courts of first, second or final instance were conducted exclusively in the Magyar language, and the official interpreters, when provided, were no longer provided gratis, as originally laid down. The Slovak leader, Father Hlinka, raised an outcry throughout Hungary when in 1906, in defending himself before a chauvinistic Magyar jury court, he declared that the Slovak peasant stood like an ox before the courts of his native land ; he was stating but the bare truth, and therein lay his main crime. It was specially laid down that the high administrative posts of High Sheriff and Vice-sheriff (*föispán* and *alispán*) should be filled by non-Magyars in non-Magyar counties ; but though the Roumanians and Slovaks respectively formed a majority varying from 66 to 96% in eleven and seven counties, not a single non-Magyar was ever appointed to such an office during the Dualist era.

Still more glaring was the educational situation. By Article 17 of Law XLIV it was laid down in theory that 'all citizens of whatever nationality living together in considerable numbers, shall be able in the neighbourhood of their homes to obtain instruction in their mother-tongue, up to the point where the highest academic culture begins.' In actual fact, throughout the Dualist period the entire *state* school system was Magyarized, and not a single state school, primary or secondary, was provided for the non-Magyars ; while parallel with this went the deliberate tendency to reduce wherever possible the scanty number of denominational schools on which alone the non-Magyar depended for instruction in the mother-tongue. In actual fact, from 1875 to 1918 the Slovaks were entirely without secondary schools, the Ruthenes in Hungary never possessed one at all, while in 1910, after forty years of Dualist rule, the Roumanians had four gymnasia (three Orthodox and one Uniate), and the Serbs a single Orthodox gymnasium. The only exception to the general dearth was that of the Saxons, who owed the possession of seven secondary schools to a long educational tradition deriving from Luther, and to their admirable autonomous regime, which, however, was trampled roughshod under foot between 1870 and 1876, in direct defiance of both of the Law of Nationalities and of the Act of Transylvanian Union. The case of the Slovaks was, however, more than usually crass, since not merely the three gymnasia which they themselves had erected at great sacrifice were dissolved, but between 1869 and 1911 their primary schools were reduced, by a deliberate government policy, from 1921 to 440 !

The Slovaks and Abstention

The makers of the Ausgleich and of the Law of Nationalities were not left to preside over its execution. Eötvös died in 1871, in the same year Andrássy gave up the Premiership and was for eight years absorbed in the duties of Joint Foreign Minister ; while the ageing Deák declined all office and, though enjoying a unique prestige as 'the wise man of the Nation,' was already a spent force when he died early in 1876. Power fell into the hands of extremer elements, and notably of Koloman Tisza, who from 1875 to 1890 ruled Hungary as the all-powerful leader of the Liberal Party, which in its turn was the mouthpiece of the 'Gentry' class politically the most conscious and active section of the nation. Tisza, like his contemporary Taaffe in Austria, was the confidant of the Crown, but in a very different and much more impersonal sense. There was between the two a tacit compact, based upon *carte blanche* for the one in home affairs and for the other in foreign and military questions. As Tisza's parliamentary backing was unassailable, save by a direct challenge to Dualism such as Francis Joseph could hardly risk, he was able to hold the Crown to its side of the bargain on practically every question. For this purpose he found the opposition of the Party of Independence—the stalwart Kossuthists of the great central plain—very convenient ; for he had his own means of keeping it within manageable bounds, and yet could use it on occasion to extract concessions over which the Crown might otherwise have boggled. For a whole generation Kossuthism performed the function of a bogey, which could always be produced out of its box when it suited the Premier of the day, and when it had served its turn, could be pressed down again by those drastic administrative methods which the authorities always had at their disposal. Foremost among these means for keeping any opposition in check were the peculiar franchise and electoral practices which were the basis of the 'Tisza System,' and which endured from 1874 till the catastrophe of 1918. The new Electoral Law of 1874 divided the voters into four main categories—property, taxation, professional and ancestral, the two first being further differentiated in town and in country. In Transylvania other standards prevailed, with the result that only 3.2% of the population enjoyed the vote, as against 7.5% in Hungary proper ; and the Croatian franchise was still narrower (in 1910, under 50,000 out of 2,600,000). Above all, the predominance secured to the ruling class by a narrow franchise, was still further entrenched by the maintenance of open voting instead of the ballot, by an elaborate system of 'electoral geometry' (with only one polling booth in each constituency), and by corruption and intimidation on a grand scale. It often happened that votes of dead men were recorded, votes were deliberately credited to the wrong candidate or conveniently 'lost' ; candidates were disqualified on the flimsiest pretexts, sometimes even expelled from the constituency or placed under arrest until all was over. The whole administrative apparatus was placed at the disposal of the Government candidates, full use was made of the gendarmerie, and even of the army—military cordons being drawn to keep obnoxious voters from the poll, or roads being suddenly closed, or veterinary restrictions imposed. At the general elections of 1896 the casualties were 32 killed and 70 wounded, in 1901 (despite the new law against corrupt and illegal practices) 7 killed and 19 wounded ; in 1910 there were fewer casualties, for the excellent reason that, according to official admissions in the

Parliaments of Budapest and Vienna, 'only 194 battalions of infantry and 114 squadrons of cavalry' were employed to enforce the Government party's will.'[1]

Thanks to this comprehensive system it became increasingly difficult for the non-Magyars to force an entry into Parliament, and they fell back upon the same mistaken policy of abstention which the Czechs had adopted towards the Reichsrat. As a result they were virtually un-represented for thirty years (1876–1906), and the Magyar chauvinists were free to work their will upon their helpless fellow-citizens.

Next to the Ruthenes the Slovaks suffered most. In 1874 their three gymnasia were closed by a Government order, and in November, 1875, the Matica Slovenská was dissolved, its endowments, buildings and collections being confiscated without the slightest attempt at justification. When the Serb deputy Dr. Polit addressed an interpellation to the Premier—urging that at least the funds should be restored to the original donors, in other words, to the Slovak nation—Tisza made his famous rejoinder : "There is no Slovak nation," an answer which rendered all further discussion impossible. Polit himself was soon afterwards elimin-ated from Parliament, declaring at one of his last appearances that he and they would meet again at Philippi—*hodie tibi, cras mihi !* As an old man he was again returned in 1906 and resumed the traditional co-operation between the Serb and Slovak groups. His friend and colleague, Svetozar Miletić, suffered a harsher fate, being tried (in defiance of parliamentary immunity) and imprisoned for his advocacy of Serbia's war of liberation against the Turks in 1876 ; after five years his reason gave way and he died in an asylum. The Roumanians also held aloof, though forming themselves into a National Party in 1881, with an advanced liberal pro-gramme very similar to others in vogue during the first half of last century.

Tisza's national policy cut both ways. On the one hand he rid himself of the nationalities as a political force. On the other he secured an almost despotic control of the two hundred odd constituencies in which the nationalities were strong and which, thanks to their stupid abstention, became virtual preserves of the Government party. A considerable portion of these seats he was able to use as rewards or baits for the carpet-baggers and ambitious *arrivistes* who flocked to his political standard, and for whom public opinion invented the sarcastic name of 'Mamelukes.' With them he was always able to vote down the Kossuthist opposition, whose main strength lay among the Magyars of the central plains. There was a brutal cynicism about his sytem, which aimed at perpetuating by all and every means the domination of the gentry class ; and this was by no means as simple as it seemed, even though the Gentry and Magnates between them seemed as yet to concentrate all the political traditions and talents available in Hungary.

What ruined all his calculations was the fact that the long period of Liberal supremacy (1875–1905) coincided with the decay of this very class. This was the result of a combination of causes—the new railway era which linked up agricultural Hungary and her neighbours with the industrial west, and the great changes which the emancipation of the peasantry in 1848 wrought upon land tenure and agricultural labour conditions, ruthlessly breaking down the old patriarchal life with its relative isolation from the main European currents. A series of bad

[1] If battalion and squadron be reckoned at 600 and 500 men on a peace footing, that means 173,000 men.

harvests in the 'nineties were the last straw, followed as they were by a steady decline in agricultural prices, owing to over-production in the world market. It was not until the twentieth century that the turn came with the new tariff system, and by this time the benefit accrued to the Magnates rather than to the Gentry. In the thirty years preceding 1905 the number of properties put up annually for sale as the result of bankruptcy grew from 9,600 to 21,100. The income on mortgaged land doubled. While the proportion of 'dwarf' holdings to small or medium holdings (in other words, holdings of an uneconomic character, not offering proper means of subsistence to peasant families) grew year by year, the number of persons engaged in agriculture decreased absolutely by about 80,000 (from 35 to 31%) and the floating agricultural proletariat went up by leaps and bounds. On the other hand, the large landowners added to their holdings, and already in 1900 owned over a third of the total arable land—or 31% of the total area of Hungary ; and if it be noted that the corresponding 'Junker' class in Germany only owned 20% of the total, it will be easy to guess the extent of political power thus concentrated in the hands of a few. Meanwhile, between 1870 and 1900 the land held under entail had increased almost sixfold (463,000 to 2,363,000 arpents) and the land held under mortmain by the Catholic Church had more than doubled (1,288,000 to 2,506,000). The unsound basis on which Hungarian agriculture rested in this period is in striking contrast with the progress of Austria, which was rapidly developing into an industrial state. While the agricultural population of Hungary rose from roughly 5,000,000 to 6,000,000 (or by 21%), that of Austria rose from 5,500,000 to 8,250,000, or by 52%.

From these and similar statistics three central facts emerge, which are as decisive for the fate of the Slovaks as for that of Hungary as a whole—the progressive decay of the Gentry, the increased power of the Magnates, and the rise of a floating agricultural proletariat, shockingly neglected, yet without influence or organization, racked by land-hunger and turning increasingly towards emigration. Koloman Tisza, himself the very personification of the Gentry class in its modern phase, set himself to console them for their lost lands by manning the bureaucracy from their ranks and by creating new posts. This tendency became chronic under his successor, and between 1892 and 1902 alone there was an increase of 37,000 ate officials. The narrow county franchise enabled them to maintain the county assemblies as a preserve of their class ; and as the competition for posts grew sharper owing to economic stress, the position worsened for the non-Magyars, who were regarded as intruders. Non-Magyars could only acquire posts at the price of national apostasy and were then looked askance upon from both sides, and tried to win favour and promotion by the usual excessive zeal of the renegade.

During this period there was a slow toning down of the historic parties. The Liberal Party stood for Dualism and the gains of 1867. The Independent Party was by now only in theory for complete separation and a Republic ; in practice it really aimed at the Personal Union, which would have left the Crown as the sole link between Hungary and Austria, and this tendency rapidly gained the upper hand after the exiled Kossuth's death in 1894. The National Party, under Count Albert Apponyi, pursued an intermediate policy of forcing the Crown, by a sort of political blackmail, into interpreting and elucidating the Ausgleich document in a sense favourable to Hungary. Meanwhile the People's Party followed demagogic clerical lines, exploiting the latent anti-Semitism inevitably provoked by the influx of Jews from Galicia and still more easterly countries, and the unnatural speed with which they not merely adopted Magyar names and pandered to Magyar prejudices, but became the ready and loud-mouthed instruments of Magyarization. It was among the Slovaks that the People's Party won adherents most easily, mainly because in their backward economic state, aggravated by social changes and Magyar chauvinism, they were peculiarly at the mercy of the ubiquitous Jew. As small trader, usurer and middleman, he dominated the whole life of the villages, then moved on to the provincial town as a budding capitalist and super-patriot, and in his final stage became the indispensable manipulator of the whole banking system and the press. There is plenty that is highly unedifying in the anti-semite movement in Slovakia, and not least the encouragement given to it by the Catholic clergy ; but it cannot be denied that the Jews exploited the Slovak masses and played the game of their Magyar oppressors, and it was not till the very eve of the Great War that the fruit of the long and arduous spadework of Slovak patriots, in building up popular banks, credit societies and co-operatives, began to emancipate the peasantry from Jewish dominance.

Tisza's own personal decline dates from 1889, when he showed himself unable to overcome Apponyi's growing agitation for the Magyar language of command in the Army. Tisza and the Andrássys, father and son, held the Liberal Party to the programme of Army unity, as in the European interest of the Monarchy ; but it thereby laid itself open to charges of lukewarm patriotism, and therefore sought a cheap popularity by whole-sale measures of Magyarization in the civil sphere, at which Francis Joseph found it only too convenient to connive. Tisza's policy towards the non-Magyars was defined on the eve of his fall by one of the ablest publicists in the Liberal Party, Gustav Beksics, as an 'endeavour to convert the historical state into a national state' by the instrument of Magyarization. "Have not the secondary schools of the nationalities," he asked an approving House, "sunk under this Government to a small and dwindling number, compared with the well-developed middle schools of the Magyar State ?" "Either Hungary will become a great national state," Beksics declared on another occasion, "or it will cease to be a state at all." Another Liberal stalwart, Béla Grünwald, who played a leading part in the suppression of the Slovak middle schools, put it on record in a much-quoted book on "North Hungary" (*Felvidék*), that 'it would involve incredible narrow-mindedness that anyone could seriously wish to be a Slovak.' 'The idea of the Magyar State' (*a Magyar állam eszme*) became the prime goal of all parties, and that brilliant playwright and editor, Eugene Rákosi (originally a Jew of the name of Krebs), devoted the rest of his life and talents to preaching 'the thirty-million Magyar State'—a dream that could only be realized if every Magyar were in some way to produce two other non-existent Magyars.

In 1892, while Dr. Wekerle, the Magyarized Swabian, was Premier, the Central Committee of the Roumanian National Party decided to exercise its legal right of petition, and addressed to the Crown a brilliant but scathing Memorandum of grievances, and to make sure of its not ending in the waste-paper basket, also published it in pamphlet form. In May, 1894, the entire Committee was brought to trial for 'incitement against the Magyar nationality' incurred in this document, and, thus after a generation of oblivion the despised Roumanians of Transylvania again found a world forum. The petition had roundly challenged the legality of the Act of Transylvanian Union, and now the party chairman, Dr. Ratziu, in conducting his defence declined to recognize the jurisdiction of the court and appealed to the civilized world. The sentences of a total of twenty-nine years' imprisonment were, according to the standards of the 'nineties, universally condemned as savagely excessive ; to our blunted senses in the Second World War, it is but fair to add, the worst illegalities of the Magyars sink into insignificance beside the daily toll of crime and terror imposed by the Nazi conquerors. Additional publicity was given to the trial when the Government ordered the dissolution of the Roumanian Party by ministerial decree. The rival activities of cultural Leagues for the defence and unity of all Roumanians or for the complete Magyarization of Transylvania, envenomed the quarrel still further. The Memorandum Trial, it should be added, brought fresh courage to the Slovaks, whose position at this time was far more desperate than that of the Roumanians, firmly rooted in the Orthodox and Uniate Church autonomy and the schools which the two Churches were able to maintain. Several leading Slovak advocates, notably Dr. Mudroň and Dr. Stefanovič, undertook to act as counsel for the defence at the Memorandum Trial, and henceforward a system of mutual defence in political trials was established between the Slovaks, Roumanians, Serbs and Ruthenes, with admirable propagandist results. Moreover, in 1895 a Congress of the Nationalities was held at Budapest, under the chairmanship of the Serb, Dr. Polit. The fact that it was allowed to meet at all was cited officially as a proof of rare magnanimity ; its demands for such reforms as universal suffrage, redistribution of the counties, as far as possible along racial lines, freedom of press, association and assembly, were of course mere window-dressing, and had not the remotest chance of fulfilment. But it laid the first foundations of a new era of co-operation and activism.

Baron Bánffy and Magyarization

The Millenary Exhibition of 1896 marked a fresh rise in the tide of Magyarization. Wekerle's successor, Baron Bánffy, held elections till then unsurpassed for violence and corruption, and the non-Magyars were still too weak to assert themselves. The People's Party, however, in its Catholic and anti-Semite zeal, wooed the Slovak masses, and its leader, Count Aladar Zichy, committed himself openly to the view that it was neither Liberal nor rational nor Christian to oppress the Nationalities, and that the Law of 1868 ought to be enforced. In many constituencies the clergy summoned the peasant masses to swear on the Crucifix that they would vote for the People's Party. Zichy's tactics were the natural outcome of indignation among the more backward sections of the community, at the so-called 'Church Laws' which had become law under Wekerle, and provided for civil marriage and state registration. Above all, divorce became possible in Hungary, while the provisions of the Roman Canon Law continued to be upheld in Austria.

But the Government held on its way, and went to unheard-of lengths by Magyarizing all the place-names, public inscriptions and notices in the entire country, and by making it legal, and advantageous, to adopt Magyar surnames, at the price of a tenpenny registration fee (hence the nickname of 'One-Crown Magyars'). Banffy did not beat about the bush, but openly declared that 'without chauvinism it is impossible to found the unitary Magyar state,' and that it was necessary, in pressing towards the goal of Magyarization, 'not to regard what stands in the way, but only to regard the aim and to push blindly forwards.' In 1898 Bánffy nipped in the bud a very promising Agrarian Socialist movement ; the troops were called out to crush the harvest strikes, and the Government kept a large reserve of foreign labourers at Mezöhegyes, ready to be despatched at a moment's notice to the aid of the landlords. In breaking the strikes the authorities relied upon the fact that the Slovak peasantry of the miserably poor northern counties (Orava, Liptov, etc.) could scarcely make ends meet unless large numbers of them took service for the period of 'field work' on the big estates of the Alföld. They received the merest pittance in wages, and like their fellows among the other non-Magyars, but also among the Magyar peasantry itself, they now took increasing refuge in emigration to the United States, where they either went under altogether, or flourished exceedingly and sent back large sums of money to their needy relatives at home.

Early in 1899 Francis Joseph found it expedient to replace the hard and tactless Bánffy by Koloman Széll, the foster son of Deák, who at once gave out the watchword of 'Law, Right and Justice,' introduced an elaborate law against corrupt practices, and discontinued the worst measures of oppression against the non-Magyars. None the less the elections of 1901 showed but little improvement ; their 'purity' is well illustrated by the fate of Count Apponyi himself, who had recently led the National Party back to the Liberal fold. At Jászberény, a purely Magyar constituency, a determined attempt was made to prevent his return, by a well-doctored register, by an illegal prolongation of the poll for thirty-six hours, and finally by the returning officer's refusal to declare Apponyi elected !

'Ex-Lex'

What brought about the fall of Széll was the increasing agitation for a separate Hungarian Army, with the Magyar language of command. Apponyi and Bánffy joined hands with the Kossuthists, and soon after the completion of the sumptuous new Parliament House on the river front of Budapest, the united Opposition carried obstruction to hitherto unheard of heights by systematically wrecking the seats and benches with their desk-lids. The Hungarian equivalent of Paragraph Fourteen —the so-called 'Ex-Lex' regime—slowly began to assert itself. In their over-confidence the Opposition forgot the ominous precedent of 1879, when Francis Joseph plunged into all the risks of a Clerical-Slav *bloc* rather than brook German-Liberal dictation on two points which throughout his entire reign he regarded as fundamental, namely Foreign Affairs and the Army. The Army Order of Chlopy, issued by him during the Galician manœuvres of 1903, was a warning to the Hungarian Opposition that interference with the prerogative of the Crown might have equally grave consequences in Hungary. The warning was defied, parliamentary life was paralysed by obstruction, and even Count Khuen-Héderváry, who brought to the Premiership all his unique experience of political repression, learned in twenty years as Ban of Croatia, found the task of appeasement beyond him.

Stephen Tisza and the Liberal Collapse

Late in 1903 the Crown selected as Premier Koloman Tisza's son, Count Stephen Tisza, of whom his own father once said that he was a fine horseman, but could not drive. He was a typical product of Hungarian Calvinism, with its rigid and fatalist creed, and of the now decaying 'Gentry' class, combining immovable principles with altogether outworn ambitions and tactics. Rudolf Sieghart, one of the men most behind the scenes of Dualism in its final phase, has said of him that 'he had something of the high infallibility of the early Puritan,' and that 'he was what the French call "austère," cool, self-conscious, correct, severe upon himself and upon others, in short, a Cromwellian nature.' An elder of the Church, yet an ardent duellist, he was too scrupulous to owe a majority to the traditional methods, and arrogant enough to believe that he could dominate the situation. In January, 1905, therefore, he fought the first relatively 'free elections' for over a generation past, and the result was a resounding defeat for the Liberal Party. The Hungarian Coalition—consisting of the Party of Independence under Francis Kossuth and Count Apponyi, the Constitutional Party under Count Julius Andrássy the younger, and the People's Party under Count Zichy—secured so great a majority that Tisza not merely resigned office, but dissolved his party, leaving a crowd of time-serving Mamelukes to pass over into the camp of the victors.

The Crisis of 1905-1906

The Crown, finding itself left face to face with the most uncompromising elements in the state, resorted to a practice which had become habitual in Austria, but which it had either not required or not dared to employ in Hungary since 1867. Francis Joseph appointed as Premier one of his own personal intimates, Baron Géza Fejérváry, a distinguished cavalry general who was the sole surviving holder of the Maria Theresa Order (for signal valour in the field), and whose entry into the political arena was an act of obedience to his sovereign and supreme commander, and at the same time of personal gratitude and devotion. His Cabinet was composed of bureaucrats whose names were quite unknown to the general public. The unconstitutional character of the new regime was trumpeted abroad by the Coalition ; but it fatally misjudged its own strength and under-estimated both the power and the resolution of the Crown. Francis Joseph had always shown himself ready to give a free hand to the Government of the day, especially in all racial matters ; but the challenge to the Joint Army touched him on the raw and roused him from his habit of half-measures. The instrument by which he had governed for more than a generation past—the Liberal Party—having broken in his hand, a new basis of government had to be found. Starting from this entirely opportunist angle, he took a momentous step that was to transform the inner history of the Monarchy. Acting for once in a way with the full concurrence of his nephew, Francis Ferdinand, he allowed Fejérváry's Minister of the Interior, Joseph Kristóffy, to place Universal Suffrage in the forefront of his programme and to appeal to the masses against the ruling caste. As a fresh proof of an attitude towards Labour such as was hitherto unknown in Hungary, the Government withdrew existing restrictions on Association and Assembly and gave full play to the Trade Union movement, while at the same time showing itself more benevolent to the nationalities.

This attitude caused acute alarm among those older Liberals who realized that the Magyar hegemony had rested first and foremost on the support of the Crown, and that the threatened alliance between the

Crown and the united forces of proletariat and nationalities was a blow struck at the very root of that hegemony. A successful struggle against the Crown was only possible if the whole nation were enthusiastically behind the national leaders, and this was not the case. Any extension of the franchise was bound to strengthen the unenfranchised workers and non-Magyars. Meanwhile the results of almost forty years of centralizing tendencies—pursued by successive Governments since 1867, now became amply apparent. The passive resistance of the counties was a declining force ; technically no County Assembly could be forced to collect taxes or to summon recruits which had not been voted by Parliament. But in practice the central executive was almost bound to win in the long run, so long as it had the backing of the military forces of the Crown. Hence local attempts to insult or resist the Royal Commissioners sent out by the Government fell altogether flat, and the country showed an ominous indifference.

In September, 1905, Francis Joseph, feeling himself strong enough to refuse the two main points of the Coalition—a national Army and a separate customs area—summoned the three party chiefs to Vienna, but as they stood firm, dismissed them after an audience lasting less than five minutes. Again the country remained quiet, and in February, 1906, Féjerváry was allowed to dissolve Parliament without issuing writs for new elections. Worse still, the Coalition having threatened scenes of violence at the final act, the Parliament building was surrounded by a strong military force (composed, it was noted, of regiments mainly recruited from Roumanian and other non-Magyar districts), and the royal decree of dissolution was read aloud, not by the Premier, but by a Honvéd officer in full uniform, Colonel Fabrizius. And yet, despite such striking and demonstrative action on the part of the Crown, the impending return of absolutism seemed to leave Hungarian public opinion distressingly cold. To the Heir Apparent it seemed as though the heaven-sent moment had come when his uncle would be forced by circumstances to undertake the first preparations for a New Order in Hungary. He, Francis Ferdinand, was resolved not to take oath to a constitution which he regarded as played out, and as endangering the whole future of the Monarchy ; he knew, however, that under the Law of 1790 he would only have a breathing space of six months in which to put through the necessary reforms. In so doing he relied upon the alliance of the masses—a little dangerous to so arch a reactionary, but inevitable—and of all the nationalities without exception, and their kinsmen inside Austria ; and he regarded the course that events were taking under his obedient mouthpiece Kristóffy as a proof that the risk could safely be taken.

Far different, however, was the attitude of Francis Joseph, who cared nothing for the nationalities, and who was far from desiring to overthrow his own Dualist creation, only wished to read a sharp lesson to the Magyars and prove to them once and for all the utter folly of quarrelling with the Crown. Moreover, the mere fact that his grim nephew wanted a new policy applied, was already a reason against its application. Realizing its danger at the last moment, the Coalition made secret overtures to the Hofburg, and on April 9, 1906, it accepted office on terms which enabled it to save its face by a few showy outward concessions, but left the Crown's essential position unimpaired. In order to secure power, the very men who had obstructed all business for four years now consented to the retention of German as the language of the Joint Army. It was agreed that the Government should be allowed to issue a manifesto setting forth the nation's constitutional rights in the army question, as a preliminary to fresh legislation ; but of this nothing more was heard. As regards their commercial and tariff programme, they let the negotiations drag on till after the date when the new foreign Commercial Treaties came into force—in other words, until a situation had been created in which separate tariffs and a separate customs area for Hungary could only have been established by a breach of international obligations. It was easy to thrust the responsibility for this delay upon the illegal Féjerváry Cabinet. Finally, the Coalition asked that the terms of the written compact with the Crown (for Francis Joseph, knowing his men, insisted on having them in writing) should remain secret. There was a double reason for this ; publication would have revealed the extent of their surrender, but also the very explicit nature of their pledge to carry through franchise reform, 'on at least as broad a basis' as the Bill drafted by Kristóffy.

The Non-Magyars and the Coalition

It was necessary to dwell in some detail upon this fateful crisis in Hungarian history, for it explains the increased bitterness of the struggle of Nationalities in the eight years that still separate us from the catastrophe. As on more than one earlier occasion, Francis Joseph found in the Nationalities of Hungary a convenient object of barter ; they were thrown to the wolves in return for a truce in the Army question. Magyarization now penetrated into every nook and cranny of public life and culminated in the Education Acts of Count Apponyi, which deliberately aimed at breaking down the last line of defence of the non-Magyars, namely, the denominational school and its control by their clergy. The full provisions of these Laws cannot be given here : their essence lay in exacting a stringent oath of allegiance from all denominational teachers, thereby strengthening the control of the state inspectors upon them : in demanding that instruction should be imparted in Magyar : in interpreting still more widely the elastic charge, 'a tendency hostile to the state' : in greatly extending the number of hours for instruction in Magyar and demanding that 'the child of non-Magyar tongue on completion of its fourth school year shall be able to express its thoughts intelligibly in Magyar, in word and writing' : teachers who failed in this task being liable to dismissal. Moreover, under the pretext of raising standards of equipment and salary, conditions were imposed such as placed many of the Church schools before the choice of bankruptcy or acceptance of state subsidies, and therefore stricter control : and the Minister of Education acquired wide powers of interference, and even the right to dissolve non-Magyar schools.

For the first time for a whole generation the Nationalities were represented in Parliament, though it is true that instead of the 198 seats which they would have held on a purely numerical basis, they only secured 26 seats (14 Roumanians, 7 Slovaks). The marked ill-will with which they were received in the House drove them into still closer alliance ; and among them were a number of young, able and courageous men destined to play a great part in the history of their respective nations. The Roumanians were led by Alexander Vaida-Voevod and Julius Maniu, both Premiers of United Roumania, and by Goldiş, Vlad and Mihali. Among the Slovaks the most active were Milan Hodža, great-nephew of

Štúr's colleague in 1848, and a future Premier of Czechoslovakia, who, as a sign of solidarity among allies, was elected in a mainly Serbian constituency in the Bačka ; Pavel Blaho, a doctor by profession, who enjoyed to a remarkable degree the confidence of the West Slovak peasantry, and Ferdinand Juriga, a Catholic priest of great eloquence and racy humour.

The Slovaks in Parliament

The Coalition set itself to terrorize the little non-Magyar phalanx : in particular a series of press trials was organized for 'incitement against the Magyar nationality,' as incurred in published articles or even in electoral addresses ; Father Juriga was sentenced to two years' imprisonment, a young advocate Milan Ivánka (whose special crime it was, as a Protestant, to have secured the votes of the Catholic peasantry) to one year, Hodža and others to shorter terms, while a young priest named Jehlička (afterwards a traitor to the national cause) was induced to renounce his parliamentary mandate, in return for a University chair. The Slovak National Party, reconstituted at St. Martin in 1905 with a programme modelled upon the Roumanian, had a more uphill task than the Roumanians because the Magyar People's Party stole some of its thunder and had the ardent backing of the Catholic clergy.

Andrew Hlinka and Černova

At the small industrial town of Ružomberok, a local Slovak doctor of Liberal and Czechophil tendencies, Vavro Šrobár, failed to secure election owing to strong official pressure from the Clericals : that he came so near success was largely due to the eager backing given to him by Andrew Hlinka, who a year earlier had become the town priest of Ružomberok and henceforth plays a prominent part in Slovak development. A fortnight later Hlinka was suspended from office by the Bishop of Spiš, on the ground of political agitation, though against ten other priests who had canvassed on the other side no action was taken. In November, 1906, it came to a trial on the usual charge of 'incitement,' and Hlinka and Šrobár were sentenced to two years' and one year's imprisonment, while fourteen of their fellow-townsmen, including another priest, received lesser sentences. In May, 1907, Hlinka was brought from prison to be tried for further incitement in his farewell greeting to his parishioners, and was condemned to an additional eighteen months. Meanwhile Bishop Párvy tried to complete Hlinka's ruin by a charge of simony : but after a long and stubborn struggle (in which it may be admitted that Hlinka was neither conciliatory nor tactful, and earned the reputation of a 'turbulent priest'), he was acquitted by the Roman Curia, after his case had aroused the very special indignation and advocacy of the influential Moravian Clerical Party.

Before his suspension Hlinka had collected funds for the erection of a new church at his own birthplace, the village of Černova : its consecration was now placed in the hands of a notorious 'Magyarone' priest, to the great indignation of the entire community. On October 27, 1907, a large crowd of peasants demonstrated against this priest and his companions, but had remained entirely passive, when the squad of gendarmes who accompanied them suddenly opened fire, and killed twelve men and three women on the spot, wounding as many as sixty. When Dr. Hodža raised the question in Parliament, he was denounced as a criminal, and the

Minister of the Interior quoted from Hodža's weekly an extract referring to the recent election of the Roumanian 'fighting priest,' Vasile Lucaciu : 'The Roumanians are not afraid of a little blood, and the result is that this nation has won. But we Slovaks are but a timid people ; we have never indulged in violence, and so our position is worse than that of the Roumanians.' In March, 1908, fifty-nine of those who had dared to survive 'the massacre of Černova' (as it came to be called, like its namesake of Peterloo) were tried on charges of 'violence against the authorities,' and received sentences totalling thirty-six years—including three years for Hlinka's own sister, a woman of fifty-seven.

'The *legal* state,' declared Baron Bánffy in this most chauvinistic of parliaments, 'is the aim, but with this question we can only concern ourselves when we have already assured the *national* state. Hungary's interests demand its erection on the most extreme chauvinist lines.' Even Koloman Széll officially declared that 'this country must first be preserved *as a Magyar country*, and then it must be cultured, rich, enlightened and progressive.' And Stephen Tisza, as Premier in 1905 had already reminded the nationalities that the Magyar nation 'had never given a binding promise to maintain the Law of Nationalities for all time, and not to alter it when conditions alter and when we perceive that through this Law we grant to our opponents rights against ourselves.' In this phrase he revealed the reason why the Law of 1868 had always remained on paper.

The Party of National Work

Despite all the grandiloquence of the Coalition leaders, no Government in Hungary since 1867 ever showed itself so complacent and accommodating as the Coalition Government towards the Crown. The key to this lay in the pledge to introduce franchise reform, 'on at least as broad a basis' as Kristóffy's project ; this meant as a minimum universal and equal suffrage for all literates, and however hedged round by checks and qualifications, was bound to strengthen the working class and the nationalities at the expense of the present privileged class. It is not too much to say that the guiding principle of all Governments between 1906 and 1914 was not how best to carry electoral reform into effect, but how best to evade it. The central factor in Hungarian political life was the struggle not *for*, but *against*, Universal Suffrage.

In proportion, however, as its successful adoption next door, in Austria, made evasion in Hungary more difficult, the need for speedy Magyarization became an obsession with the ruling class, and was pursued with special violence against the Slovaks and Ruthenes, who were least able to resist. The behaviour of Bishop Párvy in the Hlinka affair, and the treatment of Juriga, Jehlička, Tománek, Moyš and other Slovak priests by their ecclesiastical superiors, revealed the extent to which the Government had captured the Catholic hierarchy for its designs ; and year by year it was increasingly difficult for the rank and file of the clergy to maintain a patriotic attitude. Even in the Lutheran Church similar tendencies made progress ; all the Bishops of the Dualist era were Magyar or Magyarone, and of sixteen purely or predominantly Slovak Seniorates there were only six in which it was possible to elect Seniors of Slovak sentiment. The principle of 'electoral geometry' was skilfully applied by the Magyarizing party in the Church ; and after the rearrangement of the four Synods the Slovaks were placed in a minority in all four. No means were spared to reduce the number of Lutheran schools, and those clergy who still kept the flag flying were on the black list as Panslavs and traitors.

Meanwhile the key to political events lay in the backward agricultural and industrial conditions of Hungary, giving increased power to the feudal magnate class, sealing the decay of the gentry, and incidentally promoting the rise of the Jewish capitalist, advocate and intellectual. At the turn of the century there was a floating agricultural population of one and a half millions, badly housed, wretchedly paid—earning even in summer on an average only two to two and a half crowns a day (1s. 6d. to 1s. 9d.), often for a working day of sixteen hours—ravaged by alcohol in the mountain districts (especially in the Slovak Tatra) and by tuberculosis even in the rich wheat lands of the south. The unrest so sharply suppressed by Bánffy in 1898 threatened to break out again, and in 1906 the idea of importing Chinese labour for the harvest was seriously canvassed by a Government which had entertained a delegation of the British Liberal 'Eighty Club' within a year of its own agitation against Chinese labour in South Africa.

The acute unrest was reflected in the gigantic emigration figures of this period. Before 1898 emigration had averaged 25,000 a year ; in 1901 it reached 71,000, in 1903 119,000, in 1905 170,000 (including 43,000 women), and in 1907 203,000 out of a total population of 19,000,000. The stringent emigration laws of 1903 and 1908 proved quite unavailing to check either the flow of emigrants, who were almost exclusively peasants, or their shocking exploitation by the big shipping companies and the Jewish touts and agents.

In the towns of Hungary Labour was almost totally unorganized, and the process was greatly delayed by the absence of the ballot and also of any law of association or assembly. It was not till 1899 that the first congress of Trade Unions was held, and in 1902 there were still only 16,000 enrolled members, though the number grew to 71,000 in 1906 and 130,000 in 1908. The Social Democrats, who first met in congress in 1890, but then split into two small factions, first managed to breathe under the illegal regime of Fejérváry ! Factory inspection was very inadequate, hours were long (in the mines twelve hours from pithead to pithead), wages wretched ; in 1901 58% of the working class of Budapest lived in dwellings of only one room, as against 7·5% in Vienna (*before* the famous reforms of the Vienna Town Council). Insurance was entirely inadequate, and the state did not contribute anything. Even the new industrial code of 1908 upheld the antediluvian view of forbidding both strikes and lockouts, for all enterprises of public utility. If politically the Middle Ages did not end in Hungary till 1848, it might quite plausibly be argued that economically they continued till 1918. The phrase 'Extra Hungariam non est vita' made its appeal to the ruling class, and the cynic was amply entitled to add, 'aut si vita, non est ita.' It was in this strange world, hitherto so isolated from the major currents of European affairs, that the Slovaks were still living ; and it is essential to an understanding of the subsequent narrative to realize the extreme difference of *milieu* between Slovaks and Czechs, the extent to which the Czechs had in the last century before the war repaired their own backwardness under the more enlightened rule of Austria, and above all the fact that the Czechs were free to go forward at a growing pace, while the Slovaks were falling behind in the race, if not actually beginning to go backwards.

From Khuen to Stephen Tisza

By the end of 1909 the Coalition, which had swept all before it, was in steady disintegration ; and in January, 1910, Count Khuen-Héderváry again became Premier, this time with the task of reconstituting the old Liberals under the camouflage of a 'Party of National Work.' Of the elections by which he stamped a new majority out of the ground in June, 1910, it will suffice to say that they were worthy of Bánffy's example. When Parliament opened, he announced his intention of introducing electoral reform, 'on the basis of Universal Suffrage, without plural voting, but in such a form as will safeguard in the future also the character of the Hungarian state, in accordance with its 1,000 years of history.' Having thus paid lip-service to the principles laid down by the Crown, he made no further attempt to square the circle.

Early in 1910 Khuen came into violent collision with Apponyi, who revived in a new and thinly disguised form his old demands in the Army question ; but this time resistance came not only from Francis Ferdinand and the Army chiefs, but from Francis Joseph himself, who declared that he would rather abdicate than yield. It was thought expedient to have a more colourless Premier, and Dr. Ladislas Lukács therefore replaced Khuen, leaving, however, the strong man of the party, Count Stephen Tisza, in the key position of President of the House. On June 4, 1912, he carried the new Defence Bill in a frontal attack upon an almost frantic Opposition. On his orders the police entered and forcibly removed the obstreperous deputies, and shots fired at him by the Kossuthist deputy Kovács merely roused his fighting spirit. Parallel with these autocratic tendencies went the suspension of the Croatian Constitution by order of Budapest, and the appointment of Baron Cuvaj as the first of the long series of Europe's dictators. This had effects far beyond the narrow sphere of Zagreb or even Budapest, for it meant the final bankruptcy of Austria-Hungary's Balkan policy and the alienation of both Serbia and Roumania from the Monarchy. It turned the eyes of all Jugoslavs and Roumanians towards Belgrade and Bucarest, at the very moment when the Balkan League was forming, as a prelude to the ejection of the Turks from the Balkan Peninsula. These events lie outside the sphere of Slovak history, but it is necessary to insist that they altered the whole focus of the racial question and vitally affected the fate of all the non-Magyar nationalities.

During the following winter Lukács fell from power, owing to the revelations of the Opposition deputy, Désy, to the effect that the Premier had accepted a sum of three million crowns from a leading Budapest banker for purposes of electoral corruption. The court before which Lukács prosecuted Désy for describing him as 'the greatest Panamist in Europe,' held that he had proved his case, and acquitted him ! This threw all previous scandals into the shade, and made Lukács impossible. Incidentally, it threw a lurid light upon the sincerity of Lukács's Government when, on taking office, it had publicly pledged itself to Electoral Reform 'in the spirit of liberty and democratic progress, on the basis of the principle of Universal Suffrage, but in such a way as to preserve the due influence of the more developed and riper strata of society and also the unitary national character of the Magyar state.'

On June 5, 1913, Count Tisza succeeded Lukács as Premier, and there was an immediate stiffening of the regime in all directions. His speech of open encouragement to Bulgaria was understood throughout the

Balkans as an intimation that Austria-Hungary would intervene, and so contributed materially to the Bulgarian attack upon Serbia and Greece. His overtures to the Roumanians of Transylvania—which were, of course, intended to avert the defection of independent Roumania from the Triple Alliance—failed owing to his peremptory 'take it or leave it' tactics. Hardly less categorical was his denunciation of the Kossuthist flirtation with the Entente as 'disloyal.' Meanwhile at home he set himself to crush obstruction at all costs, increased the contingent for the Army, advocated Government nomination of the County High Sheriffs and Vice-Sheriffs (which meant the end of real county autonomy), and summed up his whole attitude in the words : "I would sooner let myself be crushed a hundred times by events than take upon my conscience the reproach of slackness or cowardice." His revised Standing Orders and the institution of an Armed Guard inside the House, made it easier to impose his will upon any minority ; but his Law of Electoral Reform (XIV, 1913) went through more easily, because it corresponded to the prevalent reactionary mood. It was a travesty of Universal Suffrage and openly sought to undo any slight gains to the nationalities through an increase of voters (from 1,200,000 to 1,650,000), by a fresh gerrymandering of the constituencies and by specific provisions such as raising the voting age from twenty to thirty and limiting the vote to those who had been through six classes of a primary school ! The official report introducing the Bill to the House described parliamentary reform as 'a disagreeable inheritance' : and this phrase reveals the spirit in which the Bill was conceived and given to the world. Tisza himself had the courage of his opinions and was an open enemy of democracy, holding that it would act as a poison in Hungary, simultaneously placing the Magyars in a minority and lowering the level of parliamentary life.

After passing this law Parliament became increasingly docile to Tisza, mainly no doubt because it was in his power to dissolve it and order elections under the new franchise. In actual fact, it was still in being when war broke out, and as elections then became almost impossible, it continued to sit in its unreformed form. The new franchise never came into force, and yet another Franchise Bill was introduced in the spring of 1918, was passed in an utterly mangled form as a result of Tisza's opposition, and in its turn remained on paper. Thus the Parliament of 1910 was well on in its ninth year when the first Hungarian Revolution temporarily substituted a Republic and a National Assembly for the old order.

The Slovaks in extremis

In this closing period of Dualism the nationalities were again forced into the background, their representation in Parliament being reduced from twenty-six to eight (five Roumanians—including Maniu and Vaida) and three Slovaks (Hodža, Blaho and Skyčák). The tiny group of Protestant 'die-hards' maintained its resistance at Turčiansky Sv. Martin—really more of a village than a town ; its two organs, *Národnie Noviný*, thrice weekly, and the monthly literary review *Slovenské Pohlady*, had an uphill fight and few subscribers. To the former the poet Svetozar Hurban Vajanský (1847–1916), son of the old leader of 1848, sacrificed what might have been a great career under less cramped circumstances. His romantic temperament and ardent Protestant faith led him to adopt a reserved attitude both to the Czech Clericals and to the free-thinking

Left wing at Prague (in which he included Masaryk), and at the same time, most illogically, to pin his faith to Tsarist Russia and an idealized Pan-slavism, such as left Kollár far behind. The Slovaks produced an even more considerable poet in 'Hviezdoslav' (1849–1921), a member of the minor Slovak 'gentry' family of Orszagh, who narrowly escaped from Magyarization, but being of a modest and retiring temperament, withdrew into a world of his own imagination, living and dying in his native town of Dolny Kubin. His poetry was of a very high and rarified order, and may well prove to have been instrumental in ensuring the survival of literary Slovak. None the less, the parlous state to which Slovak culture had been reduced by the impact of Magyarizing policy is strikingly illustrated by the careers of his three contemporaries, Martin Kukučin, who gave up publication as hopeless and went into voluntary exile, first in Dalmatia, then in South America, only returning to his lost country and resuming literary efforts after an interval of a quarter of a century ; J. L. Bella, who as a younger composer found conditions in Slovakia even less favourable for musical composition and joined a German orchestra in Transylvania, only returning to Bratislava after the war, as a man approaching eighty, to see the *première* of his opera *Wieland the Smith ;* and Nádaši-Jégé, who also resumed novel writing at the age of sixty after an interval of thirty years. Meanwhile the number of Slovak periodicals had dropped from forty-one in 1909 to ten in 1918, the veto upon the Matica Slovenská was stubbornly upheld, and the Catholic Society of St. Vojtěch at Trnava led a hand-to-mouth existence. All these examples are eloquent proof that the Magyarization of Slovakia was advancing by leaps and bounds, and that in another generation, especially if the Central Powers had been victorious, assimilation would have been virtually complete. The so-called 'Magyarone' spirit was spreading among the clergy and the official class, thanks on the one hand to the extreme propagandist fervour of the Magyars, but also to a weakening of fibre among the Slovaks, comparable to physical decay when nourishment is withheld. Not the least of the causes of discontent and unrest among the Czechs, while their own movement gained daily in momentum, was the consciousness that their Slovak brethren were in imminent danger of extinction, and that conditions in the Monarchy rendered them impotent to help.

CHAPTER XV

THE STRUGGLE FOR INDEPENDENCE (1914–1918)

When the fate of dynasties, regimes, states or nations is at stake, half-measures and compromises have never helped, and never will.
—Dr. Edvard Beneš.

Though the conflicts of the present day turn on questions of politics and nationality, not of religion, the memory of Hus and of the Hussite Wars has often strengthened and roused to new efforts those Bohemians who felt inclined to despair of the future of their country.
—Count Francis Lützow.

THE outbreak of the Great War found the Czechs in a mood of sullen, suspicious passivity, powerless to control the major issues of foreign policy upon which their fate depended, but better organized than ever before, a conscious democracy tirelessly devoted to piecework in the national cause—what their German neighbours called *'kleine Arbeit.'* The nobility, which in the nineteenth century had flirted with Czech nationalism, was now again almost lost, the hierarchy had become an instrument of the Government, though the priesthood had firm roots in the peasantry, and stood the strain bravely ; the Germans still dominated the higher bourgeoisie of Bohemia, though every year the Czechs redressed the balance in their own favour. The backbone of the Czech movement was an alliance between the petite bourgeoisie and the peasantry, which expressed itself politically in an expansion of Radicals and Agrarians at the expense of both Old and Young Czechs. Meanwhile the Slovaks, as we saw, had their backs against the wall. The entire upper class was Magyarized, the hierarchy worked openly for the Government, the great majority of the Catholic, and a considerable section of the Protestant, clergy were more or less consciously 'Magyarone,' all official posts, high and low, were closed to nationally conscious Slovaks. Education was in Magyar hands. Save among a small group of four hundred to five hundred families—among whom the children of the Lutheran clergy played a disproportionate part—resistance was weakening ; the end seemed in sight.

Francis Ferdinand

The causes of the Great War lie quite outside the scope of this survey, if only because the controls lay out of reach of Czech hands. But so far from being indifferent to the growing quarrel between the Monarchy and Serbia, and inside the Monarchy between Budapest and Zagreb, the Czechs had year by year drawn closer to the Southern Slavs, and there was active co-operation between the Czech and Jugoslav Clubs in the Reichsrat. In 1913 Masaryk paid a visit to Belgrade, and brought back to Vienna conciliatory messages from the Serbian Premier Nicholas Pašić ; but Berchtold received him with disdain and actually professed the belief that Masaryk was trying to make some money ! On the other hand, the murder of the Heir Apparent left the Czechs cold. They had had ample means of studying his character at close quarters, at his favourite Bohemian castle of Konopiště ; rightly or wrongly, he was regarded as rapacious and stingy, and his federalist leanings were out-weighed by his autocratic outbursts, due no doubt to the fatal disease which he knew to be gaining upon him. The fact that his wife, the Duchess of Hohenberg, Countess Sophie Chotek, came of one of the Bohemian feudal houses which had Czech leanings did not, in the eyes of the pro-gressive Czechs, atone for the narrowly clerical views which she and her husband were known to share. And on their side it could not be expected that there should be much sympathy for so fervently democratic a people as the Czechs, among whom anti-militarist and even, here and there, anti-dynastic, currents were beginning to show themselves.

The Czechs and Slav Sentiment

While in Vienna crowds sang the ballad of Prince Eugene before Belgrade, and in Budapest there was almost equal jubilation at the removal of the Archduke and the prospect of smashing Serbia, in Prague there was not a trace of warlike enthusiasm, for the excellent reason that war with Russia and Serbia was felt to be little better than civil war, or to say the very least, repugnant as an outrage upon Slav solidarity. To the Czechs Serbia was what Belgium was to Britain, but to them Russia was not merely the 'steam-roller' which might reach their own frontiers ; it was also idealized as the great Slav brother, who was resuming in favour of Serbia the role which it had played in liberating Bulgaria a generation earlier.

During the opening months of the war all political life was silenced ; breathless and perplexed, the Czechs could at first do nothing but wait upon events, in the knowledge that the fate of Bohemia would depend in no small measure upon the length of hostilities, and in any case upon many things that lay altogether beyond their control. Neither the Reichsrat nor the Diets were allowed to meet, and a stiff censorship and suspension of meetings made all expression of opinion dangerous. The General Staff, which under the Archduke Friedrich took up its head-quarters at Teschen, and was for the first two years all-powerful on the home front (in Austria, though not in Hungary), was particularly suspi-cious of Bohemia, especially when the Russians began their advance upon Cracow : it came into conflict with the Governor, Prince Francis Thun, whose measures, stringent as they were, seemed to them altogether too mild.

Kramář and Masaryk

It must be emphasized at the outset that none of the Czech leaders had pursued separatist aims before the war, if only because there was no Czech state outside the Monarchy towards which they could gravitate ; they had always clung, though with diminishing hope, to the possibility of reconstructing the Monarchy on a federalist basis. The war led them to consider more drastic solutions, and produced two main currents of opinion, represented by Kramář and Masaryk. Kramář, for all his Russophil and Neo-Slav ideas, had loyally worked for an honourable compromise between German and Czech inside Austria, and between Vienna and St. Petersburg in the international field. For him Austria-Hungary was the aggressor, Russia's defence of Serbia was fully justified, and hence war was for him the end of his allegiance to the Habsburg state. But realizing his complete helplessness in the initial stages, he was content to wait passively until the tramp of Cossack hoofs should sound on the streets of Olomouc and Brno and Prague itself. He was not in the least disturbed by the Tsarist manifestos to the Czech nation, or by the crass incomprehension shown by the Russian occupying authorities in Galicia, and was perfectly prepared to welcome a Russian Grand Duke as Governor of the Czech lands. If the war had ended with a speedy Russian victory and the overthrow of the Habsburg throne, it is certain that he would have favoured a Russian candidate for the restored Crown of St. Wenceslas.

It was at this point that his political tactics already diverged so radically from those of Masaryk, who had a no less profound knowledge of Russia (revealed in his really great book, *Russia and Europe*) but who approached all Russian problems from a more realist angle and never surrendered to the glamour of what he himself has well named 'Cæsaro-papism,' or to the mystic emotions of 'the Third Rome.' He knew the essentially democratic outlook of his own people, and foresaw that not all their Slavophil sympathies would prevent the danger of friction with the Tsarist envoys. But above all he felt profoundly convinced that a victorious issue of the war depended not on Russia, but upon the Western democracies and America, and hence, that if the Czech cause was to obtain a hearing and achieve decisive results, a long and arduous task of enlightenment must be undertaken in Paris, London, Rome and Washington.

It was under the spur of such doubts and questionings that Masaryk availed himself of his parliamentary immunity to escort his American sister-in-law from Prague to her steamer at Rotterdam, in the hope of establishing contact with his Entente friends. On the first occasion he failed, but in October he met the present writer secretly at Rotterdam, and spent two days exchanging views and information.[1] At this early stage of the war he frankly admitted complete Bohemian independence to be a maximum programme, only to be realized if the war was a long one (Kitchener's prophecy of at least three years had a great influence upon him), and he as yet assumed that if independence were once achieved, the nation would prefer a monarchy to a republic, though under a Western prince rather than a Grand Duke. He held the view that a long and sustained effort would be needed to bring home to Western opinion the true issues involved in the fall or survival of the Habsburg Monarchy and the strategic position of Bohemia ; and he inclined to the view that Bohemia could only permanently maintain herself if she bordered directly with Russia. It is not too much to say that alone among the statesmen of Europe (except perhaps Venizelos), he already had a clear picture of the new world which he wished to construct upon the ruins of the old.

On his return home Masaryk spent two months conferring with those of the Czech party chiefs upon whose discretion he could absolutely rely, laying the first foundations of the secret 'Maffia' organization and planning, down to the smallest details, the means of communication through neutral countries. His two chief adherents were Dr. Šámal (who became head of the President's Chancery in the free Republic, but eventually died in a Nazi prison), and Dr. Scheiner, President of the Sokol organization, which he and the Radical deputy Kalina already envisaged as a National Guard in the event of a Russian invasion, and therefore as the nucleus of a future National Army. In December, 1914, Masaryk again

---

[1] *See Masaryk in England*, by R. W. Seton-Watson (1943), where Professor Masaryk's War Memoranda are published in full.

went abroad, this time to Italy, where he established contacts with the Southern Slav exiles and the Russian and French Embassies. In February, 1915, he was on the point of returning, when an urgent warning came to him through the poet Machar from a secret service source in the Vienna War Office, that he would be arrested at the frontier and perhaps shot as a traitor ; and this was reinforced by Edvard Beneš, a young university lecturer in Prague with whom he had left the threads of conspiracy, and who managed to meet him at Geneva without incurring suspicion. Masaryk remained abroad, and soon after made his way, on a Serbian diplomatic passport, to Paris and London, which was to become the headquarters of the new movement ; while Beneš returned to Prague, to test and develop the Maffia as an instrument of internal propaganda, till the signal for him to join Masaryk was given.

The Czechs on the Russian Front

Meanwhile Czech detestation of the war found drastic expression in wholesale surrenders on the Russian and Serbian fronts, followed by severe Austrian reprisals. It was at first a perilous operation, for they had to run the gauntlet between German or Magyar machine-guns in the rear and suspicious Russians in front. It was only after some delay that, warned by Emanuel Voska, the American Czech arch-propagandist, Wickham Steed explained the true facts to the Russian Ambassador in London, Count Benckendorff, and got him to notify the Russian General Staff that the singing of certain songs (Hej Slovani, the Panslav hymn, and another sung to the tune of 'Poland is not yet lost') at midnight in the Austrian trenches, meant that Czech or Slovak troops were waiting to go over to the Russians. The 11th Austrian Regiment refused to march against the Serbs, and was decimated. The 36th Regiment revolted in barracks and was massacred by German troops ; the 88th, after an unsuccessful attempt to surrender, met with similar treatment from Magyar Honvéds, and the 13th and 72nd Slovak Regiments fared in much the same way. The most famous example was that of the 28th Regiment, nicknamed the 'Children of Prague,' which, on leaving for the front, marched through the capital to the tune of Hej Slovani, but added a special verse : 'We march against the Russians, but no one knows why' ; on April 3, 1915, it surrendered in a body on the Russian front, and the Teschen High Command issued an army order disbanding the regiment. But what Vienna felt as a disgrace, Prague regarded as a distinction, and defections continued, though never again in such large bodies at one time. It was incidents such as these which made it necessary to reorganize the regiments of the Joint Army on a mixed racial basis, setting one race to watch the other, and eventually to stiffen even these reconstituted regiments with German units. In the end, it was this above all else that rendered impossible any idea of a separate peace.

The Maffia

Meanwhile many thousands of Czech civilians were interned as 'political suspects,' and death sentences by courts-martial were close upon 5,000—from which it will be seen that the Heydrich Terror, though far more savage and systematic, has its precedent in the First World War. It should, however, be added that Austrian repression was far more severe in Eastern Galicia, Bosnia and Slavonia than in the Czech lands.[1] Among the Czech leaders Dr. Klofáč, the National Socialist, who passed as the most extreme of them all, was the only one to be arrested in 1914, though all were very closely watched. But on the death of Prince Thun early in 1915 the new Governor, Count Coudenhouve, was at the mercy of the military authorities, and there was a rapid stiffening. In May Scheiner and Kramář were arrested, and in July the latter's close associate Alois Rašín (a marked man through life, as one of the leaders of the Omladina in 1890, and afterwards the first Finance Minister of the Republic, and saviour of the Central European currencies). In September there were fresh arrests, as a result of the so-called 'Button Incident,' when one of the Maffia leaders, suspecting that the bearer of a message from Masaryk was really an *agent provocateur*, denounced her to the police. Among those imprisoned were Dr. Alice Masaryk, Mme Beneš, Hajek (afterwards chief of the Press Bureau of the Republic) and his wife, and the Socialist deputy Soukup. Fortunately, however, just before the net was drawn close, two men managed to escape abroad ; the first, Dr. Dürich, was a prominent Agrarian deputy, and had been chosen to co-operate with Masaryk as a representative of the parties of the Right, while the second, Edvard Beneš, enjoyed equally the confidence of the innermost ring of conspirators, and of Masaryk himself. Dürich proved to be a complete failure, and when he reached Russia from the West became the mere tool of the Tsarist reactionaries, to such an extent that he had to be formally excluded from the National Committee. But Beneš at once became Masaryk's indispensable helper, and settled in Paris as the secretary-general of the movement, while his chief made London his headquarters and devoted himself to the thorny problem of bringing home to an ignorant public and a scarcely less ignorant Government the essential facts about Austria-Hungary and its subject peoples. In their joint efforts they received powerful aid from Milan Štefánik, who soon became the third of the Czechoslovak Triumvirate in exile. Štefánik was the son of a Slovak Lutheran pastor, who already in his teens had been in trouble with the Magyar authorities, owing to his nationalistic sentiments, and finding his way to Paris, obtained a post at the Observatoire and was a member of more than one French astronomical expedition, in Tahiti and the Sahara. On the outbreak of war he became an airman in the French Army, and attracted attention by his brilliant performances on the Italian and Balkan fronts. He already had access to a number of the political *salons* of Paris, and it was through these connections that Masaryk was first received by Briand and met some of the key-men in French politics. Latterly this Ariel of the Revolution had lived largely by will-power, after recovering from a dangerous operation.

The little group had the great advantage of working untrammelled by rival intrigues, for it was of the essence of the situation that those at home must leave the widest possible latitude to those whom they trusted with the leadership abroad, and it was, of course, obvious to all that Masaryk stood head and shoulders above his colleagues, many of whom were in their early thirties. Step by step they made public their political aims. The Quincentenary of John Hus (July 6, 1915) was made

[1] The Polish Socialist leader Daszynski, in the Reichsrat in 1918, maintained that there had been 30,000 executions in Galicia alone. The Croat poet and deputy Tresić-Pavičić, speaking in the Reichsrat on October 19, 1917, gave a horrifying account of the internment camps of Arad, Nezsidér and Styria.

the occasion of a great demonstration at Geneva, where Masaryk and Ernest Denis linked up the long Hussite struggle for religious and intellectual liberty with the fight for freedom of the modern Czechs. In October Masaryk inaugurated the School of Slavonic Studies in the University of London, by a lecture upon the 'Zone of Small Nations' lying between Germany and Russia, and indicating the extent to which the political keys of the future lay within that region of Europe. In February, 1916, he gave a similar lecture on 'The Slavs in the World,' at the Sorbonne. But meanwhile, on November 15, 1915, a 'Czech Committee of Action Abroad' had issued its manifesto in favour of an independent Czechoslovak State, declaring the Habsburg dynasty to have abdicated by its submission to the Hohenzollern. 'To Russia, the great Slav nation, to England, who first established the rules of government of nation by nation, to the Italy of Cavour, Mazzini and Ferrero, to France of the Revolution, Bohemia confides her destinies.'[1] The signatories were Masaryk and Dürich, followed by the heads of all the Czech and Slovak Leagues and Societies in Europe and America ; these latter were full of zeal and sent far more than their due quota as volunteers in the Entente armies, but they were neither numerous nor influential. The only serious organ of the movement was *La Nation Tchèque*, first published in May, 1915, in Paris under the personal supervision of Ernest Denis, and after the two first years taken over by Edvard Beneš, while Denis became responsible for the new *Monde Slave*. In February, 1916, the Committee of Action was reconstructed as the Czechoslovak National Council, with Masaryk as President, Beneš as General Secretary, and Štefánik as representative of Slovakia. Though there were disagreements, some ideological, some purely personal, such as are inherent in such movements, it is true to say that there was greater unity of purpose and a clearer line of action among the Czechoslovaks than among any of the other exiled nationalities of Central Europe. Incidentally, it is well to note that Masaryk and Beneš throughout this whole period made a special point of cultivating the closest relations with the exiled Jugoslav Committee and with representative Poles and Roumanians.

Masaryk, when he set out upon his great adventure, took with him the Kralice Bible and the Testament of Comenius, asking himself in all earnestness whether it would be vouchsafed to him and to his contemporaries to 'make good, once for all, the disaster that overwhelmed us as a nation three centuries ago.' Were 'the storms of wrath' at last about to pass, and would God then restore to the Czech people rule over its own affairs ? It was in this spirit that he persevered through four years of exile, in Europe, Asia and America—consciously linking up the cause of Czechoslovak independence with the cause for which Hus and Comenius suffered. Once again the Czechs were true to type, in that they gave their confidence to leaders who combined markedly ethical principles with that sober 'realism' in politics which is poles apart from German '*Realpolitik*.' Masaryk was a man of spartan tastes, opposed to convention and indifferent to popularity, but winning many hearts by his simplicity and unflinching purpose. Nothing was too insignificant for his attention—the latest film, or novel, or sermon, the opinions of men in the street ; as he was constantly striving to read the mind of the foreign statesmen upon

---

[1] The order in which the nations are named deserves special attention : needless to say, America was still neutral and could not be mentioned, even by her own citizens.

whom his nation's fate might depend, so he drafted more than one memorandum, which was as much a warning as an analysis, intended to bring home to them the wider European aspects of the question that concerned him most.

The New Emperor

Without some such summary of the initial activities of the Czechs in exile the final triumph of their cause would be difficult to understand ; but it is not necessary to dwell upon the details of the two first years of the war inside Austria. The Czechs were of course part and parcel of the military machine, trusted less and less because of their desertions, and tied hand and foot in every sphere of life—though doubtless free enough by comparison with their position in the Second World War. Throughout 1916 the advantage lay with the Central Powers, but when Roumania joined in, Germany, as in the case of Italy, Russia and Serbia, had to provide the necessary stiffening before this fresh enemy could be driven back. This provided the final argument in favour of German-Austrian unity of Command, and Francis Joseph reluctantly accepted its necessity shortly before his death that autumn. Henceforth German troops were inserted as the 'stay-bones' of a corset, and the two armies became so inextricably intertwined as to render independent action, and above all, action for a separate peace, almost impossible, though many people on the Entente side continued to hug the illusion, and occasionally made themselves ridiculous by secret overtures. Needless to say, increased German control meant a corresponding decline in the prestige of the once almost dominant General Staff at Teschen.

The death of Francis Joseph in November, 1916, and the accession of his well-intentioned but trivial grand-nephew—'Charles the Sudden,' as he was universally nicknamed, partly as a result of his love of transacting business by telephone—rapidly changed the whole aspect of affairs. Charles's political ideas, in so far as he can be said to have had definitely formed ideas, were closer to his uncle Francis Ferdinand than to Francis Joseph, and it was among the friends of the former that he sought for men capable of occupying the key positions. The little clique at court which had so successfully isolated the old Emperor from his people, Prince Montenuovo, Count Paar and others, were replaced by Count Polzer-Hoditz and Conrad Hohenlohe, known as the 'Red Prince.' Archduke Frederick and with him the versatile Conrad von Hötzendorf, were dismissed, and Army headquarters, transplanted from Teschen to Baden near Vienna, were entrusted to General von Arz, a Transylvanian Saxon known for his devotion to German military and political traditions. On the other hand Count Heinrich Clam-Martinic—nephew of Rieger's ally of the same name —succeeded Koerber as Austrian Premier, Count Otokar Czernin, known for his federalist leanings and his seeming sympathy for the non-Magyars during his term as Austro-Hungarian Minister in Bucarest, became Joint Foreign Minister in place of Tisza's confidant, the uninspired Baron Burián : and last of all, Count Tisza himself was ousted from the Hungarian Premiership, in favour of Charles's own contemporary, the no less mediocre Count Maurice Esterházy.

Tisza and the Coronation

Before he went, however, Tisza had secured one vital decision. Thanks to his insistence, within six weeks of the death of Francis Joseph, Charles was crowned as Apostolic King of Hungary and, as the culminating point of this mystical ceremony, had taken oath not merely to preserve all territory already held, but to extend its bounds wherever possible. It thus became impossible for Charles, without breaking an oath of exceptional solemnity, to make those federalistic changes without which neither Czechoslovak nor Jugoslav unity inside the Habsburg Monarchy could be achieved. Tisza, we may assume, knew well what he was doing, and wished to prevent those men from the entourage of Francis Ferdinand with whom Charles was now surrounding himself from winning him for the daring plan which his uncle had begun to hold in readiness for a similar situation. Francis Ferdinand was credited with the intention of using the six months' respite which Hungarian law allowed to a new sovereign before he must take oath as *rex coronatus*, by pushing through drastic constitutional changes, and then inducing the reconstructed Parliament to pass the legislation without which the federalization of the Monarchy could not be effected. Tisza had now barred and bolted the doors that led to any such scheme, and thereby sealed the fate of the Dual Monarchy, as the well-meaning Charles himself realized when the state was *in extremis* and he could not obtain Hungary's sanction for a federalist transformation.

Many causes contributed to produce the fall of Tisza—the growth of an Opposition provoked by his tactlessness and hard driving ; his resistance to franchise reform, as urged upon him by Charles, his frank disapproval of the Austro-German compromise in the Polish Question, his absolute insistence that Hungary should retain control of her own food supplies in the face of growing privations in Austria and Germany. Another fundamental subject of disagreement was the young Emperor's growing resolve, based on conviction as well as tactics—to summon the Reichsrat after its three years of abeyance, and thus to provide a forum for the muzzled peoples of Austria.

To this fateful decision he was impelled by three major events of external policy. The first of these was the peace offer of the Central Powers to President Wilson a month after his re-election. This led the President to invite the rival belligerents to state their war aims, and the Entente Powers found it necessary, after two years of hesitation and guesswork, to attempt some definition of their attitude to Austria-Hungary. They were already pledged to the restoration of Belgium and Serbia and German evacuation of the occupied territory ; they now added 'the reorganization of Europe,' based upon the rights of small and great nations, guarantees against aggression, free economic development, and restoration of all provinces 'torn away by force against the wish of the inhabitants.' And this they defined in the expulsion of Turkey from Europe and the 'liberation of the Italians, Slavs, Roumanians and Czechoslovaks from foreign rule.' It was only at a much later date that the inner history of this phrase became known, though everyone acquainted with the political alphabet could at once see that something had been altered or inverted at the last moment. In actual fact, the Italians had insisted upon 'Slavs' instead of 'Jugoslavs,' owing to Sonnino's obstinate horror of Jugoslav Unity ; and as the French then very rightly argued that 'Slavs' was much too vague and general a term, they were pressed for the addition of 'Czechoslovaks,' for which Beneš had been busily working and pleading at the Quai d'Orsay. In the end, so little conversant were the *Entente* diplomats with the subject at issue, that they accepted and published the final text without realizing that to write 'Slavs' and 'Czecho-Slovaks' was like writing 'Latins' and 'Italians or Spaniards.'

Deplorable though this incident was as a symptom of Allied ignorance, it was for the Czech cause a very considerable diplomatic success—the first of a series achieved by the triumvirate, singly or collectively. For the moment, however, even this was not apparent, for as the result of extreme pressure from Vienna, and in return for fair-spoken promises, the Czech Clerical Party was induced to repudiate the Allied answer to Wilson ; and a similar attitude was taken up by the Czech Parliamentary Club, which had already sent its delegates to the coronation in Budapest. The reward for this was the reprieve of Dr. Kramář and his colleagues, then under sentence of death for treason ; and this went hand in hand with assurances that Charles intended to restore parliamentary government in Austria, and to strain every nerve for peace.

Charles Convokes the Reichsrat

Following soon upon the German peace move, two other major events forced Charles's hand—America's entry, and the Russian Revolution. As a result, in the year 1917 the War became more and more a war of ideas and of rival propagandas, centring in neutral Stockholm, to which Socialist delegates from every country in Europe flocked. The latitude allowed even by the most reactionary states to their left-wing politicians forms one of the most striking contrasts with the situation in the Second World War, in which Gestapo predominance ensures a sepulchral uniformity. In particular, Vienna thought it inadvisable to refuse passports to three of the most eminent Austrian socialist deputies, Adler, Seitz and Renner ; from Budapest none went, because no Socialist had as yet gained entrance to the Hungarian Parliament.

Charles and his advisers were not blind to the attractions which the Russian Revolution, in its earlier and liberal form, was likely to exercise upon the Austrian masses, and to the possibility that the more radical currents, as they gained in strength, might outstrip moderate counsels. Mediocre as they may have been they would never have committed the cynical blunder of the German High Command in giving the 'sealed train' of Lenin passage through their lines. But the full gravity of the situation, as seen from Vienna, is proved by the secret warning given by Count Czernin to the Emperor in March, 1917, and betrayed by devious channels to the Allies.[1] This was to the effect that Austria must endeavour at all costs to obtain an agreed, or even a separate, peace by the late summer, or she would be risking complete collapse and disaster. This, then, was the considered opinion of the Foreign Minister, based upon the most secret political and military sources ; in actual fact, Austria-Hungary managed to remain in the war for a whole year and a quarter longer than his calculations had led him to accept as possible. But in essentials he was a true prophet, for when she fell she broke into fragments and never rose again.

It was this warning that led Charles, with Czernin's connivance, to make his secret overture to the Entente through the Empress's brother, Prince Sixtus of Parma. The Prince made several journeys between

---

[1] The present writer learned the essential facts before the end of May, 1917, from a source which owed it to certain of the Czech and Croat leaders in Vienna, who, like everyone else, had their agents in Switzerland.

the Laxenburg Palace, the Elysée and Downing Street, and Charles made clear his readiness to see Alsace-Lorraine, his ally's principal booty from a former war, restored to France. But when it came to Charles himself making even a minimum of concessions to Italy, without which it was obvious that the Entente Powers could not enter upon serious discussions, he was as little disposed to yield as his grand-uncle two years earlier, when Bülow was negotiating in Rome with Sonnino. The whole overture ended as a burst bubble, though its revelation by Clemenceau in April, 1918, in response to a more than usually perfidious speech of Czernin, had the effect of high explosive upon the defences of the luckless Charles and his ministers. For a whole year after Sixtus's machinations had failed, there were Allied statesmen naïve enough to believe that Austria-Hungary could be detached from Germany : this was exemplified by the intrigue of Count Revertera with Count Armand in August, 1917, and by the secret Swiss meeting of General Smuts and Count Mensdorff in January, 1918. But in reality Charles and Czernin were on the horns of a dilemma ; even if they were ready to make concessions such as the Entente could decently fob off upon disillusioned Italy, Serbia and Rou-mania—and there was never any sign of such readiness—separate peace had become a physical impossibility. It would only have substituted war with Germany for war with the Entente. Czernin had some excuse for playing the *faux bonhomme*, though the character came to him very naturally ; for he saw that his ally's aims were altogether incompatible with a speedy peace.

The reopening of the Austrian Reichsrat on May 30, 1917, and the political amnesty which it involved, were welcomed by the Czechs, not as a step towards consolidation, which all parties had long since ceased to desire or to expect, but as an opportunity for thinly veiled revolutionary propaganda. Already the controls had been loosened, or it would not have been possible for Czech journalists to issue a protest against the censor's practice of forcing them to publish official matter without any indication of its source, still less for one hundred and thirty Czech men of letters to publish a manifesto in favour of Bohemian national rights. We may pause for an instant to picture to ourselves how the signatories would have fared at the hands of such hyænas as Heydrich or Karl Hermann Frank.

On the first day there were a series of declarations by the various parties. Staněk and Kalina spoke for the Czech Club, using phrases deliberately copied from President Wilson. They demanded 'a federal state of free national states with equal rights,' and as a corollary to this, Czecho-Slovak unity ; they repudiated all responsibility for the war ; they attacked 'the so-called Constitution' and greeted 'with boundless admiration and enthusiasm' Russia's liberation and finally declared 'before the whole world solemnly the Czech people's will to freedom and independence.' The Slovene leader, Father Korošec, speaking for Croats and Serbs also, followed similar tactics, demanding the union of all Jugo-slavs of the Monarchy under the Habsburg sceptre, as the minimum concession to the existing order. The speech from the Throne, while professing devotion to constitutional practice, insisted that the necessary decisions must rest with the Crown alone after the conclusion of peace, and that the monarch's Oath to the Constitution was being postponed 'till the foundations of a new, strong and happy Austria could be laid.' An ominous phrase about 'expanding the administrative foundations of public life, especially in Bohemia,' prompted Staněk to the bold rejoinder that a door seemed to be purposely left open so that the constitution could yet again be broken in the interests of the Germans against the non-Germans. The Germans reacted with some violence, but it was no secret that the majority of them favoured an *octroi* on centralist lines, a reconstruction of the Bohemian and Moravian Diets in their favour, the introduction of German as the language of state, and the exclusion of Galicia (with its eight million Poles and Ruthenes) from the Reichsrat with the deliberate object of placing the Czechs in a hopeless minority. The Premier proved incapable of squaring the circle ; to say that his programme was 'Austria' satisfied nobody, and his vague distinctions between a 'Länderstaat'and a 'Völkerstaat' annoyed the Germans almost as much as the Slavs. The atmosphere grew still more heated when his kinsman Count Oswald Thun made a violent onslaught against Czech treachery 'at the front and in the rear' ; and swift upon this came the news of a brilliant military action fought by the Czechoslovak legionaries under General Brusilov against their former comrades. This coincided with the Emperor's well-intentioned action in releasing Kramář under the amnesty—an action which caused a great deal of effervescence in the officers' corps and was denounced by the Chairman of the German parliamentary union as 'a grave blow against the state.' Clam was obviously unequal to his position, and on June 23 had been replaced by a Government of colourless bureaucrats led by Dr. von Seidler, who in his turn lived from hand to mouth and, without winning over the non-Germans, was criticized by the Germans as far too moderate.

The resolutions of May 30 were interpreted in Budapest as little short of a declaration of war upon Hungary, and increased the latter's inclination to use its superior stocks of food as a means of bullying Vienna, now permanently on the verge of starvation. The weak Maurice Esterházy soon gave place to Dr. Wekerle, the veteran 'Swabian' who had been responsible for the Church Laws of the 'nineties, and had again been Premier during the Coalition regime of 1906 to 1909. Behind the scenes he was now working with Tisza, and while paying the usual lip-service to Universal Suffrage, qualified his pledges of radical reform by insistence upon 'guarantees for the undisturbed development of the life of the state and of our national existence.' Behind this vague phrase was an elaborate design for coupling the franchise with a knowledge of the Magyar language, in other words, for making it a powerful instrument of Magyarization and of oligarchy.

The Magyars and Pan-Germans joined hands to wrest from the Austrian Premier a formal repudiation of federalism and in place of this the more than futile offer of national autonomy in each of the seventeen provinces of Austria, to the complete exclusion of Hungary. The Czechs retorted by refusing to enter the Commission for constitutional revision, and concluded a working alliance in Parliament with the Jugoslavs, Ukrainians and even the Poles. Individually they missed no opportunity of 'talking through the window,' as the Austrian phrase went—this time not merely to the streets outside, but across the line of hostile trenches to their kinsmen in the Entente camp. One declared the time ripe for the opening of 'Austria's "Peter and Paul" fortress,' another that real peace in Europe was impossible till 'on the ruins of the Dual Monarchy new national states shall arise' ; a third, Father Zahradník, demanded 'an independent Czechoslovak state with all the attributes of sovereignty,' and argued that the Czech problem could only be solved at the Peace Conference, not at Vienna. There were of course lively rejoinders from Budapest, and Tisza himself, alluding to the Czechs' demand for union with Slovakia, invited them to 'come and take it.' Wekerle quoted the Crown's assurances that 'autonomy' in no way affected Hungary, and turned the tables by demanding the *de facto* transfer of Dalmatia from Austria to the Triune Kingdom. The general uncertainty was still further heightened by the fact that the Economic Ausgleich, renewable every ten years, was due for revision by the close of the year 1917, and that as agreement on fundamentals between Budapest and Vienna proved impossible, a 'Provisorium' of two years was concluded, on the assumption that before it expired the conclusion of peace would have transformed the whole situation. In reality Dualism, and with it the Habsburg state itself, ceased to exist before that date.

During the remainder of 1917 and throughout 1918 there was a persistent battledore and shuttlecock across the trenches between the leaders at home and their unavowed spokesmen abroad. The most striking example of this game was provided by the Jugoslavs, with whom the Czechs were always in intimate collaboration. The Croat and Serb deputies of Zagreb clung to a legalist interpretation of the *status quo*, attended the Coronation and took their seats in the joint Hungaro-Croat Parliament, thus avoiding the complete suspension of Croatian autonomy —a purely opportunist policy, which was lacking in heroism but enabled them to save many resources for the final struggle. The Croats, Serbs and Slovenes of the Reichsrat, skilfully led first by Mgr. Krek, and then by Father Korošec, put forward full-fledged national demands and stressed their programme of unity, but took care to be loud in their professions of loyalty to the dynasty and to add some such phrase as 'under the Habsburg sceptre' to any statement of programme. And meanwhile the Jugoslav Committee in exile, in secret contact with Vienna and Zagreb, though much more sporadically than the well-organized Czechs of the Maffia, issued its manifestos in favour of the unity and independence of all Jugoslavs, in conjunction with Serbia and Montenegro, under the Karagjorgjević dynasty. No one perhaps went further than the leader of the Czech Socialists, Vlastimil Tusar, who declared that if it be treason to claim liberty and independence, then each of us is a traitor, 'but such treason is an honour, not dishonour.'

The last quarter of 1917 witnessed three momentous events which reacted upon the fate of Austria and the Czechs. In October the Germans broke through the Italian front at Caporetto, and very nearly knocked Italy out of the war ; but the very intensity of the danger rallied the most generous elements of the nation, and—what specially concerns us here— temporarily cured it of its chauvinism and made it ready to collaborate with those who desired the overthrow of the Habsburg Monarchy. One of the great difficulties had hitherto been that the Foreign Minister, Baron Sonnino, regarded this as neither practicable nor desirable, and looked askance upon the Croats, and even the Czechs and Poles, while finding the narrow and ignorant Pan-Serbism of Pašić very much to his taste ; now for the space of a year, under the spur of adversity, the Italian Premier Orlando showed vision and initiative and seemed about to win for Italy the primacy among the Balkan States. Beneš and Štefánik, we shall see, were not slow to profit by the change of atmosphere, and by their mediatory attitude helped to realize that appeasement between

Italian and Jugoslav upon which joint action against Austria-Hungary depended.

Allied War Aims and a Separate Peace

Following close upon Caporetto came the overthrow of the Russian Liberal Government, the establishment of the Bolshevik regime under Lenin and Trotsky, and the conclusion of an armistice at Brest-Litovsk on December 13. During the long peace negotiations that followed both sides pursued an elaborate and quite insincere game for position, which centred round the two famous catch-words 'self-determination' and 'No Annexations.' Trotsky's avowed aim of flinging the lighted torch of Revolution into the house of every neighbour, roused to tardy action many statesmen who had been waiting upon events, too nebulous in their own ideas to risk a definition of war aims. At the same time it served as a stimulus to the many half-gods hovering round the European Cabinets, to profit by a still fluid situation, and also to the exiled leaders, in so far as they were capable of readjusting their schemes and forestalling awkward surprises. Even now some of the Allied statesmen could not shake off the pathetic, or pitiful, illusion that Austria-Hungary could still be won for a separate peace. When President Wilson declared belated war upon Austria-Hungary on December 4, he pointedly announced that his sole desire was that the affairs of its many nations should be allowed "to rest in their own hands." On January 5, 1918, Mr. Lloyd George, in his address to the Trade Unions, agreed with President Wilson that 'the break-up of Austria-Hungary is no part of our war aims,' but that unrest was bound to continue 'unless genuine self-government on true democratic principles' were granted to the nationalities. Three days later, the President, in his famous 'Fourteen Points' speech, showed a no less ominous reserve, simply affirming that "the peoples of Austria-Hungary, whose place among the nations we wish to see safeguarded and assured, should be accorded the freest opportunity of autonomous development."[1] These two momentous pronouncements were undoubtedly influenced by the secret conversations held at Geneva in the middle of December between Count Mensdorff, the former Austro-Hungarian Ambassador in London, General Smuts, as member of the British War Cabinet and Mr. Philip Kerr (afterwards, as Lord Lothian, British Ambassador in Washington), then private secretary to Mr. Lloyd George. Mensdorff, it is but fair to say, speedily made it clear that he was not offering a separate peace, but a general peace, while Smuts in his report expresses relief that he had not mentioned the idea of separate peace—in other words, gives away the real motive which had brought him to Geneva and the extent of his failure to grasp the true situation in Europe. Incidentally, the General in going through with Mensdorff the various national problems involved, never even alluded to the Czechs, and swallowed his description of Czernin as 'a young statesman descended from the ancient royal house of Bohemia, full of lofty political idealism.' Mensdorff's report to Czernin led the latter to suggest a secret meeting with Lloyd George in Switzerland,

[1] Early in January, 1918, a report was handed to President Wilson by MM. Meyer, Hunter Miller and Lippmann, which argued that American 'policy must consist, first in a stirring up of nationalist discontent (in Austria-Hungary) and then in refusing to accept the extreme logic of this discontent, which would be the dismemberment of Austria-Hungary.' When three men of such knowledge and originality of mind thought it still possible thus to play with high explosive, it may be imagined how the amateur politicians and armchair critics demeaned themselves.

and Smuts and Kerr went back in March to discuss matters with Count Skrzynski, afterwards Polish Foreign Minister, but then acting as an Austrian diplomatist. The bubble burst in March, partly because the supreme German offensive forced the Americans to desist, but partly because in the meantime one of President Wilson's agents in Europe, George Herron, had transmitted proofs to Washington that even with the best will in the world the Emperor Charles could not break away from the German yoke. Herron during this period was the wax plate upon which the wishes, hopes and manœuvres of many accredited agents of the Central Powers were accurately recorded and transmitted to Washington—in particular Heinrich Lammasch, the international lawyer, of Vienna University, a man of high ideals and purest intentions, whose employment in such a quest was a proof of the young Emperor's sincerity, but who never had the slightest chance of success, because he was never in a position to deliver the goods. Intrigue would be too harsh a word to describe the activities either of Lammasch or his master : suffice it to say that a vital part in bringing them and Herron down from cloud-land to the stern realities of warring Europe was played by Dr. Stephen Osuský, a young Slovak lawyer from Chicago, who had come to Europe in 1916 as delegate of the Slovak League and from 1917 onwards acted as liaison officer between the Prague Maffia and the National Committee in Paris, from the key position of Geneva.[1]

The 'Epiphany' Manifesto

Fully alive to the dangers of so fluid a situation, Beneš, in the absence of Masaryk in Russia, warned his friends in Prague of the urgent need for some such manifestation as would leave the world in no doubt as to the Czech nation's will. They responded by convoking in Prague the so-called 'Epiphany Convention' (January 6, 1918) of all the Czech deputies in the Reichsrat and the three Diets of the Bohemian Crown (Bohemia, Moravia, Silesia), together with many leaders of the literary and business world. The result was a manifesto protesting against Czernin's double-dealing at Brest-Litovsk, insisting more strongly than ever upon self-determination, denouncing Hungarian treatment of the Slovaks, and demanding a sovereign state of their own, 'within the historic boundaries of the Bohemian Lands and of Slovakia.' For the first time, too, they claimed the right of representation at the Peace Conference. This was all the more serious coming, as it did, at a moment of growing economic stress and privation, when Czernin was writing to the Emperor, 'if this unexampled regime continues, it is certain that in a few weeks we shall have complete upheaval and revolution.' As a proof of solidarity with the striking workmen of German Austria, the Czech Socialists declared a general strike on January 22, and over 130,000 men came out in Prague, Pilsen and Kladno alone. The Seidler Government, affecting to regard the manifesto as 'war psychosis,' at first forbade its publication, and only desisted when it realized that it would not get a majority in Parliament for the confiscation. In the words of a German writer, this incident meant 'the end of Czech opportunism, the victory of national radicalism ; Empire and dynasty were tacitly abandoned by the Czech people, and the declining power of the Viennese Government made it

[1] Dr. Osuský afterwards became Czechoslovak Minister in Paris in 1919, and held the post until the fall of France in 1940.

tactically superfluous to mention Austria or the Habsburgs in a pronouncement containing the national demands.'

Czernin, on the horns of a dilemma, adopted the Fourteen Points in theory, while at the same time promising to 'defend the territorial *status quo* of our allies as our own,' and putting 'Strasburg and Trieste' on the same level. At all costs he must have his 'Bread Peace' for internal consumption, and so concluded a treaty with the Ukraine, but only after its Government, the provisional Rada, in Trotsky's biting phrase 'possessed no territory save their rooms at Brest.' The great drive of the Central Powers towards Kiev and Odessa gave them plenty of *Lebensraum*, but not the vital food supplies of which they stood in need. Rations in Vienna had to be reduced, while Hungary had all the food she required, and the plight of the Sudeten Germans, in their industrialized mountain lands, rapidly became far more precarious than that of the food-growing Czech lands of the central Bohemian plateau.

Masaryk in Russia and the Legions

In the meantime Masaryk had spent the year 1916 in London, studying the possibilities of propaganda in a country which still really 'knew nothing' of the Central European peoples, establishing contacts with political, diplomatic and academic circles, and chafing at the slowness of the mills of God in their English edition. The Committee's machine was set up in Paris, where Beneš and Štefánik had a less uphill task than their chief in guiding French opinion and winning official support for the solution which Beneš succinctly summed up in the title of his propagandist pamphlet, *Détruisez l'Autriche-Hongrie*.

The Russian Revolution had a decisive effect upon Masaryk, who had viewed with extreme disquietude the reactionary and ill-informed outlook of the Tsarist authorities towards Czechs and Jugoslavs alike. The Foreign Minister, Sazonov, though a man of character, was hopelessly ignorant about the lesser Slav nations and looked at everything from a narrowly Orthodox angle, being inclined to leave the Catholic Slavs—Czechs, Slovaks, Croats and Slovenes alike—to the tender mercies of Austria or (in the case of the Dalmatian coast) of Italy. He imagined the Orthodox population of Dalmatia to be situated in the south round Kotor (Cattaro), whereas in reality 80% of it was in the extreme north, bordering on the Lika ; and he actually preferred the subservient Panslavism and Panserbism of Pašić to the manly and stubborn statesmanship of the Croat leader Supilo, who wormed out of him and Gulkievich the secret of the Treaty of London, with its gross betrayal of 700–800,000 Slavs to Italy. On the other hand a small group of Tsarist Czechs at Kiev had early in the war contrived to secure an audience with Tsar Nicholas, and presented him with a map of the future Bohemia—including Vienna and Upper Austria !—and the Tsar, failing utterly to grasp the true meaning of this, vaguely expressed the hope that God would help them to realize their wishes. Masaryk's comment in his post-war memoirs was : "I, too, believe in God, but not in a Rasputinian God, and things turned out as I expected." Dürich, on reaching Russia, linked up with Koníček and his tiny group of reactionary phantasts, and still further poisoned the minds of their backers in high quarters, who, in Masaryk's words, 'confounding two different conceptions,' distrusted the Czechs at one and the same time as Liberals and as Catholics. After Sazonov's fall the Russian attitude became more negative than ever towards the lesser Slavs, and the recruitment of Slav contingents from the numerous Austro-Hungarian prisoners of war again fell into disfavour. The 'Družina' or Legion of Russian citizens of Czech race was formed in the opening months of the war, but while desertion was actively encouraged, the drafting of prisoners into special national units was frowned upon, or coupled with the impossible condition of accepting Russian citizenship. There were even proselytizing attempts in favour of Orthodoxy. Thanks to the efforts of Štefánik during a visit to Russia, permission to form a Czech D vision was at last granted, but speedily withdrawn. Dürich actually advocated the incorporation of Bohemia in Russia and the acceptance of the Orthodox faith, but this was too much even for men who gave their support to the already tottering regime of Stürmer and Trepov ! It was at this stage that he was found to have accepted money from the Tsarists, and had to be expelled altogether from the movement.

The Revolution changed everything ; several leading members of the Provisional Government, and especially the Foreign Minister Milyukov, were close friends of Masaryk and sympathized actively with the aspirations of the lesser Slav nations. They at once showed their good will by accepting Polish unity and independence, though in some kind of special relationship with Russia. Masaryk no longer had to soft-pedal when liberation or democracy were under discussion, and hoped to carry the Duma for his ideas. But he realized that his place was now in Russia, and after a farewell conference with Beneš and Štefánik, he set out for Petrograd with the full approval of the British Government, which provided him with a false passport and facilities for the perilous journey across the North Sea, and through spy-haunted Sweden. His good relations first with the Lvov, and then with the Kerensky Government did not blind him to the rapid disintegration of Russia ; and while warning his friends in the West to discount further military help, he lost no time in using the wider powers granted by the new regime to organize a regular Czechoslovak army on the Russian front. When he reached Petrograd he found that he had already been recognized as something very like dictator, 'sole representative of the Czecho-Slovak nation' in Russia. Milyukov helped him to win over the High Command, and the gallant share taken by the Czech volunteers in the battle of Zborov (July 3, 1917), the last flickering success achieved by Brusilov's armies, helped to convince many military and political sceptics. This was followed by a mass meeting in Kiev, in which Masaryk defined his programme of independence and pronounced in favour of a Republic, which 'a nation conscious and intelligent was perfectly capable of maintaining.'

Few achievements are more extraordinary than that of this exiled professor of philosophy, able at the age of sixty-eight to create a national army and throw it decisively into the political balance in the new Europe that war and revolutionary chaos were bringing to birth. As he himself has explained, he 'wanted as large an army as possible, an army really military, not political'—Czech, not Russian, in spirit, though 'definitely Russophil and knowing clearly what it was fighting for.' This army he wished to transfer to France ; the French Government had already been persuaded to adopt the proposal, and now on his arrival he obtained the sanction of the Russian Staff and arranged with the French Mission under M. Albert Thomas for a first instalment of 30,000 men, including a number of officers (Czechs and Serbs) who had fought in the Jugoslav Legions under

Russian Command during the German invasion of Roumania. Unhappily, however, during the summer of 1917 the Russian army was already in dissolution, and though the new Chief of Staff, General Dukhonin, sanctioned the formation of a second Czechoslovak Corps, and was actually thinking of himself assuming their command when he was murdered by the Bolsheviks, it was too late to carry out the operation. One small contingent was shipped from Archangel to France, but geography, that confirmed enemy of the Slavs, now left them with one solitary exit across the steppes of Asia.

The Bolshevik Revolution complicated everything ; on the Bolshevik side there were many shades of opinion—some who knew the record of the Tsarist intrigues and assumed all Czechs to be like Koniček and Dürich, others who were ready to use the Czech prisoners in Russia as something to bargain with in the final negotiations with Berlin and Vienna, and more still who reproached them for putting nationality before what is now called ideology. Masaryk's overriding object was to maintain absolute neutrality and aloofness from internal Russian feuds, and this he impressed again and again upon his men, as their only hope of extricating themselves from the vast moving bog of revolution. 'From the moment of the Brest armistice it was clear to us that our army had nothing more to do in Russia,' and when the Ukraine was recognized by the Central Powers and declared its independence, Masaryk withdrew his men from its territory and refused recognition. He was all the more cautious because even in his Russian isolation he realized only too well that the Allies had no Russian policy at all, and on many points disagreed profoundly among themselves. He dealt direct with the Bolshevik authorities, and as soon as he had secured their consent for the withdrawal of the Legionaries across Siberia, he himself left Moscow (March 7, 1918) for Vladivostok : and thence he went on *via* Tokyo to the United States, where scarcely less arduous and even more decisive action awaited him. But hardly had he left, when the first orders issued by the Soviet Command, promising all necessary facilities along the route, were revoked from Moscow, almost certainly under German influence at the period of the Peace of Brest-Litovsk. We shall see that despite renewed negotiations and a fresh promise of facilities, the door of escape again began to be closed, and in the end had to be held open by force, until this most romantic of military experiments had been completed.

The Pact of Rome

While Masaryk was organizing an army in Russia, his tireless and resourceful lieutenants were bent upon securing recognition from the Western Powers, and forming an united front with the other subject races of the monarchy. The main obstacle to this had lain in Italy's obstruction in all matters relating to the Jugoslavs ; but Caporetto had a sobering effect, and enhanced the position of Bissolati, the chief Socialist member of the Italian Cabinet, and of Salvemini and his small group of Liberals round the weekly *Unità*. From December to March a series of meetings were held between Trumbić and his colleagues of the Jugoslav Committee on the one side[1] and first General Mola and afterwards Andrea Torre, as

---

[1] Supilo had died in September, 1917, having lived to endorse the so-called 'Declaration of Corfu,' signed by the exiled Committee and the exiled Serbian Government.

delegate of a large body of Italian Senators and deputies ;[1] and the agreement reached between them enabled the Orlando Government to invite representatives of all the subject races to a Congress in Rome. Parallel with this, and as an indispensable condition of success, went the creation of the British Department of Enemy Propaganda under Lord Northcliffe, and the clear enunciation on the part of its organizers of the alternative policies which confronted the British Government. The choice, they contended, lay between (a) 'to work for a separate peace with the Emperor, the Court and the aristocracy, on the principle of not interfering with the domestic affairs of the Habsburg Monarchy, and of leaving its territory almost or quite intact,' and (b) 'to try to break the power of Austria-Hungary, as the weakest link in the chain of enemy states, by supporting and encouraging all anti-German and pro-Ally peoples and tendencies.' Mr. Balfour approved the adoption of policy B, though without committing himself finally to the view that a complete break-up of the Monarchy could be achieved ; and henceforward the propagandists of the three Western Powers and of America based their whole work upon it. Feverish last-minute efforts were made to wreck their activities, but the Congress of Rome met on April 9 on the Capitol and proved a resounding success. Orlando himself greeted the delegates, while Sonnino sulked in his corner ; Trumbić, who earned the name of 'Il Croato al Campidoglio' (The Croat on the Capitol), headed large delegations from the Jugoslav Committee and the Serbian Skupština, and among those representing the Czechoslovaks, Poles and Roumanians were Beneš, Štefánik, Sychrava, and Osuský, Skirmunt, Seyda and Zamorski, Mironescu and Lupu. They found a common programme in the words *Delenda Austria*, and saw in German domination the main obstacle to their national aspirations.

The Congress partly owed its success to a sensational event of the previous week. On April 2 Count Czernin, perhaps hoping to spoil the effect of what he must have known to be impending, delivered a speech at the Vienna Rathaus, in which he denounced those Czechs who followed 'the miserable Masaryk,' but claimed that 'the Czech people as a whole is loyal and Austrian.' For Austria-Hungary he disclaimed all desire for annexations and even denied that Germany had territorial ambitions in the East. But he was also unwise enough to accuse Clemenceau of having made peace overtures and to treat this as inconsistent with the French insistence upon Alsace-Lorraine. To this came the Tiger's sledge hammer retort : "Czernin has lied," and when Vienna tried to brazen it out, the Emperor's original letter of March, 1917, offering to discuss peace terms and admitting the justice of the French claim to Alsace, was published in Paris. Czernin fell like a stone, and was replaced by the ineffective Count Burián, whom Charles had dismissed as incompetent eighteen months earlier. But Charles himself was left in a pitiable plight, denounced as a traitor to the German cause by all Germany and large sections of his own subjects, and an object of ridicule to the non-Germans ; he was forced to visit the Emperor William at Spa, to make a public recantation and to discuss measures for tightening still further Germany's stranglehold upon the Monarchy. On all sides the incident was treated as one of the most

---

[1] The present writer, together with Mr. Wickham Steed (whose memoirs contain what is so far the only authentic account of the negotiations), Sir Arthur Evans and Signor Emanuel, were witnesses to the agreement signed at the Savoy Hotel by MM. Trumbić and Torre.

humiliating in the long history of the Habsburg dynasty, which thus took a fresh plunge towards the abyss. It also brutally tore to shreds the feeble web of peace intrigue which had done so much to confuse the issue, even though it was from the first foredoomed to failure.

Czech Agitation Inside and Outside Austria

Under the stress of this incident the Czech leaders were encouraged to convoke a meeting of notables in Prague on April 13, and in the presence of special Croat and Slovene delegates a 'National Oath' was read out by the veteran novelist Alois Jirásek and adopted by acclamation. Another sign that the spirit of resistance was rising was provided by the letter addressed by the Slovene leader Dr. Korošec to the Czech Union, accusing Czernin of gross self-deception ; 'The Czech people, like one man, has risen and demonstrated its perfect solidarity,' and the Jugoslavs were no less unanimous in holding to their fraternal union with the Czechs, which no intrigue can destroy.

The Roman Congress reverberated through the tottering Monarchy, and on May 16, the Jubilee of the Czech National Theatre, the Czechs organized in Prague a gathering planned to represent the same races as had been present on the Capitol. The Chairman was no other than Dr. Kramář, released and pardoned, and over two hundred Jugoslavs attended (including the deputies Radić, Pribičević, Pavelić[1] and Korošec) ; the Poles sent the poet Kasprowicz, the Slovaks their greatest literary figure, Hviezdoslav, and Italians and Roumanians were also present. One speech was more outspoken than the others, and all five nations pledged themselves to a united struggle for independence and democratic government. Even the Slovaks, isolated and enfeebled, began to raise their heads, and on May 24 there was a meeting at St. Martin at which resolutions were passed in favour of close accord between Slovaks and Czechs. The mere fact that such a meeting could have taken place at all was a sure sign of the disarray which recent events and the parlous state alike of the army and of the home front had caused among Hungarian chauvinists.

The Roman Congress, parallel with the exploits of the Czechoslovak Legions in Russia, reacted also in the international field. In September, 1917, Beneš had negotiated with the Italians for recognition of a separate army formed from volunteers among the Czechs captured on the Italian front ; but the Staff held out for their inclusion in the Italian Army, and it was not till after Caporetto and the Capitol that a new spirit arose, which enabled Štefánik to negotiate directly with Orlando and his War Minister, without interference from Sonnino. The result was the formation of a Czechoslovak army of 24,000 men in Italy, and the employment of its first units on the Italian front, after a ceremonious presentation of colours in the presence of five leading members of the Italian Cabinet. But even now Italian prejudices withheld similar concessions to the numerous Jugoslav officers and men who were confined at the camp of Nocera and elsewhere, and were clamouring to be allowed to serve against Austria.

In February 1918, meanwhile, Dr. Beneš reached definite agreement with the French General Staff regarding the Czechoslovak army in France,

---

[1] A prominent Croat dental surgeon, deputy of the Serbo-Croat Coalition in Zagreb, not to be confused with his namesake, the future terrorist Chief of State.

which was placed under the authority of the National Committee, with General Janin (late chief of the French military mission in Russia) as its first general. In June the first regiment left for the front, after the presentation of flags by President Poincaré and the Foreign Minister, M. Pichon. There followed Pichon's Note of June 28 recognizing the Czecho-slovak Council as 'supreme organ of the nation, and the first basis of a future Czechoslovak Government.' Well might Beneš in his War Memoirs stress this event as one of the landmarks of the Czech struggle for independence. Moreover, Poincaré's speech to the new army—which contains the first public reference to a greater Anabasis than that of Xenophon, 'an incomparable example of moral strength, endurance and patriotic faith'—aroused the interest of Balfour, who already on June 3 had been ready to recognize the Council 'as supreme organ of the Czechoslovak movement in Allied lands.' He now entered into informal discussions, with Lord Robert Cecil as intermediary; and when the Foreign Secretary raised the question how far the Czech movement could claim to speak for the nation at home, Beneš was fortunately able to point to the three demonstrations of January 6, April 13 and May 16 (see p. 297), whose representative character was amply apparent. At last on August 9 Balfour signed on behalf of Britain a document recognizing the Czecho-slovaks as 'an allied nation,' their three armies as regular belligerents, and the National Council as 'present trustee of the future Czechoslovak Government'[1] and therefore competent to exercise authority over those armies.

Meanwhile the attitude of the United States Government was under-going a still more momentous evolution, but this is better treated in conjunction with Masaryk's American visit.

Failure on the Piave

In the middle of January Austria-Hungary launched a last despairing offensive on the Piave, but it was soon clear that her soldiers had lost their powers of offensive; 'this starving, frozen, exhausted army' is the phrase employed by the distinguished soldier and author von Glaise-Horstenau, to describe its state as it emerged from a third winter of Alpine warfare. The failure of the commissariat and of supplies of military uniforms and underwear kept pace with a catastrophic deterioration in the food situation on the Austrian home front, though in Hungary, by comparison, there was something very like official hoarding at the expense of her more distressed partner. Marshals Conrad and Boroević—the former the most notable soldier whom Austria had produced since Radetzky, the latter the man who had held the Italians at bay in the long series of battles on the Isonzo—were indicated as the scapegoats of the Piave failure; but while Conrad was made a count and sent into retirement after a painful scene with Charles, it was in the end thought inadvisable to remove the famous Slav general who in holding the Isonzo for Austria felt himself also to be defending Jugoslav soil against the Italian invader. Conrad felt that he had been treated with typical Habsburg ingratitude, like Benedek and Tegetthoff before him.

In passing, attention must be drawn to another important ingredient

---

[1] The story of how the word 'trustee' was adopted as a legal compromise between two points of view, is graphically told in Wickham Steed's *Through Thirty Years*. He was the magician who drew the rabbit from the hat.

in the Austrian military failure, namely the intensive propaganda conducted from behind the Italian front by the committees appointed for
the purpose at the Rome Congress ; this took varied forms, notably that
of leaflets distributed by air, and messages and patriotic songs broadcast
by loudspeakers on quiet nights close to the enemy trenches. So effective
were the appeals to the soldiers to surrender and join their kinsmen
fighting for liberty, that on more than one occasion regiments had to be
withdrawn or transferred to other parts of the front, or even reconstructed
altogether.

The fall of Conrad was shortly followed by that of Dr. von Seidler
(July 17), who found himself equally unable to control the non-German
nationalities and his own Austrian Germans. His successor was Baron
Hussarek, of Czech origin, well known as a professor of canon law, and
a former Minister of Education, whose reactionary tendencies had earned
him the favour of the Christian Socialists. His first act was to throw
a sop to the German extremists by administrative measures portending
'Partition' (or *Zweiteilung*) in Bohemia ; but finding that this infuriated
the Czechs without really appeasing the Germans, he fell back upon a
formula even more ambiguous than those of Seidler—that 'German
course' was to be interpreted as 'Austrian course.' The Czech deputies
in the Reichsrat, fully prepared for some such governmental action, had
on July 13 coalesced in a new National Council—Národní Výbor—of
thirty members, chosen in due proportion from all parties. The selection
of Dr. Kramář as chairman was in itself a straight challenge to Vienna,
and it began its activities with the declaration that 'the whole nation
stands behind us as a united wall of steel.' Its members took a leading
part in the stormy secret debate that followed the Piave reverse. Despite
its unsatisfactory course, the Government did not dare to refuse reinforcements for the Western front. Even before August 8—the 'Black
Day' of Ludendorff's Memoirs—the Austro-Hungarian authorities felt
themselves to be entirely dependent upon Germany, while increasingly
aware that Germany was losing the war and that the Bulgarian front was
wavering. The lists were ready for the final joust.

The Czech Anabasis

In April the Czechoslovak Legions began their withdrawal eastwards,
but speedily came into conflict with the Bolshevik authorities, who,
partly under German prompting, demanded that they should surrender
all their arms and equipment. Trotsky, as Foreign Commissar, arrested
Maxa, the Czech political delegate to Moscow, officially reiterated the
demand on May 23, and actually gave orders to shoot every Czech caught
with weapons in his hand. Organized resistance began at Cheliabinsk on
May 19, and soon the Czechoslovak army was in armed control of the
enormous stretch of railway from Samara on the Volga through Omsk to
Lake Baikal and Vladivostok. Bolshevik attacks upon them drew an
ineffective protest from the Allied diplomats still in Moscow, and a
counter-protest from the German Ambassador, Count Mirbach. Masaryk
had already set off across Siberia in advance of his troops, with a view
to arranging with Japan their evacuation by sea from Vladivostok. He
was strenuously opposed to intervention in any Russian internal quarrel,
and aimed above all at bringing as many of his men as quickly as possible
to the Western front. He now repeated his instructions from the United

States, which he reached on April 29—insisting that 'our Army is a democratic one, serving democratic aims,' and that 'experience in Russia has shown us that democracy is not the equivalent of anarchy and dis-organization.' He also despatched Štefánik, now a general, and General Janin, on a joint military mission to Siberia, where General Sirový was appointed Commander-in-Chief and addressed himself to the task of extricating the more westerly Czechoslovak groups and evacuating them all to the sea. Before this could be accomplished, some of these units, under reckless and irresponsible leaders, had become involved in the final tragedy of Admiral Kolchak at Omsk.

The sound of these remote clashes echoed across the world, until it fired the imagination of the West, and Mr. Lloyd George did not exagger-at when he called it 'one of the greatest epics in history'—'a priceless service which we shall never forget.' The Anabasis had traversed five thousand miles of railway ; everything had been improvised—'the military life, traditions and amusements. . . . They were self-made men of the Revolution, types of their race . . . not military geniuses, but solid, conscientious soldiers, yearning to achieve something solid and important.' 'And not the least characteristic feature of their great adventure was the cultural apparatus which they erected—newspapers, theatre, choral societies, bands, entertainments.' Thus writes of them the man whose task it was to exploit their achievements in the West and use them as the justification of Allied recognition.

It should be added that President Masaryk, in his Memoirs, estimates the total number of Czechoslovak combatants on all three fronts at 128,000 (of whom 92,000 in Russia, 12,000 in France and 24,000 in Italy), or, if the 54,000 reserves organized in Italy after the armistice be added, 182,000.

Masaryk in America

If Masaryk and his lieutenants always contrived to be at the right spot at the right moment, this was peculiarly true of Masaryk himself when he reached the United States and quickly realized that Washington might decide the fate of his nation, if once the true situation in the Habsburg state could be brought home to the President and his entourage. In this task he was assisted by men like Colonel House, Charles R. Crane and his son Richard (afterwards first American Minister in Prague) ; he was first received by Wilson on June 19, and his influence contributed materially to the gradual but steady evolution of the President's ideas throughout that summer. The Four Principles (February 11), the Four Ends (July 4) and above all the Five Particulars (September 27) modified the Fourteen Points very materially, and especially in respect to the situation in the Danubian countries. Much of it was abstract and in-definite, but there was no escape from such phrases as 'utmost satisfaction to all well-defined national aspirations' and 'a free acceptance of the people immediately concerned' as the basis of every settlement. Throughout this period the reports of George Herron direct to the White House played a material part in convincing the President of the essential insincerity of the Habsburg state and the hopelessness of winning its people for any patchwork settlement : and here again the constant influence of Osuský upon Herron can hardly be exaggerated. While Wilson was still in-vestigating in the stratosphere, the ground had been prepared for Masaryk in a much more mundane direction by the vigorous organization of counter-espionage by Voska and others of the Czech colony in New York, Pittsburgh and Chicago. It was thanks above all to Voska that the intrigues and factory wreckings of Papen and Boy-Ed (the German military and naval attachés) and of Dumba (the Austro-Hungarian Ambassador) were brought to light. The ensuing scandal discredited the Central Powers and at the same time drew attention to the Czechoslovak national movement and its full-blooded loyalty to America.

Already on May 29 the Secretary of State, Mr. Lansing, publicly notified the Czechoslovak Council of his great interest in the discussions of the Roman Congress and intimated that 'the national claims of the Czechoslovaks and Jugoslavs to freedom enjoy the sincere sympathy of this Government.' On June 28 he went a stage further and endorsed the demands formulated at Rome : 'all members of the Slav race must be altogether set free from the Austrian yoke.' On September 3 America formally recognized the Czechoslovaks as belligerents and the National Council as *de facto* Czechoslovak Government, thus for the moment outstripping France and Britain in friendly competition.

On June 30, Masaryk attended a large meeting at Pittsburgh between the Czechs and Slovaks of America, which was destined to lead to many misunderstandings in later years. The Convention, which was signed by Masaryk and representatives of the Slovak League and other societies in America, expressed itself in favour of Czechoslovak unity, but also a considerable degree of autonomy for Slovakia inside the future Republic. As none of the signatories had any mandate to sign such a document, the final clause made the whole arrangement contingent upon its endorsement by constitutionally elected representatives of both Czechs and Slovaks at home after the war. The charges of bad faith afterwards levelled against the Czechs, and even against Masaryk himself, because they did not at once set up a separate Slovak Parliament, rested upon an obvious *non sequitur* : and the fact that a full facsimile of the original convention was so widely employed as a means of agitation among the Slovaks both of Europe and of America, was a clear proof of political immaturity and inability to interpret a more than usually explicit document. In the light of later events it is easy to see the sinister motives that prompted such men as Jehlička and Tuka. The Pittsburgh agreement was only one of a series of programmes, some of which had contemplated the union of Slovakia with Russia (this was the idea of the notorious Koníček) or with Poland, or even complete independence ; what alone gave it its importance was the signature of Masaryk.

On September 15 there was a monster meeting at the Carnegie Hall in New York, of the peoples represented at the Roman Congress ; Masaryk represented the Czechs and Slovaks, Paderewski the Poles, Hinković the Jugoslavs and Stoica the Roumanians, and their speeches did much to popularize the cause of independence among the American public. As a logical outcome of this, a solemn united meeting was held at Independence Hall in Philadelphia, where the Thirteen States had proclaimed their independence in 1776. Eleven nationalities signed the joint declaration, but by that time the rapids had been reached and the Habsburg state was on the point of death.

⤳ *Burián and Wilson*

During the late summer of 1918 a political deadlock had been reached both in Austria and in Hungary, corresponding to the military paralysis on the Piave front. This was exemplified by the growing boldness of Czech speakers in Parliament. As early as July 16 Tusar took it for granted that the war would end with the creation of a Czech state ; and next day Stranský denounced the Austria of Seidler as 'a constitutional monarchy without crown and without constitution.' On August 18 (the choice of the old Emperor's birthday seemed a deliberate challenge), another Slav Congress was held, this time under Slovene auspices at Ljubljana ; delegates from Prague attended, but the most striking feature was the prominent part played by the Catholic Clergy, notably the Prince-Bishop Jeglić. A fortnight later the Czech clergy took the hint, and issued a widely signed manifesto endorsing the 'National Oath,' and calling the Czechoslovak state 'an act of God's historic justice.'

By this time there was a panic in high quarters in Vienna. Already on August 19 Charles told General Cramon, Germany's chief liaison officer in Vienna, that unless a general peace could be reached by the end of the year, Austria would be forced to conclude a separate peace, and the Commander-in-Chief, General von Arz gave Hindenburg the same warning. For a whole month the Foreign Minister, Count Burián, tried to win his German colleague for peace overtures, and finally on September 14 issued a Peace Note to all the belligerents, in defiance of a special autograph letter of William II to Charles, warning that such action might 'seriously endanger the Alliance.' Its effect was deliberately spoilt by a speech of the German Vice-Chancellor Payer, in which among other things he affirmed Germany's intention of keeping her conquests in the Baltic states, the Ukraine and Roumania. It was at once rejected by Lloyd George, Clemenceau and Lansing, and next day the Allied offensive in the Balkans began. On September 25 Bulgaria sued for peace, and it was known that Turkey was about to follow. Austria's whole southern front became untenable, and Marshal Kövess was faced by the unpromising task of evacuating to some line behind the Danube an army already seething with revolutionary discontent. Burián himself tells us that there was a project for offering Bosnia-Hercegovina to Serbia as the price of peace, but that Vienna and Budapest could not even now agree to its surrender. The two Governments were at this moment equally removed from reality ; it was at this time that Count Tisza had the fantastic idea of visiting Zagreb, Sarajevo and Split, lecturing the local Jugoslav leaders as if they were schoolboys and threatening them that if Hungary fell she would still have time to bring down the Croats with her.

Turkey and Bulgaria, however, were completely overshadowed by Germany, who was by now in full retreat on the Western front, and recognized the necessity for an armistice. The panic-stricken Burián, on October 4, addressed a note through Sweden to President Wilson, offering to negotiate on the basis of the Fourteen Points ; he failed to realize that the President's speech of September 27 (known as 'the Five Particulars') had very materially modified the Fourteen Points, and especially the Tenth, relating to the future of Austria-Hungary. He therefore received a curt answer, referring him to the High Command so long as the armies of the Central Powers were still in occupation of *Entente* territory. On the 15th Burián, without consulting Berlin, made a speech consenting to these evacuations and praising the proposed League of Nations ; but the Entente was waiting for Germany's decision.

In this fortnight of panic the authorities in Vienna realized that there must be material changes in the structure of the Monarchy, but found themselves blocked at every turn by the *non possumus* attitude of Hungary, and of its Premier, Dr. Wekerle, whose Swabian obstinacy had increased with old age. Baron Hussarek announced to the Reichsrat his Government's intention to grant national autonomy, thereby dropping with a loud bang all his predecessors' plans for a 'German course.' But Staněk, speaking in the name of all Czech parties, left all previous declarations in the shade when he demanded that the Czechs must not be excluded from the coming peace negotiations, and would be represented by the Czech Legions! He ended with an appeal for unconditional surrender and was at once followed by Father Korošec, demanding for the Jugoslav 'full freedom or death.' A week later Hussarek frankly admitted that by accepting the Fourteen Points as a basis, Austria-Hungary had put itself on a basis incompatible with the existing structure of the Monarchy. This alarmed the Magyars, and Wekerle warned the Emperor that if he persisted on these lines, without making it clear that Hungarian integrity must not be tampered with, the Hungarian Government would cut off food supplies from Vienna! Faced by rival threats of sabotage from his two Premiers, the Emperor pressed on with his project of federalization, though he must have realized that in view of Budapest's attitude it was already stillborn. The Emperor's manifesto of October 17 to the peoples of Austria provided for four federal states—a German, a Czech, an Ukrainian and a Jugoslav, but Croatia, Bosnia and Slovakia remained outside their boundaries. By way of contrast, Western Galicia was to go to Poland, while Bukovina and Trieste (between whom there was not the remotest analogy) received a special autonomous status.

Needless to say the Czechs and Jugoslavs rejected the offer as altogether inadequate and barring the way to their attainment of unity; and in any case, they argued, their problems were now international and would have to be settled at the Peace Conference. But the Magyars were scarcely less dissatisfied, doubtless because they saw the flood-gates opening. Wekerle declared : "We are no longer faced by the same Austria with whom we came to terms in the past" ; the manifesto had invalidated the contract between the two countries, and it was thus necessary to substitute the Personal Union. Tisza, to a sceptical audience, tried to argue that Hungary's integrity was not incompatible with the Fourteen Points ; but in the same breath admitted that events had proved his enemy Michael Károlyi right, and that 'we have lost the war.' Ever since the war the Hungarian reactionaries have tried to lay the blame for disaster on Károlyi ; but General Cramon only states the bare truth in ranking Tisza among the chief 'gravediggers of the Habsburg Monarchy.[1] This phrase of his—"We have lost the war"—reverberated along the whole front and kindled sentiments at once revolutionary and despairing. In Parliament, when they were uttered, they encouraged the Slovak and Roumanian deputies, Juriga and Vaida-Voevod, to claim not merely the long withheld regional autonomy, but separate representation at the Peace Conference ; the Magyars realized in helpless frenzy that the Austrian paralysis was affecting Hungary also, and that the Croats in union with their Serb and Slovene kinsmen of Austria, were already forming their united Parliament at Zagreb.

---

[1] 'All that occurred in Hungary in those days,' writes Cramon, 'must be reckoned in the realm of war psychosis.' 'So great was the fame of Tisza,' writes Glaise-Horstenau, a no less reliable witness, 'even among the non-Magyar troops, that his words worked like a poison in their ranks.'

The avalanche gathered in force after October 21, when President Wilson's answer to Burián's note of a whole fortnight earlier was given to the world. For in it the President declared himself to be 'no longer at liberty to accept a mere "autonomy" as a basis of peace.' 'Certain events of the utmost importance' which had occurred since his 'Fourteen Points' speech, had 'necessarily altered the attitude and responsibility' of his Government. These were the American recognition of the Czechoslovaks and their Council as a belligerent nation and a *de facto* Government,' and the further recognition of 'the justice of the nationalist aspirations of the Jugoslavs for freedom.' 'They and not he,' must be judges as to what actions by the Austro-Hungarian Government would 'satisfy their aspirations and their conception of their rights and destiny as members of the family of nations.'

Dissolution

Burián himself admitted that Wilson's answer 'fell like a bomb, bursting at a stroke the framework of the Monarchy.' The *Neue Freie Presse*, the leading newspaper of the Monarchy, wrote of it as 'a blow at the heart'; 'Austria-Hungary has a Premier whose seat is at Washington; his name is Wilson, and the executor of his policy at Vienna is Baron Hussarek.' Four days later, on October 25, Burián was replaced as Foreign Minister by Count Julius Andrássy, with a mandate to make peace, and a telegram was sent to the Emperor William stressing the danger to internal order and to the dynastic principle, and Austria's inability to 'get hold of the wheel when there was no longer anything left to steer.' Dr. Wekerle had already resigned office when the news that Croat regiments had seized Fiume reached Budapest; and now his Austrian colleague Baron Hussarek was succeeded by the admirable Professor Lammasch, at a moment when his only task was to liquidate —'to supervise the peaceful transfer of business from the central to the local national governments.' Even with him the Czechs and Jugoslavs now declined to negotiate; they could not be expected to accept some half-solution, when complete independence was in their grasp. President Wilson's note was the *coup de grâce* for the Dual Monarchy, and when Andrássy replied by accepting its reference to the Czechoslovaks and Jugoslavs as a basis for armistice and peace (October 27), the Monarchy simply fell asunder; the troops poured back in thousands from every front, and within a week it was difficult for the Allies to find any authority with whom to negotiate an armistice.

Parallel with the notes exchanged between Vienna and Washington went consultations between Masaryk and the State Department. On October 18—the day after the Emperor Charles's Manifesto—the Czechoslovak National Council abroad declared itself as a Provisional Government, with Masaryk, Beneš and Štefánik as Premier, Foreign Minister and War Minister, and appointed diplomatic representatives in the Allied capitals. It followed this by a manifesto, justifying its claim on the basis of historic national rights to independence and to union between Czechs and Slovaks. It made a frontal attack upon the Habsburg dynasty and expressly denied the Divine Right of Kings, as inconsistent with the ideals of modern democracy. The Czechs had elected the Habsburgs of their own free will, and were now entitled to depose them. The new Republic, it was declared, would rest upon liberty of conscience, religion, speech, press and assembly, upon tolerance and minority rights: and the closing phrases reaffirmed the nation's belief in democracy and freedom. This act of state was almost immediately recognized by the Allied and Associated Powers and Masaryk, having done his work in America, hastened back to Europe, reaching London on November 29, and making his triumphal entry into Prague on December 21.

Meanwhile the final stage of independence had been reached in Prague itself. Acting upon the urgent warnings of Beneš, the Národní Výbor had during September scrupulously discouraged any disturbances that might give the authorities an excuse for repressions, but closed its ranks still further. A separate 'Socialist Council' had been formed in September, but its leaders Habrman and Soukup co-operated most loyally with the other parties, and at the end of that month the only group still standing aloof, the Catholic Party, now publicly condemned all idea of 'activism' on the side of Austria, and through its spokesman, Mgr Šrámek, associated itself with the aim of an independent Czechoslovak state.

As disintegration and confusion spread throughout the Monarchy, the Národní Výbor prepared, step by step, for the supreme crisis, and on October 19, in response to the Emperor's manifesto, issued the categorical statement that the Czech question was no longer internal, but international. The Vienna Government, committed to the acceptance of Wilsonian doctrine as the basis of peace negotiations, could not refuse passports to responsible Czech leaders for a meeting in Switzerland with Beneš and his colleagues of the National Council ; and on October 28 Dr. Kramář, accompanied by four other party chiefs (Staněk, Habrman, Klofáč and Kalina), the Maffia leader, Šámal, and Dr. Preiss, the chairman of the Živnostenská Banka, met at Geneva with Beneš and his three close collaborators Štrimpl, Markovič and Osuský. Kramář at first favoured a monarchy, but found himself in a minority of one and was too good a democrat to persist ; and it was speedily agreed that Masaryk was the only possible President, and that Kramář himself should form a Cabinet including representatives of all the Czech parties, together with three Slovaks (Hodža, Šrobár and Ivanka) and if possible a German Landsmann minister.

By now, however, events were assuming a breakneck pace, and on the very day of the Geneva meeting, the *Twenty-eighth October*, the Republic was proclaimed in Prague, and took over power from General Kestránek and the protesting Governor, Count Coudenhove. That all this was effected without bloodshed was due to the nerve and resourcefulness of the four leaders who had been, as it were, charged with the defence of the home front—Švehla, Rašín, Soukup and Stříbrný, representing the Agrarian, National Democrat, Socialist and National Socialist parties respectively; it was their discipline and restraint that prevented any action being taken which might have produced conflict or misunderstanding between the emigrant leaders and the people at home. It is scarcely necessary to add that this in its turn was the fruit of unwearied, vigilant and meticulous planning by the underground Maffia movement, whose concern was to preserve unity of aim and of tactics between Prague and Paris.

More difficult, but on the whole achieved with surprising success, was the agreement between the Czechs and Slovaks. The Slovak National Committee was convoked for October 29 at Turčiansky Sv. Martin, while Milan Hodža was left to negotiate with the crumbling regime in Budapest. A declaration had been drawn up denying Hungary's right of jurisdiction over Slovakia ; and some of the delegates had already started homeward, when Hodža arrived with the latest news from the outside world, and in particular Andrássy's acceptance of Czechoslovak independence in his reply to Wilson, its proclamation at Prague, and Šrobár's inclusion in the Central Prague Committee as representative of the Slovaks. With a situation changing from hour to hour, and local committees springing up in every town (as many as 110 were formed within a few days, certainly far more representative than any plebiscite could have been), it is not surprising that the procedure followed was somewhat irregular and improvised. A decade later it was asserted by Magyar propagandists—among them the traitor Tuka—that there had been a secret clause reserving to Slovakia the right to revise the position after the lapse of ten years. This story was only put about after the death of Bishop Zoch, who had played a prominent part at the meeting : it was torn to shreds by the survivors, and may be dismissed as a more than usually impudent invention. The most interesting addendum to the original resolution, accepted by universal acclamation at the time, ran thus : 'The Slovak nation is linguistically and historically a part of the unitary Czechoslovak nation. In all the cultural struggles fought by the Czech nation, the Slovaks had their share.' United, they now claimed complete independence and unrestricted right of self-determination. For the first few months there was the inevitable administrative chaos in Slovakia, owing to the flight of so many officials of the old Magyarizing school, and to the impossibility of replacing them by qualified Slovaks. But the course of events in Budapest, first under the Liberals, then under the Bolsheviks, increased in the first instance the spirit of unanimity, though there were to be regrettable lapses later on into faction and regionalism.

Let us pause for a moment to consider the causes of this phenomenal achievement. First in order undoubtedly stands the 'conjuncture' of a World War that overthrew the four great dynasties of Central and Eastern Europe and altered many frontiers—a chance such as does not recur in several centuries. But not even that would have sufficed without the brilliant leadership and initiative of Masaryk, his skill in handling men and situations and especially in selecting the right collaborators—men as yet untested but, as the event proved, equal to any emergency. No less decisive was the reaction which led him, while consciously following in the footsteps of Hus, Comenius, Havlíček and Palacký, to avoid the barren and negative policy into which the Old Czechs had allowed themselves to drift and which, in another form, Kramář was prepared to adopt under the mesmeric influence of unreformed Russia. Masaryk kept in line with the teachers of the nation without losing his ability to learn from the political thought and experience of the West, and to adapt himself to changing circumstances. Nothing shows this more clearly than his acceptance of Tsarism as a necessary ally, his change of tactics under the Provisional regime and his readiness to co-operate with the Bolsheviks when they had overthrown his real friends and upset all his most vital calculations. Parallel with this went the long struggle for recognition of his cause by the Allied Powers and America, and the success which eventually crowned his Army policy, starting as it did from unpromising and almost fantastic beginnings. Most important of all, however, was the fact that Czechs and Slovaks recognized the great leader whom

Providence had sent them, and followed him loyally through all vicissitudes.

To these factors must be added the corresponding lack of statesmanship on the part of his opponents in Austria-Hungary, the numbing influence of Francis Joseph during his long reign, his marked antipathy for the Czech cause and the many obstacles which, under the fatal Dual System, prevented men of outstanding ability from attaining to, or retaining, high office. The whole system was inimical to talent and encouraged mediocrity and slowness of decision. 'Schlamperei' and 'Gemütlichkeit' were not qualities by which a great Empire could be permanently upheld. The reign of Francis Joseph was probably, on the purely material side, the most prosperous and peaceful era in the history of Central Europe; but the Dual System contained within itself a canker that sapped those powers of resistance by which the Habsburg state had astonished Europe in the days of Frederick, of Napoleon, and of the Revolution of 1848.

CHAPTER XVI

TWENTY YEARS OF INDEPENDENCE (1918–1938)

*'Perhaps in fifty years our times will appear to people living then in such
a haze of splendour that they will almost envy us.'*
—Thomas Masaryk to Karel Čapek (1936).

It is obviously impossible, within the already swollen limits of this book, to tell the full story of the twenty years of crowded life which were vouchsafed to the Czechoslovak Republic : all that can be attempted is to describe the salient features of the new regime and the main lines of its domestic and international policy.

At the outset it ought to be admitted very frankly that Czechoslovakia rested upon two principles which are not always in harmony—on historic rights as against the old Austria, on the principle of nationality as against the old Hungary. In its origin it was a national state, the natural outcome of a long and unique historical evolution. In actual practice it was a mixed state, in which the Czechs and Slovaks represented the 'Will to the State,' while the existence of important German and Magyar minorities, which only reluctantly accepted the accomplished fact, created a problem of great delicacy, whose solution was likely to depend, and did actually depend, upon the extent to which Central Europe settled down, or relapsed into disorder, after the Great War. The new state fell, both geographically and politically, into three sections—the first Bohemia-Moravia-Silesia, the so-called 'Lands of the Crown of St. Wenceslas,' the second Slovakia, which had for a thousand years formed an integral part of the Kingdom of Hungary, and the third Ruthenia (Podkarpatská Rus), consisting of the districts of North-east Hungary inhabited mainly by Ruthenes, or Ukrainians, and enjoying a special status of their own. Though irrevocably cut off from the sea save in the lively imagination of Shakespeare, it none the less enjoyed certain great initial advantages as compared with the other Succession States. It had been subjected to a regime of severe political repression (mildness itself, it must be added, by comparison with the regime of 1939–43), but it had not been overrun or ravaged by war, like Serbia, Roumania or Poland, and it had suffered less acutely than the German provinces of Austria from food shortage and economic dislocation. It was able to make an entirely new start, shedding far more useless ballast than its neighbours. At one swoop it got rid of a hostile dynasty, emancipated itself from an aristocracy which had in the main lost contact with the national cause, and was able to eliminate from the hierarchy certain notoriously anti-national elements. This was possible because by now the Czechs possessed not only a strong national tradition and discipline, but a large educated class, and as few illiterates as their German neighbours. The numerous personnel which they inherited from Austria gave them the nucleus of a trained bureaucracy, slow-moving and easy-going, it may be, but neither inefficient nor corrupt.

Personalities in the New Republic

We have already seen what a priceless asset the Czechs possessed in three such leaders as Masaryk, Beneš and Štefánik. Of the first enough has already been said, and of the second much still remains to be said. The first great tragedy of the Republic was the flying accident in May, 1919, which cost Štefánik his life, as he was returning from Italy and was actually in sight of Bratislava, the Slovak capital, and of the crowds which were preparing to welcome him. It is highly characteristic of the poisoned weapons which were to be used in later controversies that an impudent story of his having been shot down deliberately by Czech machine-gunners should have been put into circulation, to the disgust of all sane and decent people. Štefánik was the Icarus of the movement, a legendary figure, for whom the genius of a Slovak artist, Dušan Jurkovič, has provided a massive and unique tomb on one of the highest spurs of the Lower Carpathians. Almost it may be said of him that he lived, not as other men on food and drink, but by sheer force of will and applied mathematics. The motto which fits him above all was *cogito, ergo sum*. His high idealism and fearless energy would have stood the Republic in good stead, and perhaps averted many petty misunderstandings in the days to come.

With the coming of liberty it speedily became apparent that quite a number of other men of high quality were available. For the moment Kramář was as obviously the foremost candidate for the Premiership as Masaryk for the Presidency ; with admirable patience he allowed himself to be outvoted by more radical colleagues, and at Paris his great knowledge of European diplomacy and his impassioned oratory made a certain impression. What vitiated all else, and led him to relinquish office already in July, 1919, and never to resume it, was his attitude towards the Russian problem, which he very rightly regarded as fundamental for Europe and particularly for every Slav, but which he would fain have solved by throwing the entire weight of his own nation and its greater Allies, if he could win them for such a course, into the scales against Bolshevism. This was resolutely resisted by Massaryk and Beneš, whose calculations had been seriously disarranged by the overthrow of their friends of the Liberal and Social Revolutionary regime and who never hesitated to resist Trotsky's insidious attempt to disarm the Legionaries (which would have resulted in their being handed back to the tender mercies of the German-Austrian invaders of Russia), but who at the same time believed that there was even then a basis for collaboration between the Bolshevik regime and the Western Allies. As the inheritor of the old romantic Panslavism of Rieger, Kramář not merely remained unreconciled, but, as the years passed, made less and less concealment of his profound disapproval alike of Masaryk's philosophy of state and of Beneš's conduct of diplomacy. But the overwhelming sense of the nation was against him, and his reactionary views were one of the main reasons of the dwindling influence of the National Democratic Party.

His closest party colleague, Alois Rašín, had a distinctly more revolutionary past than his chief, having been one of the ringleaders in the Omladina Trial of the early 'nineties. His outlook was, however, essentially that of a bourgeois nationalist, who combined to an exceptional degree economic theory and practice, and had the daring and energy to apply them to an altogether exceptional situation. As Finance Minister in Kramář's Cabinet he pushed through a series of currency reforms which emancipated the Czech Crown from all control by the central financial authorities of the now defunct Monarchy, and incidentally set an example to the other Succession States, which averted otherwise certain economic disaster. The main features of this reform were the stamping of all bank-notes in circulation, pending a new issue, the erection of a banking office, and a loan in gold, silver and foreign currency, as a basis for the future currency. Rašín was murdered early in January, 1923, by a young bank clerk of Communist outlook, but also deranged intellect ; but his spade-work had assured for the Republic greater financial stability, and therefore a speedier return to normalcy, than that enjoyed by any of the post-war states. After his death a very important part was played in successive Cabinets by Dr. Karl Engliš, a professor of economics at the new Brno University, and a man of moderate and balanced views, relatively un-committed to any party group : and indeed throughout the twenty years of the Republic there has never been wanting a succession of able and en-lightened financiers to whose measures the maintenance of stability was due.

Another figure who played a vital part in shaping the evolution of the new state was Antonin Švehla, leader of the Czech Agrarians—not an article of exportation, shunning publicity, almost inarticulate in the presence of strangers, drastic and explosive when occasion demanded, yet infinitely patient in his devotion to democratic ways. His successors as party chiefs, men like Malypetr and Udržal, were men of lesser calibre, but efficient manipulators of the party machine. Foremost among a number of high officials turned politicians was Jan Černý, who had proved his value as Provincial President of Moravia, and as Premier twice success-fully bridged over a period of awkward party dissensions. Among the Socialists Vlastimil Tusar distinguished himself first as Minister in revolutionary Berlin, then as Premier at the height of the ferment in 1919–20, when all was obscure alike at home and in the neighbouring states ; Habrman showed that a demagogue is sometimes capable of constructive statesmanship, while Soukup, after unwittingly playing into the hands of the police and laying bare a section of Maffia activity, after-wards atoned for it by his steadfast courage. In the final stages Kamil Krofta, as successor to Beneš as Foreign Minister, was much more than a mere mouthpiece of the new President. Special mention must be made of the group of Slovak 'activists,' Šrobár, Hodža, Blaho, Kállay, Anton Štefánek, the two Stodolas, Ruman, Slávik and others who rose nobly to the occasion and did not hesitate to improvise where all precedents were lacking. Their role will become apparent when we come to deal with the difficulties which arose in Slovakia and the reasons for the unco-operative attitude of the Clerical leader, Father Hlinka. But it may at once be pointed out that the new state achieved very considerable success in improvising out of nothing a full-fledged diplomatic service, and that among its most con-spicuous members were four Slovaks—Stephen Osuský, who during his twenty years as Minister in Paris acquired a unique knowledge of French politics and diplomacy ; Jan Masaryk, whose unconventional but arresting eloquence won him many hearts ; Bohdan Pavlů, who showed great skill in shooting the rapids of Soviet and Balkan politics, but was prematurely removed by a tragic motor accident, and Vladimir Hurban, son of the poet Vajanský, who found himself at the Washington Legation when the Munich tragedy began.

Parliament and Constitution

In the opening period everything was necessarily provisional, but three questions dominated all else—(1) the regulation of the frontiers,

(2) international recognition, and (3) the drafting of a new constitution and its ratification by the nation. The two first could of course only be solved at the Peace Conference, and this involved leaving Dr. Beneš as Foreign Minister in charge of the long and delicate negotiations in Paris : it was not until September, 1919, that he was free to set foot in the Republic which he had done so much to liberate. In the present narrative, however, it may be more convenient to give precedence to the domestic situation.

At first the centripetal forces outbalanced all others, and Kramář at the first meeting of the National Assembly expressed the nation's confidence in 'its ability to rely upon our own powers alone, and that without injustice to others. We shall count on the devotion of all towards the state, and we shall show that not only have we been able to achieve our liberty, but that we know how to promote it, and to be really free—worthy of our great past, of our traditions and of our sufferings.' This was of course fully in accord with the Declaration of Independence issued by the Triumvirate on October 18 which, not content with endorsing Wilson's principles and laying great stress upon the democratic ideal of the nation, declared that 'as the nation of Comenius, we cannot but accept the American Declaration of Independence, the principles of Lincoln and the declaration of the rights of man and of the citizen.'

It followed quite logically that Masaryk, in his first presidential message on December 23, 1918, should have begun by quoting that moving document, the Testament of Comenius, which had haunted him in exile and steeled his resolve in every trial : after three hundred years the prophecy was now fulfilled. 'Our whole history,' he declared, 'drives us towards the democratic Powers.' 'Our renaissance is the logical link between us and the democracies of the West.' 'The ideals of Fügner and Tyrš [the founders of the Sokol movement] have triumphed in our armies.' From these pronouncements there is a clear sequence of thought to the preamble of the new Constitution as finally adopted—'We, the Czechoslovak people, inspired by the desire to confirm the complete unity of the nation, to introduce just norms, to ensure the peaceful development of the homeland, to promote the general welfare of all citizens of this state and safeguard the blessings of liberty for future generations, have in our National Assembly on February 29, 1920, adopted the constitution for the Czechoslovak Republic, in the following wording :

'And we, the Czechoslovak people, do hereby declare that we shall endeavour to carry out this constitution and all the laws of our country in the spirit alike of our history and of those modern principles embodied in the watchword of self-determination ; for we wish to incorporate ourselves in the League of Nations as an educated, peace-loving, democratic and progressive member.'

In the abnormal situation resulting from the bloodless Revolution of October, 1918, a general election was out of the question, with a large proportion of the male population still out of reach and unable to vote. This difficulty was, however, surmounted by an expedient which met with universal approval and provided a thoroughly representative basis for the deliberations of the Assembly. The National Council apportioned mandates among all the existing parties, according to the number of votes polled by each at the last election to the Reichsrat, which had of course been held under universal suffrage. In the case of Slovakia this method could not be applied, because the narrow Hungarian franchise, applied with every variety of pressure and distortion, had left the Slovaks with only three deputies, and it was obviously impossible to improvise a new franchise or an administration capable of applying it. The National Council in Prague, therefore, acting upon the advice of Dr. Šrobár and the Slovak National Council, of which he was the official delegate to the central Government, nominated forty-one leading Slovaks, to whom fourteen were shortly afterwards added. This number included the President's daughter, Dr. Alice Masaryk and four recognized Czech champions of the Slovak cause (notably Mgr. Kolísek) : at a later date this was made the subject of captious criticism, but at the time it was universally accepted as a graceful compliment. Dr. Šrobár was included in the Cabinet as 'Minister for Slovakia' and set up what was in effect a sub-Cabinet of thirteen prominent Slovaks, sitting at Bratislava from January, 1919, onwards, and administering Slovakia on virtually autonomous lines.

More open to criticism, but absolutely inevitable, was the absence of representatives of the Germans and Magyars : legislation could not stand still while the minorities followed a policy of abstention and staked their hopes upon union with Austria and Hungary respectively. The result of this was that the legislation of this decisive period, when a revolutionary ferment still permeated all races and classes without exception, and when the only hope of allaying passions and restoring calmer feelings lay through the adoption of many measures that were drastic and experimental—was the exclusive work of the Czechs and Slovaks, and that the Germans and Magyars, by the time they descended from the clouds to hard realities, were confronted by a series of accomplished facts.

The essentials of this legislation may be summarized quite briefly. Currency reform, as achieved by Rašín, was the most urgent, and the thorough and practical manner in which it was carried out, not merely saved the country from internal convulsions and prepared that economic and financial recovery which made it the envy of all its neighbours ; it also was the first step towards convincing the outside world that the new state was stable, *viable* and immune from subversive influences from the East—in fact, the very opposite of what its enemies in Central Europe wished the West to believe. But not a moment was lost in other almost equally important directions. Already before the close of 1918 laws establishing the eight-hour day, unemployment insurance and a whole series of measures relative to the acute housing crisis and the protection of tenants, had been passed into law, and in May, 1919, insurance against illness had been added. A parliamentary Committee at once addressed itself to the thorny question of Land Reform, and if the Law of April 16, 1919, in which its main recommendations were embodied, represented a certain compromise between the Socialists and the parties of the Right, the result was still quite drastic enough. No less than 37.3% of all land in Bohemia, and 34% in Moravia, was in the hands of large proprietors representing less than 0.1% of the population ; and the state now obtained the right to expropriate all estates in excess of one hundred and fifty hectares, to divide among the landless peasantry or, when necessary, to augment existing 'dwarf' holdings. What distinguished this reform from the more improvised and therefore disorderly measures adopted in several other countries was the establishment of a State Land Office, which had the task of planning out methodically, year by year, the transfer of so much land, and assigning a proportionate compensation to the dispossessed owners, based on the average land prices in the years 1913–1917. Up to

1928 over 1,200,000 hectares had been definitely handed over, and the transfers were growing yearly more systematic and efficient, despite a certain amount of scandal due to the erection of so-called 'Residue Estates,' which were acquired by persons enjoying the special favour of the regime. It may safely be estimated that during the two decades of the Republic over 600,000 new small holdings were created.

Meanwhile comprehensive educational reforms were introduced. The long desired second Czech University was immediately set up at Brno and named after Masaryk, while the Slovaks acquired a university for the first time in history : from the strictly nationalistic and also from the clerical point of view the choice of the name of Comenius may be admitted as a tactical blunder, even though no name is more highly honoured in the world of education. The German University of Prague remained untouched, while two new Czech technical High Schools were erected in Prague and Brno, side by side with the German. Many technical schools of all kinds were founded—agricultural, commercial, etc. and in particular those of the type known in Germany as *'Bürgerschulen'*; while the status of the teaching profession was raised to that of civil servants. Compulsory education had been introduced in Austria in 1869 —a year before the English Education Act—and the Lands of the Bohemian Crown possessed the lowest number of illiterates in the old Monarchy (actually under 3%) ; but in Slovakia and Ruthenia the whole educational machine had been subordinated to the policy of Magyarization, and one of the most burning problems in the new Republic was, as we shall see, to renovate this machine out of all recognition at the earliest possible date.

All this was the work of the first year of liberty. That the reforms did not take a still more drastic form, and in particular that the principles of laicization in the schools were not pushed to greater lengths, was due not only to the President's consistently moderating influence, but above all to the complex character of political life and the unavoidable 'give and take' between a number of parties, no single one of which could under any circumstances hope to secure an absolute majority. The proportional arrangement on which the National Assembly rested had been reached between the famous Pětka, or Coalition of five parties—the National Democrats (Kramář), Agrarians (Švehla), Social Democrats (Bechyně), National Socialists (Klofáč, Stříbraý) and Clericals (Šrámek). The Slovak Club at first maintained a separate existence, but the disruptive forces within its ranks triumphed by the end of 1919, and while the People's Party (Ludová Strana) under Hlinka continued its lone game as the strongest single party in Slovakia, though never attaining anything like an absolute majority, the Slovak Agrarians under Hodža were alone able to preserve a sort of corporate existence inside the wider Agrarian party of the Republic as a whole.

Throughout 1919 the tide of Socialism continued to rise : the municipal elections—held under a new and ultra-democratic franchise, conferring the vote on every man and woman over the age of twenty-one, with a domicile of only three months—served as a thermometer for the composition of the future Parliament. The National Democrats, heirs of the once dominant Young Czechs, to whom the 'Key' had assigned forty-six seats and four portfolios, now fell to the fourth place, the Social Democrats and Agrarians respectively polling nearly four, and nearly three, times as many votes. This was followed by the first of many turns of the political kaleidoscope : Kramář was succeeded as Premier by the Socialist leader Tusar, and the reconstructed Cabinet turned with renewed energy to social reform. But its main efforts were devoted to the passing of the new constitution, as the first step towards normalcy.

It may be affirmed without fear of challenge that this constitution at once placed Czechoslovakia on a level with the most progressive of the small states of the West—Belgium, Holland and Switzerland—and was the only one among the new states which became a reality and stood the test of time until the floodgates were opened against it by those whose duty it was to stand on guard. It is a composite product, showing traces of influence from several quarters, and not least from America.

Political power centred in a Parliament of two Chambers, based upon universal, equal, secret and direct suffrage, and Proportional Representation. The vote is exercised by all persons of both sexes over the age of twenty-one for the Chamber, and twenty-six for the Senate. Candidates for election must have attained the age of thirty or forty-five respectively.

The Presidential Powers

It is the duty of the President to convoke Parliament twice a year, in March and October, and a majority of either House has the authority to require him to summon them within fourteen days for a special session : and if he should fail to do so, the President of either Chamber possesses legal authority to convoke them without him. The President has the right to prorogue, but not for a longer period than one month, and only once in the year. He also has the right of dissolution, but not during the last six months of his tenure of office. New elections must take place within sixty days after dissolution. There is an extremely complicated system of three successive scrutinies, so designed as to reduce to a minimum the wastage of votes, and to place a certain check upon the tendency of the already too numerous parties to split up still further into tiny fractions or splinters. The allocation of surplus votes is in the hands of a special Electoral Committee, on which all parties are represented, and which also has to investigate charges of corruption and miscounts. The scrutiny method renders necessary the formation of large constituencies, with long party lists, and this militates against as close personal contacts between electors and candidates as exist under the Western constitutions even since the advent of universal suffrage has enormously swollen the number of voters in every constituency. One unexpected provision is the abolition of bye-elections ; when a deputy dies or resigns, his place is automatically filled by the next name on the successful list in that constituency.

The President himself is elected at a joint session of both Houses, at which the standing orders of the Lower House are in operation. His term of office is seven years, and he may only be once re-elected (a special exemption from this rule was laid down in the case of President Masaryk). His principal powers are fully defined under Paragraph 64, and are, it will at once be seen, very extensive. He concludes and ratifies international treaties, and as it is explicitly laid down that treaties which result in personal or military burdens being laid upon the subject, or by which territorial changes are decided, require the consent of Parliament, it would seem to follow that other treaties, to which this interpretation cannot be given, lie entirely within the presidential sphere.

He also has the power to send back with his observations any law which Parliament has adopted ; in that event both Houses vote upon it by name, and if there is still a majority in its favour, it passes into law, or if there is a three-fifths majority in the Lower, but not in the Upper House, it must again be voted verbally, but then passes into law, overriding the Upper House. If Parliament rejects a bill introduced by the Government, the latter, but only if unanimous, has the right to refer it to a popular referendum, in which every registered elector is entitled to vote—a step to which no Government of these twenty years had occasion to resort.

Among the further prerogatives of the President are the right of addressing verbal or written messages to Parliament, giving his views upon the situation of the Republic and offering his recommendations, and the granting of pardons or pensions on his Ministers' advice. He has the absolute right to appoint and dismiss his Ministers and even to add to their number. The appointment of all university professors, judges, state officials and officers of the higher ranks is also in his hands, seemingly without reserve, though doubtless in practice through the Cabinet. He may attend, and preside at, Cabinet meetings, and may demand of any individual Minister written reports on any matter falling within his competence. He holds the rank of Commander-in-Chief. An important restriction upon his powers is the clause which states that all executive functions belong to the Government, in so far as they are not expressly assigned to the President.

Another provision, presumably intended as a safeguard against undue presidential interference, is that which establishes an Executive Committee of twenty-four members, holding office from the expiry of each electoral period till the opening of the new session, and entitled to take emergency measures.

The first clause of this remarkable document[1] proclaims that 'the people is the sole source of all power in the Czechoslovak Republic.' The above summary will already have shown that the people is assumed to exercise this power in the first instance through Parliament, but that in practice it is shared between Parliament and President. Only a long political experience, perhaps of two generations, could have revealed the relative strength of the democratic and personal forces involved. The most that can as yet be affirmed is that the First President, during a tenure of office lasting seventeen years, lost no opportunity of interpreting the constitution in a democratic sense, and that his close disciple, collaborator and successor in his three years at the Hrad upheld to the full this splendid tradition, so wholly in accord with the sentiments of the Czechoslovak people. It may safely be affirmed that the safeguards and controls against all attempts to build up dictatorial powers on the part of the President, were consciously devised by Masaryk himself, who was well acquainted with historical precedents for written documents acquiring by force of time meanings and tendencies quite alien to those intended by their authors.

The Armistice and the Frontiers

While the Republic had come into being and was bracing itself for the difficult task of setting its new house in order, events in Central Europe followed a still more breakneck course. On October 24 Italy took the offensive, when Austrian resistance had become hopeless, and when

---

[1] Preceded by the Preamble already quoted on page 316, and by ten Articles providing for the transition from the National Assembly to the new Parliament.

mutiny, starvation and chaos had permeated all ranks. An army now in full disintegration poured back towards a capital which was on the very verge of famine ; and the General Staff in desperation encouraged whole-sale surrender as at least less dangerous than the revolutionary effects of dissolution. The apotheosis of Italian victory at Vittorio Veneto, so often celebrated by the Fascist chiefs, is nothing better than an impudent myth. The fundamental fact is that when the Armistice came to be concluded on November 3, there no longer existed a central authority capable of implementing its promises. Already on October 30, the Emperor Charles had handed over the fleet to the now independent Jugoslav National Council in Zagreb, in the vain hope of saving it from the Italians and the much better grounded design of setting Italians and Jugoslavs by the ears. On October 31, while Hungary was engaged in proclaiming an independent Republic under Count Michael Károlyi, the last phantom Austrian Premier, Professor Lammasch, handed over such authority as he possessed to the newly constituted 'Staatsrat' of German Austria : for another week or so he continued to perform the functions of 'liquidator' of a now bankrupt property. Meanwhile the Joint Foreign Minister, Count Andrássy, in three brief but crowded weeks of office, had undermined the Dual System of which his great father was one of the makers, and repudi-ated that alliance with Germany which his father had concluded and which had been a foundation-stone of European policy for nearly four decades. No one took his place, and the office lapsed ; Hungary had already proclaimed her independence under Count Károlyi, the Jugoslav, Czechoslovak, Polish, Ukrainian and Roumanian districts had already seceded.

If, then, the Allies in concluding the Armistice of Villa Giusti on November 3 were negotiating with men, alike civil and military, from whose hands authority was slipping hour by hour, it is also essential to point out that they were guilty of a grave blunder in leaving the details exclusively in the hands of the Italian High Command. For General Diaz concentrated his attention upon the Alpine frontier, and made no provision for the new situation in Croatia, Serbia, Transylvania and Slovakia, with results which were soon to bear bitter fruit. It was only natural that the new Government in Budapest should negotiate with Marshal Franchet d'Esperey, advancing from the Balkan front north-wards at the head of a coalition of Allied troops ; but Franchet, dis-regarding the explicit instructions sent by Clemenceau from Paris, signed an armistice with Károlyi and Oscar Jászi at Belgrade on November 12, leaving all the territory of the Crown of St. Stephen, with the express exception of Croatia-Slavonia, under Hungarian administration. This the Károlyi Government not unnaturally tried to interpret as a guarantee of Hungarian integrity, on the basis of which direct agreements, of an autonomous or perhaps federal nature, might be concluded with Zagreb, Turčiansky Sv. Martin and Alba Iulia. The impossible[1] ⊳-shaped line of demarcation laid down for Transylvania was promptly repudiated both by the Roumanian National Council, and by the Roumanian Govern-ment, sitting at Arad, whose army, at the request of its kinsmen, marched into Transylvania : on December 1 Julius Maniu, as head of the 'Consiliul Dirigent' (or provisional Government) proclaimed union with the Old Kingdom of Roumania, while the military occupation was extended even

[1] But far less impossible than the new frontier line laid down by Ribbentrop and Ciano at the Vienna Award of 1940.

X/HCS

beyond the altogether excessive boundaries laid down by Roumania's secret Treaty of August, 1916, with the *Entente*.

How Slovakia joined the Republic

At each successive stage each nation acted for itself, in the absence of any directing hand or guidance ; and Slovakia in her turn was left in mid-air. During the first few weeks, while Magyar authority crumbled and many of the officials of the old regime took refuge in 'Rump-Hungary,' order was precariously maintained by the local national councils, taking orders occasionally from the central body at St. Martin. But it was only as the legionaries from the Italian and French fronts were repatriated that it was possible to think of military occupation, and in the interval there was a certain amount of anti-Semitic looting in the small towns of the Váh valley. Dr. Šrobár himself, as delegate of the Prague Výbor, together with Paul Blaho and Anton Štefánek, advanced as far as Senica early in November, but meeting with resistance from the remnants of the Hungarian Army, found it necessary to withdraw to Žilina, which thus became the first provisional seat of government. It was not till the last days of the year that Košice, the chief town of Eastern Slovakia, fell into Slovak hands, and Bratislava was not occupied till January 4, 1919. In the central districts a mere handful of patriots took possession of the administrative machine and as it were held on by their eyebrows until help came from farther west. This piecemeal advance coincided with a series of energetic representations made by Dr. Beneš, in his new capacity as Foreign Minister and Peace Delegate, to the Allies in Paris. The consequent delays were all the more regrettable because the Hungarian Republican Government—genuinely liberal in sentiment, but naturally enough eager to save for Hungary all the territory that could still be saved—persisted in direct negotiations with Dr. Hodža, whom the Kramář Government, at an earlier stage of development, had nominated as its diplomatic agent in Budapest, and with some of his colleagues invited from St. Martin to Budapest. Early in December the French military delegate, Colonel Vyx, at last received categorical instructions to warn the Hungarian Government that the Czechoslovak troops, against whose appearance on Slovak soil it continued to protest, were a part of the victorious Allied armies, while Kramář on his side instructed Hodža to remind Károlyi of the Supreme Council's decision in favour of Czecho-slovak unity. But the result of all this to and fro was that two quite divergent lines of demarcation were drawn in Budapest and in Paris, the former leaving Bratislava and the important Žitný Ostrov (Csallóköz, or Wheat Island) in the Danube still in Hungarian hands and preparing the way for future misunderstandings. Indeed, it was the note addressed by Colonel Vyx in March, 1919, to Budapest, demanding the evacuation of various districts situated between these two divergent lines, that was mainly responsible for the collapse of the Károlyi Government and its replacement by the Bolshevik regime of Béla Kun. This, though it was completely discredited in five months of office and then fell like a stone, not only did infinite harm in the domestic field by the excesses of Szamuely and others, but also envenomed relations between Budapest and both Prague and Bratislava, by leaving the Magyars with a lively sense of grievance.

Bratislava (Pressburg, Pozsony) now became the capital of Slovakia, despite a considerable current of opinion which would have preferred either Žilina or St. Martin, as more central and less exposed to external attack. Here was set up the so-called 'Government Office,' the administrative headquarters of the 'Ministry for Slovakia,' to whose first holder, Dr. Vavro Šrobár, special emergency powers were assigned. Under him were thirteen Referents, or heads of Government departments, forming to all intents and purposes a sub-Cabinet, well suited to deal with the abnormal problems presented by this period of transition. This initial trend in favour of a healthy decentralization was abruptly arrested by two decisive factors—the extreme shortage of qualified Slovak officials, and the series of attempts on the part of the Magyars to reimpose their rule. It was difficult enough to fill the posts of the thirteen Referents and of the Župans or Prefects of the seventeen counties taken over from Hungary ; yet it can be definitely affirmed that they rose nobly to the occasion, and that several of them—in particular Kállay, Kornel Stodola, Blaho, Štefánek, Okáňik, Bella and Ivánka—made valuable and permanent contributions to the new order. The choice was very limited, for it is a matter of common knowledge that the number of educated and nationally conscious Slovaks in 1918 did not exceed 750 to 1,000 ! In Eastern Slovakia in particular, where the Magyar regime had not tolerated the growth of a Slovak intelligentsia, hardly a single candidate for office was available. Under that regime only 35 out of 12,447 officials had had the courage or the inclination to return themselves as Slovaks, or again only 18 out of the 948 county officials, only 33 out of the 1,133 notaries, only 10 out of the 660 professors at secondary schools and not a single one out of the 464 judges and Crown law officials.

This desperate plight rendered the employment of Czech officials in Slovakia altogether inevitable ; but instead of being introduced according to plan, it was actually improvised to meet a sudden emergency. For the Magyars, realizing the extreme weakness of the new regime, tried to paralyse it altogether by organizing a general strike of the railwaymen and post office employees throughout the seventeen counties ; and disaster was only narrowly averted. In response to the urgent appeal of the Railway Referent, Kornel Stodola, several thousand patriotic Czech volunteers hurried from Bohemia and Moravia and at a moment's notice took over the vacant posts and kept the essential services running. When the crisis was over, the Magyar saboteurs could not be reinstated, but the new-comers ere long found themselves regarded as intruders, filling posts which ought to be held by born Slovaks, apparently quite irrespective of those qualifications and standards to which the authorities in Bratislava and Prague very properly attached great importance.

The strike having failed, the Magyars tried more drastic methods. On May 20 their Army invaded Slovakia from Lučenec and nearly succeeded in cutting it into two distinct halves. The Czechs held them with difficulty, but the incident roused the Council of Four in Paris to address to the Kun Government a stiff note demanding evacuation, and on June 12 to fix the Slovak-Magyar frontier. Kun's inevitable submission robbed his Government of the little prestige which it had ever possessed, and his rash attempt to recover it by attacking the Roumanians along the Tisza failed disastrously, and gave Bratianu an excuse for occupying Budapest. This brought down the Bolshevik Government with a crash, and the reactionary regime which took its place—opening with the White Terror of Horthy, Gömbös and Hejjás—was absorbed in domestic affairs and unable to challenge the situation which had arisen in Slovakia. It was not, however, till June 4, 1920, that the Treaty of Trianon stabilized the situation along the Slovak-Hungarian frontier and the long delay, due mainly to the absorption of the Powers in major problems of world-policy, did much to exacerbate the relations of two peoples who had so dramatically changed places as upper and under dog.

Ruthenia

There still remained the thorny problem of the Ruthenes of Hungary, far more isolated than ever were their Slovak neighbours—and indeed separated by mountains and forests from the mass of their Ukrainian kinsmen in Eastern Galicia, Bukovina and the Russian Ukraine. Moreover, they had been deliberately held by the Magyars in complete cultural isolation, deprived of all teaching in their own language, unrepresented in Parliament and even in the local assemblies, and seemingly ripe for final assimilation. There is a certain poetical justice in the fact that as extreme neglect and poverty drove them to emigrate in ever larger numbers, it was among these emigrants in the United States that the first demand for autonomy made itself heard. A Congress was held at Homestead (Pa.) in July, 1918, to discuss possible alternatives—full independence, which to all but a few seemed from the first impracticable, or various degrees of autonomy under Hungary, Russia or Czechoslovakia. It was to the latter that a majority inclined, in proportion as Russia disintegrated and the Ukrainian state showed symptoms of infant paralysis, while Hungary seemed doomed to fall into a series of national units. The leader of the American Uniates, Dr. Žatkovič, won over a second Congress at Scranton (Pa.) in December, 1918, in favour of union with Czechoslovakia ; he had already had an exchange of views with Masaryk before the latter returned to Europe, and he himself became the first Governor of autonomous Ruthenia, though he afterwards grew discontented at the slowness of the pace and returned to America. Meanwhile the three Ruthene National Councils which had sprung up at home in Hungary during the period of initial collapse—at Prešov, Užhorod and Hust, each starting from a different angle—found the absolute necessity for amalgamation, and issued a joint Declaration of Union with Czechoslovakia on May 8, 1919, under the somewhat clumsy and provisional name of 'Sub-Carpathian Ruthenia.' This document spoke of 'an independent state inside the Czechoslovak Republic,' 'a provisional or Ruthene *de facto* state,' under a Ruthene Minister nominated by the President, but in his turn appointing administrative and executive officials. The final statute was drawn up in Paris, and included in the Minority Treaty which Czechoslovakia signed simultaneously with the Treaty of St. Germain ; and it was also incorporated as part of the Constitutional Statute of February 29, 1920. Its essential points are a pledge of 'the widest autonomy compatible with the unity of the Republic,' a separate Diet, use of the language in education and administration, due representation in the Central Parliament, and the filling of official posts 'so far as possible by natives.' We shall see that remarkable progress was made during twenty years in this most backward, illiterate and divided province, but that what many Ruthenes regarded as the crowning obligation, the functioning of a freely elected Diet, had still been withheld when the First Republic fell in 1938. Ruthenia's main importance was strategic, whether it was to serve as a link with Russia, or as a focus for the oppressed Ukrainians beyond the mountains in Poland, or as a means of assuring contact between Czechoslovakia and Roumania. Since then there have been several turns of the political kaleidoscope, but it is safe to predict that Ruthenia will once more play a part out of all proportion to its remote and still backward status.

The Germans of Bohemia

Parallel with this development in the territories acquired from Hungary one of Dr. Beneš's main tasks in Paris was to secure a regulation of the crucial problem of the German minority, which at the first census of the new Republic (in 1921) was returned as 3,100,000 out of 13,600,000, and by 1930 had risen to 3,230,000—a lower increase than that of the other three races of the Republic.

Already on October 21, 1918, a German National Committee had been formed in Vienna and had announced its intention of negotiating with the Czechs and Jugoslavs, among whom at this late date there was little or no response. On October 29 the German deputies from Bohemia held a special meeting in Vienna and declared 'German-Bohemia' to be a part of 'the state of German Austria.' The Nationalist deputy, Dr. von Lodgmann, was elected as Landeshauptmann, and it was decided to convoke a Diet at Reichenberg, the main German centre in North-east Bohemia. The very next day another province was proclaimed under the name of 'Sudetenland'—afterwards to be used in a more comprehensive and less accurate form—with its centre at Troppau ; and in the first days of November two smaller mushroom governments sprang up at Krumau and Znaim, known as the 'Böhmerwaldgau' and 'German South Moravia.' These steps were approved by the new National Assembly in Vienna, but the rival Assembly in Prague insisted upon the historic frontiers of Bohemia. Neither Lodgmann nor the able and more moderate Socialist leader Seliger had any success with their proposed negotiations ; and indeed the supremely tactless Rašín flung at the latter's head the phrase with which Prince Windischgrätz had dismissed a Hungarian deputation in 1848—"With rebels I don't negotiate." Austria was in no state to resist the stern discouragement of the Supreme Council, and the first enthusiasm for union with Germany cooled off as the Austrians saw the chaos and financial insecurity in the Reich threatening to throw their own troubles into the shade. And meanwhile geography proved very clearly that the four scattered and detached German districts of the Crown of Saint Wenceslas might be united with Bavaria, Saxony, Silesia and independent Austria respectively, but could hardly form a single unit of government. Left to their own resources they were powerless, and by the end of 1918 Czech troops were in occupation of all four centres and the tentative Governments dissolved. This was effected almost without bloodshed, but on March 4 there were regrettable clashes and loss of life when the Czech authorities forbade their German citizens to participate in the general elections to the new Austrian Parliament.

A week earlier the Council of Four accepted the historic frontiers of Bohemia ; and at a later date considerable play was made with the fact that Dr. Beneš submitted to the Conference a series of memoranda containing exaggerations and inaccuracies. In his memoirs he has quite frankly admitted this, but it cannot seriously be suggested that their omission would have altered the decision, for the French were in an entirely intransigeant mood and opposed the slightest concessions in favour of Germany. On the other hand, too much should not be made of the fact that Masaryk and Beneš were ready to cede the Egerland in return for Glatz, and if opinion at the Conference had flowed strongly in that direction, would perhaps have accepted other frontier modifications. They would certainly have held out, and quite rightly, for the great industrial districts near the northern frontier, and probably for Karlsbad and the neighbouring spas ; and the Germans on their side, when once they saw the veto upon the Anschluss to be definite, opposed any project calculated to reduce the numbers, and hence the powers of resistance, of their kinsmen left behind in the Republic. Moreover, it was at this point that quite a number of strong economic arguments led many Germans, both employers and workmen, even those most hostile to the Czechs, to discover a common interest in maintaining Bohemian unity after eight hundred years. The unemployment and privations following upon the Depression of 1931 produced a relapse of opinion, but by 1936 the old arguments were reviving and would have made good, if the international situation had remained calm.

The Conference settles the Frontiers

On April 17 the Supreme Council gave its decision in favour of the historic frontier, and this was embodied in the Treaties of Versailles and St. Germain. Quite illogically, it made three exceptions, each, it is true, of a minor character, but well calculated to rankle in the German mind : these were two rectifications of the southern frontier at Austria's expense, near Gmünden and at Feldsberg, and the cession by Germany of the Hlučín salient in Western Silesia, where 80% of the population were Czech. The rectifications proposed by the French expert, General Lerond, and accepted by Dr. Beneš, would have reduced the number of Germans in the Republic by some 800,000 ; but the Supreme Council disliked the aggrandizement of Germany, no matter for what reason. Clemenceau's intransigeant views carried the day, and the historic argument was unwisely pushed to its extreme limit in Bohemia, while at the same moment the nationalist argument was applied with an excess of generosity all along the Slovak-Magyar frontier. On the other hand even Clemenceau felt unable to give any backing to two additional pleas introduced among the Czechoslovak claims before the Conference—a special status for Lusatia and a corridor to link Slovakia with Croatia. The former related to that sympathetic little Slav people the Sorbs (closely akin to the Wends of Brandenburg), of which considerable linguistic fragments still survived in the country north-east of Dresden, but which had formed part of Saxony since the year 1635, and could not under any imaginable circumstances have been included in the new Republic. The latter rested on the undoubted fact that all along the western borders of Hungary from the Danube southwards there were scattered Slav colonies—mainly the so-called 'Water Croats' ; but the idea that a long strip of racially mixed territory should have been assigned jointly to Czechoslovakia and Jugoslavia, with the double purpose of giving the two allies a common frontier and of isolating Hungary from Germany, was altogether too fantastic to be entertained by any of the victors. The support given by Masaryk and Beneš to these two 'stunts'—for they hardly deserve the name of proposals—was the one solitary instance of their departure from sweet reasonableness amid all the pitfalls of the Paris settlement ; and it may be assumed that they yielded to political pressure from enthusiasts at home who would take no refusal. If it be true that the adoption of a purely ethnographic frontier for Czechoslovakia 'would have left her so entirely defenceless as to be incapable of independent life,' it is no less true that the acquisition of Lusatia and the Corridor would have confronted the new state with absolutely insoluble problems of defence. The rejection of two such questionable pleas left the Conference on solid ground when it laid down 'that ethnographic reasons cannot be the only ones to be taken into account,' and quoted the inclusion of 3,000,000 Germans in Czechoslovakia as the foremost illustration of this undoubted fact.

The inclusion of three million Germans and three-quarters of a million Magyars placed Czechoslovakia high on the list of countries faced by a minority problem ; and in a much-canvassed Memorandum of May 20, 1919, Dr. Beneš forestalled criticism by undertaking to make of Czechoslovakia 'a sort of Switzerland,' in which the minorities, sharing with all its citizens universal and proportional suffrage, would also possess their own language in the schools, the local administration, and the courts of law, and have access to public office, German ranking as the second language in the state. To all this was added the perfectly proper qualification—a sort of Switzerland, 'taking into consideration the special conditions of Bohemia.' As in the case of Poland, Jugoslavia, and other reconstituted states which acquired territory from the enemy, Czechoslovakia was required by the Supreme Council to sign a special Minority Treaty, and wisely refrained from the acrimonious protests lodged by the Roumanians, Poles and Jugoslavs. But they shared their allies' annoyance at the arrogance with which the Great Powers excluded those most directly concerned from all consultation, and excluded themselves from any such undertakings as they were now dictating to the lesser Powers. Dr. Beneš was therefore among the immediate signatories of the Treaty of St. Germain on September 10, 1919, and signed the Minority Treaty on the same day. But Czechoslovakia went a stage further, and simultaneously with her new Constitution of 1920 adopted a Law of Nationalities which went considerably further than what was demanded of her by the Powers, still more what her neighbours were willing to concede. We shall see later that Czechoslovakia alone of all the lesser states can claim, with certain qualifications, to have fulfilled her obligations to the minorities.

The Teschen Dispute

A most urgent frontier dispute arose between the Czechoslovak and Polish states in connection with the little Duchy of Teschen, one of the three fragments of Silesia which Austria had succeeded in preserving from the onslaughts of Frederick the Great. In 1910 the Duchy, which had been granted in 1858 by Francis Joseph in his capacity as King of Bohemia, to his cousin Archduke Albert (the future victor of Custozza in 1866), had a total population of 426,370, of whom 233,000 were Poles, 115,000 Czechs and 76,000 Germans. What gave it its importance was that it had become 'one of the most highly industrialized and densely populated areas' in all Austria, and formed part of the Silesian coalfield. It was the output of the Teschen mines that supplied the Vitkovice ironworks and many other industries of vital importance for Moravia and for the Republic as a whole. Moreover, the railway line running through

Teschen from Bohemia (Oderberg) to Žilina was at that time a vital connecting link between the Czech districts and the whole of northern Slovakia : and though the development of transversal connections from the Morava valley to the Váh valley has diminished its importance, it still continues to be of far more vital concern to Czechoslovakia than to Poland.

In the closing period of the War this question was amiably discussed by Masaryk and Paderewski, then both in America, and it was agreed between them that it should be settled by direct friendly agreement after the war. In due course the two National Committees, Polish and Czechoslovak, which took over temporary control in Silesia after the fall of Austria, agreed upon a provisional, more or less ethnographical, frontier across the disputed zone, and the final decision was left open by both parties. In December, 1918, however, the Poles authorized elections to the Warsaw Parliament in the territory occupied by them, and in January, 1919, the Czechs retorted by occupying both Bohumin and Teschen. A Commission was appointed by the Paris Conference to investigate the dispute on the spot, and meanwhile a provisional line of occupation was laid down.

As no direct agreement could be reached at Paris, the Supreme Council in September, 1919, decided upon a plebiscite in the whole Duchy of Teschen, and also in certain disputed districts of Orava and Spiš. The Commission charged with its execution arrived in January, 1920 : but local unrest grew steadily, both sides showed an uncompromising disposition, and there were strikes and rioting. By the end of May there was a serious danger of a diplomatic rupture between Prague and Warsaw. The Council of Ambassadors in Paris, acting on behalf of the Supreme Council, urged the disputants to accept a settlement by arbitration : but this was rejected by the Czechoslovak National Assembly, while the Polish Parliament opposed the alternative suggestion of a plebiscite. Eventually, on July 11, 1920, MM. Beneš and Grabski, by joint consent, invited the Supreme Council to suspend the plebiscites and to make a decision after hearing the two parties. By the award of the four Ambassadors, announced on July 28, the Duchy was divided between Poland and Czechoslovakia, the latter retaining the town of Frýstat and the main railway line, but the town of Teschen being included in Poland. Several parishes in the Counties of Orava and Spiš were also detached from Slovakia and assigned to Poland on ethnographic grounds.

There can be little doubt that this settlement was the fairest attainable, and represented a reasonable compromise. But the Poles, despite the fact that they had acquired large tracts of non-Polish territory on every frontier on grounds of economic expediency, attached an altogether exaggerated importance to this little corner of land which meant so much to Czech industry and communications. They nursed a grievance, and twenty years later took an opportunity of reversing the decision by unilateral action, to their own subsequent undoing. This grievance, it is but fair to say, was augmented by the feeling that the Czechs had taken advantage of their weakness during the Russo-Polish War of 1920 to extract concessions and decisions which could not have been obtained in times of peace.

The Pětka and the Parties

The first general elections held under the new constitution and franchise represented the peak of Socialist influence in the control of the state (one hundred and thirty-nine seats fell to the Socialists as against one hundred and forty-six to the bourgeois groups) ; but the reconstructed Tusar Cabinet found itself increasingly between two fires—from the dwindling but still very active National Democrats on the Right and the 'bolchevisant' wing of its own party on the Left, while the Agrarians were steadily building up a solid Central *bloc*. Tusar's moderate attitude to the Germans met with little or no response in rabid Sudeten circles, and ran counter to the prevalent mood of Jingoism among the Czechs ; while his Government was blamed for consenting to a compromise in the vexed question of Teschen. The latent crisis reached its height in September, 1920, when the Left wing of the Socialists tried to force the whole party to accept affiliation with the Moscow International ; and though the attempt failed, it split the party into two and caused the fall of the Government. President Masaryk, who had submitted himself to re-election in the summer, now formed a Cabinet of officials under Dr. Černý, one of the ablest bureaucrats whom the Republic had inherited from the Austrian regime ; and when the extremists launched a general strike, which was intended to end in a revolutionary *putsch*, Černý was ready for them and liquidated the movement in three days without bloodshed—to the immense astonishment of a large section of the diplomatic corps, which had convinced itself that the Czechs were on the verge of Bolshevism.

It would lead far beyond the purpose of this book to attempt even a survey of the complex party politics of the Republic during its twenty years ; it will suffice to indicate certain fundamental trends of opinion. First and foremost stands the pronouncedly and consciously democratic outlook of the nation as a whole. The fissiparous party tendencies followed from this quite logically, and were inherent in the complex structure of the state, in the balance of rural and urban interests, of conservative and radical religious views, of language and cultural development. For it is not too much to say that between the west and east of the Republic there was a difference of several centuries, due to geographical no less than political causes. Nowhere was a more strenuous attempt made to apply the theories of proportional representation in practice, and nowhere were its inherent difficulties more clearly illustrated. At the elections of 1920 there were no fewer than eleven Czech and Slovak, seven German and four Magyar parties, but of these five had the decisive word, and their central committee of five, the so-called 'Pětka,' became the real directive force, in conjunction with the President, who used it as a pocket telescope which required constant adjustment to a new focus. This complicated balance of forces had its very obvious drawbacks from the angle of any individual party imbued with the urgency of its programme, or even merely eager to win votes by delivering the goods which it had promised ; but when once the instrument had been forged and was in skilful hands—and this was so under the 'President-Liberator' and his successor—it made for a stability rare among the states of central Europe. In the case of the Socialists this embarrassment was especially apparent, because they had already actually realized most of what was immediately realizable, while all parties were still in the stage of 'the first fine careless rapture.' But ere long it became clear to all who rejected subversive or wrecking methods, that the only choice lay between a definite Coalition of the Czechoslovak parties on a national basis—which meant the subordination of social to national aims—or the abandonment of the strictly national basis and a regrouping according to social aims. On two occasions

—in 1920 and again in 1926—the President resorted to Cabinets of officials, until the parties could be induced to regroup themselves according to the needs of a new situation.

The second general election, in 1925, weakened the Socialists at the expense of the Centre and Right, and led to the break-up of the so-called 'Red-Green *Bloc*.' In 1926, for the first time, a purely bourgeois Government was formed, under the Agrarian leader Švehla, leaving both groups of Socialists in opposition, and including—also for the first time—representatives of four out of the seven German groups and also of the Slovak Clericals. This was something of a landmark in the history of the Republic, for it meant that the principal minority was at last willing to co-operate in the building of the state, and that the largest party in Slovakia had abandoned its negative obstruction. This co-operation was obtained at the triple price of abandoning extreme centralism, of toning down anti-clerical tendencies and of stiffening tariffs in the interest of the Agrarians. In a word, decentralization, activism, protection, ecclesiastical peace, were four notable elements in the shifting of the political balance.

The far-reaching administrative reforms of 1927 had a calming effect in more than one direction. In Slovakia the exaggerated centralism of the Law of 1923—which replaced the seventeen counties of the old Hungary by six needlessly large Župas—had caused considerable dissatisfaction on purely technical as well as political grounds ; and the Law of 1927 was a welcome reversal, though it did not go nearly far enough for the fanatics of the Hlinka Party. Its main effect was to place Slovakia, as a single unit, on an equal footing with Bohemia and Moravia (Ruthenia, thanks to geographical and ethnographic reasons, had a special position of its own), and to give it a Provincial President invested with wide powers, and an elected Provincial Assembly of fifty-four members, in many respects similar to the Diets of earlier days. The district assemblies were also democratized, though the permanent officials still retained a measure of that influence which had been traditional under Hungary ; very great possibilities in the direction of local self-government were thus opened up. The more reasonable mood of Prague, as revealed in these concessions, served as an encouragement to a majority of the Germans to adopt a policy of 'activism.' Before the previous elections the 70 German deputies in Parliament had been split up as follows : 24 Agrarians (Bund der Landwirte), 12 Christian Socialists, 18 Social Democrats, 10 German Nationalists and 6 National Socialists. The two first of these now entered the Government, Professors Spina and Mayr-Harting obtaining the portfolios of Public Works and Justice ; and when the Socialists gained ground again at the elections of 1929, Mayr-Harting withdrew in favour of Dr. Czech, leader of the German Socialists, leaving 34 out of 70 Germans opposed to activism.

Religious Problems

Parallel with a slackening of the tide of Centralism the religious issue assumed a much calmer aspect. The upheaval of 1918 had been followed by a wave of anti-clerical feeling. It is not surprising that it should have found strong expression in Czechoslovakia, for throughout the old Austria —German and Czech districts alike—a large proportion of the academic and intellectual classes had become estranged from the Catholic Church, and anti-clerical feelings were especially rife in the teaching profession.

The Czechs had an additional incentive, in that the hierarchy was associated with the dynasty, which they had good reason to regard as hostile to their national cause. As a result of the Revolution, the official pressure which under the Habsburgs had been steadily exercised in favour of the Church, suddenly ceased ; the state became as it were neutral in religious questions, and the question of separation of Church and State came into the forefront of discussion. There were wholesale secessions from the Church, swelling the ranks of those who returned themselves as 'without church connection' (*Konfessionslos*). Quite apart from this, a new 'Czecho-slovak Church' was founded, whose adherents soon swelled from five hundred thousand to close on a million. After introducing marriage of the clergy and wavering for a time between the 'Old Catholics,' Orthodoxy and Evangelical Protestantism, it came down very definitely on the side of the latter, and has developed close contacts with the Protestant Episcopal Churches of the West. Its sympathies for modernist theology, of the type favoured in Germany and Scotland under the name of the higher criticism, soon subsided into a mood of calm and tolerant Protestant orthodoxy.

Meanwhile the wilder spirits were in the first two years guilty of regrettable excesses, such as the destruction of monuments associated with the Jesuit era ; this kept pace with a movement of iconoclasm directed against statues of the Habsburgs or of Hungarian national heroes. There was at one moment a design for the overthrow of St. John Nepomuk's statue on the Charles Bridge in Prague. More serious, if more justified, was the decision to remove the crucifix from the schools, and to rescind the law making divorce impossible (in Austria, though not in Hungary, the marriage laws had hitherto been identical with the Roman Canon Law). On the other hand, the Republic continued to be responsible for the Congrua (or contributions to the salaries of clergy of all recognized denominations).

The alarm eagerly spread abroad by the enemies of the Republic at what they affected to regard as symptoms of imminent Bolshevization soon subsided as it became obvious that the Catholic Church of Bohemia was fully equal to the situation and that the secession of indifferent or secretly hostile adherents, so far from being a loss, was rather of the nature of the dropping of useless ballast. The secular clergy, always patriotic and active in good works, now rose to the emergency, while the hierarchy was purged of Germanism and reaction, which had so long gone hand in hand. Archbishop Kordač, and after him Cardinal Kašpar, showed moderation and statesmanship, and such men as Mgr Zavoral, Abbot of the Premonstratensians of Strahov, were held in universal esteem. There was a last recrudescence of religious strife in the summer of 1924, when the Nuncio, Mgr Marmaggi, left Prague out of protest at the Government's participation in the Hus celebrations. But the ensuing negotiations between Prague and the Vatican led eventually to a compromise which all save the fanatics welcomed. The anti-Clericals had by this time come to see that they were not strong enough to enforce absolute separation, while Rome held it to be more politic to accept the limited but very valuable concessions offered by Dr. Beneš, who could carry the Left parties with him, rather than gamble upon the advent of some Foreign Minister of the Right, who might never materialize, but would in any case probably be repudiated ere very long.

The *modus vivendi* of January, 1928, was an honourable truce between

Church and State ; it rested on a recognition of the indisputable fact that Czechoslovakia is a predominantly Catholic country, yet that the majority of its citizens are opposed to Clerical rule and firmly wedded to religious equality and mutual tolerance. It is this peculiarly Czech mentality that explains the fact that Hus, though denounced by the Church as a heretic, is revered by many good Catholics for his national leadership, and again that many good Catholics have always preferred to record their votes for one of the purely secular parties, rather than for one whose basis is specifically Catholic. It would be a very crude mistake to estimate the number of practising Catholics in the Republic by the number of votes polled by the Clerical parties. The celebrations in honour of the Millenary of St. Wenceslas in July and September, 1929—culminating in the completion of the splendid medieval Cathedral of St. Vitus in Prague—and the ceremonies connected with the Eucharistic Congress in Prague some years later—provided eloquent proof of the strength of religious sentiment among the widest masses, and of the extent to which public sentiment, after the first stormy decade, was returning to normality. If Czechoslovakia could be described as politically an ideal half-way house between the extremes of the Right and the Left, it was partly because the Catholic Church was strong enough to prevent the complete triumph of the latter, but not sufficiently strong to establish a conservative ascendancy. Highly characteristic of the growing calm was the attempt to exalt the figure of St. Wenceslas—a prince of whom but little is known beyond his estimable character, his leanings towards a German alliance and his premature and tragic end—as a compromise candidate between the heretic Hus and the half-mythical John of Nepomuk, to whom the Jesuits in their days of triumph had assigned a role which would have greatly astonished him and his contemporaries.

Parallel with the revivification of Catholicism in the Czech lands Protestantism also made great progress. The ancient Church of the Brethren, with its fine tradition of learning and missionary zeal, was linked up with the smaller Calvinist bodies into a single whole, while the Slovak Lutherans, set free from Magyar pressure, entered upon a new lease of life. The Hus Protestant Faculty in Prague soon became a real centre of religious teaching. In the second decade of the Republic the 'Czechoslovak Church' passed from the stage of propaganda to that of consolidation and social work, while free thought, once so militant, receded into the background.

[1] It may help the reader to have before him the two religious censuses of 1921 and 1930 :

Roman Catholic	10,381,833	..	10,831,696
Greek Catholic (Uniate)	535,543	..	585,041
Czechoslovak Church	525,333	..	793,385
Orthodox	75,097	..	145,598
Jews	354,342	..	356,630
Protestants	976,156	..	1,129,758
Without church connection (Konfessionslos)	727,507	..	854,638
	13,713,172	..	14,479,565

The Protestants fall into four portions :

Church of the Bohemian Brethren	233,868
Lutheran Church of Bohemia	150,687
Lutheran Church of Slovakia	384,495
Calvinist Church of Slovakia	207,106

Friction in Slovakia

It was necessary to pay special attention to the religious issue, because nothing contributed so much to the friction that arose between Slovaks and Czechs after the brief honeymoon of the first two years. There was from the first a profound 'incompatibility of temper' between the two kinsmen, due to long centuries of Slovak isolation from Western currents, followed by two generations of assimilation and 'Magyarone' outlook. The Slovak leaders admitted in conversation that Slovakia could not be administered or successfully held against the Magyars without Czech help, yet in the same breath they denounced the Czech volunteers in their midst and put forward claims which, if conceded, would have produced immediate chaos. The Czech volunteers, who had saved the situation during the railway strike of 1919, were by now unpopular, as an obstacle to the promotion of local candidates ; their efficiency, their trade union rates and their somewhat narrow free-thinking ideas were equally distasteful to a country till then run on oligarchic lines. Yet it was absolutely impossible to find really qualified judges or high officials without either having recourse to the 'Czech Lands' or bringing down standards with a run ; and when it came to the University of Bratislava, there were only eight possible Slovak candidates for University chairs, and even of these some did not really qualify according to normal standards.

Meanwhile the personal element played an important part ; and Slovak questions were only too soon grouped round the rivalry of two men who had first entered the political arena in close accord, in their native town of Ružomberok—Father Andrew Hlinka, eloquent, passionate, a churchman of the twelfth rather than the twentieth century, and Dr. Vavro Šrobár, a doctor of progressive and even sceptical outlook, already identified with strongly Czechophil and centralist views. Fate would have it that Šrobár became the delegate of St. Martin to the provisional Government in Prague, and though he grouped around him, as Referents and Župans, most of the men who had exposed themselves in the conflict with the Magyars, there was one conspicuous absentee— Hlinka. The cause of this was that as early as January, 1919, Šrobár resisted the demands of some leading Catholic clergy that Hlinka should be forthwith appointed as Slovak Patriarch. To this Šrobár very properly demurred, on the ground that the office was not his to confer, and that any such act would embroil the new Republic in an acute conflict with the Holy See. But it was at once apparent that behind the impulsive and idolized patriot Hlinka there lurked the sinister figure of Father Jehlička, who had stood for Parliament as a Slovak nationalist in 1907 but had withdrawn from politics on orders from the Magyar Primate, and now after twelve years of silence emerged as a super-patriot. This archintriguer gradually induced Hlinka to draw apart from the Slovak Club, then to address to the Peace Conference a memorandum in favour of Slovak autonomy, and finally, in company with Jehlička, to visit first Warsaw, then Paris, in search of help against the Czechs. Before it was too late, Hlinka drew back and returned to Slovakia, leaving Jehlička to launch out upon a campaign of intrigue and calumny against the Republic and after twenty years of exile to die as a paid agent of Budapest.[1]

[1] When in 1933 Jehlička accompanied Count Stephen Bethlen on his propagandist tour to England, a letter was signed by all Slovak deputies and senators of the Prague Parliament (other than the Communist group) disowning Jehlička as a traitor to the Slovak cause.

Hlinka, who with many high qualities combined a fatal inability to judge men, directed his party, the Ludová Strana, more and more into channels hostile to Prague, and in August, 1922, issued its so-called 'Žilina Memorandum,' demanding a somewhat ill-defined 'Autonomy' for the Slovaks and accusing 'Prague' and the President himself, of a breach of faith in not executing the Treaties (in itself, of course, a deliberate misnomer, since they were in no sense treaties) of Cleveland (October, 1915) and Pittsburgh (May, 1918). The latter expressly recognized in its concluding clause that its signatories in the United States were in no way competent to bind the nation to their views, and that only the nation itself, after liberation, could decide. It is most characteristic of the strange mentality of the Slovak Clericals that in the teeth of this they continued to operate with charges of bad faith, and even to distribute facsimiles of the 'treaty,' in which, of course, the final clause could be read.

On the other hand, the situation was aggravated by the centralizing tendencies which for a time prevailed at Prague while the Socialist tide was running strongest ; and long before it turned again, in 1926, in favour of decentralization, the cleavage between the Clerical and Progressive elements in Slovakia had become stereotyped. The mischief was increased by the existence of a strong 'Magyarone' element among the Slovak Catholic clergy, which completely differentiated them from the admirably patriotic clergy of Bohemia and Moravia and rendered them hostile to what would have been a natural co-operation between the two Clerical parties of the two halves of the Republic. Behind this was the unhappy fact that Hlinka, having emancipated himself at the eleventh hour from the influence of Jehlička, now fell under the spell of the much more insidious and elusive Adalbert Tuka, who had held a chair at the Magyar University of Pressburg (Bratislava), had returned himself as a Magyar at the census of 1921, and now, though speaking his Slovak mother tongue somewhat imperfectly, became chief editor of Slovák, the official organ of the Hlinka Party and the champion of racial exclusivism and linguistic purity. Tuka's whole efforts were for years directed towards poisoning the relations between Slovaks and Czechs and maintaining a state of uncertainty which suited the Magyar propagandists of treaty revision, but no one else. In particular he persisted in repeating the legend of a secret clause in the St. Martin Declaration of October 30, 1918, limiting the sanction then accorded to a period of ten years ; in that event, unless the existing regime were thrown overboard, a *vacuum juris* would result in October, 1928, and Slovakia would be free to reconsider everything. This was water to the mill of Lord Rothermere, who in 1927 launched a reckless and ill-informed campaign for the revision of the Treaty of Trianon, and roused Magyar opinion to hysterical heights. The lengths to which adulation was carried in Hungary during the more than royal progress of Esmond Harmsworth are shown by two incidents. Eugene Rakosi, the veteran playwright and editor, drew a comparison with the Trinity : the Father, he said, had sent his only Son to Hungary, and the Holy Spirit could be seen hovering over his head ! A former Minister of Agriculture, writing in the official *Pester Lloyd*, declared that Rothermere by his articles in the *Daily Mail* (containing crass mistakes, such as must have hit him and every serious Magyar in the face) had performed a similar act to that of Luther in affixing his theses to the church door at Wittenberg ! And two of Hungary's chief assets in this campaign were Tuka and Jehlička, the former backed by all the perverse energy of the genuinely anti-Magyar Hlinka, the latter conducting his agitation from a bureau in Vienna financed by the Budapest Government.

The administrative reform of 1927 (see p. 000) was the work of the last Švehla Cabinet, in which the Agrarians were the finger on the balance. Milan Hodža, leader of the Slovak section of that party, enjoyed great influence with the Premier and wisely contented himself with instalments of autonomy won by co-operation with Prague rather than the stormy 'all or nothing' demands of Hlinka and the wirepullers of the Ludová Strana. The new Law specially affected Slovakia, for the six Župas erected in 1921 in place of the seventeen Hungarian counties, were again abolished, and new machinery was erected : a Provincial President, appointed by the Central Government, but responsible to an elected Assembly, with its own budget and an elected executive Committee enjoying certain strictly defined powers. The name of Diet was deliberately avoided, and a brake—some thought too heavy for so slight a structure—was imposed upon possible extremism by the addition of one-third of nominated members. This was a not very democratic reversion to the practice of the old Hungarian county assemblies, where one half were 'virilists' (or highest taxpayers) and certain officials sat *ex officio*. The effect was greatly to increase the importance of Bratislava, as administrative capital, and to a lesser degree of Košice as the chief town of Eastern Slovakia ; the drawbacks of concentrating in the extreme south-west corner were only too obvious, but Bratislava's position in Danubian river trade and in the grain exchange outweighed other objections.

The reform of 1927 did not of course satisfy the extreme autonomists, but it led to a considerable calming of opinion, and Mgr Hlinka, though he himself declined to enter the Government, allowed two of his followers to accept office—one of them being Father Tiso, afterwards President of Hitler's puppet Slovak state. This party, it should be noted, was always the largest single party in Slovakia, but never obtained more than a proportion varying from 25% to 40% of the total votes cast. For a brief period it now seemed as though the *modus vivendi* with the Vatican, concluded in January, 1928, would help still further to calm down ruffled feelings. The three first Slovak Bishops were appointed in 1921, and three more sees were administered by apostolic delegates ; but the revival of a Slovak Archbishopric, dormant since the days of St. Methodius, was still delayed, owing to the difficulty of redrawing the boundaries of the border sees, which were still under the jurisdiction of the Cardinal Primate of Hungary. What made inevitable a fresh breach between the People's Party and all unionist groups both in Slovakia and in the Czech lands, was Tuka's action in reviving the legend of the *Vacuum Juris* and warning his opponents that unless the constitution were modified in an autonomist sense by October 30, 1928, the existing laws would lose their validity, taxes could lawfully be withheld and the Slovaks would be free to decide their fate *de novo*. In July, 1929, Tuka was put on trial, with the party secretary Šaňo Mach, and after proceedings lasting ten weeks was convicted of espionage, betrayal of military secrets to a foreign power, planning the secession of Slovakia from the Republic, and forming 'Rodobrana' detachments to promote this aim. He was proved to have been in contact with the traitor Jehlička and the Magyar propaganda, and richly deserved his sentence of fifteen years' imprisonment. Hlinka made the grave blunder of declining to repudiate Tuka after this sentence, and paid rather cheaply for this by the loss of five seats at the general election of October,

1929. Udržal, in reconstructing his Cabinet, not unnaturally omitted the People's Party, and Tiso's place was taken by the Slovak Socialist leader, Dr. Dérer.[1]

From that day onwards Hlinka refrained from all political co-operation and, having lost Tuka as well as Jehlička, now fell under the influence of the much more astute but no less perfidious Tiso. While an irreducible minimum of fanatics immune from every argument continued to vote for Hlinka, the real political influence in Slovakia lay more and more with the Agrarian Milan Hodža (who as Minister of Agriculture maintained close contacts with the representatives of the 'Green International' of various peasant countries), and the Socialist Ivan Dérer, whose main aim was to extend and deepen the social benefits which had accrued to backward Slovakia and still more backward Ruthenia from their association with the Czech lands.

If in the third decade of the Republic the lists were set in Slovakia, and no serious internal change was to be expected save as a result of international upheaval (as actually happened in 1938), this was in no small measure due to the remarkable transformation wrought in the field of education—an achievement which has not its like in Europe, and for which much of the credit belongs to the Referent for Education, Anton Štefánek, who had in pre-war days been a secondary schoolmaster in Vienna and then became editor of two small Slovak papers in Budapest (*Slovenský Denník* and *Obzor*), as the close collaborator of Milan Hodža. We already saw that the Slovaks were deprived of their only three secondary schools as long ago as 1875, and never possessed a University till 1919. On the eve of the Great War 214,000 Slovak children were being educated in purely Magyar primary schools (and not one of the *state* schools used the Slovak language) and only 42,000 in Slovak schools. By 1918 the number of Slovak schools (all denominational) had fallen to 276, with 390 teachers and 30,000 children. Within five years of the Liberation (in the school year 1926–1927) the number had risen to 2,652 schools, with 4,354 teachers and 277,794 children ; while the Magyars were left with 695—more than double the number of schools allowed by them ten years earlier for the ten times more numerous Slovaks. Within the first year 18 Slovak gymnasia were set up and by 1928 had increased to 39, while the teachers' training colleges increased from 6 to 13. Large numbers of commercial, industrial and agricultural schools were also established. An elaborate system of kindergarten and crèches, of village libraries and singing societies was set up ; and it is to be remembered that as there were hardly any Slovak school books under the Magyar regime, new ones had to be written and printed with a minimum of delay. In addition to the University of Bratislava, which after ten years had 55 professors and a further staff of 185, there were high schools of agriculture and forestry, and academies of law and theology. In view of the reckless calumnies launched against the Czechs, special stress must be laid upon the devoted work of over 1,400 Czech teachers in the schools of Slovakia, without whose help the work of regeneration and the maintenance of certain minimum standards would have been altogether impossible. Incidentally, that work could not even have been attempted if the linguistic difference between Czech and Slovak were comparatively trifling.

[1] At these elections the Hlinka Party polled 406,000 votes, as against 678,000 of the Unionist groups (280,000 Agrarians, 152,000 Communists, 105,000 Socialists, 53,000 National Democrats, 42,000 National Socialists).

A few words must be reserved for another change in the situation of Slovakia, which though wrought among a small minority of the nation, was of the highest moral importance—we refer to the emancipation of the Lutheran Church from the tightening grip of Magyarization, and its reconstitution under freely elected Slovak Bishops, with its General Assembly, synods and seniorates purged of foreign influence and free to develop on democratic lines.

The Great Depression

Under Švehla a fair balance of party forces had been reached, and on the whole continued under his two successors, Udržal (February, 1929–October, 1932) and Malypetr (1932–1935). The system of mutual concessions enforced by the Pětka made for stability, but as an English critic has justly pointed out, it presented 'the disadvantage that the elector never knows, when he votes for a party, to what extent it will feel impelled to compromise with regard to the programme whereby it wins his vote. On the other hand, the necessity for compromise prevents radical and arbitrary changes of policy between elections, but permits of minor changes in the composition and policy of a government without a general election.'[1]

Just at the moment when the dust of domestic controversy seemed at last to be settling down, the Great Depression descended upon Europe, and an icy wind played havoc with the international trade policy which the Republic had pursued with very considerable success for just over a decade. Two able Finance Ministers, first Engliš, then Trapl, fought valiantly against the effects of this economic blizzard, and some of their colleagues shrank back from the drastic measures which alone could secure a balanced budget and avert dangerous inflation. Several times the Coalition was in danger of collapse, and was saved only by the President holding another Cabinet of officials as a sword of Damocles over their heads. With a steep decline in the export trade, the Republic had at the end of 1932 no less than 750,000 unemployed, and the situation could only be saved by drastic economies, and a highly unpopular reduction of salaries. We shall see, too, that German-Bohemia was more severely hit than any other district, and that this had inevitable political reactions. Yet, all things considered, the parties showed remarkable restraint and responsibility. On the one flank the little phalanx of thirty Communist deputies, on the other a new Fascist formation under the ambitious and scurrilous ex-Socialist, Stříbrný, tried to discredit the policy of 'the Hrad'[2] (the phrase used for President Masaryk and his faithful Foreign Minister, Dr. Beneš), but with singular lack of success. Stříbrný's gutter press never really struck roots among a people capable of appreciating the priceless benefits of such leadership, and he only discredited himself still further when he allied himself with the ex-General Gajda, who had played with the idea of a *putsch* and had been dismissed from the Army. The Malypetr Government was by 1933 firmly seated in the saddle, and the crisis seemed to be dying down. The Premier himself was the first holder of that office who had only entered politics *after* the Great War, and had shown skill and moderation as President of the Chamber. In 1935 he was succeeded by Dr. Hodža, the first Slovak to become Prime Minister, and of all the Agrarians far the most

---

[1] Edgar Young, *Czechoslovakia* (1938), p. 114.
[2] I.e. the Castle of Prague.

conversant with international affairs. His special interests lay in the direction of peasant collaboration—what was sometimes called the Green International—and again, of economic and even political co-operation between Czechoslovakia and Austria. In this he outpaced, rather than differed from, his colleague the Foreign Minister ; ever since the collusive Curtius-Schober attempt to bounce Europe into accepting an Austro-German Zollverein, as the first step towards the Anschluss, and still more since the advent of Hitler to power in Germany two years later, it was obvious that international questions were destined to overshadow, and eventually to determine, the course of domestic affairs.

Foreign Policy

To do justice to the foreign policy of Dr. Beneš would require a whole volume to itself, if only for the reason that his case is unique in modern history ; for he was in continuous office as Foreign Minister during the seventeen crowded years from 1918 to 1935, after having served an apprenticeship of three years as secretary general of the National Council, and, as if this were not enough, he retained a predominant influence over it for three further years as President, until the catastrophe of Munich. Indeed he might almost be compared with Tennyson's Brook which, though 'men may come and men may go,' flowed on its even course. Before all else, and before it was even possible for Dr. Beneš to return home from Paris, it was necessary to stabilize the frontiers ; and we have already seen that this was accomplished by the Treaties of Versailles and St. Germain, on the basis of the historic frontier, though at three points slight rectifications were made in favour of Czechoslovakia. The striking contrast between Austrian compliance and Hungarian resistance is the measure of the expansive and aggressive forces let loose during the Dualist era by the Germans and Magyars respectively against their subordinate races. The curtailment of Austria meant the loss of over three million Germans to the composite Czechoslovak Republic, and the partition of Hungary involved the assignment of roughly 1,300,000 Magyars to Roumania, 700,000 to Czechoslovakia and 500,000 to Jugoslavia—or a total of 2,500,000, including a large number of more or less assimilated Jews.[1] Yet in the one case the new situation was accepted almost at once, and no claim for restoration was ever put forward by Vienna to Prague, whereas in the other the whole world was filled with passionate agitation under the catchword 'No, No, Never.'

The break-up of the Monarchy caused violent dislocation and much suffering, especially among the middle class and intellectuals of Vienna ; but there was nothing in Austria remotely comparable with the three Revolutions, the Red and White Terrors, the onslaughts on Slovakia and Roumania, the Roumanian occupation of the capital and the two Royalist *putsches*, which convulsed Hungary within the space of less than two years. Austria indeed was the first neighbour with whom Czechoslovakia was able to establish relatively normal relations. As early as January, 1920, the Chancellor, Dr. Renner, visited Prague, and in the following April, by the Treaty of Lány, the two countries gave each other a mutual guarantee. In 1921 President Hainisch visited President Masaryk, whom he had known in the pre-war Reichsrat. In 1922 Czechoslovakia asso-

[1] This figure, it is true, was swollen by propagandists to 3,500,000, but quite erroneously.

ciated herself actively with the League of Nations' efforts to restore the
financial credit of Austria and thus diminish the internal economic crisis.
It would be going too far to speak of cordiality between Czechoslovakia
and Austria, but during the first post-war decade good neighbourly
relations had been established. It is true that the secret Austro-German
agreement, negotiated in 1931 between Schober and Curtius, with the
immediate aim of a Zollverein but the ulterior aim of political union,
administered a severe shock to Prague ; but as the Entente imposed a
firm veto and the scheme was abandoned, no permanent damage was done.
While, then, the new authoritarian regime of Dollfuss and Schuschnigg
could not be sympathetic to the democratic Czechs, its frank opposition
to the Anschluss, and to the cruder forms of Nazism, provided a certain
guarantee of common interests. In the five years before Hitler seized
Vienna, Vienna and Prague were equally aware of the growing danger
from the North and increasingly disposed to offer a common front to
aggression ; but Vienna, by its reliance upon Mussolini and by its feeble
dabbling in the doctrines of the Corporative State, had put itself into a
false position alike in domestic and in foreign policy, and had not dared to
press for Danubian union in the teeth of Italian hostility.

With Hungary Czechoslovakia's relations were frankly bad from the
very outset ; she could not agree even with such genuinely Liberal leaders
as Károlyi and Jászi, who to the last were striving to avert the detachment
of Slovakia and Ruthenia from Hungary ; and if there could be no accord
with them, still less hope was there of an accord with the rival extremes of
Béla Kun and Admiral Horthy. The long duration of the conflict, due to
the absorption of the Supreme Council in other major questions (they
eventually pushed through St. Germain and delegated Trianon to the
Council of Ambassadors), undoubtedly exacerbated it still further. It
confirmed the Magyars in the conviction that the final settlement had
rested upon vengeance and ignorance, though in reality it was fully worked
out by highly competent experts in Paris. While the counter-revolution
was still raging during the winter of 1919–20, the Czechs, Jugoslavs and
Roumanians got together and concerted joint measures against Hungarian
ambitions. The two moving spirits were Beneš and Take Ionescu. The
first definite agreement was that concluded between Czechoslovakia and
Jugoslavia on April 14, 1920 (replaced on August 31, 1922, by an open
alliance) ; it was followed a year later by similar agreements between
Czechoslovakia and Roumania (April 23, 1921) and Jugoslavia and
Roumania (June 7, 1921), which were already in preparation but were
precipitated by the ex-Emperor Charles's rash attempt at restoration.
These triple pacts, known as the Little Entente, were intended above all
to preserve the new Danubian *status quo* ; they had three quite specific
aims, in each case negative—to prevent Habsburg restoration, to prevent
territorial revision in favour of Hungary, and to prevent the Anschluss of
Austria to the Reich. So long as the three countries preserved their
independence, they never wavered in these aims. They bluntly challenged
the Legitimist contention that the Habsburg Question was a purely
internal affair of Hungary ; as the Habsburgs were sovereigns not only of
Hungary but of the whole Dual Monarchy, their return would, it was
contended, have a direct and immediate effect upon all their former
subjects, and would be a disturbing element in the general European
situation. They also pointed out quite accurately that the governing
class of Hungary, which had in former centuries been far from showing

peculiar devotion to the dynasty, was mainly interested in the return of Charles because it had come to identify Habsburg dynastic doctrine with the doctrine of territorial integrity. By his coronation oath Charles was pledged to uphold this integrity by every means, and not only not to alienate any possessions of the Hungarian Crown, 'under whatsoever right or title, but even to augment and extend them.'

Here lies the key to the very prompt and energetic action of the three Succession States in October, 1921, when Charles and Zita flew to Budapest and appealed to the loyalty of the embarrassed Regent Horthy. The three Foreign Ministers, Beneš, Take Ionescu and Pašić, addressed a stiff note of warning to Budapest, to the effect that restoration would be regarded as a *casus belli* and would be met by their immediate mobilization, and announced their resolve to take action such as would ensure 'the final settlement of the Habsburg question in Hungary.' Faced by such an attitude and the popular excitement in all the neighbouring countries (it was on this occasion that the students of Bratislava University, led by ex-Legionaries, demolished the famous marble statue of Maria Theresa, as a proof that Slovakia would never tolerate Habsburg restoration), the Regent declined to yield up the throne to its legitimate owner, and the unhappy Charles was deported on a British destroyer and sent to Madeira, where he died of despair rather than illness, less than nine months later. On this occasion Beneš addressed a weighty note to the Council of Ambassadors, reminding it of previous commitments in the question and of Hungary's failure to disarm and her disregard for the Council in the Burgenland dispute, and asking for definite measures against Hungary as a necessary preliminary to demobilization. This led the Council to exercise tardy pressure, and the Hungarian National Assembly adopted a Law not merely abrogating the sovereignty of Charles, but permanently excluding the House of Habsburg, and undertaking not to select a candidate for the vacant throne without previous consultation with the Great Powers.

It was, of course, France who went farthest to meet the wishes of the Little Entente, and who has, with some exaggeration, but by no means without reason, been accused of building up a group of satellite Powers to the east of Germany, and thus preventing a return to normal conditions in Central Europe as a whole. Beneš in particular has been depicted as the docile tool of France, and it is certainly true that he and Masaryk favoured the closest relations with France, all the more so as America resumed her isolation and Britain insisted upon drawing political distinctions between East and West, while Russia was passing through a series of convulsions and was neither willing to enter the League system nor would as yet have been accepted if she had so desired. Under such circumstances it is difficult to conceive what other course Czechoslovakia could safely have adopted, and it is seldom that the most captious critic puts forward any concrete alternative. It is, however, altogether untrue that Masaryk and Beneš pursued a policy of subservience to France ; on the contrary, while emphasizing their Western orientation and their entire loyalty to their former allies, they resisted even the personal pressure exercised by Marshal Foch during a visit to Prague, with the result that the Treaty of Alliance concluded between Prague and Paris in January, 1924, was framed upon purely defensive lines, avoiding all possibility of aggression and laying very special emphasis upon its strict compatibility with the League Covenant. On her side France went farther to meet the

Czechs than ever before, consenting to a mutual guarantee against attack, promising joint action to prevent Habsburg or Hohenzollern restoration, endorsing anew the veto upon the Anschluss, and undertaking not to conclude any future treaty without informing them in advance. While pursuing this openly Francophile line, and encouraging Jugoslavia to follow his example, Beneš used all his influence in Belgrade to hold her statesmen back from commitments such as might give offence in Rome or render an Italo-Jugoslav *détente* more difficult.

The policy of 'regional agreements' pursued by Prague during these years, which found its main expression in the Little Entente, was the logical outcome of a diplomatic situation in which first America 'drew out' altogether from European complications, and then Britain sought to limit her commitments by drawing hard and fast distinctions, of a most dubious character, between security in the West and security in the East. The Powers which were moving in the direction of Locarno gave their encouragement to the Little Entente, as one form of the 'regional agreements' which they conceived as a substitute for further commitments. A regrettable exception was provided by Italy, whose selfish policy it was consistently to prevent union among the Danubian states, and in particular to exploit Hungary's revisionist ambitions as a heaven-sent (or rather hell-sent) instrument of discord.

To Masaryk and Beneš, from the very outset, the policy of strengthening and extending the Little Entente was an elementary precaution, of a mainly conservative and negative character. Much more important was the role assumed by Czechoslovakia in the struggle for a new international order—a struggle at once constructive, democratic and essentially pacific. Mr. Lloyd George in his memoirs has expressed regret that at the Peace Conference Czechoslovakia was represented, 'not by her wise leader President Masaryk,' but by the 'impulsive, clever, but much less sagacious and short-sighted politician Dr. Beneš,' and has clearly implied that his regret applied also to the series of conferences in the immediate post-war period. This rests upon an unhappy misunderstanding which arose at the abortive Conference of Genoa in 1922, whose failure Mr. Lloyd George felt very keenly, but for which it is not fair to hold Dr. Beneš so largely responsible. Behind his tart verdict upon Beneš, however, there is the profoundly erroneous assumption that it is possible to distinguish between Masaryk and Beneš. In reality there has rarely been in modern history (since the strangely different alliance of Francis and Metternich) a partnership so close and so harmonious as that between the President Liberator and his eventual successor. In tactical approach, in the externals by which superficial observers judge these things, there was an obvious divergence, but the union of hearts, the identity of aims and of principles, can hardly be exaggerated, and if the verdict of history goes against the one, it will have to go against the other also. This had to be stressed at some point in the narrative, and it is perhaps best to relate it to the role played by Beneš at Geneva, with the whole-hearted approval of his chief.

Dr. Beneš and the League

Dr. Beneš first came into prominence in the international sphere at the Conference of Genoa, in 1922, when he unsuccessfully advocated a Franco-British Guarantee pact. The ultimate cause of failure was the deep-seated divergence of views between Paris and London in the burning question of reparations, which continued to block the way to Germany's readmission to the comity of nations. Beneš's early efforts to convince the Great Powers were unsuccessful, but he was prepared to bide his time. In 1924 he was again in the forefront of the controversy and, in conjunction with the Greek statesman Politis, helped Ramsay MacDonald and Herriot to draft the famous Protocol, whose adoption by the League might have altered the course of history. In his speech as *rapporteur* before the Assembly Beneš insisted that 'effective guarantees and the promise of assistance are not only a necessary condition, but also an inevitable consequence of arbitration.' The Geneva Protocol was taken up by Briand in the name of France, and after some hesitation accepted by the Labour Government. But during the winter MacDonald gave place to Baldwin, and the combined influence of the Conservative Party and of the Dominion Governments, who looked askance upon fresh European commitments, led the new Foreign Secretary, Austen Chamberlain, to draw back from the Protocol and to advocate regional agreements as supplementary to the Covenant of the League. With a perspective of nearly twenty-five years we may marvel at the blindness of our statesmen in the post-war era. What Count Skrzynski, the Polish Foreign Minister, said on March 20, 1925—'A Western Pact without guarantees in the East is like having a house full of beautiful tapestries and taking precautions for them only, abandoning all the objects in the neighbouring rooms to the danger of fire'—sounds to us in 1943 as a self-evident commonplace ; but at the time it was rejected with horror by large sections of public opinion and by our acknowledged leaders.

The Geneva Protocol, then, which Czechoslovakia had been the first state to ratify, was consigned to limbo, and in October, 1925, the much-heralded and ably advertised Locarno settlement was substituted ; while one end of the new dam was equipped with all the most modern machinery and received constant attention, the other end was left in an incomplete and leaky state, sometimes patched up as the result of a sudden panic, but increasingly undermined and ready to crack at every join when once a certain pressure was applied. In 1939 the pressure of pent-up waters which the wiseacres of Locarno had ignored, burst the eastern dam, and instantly involved the whole of Europe in ruin. That unflagging champion of the League, Lord Cecil, in his Memoirs, records his belief that Locarno was never popular, since 'perhaps the common people, with their remarkable political sense, recognized that a particular arrangement of this kind could not be the basis of a lasting security for peace. . . . Europe may perhaps be separated for peace purposes from the rest of the world, though this would not be easy. But no smaller area can be so treated.' The 'No Commitment Policy,' aimed at escaping from European entanglements, had exactly the opposite effect, and this 'senseless system', as Lord Cecil calls it, was the main cause of the Polish War.

Beneš again showed his usual resilience. Forced to submit with a good grace to the decisions of the greater Powers, he received as a consolation prize a Franco-Czechoslovak Treaty of mutual guarantee, promising 'immediate aid' in the event of 'unprovoked attack' ; and this remained as one of the buttresses of his whole policy, until the day in 1938 when France, under British promptings, but hardly needing any encouragement, declined to redeem her word. Meanwhile he adhered to the view that questions of limitation of armaments and security could not be silenced by the failure of the Protocol, but would continue to force themselves upon the general attention, and in the eight years that separated Locarno from the opening of Hitler's offensive against the Geneva system, he was more untiring than ever in his activities at Geneva, in particular at the Disarmament Conference. To him the 'Covenant was 'a real product of intellectual, political and cultural development, achieved by stages through three great revolutions, the English, the American and the French'; it was 'a mark of political and social progress, the realization of a new international life, a new order in morals and in politics, the culminating point of the new ideology of the last two centuries.' Hence in all his efforts he was almost equally prompted by a profound and sincere sympathy for that greatest of all political experiments, the achievement of a new international world order, and by a prophetic insight into the grim alternative that would face the smaller states, and very particularly so vulnerable a country as his own, in the event of final failure at Geneva. This is an entirely adequate (and to all who trouble to study the facts, entirely convincing) explanation of Dr. Beneš's motives, but to the cynic and the propagandist they remained a mystery; for there are none so blind as those who will not see.

No great prescience was required for a statesman living so close to the main nerve centres of Europe to take alarm at the Great Depression of 1931, the spread of unemployment and unrest in the Reich and its effect upon his own country; and the collapse of the Creditanstalt in Vienna came as a salvo of warning from his nearest neighbour's house. It is, however, right to note in passing that Dr. Beneš was one of the very first to take alarm at Japanese aggression in Manchuria and China and the failure of the League to impose sanctions. The advent of Hitler to power and his withdrawal from the League only six months after Japan's open defiance and secession, reacted very promptly upon the foreign and domestic policy of Czechoslovakia; for as we shall see, Nazism found a Trojan horse in the new Sudeten German Party, while the Little Entente and Poland began anxiously to take stock of the changing situation in Europe. Ever since the Curtius-Schober design for a German-Austrian Zollverein had met with the veto of the Western Powers, a series of projects for Central Europe were propounded, the most notable being that of the ex-Premier Tardieu, but each time wrecked by Mussolini. It was increasingly clear that Europe was moving away from democratic League principles and free participation of the smaller Powers, towards the establishment of a narrow 'directorium' of the Great Powers, and even then, of course, to the exclusion of Soviet Russia. In February, 1933, the Little Entente, under Beneš, Titulescu and Jevtić, signed a new Pact of Organization at Geneva, which provided for a permanent Council of the three Foreign Ministers, meeting at least three times a year, and an Economic Council for the co-ordination of trade interests. Their treaties of alliance were renewed for an indefinite period, unless special notice were given; and each state undertook to conclude no further unilateral treaty or trade agreement without consultation and consent of its allies. Great stress was laid upon registration with the League and upon the invalidity of any decision conflicting with the terms of the Covenant. This essentially unaggressive Pact was greeted with violent hostility in Italy and Hungary, who regarded it, not without justice, as a check to their revisionist designs.

Unfortunately the parallel design of a *rapprochement* with Poland came to nothing. Marshal Pilsudski, well aware of the predatory instincts of Hitler, would have been ready to join France in common action against the dictator ; but finding her shrink from a preventive war for fear of offending Britain, he made his own bargain with Berlin in January, 1934, and henceforward played a lone game. This game succeeded so long as his ruthless but brilliantly constructive mind was there to direct it, but under Colonel Beck it soon degenerated into complete cynicism, ending in blackmail and bankruptcy. One result was a considerable deterioration in the relations of Warsaw and Prague, the former never being able to escape from the illusion that Poland was a Great Power, and therefore entitled to greater consideration than Czechoslovakia. There was also a strong element of pique, due to Poland's exclusion from the discussions which led to the Four-Power Pact, the scarcely concealed intention of which was to prepare the way for treaty revision by placing France in a minority and leaving the balance in Italy's hands. Dr. Beneš, speaking in the name of the Little Entente, delivered the frankest speech of his career, making it quite clear that he and his colleagues saw in the proposed Pact the design of a new Balance of Power, calculated to weaken France in Europe as a whole, and to weaken the Little Entente and Poland in Central Europe in particular. He even went so far as to warn Sir John Simon that frontier changes could only be imposed by force of arms.

This moment represented the height of co-operation between Beneš and that brilliant, if sometimes erratic, Roumanian statesman Nicholas Titulescu, who made a tour of the south-eastern capitals as a preliminary to the signature, on February 4 in Athens, of a Balkan Entente, between Jugoslavia, Roumania, Greece and Turkey. Its mutual guarantee of frontiers against outside aggression was declared not to be valid against a Great Power—which was an indirect way of saying that Greece was not bound to help Jugoslavia if attacked by Italy. But the Pact had the effect of adding the weight of Turkey and Greece to that of Jugoslavia and Roumania in the case of the Hungarian frontiers, and of ringing round Bulgaria in such a way as to render aggression quite hopeless except with the active help of a Great Power. Czechoslovakia, though of course not directly concerned, was indirectly strengthened by the new Pact and gave it her full support.

In March, 1934, Mussolini countered with the so-called 'Rome Protocols,' in which Hungary under General Gömbös and Austria under Dr. Dollfuss were featured as the vassals of Italy, tied down in such a way as to block any project of Danubian union save on Italy's terms. To this France countered in her turn by sending her new Foreign Minister, Louis Barthou, on a round of Balkan visits, during which he encouraged anti-revisionists to expect French backing. This had a still more ambitious sequel in his attempts to bring Russia back into the Commonwealth of Nations, and to set up an Eastern Pact of mutual guarantee, corresponding to the Locarno arrangements for Western Europe. Simultaneously with this King Alexander addressed himself with considerable success to the task of winning Bulgaria for inclusion in the Balkan Entente, and thus establishing a solid peace front of five of the six south-eastern states.

Europe was already marshalling her forces in two hostile camps, and the quadruple series of murders most foul, in each case directly incited by the rulers of a foreign Power, showed those who were not still blind to reality—unhappily a minority among those in authority—that the control of large parts of the Continent was in the hands of bandits, whose aim it was to overthrow the whole existing order. Mussolini had stood behind the forcible destruction of Viennese Socialism and was now financing and training the Croat 'Ustashi' terrorists. On the 'Thirtieth of June' Hitler and his accomplices Göring and Goebbels staged a cold-blooded and treacherous massacre for which there is no parallel in European history since the night of St. Bartholomew. On July 25 their henchmen murdered the Austrian Chancellor Dollfuss in circumstances of still greater brutality, but bungled the seizure of power and left Hitler no choice but postponement, especially as Mussolini was massing troops on the Brenner and the Nazi army was quite unprepared. On October 9, however, Mussolini's hired assassins Pavelić, Kvaternik and others (the men to whom Hitler in 1941 entrusted the government of Croatia), successfully assassinated King Alexander at Marseilles and by a lucky stroke also rid themselves of Barthou, the last French Foreign Minister capable of a European conception and possessing the courage and energy to put it into effect. Jugoslavia rallied round the Regency, and Mussolini had to recognize that she was not yet on the point of dissolution. But in every Balkan capital it was now obvious that Germany and Italy were controlled by men who would stick at nothing and with whom it admirably suited the military caste to co-operate ; that that 'third alternative' of 'competition in armaments' which Mr. Baldwin had refused to contemplate as recently as November, 1933, was now once more a reality, but that neither France nor Britain was prepared to face the facts, to take the necessary precautions, or even to warn their all too somnolent peoples. No one was more alive to the situation than Dr. Beneš who made to Lord Cecil in May, 1933, the remarkable forecast that Hitler's aim was 'to absorb Austria and Czechoslovakia, to create an independent Ukraine as counterpoise to Russia and Poland, to suppress the Danzig Corridor and reduce Poland to subservience.'[1] He at least was not blind, nor did he fail to give warning in the capitals of Western Europe.

The death of Barthou was a serious blow to the cause of stability, the more so as his successor was Laval, not yet a quisling sold to the service of France's mortal enemies, but certainly notorious as a cynic and a corruptionist. Nothing illustrates more clearly the speed with which the balances in Europe were being readjusted than the fact that two such men as Barthou and Laval presided over the admittance of Soviet Russia to the comity of nations at Geneva—that comity from which, until her coming, a majority of the seven Great Powers had either held aloof, or withdrawn. As the two Powers most hostile to Russia—Japan and Germany—were the chief opponents of the League, and the chief promoters of rearmament, it suited Russia very well to abandon her former hostility to the League, and it also suited the Western Powers to invite her ; and under the stimulus of June 30 and July 25 the ceremony took place in September. Mr. Litvinov defined the common aim of its members as 'the organization of peace,' and it became obvious that for the present, at any rate, Russia looked to the collective system rather than to World Revolution as her chief instrument of defence. The winter was spent in further efforts to bring to birth an Eastern Pact of Mutual Guarantee, to which Russia, Poland, the Baltic States, Czechoslovakia *and Germany* would be parties, with the benevolent approval, though without the participation, of Britain and Italy. It gradually became obvious that Hitler was opposed to anything likely to stabilize the *status quo* in the East and was using the Bolshevist bogy as camouflage for his designs ;

[1] *A Great Experiment*, p. 247.

and indeed by the spring he was violently attacking the whole idea of such a Pact as a hostile manœuvre, and had induced the short-sighted Polish Government to share his aloofness and deal only direct with Berlin. Undeterred by his anger, a Franco-Soviet Pact was signed on May 2, 1935, without Germany, but only after the text had been approved by the British Government as following strictly defensive lines and complying with the Covenant—Russia offering to Germany the same guarantee now given to France, and France to Germany the same now given to Russia. The Pact expressly stated that France and Russia 'continue to regard as desirable' the signature of a Treaty of Assistance between themselves and Germany, in other words, placing it at any moment within Germany's own power to put an end to her alleged 'encirclement." That the Pact was strictly defensive and reflected Genevan principles, cannot be denied ; but the fact remains that Germany by her own action had reconstituted the pre-war Franco-Russian Alliance.

This Pact was followed on May 16 by a similar Pact between Czechoslovakia and Soviet Russia, the obligation being, however, in this case limited to cases in which France had already come to the aid of the attacked country under her treaties with Moscow or Prague. Thus Czechoslovakia, and especially her Foreign Minister, shared with France the full blast of Hitler's displeasure when a week later he denounced the Pact as a military alliance, introducing a new and incalculable factor from Eastern Europe and Asia into the European balance of power. He even treated the Bolshevization of France as a possibility, in which event, he argued, France and Russia would be controlled 'from one headquarters in Moscow.' It is hardly necessary to point out that all his phrases about a disturbed balance of power were utterly disingenuous ; its maintenance was the main object of the two Pacts, and therein consisted their enormity to the man bent upon radically altering the status of all his eastern neighbours. Thus for good or for evil Dr. Beneš, in his last year of office as Foreign Minister, found himself in the very forefront of the European conflict. His whole policy had hitherto rested upon support of the League, and regional agreements as a supplement to its deficiencies. He now made his Pact with Russia as a form of reinsurance, intended to fill the gap left by the Locarno reservations, and also as a logical sequel to his and Masaryk's profound conviction that Czechoslovakia could not permanently keep her full independence without intimate relations with Russia. And now, at the end of long years of effort in the service of the League, he was elected Chairman of the Assembly at one of the most crucial and delicate moments in its history, when Mussolini was on the point of invading Abyssinia and when Sir Samuel Hoare, by his famous speech of September 11, 1935, rallied the League in defence of 'collective security.' But between the day when fifty nations accepted British leadership against the naked aggression of Italy and that other day when the peace proposal that has for ever linked together the names of Hoare and Laval, broke the back of the League and rendered a new war inevitable, the domestic situation in Czechoslovakia had urgently recalled Dr. Beneš to another sphere. For the next three years his part in international affairs was to be as active as ever ; but it was no longer as delegate to Geneva, but as successor to the presidential office.

CHAPTER XVII

MUNICH AND AFTER

If the trumpet give an uncertain sound, who shall prepare himself to the battle ?

Am I my brother's keeper ?

IN the course of 1935, President Masaryk, who had held the high office of President for seventeen years of tireless and exacting work, and was now eighty-five, realized that his powers were failing, and was still able —one more sign of the innate greatness of the man—to recognize the psychological moment for his resignation. On previous occasions of illness he had made it clear that he regarded Edvard Beneš as his obvious successor, and now, in an international situation so fluid and so dangerous, he was more than ever insistent. It is hardly necessary to point out that if Beneš had retained the post of Foreign Minister throughout sixteen changes of Cabinet, this was due to Masaryk's resolute backing and to the complete unanimity of mind and heart that prevailed between the two men. Once, in conversation with that versatile writer, the late Karel Čapek, Masaryk had said 'Without Beneš we should not have a Republic' ; and now he did not hesitate to throw his whole prestige into the scale in favour of Beneš. Kramář, by this time in the background and in failing health, continued his irrevocable hostility to both Masaryk and Beneš, accusing them of subservience to Soviet Russia ; but he had no alternative policy to suggest, in the situation towards which Europe was once more so rapidly drifting. It was under his influence that the National Democratic Party most unwisely challenged the election of Beneš. Their candidate, Professor Němec, only obtained 24 votes, and Dr. Beneš was elected by 340 to 24 (with 76 abstentions, mostly from the German opponents of activism). In his farewell address the President-Liberator pointedly reminded his listeners, in a phrase redolent of his lifelong philosophy, that 'States are preserved by those ideals to which they owe their origin' ; and at another point he placed most prominently among the *desiderata* of any future government 'a good foreign policy, and at home justice to all citizens of whatever nationality.'

As events proved, President Masaryk had left himself the narrowest of margins ; at the final ceremony he had a slight stroke, and only concluded his speech with an effort. He lived two more years in tranquil retirement at the Castle of Lány, full of concern at the state of Europe, but confident that he was leaving the conduct of affairs in competent hands. He died on September 14, 1937, and his funeral was marked by scenes of grief and affection such as no one who witnessed them can ever forget. The new President, in the funeral oration which he delivered before the diplomatic corps and the political and cultural *élite* of the nation, deliberately stressed the inescapable choice, which, in Masaryk's belief, events were forcing upon the nations of Europe—the choice between Jesus and Cæsar. This was only the first of a series of messages which Dr. Beneš addressed to his people, in the true tradition of the President-Liberator.

Crisis in Europe

In the period following the election events in Europe continued their headlong course, and the new President's first concern was with foreign policy. At first the Premier, Dr. Hodža, retained the portfolio of Foreign Affairs in his own hands, and for this he possessed very special qualifications—for instance, his many contacts with Roumania and Jugoslavia, dating from those pre-war days when he sat in the Hungarian Parliament; his cordial relations with Poland; his interest in the peasant movement loosely described as the 'Green International'; and not least his many contacts with leading Austrians, who were only too happy to have to deal with a Slovak who knew and loved his Vienna rather than with the more unbending and intractable Czech. As, however, the Hitler regime grew ever more aggressive, and as the problem of the German minority inside the Republic acquired renewed intensity, it became necessary for the Premier to concentrate upon domestic affairs—here again, as a Slovak, he had a certain advantage in dealing with the Germans—and to appoint a new Foreign Minister. This was the distinguished historian Kamil Krofta, who after serving as Minister in Rome and Berlin, had since 1927 been Permanent Chief of the Foreign Office, and had won general recognition for his powers of application, his unruffled calm and sweet reasonableness.

During the first half of 1936 the international situation was dominated by the burning questions of rearmament and sanctions; on March 7 Hitler reoccupied the Rhineland with complete impunity, on May 9 Mussolini annexed Abyssinia to the new 'Impero Romano,' and on July 4 sanctions were withdrawn. Confronted by these proofs that the two Dictators, with their Spanish 'Ersatz,' General Franco, had got the Western Powers on the run, Czechoslovakia roused itself to fresh exertions. In January, while Italy was still in difficulties in Africa, the Austrian Chancellor, Dr. von Schuschnigg, paid an official visit to Prague and seemed to be moving in the direction of some general Danubian accord. But in proportion as Mussolini recovered, he was able to exercise a restraining influence upon Vienna; and the Austro-German pact of July 4 represented Austria's relapse into subservience to the two Dictators. Mussolini took his revenge against Prague by pronouncing himself more openly than ever before in favour of Hungarian revision.

Throughout this period the Little and Balkan Ententes were correspondingly active, and there was an exchange of state visits between President Beneš, King Carol and the Prince-Regent Paul. On the anniversary of Roumanian and Jugoslav unity there was a joint session of the Parliaments of the three northernmost Allies, and there was much talk of solidarity. A welcome supplement was added in the Bulgaro-Jugoslav Pact 'of eternal and indissoluble peace and friendship' (January 23, 1937), which seemed to fill the one really awkward gap in the general Balkan arrangement. But there was more than one fly in the ointment. King Carol, who during the ensuing two years maintained a loyal and courageous foreign policy towards his allies, and in particular towards Czechoslovakia, committed the blunder of dismissing his able and enlightened Foreign Secretary Nicholas Titulescu, thereby tearing the delicate web of negotiation with Moscow. Moreover, he far outweighed any merits of his foreign policy by playing a reactionary and totalitarian domestic policy, which disintegrated the old parties and merely opened the door to the irresponsible banditry of Codreanu and the Iron Guard. Meanwhile Jugoslav policy gradually assumed an attitude of reserve towards Prague, Paris and Moscow ; Prince Paul's two chief advisers, the cynical and utterly opportunist Stojadinović and the reactionary clerical Korošec, shared the obsessions of his Greek kinsfolk with regard to 'the Red Danger' and 'the Popular Front.' The Italo-Jugoslav Pact of March, 1937, was in itself unexceptionable, but the fact that it was concluded without any previous reference to Jugoslavia's allies was a direct violation of the Little and Balkan Entente statutes, and was widely interpreted as a hint of secession, administered on the prompting of Mussolini. It must unhappily be added that a further incentive to disintegration was pro- vided by the flabby attitude of the Western Powers towards Italo-German intervention in Spain. To conclude a 'Gentleman's Agreement,' and to allude to so discreditable an arrangement under that name, was to make nonsense of all the high Genevan professions of faith and to warn the lesser Powers of the south-east to fend for themselves. During the winter of 1937 it became obvious to Hitler that the Western Powers, who had shrunk from fulfilling their League obligations in defence of Spain against the most naked aggression would be equally reluctant to defend Austria from invasion, even though she was in a peculiar degree the creation of Versailles and the ward of the League. Indeed, Lord Halifax, during a visit to the Sports Exhibition in Berlin, confirmed Hitler in the belief that Britain and France would not go beyond diplomatic protests, and that the Anschluss would leave them talking.

Activism, National Socialism and Henlein

The rise of Hitler to power and the rapid transformation of the Third Reich into an aggressive, totalitarian state inevitably reacted upon the relations of Czechs and Germans inside the Republic and arrested the process of stabilization of which 'Activism' was both cause and effect, and which had survived the serious shock administered by the Great Depression. The key to the situation which now arose is to be found in certain very simple but fundamental facts which were only too often overlooked in the West. The events of 1918 meant that in the Czech lands majority and minority changed places, and while this met with the virtually unanimous approval of the Czechs, it was highly distasteful to the Germans, who resisted, and would have resisted much more resolutely but for the utter prostration and helplessness both of the Reich and of Austria. Moreover, Bohemia was the original home of German nationalism in its most rabid form, as expounded by Georg von Schönerer, Karl Hermann Wolf and other fanatics ; for the half century preceding the Great War there had been a growing divergence of political outlook between the Sudetian and Alpine Germans, the latter being 'Black and Yellow' or 'Habsburg' in feeling and desiring the survival of the Monarchy as a Great Power, whereas the former[1] turned with growing fanaticism and intolerance of phrase towards Berlin, in whom they saw the champion of a Greater Germany dominating the Continent, as a first step towards world hegemony. This explains why the Czechs, for all their traditional

[1] It is, of course, quite inaccurate to apply the term 'Sudetian' to the Germans of the Bohemian Forest or the Giant Mountains : it only belongs to those of the Sudeten range in North-east Moravia. But for purposes of convenience 'Sudeten,' was used as a generic term, covering all Germans of the Bohemian Lands, in contrast to the ' Alpenländer' of the old ' hereditary provinces.'

antagonism to the Habsburg dynasty, might have found common ground with the Alpine Germans but for the influence of the Sudetians, and why, after the fall of the dynasty, Vienna and Prague were slowly moving from a perfunctory *détente* to a real working agreement. In a word, Nazism was the natural expression of the Sudetian philosophy, the Austrian Republic that of the Alpine lands.

Hitler has paid tribute to Schönerer as the true forerunner of National Socialism, but has criticized both 'Ritter Georg' and the in every way superior Lueger as having failed as judges of human character, and the whole Pan-German agitation as having sunk to the level of 'Bourgeois, well-behaved, mildly radical' *(vornehm, gedämpft radikal)*. He quite unjustly condemns the Austrian Parliament as 'a swamp of general corruption' to address which is like 'casting pearls before the well-known animals.' It would be easy to cull from the speeches of Wolf, Iro and other pioneers a mass of abusive statements which bear no resemblance to pearls, but were admirably suited as food for swine. But if these men paved the way, the first to give concrete expression to the future Nazi doctrine was the German Workers' Party *(Deutsche Arbeiterpartei)*, founded in 1904 by a few unknown radical stalwarts, Knirsch, Krebs and Jung, reconstituted in 1909 as the 'German Social Party' *(Deutsche Soziale Partei)*, and again reconstituted in May, 1918, as the German National Socialist Workers' Party *(Deutsche Nazionalsozialistische Arbeiterpartei*, or DNSAP). These extremists, in the last Austrian Parliament of 1917, were openly clamouring for a Greater German Empire, with Austro-Hungarian domination over the Balkans and of course due subordination of all Slavs, while in its domestic policy a prominent item was nationalization on anti-capitalistic and anti-semitic lines. After the collapse of the monarchy and the occupation of 'German-Bohemia' by the Czechs with the endorsement of the Peace Conference, we saw that the Germans split into seven parties, and adopted an attitude of sullen negation towards the state ; but from 1927 onwards, partly owing to the shift towards the Right inside the Czech governing Coalition of parties, partly owing to the contrast in economic development between Czecho-slovakia and Germany, and partly owing to the trend towards decentralization exemplified in the Administrative Reform of 1926-1927, an activist policy was adopted by an important section of German opinion, and henceforth there were always two, and sometimes three, German members of the Cabinet. It should be noted that already at the election of 1925 the German Agrarians, Christian Socialists and Liberals polled between them 900,000 votes against only 250,000 from the Opposition parties ; in 1929 the two first polled 744,000, the Social Democrats (who not long after joined the Government) 506,000 and the Opposition 380,000. But there remained a remnant of irreconcilables and die-hards, with the ill-defined watchword *'Schule, Scholle, Arbeitsplatz'* (school, soil, working-place), demanding that all Sudetians should form a separate unit or *Volksgruppe* with its own control of culture and education, and that the solidly German districts *(das geschlossene Siedlungsgebiet*—an entity which had stubbornly defied the efforts of two generations to define it) should have autonomy, with a Diet of its own, and with German as its official language, and employing German officials only.

The Great Depression hit the Sudetian districts with special severity and the consequent unemployment and suffering served as automatic recruiting agencies for the extremists, who were in permanent contact

with their opposite number, the National Socialists of the Reich. Taking
a leaf from Hitler's book, they formed an organization called *Volkssport*
for youths over twenty-one, modelled exactly on the Storm Troops of the
Reich ; and the *Kameradschaftsbund* (or *K.B.*), founded as early as 1926
by three young Sudetians, Heinrich, Rutha, and Walther Brand, under
the neo-romantic influence of the Viennese professor Othmar Spann,
also came rapidly to the front. In its essence, it was a decisive turn away
from Liberalism, but though turning to the Middle Ages in order to
borrow certain ideas from the guild system, it pointedly ignored the
Church ; above all, it rested upon Germany's mission to unite all Germans
and in particular to reclaim Bohemia for that German spirit which was
one day to bring recovery to the whole world. *'Einmal wird am deutschen
Wesen die Welt genesen.'* Yet another organization called *Bereitschaft*
(readiness), with its headquarters at Olomouc, sought to strengthen
cultural contacts with the new Reich, whose plans now so obviously
followed the old Pan-German lines. Naturally enough it was the headstrong youths of the *Volkssport* who sailed nearest the wind ; and it will
remain a moot point whether the trial of seven of its student ringleaders
in 1932, on the charge of planning armed rebellion on behalf of a foreign
Power whom it was quite superfluous to name, was a necessary and
legitimate measure of Czech defence, or merely added oil to the flames.
As no arms could be discovered, the original charge had to be dropped,
but the accused having openly endorsed the twenty-one points of Hitler's
programme (the first of which demands the union of all Germans in a
Great German state), three of them were sentenced to two and a half
years for conspiring against the Republic. The public prosecutor was
inane enough to argue that the lack of all trace of weapons made the
affair all the more suspect. This incident was greatly exploited against
the activists, who were accused of complaisance to the Czechs and failure
to vindicate German rights. It coincided with Hitler's advent to power,
which galvanized the German minorities in twelve European countries,
and none more effectively than that of Bohemia.

Late in 1933 the National Socialist Party forestalled its dissolution
by voluntary liquidation, and several of its chiefs escaped across the
frontier ; the German National Party also wound itself up. This led to
fierce recriminations and threats in the Reich, but it was easy to point
out that a savagely totalitarian regime could hardly object to a neighbouring state discouraging a movement which aimed at its own *Gleichschaltung* or even elimination, and that similar measures were being
applied in Austria, but on far more drastic lines. Mussolini, in particular,
after encouraging Dollfuss to suppress the Socialists, could hardly protest
if he or Schuschnigg turned their attentions to the far more dangerous
Nazi movement in Austria.

The next turn of the kaleidoscope was the formation on October 1,
1934, of a new German party, the German Home Front (*Deutsche Heimat-
front*) under the auspices of Konrad Henlein, a man of thirty-five, known
only as a collaborator of the *K.B.* chiefs, and himself head of the German
Gymnastic Federation (*Turnverband*) of the Republic. In 1931 he had
published an article declaring 'war to the death on liberalism, even behind
the disguise of the cult of personality. Disciplined mass units rule the
present—Fascism, the Heimwehr, the Hitler movement ; for men wish
to be led in manly fashion. . . . We all know that an un-German parliamentarism and party system, which divides our people into inorganic

parts, will and must break down.' But in the party programme which he proclaimed at Böhmisch Leipa (Česká Lípa) in October, 1934, he struck a much milder note. He acclaimed the principle of leadership and assumed the part himself ; but he repudiated Pan-Germanism and Pan-Slavism equally, as leading inevitably to war ; he insisted that Fascism and Nazism alike lost their natural *raison d'être* at the Czechoslovak frontiers ; he declared against Treaty revision and Habsburg restoration, and he declared that 'we shall never renounce liberalism, i.e. unconditional respect for individual rights.' In the same way he argued with great fervour that loyalty to the race and to the state were not mutually exclusive, he repudiated the idea of 'a Sudeten German Parliament or anything like it,' and he drew a distinction between an irredentism due to 'ideological contacts' and one due to economic developments—thereby implying that remediable economic distress was the main cause of the unrest in German Bohemia. He concluded by offering 'openly and honourably the hand to peace.'

There was an uncomfortable discrepancy between these siren notes and the totalitarian methods of agitation developed during the elections of 1935 ; the fact that the chosen 'Leader' of the new party ostentatiously refrained from seeking election aroused hostile comment, and was taken as a slight to the parliamentary system. There was a constant insistence on the conception of *Volksgemeinschaft* as blending nationality, spirit, blood and culture and subordinating to it the hitherto prevalent conceptions of the state. Thanks largely to backing from beyond the frontier, Henlein won a resounding victory at the polls, resembling *in parvo* that of Hitler two years earlier. Out of 72 German seats he secured 44, with 1,249,000 votes, or 62% of the German electorate ; the German Agrarians and Christian Socialists lost about half their following, and the Social Democrats dropped from 506,000 to 299,000. To emphasize its essential unity of purpose, the victors assumed the title of 'Sudeten German Party (S.d.P.), implying that the Activists represented nothing. And in all seriousness activism had suffered a staggering blow, and was henceforward on the defensive.

During 1936 there was an anxious pause. The so-called Machnik Decree, by which the War Minister placed restrictions on the type of clerk employed by firms working on national armaments or defence work, was followed by a new State Defence Law, militarizing a zone immediately inside the frontiers of Bohemia, constructing 'Maginot' fortifications, restricting the movements of strangers and taking precautions against espionage. Quite inevitably, all these measures caused more dislocation among the Germans, who lived mainly on the periphery, than among the Czechs ; and the dissatisfaction thus engendered enabled Henlein to conduct a cautious, but quite unmistakable campaign for substituting a German for a Russian or Western orientation. There was much disingenuous talk about the country of Herder, Lessing and Goethe, as if they and all that they stood for were not in process of elimination in the country of Hitler, Göring and Röhm. In the summer President Beneš paid a series of visits to the German districts and declared himself in favour of 'direct, open and legal discussion, without pressure and without threats' between Czech and German ; but he did not succeed in arresting the steady drift from Activism into the camp of the crypto-Nazis. Two months earlier (June 21, 1936) Henlein had felt himself strong enough to reject as inadequate not only the existing Minority Law, but the whole theory upon which it rested. There must be protection not only to individuals, but to whole national groups ; 'every people and its responsible leaders must be acknowledged to be solely responsible for the adjustment of their own national status.' Pushed logically home in conjunction with a totalitarian interpretation of the state, this would have made Hitler the supreme arbiter of Sudetian destinies, and created a state within the state. An agreement reached on February 18, 1937, between the Hodža Government and the Young Activists, led by Wenzel Jaksch and Gustav Hacker, promised a more equitable apportionment of official contracts as between Czechs and Germans, and a stiffening up of minority practice under the existing laws : but of necessity, this did not go to the root of the matter. With reckless exaggeration it was claimed by the Henleinists that the Germans had 'about 44,000 state posts too few' (this of course included all sorts of minor jobs in the postal and railway services).

The best test of the status of the German citizen in the Republic is that provided in the educational statistics. Early in 1936 Henlein had publicly complained that in defiance of the minority treaty the Germans did not possess a due proportion of schools. But it was shown that in the previous school year, out of a total of 343,000 and 89,000 German children in primary and higher primary schools, all save 10,000 and 6,000 respectively attended schools where the language of instruction was German. It was also pointed out that most of these Germans in Czech schools had been freely sent by their parents to learn the other main language of the country, and that for the same reason a certain number of Czech children attended German higher primary schools. The controversy was thus reduced to a question of a tiny minority of 3% to 5%, and the insinuation that Czechization was being pursued in the schools of the Republic was blown sky-high. It is important to add that in the higher spheres of education the Germans occupied an equally favourable position ; they had in 1935, 80 secondary schools, 10 training colleges, 52 agricultural schools, 48 commercial academies, 98 technical and industrial schools, a university, 2 technical high schools, academies of music and art and two seminaries.

In 1937 Henlein struck a somewhat shriller note than before, demanding, without defining 'complete Sudetian autonomy,' and warning the Czechs that they must make good all the wrong they had done the Germans since 1918, and must not drive them to desperation. In April his colleagues (he still held aloof himself) laid draft proposals before Parliament amounting to little short of creating a state within the state. Each 'national organization' was to constitute a legal personality and elect its own 'sprecher' or speaker. Various provisions sought to stereotype the relations between the various nationalities, by setting up a national register or *Kataster* and prohibiting any change. The whole document, though moderately worded, implied the adoption of a rigid totalitarianism in each racial group ; and its adoption would automatically have wiped the Activists out of existence. Nothing further came of it, for the simple reason that it was intended from the first as a piece of propaganda. At the same time a somewhat lurid light was thrown upon the central management of this authoritarian party by the disgrace of one of Henlein's chief lieutenants, Walther Brand, before a Court of Honour, and by the arrest of another of the innermost ring, Heinrich Rutha, on homosexual charges reminiscent of such Nazi stalwarts as Röhm and Heines. Meanwhile the Nazi propagandist machine poured forth its scurrilities against the Czechs, invented, and placed in every capital of Europe, impudent stories of Soviet airfields in the Republic and other equally false stories of wholesale ill-treatment of a long-suffering German population by a brutal Czech police. But there were other ingredients in an elaborate technique : Gestapo agents kidnapped German political refugees in the Republic and spirited them across the frontier, or murdered them in their places of refuge, and in this and in a score of other ways intimidated the Activists. They lost no occasion of warning them of what was in store for those who took the side of collapsing Czech democracy and its judæo-plutocratic allies against the future master of Europe. The Nazi voice, then as now, was capable of modulation, and while the *Völkische Beobachter* fulminated, Henlein himself paid visits to London and cooed like any sucking dove.[1] He found there so complete a failure to grasp the implications of the situation (Paris he did not deign to visit, and it could be ignored if once London could be detached), that he was encouraged to send an open letter to President Beneš in October, 1937, maintaining that the Sudetian cause enjoyed sympathy in London, and that if the grant of autonomy were further delayed, the President would be responsible for the damage to European peace. This was too much for Prague, especially when launched parallel with fresh streams of calumny and abuse from the Reich : wild talk of an impending revolt was tested by a deliberate postponement of the municipal elections. Then followed an ominous lull, while the Führer again turned his attention to Austria. The Hodža Government genuinely took up the problem of implementing the undertakings of February, 1937 ; but the pace was slow and the difficulties were many—on the one hand a lack of otherwise qualified persons speaking both Czech and German—which was a measure of the watertight compartments in which the two races lived—and on the other the impossibility of dismissing large numbers of old officials to make way for those with full linguistic qualifications. There was also the political difficulty (in some ways the most insuperable of all) that in effect the Czechs were being asked to reward their Activist friends for ten years of loyal co-operation by giving their places to those whose occasional fair-spoken phrases could not conceal their blazing hostility to democracy and all its works. Stripped of all verbiage, Henlein's full demands amounted to this—that Czechoslovakia should admit the Trojan Horse of totalitarianism, but at the same moment renounce her purely defensive treaties with Soviet Russia and France, thus really surrendering to Berlin the control of her whole domestic and foreign policy. This would obviously mean, and was intended to mean, the end of the Republic, as created and upheld by Masaryk and Beneš.

The Anschluss

Superficial observers had hailed the agreement of July 11, 1936, between Austria and Germany as putting an end to the dangerous agitation set on foot in Austria by a compact Nazi minority and fomented by ample funds and instruments of terrorism. In reality it was merely a truce to lull the West into a false security while the Axis Powers flung more men and munitions into the Spanish struggle and finally turned the scale against the Spanish Republic. Already a whole year earlier Mr. Chamber-

---

[1] The present writer's experience of Henlein's London visits can be found in Appendix v.

lain had shown his complete indifference to the moral issues involved by concluding a 'Gentleman's Agreement' (save the mark !) with Mussolini on the very day that 4,000 Italian troops were landing at Cadiz. In the late summer the activities of Italian and German submarines in the Mediterranean had provoked a flicker of temper in the somnolent British lion, and Mr. Eden had been allowed to take a firm line at the Nyon Conference, with the result that Mussolini immediately drew in his horns. But at the end of October, when Mussolini published a casualty list of the Italians fallen in the Spanish War and himself distributed medals, he saw that the lion was again asleep, and drew the conclusion that Britain and France were either indifferent to the high principles which they were constantly announcing, or too timorous to act upon them, and that he would do well to throw in his lot finally with Germany and fling out of the League altogether. He also saw no less clearly that the abandonment of his vassal in Vienna was the price which he must pay for full German backing of Italy in the Mediterranean : with his eyes bent upon a new Impero Romano in Africa, he was ready to accept the inevitable corollaries of Austria's downfall, namely the ruin of Czechoslovakia, for which he cared nothing, and German infiltration of Hungary and the Balkans.

This brief incursion into diplomatic history may seem both tendentious and beside the point ; reflection will show that it provides the key to the happenings of 1938–1939. For it was in the winter of 1937 that Hitler initiated that policy of 'One by One' which he pursued with such success —at first bloodlessly, then with the sure aim of the long-practised thug, but finally with less and less effect, as the survivors were driven by self-preservation to form a common front against him. It is necessary always to insist upon the extent to which we ourselves are responsible for the ruin that has come upon us all.

At the turn of the year Hitler was crouching to spring at a fresh victim, though the victim itself remained blind till a very late hour and though its friends shut their eyes more tightly than ever. There were already signs in the background that something was imminent. Hitler postponed his annual account of his stewardship from January 30 to February 20, and in the interval thus gained introduced a purge among the higher generals, placed the Foreign Office in the hands of that reckless and overweening amateur Joachim von Ribbentrop, and removed the subtly perfidious Franz von Papen from the Embassy in Vienna. His plans had been seriously dislocated by Schuschnigg's arrest of Dr. Tavs, one of the leading Nazi plotters in Austria (January 26, 1938) ; and in high dudgeon he summoned the Austrian Chancellor to his Alpine Valhalla at Berchtesgaden, *ad audiendum verbum*. What was Schuschnigg's naïve amazement to find that Hitler, so far from offering co-operation in the repression of terrorism such as might disturb the improving relations between the two countries, browbeat and abused him and threatened the immediate invasion of Austria unless his ultimatum were accepted within three days. Seyss-Inquart and Guido Schmidt, whom Schuschnigg had to admit to his Cabinet as Minister of the Interior and Foreign Minister, were to escort the Trojan horse within the walls of Vienna. Hitler's delayed speech, with its demand for colonies, its flat rejection of internationalism and the League, and its abuse of Soviet Russia, also contained pointed allusions to the ten million Germans (i.e. six and a half in Austria three and a half in Czechoslovakia) who had been denied the right to join the Reich, in defiance of the principle of self-determination. So fatuously blind to what was taking place were Mr. Chamberlain and M. Daladier, that the former dispensed with the services of Mr. Eden within a few hours of Hitler's Reichstag menaces, thereby convincing Ribbentrop that his master could do what he liked with London and Paris.

At the twelfth hour Schuschnigg was at last fully alive to the danger, and consented to a Coalition of Clericals and Socialists and an immediate plebiscite. Within a few days it was abundantly clear to friend and foe alike that Austria would rally overwhelmingly in favour of the Coalition and reveal the Nazis as a hopelessly outnumbered minority. This had to be prevented at all costs ; and hence on March 11 the German Army poured across the Austrian frontier, seized Vienna and incidentally, by the suddenness of its treachery, caught all Hitler's opponents like rats in a trap, thus destroying the possibility of a Government in exile. The Gestapo lost not a day in installing their Terror in Vienna, not only against the Jews but against all independent-minded Austrians from Right to Left ; and on April 10 the plebiscite rigged by order of the Führer among a people from whom he had expected an adverse vote of 80%, resulted in a totalitarian poll of 99% in his favour ! They also revealed the care with which all kinds of details had been prepared in advance—the printed lists of thousands of suspects, the lavish Nazi bunting supplied for decoration, the accommodation for 700 invading aircraft, and so on. Perfidy could go no further.

In passing it is worth drawing attention to a curious trait of Hitler and his gangsters ; in the midst of action which sets every conception of law and order, of religion and plighted word, at open defiance, they must needs stop to imitate the free institutions which they are never tired of abusing. The Austrian plebiscite was as pitiable a farce as the Reichstag Trial, as arbitrary as the executions and shameless plunder in which they have since indulged in half the countries of Europe : why then not dispense altogether with legal, or constitutional or indeed moral forms and follow the 'sic volo, sic jubeo' of the most untrammelled tyrant since Zenghis Khan ? In June, 1934, he justified the cold-blooded murder of his old comrades by declaring that "in those twenty-four hours the Supreme Court of the German people was I," and the whole German nation, by its terrified silence, made itself the accomplice of his guilt. By his treatment of Austria he had added perjury to murder ; for in the most important of all his speeches (May 21, 1935) he had pledged himself not to annex Austria, and now he was breaking both it and his later pledges of July 11, 1936, and February 12, 1938.

At the critical moment all had not been well with the German army of invasion ; along the main roads through Linz to Vienna there had been little short of chaos, and if the Czechoslovak Army, whose military preparedness was well known, had been encouraged to intervene, the result might have been as surprising as that which would have followed Franco-British resistance to German invasion of the Rhineland. There were no illusions at that moment in Berlin ; and General Göring thought it advisable to summon the Czechoslovak Minister in Berlin, and give him the explicit assurance that Germany entertained no aggressive designs upon Czechoslovakia, and had therefore withdrawn her occupying forces to a distance of fifteen kilometres from the Bohemian frontier. Baron Neurath also told him that Germany considered herself bound by the German-Czech arbitration Convention of October, 1935, and these assurances were pointedly taken up by Mr. Chamberlain and Lord Halifax.

President Beneš and his advisers were not foolish enough to believe in Göring's good faith, and did all in their power to prepare their army for the now inevitable struggle. But they hesitated to act alone, at a moment when neither the statesmen of the West nor public opinion were really alive to the issues involved. The Duce had already been squared, and Russia was rightly suspicious of everyone and playing for time.

Mr. Chamberlain, happily rid of Mr. Eden, proceeded to negotiate with Italy—showing a strange indifference to the moral issues involved in the extinction of a country towards whom Britain and the League were peculiarly bound in honour. He also betrayed his naïve belief that man-eating tigers can be appeased by scraps of paper. He spoke of 'a new situation' created in Europe, of 'intensified insecurity,' but soon made it clear that not knowing what to do he would do exactly nothing. In France the parties were more interested in mutual mud-slinging than in the fate of Central Europe : important sections of the *grande bourgeoisie* merely saw in Czechoslovakia the allies of Bolshevism, and completely ignored the probable effects of the disappearance of Austria and Czechoslovakia upon the strategic situation in Europe, and therefore upon France's immunity from attack. Even Moscow, for all its realist grasp of European strategy, and for all its desire to save Bohemia, that most westerly bastion of Slavdom, was not prepared to draw upon itself the whole striking force of the German Army, and therefore preferred to win the longest possible respite for military armament. Faced by the rapid disintegration of the Versailles and Geneva system, the Czechs stood to arms, and were ready to sell their lives dearly, avoiding meanwhile all acts of provocation.

The Collapse of Activism

Henlein and his followers drew their own deductions when they saw that the Western Powers were left talking while Hitler marched ; their open jubilation led to an undignified stampede of the Activists into the S.d.P. camp. Dr. Spina resigned, and died soon afterwards ; only the Socialists stood firm, since for them, as for the Communists, there could be no compromise with the totalitarians. Rendered still bolder by this, Henlein on April 29 issued the so-called Karlsbad Points on the basis of which 'the legal order of the state must be reconstructed.' He was no longer content to claim full equality of status between Czech and German, full self-government for the German districts and the appointment of German officials in German areas ; these had already been conceded in theory. But he also demanded the recognition of the Sudetian Germans as 'a legal personality' and their right to confess 'German political philosophy'—in other words, National Socialism. This, if conceded, would have involved the erection of a state within the state—a totalitarian sub-state within a democratic state. At the same time he made it quite clear that he desired a revision of Czech foreign policy and the abandonment of any attempt to make of Czechoslovakia 'a bulwark against Germanism,' thus in effect asserting the right of a minority to reverse the whole system upon which the home and foreign policy of the Republic had rested since its foundation. While watching the effect of his new tactics upon both Czechs and Germans, Henlein again visited London, and although warned by Mr. Churchill and other political realists not to draw rash conclusions as to Britain's attitude towards Continental complications, he returned home convinced by the entourage of the Prime Minister, and by *The Times* and *Observer*, that Britain was not interested in Czechoslovakia and that the Czechs would have to choose 'between autonomy and separation.' It was at this very time that Mr. Chamberlain, at a private luncheon to American and Canadian journalists, gave it as his opinion that for geographical reasons neither France nor Russia, still less Britain, could fight for the Czechs and that Czechoslovakia, not being a homogeneous country, 'could not survive in its present form,' and had therefore better make the best terms it could with Hitler.

Chamberlain and 'Appeasement'

The gist of this, when published in the *Montreal Star*, and reinforced by Lord Halifax's view that peace stood higher than 'devotion to some high purpose,' and that Italy's conquest of Abyssinia should therefore be recognized, certainly contributed to the overweening confidence with which Hitler, on May 21, after consulting his colleague Mussolini, concentrated troops on the Bavarian and Saxon frontiers for a lightning attack upon Czechoslovakia. Prague replied with a partial concentration of forces, which went so smoothly and rapidly as to render mobilization unnecessary, and its timely warnings drew statements of a more than usually firm character from the British and French Governments. A spokesman of the Quai d'Orsay went so far as to say that 'if Germany crosses the Czech frontier, that will automatically start war, and France will furnish help to the uttermost.' For the moment the conflict was averted, but the Czechs, though attending with even more than usual fervour the splendid Sokol celebrations, were braced to a sense of imminent danger by periodic blasts of propaganda from the Reich, by denunciations of the Czechs as friends of 'the Kremlin murder rabble,' and by threats to the Activists of the fate that awaited them. It subsequently became known that Hitler on May 28 summoned the chief party and Army leaders, and intimated to them his firm resolve to occupy the Sudeten lands by the beginning of October at the very latest.

On the Czech side it has been very frankly argued that the Hodža Government made a mistake in not following up the *détente* of May 21 by the immediate promulgation of a new Plan, such as would have robbed the S.d.P. of its main arguments, and confronted Hitler with an agreed settlement. It may, however, be doubted whether this criticism is really valid, for on the one hand neither Dr. Hodža nor President Beneš, however eager to be conciliatory, could carry the Czech public beyond a certain point of concession to men whom they so profoundly distrusted as the smooth-faced Henlein and the rabid, cynical, Frank ; and on the other hand, and above all else, it was no longer a matter of speculation, but of common knowledge, on the basis of their acts and speeches, that Hitler and his henchmen did not want self-determination, autonomy, racial equality or democratic rights, but conquest, domination, and the complete denial to the Czechs of all those things for which they clamoured before the face of a still gullible Europe. In view of this fundamental fact it is utterly misleading to speak of the failure to reach agreement as due to President Beneš or to his disagreement with Dr. Hodža. The two men differed profoundly in temperament and outlook, and as exiles they were destined to fall still farther apart ; but it can be categorically asserted that up to the Allied ultimatum of September 17 they saw eye to eye, worked loyally together, and stood equally committed to concessions which we may condemn in retrospect not as inadequate, but as excessive, and as creating a state within the state.

The Runciman Mission

On the eve of the May crisis the British and French Governments had urged Prague to make concessions 'to the utmost limit of possibility,' and late in May had suggested an international committee of enquiry, but met with a flat refusal from Berlin. But during the British Royal visit to Paris on July 19 the two allies agreed upon a purely British enquiry, presumably on the ground that Britain, not being an ally of the Czechs, would be better able than the French to view the internal situation with the necessary impartiality. At the close of the parliamentary session, therefore, Mr. Chamberlain announced his decision to send Lord Runciman to Prague—'not in any sense as an arbitrator . . . but as an investigator and mediator . . . acting only in his personal capacity.' Prague, which had not even been consulted beforehand, was not unnaturally alarmed at the decision and still more at the Prime Minister's assertion that Lord Runciman was being sent 'in response to a request from the Government of Czechoslovakia'; for this was a direct misstatement. Another disturbing feature was the Prime Minister's definition of Lord Runciman as 'a person with the necessary experience and qualities'; for it was notorious that he had no previous acquaintance whatsoever with the country, its personalities, its problems and its languages. Another phrase in the same speech, to the effect that there was 'throughout the Continent a relaxation of that sense of tension which six months ago was present,' revealed the extent to which Mr. Chamberlain was suffering from illusions. Without going further afield in Europe, the appointment instantly stiffened the Henlein party, and greatly increased the tension in the Republic, not least between the S.d.P. and the Social Democratic Activists. Meanwhile Lord Halifax, speaking in the House of Lords, quoted Lord Runciman's own remark on his appointment: 'You are setting me adrift in a small boat in mid-Atlantic,' and endorsed it as an accurate description—thereby revealing an astonishing naïvety on the part of both men. If the mission was not already foredoomed to failure, Lord Runciman's practice of spending his week-ends with feudal magnates known to be coquetting with Nazism would have sufficed to prejudice public opinion against him. He even committed the blunder of first meeting Henlein at the Castle of Prince Max Egon Hohenlohe, who was not even a Czechoslovak citizen. The S.d.P., backed by the Gestapo and the Nazi press, continued to create incidents and incite its members to defend themselves against 'acts of provocation.' On September 2 Henlein paid his first open visit to Hitler, and an official German *communiqué* announced that he had gone 'at Lord Runciman's desire,' and that 'complete unanimity' had marked the meeting. Small wonder that the Czechs began to wonder whether London and Berlin were uniting against them.

During the recess Sir John Simon officially voiced the anxiety of the British Government, and its Ambassador in Berlin, on instructions, gave no less than four times the warning that Germany's military preparations might endanger not only the success of the Runciman mission, but even the peace of Europe. But as so often in these twenty years, in proportion as the one ally's tone grew firmer, that of the other seemed to falter ; in July Daladier had gone much further than Halifax was prepared to go ; in September Bonnet began to draw back, and while issuing to the French press a *démenti* of any renewal of pledges towards Czechoslovakia, warned Prague that France could not 'march' unless certain that Britain was at her side.[1] With this background in Europe, negotiations between the Czechs and Sudetians dragged on without the possibility of added momentum from Hodža, Beneš or Runciman. But on September 5 President Beneš, on the insistence of Lord Runciman, offered to the Henlein party the so-called Fourth Plan, which, in the words of the latter's own subsequent report on his Mission, 'embodied almost all the requirements of the Karlsbad Eight Points, and with a little clarification and extension could have been made to cover them in their entirety.' For the next week the Mission did what it could to promote a compromise between the Government and Henlein, though genuinely, if belatedly, aware that 'a breath might upset the card house' in which they were living.

This fatal breath came in the form of a leading article in *The Times* of September 7, which, after summarizing very fairly the course of the dispute, and admitting that 'no central government would still deserve its title if it did not reserve in its own hands Defence, Foreign Policy and Finance,' suddenly went off at a tangent and wrote as follows : 'If the Sudetians are not satisfied with the last Czech offer, it can only be inferred that they do not find themselves at ease within the Republic. In that case it might be well for the Czechoslovak Government to consider whether a solution should not be sought on some totally different lines, which would make 'Czechoslovakia an entirely homogeneous state by the secession of that fringe of alien populations who are contiguous to the nation with which they are united by race.' In other words, the view put forward by Chamberlain to the American journalists in May—that Czechoslovakia could not survive 'in its present form'—emerges in *The Times* in an authoritative and inspired call for surrender, behind the back of a Mission which had been sent to Prague to work for an intermediate solution. Official denials were at once issued by the Foreign Office and even by No. 10 Downing Street, but the mischief was already done, and Berlin and its Sudetian tools were now fully convinced that the article had the approval of the British Prime Minister. Their stiffening attitude was reflected in Hitler's speech at the Nürnberg party rally on September 12, in which he fulminated against 'this Beneš' and accused him of 'torturing,' and planning the 'extermination' of, the Sudetian Germans. Two days later Henlein and Frank publicly rejected both the Fourth Plan and even their own Karlsbad Points, then proclaimed an openly separatist programme without even waiting to consult their party executive. On September 15 Henlein fled to the Reich, leaving the rank and file to do the fighting, and declaring on the wireless : "We wish to live as free Germans ! We want to go home to the Reich." Two days later, as a self-revealed traitor, he was denouncing 'the Hussite-Bolshevik criminals of Prague,' and revealing by every word and action the perfidy of his attitude towards Runciman and Chamberlain. This combination of perfidy and cowardice on the part of the Leader caused an immediate

[1]On the 4th, it is true, he publicly declared "France will in any case remain faithful to her agreements and treaties."

revulsion of feeling and a considerable rally to the Activist cause : the Socialist leader Wenzel Jaksch launched an appeal 'to all men of good will' to defend the common patrimony of Czech and German. A group of a dozen of the great feudal magnates of Bohemia—Kinsky, Lobkowicz Schwarzenberg, Kolovrat, Sternberg, Czernin and others—waited on the President to assure him of their loyalty. By the night of Saturday the 17th calm reigned throughout the Republic, calm as complete as after the crisis of May 21 ; members of the Runciman Mission were able, from their personal experience, to explode the myth of Czech atrocities, and a week of normal development would have completely unmasked and discredited Henlein and his lieutenants.

Chamberlain and Hitler

Unhappily events took an entirely different turn, owing to the arbitrary and ill-advised action of the British Prime Minister. Seemingly indifferent to the merits of the case, and having apparently made up his mind in advance to hand over to Hitler more than the Czechs would ever voluntarily concede, he did not trouble to take with him either the Foreign Secretary or one of his permanent officials, but preferred to rely upon Sir Horace Wilson, who shared his own profound ignorance of European politics. He actually dispensed with his own interpreter when talking to the dictator. He did not even wait to consult his own emissary to Prague, but flew to Berchtesgaden on September 15 and talked to Hitler while Runciman was on his way from Prague to London. The Prime Minister came intending to negotiate a compromise, but found Hitler 'prepared to risk a world war rather than wait.' In Mr. Duff Cooper's words, 'he was met by an ultimatum' and made no alternative suggestion, but merely 'returned with proposals wrapped up in a cloak called self-determination.'

In his conduct of foreign policy, Mr. Chamberlain had to all intents superseded the Foreign Office, then under the able direction of Sir Robert Vansittart.[1] This did not pass unchallenged. A number of clear-sighted and courageous men, of whom Mr. Churchill was the most eminent, and many of whom afterwards became members of his Cabinet in the Second World War, were indignant at the then Prime Minister's undemocratic and unconstitutional methods. Mr. Eden voiced this feeling on September 26, when he declared, "The conviction is growing that continued retreat can only lead to ever-widening confusion." For the moment, however, the big battalions were against them, and bore them down.

Although, however, the fateful decision was taken without Lord Runciman, it is essential to the narrative to point out that he also, on the eve of his departure from Prague, had reached conclusions which amounted to a complete *volte-face*. Having accepted the constitutional and territorial integrity of Czechoslovakia as the basis of his mediation, having eventually accepted the Fourth Plan as perfectly just and workable, and as compatible with the Sudetian programme, and having laid the full blame

[1]'In the late summer of 1938, during the Munich crisis,' writes Mr. George Glasgow in *Contemporary Review* for June, 1943, 'Chamberlain took negotiations into his own hands, *even going to the length* of telegraphing directions to Sir Nevile Henderson to communicate only with No. 10 Downing Street, and not with the Foreign Office across the road.' As this seemed to me an overstatement (though of an essential fact which was no secret at the time), I asked Mr. Glasgow who was his authority for so categorical an assertion. He informs me that it was no other than Mr. Chamberlain himself who told him of these instructions : and he allows me to quote him to this effect.

upon Henlein and Frank for the breakdown of negotiations, he suddenly advocated 'a policy of immediate and drastic action'—i.e. 'the transfer of predominantly German districts' to Germany, without control or plebiscite. Yet within a few sentences he went on to admit that a hard and fast separation of German and Czech was impossible, that 'economic connections are so close that an absolute separation is not only undesirable but inconceivable,' and that 'history has proved that in times of peace the two peoples can live together on friendly terms.' The contradiction inside the one document is so crass as to have evoked the theory that certain passages had been interpolated by some other hand : the alternative is less sensational, but certainly does not suggest clearness of vision on the part of Lord Runciman.[1] His proposals amount to a cynical abandonment of close upon a million Czechs to Germany, to say nothing of the half million or more German Socialist stalwarts, to their deadliest enemies, and this as an alleged improvement upon existing minority legislation, which, though it might require amplification, admittedly went further than that of any other country in Central or Eastern Europe. Indeed not the least of the enormities of which the Mission was guilty, was its failure to consult the Activists, and in particular the Socialists led by Herr Wenzel Jaksch, whose able and detailed memoranda were never taken seriously.

The proposals culminate in the suggestion that 'the Czechoslovak Government should so remodel her foreign relations as to give assurances to her neighbours that she will on no account attack them . . .'' and that the Powers should 'guarantee assistance in the case of unprovoked aggression against her.' Mr. Fish Armstrong's comment goes to the root of the whole matter :—'What Lord Runciman was in fact urging was that Czechoslovakia be required to abolish political liberties, suppress free speech and co-ordinate the press under a totalitarian regime, relinquish her ties with France and Soviet Russia, give up her responsibilities as a 'grown-up' member of the League, accept in return a guarantee by 'the peaceful Powers,' whoever they might be, and enter the German economic system.'[2]

The Anglo-French Diktat

On Friday, September 11, Chamberlain returned to London, and on Sunday was joined by Daladier and Bonnet. Between them, in almost indecent haste, and without even informing, much less consulting the Czechoslovak Minister, Mr. Jan Masaryk, they drafted the so-called 'Anglo-French Plan,' which went even farther than the Runciman report, by throwing over all idea of a plebiscite and proposing the immediate transfer to the Reich of all districts containing over 50% of Germans.[1]

Runciman only went so far as to suggest "self-determination at once" in "frontier districts where the Sudetian population is in an important majority." The Anglo-French Plan completely overlooked the fact that by this definition it might in many places be handing over a forty per cent German minority of socialist activists to its deadliest foe. It may be doubted whether it either thought or cared. The details would be settled

[1] Incidentally, it is widely believed among the Czechs that the stubborn silence and retirement into which Lord Runciman has withdrawn, is due to remorse at discovering too late the trap into which he was led, and his own share in precipitating disaster, and at the same time to resentment at the way in which he was used by his own chief as a mere tool in a preconceived strategic plan.

[2] *When there is no Peace*, p. 67.

by 'some international-body' and a general guarantee of the new frontier 'against unprovoked aggression' would be substituted for the treaties with which France and Britain were proposing to dispense. Well might Dr. Osuský complain bitterly that his country had been 'sentenced without even being heard,' by those on whose plighted word it had relied. Direct transfers would be entrusted by the amateurs of London and Paris to lesser amateurs on the spot.

There was consternation, and also intense indignation, in Prague at the callous way in which the Great Powers were using Czechoslovakia as a scapegoat. The note which the Hodža Cabinet wrote in answer to the Plan (and which, incredible as it may seem, was withheld from publication in London and Paris),[1] tried to bring home to its authors the enormity of the precedent thus adopted. The most democratic state east of the Rhine was being peremptorily ordered, by an ally and a friendly Power, almost at a moment's notice, to submit to drastic frontier revision without reference to Parliament. This would inevitably 'affect the democratic regime of the country and its juridical system,' would place it at the mercy of Germany and would involve political changes in Central and Southern Europe so profound as to destroy the whole existing balance of forces. This 'supreme appeal'—which subsequent events have justified to a terrifying degree—was simply brushed aside, and during the night of September 21 the British and French Ministers, Mr. Newton and M. de Lacroix, received telephonic instructions to make an immediate *démarche* and to insist that the Prague Government should withdraw its note 'and urgently consider an alternative that takes account of realities.' This urgency was due to the fact that Chamberlain had already arranged to pay a second flying visit to Hitler, this time at Godesberg.

The Midnight Ultimatum

At 2 a.m. the British and French Ministers, Mr. Newton and M. Delacroix, were received by President Beneš, and the former handed to him the British reply to the Czechoslovak Note. This document opened with the categorical statement that the Czechoslovak Note 'in no way meets the critical situation which the Anglo-French proposals were designed to avert,' and would, in London's opinion, if made public, lead to an immediate German invasion. The Prague Government was therefore urged to withdraw it and 'urgently consider an alternative that takes account of realities.' By persisting in its adherence to the note, they would make a second visit of Chamberlain to Hitler useless and bring about a situation for which His Majesty's Government could take no responsibility. The Czech proposal of arbitration was brushed aside as obviously inacceptable to Germany.

This was supplemented by a still more categorical statement of the French Minister, which culminated in the phrase : 'If the Czechoslovak Government is unable to accept forthwith the Franco-British proposals' and rejects them, and 'if war results, it is Czechoslovakia who will be responsible for it, and France will not associate herself with it (*ne s'y associera pas*).' At the President's request this was confirmed in a written communication before mid-day. After affirming that the Franco-British

---

[1] It was first published in English by the present writer in his *Munich and the Dictators*, and by Mr. Fish Armstrong in *When there is no Peace*—in each case as a special Appendix.

démarche was regarded in Paris as the sole means of arresting a German invasion of Czechoslovakia, it went on to argue that by rejecting the proposal of the two Governments Czechoslovakia would be 'taking the responsibility of causing Germany to resort to force.' It would thereby 'violate the solidarity established between France and Britain,' and thus rob French assistance 'of all practical efficacy.' M. Bonnet, it was added, had 'already given indications in this sense' to M. Osuský as early as July, and finally on September 20. Hence Czechoslovakia, in persisting, would be 'taking a risk from which we are conscious of having saved her, and should herself understand the conclusions which France has the right to draw if Czechoslovakia does not immediately accept the Franco-British proposal.'

Translated from diplomatic verbiage into plain speech, this meant that the French and British had decided to offer Germany a cession of Czechoslovak territory, over the head of Prague ; that if Czechoslovakia rejected the proposals dictated to her, she would be held responsible for war by her own ally and by that ally's friend. The phrase relative to 'Franco-British solidarity' could only mean that Britain was resolved not to take part in such a war and would therefore leave France to face Germany alone ; and as this would destroy the value of French assistance to Czechoslovakia, the latter must realize that France also would not go to war.

Conscious of the peculiar infamy involved in abandoning an ally whom they had repeatedly encouraged—not to say incited—to resist German demands, MM. Daladier and Bonnet put about the deliberately false statement that the Czechoslovak Premier Dr. Hodža or President Beneš himself—the story has several versions—had on their own initiative asked Paris to present an ultimatum, in order that they might the more easily convince Czechoslovak opinion that surrender was inevitable. Both statesmen gave categorical and convincing denials, but Bonnet continued the campaign of calumny in the scurrilous but influential Hitlerite organ *Gringoire*.

This midnight interview, which for sheer tragedy has taken its place in Bohemian history with the Defenestration of 1618, was followed by a Cabinet meeting at which stock was taken of the desperate situation —France repudiating the pledges which she had vigorously reaffirmed no less than thrice during the current year ; Britain not legally bound, but doing all in her power to encourage French repudiation, even to the extent of threatening to break her own pledge to France if France stood by her treaty with Czechoslovakia ; Russia only bound in the event of France honouring her word ; Roumania and Jugoslavia bound to help against Hungary, but not against Germany, and in any case not in a position to be effective if the Western Powers held aloof ; Jugoslavia indeed, under Prince Paul and Stojadinović, drawing daily closer to the Axis ; Italy working for the partition of Czechoslovakia ; Poland and Hungary preparing to stab in the back. President Beneš had, it is true, categorical assurances that Soviet Russia, in response to a direct appeal, would intervene, no longer on the basis of treaty pledges, but simply to save a kindred Slav nation in distress. It must, however, be added that Moscow never attempted to define the exact manner in which such assistance would be made effective. But even in their despair the Czech statesmen shrank back from the consequences of such a decision, realizing that this would have enabled the Nazis to proclaim an ideological Holy

War against Bolshevism, thereby paralysing opinion in the West and putting Czechoslovakia in the firing-line between the two camps.

The Government submitted, and then set itself to explain to a stupefied nation that it had been 'exposed to pressure for which there was no precedent in history, and which amounted to a *"Diktat"* such as is imposed upon a vanquished people. But we are not a vanquished people. We submitted in order to avoid greater losses, misery and bloodshed. We are sacrificing ourselves to save peace, as Christ sacrificed Himself to save humanity.' Dr. Hodža resigned, and was succeeded as Premier by General Sirový, the Inspector-General of the Army, to whom public opinion somewhat mistakenly looked as the strong and silent man, a modern Žižka, capable of saving his people.

Godesberg

On September 22, having enforced Czech submission 'with indecent haste and ruthlessness' (Mr. Amery's words in the Munich debate), and refused to summon the British Parliament, Mr. Chamberlain flew to Godesberg, only to find himself confronted by 'a totally unexpected situation.' Hitler's demands had of course risen in the interval, and now included total evacuation, within a week, of all the districts indicated on a map drawn by his military advisers and now laid before his visitor, and an early plebiscite in other areas, 'to be more exactly defined later.' This was too much even for a statesman bent upon a settlement at all costs ; we have his own word that he 'bitterly reproached' Hitler 'for his failure to respond,' and described his terms as 'an ultimatum rather than a memorandum.' For the first and last time during the crisis he showed some consideration for the Czechs, by informing them that London could no longer uphold its advice against mobilization. That same evening Czechoslovakia mobilized, and extraordinary scenes of enthusiasm and sober resolve were witnessed in every town and village of the Republic. In Paris Daladier reaffirmed France's resolve to fulfil her obligations if Czechoslovakia were attacked ; in Geneva Litvinov reaffirmed Russia's loyalty to her obligations ; in Moscow the Polish Chargé was warned that if Poland attacked Czechoslovakia, Russia would regard the Russo-Polish Treaty of non-aggression as null and void. On the other side, Henlein's fugitive lieutenants were allowed by Goebbels to broadcast the foulest abuse against the 'bandit state' ; to this Hitler added, in a speech at the Sportpalast, hysterical personal diatribes against Beneš. 'Two men confront each other : there is Beneš, and here am I. . . . We do not want any Czechs : our demand for the Sudetens is irrevocable . . . Beneš has it in his hands to choose either peace or war. He will accept my demands or we shall go and liberate our Germans.' And among the countless listeners who heard him roaring like a wild animal, and heard the fanatic responses of his audience, there were some who interpreted Hitler's 'simulation of madness' as the 'supreme bluff' directed against the feeble nerves of British and French Ministers.

The Lists are Set

On September 27, undeterred by a special message from the Prime Minister, conveyed by Sir Horace Wilson, Hitler announced that unless the Godesberg demands were accepted by 2 p.m. German mobilization would at once begin. Among all his crudities of speech, nothing was more insulting than the passage in which he spoke of Germany's 'will to peace' with Britain, and hoped that 'those who are of the same will will gain the upper hand in the British people.' If it meant anything, this meant that, as Mr. Eden had had to go because he was unacceptable to the Axis, so now Mr. Chamberlain, unless he showed complete subservience, would also be regarded as an obstacle. That evening Chamberlain broadcast to the nation, protesting his inability to understand how Englishmen could be on the verge of war, 'because of a quarrel in a far-away country between people of whom we know nothing.'[1] Then, with almost unbelievable naïvety, he admitted that after Berchtesgaden he had forced upon the Czechs proposals which gave Hitler 'the substance of what he wanted,' upon which the Führer had promised that 'after this Sudeten German question is settled, that is the end of Germany's territorial claims in Europe ' ! He felt bound to say that he found Hitler's attitude 'unreasonable,' but at once went on to offer him a British guarantee of Czech fulfilment—presumably to be enforced by yet another *Diktat*—and to state his readiness to pay a third visit to Germany, in search of the appeasement that eluded all his efforts. As if to ensure that Hitler should remain unyielding, he added that he could not involve 'the whole British Empire, simply on her (Czechoslovakia's) account.' Only if one nation 'had made up its mind to dominate the world by fear of its force' would he feel justified in going to war ; and his whole tone implied that he did not believe this of Hitler. None the less, four hours later the mobilization of the British Fleet showed that there was some sense of reality left in high quarters in London.

On the same day President Roosevelt added a warning to Hitler against 'provoking a war as unnecessary as it is unjustifiable,' and suggested the holding of a conference of all nations directly concerned 'in some neutral spot.' The President, with a clear vision that contrasted with the groping blindness of Chamberlain and Daladier, had already on August 18 warned his people that 'We in the Americas are no longer a far-away Continent to which eddies of controversy beyond the seas could bring no interest or harm. They had become 'vital factors in world-peace, whether we choose or not.' His Secretary of State, Mr. Cordell Hull, had rightly argued that 'when freedom is destroyed over increasing areas elsewhere, our ideals of individual liberty, our most cherished political and social institutions, are jeopardized.' A fortnight later the American Ambassador in Paris, Mr. Bullitt, taking his cue from these utterances, declared that 'if war breaks out in Europe once more, no man can say or predict whether or not the United States would be involved in such a war.'

Meanwhile the evacuation of Paris had already begun ; Russia advised Prague to appeal to the League under Article XI or XVI, and was preparing for action (though circumspectly, so as to give no excuse for the launching of an anti-Bolshevist campaign in the West); there were obvious signs of Italy and Spain leaning towards neutrality, Poland began to doubt the wisdom of her blackmailing policy, and Hungary played a waiting game. Roumania remained absolutely loyal, Jugoslav and Bulgarian opinion were at one in sympathy for the Czechs. Germany stood alone, and it was believed at the time in specially well-informed quarters that the Army Chiefs strongly urged the Führer against the risk

[1] In the version given to America by the Columbia Broadcasting Corporation, this phrase inaccurately runs, 'people of whom we *need* know nothing.'

of war, and that they had been influenced in this by M. Litvinov's outspoken speech at the League Assembly a week earlier, in which he advocated collective action and announced not only the readiness of the Russian army chiefs to confer with the French and Czech staffs, but even Russia's intention of joining the French in defence of Czechoslovakia. It is not too much to affirm that the attitude of Russia was clear and consistent throughout the crisis, whereas that of the two Western Powers was inexplicable on any other showing than that from the first they had no intention of helping Czechoslovakia, for otherwise their neglect of the first steps towards military co-operation in case of need would have been sheer insanity.

Chamberlain Goes to Munich

On September 28 Chamberlain gave the House an account of his policy. He announced his Government's willingness to join in a general international guarantee of the new Czechoslovak boundaries against aggression 'in place of the existing treaties with France and Russia, which involve reciprocal obligations of a military character.' He tacitly admitted that this drastic reorientation had been forced upon Prague without any pretence at consultation. He insisted that the Government was thus 'accepting a completely new commitment,' but failed to explain what value such a guarantee could offer in a radically transformed Europe. In view of his failure to implement the pledge a few weeks later, it must be assumed that he either had not thought out the meaning of his offer, or had never meant it seriously. He closed his speech by the sensational announcement that he had sent 'the last, last, message' to Hitler, actually offering to discuss with him in Berlin an arrangement which would give him 'all essentials without war and without delay,' and that Hitler had invited him, with Mussolini and Daladier, to Munich next day. The scene that followed has been accurately described as an outburst of 'mass hysteria.'[1] All discussion or caution went by the board. The Foreign Secretary, Lord Halifax, was spared the deadly humiliation of ratifying his chief's surrender, and Mr. Chamberlain flew to Munich, accompanied by Sir Horace Wilson, Mr. Strang and Mr. Ashton-Gwatkin, who was specially qualified as the official adviser to the Runciman Mission.

At Godesberg there had still been some pretence of consulting the Czechs, or at least notifying them of decisions or listening to their arguments. At Munich the British Prime Minister showed more plainly than ever before his disregard for their rights and interests, by consenting to their exclusion from the discussions. This embargo was applied not only to the Little Entente and to Poland, but to Soviet Russia, whose banishment from the councils of Europe was a major aim of the Axis Powers. Daladier found himself in a minority of one and lacked the courage to resist. Thus the Munich Agreement was pushed through with indecent haste and without the slightest attempt to check off either the facts or the arguments upon which the decisions were based. Its terms can be summed up quite briefly. Evacuation of the Sudeten lands was to be

---

[1] The present writer witnessed this scene from a seat 'under the clock,' with a full view of the Conservative benches. He watched many members cheering and waving their papers, some actually weeping with emotion and relief. He will never forget the grim, set faces of three men (there doubtless were others), who held aloof from the demonstration, realizing the dire consequences which the House was preparing for itself: they were Mr. Churchill, Mr. Eden and Mr. Amery. He will remember the scene as the most humiliating in all his experience.

carried out in four stages, the first beginning as early as October 1, the fourth being completed on October 7, according to lines indicated on a map supplied by the German General Staff. Then an international Commission of the four Powers together with Czechoslovakia was to lay down 'the conditions governing evacuation and to define forthwith the remaining territory of preponderantly German character,' in time for this also to be occupied by October 10. All 'existing installations' in the surrendered territory, whether fortifications or factory plants, were to be handed over intact—in other words, the Czechoslovak Army was to place itself, bound hand and foot, at the mercy of Nazi Germany. The Commission was then to determine what other territories should be submitted to a plebiscite, not later than the end of November, and its concluding function would be to carry out the final delimitation of frontiers.

The Munich Diktat

While the Big Four prepared their new 'Diktat,' the two Czech representatives at Munich, MM. Mastný and Hubert Masařík, who reached Munich by air at 4.30 p.m. on Thursday, September 29, were met by Gestapo agents, escorted to their hotel, and kept waiting till 10 p.m., before Mr. Gwatkin was able to show them a map indicating the new frontiers. "If you do not accept," he told them, "you will have to settle your affairs alone with Germany." Finally, they were admitted, at 1.30 a.m. on September 30 to the presence of Chamberlain, Daladier and their discomfited officials, Hitler and Mussolini not having deigned to wait. In the words of M. Masařík's report, 'The French were visibly embarrassed,' and seemed to realize their loss of prestige. But Mr. Chamberlain 'who was constantly yawning, without the least sign of embarrassment, would hardly listen to Czech enquiries or objections.' It at once transpired that there was no intention of submitting the plan to Prague or even listening to its views ; the four statesmen regarded the plan as already accepted, and Prague was curtly informed by telephone that it must send its delegates to the International Commission to Berlin by 5 p.m. on that very day at latest, and by the next day the officer whose duty it would be to fix with the Germans the details of evacuation of the First Zone.

Godesberg and Munich

Chamberlain, in justifying himself before the House, spoke of the Godesberg Memorandum of Hitler as 'in fact an ultimatum' and as 'inacceptable terms' ; but he stressed the difference between it and the final Munich Agreement, and argued that 'on the difference between these two documents will depend judgment as to whether we were successful in what we set out to do, namely to find an orderly, instead of a violent, method, of carrying out an agreed decision.' On this basis he stands utterly condemned.

(1) The principle of 'international supervision' was thrown to the winds, the time-limit before actual occupation being made so short that the Czechs had to surrender not only their line of forts, but all their innermost military secrets. This was, of course, the reason for German insistence, but when warned of this, Chamberlain and Daladier turned a deaf ear. Incredible as it sounds, Czechoslovakia was forced to surrender her main defences before the future frontier had been fixed, and without any guarantee that a discussion of details would be allowed.

(2) If the Godesberg line took in certain areas not predominantly German, the Munich line assigned to Germany further predominantly *Czech* areas.

(3) The Berlin Commission, in fixing the Fifth Zone, disregarded the principle of ceding only districts with over 50% of Germans ; in Northern Moravia 254 Czech communes, with 221,000 Czechs and 14,500 Germans, were made over to Germany, and in Southern Moravia 38, with 54,000 Czechs and 16,500 Germans. No fewer than 719,000 Czechs in all were assigned to Germany (leaving 6,476,000 Czechs and 250,000 Germans inside the torso). More monstrous still, on November 22 it transpired that Germany was to receive a Sixth Zone never even mentioned at Munich, which contained 70 more villages, with at least 60,000 more Czechs. The main railways connecting Prague with Brno, and both cities with the industrial centre of Moravská Ostrava and with Slovakia, were cut at nine places in all, thus securing to Germany a strategic and economic stranglehold over the country.

(4) The original proposal for a plebiscite in certain areas, to be defined by the Commission, was discarded in favour of 'direct transfer' on Godesberg lines.

(5) The facilities for evacuation of persons and property from the transferred areas were abandoned, and only two days elapsed before the announcement of the line of the Fifth Zone and its actual occupation by German troops.

(6) The provisions for opting during a period of six months, were simply allowed to lapse.

(7) ' The new system of guarantees,' it was claimed by Chamberlain, would give Czechoslovakia 'a greater security than she has ever enjoyed in the past.' It is difficult to believe that this was sincerely meant, for when, on the second day of the debate, Sir Thomas Inskip spoke of the Government's 'moral obligation to treat the guarantee as being now in force,' the Premier next day denied that it was in operation, and never did anything to make it effective.

Poland's Seizure of Teschen

At Munich the main subject of discussion was of course the Sudeten question, but it was agreed that the territorial claims of Poland and Hungary should also be considered at an early date. On September 30, while Czechoslovakia was actually on the operating table, the Polish Foreign Minister, Colonel Beck, sent a peremptory note to Prague demanding immediate cession of the Teschen district ; the Prague Government was not in a position to resist, and by October 10 the Polish Army was in possession of its uttermost claims. If it had limited itself to the district which had caused the dispute between Czechoslovakia and Poland in 1918, and whose population was predominantly Polish, a reasoned case could have been presented, though even then Poland's action could have been criticized as unchivalrous to the last degree. But unhappily Colonel Beck, instead of contenting himself with the linguistic or ethnographic boundary, proceeded to annex a number of more westerly districts, which were incontestably Czech, and to which Poland had never laid claim ; and during November he helped himself to additional territory both in Czech-Silesia and in Slovakia. The total territory seized by Poland contained 77,000 Poles, with 20,000 Germans and 132,000 Czechs. It included the key railway junction of Bohumín (Oderberg), and the greater part of the coal-mines and industries of Ostrava and Karvinna. Thousands of Czechs were expelled with quite unnecessary cruelty, and the Czech schools were at once closed. By this action the ruling clique of Poland not merely stultified the principles on which her own claims rested, but displayed peculiar perfidy towards a sister-nation in her bitter need, and a degree of short-sightedness which all too soon was to be dearly paid for. At the time there was much loose talk about the need for an improved strategic frontier to hold Germany in check; but when it came to war in September, 1939, the new lines were overrun by the Germans within the first twenty-four hours.

'Peace with Honour'

What has paradoxically been called the Munich 'Settlement'—more accurately described by Mr. Fish Armstrong as 'Peace when there is no Peace'—was achieved by five successive ultimatums—two presented by Germany to Britain and France, and three by Britain and France to Czechoslovakia. It was described by Mr. Chamberlain as 'Peace by Agreement' and 'Peace with Honour,' but if this be accurate, words lose all their meaning, for there is no more abject surrender in all British history; it was reached by dictation, not agreement; and it will always remain a moot question whether it was more dishonourable for France to violate her treaty with Czechoslovakia or for Britain to drive her to repudiate. It was conducted throughout on undemocratic lines, Parliament being confronted at each decisive stage with an accomplished fact; the Premier's acceptance of the Munich invitation was launched with such dramatic skill as to stifle all question or discussion, and when next Parliament could meet and supposed itself to be engaged in a decisive debate, the fate of Czechoslovakia was already irrevocably sealed, and German troops were actually marching in while Members talked in Westminster. Viewed from the Czechoslovak angle it was a Diktat more peremptory than that addressed by Austria-Hungary to Serbia after the murder of the Archduke, and not by an outraged enemy, but by an ally and a friend. Moreover, it was framed in open defiance of the whole Czechoslovak constitutional position, and in such a way as to make it impossible to consult the Prague Parliament or public opinion.

There was, however, a still wider aspect of the Munich 'settlement.' No other than Mr. Churchill described it as 'total and unmitigated defeat,' and Mr. Duff Cooper reminded the House that Hitler had got away without fighting 'by well-timed bluff, bluster and blackmail.' In the words of Mr. Richard Law we had 'obtained by peaceable means what we had fought four wars to prevent happening, namely the domination of Europe by a single Power.' The Premier's 'policy of scuttle and defeatism,' said Sir Archibald Sinclair, was merely storing up for a future Government 'the hard choice between war and complete submission to the Dictator's will.' We had, in fact, submitted to the very danger which, in the words of Sir Edward Grey, we so narrowly escaped in 1914—'the danger of sitting still while Germany conquered Europe.'

What the Western Powers sanctioned at Munich was not the fulfilment of self-determination, but the surrender of a key position to the Pan-Germans. The frontier of Bohemia, one of the oldest in all Europe, and never altered even in the darkest days of national eclipse, ceased, at one stroke, to be defensible, and the whole Danubian area was at the mercy of Germany. The Czechoslovak Army, for the moment, remained in being, but most of its defensive positions were lost, its material resources—especially in coal—were seriously curtailed, and Germany obtained the right to build a strategic arterial road connecting Breslau and Vienna, and cutting in half what remained of the Republic. In terms of European strategy, the best small army in the world, with a total strength of 1,500,000 men and 2,000 planes, was entirely immobilized and threatened with speedy destruction. In the event of war, France and Britain had in their folly thrown away the help of between thirty-five and forty-five divisions, to say nothing of air bases within striking distance of Leipzig, Munich and Berlin. Moreover, their abandonment of the last free democracy east of the Rhine was at one and the same time a deadly blow to democratic institutions inside the Republic, a direct encouragement to Nazi tendencies in all the smaller states, especially in the Balkans, and a rebuff to the principles of the League, to which Czechoslovakia had shown such loyalty for twenty years. For France it meant the collapse of her whole system of alliances and a radical change in the balance of forces on the Continent. For all, it meant that the democratic ideology was being driven more and more on to the defensive, and that the democratic Powers were associating themselves with the Axis's open contempt for the sanctity of treaties.

What enlightened opinion in the New World thought of Munich may be inferred from a brief statement made on September 28, by President Roosevelt's secretary, Mr. Early. Munich, he said, did not correspond to the intentions of the President, who had envisaged, not 'a Directory of Four,' but a conference of all the countries interested—that is to say, Czechoslovakia, Poland, Russia and Hungary as well as the four Great Powers—and considered that the meeting should have been held in a neutral country. Small wonder that after Mr. Chamberlain's surrender America should have withdrawn into a disgusted isolation.

The Role of France

It was inevitable that in a book intended for English readers the decisive part played by Britain in the overthrow of Czechoslovak independence should be given due prominence. But it is now no less essential to redress the balance by summarizing the still more humiliating and perfidious conduct of the French Government. At the moment so skilfully selected by Hitler for the invasion of Austria, France was without a Government, but one of the first steps taken by M. Paul-Boncour as Foreign Minister in the newly-formed Cabinet of M. Blum was to renew in the most positive form French obligations towards her Czechoslovak ally in the event of a similar attack upon her. This Cabinet, however, barely survived for a month, and on April 10 was replaced by M. Daladier as Premier, with the sinister figure of M. Georges Bonnet as Foreign Minister. The new Premier in his first public declaration laid great stress on France's 'fidelity to all existing pacts and treaties' and was naturally more explicit to the Czechoslovak representative. But there is strong reason to believe that between them Daladier and Bonnet had already resolved to recast French foreign policy, and were planning to draw back from Central Europe, to liquidate or abandon their obligations to Czechoslovakia, the

Little Entente and Soviet Russia and even to evade their commitments under the League Covenant, with a view to concentrating their efforts upon the maintenance of the French Empire. It was upon these terms that Foreign Affairs were offered to Bonnet, after other more reputable statesmen had rejected them as unacceptable ; and it is characteristic of the man that one of his first steps was to assure the Czechoslovak Minister, Dr. Osuský, that no change in foreign policy was contemplated Yet by the end of the month, when Daladier and Bonnet visited London, they were agreed that pressure should be applied to Prague, even at the risk of Henlein and his party acquiring the position of a state within the state. During the British Royal Visit to Paris in July these designs assumed a more concrete shape ; the French Ministers became more fully aware of the negative and timid policy of the Chamberlain Government, and were thus encouraged to believe that they could act with impunity so far as Britain was concerned. None the less, M. Daladier on July 12 reaffirmed more categorically than ever France's 'solemn undertakings' towards Czechoslovakia, which 'cannot be evaded.' The first hint of a change was conveyed by M. Bonnet on July 27, to the effect that France could not 'march' unless Britain were at her side. But already the leading French diplomatists had been called back to Paris to discuss the changed situation and to receive new instructions ; and one of them, on returning to his post, called his staff together and informed them as a dire secret that Paris had decided to leave Prague to its fate, adding with a mixture of melancholy and cynicism, 'C'est fini, mes amis.'

Yet throughout the summer the French Government continued to conceal its veritable intentions and to reaffirm its loyalty. Specially notable was Daladier's answer to President Roosevelt's appeal of September 26, in which he declared that France would be 'faithful to the spirit and to the letter of our engagements.' During the fateful visit of Daladier and Bonnet to London on the 17th, the latter had given to Lord Halifax a most misleading summary of the considered views of General Gamelin as Chief of Staff—in effect, omitting the military pros and underlining the cons of a steadfast policy.[1]

Most damning of all, however, was the attitude of the French Government to the *communiqué* issued by Lord Halifax on the night of Hitler's Sport-Palace speech, stating that if despite all Chamberlain's efforts for peace Germany should attack Czechoslovakia, 'France will be bound to come to her assistance, and Britain and Russia will certainly stand by France.' This memorable declaration was intended to prevent a repetition of the situation of August, 1914, when Sir Edward Grey's delay in pronouncing himself until Parliament had expressed its opinion, was (most unfairly) treated as a failure to prevent war. This time, instead of arousing the gratitude of French opinion, it was treated by a large section of the French press, with the direct encouragement of M. Bonnet himself, as a bundle of *fausses nouvelles* put out by Sir Robert Vansittart, 'the chief of the War Party at the Foreign Office' and 'endorsed by an obscure underling.'[2]

The campaign against 'the soi-disant *communiqué* of the F.O.' was

[1] As an immediate consequence of Munich, Bonnet ejected M. Comert from the Press Bureau of the Quai d'Orsay, and sent M. Massigli to the distant, if important, post of Ankara, leaving M. Leger in the same sort of isolation to which his British opposite number, Sir Robert Vansittart, had already been reduced.

[2] These are the words of the well-known defeatist writer, Pierre Dominique, in his book *Après Munich*.

continued by the *République*, the *Liberté*, the *Matin* and other journals, the latter denouncing it as 'a clever lie,' though it was known to have been issued with the full approval and authority of Lord Halifax himself. It was not till October 24 that Bonnet, who had meanwhile dismissed his own press chief, M. Comert, at the instance of *Gringoire*, and the Nazi press, found it convenient to admit the *fausses nouvelles* to have been perfectly accurate. The lie had been given 'time on its own wings to fly,' and the mischief was already done.[1]

In the light of these facts, which could easily be amplified, it is not possible to acquit the rulers of France of bad faith and evasion, whereas Mr. Chamberlain was merely unimaginative and impervious to facts.

The Second Republic

In striking contrast to the pitiable blindness of Mr. Chamberlain and to his stubborn indifference to the moral issue—in Lord Vansittart's words—'an honest man endowed with more confidence than knowledge'—there was one British statesman who never swerved in his condemnation of Munich and of all its works. During the baleful Munich debate Mr. Churchill said : "All is over. Silent, mournful, abandoned, broken, Czechoslovakia recedes into the darkness. . . . I venture to think that in future the Czechoslovak state cannot be maintained as an independent entity. I think you will find that in a period of time which may be measured by years, but may be measured only by months, *Czechoslovakia will be engulfed in the Nazi regime.* . . . The whole equilibrium of Europe has been deranged, and the terrible words have for the time being been pronounced against the Western democracies, 'Thou art weighed in the balance and found wanting'."

He was only too true a prophet, and it remains for us to summarize the main events during the five months of twilight and transition that separated the Munich surrender from Hitler's decision to complete his conquest by a fresh breach of faith.

In this period the process of disintegration was continued from within, all the worst and most time-serving elements coming rapidly to the surface, and inevitably finding a certain number of malcontents ready to play, consciously or unconsciously, into the enemy's hand. Perhaps the most striking example of this was the role of Colonel Emanuel Moravec, the leading Czech military critic, who had gone further than any other writer in expounding the strategic significance of Czechoslovakia as a check upon German ambitions, but who now executed a complete *volte face*, denounced the treachery of the Western Powers and argued the necessity of accepting hard facts and throwing in the nation's lot with triumphant Nazi Germany. His later behaviour has been so odious and inhuman that we are apt to forget the provocation under which he acted. There were others who concentrated upon calumniating Beneš and laying all the blame for disaster upon his and Masaryk's twenty-years' policy of devotion to democratic ideas and the League of Nations. On October 5 the President resigned, recognizing in his farewell address that his strongly democratic views might be 'an obstacle to the necessary development' of the reconstructed state. 'The culture of our nation,' he declared, 'will become stronger. The top of the tree is cut off, but the trunk remains. Let us descend to the roots. Some time the tree will put forth new leaves.'

[1] For further details, see Alexander Werth, *France and Munich*.

A sure instinct led Dr. Beneš to leave the country and to brace himself for a second and no less strenuous exile. Moreover, cruel as was the injustice which he and his people had suffered, he was far-sighted enough to set his main hope upon the two English-speaking democracies, believing that eventually the scales would fall from their eyes, and they would stand forth in defence of liberty and of small nations.

Slovakia and the Vienna Award

His departure was a signal for centrifugal forces eagerly encouraged from outside the new frontiers. At the very moment when the Germans were occupying the Fourth Zone, a meeting of the various Slovak parties took place at Žilina, and at the instance of the Slovak People's Party (the Ludová Strana), whose veteran leader, Monsignor Andrew Hlinka, had died in August, 1938, demanded that 'government and executive power in Slovakia should repose in a Slovak Government of five Ministers,' who would at the same time be members of the joint Cabinet in Prague. Foreign Affairs, National Defence and State Loans would be the only matters left to the central authorities. As Prague had been reduced by events to an entirely passive role, the new Slovak Government was set up on October 7, under Hlinka's successor, Father Tiso ; and Slovakia's example was followed four days later by 'Carpathian Ruthenia,' which now claimed its much overdue provincial Diet, according to the terms laid down in the Treaty of St. Germain, but never put into practice owing to the admittedly backward and disunited conditions that prevailed. The new autonomy began badly, for the Ruthene Premier, Andrew Brody, appointed on October 11, was after only fifteen days arrested on a charge of treason, having plotted with one member of his Cabinet for the union of all Ruthenia with Hungary.

This internal chaos was rendered still greater by the impatience of Hungary, the only one of the claimants who had not yet received a share of the spoils. The question became acute at a moment when Prague and Bratislava were still far from agreed among themselves as to which should conduct negotiations with Budapest. In actual fact, Tiso met the Hungarian delegates, Kánya and Teleki, who, finding him adamant, went off hot-haste to see Hitler, in the hope that he might impose a settlement upon the refractory Slovaks. Direct negotiations were twice renewed and twice broken off, and by the end of the month an armed conflict seemed inevitable, even though the Slovaks could only have hoped to resist the Hungarians with the help of the Czechs whom they were already engaged in evicting from Slovakia with every mark of indignity. As a last resort it was agreed to refer the dispute to Axis arbitration. The other two signatories of Munich were pointedly ignored, though it had of course been originally intended that all four should decide the frontiers towards Poland and Hungary no less than towards Germany. London and Paris swallowed without a word what was on the one side a deliberate insult, but on the other a neglect of obligations solemnly undertaken.

The first Vienna Award (November 2, 1938) rejected the Magyar claims to Bratislava and Nitra, without the former of which a Slovak state could not have continued to exist ; but at every other point Herr von Ribbentrop and Count Ciano weighed down the scales in favour of Hungary. For the restoration of the Danube island (Csallóköz, Žitný Ostrov) a good ethnographical case could be made out, though it meant reducing Slovakia's access to the Danube to a few kilometres near Bratislava itself. Again, on a purely ethnographic basis the Magyars were entitled to recover the towns of Rimavska Sobota and Rožnava, though the result was to render communications by road and rail impossible along the whole southern border. But by the cession of Košice Slovakia was deprived of her second capital, the only possible economic and cultural centre for the whole eastern half of the country. It had flourished exceedingly under the Republic, and its population of 24,000 in 1880 and 44,000 in 1910, had risen by 1930 to 70,000 of whom only 11,000 were Magyars. Still more scandalous was the treatment of Ruthenia, whose administrative and cultural capital, Užhorod, and its second town, Mukačevo, were transferred to Hungary, the result being to deprive the tiny state not only of its business centre and main machinery of state, but also of its main arable area and its transversal railway and road communications. The new Government, under Monsignor Vološin, was thus forced to set up its new capital in Hust—a glorified village lacking in all the requirements even of the remotest county town. The First Vienna Award (as also the Second, which in 1941 partitioned Transylvania) was 'an economic monstrosity' of the first order, which remains inexplicable unless we assume either complete incompetence on the part of its authors, or the deliberate intention of creating a running sore and rendering appeasement impossible. In the territory thus assigned to Hungary there was a population of 853,000 (503,000 Magyars, 272,000 Slovaks, 38,000 Ruthenes).

Dr. Tiso protested vigorously, but of course quite vainly, and maintained, with some exaggeration, that Hungary would now have a Slovak minority of 20% in contrast to the 6% Magyar minority in Czechoslovakia. It might have been supposed that he would recognize cause and effect in the downfall of the First Republic and the series of partitions that followed, and would moderate his separatist attitude. In actual fact negotiations for the extension of autonomy continued between Prague, Bratislava and Hust till November 22, when the new constitutional laws for Slovakia and Ruthenia were accepted by the central Parliament. The balance between the four provinces was now more top-heavy than ever. Eighty per cent of industry was now in the Czech lands, as against 17% and 3% in the other two provinces. Slovakia's share in the national income, and again her share in capital savings, were barely one-tenth of the whole.

The Last Agony

It was only after these far-reaching changes that Parliament proceeded to fill the presidential vacancy. The successful candidate was Dr. Emil Hácha, President of the Supreme Administrative Court, an elderly judge of unquestioned integrity, known to hold sober and conservative views, but also to have no political experience ; he was elected by 272 out of 312, the Communists and the Germans holding aloof. His election was followed by the resignation of the Premier General Syrový, of whom it is scarcely a criticism to say that he was unequal to an utterly impossible situation. His successor was Rudolf Beran, for many years Secretary-General, and now President, of the Agrarian Party, who had for the last two years coquetted with the Henlein Party, and who now gave rein to his reactionary tendencies, while seeking a convenient scapegoat in the exiled Beneš. It was decided to uproot the complex party system of the free Republic and to force all voters into one or other of two composite groups—the Party of National Unity, comprising the Agrarians, Clericals, Small Traders and Fascists, the Party of Labour comprising the Socialists and the Left of the National Socialists. The Social Democratic Party had already formally broken away from its international affiliations ; the Communist Party was soon afterwards dissolved, and a decree made it illegal to form any new party without the direct sanction of the Government. A very drastic Enabling Act was passed, authorizing the President to change even vital constitutional laws by personal decree, thus inaugurating 'a system of authoritarian democracy.' New elections were soon regarded as superfluous. An altogether artificial situation thus arose, for the Government had but little prestige and a precarious majority, yet the Opposition, by common consent, did not dare to press home its criticism, lest its own victory might precipitate the fresh intervention for which Berlin was preparing.

The agony through which Czechoslovakia passed in the closing months of 1938 can hardly be described ; and it was aggravated by the spectacle of the applause bestowed by the Western public upon the statesmen of Munich, and the proof thus afforded that they failed to understand the elements of the European situation, or what awaited them all in the very near future. These feelings were voiced by the address of the Presidents of the two Houses to the British and French Parliaments ; here it was pointed out that Czechoslovakia 'under tremendous pressure' sacrificed boundaries which had held for a thousand years, and now found that the principles of the settlement were not being carried into effect. 'We appeal to them to understand the moral revolution which caused the punishment of a nation that desired nothing more than to fulfil its obligations, a nation which had faith in the high principles of human co-operation, which committed no other wrong than the desire to live in its own fashion in the cultural community of nations and states. We bequeath our sorrow to the French and British peoples.' The 'moral revolution' of which they spoke provoked many suicides, not only among the Jews, but in wide intellectual circles. Karel Čapek's always fragile health gave way, and he did not live to see the final disaster. The poet Hora addressed to the maturer part of the nation a poignant appeal to live 'strenuously and sincerely' for the sake of the rising generation, and to provide by its unity the bridge across which their youth might pass to life and work. Little, alas, did he realize that it would be the dominant aim of the victor to deprive the whole younger generation of Czechs of all opportunities of education and culture.

During January and February British and French statesmen reverted to a mood of false optimism, and did not even profit by the respite obtained, in order to make good the alarming gaps in their armaments. Mr. Chamberlain paid an official visit to Mussolini, and publicly recognized the King as Emperor of Abyssinia. Sir Samuel Hoare denounced the Government's critics as 'jitterbugs,' and as late as March 9 was talking about the coming of a Golden Age in Europe, to be established by the three dictators and the two Prime Ministers working in harmony. On March 13, when the crisis was already upon us all, The Times actually referred to 'the knowledge that Germany has completed those demands upon her neighbours which . . . they had failed to satisfy while the way of orderly settlement was still open.' Within two days of this Hitler invaded Czechoslovakia and proclaimed its annexation to the Reich.

The subservience of the Beran Government to Berlin, great as it was, could not satisfy Hitler. The deputy Kundt, as leader of the considerable German minority still left inside the Czech Republic, was encouraged to claim what amounted to 'a state within the state' and to create as many artificial 'focal points of German culture' as possible. Germans from the districts handed over to Germany were ordered from Berlin to continue their studies at the German University of Prague, and to make it a centre of aggressive Nazism. They now had far more schools than their number justified, but there was no question of parity for the transferred Czech minority in the Reich. Kundt went so far as to demand for the Germans still remaining the restoration of all the privileges enjoyed by the original German immigrants of the Middle Ages !

Meanwhile Dr. Chvalkovský, who had succeeded Dr. Krofta as Foreign Minister, was summoned by Hitler and Ribbentrop, and curtly informed that the Czechs must draw the consequences from their defeat. All remnants of the Beneš regime must be liquidated, especially in the bureaucracy, the Army and the Press ; Kundt's demands must be fully satisfied ; radical measures must be taken against the Jews ; the Army must be reduced ; and Czechoslovakia, repudiating all her former alliances, must officially join the Anti-Comintern Pact and the Axis.

It would be obviously unjust to suggest that Beran and Chvalkovsky consented gladly to this 'liquidation,' or were blind to the shameless economic exploitation which was following closely on the heels of political subjection ; but Germany had them by the throat, and they could only play for time and profess their desire for 'good neighbourly relations.' 'We must not toy with fate,' said Chvalkovský on February 20, 'if Munich is not to become the prelude to a new catastrophe.'

Slovakia Secedes

By March Hitler had decided to complete the liquidation of Czechoslovakia ; the last outposts of the Bohemian Salient had to fall before his strategists could feel ready for the next advance, whether it were against Poland or through a menial Hungary to the Balkans. The Sudeten question, having been 'solved,' no longer provided a pretext for intervention and an instrument for throwing dust in the eyes of Western statesmen ; but new weapons of anarchy lay ready to his hand in Slovakia and Ruthenia.

Two months after the establishment of 'autonomy,' the Slovak extremists brought back to Bratislava Professor Vojtěch Tuka, who had served seven years' imprisonment for his subversive activities, and had latterly been under house arrest at Plzen. He and his chief lieutenant, Šaňo Mach, openly agitated for 'complete independence and the sovereignty of the Slovak state,' and even for the transfer of certain Slovak districts in Moravia to the new state. They had the help of the 'Hlinka Guard,' a very inferior and undisciplined imitation of the Nazi S.A. They launched an anti-Semitic campaign, with the double purpose of pleasing Hitler and rousing the more irresponsible elements in Slovakia. They also encouraged, because they could not prevent, the totalitarian agitation of Karmasin, leader of the German minority and Secretary of State in the Slovak Cabinet. The official Slovák of March 7 announced that 'the new Slovakia has sincerely taken its place by the side of those great nations which have begun the struggle against Judæo-Marxism.'

In the first week of March, 1939, the separatist movement both in Slovakia and Ruthenia came rapidly to a head, the Bratislava Cabinet declining to make a public declaration of loyalty to the Republic, but none the less expecting the Central Government to raise a loan to replenish their empty coffers, a separate Slovak army, and separate diplomatic representation abroad. President Hácha and the Beran Government summoned their last energies, and for the moment forestalled open secession by dismissing Mgr Tiso and his Cabinet, disarming the Hlinka Guard and occupying the Government offices in Bratislava and other towns. Before acting thus President Hácha, true to his policy of co-operation with Germany, had consulted the Wilhelmstrasse, and had been encouraged to proceed. Yet at that very time the most extreme member of the Tiso Government, Durčiansky, having fled to Vienna, was organizing a violent radio campaign in favour of secession, with the help of the Nazi Governor of Austria, Herr von Seyss-Inquart (now Governor of Holland). For two days Tiso's legally appointed successor, Karel Sidor, held office and co-operated with Prague; but on March 13 Tiso himself contrived to escape from the Jesuit seminary where he was under police supervision, joined Durčiansky in Vienna and flew with him to Berlin for an interview with Hitler. He returned by air to Bratislava with the Führer's instructions to summon the Slovak Diet and obtain from it a 'unanimous' vote of independence. No sooner said than done; on March 14 Tiso resumed the post of Premier, consoling Sidor with the Legation to the Vatican; Durčiansky, as yet the chief exponent of a Germanophil policy, became Foreign Minister, and the Magyarone traitor Tuka, Vice Premier. Within twenty-four hours of the mock declaration of independence, Tiso slavishly placed the new state 'under the protection of the Great German Reich,' an offer which was curtly accepted the next day with the ominous words: 'I herewith take over the problems of the Slovak state.' *Slovák*, the Government's official organ, amid its exultations over the event, was brazen enough to write as follows: 'How the Czechs arrange their further state existence is their own affair. Undeniably we must thank them for having helped us in many ways, and we must also admit that without them we should not have gained our freedom twenty years ago. This is a historical fact, and only an unjust man would wish to deny it.'

The Collapse of Ruthenia

The action of the Slovaks left the third federal unit, Ruthenia, completely in the air and cut off from all possibility of Czech help. Mgr. Vološin and his phantom Government therefore proclaimed their independence, and, like Tiso, appealed to Hitler for help. But this time there was no response, and already on March 14 the Hungarian Government sent an ultimatum to Prague, recognizing Slovakia's new independent status, but demanding the withdrawal of all Czech troops from Ruthenia within twenty-four hours, and fixing a time-limit of twelve hours for reply. Prague had no choice but to submit, and Budapest, without troubling even to discuss matters with the Hust Government simply invaded the little province and drove its few organized defenders into the mountains or over the frontier. The Magyars gave no quarter to those who resisted, and there were summary executions outside the Hust Hotel which had been the temporary seat of government. The Slovaks did not dare to intervene, knowing themselves to be incapable of resisting a Magyar invasion. While the Poles were delighted to see the end of a regime which, however primitive, might have served as a rallying point for Ukrainian nationalism, the Germans were not sorry to see the liquidation of the impossible experiment which Ciano had foisted upon them at the Vienna Award. Even the Roumanians, though they regretted the loss of direct communications with Czechoslovakia, were glad enough that the junction of the Hungarian and Polish frontiers should have interposed a territorial barrier between themselves and the Reich.

The fate of Ruthenia provided conclusive proof, if proof were still needed, that all idea of settlement on a racial basis had been abandoned, and that strategy took precedence over self-determination. The transformation wrought by the Czechs since 1919 in the most scandalously neglected nationality of pre-war Hungary never received the attention which it deserved from Europe. Yet it was one of the most remarkable and successful political experiments of the post-war period, and a new generation, trained in their own schools and nationally conscious, was growing up and taking every year a greater share in the government of the little province. Now it has been flung back into the morass of neglect, exploitation and Magyarization from which it had been extricated, and this without the slightest pretence at popular consultation.

The End of Appeasement

While these events in the Eastern half of the Republic paralysed the action of the Central authorities, Berlin suddenly showed its hand by launching a fresh radio campaign against the 'Czech Terror,' and to mass troops along the frontier. Next day the occupying troops were puzzled to find everywhere complete calm and exemplary order and asked in vain to be shown the dead and wounded victims of the entirely imaginary terrorists. On March 14, the very day when Chamberlain stated in the House of Commons that the promised guarantee to Czechoslovakia only held good in case of an unprovoked attack, but that 'no such aggression has yet taken place,' President Hácha, on orders from Hitler, left for Berlin, accompanied by his Foreign Minister. On arrival he learned that Moravská Ostrava had already been occupied by German troops. At 1 a.m. on the 15th they were received by Hitler, Ribbentrop and Göring, and curtly informed that the Führer had decided upon the complete military occupation of the Czech lands, and that if they did not instantly submit, Prague would be bombarded by eight hundred planes which were already in readiness. At four in the morning the phantom President signed a declaration that 'in order to secure final pacification, he placed the destiny of the Czech people and country with confidence in the hands of the Führer of the German Reich.' Hitler then issued a proclamation brazenly denouncing 'the unbearable regime of terrorism' still conducted by the helpless Czechs against the triumphant Germans—behaviour which, if it continued, 'must destroy the last vestige of order in a territory in which Germany is vitally interested.' In passing, he spoke of Bohemia as having for over a thousand years belonged to the German Reich—a statement which for crudity and misrepresentation has few equals in history, and needs no refutation for the readers of this volume. He had therefore ordered invasion, as a preliminary to disarming 'the terrorist gangs' and establishing a new order 'which will do justice to a thousand years of history and to the practical needs of the German and Czech peoples.' Hácha had come prepared to accept the most drastic terms including even a military alliance, a common foreign policy and a customs and currency union ; but these demands went far beyond his gloomiest anticipations.

Long since robbed of all possibility of resistance, the Czech population could not conceal its despair and fury. Events were only too soon to impose on every man, woman and child the urgent need for veiling their true sentiments behind an impassive mask. Hitler added insult to injury by spending the night of the 15th in the Castle of Prague, where for twenty years Masaryk and Beneš had replaced the fallen House of Habsburg, and by selecting Henlein, of all men, to act as his first deputy in Bohemia. Here too, he proclaimed 'the Protectorate of Bohemia and Moravia' as henceforth belonging to the Great German Reich. After a brief interval Baron Neurath, once Nazi Ambassador in London, and afterwards German Foreign Minister, was appointed to the office of Protector, to which that of President was definitely subordinated. Of Neurath it must be said that while he preserved the diplomatic forms of the Second Reich, his cynicism and powers of negation were boundless. He consciously sinned against the light, knowing the full extent of Nazi degradation and exploiting it to his own ends. The real driving force behind him, however, was Karl Hermann Frank, the most brutal and fanatical of all Henlein's supporters ; Henlein himself became Gauleiter for the detached Sudeten districts, but was soon allowed to fall into relative obscurity. It should be superfluous to point out that President" Hácha had no authority to sign away his country's independence, that he acted in direct defiance of the Czechoslovak Constitution, and that the Protectorate rests upon naked violence and violates a whole series of solemn promises and assurances. Above all, it runs directly counter to those claims of self-determination and minority rights which the Nazi leaders so insistently proclaimed so long as the Trojan horse was still outside the walls of the fortress.

Towards the end of March, Hácha, on instructions from Hitler, nominated a 'Committee of National Trusteeship' of fifty duly subservient members. Parliament was dissolved, and did not meet again ; the party system was suspended, and on April 1 the two surviving parties were fused into a single totalitarian party. The Nürnberg racial laws were adopted, the last vestiges of press freedom were destroyed. The Republic of Masaryk and Beneš had ceased to exist ; but these initial measures were only the herald of far worse things to come. The short-lived Munich settlement had been torn to shreds by its principal signatory, and with it the policy of appeasement had perished ignominiously, though neither London nor Paris had the courage to lift a finger. A new and iron age already cast its shadows across Europe, and the democracies began to pay the price of their earlier lack of principle. But the end is not yet.

EPILOGUE

'The philosophy of Power is a barbaric, inhuman and absurd philosophy.'
—Dr. Edvard Beneš, in Chicago.

WE have reached one of the great landmarks in Bohemia's chequered history—like those Giant Mountains that raise their jagged peaks to heaven in protest against perfidy and brutal conquest. It would be equally impossible to break off the narrative at this point and to treat in any detail the tragedy that followed. It must suffice to sketch in outline the 'New Order' imposed by Hitler upon the once flourishing Czech lands, in anticipation of an all-embracing continental *Raubwirtschaft*. On September 26, 1938, while the Western Powers were seeking to cover up their pusillanimous surrender by the catchwords of appeasement and self-determination, Hitler declared : "The Sudetens are the last territorial demand I shall make in Europe. I have no further interest in the Czech State, and I can guarantee it if necessary. We want no Czechs at all." Within a week of this he had annexed a million Czechs to the Reich, to say nothing of hundreds of thousands of unwilling German Activists ; and within five months he had decided to swallow the entire Czech nation. For the moment the pretence of German unity and self-determination still figured as the overriding necessity that prompted him ; Bohemia had to be protected against Bolshevism, and the Czechs themselves requested his help. This was a reference to the almost incredible midnight scene when Göring and Ribbentrop chased the wretched President Hácha round the table till he signed the document of surrender, while hundreds of German bombers awaited the signal to reduce Prague to ruins.[1] A year later his chosen mouthpiece, Joseph Goebbels, warned a deputation of Czech journalists that the Bohemian Protectorate was irrevocable, that 'the concept of the freedom of any nation depends on circumstances,' that the Czechs would do well to avoid the fate of Rotterdam and to 'secure all the advantages which the Great German Reich can offer,' by close collaboration. On March 4, 1941, the fair-spoken Henlein, now Sudeten Gauleiter, and no longer bound to dissemble, lectured in Vienna on his work for the spread of Nazism in the defunct Republic, and on his secret contacts with 'the National Socialist Revolution' in Germany. He claimed that as 'true followers of our Führer,' they had waged 'the struggle under camouflage, by methods which seemed legal.' The speech culminated in a passage which defined his main aim as leader of the S.d.P. as 'the political task of destroying Czechoslovakia, as a bastion against the Reich.'[2]

On October 2, 1942, one of Henlein's subordinates, the Sudeten writer, Ernst Frank, declared that 'the fate of Europe depends on lasting reconciliation between Bohemia-Moravia and the Reich.' And on October 18, 1942, Karl Hermann Frank, Secretary of State to the Protector (speaking at the rechristening of the Masaryk Embankment by the name of the butchered Butcher Heydrich), declared the Bohemian Protectorate to be 'an inalienable component within the frontiers of the Reich,' and prophesied 'the complete mental, and spiritual reconquest of its people

[1] See the French *Documents diplomatiques*, 1938–1939, No. 77—M. Coulondre's report of March 17, 1939 to Paris.
[2] See Appendix V.

381

for the Reich idea.' The murder was out ; the farce of self-determination was no longer kept up ; Germany needed the Protectorate as a key to her mastery of the Continent, and intended to hold it ; and there was an added zest in the fact that Mr. Chamberlain and the champions of appeasement had been so thoroughly duped.

From Neurath to Heydrich

At first the resentment and resistance were intense, concentrated and universal, and perhaps all the more universal because of a feeling of utter impotence. The summer of 1939 was spent by Baron Neurath and his sinister understudy K. H. Frank, in preparing the machinery of repression ; and soon after the outbreak of war and the downfall of Poland the first stage of the Czech Terror opened. But already as early as March 14, 1939 —two days before Hitler's seizure of Prague—a decree had been issued in his name establishing German special courts in Prague and Brno without troubling to await the formal erection of the Protectorate a day later. The Protector thus acquired absolute power to override at pleasure all legislation passed by the Republic in its twenty years of life.

The intense feeling lavished by the Czech public upon the centenary funeral celebration of the poet Macha—in a certain sense the Czech equivalent of Keats—created dangerous illusions ; and when an attempt was made to celebrate the twenty-first anniversary of the Republic on October 28, 1939, there were disturbances and bloodshed, which recurred at the funeral of the student Opletak. The spirit of the rising generation, and especially of the Universities, had to be broken, and on November 16 a large force of Gestapo and S.S. men arrived in military lorries, conducted a ferocious 'razzia' against the students in the Prague hostels, shot, mangled and raped at will, and deported over two thousand of the survivors to Dachau and Buchenwald, from which the less fortunate eventually returned home as moral and physical wrecks. Then all the Czech Universities were closed down for three years, and the vindictive Frank openly boasted that they would never reopen so long as Germany remained the master. This was soon followed by a systematic looting of scientific equipment and its transfer to the Reich. Hundreds of secondary and primary schools were shut down, leaving 6,000 out of the 20,000 Czech teachers unemployed, and forcing the schools that remained to put eighty or ninety, instead of thirty children, in a single class. Within a year the number of pupils admitted to secondary schools had been reduced by half. Needless to add, the numerous Czech minorities in the Sudeten districts annexed outright by the Reich were altogether deprived of every kind of school—yet another proof, if proof were needed, that Henlein, who had won the sympathy of British appeasers by his clamour for an exact proportion of Czech and German schools (at a time when the Germans of Bohemia possessed 3,000 primary and 80 secondary of their own), now showed the most shameless indifference to the fate of his Czech victims.

Meanwhile von Gregory, formerly the German press attaché in Prague, was appointed head of the new 'Press Control Service' of the Protectorate ; by his own acknowledgment he was the murderer of Formis, the refugee radio expert who till 1937 gave anti-Nazi broadcasts on a secret transmitter. This man now set up a press dictatorship inside Bohemia, which reduced news and opinion to a farce, suppressing newspapers and ejecting journalists wholesale and actually forcing the surviving editors and their staffs to put their signatures to every imaginable kind of article, written or commanded by the Gestapo under pain of dismissal or internment. Parallel with this went a ban upon Czech patriotic literature, and holocausts of books and periodicals such as threw Jesuit practice in the seventeenth century utterly into the shade. These restrictions have been partially countered by a remarkable outburst of poetical and musical talent, but culturally the whole nation is in heavy shackles.

Needless to say, the Churches have been in the forefront of Nazi persecution, and the most drastic methods have been employed to check the undoubted religious revival. Pilgrimages to such famous shrines as Stará Boleslav, Hostýn and Velehrad have been altogether forbidden. Many of the most eminent clergy have been arrested, sent to concentration camps, treated with the utmost barbarity and even deprived of their breviaries. Most of the monastic orders have been dissolved, and Church property and buildings appropriated. The Catholic Press has ceased to exist, and the flourishing Catholic Orels (the 'eagle' gymnastic societies) have shared the fate of the Sokols. The Czechoslovak Church has been placed under a special ban, owing to its democratic tendencies. The election of a successor to the Patriarch Prohazka has been forbidden. The Gestapo has set up a special control upon preaching from its pulpits. One of its leading clergy, Professor Uher, and a pastor of the Brethren, Dr. Šimek, with his wife, have been executed as hostages. The small Orthodox Church of Bohemia has been altogether dissolved, and Bishop Gorazd and two of his clergy executed, on the unproved charge of sheltering Heydrich's murderers.

All political parties were forbidden from the outset, but at the instance of the phantom President Hácha a new non-party organization, called 'Národní Souručenství' was formed, and all Czechs were urged to join it. For lack of anything better, and as a means of demonstrating their distinctively Czech nationality, no fewer than four million people joined it, but under its obscure and subservient head, Mr Foušek, the movement (if a stagnant pool can be said to have movement), speedily languished, until the arch-Quisling Moravec declared it to be 'incapable of ideological regeneration' but treated it as not even worth disbanding.

A distinction was drawn between the *Reichsbürger*, citizens of the Reich, including everyone of German extraction, and *Staatsangehörige*, consisting of the second grade nations, Czechs and Jews. The Germans, it is worth noting, never missed an opportunity of showing their contempt for equality or tolerance in any conceivable form, and of repudiating all the principles which their propagandists had poured into the ears of Western sentimentalists. Needless to add that the whole system of social legislation and trade unionism, which had made of Czechoslovakia one of the most enlightened states in Europe, went by the board under the ruthless orders of Walter Bertsch, a Reich German intruded as Minister of Economics by the Protector Neurath. Bertsch, on March 8, 1941, clearly announced Hitler's 'decision to adapt the economy of the state to the war necessities of the Reich, and to exploit it for this purpose. All individual desires must be subordinated to this.' There must be an end of fixed working hours and other working-class liberties, and all able-bodied men must be liable to industrial mobilization in the interests of Germany ; while the resources of all the Czech banks and business firms, and also of private owners of property, must be exploited to the uttermost degree. Nowhere has the system of Organized Plunder (*Raubwirtschaft*) by which the Nazi leeches have drained the lifeblood of the Continent, reached greater lengths than in the Protectorate ; but an attempt even to summarize its enormities would speedily exceed the present limits.[1]

For the first eighteen months passive resistance was almost universal in the Protectorate, fostered on the one hand by the underground movement, in secret contact with the Czech exiles in London, and on the other by the feeble President Hácha and his phantom Cabinet—headed by General Eliáš and several other genuine patriots who held on to distasteful and dangerous office, in the belief that they could here and there ward off still worse disasters. But in the autumn of 1941 Hitler was roused to still more drastic measures. It was the moment when the first offensive against Russia had reached its height, and when the apparent imminence of victory roused him to arrogant fury against all who dared to doubt his omnipotence. On September 27, 1941, Baron Neurath was suddenly replaced as Protector by Reinhard Heydrich, Himmler's most trusted lieutenant in the Gestapo, an energetic young thug of thirty-seven, who had earned a reputation for brutality and sadism such as few even among the Nazis could rival. He immediately proclaimed a state of emergency, sent the Premier, General Eliáš, to prison, set up courts of summary jurisdiction, in which the so-called judges were mostly Gestapo officials brought from Berlin headquarters, and instituted a veritable reign of terror, whose chief aim was to discover the chiefs, and once for all to destroy the machinery, of the underground movement and its contacts with London and Moscow. In the first 105 days of his rule 394 persons were sentenced to death, and 1,134 handed over to the Gestapo and reserved for a dreadful fate which we can still only surmise. Among his other achievements were the dissolution of the Sokols, the cancellation of pensions to the Legionaries, the transfer of the Parliament buildings to a German musical society, the seizure of the Crown jewels of Bohemia, and a far-reaching purge in the administration under the Prussian official Walter Bertsch, who now entered the Cabinet side by side with the new Quisling of Bohemia, Colonel Emanuel Moravec. Moravec, for some years the foremost military critic of Czechoslovakia, was a man of no small ability, but of unbalanced and venomous temper who, after expounding the doctrine of Germany as the foe, and of Czechoslovakia as the strategic bulwark of Central Europe, in 1939 switched recklessly over to the opposite extreme of a complete identification of interests between Bohemia and the Reich.

Heydrich's regime lasted almost exactly eight months ; on May 27, 1942, he was attacked and mortally wounded when driving to his office through a hilly suburb of Prague. The place and time were thought out to a nicety, and despite the offer of gigantic money rewards (10 million crowns) and all the frantic efforts of the Gestapo, his murderers (or, as the Czechs prefer to put it, those who carried out the death sentence against one of the blackest criminals of his time) have never been discovered. Some weeks later the secret police raided the church of St. Charles Borromeo (a disused monastic church which had been assigned to the small Orthodox community of Prague), and announced that among those who met their death in the skirmish that ensued were also

[1] See Chapter IV of *Four Fighting Years*—entitled 'Plunder as a Policy.'

Heydrich's two assailants. There is, however, good reason to believe that the real culprits escaped, that the Gestapo claimed a 'kill' for obvious reasons of prestige, and that the execution of Bishop Gorazd and two of his priests was a pitiful expression of the savagery in which Hitler indulges when thwarted.

Heydrich's successor, Daluege, one of Himmler's most trusted and most ruthless lieutenants, brought the Czech Terror to its culmination. Between May 28 and July 3 there were no fewer than 1,288 executions, and between that date and December, 653 more were added.[1] The victims were drawn from every rank and class of society, from every profession and creed, but were united in a common Czech patriotism and in the consciousness of martyred innocence. Among so many others it is almost invidious to mention the former Premier General Eliáš, the poet Vančura, and Dr. Šrom, once Consul-General in Vienna and Moscow. Sometimes whole families were shot together and thus exterminated ; girls with their mothers and men of eighty calmly faced the firing-squads. But the supreme example of German rage and miscalculation was the decision to wipe out the population of the villages of Lidice and Ležaky, the Gestapo alleging that they had helped to hide Heydrich's assailants in the neighbouring forest. It was announced that the men had been summarily shot, the women placed in concentration camps, and their children torn from them and sent to Nazi schools. A year later it transpired that in reality men, women and children had been massacred together, 'in one red burial blent.' But what little is known of their fate had sufficed to fire the imagination of the outside world ; the name of Lidice was given to more than one township in the New World, and it became a symbol of resistance and future liberation. In the words of Colonel Knox, the American Secretary for War, Hitler had not 'extinguished Lidice,' but 'given it life everlasting.'

In 1943 the terror has slightly abated, having developed into a long-drawn and stubborn trial of strength, between Czech and German, waged with an intensity for which there is no precedent under the more civilized dominion of Austria. On the one hand the Germans are resolved to plunder and drain dry, to make education and culture impossible for the Czechs, to link them up so intimately with the Reich that nothing will ever avail to free them ; and they are only deterred from yet more drastic repression by their urgent need for Czech hands for unwilling labour in the service of the Reich, and by the need for Bohemian factory sites, where German industry can dig itself in at a respectful distance from Allied bombers. On the other hand the Czechs use every ingenious device to evade, to delay, and where possible to sabotage and destroy. They are well aware that in the event of a German victory they will be deported wholesale from the Bohemian salient to the steppes of a conquered and desolated Russia, and they are grimly husbanding their resources, planning recuperation and retribution down to the smallest details, and waiting till the long-delayed signal sounds.

In all this, Slovakia has been a backwater of ignominy and subservience. President Tiso, who has brought dishonour upon the priestly cloth by his connivance with Nazi blood-lust, and his Premier Bela Tuka, whose condemnation for treason and espionage in 1929 earned him in certain quarters a martyr's halo, but who now openly boasts of his former con-

---

[1] The German People's Court in Prague officially gave the number of executions between January 1 and June 1, 1943, as 281, thus making an admitted total of 2,222.

tacts with Budapest and Berlin, watch each other uneasily, knowing that neither is strong enough to stand alone, and that by now most Slovaks regard their regime as a blot upon its scutcheon which the nation will never be able to erase. To-day the Catholic clergy of Slovakia are only too conscious that Tiso and Tuka, who so successfully duped their once venerated leader, Andrew Hlinka, have become the mere instruments of Nazi domination, that their once great influence over the peasantry has been fatally compromised, and that Slovakia has been handed over body and soul to Nazi economic and cultural exploitation. The wholesale evacuation of 76,000 Jews to certain death in the Nazi slaughter-houses in Poland, and the theft of their property by the puppet state and some of its high-placed officials, evoked a certain revulsion of feeling in the country ; and it is a solace to record the courageous protest of the two Lutheran Bishops Čobrda and Stephen Osuský, the refusal of the Church Assembly to repudiate their action, and the no less indignant attitude of individual Catholic bishops and priests. This, and the pitiable fiasco of the Slovak Army in Russia, which it was eventually found expedient to withdraw from the front, revealed the gulf that separates the nation from the tiny and corrupt governing clique.

The Government in Exile

The pitiable interlude of the Second Republic did at least afford a short breathing-space, during which some of the most outstanding personalities of Czechoslovakia were able to escape abroad and brace themselves for the supreme struggle. Above all, President Beneš, soon after his resignation, settled in London and began to build up around him—very much as Masaryk and he had done twenty years earlier in Paris—a centre and focus of national resistance. For some months he remained in strict seclusion, recruiting from the intense physical strain of the long crisis : but early in 1939 he had already recovered sufficiently to accept the special chair which was offered to him at Chicago University. It was there that he launched the first public protest against Hitler's perjury in occupying Prague. In Washington, London, Paris and Moscow the Czechoslovak diplomatic representatives declined to hand over their legations to the conqueror, and the four governments to which they were accredited gave them full backing in this attitude : but in most of the smaller countries pressure from Berlin proved irresistible. From the very first, however, Dr. Beneš upheld the principle of legal continuity from the First Republic, and set himself to organize a body of opinion such as could not be disregarded. When war broke out in September there were already enough Czechoslovak volunteers in France to form the nucleus of an army, and thanks to the insistence of men like Mgr. Šramek and Dr. Osuský the French Government on October 2 signed an agreement with the newly constituted National Committee under whose authority Generals Ingr and Viest were placed, subject of course to arrangements with the French High Command. But M. Daladier—partly, it is believed, from fear of offending Mussolini—declined to recognize the Committee even as a Provisional Government, and when Dr. Beneš went over to Paris in the hope of negotiating a compromise, he was not received by the Premier. This was all the more marked as the Austrian pretender, Archduke Otto, was twice received by Daladier in that very week.

With the fall of France in July, 1940, the plight of the Czechoslovak and Polish exiles on French soil became truly desperate ; and complete disaster was only averted by the energy of the British Government and the untiring efforts of the Royal Navy in rescuing the remnants of the two armies and a large number of civilian refugees who had found their way to Bordeaux or Provence. This successful action served in no small measure to diminish the shame of Munich.

In July, with the sanction of Lord Halifax, the Czechoslovak National Committee established itself in London as a Provisional Government, consisting of Dr. Beneš as President of the Republic, a Cabinet of twelve Ministers under Mgr. Šramek, and a State Council in which all political parties and groups were to be represented and which performed the democratic function of educating opinion and ventilating grievances.

The portfolio of Foreign Affairs was assigned to Mr. Jan Masaryk, who had for many years represented his country as Minister in London with signal success and originality. Despite the consistently benevolent attitude of Mr. Churchill and Mr. Eden towards the Czech cause, it still proved impossible to overcome the reluctance of certain official quarters to accept the Czech view that events had effectually liquidated the Munich settlement. The legalists upheld the amazing view that the settlement of 1938 remained valid until its signatories (i.e. Germany and Italy, no less than fallen France) declared it to have terminated. To the Czechs, on the other hand, from the standpoint of internal policy, it was all-important that the continuity between the First Republic and the exiles should be formally recognized by their greater Allies. A more reasonable objection to unrestricted recognition was the steady refusal of the British Government, even in the case of countries towards which it had assumed a guarantee, to commit itself to the exact restoration of pre-war boundaries, and this the Czechoslovak Government accepted as reasonable, while arguing that such a proviso need not preclude the wider recognition.

What did more than anything else to undermine these pettifogging arguments was Hitler's attack upon Russia, which was promptly followed by the Anglo-Soviet Alliance and Moscow's unreserved recognition of Czechoslovak independence, coupled with a pledge of non-interference in her internal affairs. On July 18, 1942, full British recognition was accorded to the Czechoslovak Government, and President Beneš's status was put on a par with that of other heads of states ; and yet the pedants upheld their reserve as to legal continuity, being doubtless encouraged in their obstinacy when on July 19 Washington contented itself with according provisional recognition.

It was not until August 5, 1942, that this altogether unnecessary trial of strength behind the scenes was terminated by an exchange of Notes between Mr. Eden and Mr. Masaryk, culminating in an absolutely explicit repudiation of the whole Munich settlement. As in the previous year, the attitude of the Soviet Government had provided a certain stimulus ; for M. Molotov, on his way home from Washington to Moscow, had called upon President Beneš and not merely condemned Munich root and branch, but "took his stand upon the pre-Munich frontiers of Czechoslovakia," and went out of his way to include Ruthenia, which some people had suspected Russia of claiming for herself. By this time it was obviously impossible for Britain to lag behind indefinitely, and her statesmen, by the agreement of August, 1942, showed a generous and broad grasp of the issues involved. The satisfaction of the Czechoslovak Government at this tardy liquidation of Munich was all the greater because it followed logically upon the Anglo-Soviet Treaty of Alliance of June 11, 1942—an event unprecedented in the whole history of British foreign policy. The United States Government, which had never recognized, and indeed had openly disapproved, the Munich settlement, none the less still hesitated to recognize the Czechoslovak Government as more than provisional; but in June, 1943, it swept all reserves to the winds and, with the hearty approval of American opinion, gave President Beneš an official welcome of more than usual emphasis.

The autumn of 1943 finds the Czech people ground beneath a tyranny more savage than any in its long history—helpless against wholesale plunder, condemned to forced labour on a large scale, deprived of most of the cultural values which the last five generations had created under Austria, and unable to hand on the torch of liberty and knowledge to their children, exposed to torture and decimation, though not as yet to the systematic massacres of which their Polish, Serbian and Russian kinsmen have been the victims. Yet nothing has availed to quench the nation's burning faith in its survival and in its future mission in a liberated and peaceful Europe. All ranks and ages stand braced and eager for the hour of supreme effort, when, as Comenius prayed three centuries ago, God shall again lift the clouds of wrath from the Czech nation.

Pour maintenir le glorieux héritage que leur ont légué leurs héros et leurs martyrs, les Tchèques sont prêts, si l'heure fatale sonne, aux suprêmes sacrifices. Vainqueurs ou vaincus, ils auront laissé au monde un grand exemple, et ils seront les créanciers de l'humanité.

ERNEST DENIS.

APPENDIX I

PREMYSLIDES AND HABSBURGS

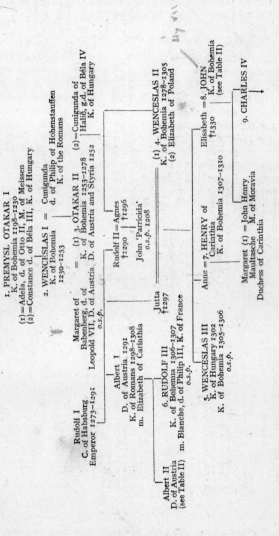

1. PREMYSL OTAKAR I
K. of Bohemia 1198–1230
(1) = Adela, d. of Otto II, M. of Meissen
(2) = Constance d. of Béla III, K. of Hungary

2. WENCESLAS I = Cunigunda
K. of Bohemia   d. of Philip of Hohenstauffen
1230–1253   K. of the Romans

Margaret of = (1) 3. OTAKAR II (2) = Cunigunda of
Babenberg, d. of   K. of Bohemia 1253–1278   Halič, g.d. of Béla IV
Leopold VII, D. of Austria, D. of Austria and Styria 1252   K. of Hungary
o.s.p.

Rudolf II = Agnes
†1290   †1296

John 'Parricida'
o.s.p. 1208

Rudolf I
C. of Habsburg
Emperor 1273–1291

Albert I
D. of Austria 1291
K. of Romans 1298–1308
m. Elizabeth of Carinthia

(1) 4. WENCESLAS II
K. of Bohemia 1278–1305
(2) Elizabeth of Poland

Jutta
†1297

6. RUDOLF III
K. of Bohemia 1306–1307
m. Blanche, d. of Philip III, K. of France
o.s.p.

5. WENCESLAS III
K. of Hungary 1302
K. of Bohemia 1305–1306
o.s.p.

Anne = 7. HENRY of
Carinthia
K. of Bohemia 1307–1310

Elisabeth = 8. JOHN
†1330   K. of Bohemia
(see Table II)

9. CHARLES IV

Margaret (1) = John Henry
Maultasche   M. of Moravia
Duchess of Carinthia

Albert II
D. of Austria
(see Table II)

APPENDIX II

HOUSES OF LUXEMBURG, JAGIELLON AND HAPSBURG

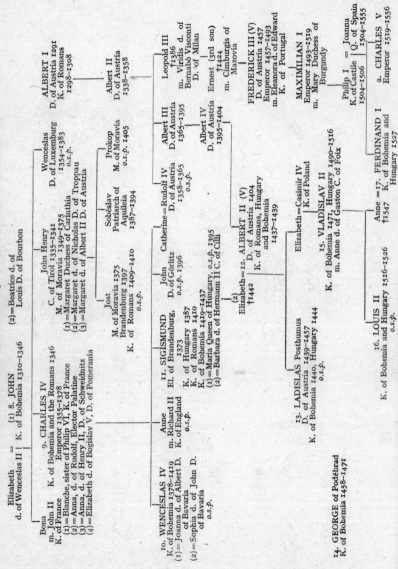

APPENDIX V

Henlein in England

The Sudetian German agitation, led by Konrad Henlein, was the Trojan Horse of the whole European tragedy. It was used with great skill to delude sentimental public opinion in the West, which imagined itself to be vindicating the principle of self-determination, when in reality it was playing straight into the hands of blatant Pan-Germanism.

It is of no little importance that this incident should be clearly understood, beyond all possibility of recurrence : and it is for this reason that I am adding to this book my own personal experience of Henlein's perfidy.

(1) I first met him in London on December 9, 1935, when he lectured at Chatham House. On the following evening I had a triangular conversation of four hours with him and Colonel Graham Christie, on the basis of which I drew up a full memorandum—mainly to place the facts on record, for I only showed it to a few friends, and never published it. I may now quote from it the following summary of Henlein's main lines of argument.

'He accepted the existing Constitution, treaties and Minority Treaty as a basis of agreement between Czechoslovaks and Sudetian Germans. He ruled out not only all question of German Bohemia (either as a whole or in part) uniting with Germany, but also admitted the impossibility of separating the Czech and German districts, and insisted on the essential unity of the Bohemian Lands throughout history and no less today. He did not put forward any scheme for the "Zweiteilung" of the Bohemian Lands.

'He expressly declared Revision of Frontiers to be no solution and used language on the subject of minorities which I found to be practically identical with my own published views. He rejected Pan-Germanism and Pan-Slavism as equally catastrophic.

'He declared the totalitarian principle to be untenable, and declared in favour of "an honest democracy." "We want a democracy such as is recommended by Masaryk." He repudiated anti-Semitism, affirmed that there was no Aryan Paragraph in his party programme, and while admitting that many of his followers held the other view, claimed that he had more than once roused their criticism by defending the Jews. While laying great stress on his general German sympathies, he denied "Nazism" or "Hitlerism" to be a doctrine suitable for exportation.'

On the subject of relations with Germany, 'he said very frankly that he had been repeatedly pressed to make a public attack on Hitler and the Third Reich, but that this was too much to ask. He was a keen believer in German cultural unity and racial kinship, but repudiated the Pan-German idea in any political form, and regarded the Nazi programme as unsuited for exportation beyond the frontiers of the Reich.

'When he treated Pan-Germanism and Pan-Slavism as more or less equal dangers, I argued that the latter was dead except as a general underlying sentiment such as would deter any Western or Southern Slav from entering an open conflict with Russia. If (so I argued) he in his turn claimed that to ask the German citizen of a Slav state to fight against Germany would be too much, I personally would accept such a view ; but I feared that a new Pan-Germanism was forming in the Third Reich which aimed at the conquest of Slav territory. He dissociated himself from such a view, but did not pursue the subject further.

'(2) I again met Henlein in Prague in January, 1936, and twice discussed with him at great length the whole subject of German-Czech relations. We talked on the agreed basis of "(1) the indivisibility of the Bohemian lands ; (2) the possibility of a settlement within the framework of the Czechoslovak constitution ; (3) repudiation of the totalitarian principle and of anti-Semitism ; (4) denial of all connection with Herr Hitler ; (5) insistence that Pan-Germanism and Pan-Slavism must lead with equal certainty to a catastrophe, and (6) acceptance of the democratic principles of Masaryk.'

He also arranged that I should meet his chief political assistants, and I thus had a conversation of three hours with six of them together, (Walther Brandt, H. Rutha, Kundt, Sebekowsky, K. H. Frank, Sandler), conducted on the same basis, but ranging freely over a wide field of home and foreign politics. There was one of the six whose name I did not catch, and who differed from all the others by his mocking, negative and intransigeant attitude : it was only later that I identified him as Karl Hermann Frank, afterwards the notorious understudy of Neurath and Heydrich.

At my invitation Henlein commissioned one of his deputies to write an article entitled 'The German Minority in Czechoslovakia,' in No. 41 of the *Slavonic Review* (Jan., 1936).

In view of what has since happened, this article makes singular reading. It states that 'Henlein desires the establishment of equal rights between civilized peoples, a peaceful settlement between all the nationalities of the State, and the full enforcement of equal rights for all citizens.' Henlein's party, he claimed, 'upholds the view that national loyalty (*Volkstreue*) in no way conflicts with State loyalty (*Staatstreue*), and that the principles laid down in the Constitution, in the Peace Treaties and in the Minority Treaties are capable of practical fulfilment for all citizens without distinction.' Yet four years later this same man had become the Champion of the Herrenvolk, and as Gauleiter of the territory illegally annexed by Hitler, was ruthlessly denying to the large Czech minority all the rights which he had claimed from the Czechs, and in addition, many rights which Europe before the coming of Hitler had been accustomed to take for granted.

(3) In the summer of 1938 Henlein again visited London and spoke at Chatham House, but on condition that his address should not be published. He was fairspoken as ever, but both obscure and evasive on the subject of his entering Parliament as the representative leader of his party (which for two years he had steadily refused to do) : and when I asked him whether the line which he was advocating would not *ipso facto* involve a complete reversal of the foreign policy hitherto followed by the Republic, and the repudiation of its treaty obligations towards France and Russia, he simply replied that he was not in a position to give any answer whatever to such a question. This was enough for me, and I made no attempt to discuss matters further with him, either in London or during my last visit to Prague in July, 1938. He continued his fairspoken tactics during August in talking with members of the Runciman Mission and even wheedled Lord Runciman into recommending his visit to Hitler : and then on September 14, on Hitler's orders, he suddenly threw off the mask, fled to Germany and proclaimed his adherence to a full-fledged separatist programme. This tale of perfidy should be ever present in the minds of those who will have to deal with the Sudetian Germans after the war.

BIBLIOGRAPHY

This bibliography fulfils the strictly limited purpose of showing the English reader what is available in his own language, together with a selection of the most important works in French and German—it being assumed that he cannot read Czech sources, and that their inclusion would completely alter the proportions and scope of any such list. It is, however, essential to remind the reader at the outset that in the last thirty years much valuable historical work has been produced by such men as Pekář, Novotný, Nejedlý, Kybal, Krofta, Šusta, Bartoš, Odložilík and others, some of which will, it may be hoped, be made available to the English-speaking world when peace returns.

I. General Histories.

Palacký, F. *Geschichte von Böhmen.* 5 v. in 10. Prague, 1844–1867.
Epoch-making in its day, and still authoritative, though now out of date on many points. Ends at 1526.

Denis, Ernest. *Huss et la guerre des Hussites.* Paris, 1878. *La Fin de l'Indépendance bohême.* 2 v. Paris 1890. *La Bohême depuis la Montagne Blanche,* 2 v. Paris, 1903. Brilliantly written and based on original sources.

Lützow, Count Francis. *Bohemia* (second edition in 'Everyman' series. L., 1919). Much the best short history, but very slight after 1792.

Maurice, F. D. *Bohemia* (Story of the Nations series). L., 1896. Readable, written from the standpoint of the Brethren. Slight after 1792.

Krofta, Kamil. *Short History of Czechoslovakia.* L., 1935.

Prokeš, Jaroslav. *Histoire tchèchoslovaque.* Paris, 1927. Up to 1918.

To these should be added the standard works of two Austrian and two German Bohemian historians.

Krones, Franz. *Handbuch der Geschichte Oesterreichs.* 4 v. Berlin, 1880.

Huber, Alfons. *Geschichte Oesterreichs.* 5 v. (to 1637). Gotha, 1885–1896.

Bachmann, Adolf. *Geschichte Böhmens.* 2 v. (to 1526). Gotha, 1899.

Bretholz, Berthold. *Geschichte Böhmens und Mährens.* 4 v. Reichenberg, 1921–1925.

The reader may also be referred to some of the standard German histories, especially in the two great series edited by W. Oncken and Zwiedineck-Südenhorst respectively—those of F. v. Bezold (1517–1618), M. Ritter (1555–1648), G. Winter (1618–1648), B. Erdmannsdörffer (1648–1740), R. Koser (on Frederick the Great), W. Oncken (1780–1815), K. Heigel (1786–1806), Zwiedineck-Südenhorst (1815–1871).

On the early period (Chapters I–III) see Krofta, chapters in the *Cambridge Medieval History,* vols. vi and vii : 'Bohemia to the extinction of the Premyslides' and 'Bohemia in the Fourteenth Century.' Of great importance and value is Mgr. F. Dvorník's *Les Slaves, Byzance et Rome au ixe siècle.* On Charles IV, Dom Bede Jarrett, *Charles IV* (L., 1932) ; W. T. Waugh, 'Charles IV' (*Cambridge Medieval History,* vol. vii).

On Hus, see A. H. Wratislaw, *John Hus* (L. 1882) a real pioneer volume, but above all Count Francis Lützow's attractive book, *Master John Hus* (L., 1909) Dr. Workman's edition of Hus's Letters, in translation and his *The Age of Hus* ; a new and much-revised edition of J. Loserth's *Hus und Wiklif* (Prague, 1884, 1926) ; R. R. Betts, 'English and Czech Influences on the Hussite Movement' (*Transactions of the Royal Histor. Society,* vol. xvi) and 'John Hus' (*History,* April, 1939). Also O. Odložilík, *Wyclif and Bohemia* (Prague, 1937), and 'Wycliffe's Influence on Central Europe' (*Slavonic Review,* vol. vii).

On the Hussite Wars, Count Francis Lützow, *The Hussite Wars* (L., 1914) ; F. v. Bezold, *König Sigismund und die Reichskriege gegen die Hussiten,* 3 small v. (Munich, 1872) and *Zur Geschichte des Hussitentums* (1874) ; G. Voigt, *Papst Pius II* (3 v., Berlin, 1854), and A. Bachmann, *Böhmen unter König Georg von Podiebrad* (Prague, 1878). So long as Pekář's great life of Žižka and other books on fifteenth-century Bohemia remain inaccessible to Western readers, the scales are hopelessly weighed down against the Czechs.

Chapters VI–VIII. Mention may be made of certain standard works on the Habsburg sovereigns, especially H. Ullmann, *Maximilian I* (2 v., Stuttgart,

1884) ; F. Buchholtz, *Geschichte der Regierung Ferdinands I* (8 v., Vienna, 1831–1839) ; F. v. Hurter, *Geschichte Kaiser Ferdinands II* (11 v., Schaffhausen, 1857–1864).

Special attention is drawn to the works of a native Bohemian historian, Anton Gindely, thorough and scientific, but dry and over-cautious, doubtless owing to the transitional period in which he lived—*Rudolf II und seine Zeit* (2 v., Prague, 1868) ; *Geschichte der Gegenreformation in Böhmen* (Leipzig, 1894) ; *Geschichte des 30 jährigen Krieges* (4 vols., Prague, 1880) ; *Geschichte der Böhmischen Brüder* (2 v., Prague, 1857)—his best book.

On Wallenstein, there is a huge literature, from which may be selected : L. v. Ranke, *Geschichte Wallensteins* (Leipzig, 1869) ; Gindely, *Waldstein bis 1630* (2 v., Prague, 1886) ; T. Bílek, *Beiträge zur Geschichte Waldsteins* (Prague, 1886) ; J. Pekař, *Wallenstein* (2 v. in German translation, Berlin, 1937), the fullest and perhaps the most impartial ; admirably written. See a short article on the Wallenstein problem, by V. Valentin, in No. 40 of the *Slavonic Review*.

On Comenius see C. J. Wright, *Comenius and the Church Universal* (L., 1940), including a full translation of 'The Bequest of the Unity of Brethren' ; S. S. Laurie, *Comenius* (Cambridge, 1904) ; J. Jakubec, *Comenius*, foreword by T. G. Masaryk (Prague, 1928) ; *Comenius in England*, by R. Fitzgibbon Young, with a mass of interesting documents relating to Comenius' English visit (Oxford, 1932) ; *The Teacher of Nations : Comenius 1641–1941*, edited by J. Needham (Cambridge, 1942) ; O. Odložilik, *Komenský* (Czechoslovak National Council of America, Chicago, 1942) ; J. Kvačala, *Comenius, sein Leben und seine Schriften* (Leipzig, 1892) ; and more recently, Anna Heyberger, *Comenius ; sa vie et son œuvre* (Paris, 1938). Mr. Young has also published brochures on *Comenius and the Indians of New England* (1929) ; *A Bohemian Philosopher at Oxford, George Ritschel* (1925) ; *A Czech Humanist in London, Rokyčansky* (1930) ; Count Lützow translated *The Labyrinth of the World* (in the Temple Classics).

On the second half of the seventeenth century there are the two studies, written in a definitely Habsburg sense, M. Koch, *Geschichte des deutschen Reiches unter Ferdinand III*, and Oswald Redlich, *Geschichte Oesterreichs unter Leopold I : 1657–1705.* (Gotha, 1921.)

On the history of Austria and its subject peoples there is literally nothing of any value in English. The elaborate History of the House of Habsburg by Archdeacon W. Coxe was from the first worthless, and is only quoted because of the absolute lack of any alternative. For the eighteenth century we have the vast and solid work of Alfred v. Arneth, *Geschichte Maria Theresias* (10 v., Vienna, 1863–1879), and there are also A. Wolff, *Oesterreich unter Maria Theresia* (Berlin, 1884), and Guglia, *Maria Theresia* (2 v., Munich, 1917). But Bohemia is very superficially dealt with in all three.

Joseph II still awaits his biographer. Hitherto the best books on him are by the Russian Paul Mitrofanov (2 v., Vienna, 1910) and the American, S. K. Padower, *The Revolutionary Emperor*. J. F. Bright's *Joseph II* (L., 1897) is very slight. Joseph's correspondence with his mother, his brother Leopold and his sister Marie Antoinette, Prince Kaunitz, Catherine the Great and others, has been published in a series of volumes by Arneth and Adolf Beer.

Here for the first time the English void is filled by Professor R. J. Kerner's admirable *Bohemia under Leopold II* (New York, 1932).

For the first period of Czech rebirth it is well to consult Count Lützow's *History of Bohemian Literature* (L., 1907) and *The Historians of Bohemia* (L., 1905).

On Metternich there are the monumental biography of H. von Srbik (2 v., Munich, 1925), and monographs of Algernon Cecil (L., 1933) and E. L. Woodward (L., 1928). For the whole reign of Francis the two best authorities are Anton Springer, *Geschichte Oesterreichs seit 1809* (2 v., Leipzig, 1863), who began as a Bohemian Liberal, of federalist views, then moved steadily away from Palacký and the Czechs, but has written a work of originality and permanent value ; and Viktor Bibl, *Der Zerfall Oesterreichs* (2 v., Vienna, 1922), the first of which rests on many important new documents from the Vienna Archives, and is admirably composed, whereas the second is a hurriedly written and unreliable 'pot-boiler.'

For the period from 1848 to 1853 see H. Friedjung, *Geschichte Oesterreichs* (2 v., Stuttgart, 1903–1912, unfinished). Joseph Redlich's splendid torso, *Das osterreichische Staats-und Reichsproblem* (2 v., Leipzig, 1920–1926), reaches to 1867, and will always remain an indispensable source, full of new documents. Richard Charmatz, *Oesterreichs innere Geschichte* (2 v., Aus Natur und Geisteswelt), goes to 1907 and is supplemented in *Oesterreichs äussere und innere Politik* 1845–1914 in the same series, which also contains his very useful and readable *Geschichte der auswärtigen*

Politik Oesterreichs im xixten Jahrhundert (2 vols., 1912). K. Rogge's *Oesterreich seit Világos* (3 vols., Leipzig, 1872) and *Oesterreich seit der Katastrophe Hohenwart-Beust* (2 v., 1879), though ponderous and only half digested, fills what otherwise remains an awkward gap. An indispensable source for Austrian Parliamentary life is Gustav Kolmer, *Parlament und Verfassung in Oesterreich* (8 v., Vienna, 1903–1911). For the rise of Austrian Socialism see L. Brügel, *Geschichte der oesterreichischen Sozialdemokratie* (5 v. Vienna, 1925).

Invaluable for a study of the question of languages and nationalities are the two documentary collections of Alfred Fischer—*Das Osterreichische Sprachenrecht* (Brünn 1901) and *Materialien zur Sprachenfrage in Osterreich* (*ibid.* 1903).

Austria is less rich than Germany in Memoirs and biographies, but special mention must be made of E. von Wertheimer's *Graf Julius Andrássy* (3 v., Stuttgart, 1910), Ernst von Plener's *Erinnerungen* (3 v., Stuttgart, 1911–1921), and Rudolf Sieghart's *Die letzten Jahrzehnte einer Grossmacht* (Berlin, 1932).

What will probably always remain the standard work on the Ausgleich, its theory and its working, is Louis Eisenmann's *Le Compromis austro-hongrois* (Paris, 1904). A convenient summary by R. W. Seton-Watson—'The Ausgleich of 1867' —will be found in the *Slavonic Year Book* for 1940.

On Francis Joseph see the admirable surveys by Joseph Redlich (L., 1929), K. Tschuppik (L., 1930, introduction by R. W. Seton-Watson) and Margutti, *Vom alten Kaiser*, by one of his aides-de-camp (Leipzig, 1921), and *Francis Joseph*, by Eugene Bagger (New York, 1927). On Francis Ferdinand see the biographies by Leopold von Chlumetzky (Berlin, 1929), T. von Sosnosky (Munich, 1929) and Maurice Muret (Paris, 1936). On Charles see Count Polzer-Hoditz, *Kaiser Karl* (Leipzig, 1929) and R. Fester, *Die Politik Kaiser Karls* (Munich, 1925), the first a defence by one of the innermost ring, the latter a ferocious onslaught from the angle of the Reich. More balanced is General v. Cramon's *Unser Bundesgenosse im Weltkriege* (Berlin, 1922).

Special mention should be made of two books—H. Wickham Steed, *The Hapsburg Monarchy*, which appeared in 1913 and will always remain a brilliant diagnosis of the situation on the eve of the War. It is a clear and searching analysis, based on close psychological study. It is still quite indispensable, and contains two specially notable chapters on the Jews in Austria and on foreign policy up to 1909. In 1941, A. J. B. Taylor filled a long-felt want in English by his admirable survey *The Habsburg Monarchy*, a history of the period from 1815 to 1919. But it is no more than a preliminary essay, and 1848 is reached on page 52 (out of a total of 300).

On Slovakia under Hungary, see R. W. Seton-Watson, *Racial Problems in Hungary* (L., 1908 with many documents and full bibliography) ; E. Denis, *Les Slovaques* (Paris, 1915), a war improvisation ; E. Sayous's *Histoire des Hongrois*, admirably written from the Magyar angle, hardly mentions the Slovaks. For constitutional problems see H. Marczali, *Ungarische Verfassungsgeschichte* and *Verfassungsrecht* (Tübingen, 1910 and 1911).

On the racial question see Bertrand Auerbach, *Les Races et les Nationalités en Autriche-Hongrie* (Paris, 2nd edition, 1917). It is impossible here to quote the endless pamphlets. Reference has already been made in the text to *Sollen wir Magyaren werden ?* (Carlstadt, 1833) ; Count Leo Thun, *Die Stellung der Slovaken in Ungarn* (Prague, 1843) ; Rudolf Springer (Karl Renner) *Grundlagen und Entwicklungsziele der Oesterreichisch-ungarischen Monarchie* (Vienna, 1906) ; Aurel Popovici *Die Vereinigten Staaten von Gross-Oesterreich* (Leipzig, 1906) and Otto Bauer, *Die Nationalitätenfrage und die Sozialdemokratie* (Vienna, 1907).

Kollár's famous tract *Ueber die literarische Wechselseitigkeit* (Leipzig, 1842) and Šafařik's more serious *Slavische Altertümer* (Leipzig, 1839) both appeared almost simultaneously in Czech and German.

Several useful Slovak monographs recently appeared in French—H. Tourtser, *Louis Štúr et l'idée de l'Indépendance slovaque* (Paris, N.D.) ; J. Oberuč, *Les Persécutions des Luthériens en Slovaquie au* xviieme *siècle* and *Mathieu Bel, un Piétiste en Slovaquie au* xviiieme *siècle* (Strasbourg, 1936).

The *Slavonic Review* contains several valuable contributions on Slovakia—e.g. A. Pražák, 'Slovak Sources of Kollár's Panslavism' (No. 18). 'The Slav Congress of 1848 and the Slovaks' (No. 19). 'Czechs and Slovaks in the Revolution of 1848' (No. 15). 'Czechs and Slovaks after 1848' (No. 16). J. Hanák, 'Slovaks and Czechs in the early Nineteenth Century' (No. 30).

The Great War

First must come the authoritative memoirs of Masaryk and Beneš—T. G. Masaryk, *The Making of a State*, edited by H. W. Steed (L., 1927) ; Karel Čapek, *President Masaryk tells his Story* (L., 1934) ; R. W. Seton-Watson, *Masaryk in England* (Cambridge, 1943), containing original memoranda and letters ; Emil Ludwig, *Gespräche mit Masaryk* (Amsterdam, 1934) ; Edvard Beneš, *My War Memories* (L., 1928) and *Democracy To-day and To-morrow* (L., 1939). There are a number of quite useful biographies, those of Masaryk by C. J. C. Street (1930), Paul Selver (1938, much the fullest), D. Lowry (1935), Otto Strasser (Zürich, 1938). This last deserves very special attention, coming as it does from such a man at such a moment. Those of Beneš are by Godfrey Lias (1940), P. Crabbitès (1935), A. Werner (Prague, 1937), J. Papoušek (in German, Prague, 1937), E. B. Hitchcock (1940). See also a collection of essays entitled *Masaryk Staatsmann und Denker* (Prague-Orbis, 1940).

The fall of Austria can best be studied in the very impartial books of Colonel E. Glaise von Horstenau (formerly head of the Kriegsarchiv in Vienna, afterwards became an active Nazi) *The Collapse of the Austro-Hungarian Empire* (L., 1930) and of Oskar Jászi, the courageous champion of non-Magyar rights in pre-war Hungary, Minister in the short-lived Károlyi Government, since 1922 an American citizen, professor at Oberlin—*The Dissolution of the Habsburg Monarchy* (Chicago, 1929).

Karl Friedrich Nowak, in *Der Sturz der Mittelmächte* (Munich, 1921), and *Chaos* (Munich, 9123), gives a vivid picture from the Austrian angle, based partly on information supplied by Marshal Conrad. J. Opočenský, *Umsturz in Mitteleuropa* (Dresden, 1931) gives the best and fullest Czech account, while Emil Strauss, in *Die Entstehung der Tschechoslovakischen Republik* (Prague, 1930), gives that of a Liberal Sudeten-German, rallied to the Republic. F. Kleinwächter, *Der Untergang der ö-u. Monarchie* (Leipzig, 1930), also deserves mention, as the view of an unusually detached Austrian. An invaluable and indispensable source for the Czech Emigration is the file of *La Nation Tchèque*, edited by E. Denis from May 1, 1915, to April 15, 1917, and then issued in a new form under the editorship of Dr. Beneš, till November 15, 1918 (six more numbers were issued by I. Markovič and H. Jelinek, and it was wound up in August, 1919).

Louise Weiss in *La République tchèchoslovaque* (Paris, 1919, preface by Beneš) gives a short sketch of the new state as constituted at Paris.

For the Peace Conference in its bearings upon Czechoslovakia see Beneš's *Memoirs* (as above). H. W. V. Temperley's *History of the Peace Conference* (6 v., 1921–1923), but especially vol. iv. See also the official Czechoslovak memoranda (with maps) issued by Dr. Beneš under the heading *Les Tchecoslovaques : leur Histoire et Civilization, leur lutte et leur travail, leur rôle dans le Monde*, and a series of official memoranda published in 1922, dealing especially with the ethnical minorities and agrarian reform.

A good deal of scattered material on the part played by the Czechs is to be found in Stannard Baker's *Woodrow Wilson*, Colonel House's *Intimate Papers* (edited Charles Seymour), Mr. Lloyd George's *War Memoirs*, Lansing's *Memoirs*, David Hunter Miller's elaborate diaries and Harold Nicolson's brilliant Study on *Peace Making* (L., 1921).

Twenty Years

There is no general history of Czechoslovakia between the two Wars, but there are a number of excellent small books, of a more or less official character, which do not, however, pretend to cover the ground. Four deserve special recommendation —J. Papoušek, *The Czech Nation's Struggle for Independence* (1928), J. Borovička, *Ten Years of Czechoslovak Politics* (1929), J. Chmelář, *Political Parties in Czechoslovakia* (1921), J. Hoch, Les Partis Politiques (1935).

Much light upon Czechoslovak foreign policy may be obtained from the two books of Robert Machray, *The Little Entente* (L., 1929) and *The Struggle for the Danube*, 1929–1938 (L., 1938), and of course from the principal speeches of Dr. Beneš, which were printed periodically in French and English in a convenient form (by Orbis), but never collected in one volume.

On Slovakia see R. W. Seton-Watson, *The New Slovakia* (Prague, 1924) and *Slovakia Then and Now* (L., 1932), a collection of essays on modern Slovakia by twenty-five eminent Slovaks, with an introduction by R. W. Seton-Watson. These should be supplemented by C. A. Macartney, *Hungary* (L., 1933), and *Hungary and her Successors* (Oxford, 1935)—a study of the Trianon settlement. The full-blooded Hungarian point of view will be found in *Justice for Hungary* (by Count Albert Apponyi, Emil Nagy and others (Budapest, 1925) ; Count Stephen Bethlen, *The Treaty of Trianon and European Peace* (L., 1934) ; and Lord Rothermere, *My Campaign for Hungary* (L., 1939).

The best short account of the Czech-German dispute is to be found in Elizabeth Wiskemann's *Czechs and Germans* (Oxford, 1938). See also Gustav Peters, *Der neue Herr von Böhmen* (Prague, 1937—grudging, but not violent) ; R. Jung, *Die Tschechen* (Berlin, 1927—rabid) ; Hans Krebs, *Kampf in Böhmen* (Berlin, 1936—uncompromising). Also P. Molisch, *Geschichte der deutsch-nationalen Bewegung in Oesterreich* (Jena, 1926) and *Die Sudetendeutsche Freiheitsbewegung in den Jahren* 1918–1919 (Vienna, 1932). *Konrad Henlein spricht* (Karlsbad, 1937) contains his official programme.

Moderate and reliable Czech treatment of the controversy will be found in K. Krofta, *Das Deutschtum in der tchechoslovakischen Geschichte* (Prague, 1935) and J. Chmelář, *The German Problem in Czechoslovakia* (Prague, 1936).

Miss Lucy Textor's excellent *Land Reform in Czechoslovakia*, published in 1923, has, of course, long ceased to be up to date.

MUNICH AND AFTER

The chronology of the crisis will be found in R. W. Seton-Watson's *From Munich to Danzig* (L., 1939) and Hamilton Fish Armstrong's *When there is no Peace* (New York, 1939). From the Czech side the fullest and most authoritative book is *Munich and After*, by Hubert Ripka.

Other books on the crisis are G. R. Gedye, *Fallen Bastions* ; F. Borkenau, *Austria and After* ; Jonathan and Joan Griffin, *Lost Liberty ?* ; Maurice Hindus, *We Shall Live Again* ; A. Henderson, *Eye-witness in Czechoslovakia* ; Edgar Young, *Czechoslovakia* ; Sheila Grant Duff, *Europe and the Czechs* (Penguin)—all in 1939.

In French there are books by Fabre-Luce and Barthélemy (the Vichy Minister of Justice), over which it would be merciful to draw a veil. Of special value is Alexander Werth's *France and Munich*.

For the period subsequent to 1939 the reader may be referred to Sheila Grant Duff, *A German Protectorate* (L., 1942) ; E. V. Pelényi, *Germany's First European Protectorate* (L., 1941) ; the official *Two Years of German Oppression* (1941), and the most recent of all, *Four Fighting Years*, also official—a terrifying and all too convincing survey. The Royal Institute of International Affairs has just published a valuable collection of the main documents as yet available on the Austrian Anschluss and the Munich Crisis, in *Documents on International Affairs*, 1938, vol. 2, ed. Monica Curtis (Oxford 1943).

INDEX